THE UNIVERSITY OF
WINCHESTER

Martial Rose Library
Tel: 01962 827306

To be returned on or before the day marked above, subject to recall.

THE

BACCHAE OF EURIPIDES

WITH

CRITICAL AND EXPLANATORY NOTES

AND WITH NUMEROUS ILLUSTRATIONS
FROM WORKS OF ANCIENT ART

BY

JOHN EDWIN SANDYS, Litt. D.

FELLOW AND TUTOR OF ST JOHN'S COLLEGE, AND PUBLIC ORATOR
IN THE UNIVERSITY OF CAMBRIDGE,
HON. LITT.D. DUBLIN,
EXAMINER IN GREEK IN THE VICTORIA UNIVERSITY AND IN THE
UNIVERSITY OF LONDON.

FOURTH EDITION.

Cambridge:
AT THE UNIVERSITY PRESS.

LONDON: C. J. CLAY AND SONS,
CAMBRIDGE UNIVERSITY PRESS WAREHOUSE, AVE MARIA LANE.
GLASGOW: 50, WELLINGTON STREET.
1900

CAMBRIDGE UNIVERSITY PRESS
Cambridge, New York, Melbourne, Madrid, Cape Town,
Singapore, São Paulo, Delhi, Mexico City

Cambridge University Press
The Edinburgh Building, Cambridge CB2 8RU, UK

Published in the United States of America by Cambridge University Press, New York

www.cambridge.org
Information on this title: www.cambridge.org/9781107620988

© Cambridge University Press 1880

First edition 1880
First published 1880
Second edition 1885
Third edition 1892
Fourth edition 1900
First paperback edition 2013

A catalogue record for this publication is available from the British Library

ISBN 978-1-107-62098-8 Paperback

PREFACE.

For my earliest interest in the celebrated, though
often far from easy, play, a new edition of which is
here offered to the public, I am indebted to the fact
that, some fifteen years ago[1], in common with many
other students in this University, I had the advantage
of attending a course of lectures upon it, by the
Reverend W. H. Thompson, afterwards Master of
Trinity College, who was at that time Regius Professor of Greek. Those who shared that advantage
will long remember his happy renderings, and his
brief and pointed criticisms, which had the rare merit
of being sufficient for their immediate purpose, while
at the same time they were calculated to stimulate
the student to further investigation on his own account.

The impulse thus given to the study of the play
led to my continuing to devote attention to it, after
taking my degree, and to my including it from time
to time, in and after 1869, among the subjects of my
College lectures. After a while, it occurred to me
that the materials thus collected might serve as a

[1] 1864.

foundation for an edition of the play ; and, finding
from the Master of Trinity that there was no prospect
of his editing it himself, I began under his kind en-
couragement to prepare to do so. My notes, however, had not proceeded further than the first 433
lines of the play, when they were laid aside for other
editorial work, shortly after the publication in 1871 of
Mr Tyrrell's edition, which, together with Mr Paley's
already existing commentary on all the plays, appeared likely, for some time to come, to meet the
wants of English students. In the course of last year,
however, finding myself attracted once more to my
original purpose, I set to work afresh, and devoted the
summer of that year to recasting, or rather, entirely
rewriting, the notes which I had already prepared,
and also to reducing into some sort of order the
materials collected for the remainder. To do this,
and to get the explanatory notes into type, was the
holiday-task which I set myself for the summer vacation of 1879, the claims of University and College
duties in term-time rendering it otherwise nearly impossible to prepare a work like the present, which,
limited as it may seem in compass, has involved a
not inconsiderable amount of labour, even apart from
what appears on the surface. Indeed, it could hardly
have been undertaken at all, but for the existence of
that excellent institution, the University Long Vacation,—an institution against which a few bold hands
have been lately lifted, but which nevertheless, in the

form in which we are familiar with it in the Colleges of Cambridge, where residence under due limitations is allowed but not enforced, has a value, for teachers and learners alike, which it would be difficult to over-estimate.

My endeavour throughout has been to supply, in a convenient and comprehensive form, a kind of hand-book to the criticism, interpretation and archaeo-logical illustration of the play, which should be inter-esting and instructive to the student, whether at School or College, and also to some extent useful to the more advanced scholar. The short introductory essays with which the volume opens, include a sketch of the closing years of the poet, and some account of the points of interest whether in mythology or in art, in dramatic or in textual criticism, which are connected with this, perhaps, his latest work. In the critical notes at the foot of the page, which, for obvious reasons of general convenience, are written in Latin, the manuscript readings are recorded, together with all the conjectural emendations that appeared for any reason to deserve notice, and also the principal varia-tions occurring in the text as printed in nine previous editions. In settling the text, I have endeavoured to decide in each case to the best of my judgment according to the evidence before me, with the result of finding myself on the whole in closer agreement with the second editions of Kirchhoff and Nauck than with those of any other editor. In the explanatory notes, at the end of the book, due acknowledgment is made of all my more important obligations to others, and of many even of the less important. Further, I have, as far as possible, gone on the principle of quoting parallel passages in full, instead of contenting myself with a bare reference, considering the former course not only more convenient to the reader, but also fairer in every way, as by this means any argument that rests upon a quotation can at once have its due weight assigned to it,—neither less nor more. Those who have ever had to spend much time in looking up references will, I think, agree with me in holding that few things are more vexatious than to find a particular opinion on a doubtful point supported by an array of references which may or may not be relevant, but all of which have to be tested in detail before any further advance can be made. As a matter of fact, few people take the trouble; and those who do, find themselves often discouraged by their experience from continuing to make the attempt.—It may be added that the short pieces of translation occasionally given in the notes are, in the case of the dialogue of the play, extracted from a rendering of that portion in blank verse, which I prepared for my use in the lecture-room.

In the explanatory notes, a number of *adversaria* by R. Shilleto (1809—1876), whose name is here gratefully recorded by one of his many private pupils, are now printed for the first time from his interleaved

copy of the *Poetae Scenici* in the Cambridge University
Library, as well as a few conjectures and other notes
by the same scholar, for some of which I am indebted
to the Rev. A. J. Tuck, Assistant Master at Upping-
ham School, who attended his lectures at King's
College. I have also the pleasure of thanking the
Rev. W. H. Thompson, D.D., Master of Trinity College, and J. S. Reid, Esq., Fellow of Gonville and
Caius, for kindly placing their own conjectures at my
disposal. A few suggestions of my own, which I
venture to submit to the judgment of scholars, will
be found in the notes on the following lines: 126,
135, 147, 209, 251, 278, 327, 550, 1002, 1008, 1157,
1207, 1365. In the case of one or two of them, it
is some slight gratification to find them to a certain
extent confirmed by their having independently occurred to others.

I have endeavoured throughout to devote particular attention to points of archaeological interest
and especially to the illustration of the play with the
help of monuments of ancient art. Under the new
scheme for the Classical Tripos, one of the special
subjects in which students will be able henceforth to
obtain distinction, after taking honours in pure scho-
larship, is Classical Archaeology, including ancient
art and mythology, with certain prescribed portions
of the wide province of topography and antiquities;
and provision is already being made by Professorial
and other teaching for the due instruction of students

in that department. Thus any Cambridge scholar who in future years undertakes a work similar to the present will happily be able to start with the advantage of a systematic study of ancient art which has only to a limited extent fallen to the lot of the present editor. On the general subject, however, I have had the pleasure of attending some of the lectures given by Professor Colvin, and by Dr Waldstein, and it will be observed that one or two incidental points in the Introduction are due to the former. But, for my special purpose, I have naturally found it necessary to rely in the main, on the study either of the actual monuments of ancient art or published representations of them, besides constantly consulting the somewhat scattered literature of the subject, a conspectus of which, so far as it has come within my own knowledge, is given at the end of the Introduction. Among the archaeologists of the last generation, to whose works I am thus under special obligations, are Otfried Müller and Otto Jahn. In the case of living authorities on ancient art and archaeology, my thanks are due to Jahn's distinguished nephew, Professor Michaelis of Strassburg, for drawing my attention to one or two recent German contributions towards the archaeological illustration of points immediately connected with the play, and in particular for enabling me to supply a more accurate copy of one of the sculptured representations of the death of Pentheus, than those hitherto published: to C. T. Newton, Esq., C.B., honorary

PREFACE.

D.C.L. and LL.D. of Oxford and Cambridge respectively, for indicating several of the subjects suitable to my purpose, among the treasures of art entrusted to his keeping in the British Museum: and to the Reverend C. W. King, Senior Fellow of Trinity, for allowing me to consult him on the particular province of ancient art in which he is a recognised master. I am further specially indebted to Messrs George Bell and Sons, the publishers of Mr King's *Antique Gems and Rings* (1872), for allowing electrotypes to be taken for this book from woodcuts used in that admirable work; eleven of the illustrations (including a gem in the Fitzwilliam Museum, originally engraved for the Syndics of the University Press) are, with the author's kind concurrence, borrowed from the comprehensive series there published. The remaining twenty-one have been prepared expressly for this volume by Mr F. Anderson, the skilful artist and engraver engaged in the establishment of Messrs R. Clay, Sons, and Taylor. A full description has been given, not only of all the thirty-two illustrations here selected (with an indication in each instance of the source from which it is derived); but also of other works of art connected with the play, which though not included in this selection, nevertheless deserve particular attention for their archaeological interest. Specialists in this department may perhaps find little that is entirely new to them in these illustrations, but I have had in view the needs of the large body of those

PREFACE.

who take a general interest in such matters, but to whom the copies of monuments of ancient art hitherto published are often somewhat inaccessible, owing partly to their being generally confined to works that can hardly be consulted except in our larger public libraries. Several of the illustrations, however, are, I have reason to know, more accurate than those that have appeared elsewhere; and I may add in conclusion that a terracotta lamp from Cyprus (on p. 238) as well as a gem lately found in the north of England (opp. p. clv) are here figured and described for the first time. For placing in my hands the originals of both of these, I have the pleasure of thanking the Reverend S. S. Lewis, F.S.A., Fellow and Librarian of Corpus Christi College.

J. E. SANDYS.

Cambridge,
July 31, 1880.

PREFACE TO SECOND EDITION.

A NEW edition of this volume having been called for at an unexpectedly early date, I have availed myself of the opportunity thus afforded to submit the whole to a careful and thorough revision. In so doing, I have endeavoured to give due consideration to all the criticisms on the former edition with which I have been favoured by scholars at home and abroad. I am especially indebted to the writers of the able and suggestive . reviews which appeared in the *Philologischer Anzeiger* 1881, pp. 13 —21 (Dr Wecklein); the *Pädagogisches Archiv* 1881, pp. 426—434 (Dr L. Schmidt); the *Academy* for 13 Nov. (Mr Paley) and 2 Oct. 1880; the *Athenaeum* for 11 Dec. 1880, and the *Spectator* for 15 Jan. 1881. I am also bound to express my thanks to the writers of the articles in the *Saturday Review* (13 Nov. 1880), the *Guardian* (27 April, 1881), the *Scotsman* (22 Oct. 1880), the *British Quarterly Review* (No. LXXIII, p. 221, 1881), and in *Notes and Queries* (27 Nov. 1880). I have further the pleasure of acknowledging my obligations, amongst others, to Professor Michaelis of Strassburg for his valuable advice and assistance on some points of archaeological detail; to Professor

Mayor for kindly supplying me with several interesting *addenda*, together with a list of all the *corrigenda*
which his practised eye had been able to detect in
my former edition; and to Mr Jerram, editor of the
Alcestis and *Helena* of Euripides, for not a few references to parallel passages, and other useful an-
notations on the earlier part of the play.

It only remains for me to state the principal
points in which the present edition differs from its
predecessor. Six additional representations of the
subject of the play, as treated in ancient art, three
of them from vase-paintings and the remaining
three from sculptured reliefs, are now included
among the woodcuts. They may be found between
pages cviii and cxvi of the Introduction. The
descriptions of these and other examples of the
artistic treatment of the death of Pentheus in the
part of the Introduction just referred to, have been
re-arranged and enlarged to the extent of about
five pages of letterpress. Some additional remarks
on the horned type of Dionysus have been inserted
on pages cxxxix—xliii; and pages cxxxviii—ix of
the former edition, describing various representations
of the Triumph of Agave, have been transferred to
more appropriate places on pages cxvi, cxvii, cxviii
of the Introduction. On pages cliv and clv several
new items have been added to the list of dissertations,
&c., bearing either on the textual criticism or the
archaeology of the play. In four passages (lines 207,

406, 981 and 1007), the text has been altered in accordance with emendations proposed by Mr Munro, Meineke, Dr Thompson, and Dr Wecklein respectively; and a few other emendations are now recorded in the critical notes to lines 209, 372, 506, 678, 860, 1060, 1125. In the explanatory notes many additional details have been inserted. Such new matter has sometimes been worked into the body of the notes (as in the notes on lines 1341 and 1350); but, in a far greater majority of instances, it has taken the form of brief references inserted at the end of the paragraph to which they belong. Owing however to the book having been stereotyped, such insertions could not in all cases be incorporated in the text of the notes; and many of them have accordingly been placed at the foot of the page, while a few for which room could not even thus be found, have been relegated to the Appendix. The latter also contains an account of a hitherto unpublished text of the play, by George Burges, with a selection from his very numerous and often needless emendations, together with some other proposed corrections of the text which have appeared since the publication of my former edition[1].

Lastly, a visit to Florence during the Easter vacation of the year 1883 has enabled me to revise and correct the *apparatus criticus* of this edition by reading through the whole of that portion of the play which is contained in the Laurentian manuscript. All the

---

[1] These last are now included in the critical notes (1892).

readings hitherto ascribed to this manuscript have thus been verified afresh; several inaccuracies of statement respecting them have been removed; and direct evidence as to the text has been substituted for some inferences formerly drawn from the silence alone of previous collators. The requisite alterations have accordingly been made in the critical notes on lines 107, 135, 151, 202, 292, 347, 398, 525 and 631; while most of the points to which my attention was drawn in examining the manuscript are recorded on p. 268—9.

During the same visit, I endeavoured in vain to find the original of the alleged 'Florentine gem' engraved on p. 122 and described on page cl. By the kind assistance, however, of Professor L. A. Milani, the accomplished and obliging keeper of the Etruscan and Classical antiquities, which have been admirably rearranged in their new home in the *Via della Colonna*, I have been enabled to give on page 258 some account of the probable origin of the engraving to which I refer. I may add that the same authority proposes shortly to publish a hitherto unnoticed illustration of the passage of this play where Dionysus is associated with the goddess of Peace (416—420), which will be looked forward to with interest by scholars and archaeologists. I only regret that I feel myself precluded for the present from giving any account of the work of art to which I allude, or from including a copy of it among the illustrations to this volume.

J. E. S.

April, 1885.

PREFACE TO THIRD EDITION.

THE *Text* of this edition is the same as that of its immediate predecessor. There is, however, one passage in which I might perhaps have been justified in introducing an alteration on the strength of evidence which was not accessible to me when the work was first published in 1880. In line 1084, the manuscript reading, εὔλειμος νάπη, presents us with an epithet which is not found elsewhere. The author of the *Christus Patiens*, who frequently borrows from this play, has ὕλιμος νάπη. But this alone was not enough to turn the scale, as ὕλιμος was quite as rare a word as εὔλειμος; accordingly, of all the editors Dindorf alone accepted ὕλιμος. The point of interest is that we now find this very word in a fragment of the *Melanippe* of Euripides, discovered in Egypt in 1879 and published in 1880, which contains the phrase, ὄρεος ὑλίμῳ νάπη (Eur. *Frag.* 495, 34 in Nauck, *Tragicorum Graecorum Fragmenta*, ed. 2, 1889). The evidence in favour of ὕλιμος is thus materially strengthened.

In the *Critical Notes* I have incorporated all the more important suggestions that have been proposed since the publication of the last edition. I have also included the conjectures of the Dutch critics, Naber and Hartmann, which were formerly printed in the Appendix. The readings of the Palatine manuscript in the Vatican Library, which alone contains the whole of the play, have been verified by a personal examination of the manuscript during a visit to Rome in the Easter vacation of 1887. The only other authority for the text, the manuscript in the Laurentian Library at Florence, I had already examined in 1883.

The work of art in the Museum at Florence, which I saw during the same visit, and to which I could only vaguely refer in the preface to my second edition, has since been published in the *Bullettino* of the German Imperial Archaeological Institute for 1890. I have to thank the author of the elaborate article, which accompanies its publication, for courteously sending me a copy. The work in question is a bronze relief on a circular mirror-case found on Etruscan soil at Corneto-Tarquinia. The photograph appended to the article shews that the design includes several figures. One of these is identified as Eirene seated, with the infant Plutus holding a cornucopia on her knee; while the youthful form gazing wistfully at her is held to be none other than Dionysus. The design in general may, serve as an illustration of the following lines in one of the choruses of this play :—

> ὁ δαίμων ὁ Διὸς παῖς
> χαίρει μὲν θαλίαισιν,
> φιλεῖ δ' ὀλβοδότειραν Εἰ-
> ρήναν, κουροτρόφον θεόν (416—420).

PREFACE TO THIRD EDITION.

In the *Introduction*, the bibliographical account of the *Literature of the Play* (pp. clii—clv) has been brought up to date. The *Commentary* has been revised, and the *Supplementary Notes* enlarged by the addition of several valuable criticisms which have been contributed to the *Classical Review* by various scholars. In two of these notes, those on lines 145 and 1163, I have now been enabled to quote the rendering which commended itself to the judgment of the late Dr Thompson in his professorial lectures. These quotations are taken from his own copy of Elmsley's edition, for the gift of which I am indebted to the kindness of Mrs Thompson.

I cannot conclude without adding that, since the publication of the second edition, I have received from India a large number of *Corrigenda* for which I have to thank Mr K. Deighton, the late Principal of the Agra College, whose editions of several of Shakespeare's plays are widely known. These *Corrigenda* have materially aided me in my endeavour to ensure that, in point of typographical correctness, the present edition should be more worthy of the favour which has been generously extended to both of the preceding editions by scholars at home and abroad.

J. E. S.

February, 1892.

PREFACE TO FOURTH EDITION.

SINCE the last issue of the present work, two of the eminent scholars, who edited this play before the appearance of my first edition in 1880, have published new recensions of the text. Professor Tyrrell's edition of 1871 has thus been succeeded by that of 1892, and Wecklein's of 1879 by that of 1898, including an *Appendix* (of fifteen pages) *coniecturas minus probabiles continens.* In the *Critical Notes* I have endeavoured to indicate all the points of any importance, in which their present texts differ from those of an earlier date. In this and other ways, slight alterations have been introduced into the critical notes on nearly fifty pages of the text. In my own *Text* the only changes are the substitution of the reading of one of our two MSS, κτύπου, for that of the other, κτύπους (l. 513), and of ὕλιμος for εὔλειμος (l. 1084). In the *Introduction* I have inserted a short description of a painting representing the fate of Pentheus, found at Pompeii in 1894—5 (p. cxv *b*). Several new items have been added to the conspectus of the *Literature of the Play*, pp. cliii–v. The rest of the work, including the *Commentary*, remains unaltered.

J. E. S.

May. 1900.

LIST OF ILLUSTRATIONS.

* *The 27 woodcuts marked thus have been prepared expressly for this work by Mr F. Anderson.*

LIST OF ILLUSTRATIONS.

CONTENTS.

INTRODUCTION.

§ 1. *The legend of Dionysus.*

THE story of the birth of Dionysus, in its simplest
form, is as follows: Semele, daughter of Cadmus
king of Thebes, being beloved by Zeus, was beguiled
by the jealous Hera into asking him to visit her, as
he visited Hera herself, in the full glory of his godhead. He accordingly appeared before her in all
his majesty as the god of thunder; Semele, over-
powered by his presence, was struck dead by his
thunderbolts; but in her death she gave untimely
birth to a child, whom Zeus, its father, rescued from

the lightning-flames and hid in the hollow of his thigh, until its time of birth was fully come. On the second birth of the infant god, his father sent him by the hands of Hermes to the nymphs of Nysa, who brought him up in a cave among the dells of that mountain, and, as a reward for their ministrations, were placed by Zeus among the stars, under the name of *Hyades.*

The name of Dionysus was supposed in ancient times to be derived from that of Zeus his father, and Nysa, the haunt of his earliest days[1]. Nysa is first mentioned in connexion with the legend of Lycurgus, king of Thrace (*Iliad* VI 133); but many other places of that name are referred to by ancient authorities, in Phocis and Euboea, in Egypt and Arabia, in Ethiopia and India, all of them associated with the worship of Dionysus (note on l. 556). The name may be connected with a rare word meaning "trees[2]," and it would be therefore particularly appropriate as the designation of a well-wooded spot : this view is supported by the fact that in one of the minor Homeric hymns, the infant god in the dales of Nysa is described as making the woodland his favourite place of wandering[3]; and it may also be illustrated by the word δενδρίτης, which was one of the many epithets under which the god was worshipped[4].

---

[1] Diodorus Siculus III 64, ἀπὸ τοῦ πατρὸς καὶ τοῦ τόπου.

[2] Pherecydes in Schol. Arist. Panath. 185, 3, p. 313 ed. D., νύσας (*v. l.* νύσσας) ἐκάλουν τὰ δένδρα.

[3] Homeric hymn 25 (26), 8, φοιτίζεσκε καθ' ὑλήεντας ἐναύλους.

[4] Plutarch, *Moralia* II p. 675 F (*Symp.* III § 4), Διονύσῳ δὲ δενδρίτῃ πάντες ὡς ἔπος εἰπεῖν Ἕλληνες θύουσιν. See *Appendix*, p. 253.

The popular legend of his second birth was long ago a stumblingblock to the scepticism of the Theban king who denied his divinity[1]; and, if it remains unexplained, it may still continue to be a cause of offence, more especially to those who acquiesce in the belief that the vulgar legends of Greek mythology were the offspring of little better than an inventive, and somewhat disordered, imagination. It has therefore been suggested[2] that the very uncertainty of the position of Nysa on earth is an indication that, in its original form, it must be traced to those clouds of heaven which are the ultimate source of no unimportant portion of the mythology of the Aryan nations; the trees of Nysa must, in fact, be looked for in the same region as the great ash-tree of Teutonic legend whose branches embrace the whole world[3]. The story of the birth of Dionysus thus resolves itself into nothing more than a rude personification of the powers of nature; the rain-cloud, big with tempest, is his mother, while his father is the sky that enfolds in its embrace the gathering storm. The short and sudden shower

[1] *Bacchae*, 242—5.

[2] Wecklein's ed. of the *Bacchae* (1879), *Einleitung* p. 1.

[3] *Yggdrasill:* Cox, *Mythology of the Aryan Nations*, II 18. Wecklein himself refers to A. Kuhn, *die Herabkunft des Feuers und des Göttertranks* [Berlin, 1859], p. 24 ff., p. 131 ff. Kuhn, it will be remembered, is a leading exponent of what has been called the 'meteorological,' as contrasted with the 'solar,' theory of Comparative Mythology. Max Müller, in maintaining the latter, assigns 'a proportionately small space to meteorological phenomena, such as clouds, thunder, and lightning' (see his *Lectures on the Science of Language*, Series II. ed. 1864, p. 517, to end of lecture xi).

which, after a flash of lightning and a clap of thunder, is discharged by the bursting cloud, and falls to earth before its time, is crudely described as the untimely birth of Ὕης, the Rain, from Ὕη, the Cloud; the former is only another name for Dionysus, and the latter for Semele, while his nurses are the Ὑάδες, the nymphs of rain[1]. Again, the passing shower is carried up once more in mist and vapour to the sky, and in due time falls to earth again, in a fertilizing and abundant rain[2]. Thus, Dionysus is the offspring of the clouds descending in the storm; is, in fact, the blending together of the watery and the fiery elements in nature. In this union of moisture and warmth, which fosters the fruits of the earth, displays its strength more especially in the fiery juice of the vine, and shares its domain with the power that presides over the ripening corn, we recognise the peculiar characteristics of the gentle and genial, as well as the stimulating and inspiring influence of Dionysus[3].

[1] *Etymologicum Magnum* under Ὕης: ἐπίθετον Διονύσου. ὁ δὲ Φερεκύδης τὴν Σεμέλην Ὕην λέγει καὶ τὰς τοῦ Διονύσου τροφοὺς Ὑάδας (Wecklein, *u. s.*, p. 2). Cf. Ruskin's *Queen of the Air*, i 30.

[2] Wecklein, however, prefers regarding the story of the god being hidden in the thigh of Zeus, as only a second mode of representing the origin of Rain, which has been combined with the first. The legend of Dionysus being hidden in the thigh of Zeus is compared by Kuhn, *u. s.* p. 167, with the Indian account of *soma* (see p. xiii), entering the thigh of Indra. For Greek attempts to rationalise the legend, see Diodorus Sic. III. 62 (also on Δ. πυριγενὴς, Strabo XIII iv § 11 and V iv § 8).

[3] Plutarch *de Iside et Osiride* § 35 (quoted by Wecklein), [*Moralia* p. 365 A], ὅτι δ᾽ οὐ μόνον τοῦ οἴνου Διόνυσον, ἀλλὰ καὶ πάσης ὑγρᾶς φύσεως Ἕλληνες ἡγοῦνται κύριον καὶ ἀρχηγὸν, ἀρκεῖ Πίνδαρος μάρτυς εἶναι, λέγων· Δενδρέων δὲ νομὸν Διόνυσος πολυγαθὴς αὐξάνοι, ἁγνὸν

A partial parallel to this may be found in the ancient Indian mythology. According to the Rig Veda (ix), the exhilarating juice of the soma-plant[1], of which all the gods are eager to partake, plays an important part in bracing Indra for his conflict with the hostile powers of the atmosphere. Soma is also the god who animates this juice, an intoxicating draught which takes a conspicuous place among the sacrifices of the Vedic age[2]. 'The simple-minded Arian people,' says Professor Whitney, 'whose whole religion was a worship of the wonderful powers and phenomena of nature, had no sooner perceived that this liquid had power to elevate the spirits, and produce a temporary frenzy, under the influence of which the individual was prompted to, and capable of, deeds beyond his natural powers, than they found in it something divine: it was to their apprehension a god endowing those whom it entered with god-like powers[3].' Soma 'dispels the darkness,' and 'lights up the gloomy nights,' he is 'the priest of the gods, the leader of poets, a *rishi*[4] among sages, a bull among wild animals, a falcon among kites, an axe in the woods'; as an

φέγγος ὀπώρας (fragm. 125). To this may be added *id.* p. 675 *Symp.* III § 4, ἀμφότεροι γὰρ οἱ θεοὶ (Poseidon and Dionysus) τῆς ὑγρᾶς καὶ γονίμου κύριοι δοκοῦσιν ἀρχῆς εἶναι.

[1] *asclepias acida* or *sarcostemma viminale.*

[2] Muir's *Sanskrit Texts* vol. 5, sect. xvi, p. 258, Kuhn *u. s.*, pp. 56 ff., 118 ff. Cf. line 284 of the play, οὗτος θεοῖσι σπένδεται θεὸς γεγώς.

[3] *Journal of American Oriental Society* II, 299 (quoted by Muir).

[4] The title given to the seven sages of ancient Hindu tradition. 'In its widest meaning the word was taken to denote the priestly bards who conducted the worship of the gods' (Cox, *Mythology of the Aryan Nations*, I p. 413).

object of adoration he is associated with *Agni*, the
divinity of Fire[1].

Even in his transformations into serpent, bull, bear,
lion or panther, by a coincidence which may, of
course, be merely accidental, Dionysus finds his
counterpart in the monstrous shapes assumed by the
changing clouds, whether as described in the *Nubes*
of Aristophanes (347), 'Centaur or pard or wolf or
bull': or as in the familiar lines of Shakespeare:

> 'Sometime we see a cloud that's dragonish;
> A vapour sometime like a bear or lion,
> A tower'd citadel, a pendent rock,
> A forked mountain, or blue promontory
> With trees upon 't, that nod unto the world,
> And mock our eyes with air: thou hast seen these signs;
> They are black vesper's pageants[2].'

Passing, however, from this cloud-land of uncertain
speculation, and returning to the traditional legend of
Dionysus, in the shape in which it was familiar to the
Greeks themselves in historic times, we find that, at
Delphi, the god whom we have just described as the
offspring of the sky and the rain-cloud, was closely
associated with the god of sunshine, Apollo. On the
two pediments of the Delphic temple, the art of the
sculptor represented the setting of the sun, and the
birth of Apollo, together with the forms of Dionysus
and his attendant *Thyiades;* while the heights of
Parnassus were not sacred to the sun-god alone, but
were also the favoured haunt of Dionysus. The
immediate surroundings of the central sanctuary of
Hellenic religion had the appearance of a vast natural

---

[1] Muir, *u. s.*, pp. 267, 269.   [2] *Antony and Cleopatra*, IV. 14.

theatre[1], closed by the semicircular range of the
Phaedriades, and, for the greater part of the day,
those resplendent rocks, facing nearly south, reflected
the full rays of the sun on the temple of Apollo[2]; but
at sunset, when the light had left their lower portions,
those brilliant cloud-effects were seen, which poetic
fancy called the torches held aloft by Dionysus, as
he leaped along the ridges of Parnassus; while the
sun-beams, darting athwart the two peaks, to the east
and to the west of the Castalian fount,

> 'translucent, pure,
> With touch etherial of Heaven's fiery rod,'

were described as the shooting and brandishing of the
wand of Dionysus[3].

Confining ourselves mainly to the details of the
legend which are recognised by Euripides himself,
we find Phrygia mentioned as one of the god's earliest
homes. He grew up under the care of the goddess
Rhea, or Cybele, who taught him the mysteries on
mount Tmolus in Lydia; from her sacred rites the
Phrygian flute was borrowed, to be blended in his
worship with the sound of the *tympanum* which is
described by our poet as the joint invention of herself
and Dionysus (l. 59). He discovers the vine and
spreads its cultivation over many lands, visiting Egypt,
Syria and Arabia and other parts of Asia : according
to a form of the legend, unrecognised by Euripides,
which became popular after the eastern conquests of

---

[1] θεατροειδὲς (Strabo IX p. 418).   [2] Mure's *Tour in Greece.* I p. 188.

[3] See notes on lines 306—308. The line quoted above from the
Samson Agonistes, I need hardly say, does not refer to Castalia in its
original context.

Alexander, he advanced in triumph even to distant India[1]. Wherever he went, he was attended by a band of followers who, in the earlier legend, were either the nymphs who had nursed him, as related in the Homeric hymn, or the *Charites*[2] whom comparative mythology identifies as the shining steeds of Dawn, though Hellenic legend never represents them except as graceful beings of human form[3]. As time went on, this simple company was expanded, by the imagination of poets and artists alike, into a multitudinous troop, including the goat-footed Pan, the sage Silenus, the frisky Satyrs and the frenzied Maenads. Wherever he went, his votaries arrayed themselves in a fantastic garb; wearing the skin of the fawn or of the panther (note on l. 24), crowning themselves with the leaves of the vine, the ivy, or the *smilax* (107), sometimes even entwining serpents around their hair or about their limbs (102). They took into their hands the rod of the *narthex* or giant fennel (113); or the *thyrsus*, the light wand swathed with ivy and capped with a fir-cone, which was the special badge of Bacchic worship (25). In their dances by night, they waved about the pinewood torch (146), while the

---

[1] Nonnus *Dionysiaca* l. 36. Curtius, *Alex.* VIII 10 § 11 (*ad Nysam urbem pervenit*). *a Libero patre conditos esse dicebant: et vera haec origo erat. sita est sub radicibus montis, quem Meron incolae appellant. inde Graeci mentiendi traxere licentiam, Iovis femine Liberum patrem esse celatum.* His Indian conquests appear as early as Antimachus (Dio. Sic. III 65).

[2] l. 414, ἐκεῖ Χάριτες. Cf. Plutarch *Qu. Gr.* 36, σὺν Χαρίτεσσιν (quoted in note on l. 100), and Pausanias V 14 (end), (at Olympia) πρὸς τῷ τεμένει τοῦ Πέλοπος Διονύσου μὲν καὶ Χαρίτων ἐν κοινῷ, μεταξὺ δὲ αὐτῶν Μουσῶν καὶ ἐφεξῆς τούτων Νυμφῶν ἐστι βωμός.

[3] Max Müller, *Lectures on Language* II pp. 369—376, 383.

flute (128, 380) and the *tympanum* (59) were among their characteristic instruments of music.

Breaking loose from the ordinary duties of everyday life (118), they held their revels on the hills, rapt into a state of wild and ecstatic enthusiasm which, with its frolics in the open air, amid the sights and sounds of nature, recalled the careless happiness of a by-gone time, before the advance of civilisation had robbed life of its romance[1]. They rejoiced in the pursuits of the chase, hunting the wild goat to the death, rending their prey in pieces as it quivered in their grasp, and feasting on the raw flesh of their victim. At the touch of their rods, as the poet tells us, springs of water leaped forth from the stricken rock, fountains of wine shot up from the earth, and marvellous streams of milk oozed from the soil, while honey dropped from their ivied wands (147, 700—711)[2]. As contrasted with marvels such as these, suggested by the poet's imagination, we find that regular festivals in honour of the god were held in alternate years, under the name of *trieterica*, on Parnassus, and elsewhere ; in Attica, where these *trieterica* were never introduced, the worship of Dionysus was, in historic times, celebrated in simple country-festivals of rude

[1] ad naturae integritatem castitatemque et aurei saeculi felicitatem redire videbantur qui illa celebrabant, et cum feris quandam communitatem inibant (Hartung, *Euripides restitutus* II 551). For a prose poem on the subject, see Maurice de Guèrin's *la Bacchante* p. 391 ff.

[2] At the festivals of Dionysus these marvellous streams may have been produced by mechanical means, as suggested by Hero *de automatis* p. 247 ed. 1693, ἐκ μὲν τοῦ θύρσου τοῦ Διονύσου ἤτοι γάλα ἢ ὕδωρ ἐκπιτυσθήσεται· ἐκ δὲ τοῦ σκύφους οἶνος ἐκχυθήσεται ἐπὶ τὸν ὑποκείμενον πανθηρίσκον κ.τ.λ.

rejoicings over the gathering in of the vintage; as well as in the feast of the wine-press called the Lenaea, in the ancient festival of the new-wine known as the Anthesteria, and chiefly in that of the great Dionysia,

> With its Bromian mirth, at the coming of spring;
> With the strife of its choirs, as they cheerily sing;
> With its Muse of the flute deep-murmuring. Ar. *Nubes* 311.

While, in Attica, his worship was thus blended with the refining influences of poetry and music, the wilder extravagances of his ritual seem to have lingered long among the barbarous tribes of Thrace.

Lastly, the legend told of the vengeance that visited all who opposed the worship of the god, and of this vengeance the two most signal instances were the fate of the Thracian king, Lycurgus, and the Theban prince, Pentheus. In the case of the former, all the revel-band of the god were captured by the king, but the women were soon set free: the land ceased to bear fruit, the king was struck with madness, killed his own son by mistake, and himself came to an untimely end, torn in pieces by horses at the bidding of Dionysus. After this, Dionysus, passing through Thrace without further resistance, returns to Thebes, the city of his birth, drives the women out of their homes, and makes them hold revel on Cithaeron, to the indignation of Pentheus, their youthful king, who is bent on putting a stop to the scandal and asserting his authority; he is lured out to the hills by Dionysus; where his mother, Agave, under the influence of Bacchic transport, mistaking him for a wild animal of the chase, tears him in pieces, and thus unwittingly kills her unhappy son.

§ 2. *The legend of Dionysus in Greek literature down to the time of Euripides.*

The earlier *Epic poetry* supplies us with a striking passage on the story of Lycurgus, king of Thrace, whose life, like that of Pentheus, is cut short by his hostility to Dionysus. It occurs in the episode of Glaucus and Diomede, where the former refers to the legend in the following terms :

> Against the gods of heaven I dare not fight,
> No! for e'en Dryas' son, Lycurgus strong,
> Lived not a long life, when he warred with heaven.
> He, on a day, from Nysa's haunts divine
> Drave forth the nurse-nymphs of mad Dionysus,
> Who all to earth flung down their holy gear,
> Struck by the ox-goad of the ruthless king.
> The god, affrighted, plunged beneath the wave,
> Where Thetis in her lap enfolded him
> Dazed by the king's rebuke. With *him* the gods
> Who lightly live were wroth, and Cronus' son
> Smote him with blindness. Aye! he lived not long,
> When once at war with all the immortal gods. *Il.* VI 129—140.

Elsewhere in the *Iliad*, Dionysus 'son of Semele' is described as a 'joy to mortals' (XIV 325, χάρμα βροτοῖσιν); when Andromache rushes forth from her loom to learn the fate of Hector, the poet compares her to a wild maenad (XXII 460, μαινάδι ἴση)[1]; the flute, which was a special characteristic of the worship of Dionysus, is only mentioned twice, once in the description of the marriage-feast in the Shield of Achilles (XVIII 495, αὐλοὶ φόρμιγγές τε), and again, of the music of Ilium heard in the Grecian camp by the sleepless Agamemnon (X 13, αὐλῶν

[1] Cf. Lobeck's *Aglaophamus*, 284—298.

συρίγγων τ' ἐνοπήν)—a passage which suggests the obvious remark that Homer assigns that instrument, not to the Greeks, but to the Trojans only[1]. In the *Odyssey* we find a passing allusion to the death of Ariadne (XI 325, Διονύσου μαρτυρίῃσιν); and the golden urn, mentioned in XXIV 74, is called the gift of Dionysus and the handiwork of Hephaestus, but the wine given to Odysseus in *Od.* IX 197 is mentioned as the gift, *not* of Dionysus, but of Maron son of Euanthes, priest of Apollo. Hesiod gives us little more than a general reference to the son of Zeus and Semele, Διώνυσος πολυγηθής (*Theog.* 941)[2], and Herodotus, who refers to his worship in Arabia, mentions him, with Hercules, and Pan, as the most recent of all the gods (II 145)[3].

From these meagre references we gladly turn to a passage of special interest, in connexion with his marvellous transformations. One of the Homeric hymns (VII) tells us how, on a day long ago, Dionysus, son of famous Semele, once appeared in the form of a youth in the bloom of life, standing on a head-land by the sea, with a purple robe around his shoulders, and his dark hair flowing adown his neck, when he was seized by some Tyrrhenian sailors who took him for a king's son and carried him off in their vessel, hoping for large ransom for him. They try to bind him fast, but the chains fall away from his hands and his feet, while he sits smiling at them with his dark-blue eyes. The helmsman alone pro-

---

[1] Cf. the statement criticised by Eustathius on *Il.* XVIII 495, φασὶν οἱ παλαιοὶ ὡς οὐδαμοῦ αὐλοὶ παρ᾽ Ἕλλησιν. See also Lobeck's *Aglaophamus*, p. 298 note. [2] Sc. *Herc.* 400 (ὅμφακες) οἷα Διώνυσος δῶκ ἀνδράσι χάρμα καὶ ἄχθος. [3] The testimony of Herodotus is discussed in Brown's *Dionysiak Myth* I pp. 163—226.

testing against the wrong, they sail away under a fair wind, with the captive youth, when suddenly throughout the dark ship a fragrant stream of wine gushes forth, the sail is entwined with a vine and fringed with clusters of grapes, the mast is hung with dark ivy, and with blooming flowers and beautiful berries, and the rowlocks are all wreathed with garlands. The youth now changes himself into a roaring lion, while, in the midst of the vessel, he conjures up a shaggy bear; the lion seizes the captain, while all the crew are driven into the sea and turned into dolphins—all save the good helmsman, to whom the youth in pity reveals himself as Διόνυσος ἐρίβρομος, and to whom he gives his gracious benediction. This adventure, one of the most poetical episodes in the legend of Dionysus, was also a favourite subject in ancient art, the best remaining example of which is the frieze of the choragic monument of Lysicrates, a cast of which may be seen in the British Museum[1].

Dionysus was also a favourite theme of *Lyric Poetry.* In contrast with the grave and sober music of the *Paean* of Apollo, we there have the wild and tumultuous strains of the *Dithyramb* of Dionysus, which was specially devoted to celebrating the birth of the god[2].

One of the many victories of the Acamantid tribe in a dithyrambic contest is the theme of an epinician epigram by Simonides (150 = 205); and among the

[1] See also Gerhard's *auserlesene Vasenbilder* I taf. 49, and *Archäologische Zeitung* 1874 taf. 5; cf. Philostratus *im.* I 19.

[2] Note on l. 526.

fragments of Archilochus is the following couplet referring to the dithyrambic song:

ὡς Διωνύσοι᾽ ἄνακτος καλὸν ἐξάρξαι μέλος
οἶδα διθύραμβον οἴνῳ συγκεραυνωθεὶς φρένας.

Pindar refers to Arion's improvement of the dithyramb as one of the glories of Corinth[1], he also alludes to the god's ivy crown (fragm. 103*), and to the worship of Διόνυσος δενδρίτης (fragm. 125)[2]; among the glories of his own Thebes, he mentions τὰν Διωνύσου πολυγαθέα τιμὰν (fragm. 5), and χαλκοκρότου πάρεδρον Δαμάτερος εὐρυχαίταν Διόνυσον (*Isthm.* VI [VII] 5). He further tells of the large recompense given to the daughters of Cadmus for all their sorrow, ζώει μὲν ἐν ᾽Ολυμπίοις ἀποθανοῖσα βρόμῳ κεραυνοῦ ταννέθειρα Σεμέλα, φιλεῖ δέ μιν Παλλὰς αἰεί, καὶ Ζεὺς πατὴρ μάλα· φιλεῖ δὲ παῖς ὁ κισσοφόρος (*Ol.* II 28)[3]; and, in the only fragment of his dithyrambs which has been preserved in any considerable length, he describes himself as πορευθέντ᾽ ἀοιδᾷ δεύτερον ἐπὶ κισσοδέταν θεόν, τὸν Βρόμιον τὸν ᾽Εριβόαν τε καλέομεν, closing with the line ἀχεῖται Σεμέλαν ἑλικάμπυκα χοροί[4].

The Greek *Drama*, as is well known, owed its origin to the dithyrambic choruses in the festivals of Dionysus, who was in fact the patron-god of the stage; the theatre at Athens was the 'theatre of Dionysus,' his altar stood in the centre of the 'or-

---

[1] ταὶ Διωνύσου πόθεν ἐξέφανεν σὺν βοηλάτᾳ χάριτες διθυράμβῳ;

[2] δενδρέων δὲ νομὸν Διόνυσος πολυγαθὴς αὐξάνοι, ἀγνὸν φέγγος ὀπώρας.

[3] See the exquisite Etruscan mirror in Müller-Wieseler, I lxi 308.

[4] For the minor lyric poets see Brown's *Dionysiak Myth* I 86—89.

chestra,' the middle stall in the foremost row of reserved seats was assigned to the priest of that god, and is still to be seen carved with the inscription, ΙΕΡΕΩΣ ΔΙΟΝΥΣΟΥ ΕΛΕΥΘΕΡΕΩΣ.[1] Hard by the theatre, was the most ancient sanctuary of Dionysus. When the traveller Pausanias visited Athens, he saw, within the sacred enclosure, two temples and two statues of Dionysus, one surnamed *Eleuthereus*, which was made of wood and received its name from the country *deme* of Eleutherae, the other made of ivory and gold, the work of Alcamenes. 'Here also,' he adds, 'are pictures representing Pentheus and Lycurgus being punished for the wrongs they had done to Dionysus[2].'

Tragedy, in particular, in its earlier forms, was in many ways connected with the god. His adventures were often the subject of the set speeches that were interspersed between the choral odes, and when the Tragedy of Thespis had established itself, before Comedy had come into existence, the populace, discontented with the serious style of the new dramatic exhibitions, and resenting the introduction into the performances, of other heroes than the familiar and favourite Dionysus, are said to have expressed their indignation at what they regarded as irrelevant matter in the clamorous protest, which afterwards became proverbial, τί ταῦτα πρὸς τὸν Διόνυσον;[3]

[1] Engraved in Haigh's *Attic Theatre*, p. 308.

[2] Pausanias 1 20 § 3, and 38 § 8 (Leake's *Athens* I p. 137).

[3] Plutarch *Sympos.* 1 1, Zenobius p. 40, and Suidas quoted in Donaldson's *Theatre of the Greeks*, chap. v. p. 69. He appears as the inventor of tragedy, holding a tragic mask in his left, and being crowned by Νίκη, on a vase in the British Museum, no. 1293.

To Thespis himself is attributed a play called the *Pentheus*, but the only line quoted as coming from it (ἔργῳ νόμιζε νεβρίδ' ἔχειν ἐπενδύτην) is probably to be ascribed to a pupil of Plato[1].

In *Aeschylus*, the doom of Pentheus is the subject of a well-known passage in the prologue of the *Eumenides*, where the Pythian priestess refers to the god, as having taken possession of the heights of Parnassus as his favoured haunt, after compassing the death of the Theban king:

> The Nymphs I worship, near the vaulted cave
> Corycian, home of birds and haunt of gods;
> And Bromius, I remember, guards the spot,
> Since erst that god, leading his Maenad host,
> Dealt death to Pentheus, like a hunted hare[2].

The same poet wrote a set of four plays on the doom of Lycurgus, known as the tetralogy of the Λυκουργεία, consisting of the 'Ηδωνοί, Βασσαρίδες, and Νεανίσκοι, followed by the satyric drama, Λυκοῦργος[3]. Among the fragments of the first play, we find a description, by a Thracian chorus, of the strange music of the god's retinue, the thrilling flute, the clanging cymbals, the twanging lute, the drum reverberating like subterranean thunder, and the deep tones of some other instrument unseen, whose sound resembles the bellowing of a bull (fragm. 55, partly quoted in note on l. 59). Just as in the *Bacchae*, so here, Dionysus is captured and brought before

---

[1] Heraclides Ponticus (Diogenes Laertius v § 92, referred to by Wecklein).

[2] *Eum.* 22—27, quoted on l. 559.

[3] *Scholium* on Ravenna MS of Aristophanes, *Thesm.* 135.

the king, who, like Pentheus, asks his girl-faced prisoner whence he came [1]. When the god reveals himself, the palace of Lycurgus, like that of the Theban
king, 'reels like a bacchanal inspired' before his
presence [2]. Lastly, the long-trailing robe, or *bassara*,
which gives the name to the Bacchanals who form
the chorus of the second piece in the trilogy, is referred to in the lines :

> ὅστις χιτῶνας βασσάρας τε Λυδίας
> ἔχει ποδήρεις (64 *b*).

Of the second play, we learn that it included an
account of the attack of the *Bassarides* on Orpheus,
who instead of honouring Dionysus adored the sun-
god Apollo, climbing the Pangaean mount betimes,
to do his reverence to the rising sun. They tore
him in pieces, and scattered his limbs abroad, every
one from its fellow (like those of Pentheus in our play);
but the Muses came and gathered them all together
and buried them. The few remaining lines are too
trivial to detain us; in one of them we have a reference to a 'bull goring' (22 *b*, cf. *Bacchae*, 743), in
another to a 'murky flame smouldering on an altar'
(22 *a*).

In the third play, in which the Thracian king
appears to have paid with his life the penalty of
opposing Dionysus, and yet to have been honoured
side by side with that god after his death, we find
little of special interest beyond the line describing

---

[1] Fragm. 56, quoted in note on l. 460.

[2] Fragm. 64 *a*, quoted in note on l. 726.

the breezes that play in the cool and shady haunts
of the gods: αὔρας [v.l. σαύρας] ὑποσκίοισιν ἐν ψυκτη-
ρίοις.

The fragments of the satyric drama at the close
of the tetralogy contain nothing that is of any
importance for our purpose[1].

There was also a trilogy of Aeschylus, on the
doom of Pentheus, which probably consisted of the
following pieces : (1) Σεμέλη ἢ ὑδροφόροι, (2) Βάκχαι,
(3) Πενθεύς. One of the fragments of the first apparently refers to the alleged death of the son of Semele
by the thunderbolts of Zeus[2] ; another to the
'Thyiades that banquet on raw flesh[3].' From (2),
which is sometimes identified with (3), not a single
fragment has been preserved; from the *Pentheus*,
we have only a solitary line (μηδ' αἵματος πέμφιγα
πρὸς πέδῳ βάλῃς), alluding possibly to the bloodless
victory over the Bacchae which Dionysus bids the
king look forward to, as the result of his espial (cf.
804, and contrast 837). His death was referred to
in another play called the Ξάντριαι, the title of
which was formerly understood of the Bacchantes
tearing their victims in pieces,—a meaning suggested
by the use of the verb ξαίνειν in a passage of Philostratus describing the rending asunder of the limbs

---

[1] They happen to include one of the earliest references to malt
liquor, or barley mead (123, κἀκ τῶνδ' ἔπινε βρῦτον ἰσχναίνων χρόνῳ
κἀσεμνοκόμπει τοῦτ' ἐν ἀνδρείᾳ στέγῃ).

[2] Ζεὺς ὃς κατέκτα τοῦτον, cf. l. 244.

of Pentheus[1]. It appears simpler, however, to take it in the more obvious sense of 'the wool-carding women[2].' In the *Bacchae* we read of *all* the women being driven from the looms to the mountains by the frenzy inspired by Dionysus (118, 1236); and in the earlier treatment of the same, or at any rate a similar, subject by Aeschylus, the chorus may possibly have consisted of the sober and stay-at-home women who went on working with their wool instead of joining the revels on the hills. It has been ingeniously suggested that the play may have referred, not to the story of Pentheus, but to another part of the legend of Dionysus, the 'wool-carders' being in this case the daughters of Minyas, who, when the worship of Dionysus was established in Boeotia, after the death of Pentheus, instead of taking part in the orgies in Cithaeron, remained in their home engaged in spinning and weaving wool, and were duly punished by the god for their neglect of his rites[3].

---

[1] Quoted on l. 1136 (so Elmsley, p. 15).

[2] *mulieres lanificae; Od.* XXII 423, εἰριά τε ξαίνειν, Eur. *Or.* 12, στέμματα ξήνασα (of one of the Parcae).

[3] Ovid *Met.* IV 1—54; 329—415, esp. 32—35, *solae Minyeides intus, intempestiva turbantes festa Minerva, aut ducunt lanas, aut stamina pollice versant, aut haerent telae, famulasque laboribus urgent.* This interpretation of the name Ξάντριαι is supported by Wecklein, who quotes Böckh, *Graec. trag. princ.* c. iii, and assigns the play to the same trilogy as the (Διονύσου) τροφοί and the 'Αθάμας. According to the legend as related in Apollodorus (III 4 § 3), Zeus, when Dionysus had been born from his thigh, sent the infant by the hands of Hermes to be brought up by Semele's sister Ino and that sister's husband Athamas. Both of them were struck mad by Hera, Athamas mistook one of his sons for a lion's cub (cf. fragm. 4 *a*, βρυαζούσης λεαίνης, and Ovid *l. c.* 513, *cum gemina...prole leaena*), while Ino slew the other.

But however this may be, we may be sure that
the death of Pentheus was either incidentally or fully
referred to in the tragedy, and that it took place,
as in our own play, on mount Cithaeron[1]; and it is
highly probable that the 'stakes of pine in flame
enfolded,' mentioned in one of the fragments[2], were
the torches used by the Bacchae in their attack on
the intruder Pentheus, in exactly the same manner as
is represented on a work of ancient art figured on a
subsequent page (lxxxviii).   Thus it would appear
that the *manner* of his death, as referred to by Aeschylus, was somewhat different to that which is related
by Euripides.   In the same play Lyssa, the goddess
of Madness, appears in person, as in the *Hercules
furens* of our poet, and incites the Bacchae in a
stirring speech in which she apparently compares the
frenzy she inspires with the convulsions caused by
the scorpion's sting[3].   Another fragment tells of a
place 'unlit by ray of sun or moon'; words which
possibly describe a gloomy dungeon like that in
l. 510 (σκότιον κνέφας).

As we leave these few fragments of Aeschylus on
the worship of Dionysus, we may well remark, with

---

[1] Schol. on Aesch. *Eum.* 24, νῦν φησιν ἐν Παρνασῷ εἶναι τὰ κατὰ
Πενθέα· ἐν δὲ ταῖς Ξαντρίαις ἐν Κιθαιρῶνι.   The former part of this note
is clearly wrong, as Aeschylus in the *Eumenides* says nothing of the
place where Pentheus was slain, but only alludes to the god's making
the Corycian cave on Parnassus his haunt, *after* putting the Theban
king to death (doubtless, as in the *Xantriae*, on Cithaeron).

[2] Pollux : τὰς μέντοι λαμπάδας καὶ κάμακας εἴρηκεν ἐν Ξαντρίαις
Αἰσχύλος ' κάμακες πεύκης οἱ πυρίφλεκτοι ' (fragm. 167).

[3] Fragm. 165.   Eur., in l. 977, speaks of the 'hounds of Lyssa.'

Milman, that 'the loss of these Aeschylean tragedies is to be deplored more than that of any of the poet's works, except perhaps his *Niobe*. What must they have been, with his lofty fearlessness of religious conception, his massy power and grandeur, and his lyric language unrivalled in its rude picturesqueness?' 'We would willingly know, too,' he adds, 'how such a subject could have been treated by the grave and reverent Sophocles[1].'

Among the lost plays of *Sophocles* is one called the Ὑδροφόροι, which may possibly have been, like the play of Aeschylus already mentioned, an alternative title for a Σεμέλη; but hardly anything remains to indicate its subject, except the bald statement that the author there used Βακχᾶν in the same sense as Βακχευτάν. His son, Iophon, wrote a *Pentheus* and a *Bacchae* (unless indeed these plays were identical), and a play of the latter name was included in the tetralogy with which Xenocles was victorious over Euripides in the year 415 B.C.[2] Sophocles himself, in his extant tragedies, has a few graceful passages

---

[1] *Agamemnon and Bacchanals*, p. 96.

[2] Aelian *Var. Hist.* II 8, κατὰ τὴν πρώτην καὶ ἐνενηκοστὴν Ὀλυμπιάδα, καθ' ἣν ἐνίκα Ἐξαίνετος ὁ Ἀκραγαντῖνος στάδιον, ἀντηγωνίσαντο ἀλλήλοις Ξενοκλῆς καὶ Εὐριπίδης. καὶ πρῶτός γε ἦν Ξενοκλῆς, ὅστις ποτὲ οὗτός ἐστιν, Οἰδίποδι καὶ Λυκάονι καὶ Βάκχαις καὶ Ἀθάμαντι Σατυρικῷ. τούτου δεύτερος Εὐριπίδης ἦν Ἀλεξάνδρῳ καὶ Παλαμήδει καὶ Τρωσὶ καὶ Σισύφῳ Σατυρικῷ. γελοῖον δὲ (οὐ γάρ;) Ξενοκλέα μὲν νικᾶν, Εὐριπίδην δὲ ἡττᾶσθαι, καὶ ταῦτα τοιούτοις δράμασι. τῶν δύο τοίνυν τὸ ἕτερον· ἢ ἀνόητοι ἦσαν οἱ τῆς ψήφου κύριοι καὶ ἀμαθεῖς καὶ πόρρω κρίσεως ὀρθῆς, ἢ ἐδεκάσθησαν. ἄτοπον δὲ ἑκάτερον καὶ Ἀθηναίων ἥκιστα ἄξιον. On the small number of victories won by the greatest dramatists, v. Meineke *Com. Frag.* ii 904.

referring to the legend of Dionysus. In the *Oedipus Tyrannus*, for example, the god is invoked as follows by a Theban chorus:

"We call on the god of the golden crown (χρυσομίτραν), whose name is linked with the name of our land, the ruddy (οἰνῶπα) boisterous Bacchus, the comrade of the Maenads; we call on him to come, and flash his flaming brand, against the war-god whom the gods disown." (211—215.)

At a later point in the same play, the Chorus, while musing on the birth of Oedipus, wonders whether he is the offspring of one of the gods, of Pan or Apollo or Hermes;

"or haply the Bacchic god, who dwells upon the mountain-peaks, received him as a gift from one of the Nymphs of Helicon with whom he loves to sport." (1105.)

Again, in the *Oedipus Coloneus*, the representation of which by the poet's grandson, in B.C. 401, belongs to a date later than the *Bacchae*, (though it was written possibly many years before,) the choral ode, which the familiar anecdote connects with the author's declining years, describes, as a haunt of Dionysus,

"the gleaming Colonus; where down in the fresh green dells the clear-voiced nightingale most loves to sing, true evermore to the purpling ivy and to the god's own sacred leafage, with its unnumbered fruit inviolate, that knows no heat of sun, no blast of storm; where Dionysus, lord of revel, wanders, dancing around the nymphs divine who nursed his youth." (670—680.)

In the earliest of his plays whose date is known, the *Antigone* of 440 B.C., we have the following reference to the legend of Lycurgus:

"Fast bound, besides, was Dryas' son, the Edonian king of temper keen, who, for his bitter taunts, was enchained in a dungeon of rock, by the will of Dionysus. So dread is the full bloom of wrath that issues from madness like his; but at last he learnt that in all his frenzy, 'twas the god himself that he was taunting with bitter tongue; for he fain would have quelled the dames inspired, and quenched the Evian torch, and vexed the heart of the Muses to whom the flute is dear." (955—965.)

The parallel story of Pentheus is, however, never referred to by Sophocles; to have devoted a whole tragedy to a theme into which the wild enthusiasm of Bacchanalian revelry must necessarily have largely entered, would perhaps have been hardly in keeping with the calm and serene composure which is one of the main characteristics of that poet's temper. But we may well regret that the legend of Dionysus was not more fully handled by one who could write the brilliant ode in the *Antigone*, where the god is summoned to the relief of the plague-stricken place of his birth. It is a perfect mosaic of happy allusion to his varied attributes, to his favoured haunts and to his wide-spread worship; and, as many of these points will meet us again in the play which we are about to study, we may close this brief review of the literary treatment of the legend before the time of Euripides with an attempt to render the ode in question (1115—52).

> Hail, thou god of many names,
>   Pride of Theban Semele,
> Born to Zeus mid lightning flames,
>   Strength of glorious Italy!
> O'er Deo's dells thy power presideth,
>   Where Eleusis welcomes all;
> Where Ismenos softly glideth,
>   Bacchic god, on thee we call;
> In Thebes, the Bacchant's home, to dwell thou deignest,
> And o'er the brood of the fierce dragon reignest.

O'er the double-crested height,
  Where the nymphs Corycian roam,
Looks on thee the lurid light,
  Where Castalia falls in foam.
Nysa's hillside ivy-clad,
  And the bright Euboean shore,
Green with vines, with clusters glad,
  Haply soon shall waft thee o'er.
Oh ! haste to Thebes and all her calling streets;
A people's holy cry thy coming greets.

  Far above all towns that be,
  Thebes is honoured most by thee,
  And Semele, the thunder-slain ;
E'en now, when all our thronging town
With dire disease is stricken down,
Speed hither, speed ! with healing in thy train,
O'er high Parnassus, or the moaning main.

  Leader of the heavenly quire
  Of dancing stars that throb with fire !
  Shine, son of Zeus ! upon our sight,
Thou ruler of the midnight voices,
  Thou king, whose Thyiad-band rejoices
In madding dances all the live-long night,
Iacchos praising, lord of their delight.

§ 3. *Euripides in Macedonia.*

While we are told of Sophocles that, so strong was his love for Athens, that none of the kings, who invited him to their courts, could induce him to leave his country[1]; the closing years of Euripides, like those of Aeschylus at the court of Hiero, were spent far away from the land of his birth. He was weary, perhaps, of scenes of domestic discomfort; he had been persecuted in the *Thesmophoriazusae* by the taunts of that licensed libeller, Aristophanes; and the shadows of unpopularity were possibly already gathering round his friend, Socrates[2], while Alcibiades, in honour of whose Olympic victory he had composed a song of triumph[3], was now a condemned exile. Accordingly, the aged poet retired from Athens. He visited, in the first instance, Magnesia, where he was received with special distinction[4], and where we may fancy him looking from the shores of the Pagasaean bay toward the pine-woods of mount Pelion, and recalling the prologue of his own *Medea:*

> Oh! that the Argo ne'er had winged her way
> To Colchis, 'twixt the blue Symplegades;
> Nor the cleft pine e'er fall'n in Pelion's glens.

[1] οὕτω φιλαθηναιότατος ἦν. *Vit. anon.*

[2] Diogen. Laert. *Socr.* II 5, ἐδόκει δὲ συμποιεῖν Εὐριπίδῃ. ὅθεν Μνησίλοχος οὕτω φησί· Φρύγες ἐστὶ καινὸν δρᾶμα τοῦτ' Εὐριπίδου, | ᾧ καὶ τὰ φρύγαν' ὑποτίθησι Σωκράτης. Aelian *Var. Hist.* II 13, ὁ δὲ Σωκράτης σπάνιον μὲν ἐπεφοίτα τοῖς θεάτροις, εἴ ποτε δὲ Εὐριπίδης ὁ τῆς τραγῳδίας ποιητὴς ἠγωνίζετο καινοῖς τραγῳδοῖς, τότε γε ἀφικνεῖτο...ἔχαιρε γὰρ τῷ ἀνδρὶ διά τε τὴν σοφίαν αὐτοῦ καὶ τὴν ἐν τοῖς μέτροις ἀρετήν.

[3] Plutarch *Alcib.* xi.

[4] *vit. Eur.* (in Nauck's ed. p. v, l. 21), μετέστη δὲ ἐν Μαγνησίᾳ καὶ προξενίᾳ ἐτιμήθη καὶ ἀτελείᾳ.

From Magnesia he proceeded to the court of Archelaus, king of Macedonia. Socrates himself was also invited by that king; but, true to himself, he declined the compliment, on the ground that it was as degrading to accept a favour when unable to return it, as to receive an injury when incapable of requiting it[1]. The philosopher may well have had other reasons for refusing the invitation, as he was doubtless aware of the career of crime by which the king had won the throne. A graphic description of that career is, at any rate, to be found in a dialogue between Socrates and Polus, in the following passage from the *Gorgias* of Plato:—

'*Polus.* You see, I presume, that Archelaus the son of Perdiccas is King of Macedonia. *Socr.* Well, if I don't, I hear of him, at any rate. *Polus.* Is he happy, then, in your opinion, or wretched? *Socr.* I don't know, Polus, for I have not the honour of his acquaintance. *Polus.* What then? Do you mean to say you could find it out, by making his acquaintance? Don't you know already, that he is happy? *Socr.* No, indeed, I don't. *Polus.* Then it's clear, Socrates, that you will say that you don't know that 'the Great King' is happy either. *Socr.* And if I do, I shall be speaking the truth; for I don't know what is his condition in regard to mental cultivation and moral character. *Polus.* How then? Does happiness consist in this alone? *Socr.* Yes, according to *my* view, Polus; the man or woman who is gentle and good, I say, is happy, and one that is unjust and wicked is miserable. *Polus.* Then, according to *your* account, the said Archelaus is miserable. *Socr.* Yes, my friend, if he is unjust he is. *Polus.* Why, of course, he is unjust; he had no claim at all to the throne which he now holds, as he was the son of a woman who was the slave of his father Perdiccas' brother, Alcetas; and therefore in strict *right*, he was himself the slave of Alcetas; and, if he had wanted to do what was 'right,' he would have been

---

[1] Ar. *Rhet.* II 23 § 8, Σωκράτης οὐκ ἔφη βαδίζειν ὡς Ἀρχέλαον· ὕβριν γὰρ ἔφη εἶναι τὸ μὴ δύνασθαι ἀμύνασθαι ὁμοίως εὖ παθόντα ὥσπερ καὶ κακῶς. Stobaeus 97 p. 522. Diog. Laert. II 5 § 9.

the slave of Alcetas, and 'happy' according to your account; but, as it is, he has become unspeakably miserable, for he has committed acts of the gravest injustice.   In the first place, he invited to court this very same master and uncle of his, on the pretence of intending to restore him to the throne which Perdiccas had usurped; and after entertaining him and his son Alexander, his own cousin, about the same age as himself, and making them drunk, he stowed them away in a carriage, drove them off by night, killed them both and made away with their bodies.   And, after all this wickedness, he never discovered that he had made himself the most 'miserable' of men, he never repented of what he had done; he did not choose to make himself 'happy' by bringing up, as he was bound to do, his brother, the true son of Perdiccas, a boy of some seven years of age, to whom the throne rightly belonged, and by restoring to him his kingdom.   No! far from it; not long after, he threw him into a well and drowned him, and then told his mother Cleopatra, that he had tumbled in, just as he was chasing a goose, and had so come by his death.   Accordingly, as he is now the greatest criminal in Macedonia, he is doubtless the most 'miserable' of all the Macedonians, and not the happiest; and I dare say there are a good many people in Athens, who, with *you* at their head, would rather change places with any Macedonian you please to name, than with King Archelaus[1].'

Antecedents such as these may well have deterred Socrates from presenting himself at the court of the king; Euripides, however, poet and philosopher in one[2], accepted the invitation which the philosopher declined.   For, in justice to this most 'unjust' Archelaus, we are bound to admit that he appears to have governed well the kingdom that he had won by crime, thus proving an exception to the rule laid down by Tacitus, *nemo unquam imperium flagitio quaesitum bonis artibus exercuit*[3].   He built fortresses, developed the means of communication between various portions of

---

[1] Plato *Gorgias* 470 D—471 D (mainly from Cope's translation).

[2] Vitruvius viii, praef., *Euripides, auditor Anaxagorae, quem philosophum Athenienses scenicum appellaverunt.*

[3] *Hist.* 1 30.

his territory, and equipped himself with an ample
supply of horses and arms, by which the military
resources of his dominion were improved to a greater
extent by himself alone than by all his eight prede-
cessors put together[1]. He not only did all this, but
(like the Elder Dionysius not long after) he also
became a distinguished patron of art and literature.
His palace was lavishly embellished with paintings by
Zeuxis[2], who presented his patron with a picture of
Pan for which he would accept no remuneration, on
the ground that the work was beyond all price[3]. As
a descendant of the Heracleid Temenidae of Argos,
the king may have feasted his eyes on pictures by that
artist representing the exploits of Hercules, his heroic
ancestor[4]; the patron of the poet of the *Bacchae* may
have had his walls adorned with those pendent grapes,
in painting which, according to the familiar story,
Zeuxis was unrivalled[5]. Either at Aegae, the ancient
capital, or at Dium on the sea-coast, the king established 'Olympian' festivals in honour of the Muses[6].
At his court was the tragic poet Agathon, the first to
set the pernicious precedent of introducing into his plays
choral odes which had no connexion with the plot[7],—
Agathon, the genial host of Plato's *Symposium*, who was

[1] Thuc. II 100.

[2] Aelian *Var. Hist.* XIV 17 (at the cost of 400 *minae*).

[3] Pliny *Nat. Hist.* XXXV § 62.

[4] Such as *Hercules infans dracones strangulans*, painted by Zeuxis,
apparently however for Agrigentum (Pliny *u. s.*).

[5] Pliny *u. s.*, § 66.

[6] See note on l. 409.

[7] Aristot. *Poet.* 18, 22, ἐμβόλιμα ᾄδουσι, πρῶτον ἄρξαντος ᾿Αγάθωνος
τοιούτου.

complimented by Euripides himself, while reclining at
the king's table with his brother poet, as 'handsome
not only in the spring-time, but also in the autumn of
life[1].' There too, was the famous musician and dithyrambic poet, Timotheus, who, when hissed off the
stage for his bold innovations, had been re-assured
by Euripides with the prediction that 'he would soon
have the theatres at his feet[2].' And there, also, was
Choerilus, the writer of the great epic on the wars of
the Greeks with Xerxes and Dareius[3].

In this goodly company, Euripides composed a
play to which, in compliment to his patron, he gave
the name of 'Archelaus'[4]; and it was almost certainly
at the court of that king, that he either wrote the play
which is now before us, or, at any rate, gave it the last
finishing touches. This conclusion is rendered highly
probable by its complimentary references to the haunt
of the Muses in Pieria, which was part of the king's
dominions ; to the hallowed slope of Olympus, the
most prominent object in the Pierian landscape (ll.
409—415); and to the 'swift stream' of Axius (568),
which after bursting its way through what is known
as the Iron Gate between the Scardus and Orbelus

---

[1] Aelian *Var. Hist.* XIII 4, οὐ γὰρ μόνον τὸ ἔαρ τῶν καλῶν καλόν
ἐστιν, ἀλλὰ καὶ τὸ μετόπωρον.

[2] Plutarch, *an seni sit gerenda respublica* xxiii. § 4, p. 795 c—d.
Τιμόθεον Εὐριπίδης, συριττόμενον ἐπὶ τῇ καινοτομίᾳ καὶ παρανομεῖν εἰς
τὴν μουσικὴν δοκοῦντα, θαρρεῖν ἐκέλευσεν, ὡς ὀλίγου χρόνου τῶν θεάτρων
ὑπ' αὐτῷ γενησομένων. He composed a dithyramb on ' the travail of
Semele,' Boethius, *de musica*, I I. See also Plut. *apophth.* p. 177.

[3] Athenaeus VIII p. 345 E.

[4] *vit. Eur.*, Nauck, p. vi, l. 23, χαριζόμενος αὐτῷ δρᾶμα ὁμωνύμως
ἔγραψε.

ranges, and passing through the great upland plain of
Pelagonia, one of the primitive seats of the Macedonian
race, becomes the principal river of Macedonia itself,
finding its way at last into the Mediterranean at the
head of the gulf of Therma[1]. The poet also refers, in
terms of praise, to the less important stream of the
Loidias (571), one of whose tributaries rises near
Aegae, or Edessa, the ancient capital of the Macedonian kingdom. Aegae is the modern *Vodhená*,
a place remarkable for the strategic importance of its
position and the beauty of its surroundings, standing
as it does at a point commanding communication with
the upper country, and now traversed by a 'clear river
which descends from the upper part of the valley and
divides into a number of smaller streams which pass
through the town, and plunge at various points down
the steep rocks[2].' The prospect from its terraces extends over the plain of lower Macedonia which is
celebrated by Euripides as 'the land of noble horses,'
'fertilized by fairest waters' (571—5). About halfway between Aegae and the sea were the low hills
and the widespread marshes, which marked the site
of Pella[3], destined ere long to become the capital of

[1] Tozer, *Geography of Greece*, pp. 200—202.

[2] *id.* p. 203. Curtius, *H. G.* v 21. Abel, *Mak. vor Philipp*, 110—5.

[3] It is often stated by modern writers that Euripides spent the last
years of his life at Pella, and not, as seems more natural, at Aegae, the
capital (apparently) of Archelaus. The evidence of late authorities,
writing at a time when the fame of the earlier capital had been eclipsed
by that of the later, appears to me almost worthless in such a matter.
Nothing more than a tomb in Macedonia need be meant in the anonymous epigram which closes with the couplet: ἀλλ' ἔμολες Πελλαῖον
ὑπ' ἠρίον, ὡς ἂν ὁ λάτρις Πιερίδων ναίῃς ἀγχόθι Πιερίδων (*Anthol. Pal.*

one of the successors of Archelaus, Philip of Macedon, and to be the birthplace of Alexander the Great; while to the south, the landscape was closed by the mighty mass of the snowy Olympus.

Whether the play, written in whole or in part among the surroundings above described, was actually represented at the court of Archelaus, is a question on which we have no evidence. We may, however, observe that the theme selected would have probably found an appreciative audience in Macedonia. The subjects of Archelaus would be well acquainted with the story of Lycurgus, king of the adjoining district of Thrace; and the legend of Pentheus, the Theban parallel to the Thracian story, would have the advantage of being less trite and familiar to the Macedonian people. Further, the worship of Dionysus would seem to have met with an enthusiastic reception among the wild tribes of that region; this may be concluded from the terms in which Plutarch in his life of Alexander introduces an anecdote of Olympias, belonging to a date about fifty years after that of this

---

VII 44). The only other writer, so far as I can find, who mentions Pella in connexion with Eur., is Suidas s. v. Εὐριπίδης : καὶ τὰ ὀστᾶ αὐτοῦ ἐν Πέλλῃ μετακομίσαι τὸν βασιλέα. Pella, which, in the time of Philip's father Amyntas (B.C. 392), is extolled as μεγίστη τῶν ἐν Μακεδονίᾳ πόλεων (Xen. *Hell.* v 2 § 12), is depreciated by Demosthenes as being, at the accession of Philip himself, a χωρίον ἄδοξον καὶ μικρόν,—in comparison, that is, with its later fame, and in contrast, as the context shews, with the glory of Athens (*de cor.* p. 247). Abel *u. s.* p. 198, says : *unter Archelaos trat diese Stadt, soweit es irgend möglich war, an die Stelle von Edessa:* but I can find no clear authority for this statement. See *infra* p. cxxxvi. See also Leake's *Northern Greece*, iii 258—279.

play. 'All the women of this region,' he remarks, 'being of old time under the influence of the Orphic rites and the orgies of Dionysus, and bearing the name of Κλώδωνες and Μιμαλλόνες, have customs similar in many respects to the Edonian and the Thracian women near mount Haemus. But Olympias, who more than the rest affected these wild raptures and carried her enthusiasm to a still stranger pitch (βαρβαρικώτε-ρον), was wont to carry about in the revel-bands huge tame serpents, which often crept out of the ivy and the mystic baskets, and entwined themselves round the sacred wands and garlands of the women, to the terror of the men' (II § 5). It was on such an occasion as this, that Olympias, the mother of Alexander, first won the admiration of Philip of Macedon.

In Macedonia Euripides died, in B.C. 406, in the seventy-fifth year of his age[1]. The strangest legends were told of the manner of his death, possibly invented by the comic poets of his own time, or the scandal-mongers of a later generation, who, wilfully confound-ing (it may be) the fate of the poet with that of Pentheus in this, perhaps his latest, play, described him as having met his end by being torn in pieces by some infuriated women. According to another equally improbable story, indignantly denied in a well-known epigram, he was worried to death by the dogs of Archelaus[2].

He was buried near the town of Arethusa in the pass of Aulon, at a spot where two streams met, one

---

[1] Diodorus XIII 103 (Nauck *Eur.* p. x, note 3).
[2] *Anth. Pal.* VII 51, οὔ σε κυνῶν γένος εἷλ', Εὐριπίδη, κ.τ.λ.

of them famed for its healthful water, while it was
death to drink of the other[1]. His tomb was struck
by lightning, a distinction which it shared with that of
the Spartan lawgiver Lycurgus[2]. At Athens, on hearing
of his death, Sophocles, we are told, put on mourning
himself, and at a public representation in the theatre
ordered his actors and chorus to lay aside their crowns;
and all the people wept. His countrymen, who in
vain pleaded for his remains, built a cenotaph in his
honour, which was seen in the second century of our
era by the traveller Pausanias as he made his way
from Peiraeus to Athens along the ruins of the long-
walls of Conon[3]. It stood near the monument of one
whose style had many points in common with that of
Euripides, the comic poet Menander, and it bore the
following inscription, attributed to the historian Thu-
cydides, but composed more probably by the poet
and musician Timotheus:

μνῆμα μὲν Ἑλλὰς ἅπασ' Εὐριπίδου· ὀστέα δ' ἴσχει
  γῆ Μακεδών, ἥπερ[4] δέξατο τέρμα βίου·
πάτρη δ' Ἑλλάδος Ἑλλὰς, Ἀθῆναι· πολλὰ δὲ Μούσας[5]
  τέρψας, ἐκ πολλῶν καὶ τὸν ἔπαινον ἔχει.

(Anth. Pal. VII 45.)

Euripides, all Hellas is a monument to thee;
Thy bones hath Macedonia, that saw thy latter days,
And yet, thy home was Athens, the heart of Hellas she,
And thou, the Muse's darling, hast won the meed of praise.

[1] Ammianus Marc. 27, 4, 8; Pliny *Nat. Hist.* 31, 19; Vitruvius 8,
3 (Nauck *Eur.* p. xxi).
[2] Plut. *Lycurg.* 31.   [3] Pausanias I 2, 2.
[4] ms. ἥ γὰρ, al. τῇ γὰρ.
[5] al. μούσαις (thou, whose Muses charmed us).

S. B.   *d*

Another epigram refers as follows to his burial in Macedonia, and bids the poet rest assured that his fame will rival that of Homer:

χαῖρε μελαμπετάλοις[1], Εὐριπίδη, ἐν γυάλοισι
  Πιερίας τὸν ἀεὶ νυκτὸς ἔχων θάλαμον·
ἴσθι δ' ὑπὸ χθονὸς ὤν, ὅτι σοι κλέος ἄφθιτον ἔσται
  ἴσον Ὁμηρείαις ἀενάοις χάρισιν.

(VII 43.)

> Though, 'mid Pieria's dells of leafy gloom,
> In endless night thou sleepest in the tomb,
> Rest sure, though laid in dust, thy fame for aye
> Shall rival Homer's charms that never die.

[1] Lobeck's emendation for μελαμπέπλοις.

TERRACOTTA RELIEF IN THE BRITISH MUSEUM.

§ 4. *The Bacchae of Euripides : an outline of the play, with some account of its representation on the stage.*

After the death of Euripides, his son or nephew, who bore the same name, exhibited the *Bacchae*, together with the *Alcmaeon in Corinth*, and the *Iphigeneia in Aulis*[1]. No ingenuity, however, is ever likely to find any point in common which would justify the three plays being regarded as a trilogy in the ordinary acceptation of the term[1]. It is probably this trilogy to which the prize was awarded after the poet's death[2].

It may be added that the date of its representation was almost certainly after that of the *Ranae* of Aristophanes, which, as is well known, was brought out in B. C. 405, shortly after the death of Euripides and Sophocles. Had the *Bacchae* been exhibited before the *Ranae*, the latter would inevitably have contained some reference to the former, especially as the character of Dionysus is common to both, and several points in the play of Euripides would lend themselves readily to the criticism of the comic poet[3].

The *persons* of the play are

DIONYSUS, a god in the likeness of man, son of Zeus and Semele, daughter of Cadmus.

---

[1] Schol. Ar. *Ran.* 67, αἱ διδασκαλίαι φέρουσι τελευτήσαντος Εὐριπίδου τὸν υἱὸν αὐτοῦ δεδιδαχέναι ὁμώνυμον ἐν ἄστει Ἰφιγένειαν τὴν ἐν Αὐλίδι, Ἀλκμαίωνα, Βάκχας.

[2] Suidas, νίκας ἀνείλετο τέσσαρας περιών, τὴν δὲ μίαν μετὰ τὴν τελευτήν, ἐπιδειξαμένου τὸ δρᾶμα τοῦ ἀδελφιδοῦ αὐτοῦ Εὐριπίδου.

[3] Cf. Boeckh, *Graec. tragoed. princ.*, p. 306.

d 2

TEIRESIAS, an aged prophet.

CADMUS, founder, and sometime king, of Thebes.

AGAVE, one of the daughters of Cadmus.

PENTHEUS, king of Thebes, son of Agave.

THE KING'S ATTENDANT.

FIRST MESSENGER, a herdsman.

SECOND MESSENGER, one of the King's attendants.

CHORUS of Asiatic women, worshippers of Dionysus.

As there are only three actors, the *cast* of the play would probably be as follows:

First Actor (πρωταγωνιστής), Dionysus and Teiresias.

Second Actor (δευτεραγωνιστής), Pentheus and Agave.

Third Actor (τριταγωνιστής), Cadmus, Attendant, First and Second Messengers.

This arrangement enables us to assign to the first actor a leading part throughout the play, including the delivery of the opening speech. The famous actor Theodorus, as we learn from Arist. *Pol.* IV (VII) 17 § 13, always made a point of taking the opening part, because it ensured his winning the attention of the audience at the very outset. The *rôle* of Agave, though comparatively short, would require good acting, and it is possibly this that has led Wecklein to assign Agave and Pentheus to the πρωταγωνιστής. There is no difficulty in giving the Second Messenger's speech to the Second Actor; this would be quite consistent with the suggestion referred to in the note on l. 1153, where the parts of the Second Messenger and Agave are assigned to the same player; it also harmonizes with the combination of parts incidentally implied in the anecdote of the recital of a scene from this play in the Parthian camp on the death of Crassus (note on 1169). The arrangement proposed in Donaldson's *Theatre of the Greeks,* p. 296, is somewhat different:

'*Protagonist:* Dionysus, Teiresias, and the second messenger.
Deuteragonist: Cadmus, servant, first messenger.
Tritagonist: Pentheus, Agave[1].'

Throughout the play, the *Scene* is laid before the palace of Pentheus in the Cadmeia, the citadel of Thebes in the northern part of the town, the direction furthest removed from Cithaeron where the Bacchanals are holding revel. The towers of Thebes are referred to in the course of the play (172), but we need not suppose that the scenery included any representation of them. The mechanical contrivance known as the *periactos* is visible at each of the two extremities of the stage; the *periactos* on the spectators' left conventionally indicating the direction of the road to foreign and distant parts, while that on the right denotes the way to the town and to the neighbouring range of Cithaeron, which would naturally be reached by going through the town and leaving it by the

---

[1] Compare the same scholar's edition of the *Antigone,* p. 20.

Electran gates¹. The palace is a building in the Doric style, with its columns supporting an entablature, in which the triglyphs, characteristic of that order, may be seen (591, 1214). Near the palace is the monument of Semele, marking the place where she was struck dead by lightning,—a spot fenced off from profanation and mantled over with a clustering vine ; over it a dull flame is flickering which will be kindled into brightness as the action of the play advances (594—9, 623), while around it are the still smouldering ruins of the house in which she was slain.

πρόλογος (1—63). The prologue is spoken by the god Dionysus, who enters from the left of the stage. He appears in the form of man, disguised as one of his own votaries, as leader of a revel-band of women whom he has escorted from Lydia, and who form the *Chorus* of the play. In his hand he holds the *thyrsus* (495), his hair falls in long ringlets down his neck (493, ἁβρὸς βόστρυχος, and 235, 455) ; he has a flushed cheek

¹ The περίακτοι (sc. θύραι) appear to have been 'revolving doors in the form of a triangular prism, which stood before the side-doors on the stage and by turning round on a pivot indicated the different regions supposed to lie in the neighbourhood of the scene'; *Theatre of the Greeks*, p. 239. Julius Pollux, IV § 126, παρ' ἑκάτερα δὲ τῶν δύο θυρῶν τῶν περὶ τὴν μέσην, ἄλλαι δύο εἶεν ἄν, μία ἑκατέρωθεν, πρὸς ἃς αἱ περίακτοι συμπεπήγασιν· ἡ μὲν δεξιὰ (on the right of the stage, i.e. the left of the spectators,) τὰ ἔξω πόλεως δηλοῦσα, ἡ δ' ἀριστερὰ τὰ ἐκ πόλεως· μάλιστα τὰ ἐκ λιμένος... εἰ δὲ ἐπιστραφεῖεν οἱ περίακτοι ἡ δεξιὰ μὲν ἀμείβει τόπον· ἀμφότεραι δὲ χώραν ὑπαλλάττουσι. τῶν μέντοι παρόδων ἡ μὲν δεξιὰ (on the right of the spectators) ἀγρόθεν (al. ἀγορῆθεν), ἢ ἐκ λιμένος, ἢ ἐκ πόλεως ἄγει· οἱ δὲ ἀλλαχόθεν πεζοὶ ἀφικνούμενοι, κατὰ τὴν ἑτέραν εἰσίασιν. On this difficult passage, see Wecklein's *Scenische Studien* (*Philologus* 31, p. 447), and A. Müller *ib.* 35, p. 324 ff. also id. *Bühnenalterthümer*, § 13, and Haigh's *Attic Theatre*, p. 181.

(438), languishing eyes (236), and a fair and delicate form of almost feminine loveliness (353, θηλύμορφος, and 457). In other respects he is represented in the dress and other accessories common to all the retinue of the god,—the ivy-crown on his head, the fillet on his brow, and the skin of the fawn or panther slung across his chest (see notes on 106, 833 and 24). Like any other actor in Greek tragedy, he wears the long striped tunic reaching to the ground[1]; and, over this, a loose upper robe. Towards the end of the play, when he reveals himself as Dionysus, he will assume the attire conventionally appropriated to that god, when represented on the stage,—a long robe of saffron colour, bound about the breast with a broad girdle of varied hue[2].

In the first part of the prologue (1—54) Dionysus states his object in coming to Thebes in human disguise. He has triumphantly established his worship in the lands of the East, and he now comes to the city of his birth, resolved on manifesting his divinity in a signal manner to the Thebans, and chiefly to his own mother's sisters, Ino, Autonoe and Agave, and to Agave's son, the young king, Pentheus. He has inspired all the women of Thebes with madness, and driven them forth, with the daughters of Cadmus, to hold their revels on Cithaeron. If Thebes does violence to his votaries, he will give them battle at the head of his Maenads.

---

[1] Pollux, IV § 116, ἐσθῆτες μὲν τραγικαί, ποικίλον (οὕτω γὰρ ἐκαλεῖτο ὁ χιτών) κ.τ.λ.

[2] Pollux, IV § 117, ὁ δὲ κροκωτὸς ἱμάτιον· Διόνυσος δὲ αὐτῷ ἐχρῆτο, καὶ μασχαλιστῆρι ἀνθινῷ, καὶ θύρσῳ.

At this point the *Chorus*, a band of fifteen Asiatic
women, who have attended the speaker of the prologue in his wanderings, after passing along the *para-
scenia* or side-buildings of the stage, and through the
entrance called the *parodos*, has just come in full view
on the side of the *orchestra* which lies to the left of
the spectators. They appear in the garb characteristic
of Bacchanals; crowned with wreaths of ivy and with
the gay *mitra*, the Bacchic head-dress; robed in the
long tunic which falls to their feet (χιτὼν ποδήρης),
and is bound by a bright girdle; the dappled fawnskin is flung across the shoulder; all of them appear
to be barefooted (863); some of them are waving the
thyrsus, while others are beating the *tympanum*.

After a slight pause, while the *Chorus* are coming
into sight, Dionysus, whom they regard as only their
escort in travel and not as their god, in the latter part
of the prologue (**55—68**) addresses them from the stage,
calling upon them to beat their drums before the
palace, that all Thebes may come and see. while he
himself goes to join the revels on Cithaeron. [*Exit*
Dionysus by the right-hand *periactos*.]

πάροδος (**64—169**).[1] The object of the first Choral ode
is to give a brilliant and life-like picture of the Dionysiac worship in its purer forms. In the first two
strophes (64—71), recited perhaps by the *coryphaeus*
alone[2], solemn silence is called for, in language like

---

[1] Defined by Aristotle, *Poet.* 12, as ἡ πρώτη λέξις ὅλου χοροῦ, and so
termed because it was recited by the chorus immediately on reaching
the *orchestra* from the side entrance.

[2] As suggested by Wecklein on l. 64.

that of the priests of Eleusis, as a prelude to the praise of the mystic rites of Dionysus. They sing the story of his wondrous birth; they summon Thebes, his birthplace, to join his worship; they tell of the origin of the Bacchanalian music. The Epode describes the joys of the chase and the dance, and the frolics of the Bacchae on the hills.

ἐπεισόδιον¹ πρῶτον (170—369). *Scene I. Teiresias and Cadmus.* The action of the play now begins. On the right of the stage, enters from the city of Thebes the blind and aged prophet Teiresias. Unlike the Teiresias of other plays, he has none to guide him, being brought safely on his way by the invisible god, Dionysus, whose worship he has accepted. He is covered with 'the net-like woollen robe' generally worn by soothsayers when they appear on the stage². Over this he has thrown the Bacchic fawn-skin; instead of the prophet's chaplet³ he wears the ivy-crown; instead of the laurelled staff of Apollo's seer, he carries the *thyrsus* swathed with ivy.

He has an appointment with Cadmus, who comes out to meet him from the door of the Palace. The two old men have both of them agreed to go out to Cithaeron, dressed in the garb of Bacchanals, there to honour Dionysus in the dance.

---

¹ 'All that part of a tragedy which is included between two *entire choral odes*' (Arist. *Poet.* 12).

² Pollux, IV § 116, τὸ δ' ἦν πλέγμα τι ἐξ ἐρίων δικτυῶδες περὶ πᾶν τὸ σῶμα, ὃ Τειρεσίας ἐπεβάλλετο ἤ τις ἄλλος μάντις.

³ μαντεῖα στέφη, *Ag.* 1265 (Wecklein, p. 15).

Scene II (**215—369**). Pentheus, whose approach is noticed by Cadmus, suddenly comes back from abroad, entering the stage from the left. As king, he is represented with diadem and sceptre and with a purple *xystis* over the bright *chiton*[1]. His youth is indicated by an appropriate mask which has additional dignity given to it by the elevated frontlet called the ὄγκος. He is much excited by having just heard that a handsome stranger from Lydia has led all the women of Thebes to leave their homes in wild excitement, and hold revels and dances on Cithaeron. He denounces the stranger as a gross impostor, and the revels as a discreditable scandal. He has already ordered the imprisonment of some of the women, and he resolves on slaying this impostor, who is trying to make out that the babe who died at its birth, when its mother Semele was slain, was actually a god, Dionysus.—Up to this point, his speech is a kind of second prologue; he now (at line 248) catches sight of the two old men in their fantastic garb; he implores Cadmus to give up the new worship, and taunts Teiresias with having joined it from interested motives. The Chorus briefly protests; the prophet then expounds at length the true meaning of the story of the god's birth, claims for him a share in the prerogatives of the deities already accepted by Hellas, foretells the establishment of his worship at the shrine of Apollo at Delphi, and closes his speech by hinting darkly at an impending doom (327). The king is

[1] Possibly the fact that he had just returned from a journey was indicated by his appearing in the garb of travel, instead of the full *insignia* of royalty (Pfander on Eur. p. 29).

unmoved either by the predictions of Teiresias or the entreaties of Cadmus. To annoy the prophet, he orders some of his attendants to go and demolish his place of augury, while he sends others to the hills to capture the 'Lydian stranger.' [*Exeunt* Cadmus and Teiresias, by the right of the stage, for Cithaeron. The king apparently remains before his palace await-ing the return of his messengers, unmoved by the presence of the Chorus.]

στάσιμον[1] πρῶτον (370—431). The impious language of Pentheus leads the Chorus to invoke the goddess of Sanctity, wronged as she is by his insolence towards the divinity who rules the banquet and the dance, is merry with the flute and drives dull care away. Blasphemy and folly such as his can only end in disaster: there is a wisdom which is false wisdom, and an overweening ambition cuts short the days of man. Forbidden to hold their revels in Thebes, they long to leave for Cyprus or Pieria, where a welcome would await the worship of their god. Dear to him is Peace, and he gives of his bounty to rich and poor alike, hating none but him who cares not for the bliss that *he* bestows. True wisdom, they declare in con-clusion, is to refrain from the shallow conceit of those who affect to be wiser than their neighbours, and to be content, instead, with what is sanctioned by popular use and by common sense.

ἐπεισόδιον δεύτερον (434—518). The king's messengers,

---

[1] i. e. an ode sung, not while the chorus is *stationary*, but after it has taken up its position before the altar of Dionysus, ὅταν χορὸς στὰς τι κατάρχεται λέγειν (Euklides), quoted in Wecklein's *Scenische Studien u. s.* p. 462. The epithet does not exclude the movements of the dance.

entering by the right of the stage, now return from their quest. They bring with them the 'Lydian stranger' with his hands tied behind his back; and they tell the king that their prisoner had cheerfully yielded himself to them without resistance. They add that those of the Bacchae who have been already imprisoned, have had their bonds broken asunder in some strange and supernatural manner, and are now off in full career to join their companions on the hills.

The Stranger now stands loosed before the king, who scans his handsome form, questions him on his antecedents, and on the mysteries of his ritual. At every point he is met by a calm reply. He threatens to cut off his dainty locks, to rob him of his *thyrsus*, and to put him into prison; all his threats are received with dignity by one who stands assured that his god will release him at his will, and is actually present all the while, though unseen by the impious Pentheus. The king orders his attendants to seize him once more and shut him up in the darkness of the stables; he also threatens to sell as slaves the Asiatic women who have accompanied him, or else 'to stop their thumping and their drumming fingers, and keep them as his handmaids at the loom.' The Stranger warns the attendants not to touch him; and of his own accord marches off to the proposed place of imprisonment, declaring that, in requital for this wrong, the king will be pursued by the vengeance of that god whose very existence he denied[1].

---

[1] The prison may have been represented towards the left of the Palace (εἱρκτὴ δὲ ἡ λαιά, says Pollux, IV § 125); and Pentheus, finding

στάσιμον δεύτερον (519—575). The king's denial of the divinity of Dionysus and his maltreatment of the leader of his revel-band, lead the Chorus to invoke Dirce, the nymph of the Theban fountain in whose waters the new-born god had been dipped. They predict that their god's worship, though now rejected, will ere long find a place in her heart. They also call upon Dionysus himself, in whatever favoured haunt he may be wandering, to come and rescue their companion and themselves from the godless monster who is persecuting them.

ἐπεισόδιον τρίτον (576—861). *Scene* I (576—603) κομμὸς *between the Chorus and Dionysus.* The prayer of the Chorus is heard ; they are startled by a voice calling from the prison, announcing itself as the voice of their god. While they once more invoke him, the solid ground is shaken by an earthquake, the entablature of the palace appears to part asunder, and the flame that has been playing round the monument of Semele flashes into new brightness. The Chorus fall awestruck on the ground.—*Scene* II (604—641). To their joy, their companion now comes forth from the palace bidding them rise again in reassurance, while he tells them his adventures in the prison. Pentheus, so far from having succeeded in binding him, had seized a bull, which, in his gathering infatuation, he had mistaken for his prisoner, and had been hard at work

his attendants awestruck at the Stranger's presence, appears himself to have followed the prisoner with the intention of putting him in bonds (616). Wecklein, however, *Scenische Studien u. s.*, p. 444, understands εἱρκτή as an *ergastulum*.

trying to tie his cords about the captured beast, when
the shaking of the palace and the flashing of the flame
on Semele's tomb made him think the place was on
fire : he had called aloud to his servants, but they
had striven in vain to quench the flames ; he had
given chase to a phantom, and had been stabbing the
bright air with his sword, supposing all the while that
it was his prisoner whom he was killing. The latter,
meanwhile, had quietly stepped outside the palace to
reassure his friends and to meet all the king's bluster
and fury with a calm and sober self-control.—*Scene* III
(642—659). Pentheus bursts out of the palace and is
astonished to find his 'prisoner' outside. The latter,
after a short encounter with the king, draws his attention to a messenger coming with news from Cithaeron.

Scene IV (660—786). The Messenger enters on
the right. He is a herdsman, and is therefore, as it
seems, represented with wallet and staff, with a goat-
skin flung over him, and with an appropriate mask[1].
He has seen the women of Thebes resting under the
trees of Cithaeron; the lowing of his oxen had awak-
ened them and they had all started up, donned their
Bacchic garb, and refreshed themselves with marvellous streams of water and wine, milk and honey.
Disturbed in their sacred rites by the herdsmen who
had resolved on capturing the king's mother to win
favour with the king, they had put the intruders to

---

[1] Pollux, IV § 137, πήρα, βηκτηρία, διφθέρα, ἐπὶ τῶν ἀγροίκων...ὁ
μὲν διφθερίας ὄγκον οὐκ ἔχων, περίκρανον ἔχει, καὶ τρίχας ἐκτενισμένας
λευκάς, πρόσωπον ὕπωχρόν τε καὶ ὑπόλευκον καὶ μυκτῆρα τραχὺν, ἐπι-
σκύνιον μετέωρον, ὀφθαλμοὺς σκυθρωπούς.

flight, had rent and mangled the herds of cattle, and had scoured the plains below, harrying everything right and left, and turning to flight with their weak weapons the lances of armed men who opposed them. In conclusion, he urges the king, after this display of miraculous power, to receive into the state the new divinity, the god of wine and love and every other joy.—The king, indignant at the discredit which the conduct of these women is bringing on his rule, orders his troops to muster at the Electran gates on the way to mount Cithaeron.—*Scene* v (787—861): *Dionysus and Pentheus.* The Lydian stranger warns the king that ordering out his forces can only end in their being put to rout; he even offers to bring the women to the palace without resorting to force of arms, but his offer is declined by Pentheus who suspects a plot. Suddenly a bright thought strikes the Stranger (810), he resolves on tempting the king to go and see the revels in person, and the latter, thinking he cannot do better than view the scene of action before joining in pitched battle, is impelled by his growing delusion to give his consent and even to allow himself, with some misgiving, to assume the disguise of a woman, and go to Cithaeron to spy out the doings of the Maenads. Pentheus enters the palace to robe himself (846), while the Stranger remains on the stage, assuring the Chorus, that the prey is now in their toils, and calling on Dionysus to implant in the king's mind a strong delusion which should draw him onward to his doom. He then joins Pentheus within the palace, to help in arraying him for his adventure.

στάσιμον τρίτον (862--911). The Chorus, with the hope of deliverance now rising before it, wonders whether it will ever join again in the night-long dance bounding like the hunted fawn that has escaped the chase and found refuge in the shadowy woods and river-lawns in whose solitudes she delights to disport herself. Then, in graver strain, they dwell upon the doom which slowly but surely is hunting down the impious one, the despiser of a worship upheld by use and grounded in nature. After a refrain, on the joy of vanquishing one's enemies, which is twice sung by both divisions of the Chorus, they end by extolling the happiness of rest after toil, and by vaguely alluding to the varied issues of mortal hopes.

ἐπεισόδιον τέταρτον (912—976). [From the palace enters Dionysus, shortly followed by Pentheus in woman's garb.] The king, in his ever-increasing delusion, fancies that he sees two suns and a double Thebes, and that his escort resembles a horned bull. The guide is allowed to put the last touches to the king's toilet, and, after an interchange of conversation in which the king's lightmindedness is still further shewn and in which nearly every remark that he makes is answered by the Stranger in terms of bitter irony, they leave the stage together for Cithaeron. Both alike are exulting in the prospect of an approaching victory, while the Stranger calls on Agave, and her sisters on the hills, to stretch forth their hands at the coming of the king to a glorious contest. [*Exeunt* by the right *periactos.*]

στάσιμον τέταρτον (977--1023). The Chorus, taking up
the appeal to Agave with which the scene on the
stage has just closed, calls on the ' hounds of Frenzy '
to incite the daughters of Cadmus to take vengeance
on the spy, predicting that his own mother will be
the first to visit with punishment the godless, lawless,
reckless profaner of the god's mysteries. After moralising on the sober and reverent temper, as contrasted
with the false affectation of wisdom, they close by
imploring their god to appear in one of his many
forms, and fling his toils about their foe.

ἐπεισόδιον πέμπτον (1024—1152). By the right of the
stage enters one of the king's attendants. He announces the catastrophe which has meanwhile taken
place on Cithaeron. In answer to the eager questionings of the Chorus, he tells how Pentheus and the
Stranger and himself had reached the rock-girt glen
where the Maenads were holding holiday; how Pentheus had mounted a fir-tree, to spy out their revels;
how, when the Stranger had vanished, a voice was
heard from heaven, calling on them to avenge themselves on the intruder; how Agave in her madness,
mistaking Pentheus for a beast of the chase, had, with
the help of the rest, uprooted the tree, so that he was
thrown to the ground, where she attacked him, while
he in vain implored her to spare her son; and lastly,
how the mother had, with her sisters, tcrn all his
limbs asunder. The attendant withdraws, announcing the speedy approach of Agave and concluding
by briefly moralising on the wisdom of a sober and
reverent piety.

The Chorus breaks out into a short ode of exultation (**1153—1164**), at the close of which appears, from
the right of the stage, Agave, attended by some of
her companions (1168, κῶμος, 1381, πομποί). She is
dressed in Bacchic attire, her eyeballs are rolling
wildly, and on the point of her thyrsus she bears the
head of her son, which she displays to the Chorus as
the head of some wild beast which she has captured.
While Agave glories in her victory, the Chorus reply
in strains of exultation intermingled with words of
pity. She then calls on all Thebes to wish her joy of
her prowess; she asks for Cadmus and for Pentheus
whom she misses, and whom she wants to come and
nail up the spoils of her chase over the door of his
palace.—The ἔξοδος (**1165—1392**) has meanwhile begun.

Cadmus, who had heard of his daughter's deed
of horror, just as he was returning from the mount
with Teiresias, now enters from the right of the stage,
with his attendants bearing the mangled limbs of
Pentheus, which he has gathered together, with much
toil, among the rocks of Cithaeron. He sees Agave,
still exulting in her prey, and little by little recalls her
to her senses, till at last she knows that the head of
the 'lion' is in truth the head of her son (1284). Cadmus, after explaining how she had come to kill him,
makes a speech of lamentation over the fate of his
grandson, which was followed by a corresponding
speech on the part of the mother; nearly all of this
lament has unhappily been lost, but it may be re-
covered in some small measure by the help of the
cento from the plays of Euripides, known by the
name of the *Christus Patiens* (see note on l. 1329).

Dionysus appears once more, now no longer as the Lydian stranger unrecognised by the rest, but in all the glory of his godhead[1]. In a speech whose earlier portion has not come down to us, he foretells the destinies of Cadmus and his wife, both of whom are to be changed into serpents in Illyria, and, after various adventures, to enjoy happiness at last. He also announces that Agave and her sisters, having the guilt of bloodshed upon them, must leave the land. Then follows a pathetic parting between Cadmus and his daughters ; Agave and her sisters now leave the stage in the direction opposite to Cithaeron ; Cadmus enters the palace by the middle door ; and, while the audience are rising, the play closes with some conventional anapaests sung by the Chorus as they march off from the orchestra, by the same side as they entered it, namely by the *parodos* to the left of the stage.

[1] It has been suggested that as an indication of his divine character, he probably appeared 'surrounded by clouds on the balcony of the scene,' Donaldson, *Theatre of the Greeks*, p. 296.

§ 5. *On the dramatis personae, the Choral Odes and the Messengers' speeches.*

It will be seen from the preceding outline that the development of the play falls into two distinct portions ; ascending by three successive stages in the first three 'episodes,' culminating at the point where the turn in the fortunes of the two principal characters begins (l. 810), and descending in three corresponding stages to the close of the tragedy[1]. In the language of the Poetics of Aristotle, 'all that is between the beginning of the piece and the last part, where the change of fortune commences,' is called the δέσις ; 'all between the beginning of that change (τῆς μετα-βάσεως) and the conclusion ' is the λύσις (chap. xviii). In the present instance, the tragic emotions of terror and pity, so often referred to in that treatise, are alike brought into play, the former by the awful end of Pentheus, the latter by the unhappy fate of Agave. When a friend kills a friend, or when the mother slays her son, it is in cases such as these that our pity is excited, and 'such incidents,' says Aristotle, 'are the proper subjects for the poet's choice.' 'To execute such a deed through ignorance and afterwards to make the discovery' is the kind of ἀναγνώρισις to which the same critic assigns a special preference;

---

[1] This symmetry of division is noted by Wecklein, *Einleitung*, p. 11, whose six stages are, however, slightly different to mine, as he begins the ἔξοδος at l. 1024. But, if we count 1153—64 as a ' choral ode,' the definition of ἔξοδος in Ar. *Poet.* 12, as 'that part which has no choral ode after it,' compels us to begin the ἔξοδος at 1165 (or 1168), and to treat 1024—1152 as a fifth ἐπεισόδιον.

'for thus,' as he remarks, 'the shocking atrociousness (τὸ μιαρὸν) is avoided, and, at the same time, the discovery has a striking effect' (xiv).

The play brings before us a conflict between divine power claiming its due recognition, and human arrogance that denies that claim. In this conflict, but for the disguise assumed by *Dionysus*, the contest would have been too unequal to admit of any tragic interest. As it is, he is brought face to face with Pentheus,—man matched against man, the apparently helpless prisoner calmly confronting the passionate and overbearing king. His character as a god incarnate is admirably sustained throughout ; under the veil of humanity, the suffering and patient deity maintains a serene composure, strong in the consciousness of ultimate victory. The effect of his encounters with the king seems to ourselves, perhaps, to be marred by the clever word-fence, which was doubtless dear to the Greek audience for which the play was intended, and by a cruel irony which appears to impair the dignity of his character. Irony, in itself, is quite consistent with dignity, and one of the loftiest types of humanity recognised by Aristotle, that of the μεγαλόψυχος, though frank and direct in his general discourse, is apt, 'with the many,' to resort to irony. But, however interesting the irony of Greek tragedy may be to an audience that is in the secret of an impending doom, it is nevertheless a heartless mockery of the wretch whom it deludes to his destruction ; and it is inexcusable except so far as it supplies the means of inflicting a sharp lesson on

arrogance, like that of Pentheus. With an audience
that is familiar with the plot, it has undoubtedly the
dramatic interest of setting up a clear contrast between
the present delusion in which self-conceit, like his, is
enfolding itself, and the rapidly approaching crisis in
which that delusion will be rudely stripped off[1].

Pentheus is a less interesting character. The
poet does not intend us to regard him as a martyr
to the cause of abstinence; and any pity that we
feel for him is far less than is inspired by the fate
of a Hippolytus. With headstrong impulse, and
arrogant bluster, the youthful king declines to listen
to the warnings of older men like Cadmus, and the
still more antiquated Teiresias, who, old as they are,
shew themselves eager to welcome the new worship.
And so he goes onward to his doom, hopelessly
entangled in a fatal infatuation. It is a redeeming
point in his character that, on hearing that all the
women of Thebes are holding revel in Cithaeron,
groundless as his anxiety proves to be, he is jealous for
their honour, and sensitive of the scandal involved in
such a departure from the ordinary decorum of their
secluded lives. And it is just because he is a mixed
character, with good and bad points alike, that his
death is a fit subject for a tragedy. For, whether in
real life or on the stage, an utter villain may meet his

---

[1] There are some good remarks on tragic irony in Mr Gilkes'
School Lectures on the Electra of Sophocles, 1879, p. 59, a book which
ought to be in the hands of all who desire to read that play with profit.
Thirlwall's essay on the 'irony' of Sophocles is well known to every
scholar; there are some strictures on it in Prof. Campbell's Sophocles,
pp. 111—118 = pp. 126—133, ed. 2.

doom without arousing in us either of the tragic emotions of terror or of pity. It is the misfortunes of characters who have enough of good in them to be interesting, that excite our feelings by arousing in us commiseration for their sufferings, and inspiring us with awe at the contemplation of their doom[1].

The aged *Cadmus* is an adherent of the new creed, whose motives, however, for acknowledging the divinity of Dionysus, are not of the highest order. Blended with other reasons, it is a kind of family pride that makes him suggest, that even if his daughter's son were *no* god, it would be best to call him so, for the credit of the house. Hence, near the end of the play, where all the characters have their doom dealt out to them, Cadmus, though assured of an ultimate happiness which appears to cause him but little elation, has in the meantime his due share of troubles allotted him.

Teiresias has a dignified part assigned to him as the exponent of the true meaning of the legend of Dionysus, and as the foreteller of his future greatness. There is further a special fitness in the prophet of Apollo being foremost in welcoming a deity whose worship was afterwards so closely associated with that of the god of Delphi. The conservative tone in which he refers to the time-honoured traditions of the ancestral religion (in l. 200 ff.), though dramatically appropriate in the lips of the aged soothsayer, is not exactly in keeping with the position he himself takes up in accepting the new divinity. For, by an inversion

[1] Ar. *Poet.* 13; Matthew Arnold's *Merope*, p. xxxiii.

of the common contrast, while the youthful Pentheus
plays the part of the conservative in his mistrust of
novelty, it is the aged Teiresias who proves himself
more tolerant in his religious comprehensiveness.

Agave, who is the unconscious instrument of the
vengeance of Dionysus, is herself punished by the
god for her rejection of him, by being inspired with a
frenzy that leads her unwittingly to slay her son.   In
the delineation of that frenzy, blended as it is with
the partial sanity which is one of the most painful
characteristics of mental delusion, the poet justifies
the remark of the ancient critic who mentions the
passion of madness as one in the treatment of which
he specially excelled[1].   But it is a matter of some surprise that, while the laws of Greek Tragedy strictly
prevented all deeds of horror, such as the slaying of
Pentheus, from being represented on the stage, and
left them to be only recited in a messenger's narrative, an Athenian audience should nevertheless have
tolerated the exhibition of the head of a son by the
mother who had killed him.   The horror is, however,
partly diminished by her own unconsciousness, while
the same cause heightens the pity inspired by her
fate.

At first sight, it would appear that the play might
well have ended with the speech of Cadmus over the

---

[1] [Longinus] περὶ ὕψους XV § 3, ἔστι μὲν οὖν φιλοπονώτατος ὁ Εὐριπίδης δύο ταυτὶ πάθη, μανίας τε καὶ ἔρωτας, ἐκτραγῳδῆσαι, κἀν τούτοις, ὡς
οὐκ οἶδ᾽ εἴ τισιν ἑτέροις (εἴ τις ἕτερος, Stanley), ἐπιτυχέστατος, οὐ μὴν
ἀλλὰ καὶ ταῖς ἄλλαις ἐπιτίθεσθαι φαντασίαις οὐκ ἄτολμος.   See n. on
l. 1214.

body of Pentheus, which closes with a couplet briefly
expressing the moral of his doom :

εἰ δ' ἔστιν ὅστις δαιμόνων ὑπερφρονεῖ,
ἐς τοῦδ' ἀθρήσας θάνατον ἡγείσθω θεούς (1326).

But it is probably just because the feelings of horror
have been too strongly excited, that the god himself
appears, to allay these disquieting emotions as well as
to assert the divine power which has been partially
in abeyance, to mete out due recompense to all, and,
even in the punishment of Cadmus, to assure him of
compensating consolations. It is for this reason also
that, just as in a Greek speech the peroration is
usually calmer than the immediately preceding portion, so the final scene, that here closely follows a
passage of highly-wrought excitement, is one of
tender and somewhat common-place farewells.

Another reason, why the play cannot really close
at the point above-mentioned, is to be found in the
law of symmetry which is a leading principle in
Greek poetry as well as in Greek art. The balance
of the composition requires the speech of Cadmus to
be followed by a corresponding speech of Agave.
Nearly all of the latter, and a great part of the subsequent speech of Dionysus, have unfortunately been
lost. This loss may, of course, have been due to
accident alone ; a single leaf in the manuscript from
which our only copy of the latter half of the play
was transcribed, may have been torn out, simply
because it was near the close of the volume ; but it
may also be worth suggesting that the end of the

play may have been mutilated in that earlier *codex* by one who was unconscious of the dramatic purpose of the speeches of Agave and Dionysus.

The *Choral Odes*, unlike those of many other dramas of Euripides, are here, as in a piece of the same date, the *Iphigeneia in Aulis*, closely connected with the action of the play. This may be readily seen by referring to the outline sketched in the previous section. They also shew a certain inter-dependence on one another; thus, the allusions, in the first *Stasimon*, to the places where Dionysus is worshipped, find their echo in the reference to the god's own haunts in the second; the longing for liberty expressed in the second is after an interval caught up by a similar strain in the third; while the moral reflexions of the first are to some extent repeated.in the last. It is doubtless undramatic for the king, after ordering his attendants to capture all the Theban revellers they can find, as well as the Lydian stranger, to allow a band of Asiatic women to go on beating their drums, and dancing and singing unmolested in front of his own palace[1]. But the poet appears to have been conscious of this difficulty, as he makes Pentheus *threaten* to put a stop to it (l. 5 10—14, cf. 545, 1036) ; and the king is only prevented from actually doing so by his anxiety to capture the Lydian stranger ; but as soon as he has succeeded in this object, he becomes hopelessly entangled in toils that leave him no chance of carrying out his threat.

---

[1] Mahaffy on Eur. p. 84.

Had Pentheus put the Chorus into prison, the play would have at once collapsed ; and we may fairly allow a position of privilege to so essential a portion of the conventional surroundings of a Greek tragedy. The only other course would have involved having a chorus that was either coldly neutral, or actually hostile to the worship of Dionysus, and therefore out of harmony with the object of the play. A chorus of aged Thebans, for instance, might have required no departure from dramatic probability, but it would have been a poor exchange for our revel-band of Oriental women, gaily clad in bright attire and singing jubilant songs, as they lightly move to the sound of Bacchanalian music.

The choral metres, a conspectus of which is given at the close of the volume, are all of them admirably adapted to give expression to the varied emotions of the votaries of Dionysus. The Trochaic passage, in ll. 604—641, is well suited as a transition from the hurried excitement of the preceding scene, to the quieter Iambic verses which immediately follow it. The Iambic lines, in general, are remarkable for the large number of resolved feet, which is one of the marks of the poet's later manner[1].

The composition of *Messengers' Speeches* is one of the points in which Euripides excels ; and in the

---

[1] This, as remarked by Hermann, is a characteristic of all his plays that belong to a later date than Ol. 89 or 90 [B.C. 424—417], *e. g.* the *Troades* of 415, and the *Orestes* of 408. Of the versification of the *Bacchae*, according to Hartung's *Eur. rest.* ii p. 512, *observatum est a quibusdam senarios plus minus* 50 *primum pedem anapaestum habere, et in* 950 *versibus solutiones* 368 *esse.*

present play we have the advantage of two such passages, in which the revels on Cithaeron and the death of Pentheus are described in narratives which are, perhaps, unsurpassed in Greek tragedy for radiant brilliancy, energetic swiftness and the vivid representation of successive incidents, following fast on one another.   In listening to the first speech, we find ourselves in a wonderland where all is marvellous, and we feel that here, at any rate, we have one who, like Aristophanes in his lighter moods, would have been able to appreciate a creation of the fancy like the *Midsummer Night's Dream* of our own poet. Of both the messengers' speeches we may almost say, as has been finely said of the dramas of Calderon, that 'the scenery is lighted up with unknown and preternatural splendour[1].'

The account of the catastrophe in the second speech is remarkably vigorous.   The quiet passage in its earlier portion, telling of the king and his attendant and their mysterious guide, stealing in silence along the glades of Cithaeron, with the few following touches of description pleasantly representing to us the glen with its rocks and rivulets and overshadowing pine-trees, has, it will be observed, the dramatic effect of heightening by force of contrast the tumultuous excitement attending the deed of horror which is the subject of the latter part of the messenger's recital. For the effect thus produced, we may compare the scene near the end of the first part of Goethe's *Faust*,

---

[1] Ticknor's *Spanish Literature* xxiv, Vol. II p. 410, ed. 1863.   Cf. Symonds' *Studies of the Greek Poets*, 1873, p. 211, 231.

where, shortly before the tumult of the wild revels
of the *Walpurgisnacht*, we find Faust quietly talk-
ing to Mephistopheles about the charm of silently
threading the mazes of the valleys, and of climbing
the crags from which the ever-babbling fountain falls,
when the breath of spring has already wakened the
birch into life, and is just quickening the lingering
pine[1]. We have a similar instance of repose in
Shakespeare in the short dialogue between Duncan
and Banquo just as they approach the gates of
Macbeth's castle (*Macbeth* I. vi. 1—9) ; upon which it
was well observed by Sir Joshua Reynolds that ' their
conversation very naturally turns upon the beauty of
its situation, and the pleasantness of the air : and
Banquo observing the martlets' nests in every recess
of the cornice, remarks that where those birds most
breed and haunt, the air is delicate. The subject of
this quiet and easy conversation gives that repose so
necessary to the mind, after the tumultuous bustle of
the preceding scenes, and perfectly contrasts the scene
of horror that immediately succeeds[2].' Another instance of the ' lull before the storm ' is noticed by a recent writer on Calderon, in 'the pretty pastoral scene'
in the play called the *Hair of Absalom* where the
sheep-shearers are pleasantly conversing with Tamar
just before the arrival of Amnon and his brothers[3].

---

[1] *Im Labyrinth der Thäler hinzuschleichen, Dann diesen Felsen zu
ersteigen, Von dem der Quell sich ewig sprudelnd stürzt, Das ist die
Lust, die solche Pfade würzt! Der Frühling webt schon in den Birken,
Und selbst die Fichte fühlt ihn schon !* Part I, Act IV, Scene 5, *init.*

[2] *Discourse* viii, in vol. I, p. 442, of his Works, ed. 1835.

[3] Calderon, by E. J. Hasell, p. 20; *id.* by Trench, ed. 2, p. 55. -

The Second Messenger's speech was referred to
by Humboldt as a 'description of scenery disclosing
a deep feeling for nature,' but, as remarked elsewhere
(p. 211), the line and a half on the

> ' rock-girt glen, with rivulets watered,
> with stone-pines overshadowed,'

is nearly all that we there find to prove that the poet
was fully capable of appreciating and describing the
picturesque element in nature, had it suited his purpose to do so at greater length. As it is, a few
touches suffice to give a clear and vivid impression of
the kind of scene intended by him, and all more
elaborate details would have been obviously out of
place ; for of this, as of all the master-pieces of Greek
literature, the remark of Lessing holds good, ' that it
is the privilege of the ancients never in any matter to
do too much or too little' (*Laokoon*, preface). The
elaborate word-painting of Shelley, in Beatrice's
description of the gloomy chasm appointed for her
father's murder (*Cenci* III 1, 243—265), impressive as
it is to the reader who has time to linger over its
details in the solitude of his room, would have been
utterly out of place in any play intended for representation on the stage. For comparison with the
above passage, we can only quote the few following
lines :

> ' High above there grow,
> With intersecting trunks, from crag to crag,
> Cedars, and yews, and pines ; whose tangled hair
> Is matted in one solid roof of shade
> By the dark ivy's twine.'

But, as a whole, it would certainly have been regarded by any Greek tragedian as unsuitable for delivery before an enormous audience, like that which assembled in the theatre of Dionysus ; as ' it is impossible for a thousand people at once to be sentimental and tender on the beauties of nature[1].' It may also be noticed that Shelley's description, with which the present passage has before now been unfavourably contrasted[2], is not true to the facts, as it does not really correspond to the actual scenery on the way to the castle of Petrella, which he had never visited ; whereas the few touches of topographical detail given in the above passage are not only beautiful in themselves, but have also the advantage of being in strict accordance with the natural scenery of Cithaeron. In some respects, it is true, the taste for the picturesque among the Greeks was different from that of modern times ; but as regards Euripides in particular, it would be easy to quote not a few passages which, even in a modern poet, would be considered picturesque in an eminent degree (e.g. the sunrise scene in the *Ion*). It is, however, worth while to observe that the most telling touches of description in the *Hippolytus*, where Phaedra longs for ' the pure draught from the dewy fountain,' for ' rest beneath the black poplar in the leafy meadow,' for ' a ride among the woodland pines or over the sands unwashed by the wave,' are all of them put in the lips of a love-sick woman ; and, for all this, she is rudely rebuked by her common-

---

[1] W. G. Clark, *Peloponnesus*, p. 123.
[2] By Cope in *Cambridge Essays*, 1856, p. 137.

place nurse, who, reflecting perhaps the ordinary Athenian feeling in such matters, warns her mistress that it would be unsafe to express such longings as these in public, as they would at once be set down to a disordered imagination. In the present play, the occasional outbursts of admiration for the beauties of nature are probably intended to be characteristic of the enthusiasm of the votaries of Dionysus, whose favourite haunts are to be found in the woodland solitudes and on the lonely hills (e.g. lines 38, 135, 874)[1].

---

[1] On the general subject of the Greek view of the picturesque in nature, see further, in Ruskin's *Modern Painters*, part IV, chap. xiii.; Cope in *Cambridge Essays* for 1856, '*On the taste for the picturesque among the Greeks*'; W. G. Clark's *Peloponnesus*, pp. 118—124; and Woermann, *Ueber den landschaftlichen Natursinn der Griechen und Römer*, München, 1871, pp. 130, esp. pp. 42—50; also A. Riese, *die Entwicklung des Naturgefühls bei den Griechen*, Kiel, 1882.

§ 6. *On the purpose of the play.*

On a superficial view, it might appear that the object of the play is nothing more than the glorification of the god whose worship was intimately connected with the origin and development of the Greek drama ; but a more careful examination shews that there are also indications of a less obvious kind, pointing to an ulterior purpose. Among such indications it has been usual to quote one of the speeches of Teiresias, with its protest against rationalising and philosophising about the gods, and its declaration of acquiescence in the traditions of the popular faith (200 ff.). But, as appears from passages in other plays, the poet had no great love for prophets and soothsayers ; and, in the present instance, he allows the taunt of interested motives which is flung at Teiresias by Pentheus, to remain unanswered by the former (n. on 257). Accordingly, we cannot unreservedly accept the prophet as the spokesman of the poet's opinions ; and we shall, here as elsewhere, look more naturally for these in the choral odes. The chorus in Greek tragedy is, again and again, the interpreter to the audience of the inner meaning of the action of the play ; and the moral reflexions which are to be found in the lyrical portions of the *Bacchae* seem in several instances to be all the more likely to be meant to express the poet's own opinions, when we observe that they are not entirely in keeping

S. B.   *f* with the sentiments which might naturally have been expected from a band of Asiatic women. We are told, for example, that 'to be knowing is not to be wise'; that, in other words, it is folly to be wise in one's own conceit (395); that the true wisdom consists in holding aloof from those who set themselves up to be wiser than their fellows, and in acquiescing contentedly in the common sense of ordinary men (427). The sober temper is commended (1002), the gentle life extolled (388), and practical good sense preferred to the pretence of superior intelligence. Dionysus himself, at the end of one of his speeches, calls it a mark of true wisdom to cultivate a sage and easy good-temper (641). Lastly, at the close of the Second Messenger's speech, in the few sententious lines which, with their didactic moralising, appear to fall rather flat after the swift and energetic account of the catastrophe[1], we are told that, for mortal men, the highest wisdom is to be found in 'sober sense and awe of things divine.'

What are we to make of all this? In these denunciations of τὸ σοφὸν, are we really listening to the pupil of Anaxagoras, to him whom his Athenian admirers called the 'philosopher of the stage[2],' to the most book-learned of the great Tragic writers of

---

[1] Bathos of this kind is unavoidable whenever the didactic style of poetry follows closely on an instance of a higher type. This is well shewn by the moralising refrain at the close of the successive stanzas in one of Wordsworth's poems of the imagination, called 'Devotional incitements.' For this illustration I am indebted to Professor Colvin.

[2] Athenaeus IV p. 158 E, ὁ σκηνικὸς οὗτος φιλόσοφος, Vitruvius, Book VIII, Preface.

antiquity, who, in the phrase of a hostile critic, is made
to describe himself as 'from the scrolls of lore distil-
ling the essence of his wit[1]'? Is the poet who here
upholds the honour of Dionysus, and maintains the
belief in his divinity, the same as he who, elsewhere,
allows his characters to rail unrebuked against the
legends of the popular mythology, and even to deny
the wisdom of Apollo, the justice of Athene, the
righteousness of Zeus[2], and to speak in vague terms
of the very existence of the greatest of the gods[3]?

A partial solution of the difficulty is not far to
seek. Euripides, like others who have hesitated in
accepting unreservedly the tenets of a popular creed,
had in his earlier writings run the risk of being misunderstood by those who clung more tenaciously to
the traditional beliefs. His political enemy, the ultra-
conservative Aristophanes, had unscrupulously set
him down as an atheist[4], though, all the while, it
would appear that he had only striven for the recognition of a higher type of the divine than that which
was represented in the current mythology of the day.
Hence our play, with its story of just doom falling on
the 'godless' Pentheus (τὸν ἄθεον, 995), may be
regarded as in some sort an *apologia* and an *eirenicon*,
or as, at any rate, a confession on the part of the poet
that he was fully conscious that, in some of the simple

---

[1] Ar. *Ranae* 943, 1410 : Athen. I p. 3 A.

[2] *El.* 1246, *Andr.* 1165, *H. F.* 342—7, *Iph. T.* 570, *fragm.*
268, 1030 Nauck's *Eur.* p. xxx).

[3] *Tro.* 884, *fragm.* 483 and 904 (*ibid.*).

[4] *Thesm.* 450, νῦν δ' οὗτος ἐν ταῖσιν τραγῳδίαις ποιῶν τοὺς ἄνδρας
ἀναπέπεικεν οὐκ εἶναι θεούς.

legends of the popular faith, there was an element of sound sense which thoughtful men must treat with forbearànce, resolved on using it, if possible, as an instrument for inculcating a truer morality, instead of assailing it with a presumptuous denial. Possibly also, 'among the half-educated Macedonian youth, with whom literature was coming into fashion, the poet,' as has been suggested by a recent critic, 'may have met with a good deal of that insolent second-hand scepticism which is so offensive to a deep and serious thinker, and he may have wished to shew them that he was not, as they doubtless hailed him, the apostle of this random speculative arrogance[1].'

It was one of our own countrymen, the accomplished Tyrwhitt, who was apparently the first to suggest that the play was a kind of *apologia*, intended to meet the charges of impiety which had been brought against the poet and his friends ; a view which is also taken by Schoene in the introduction to his edition (p. 20). Lobeck, in his *Aglaophamus*, goes further than this, in regarding it as possibly inspired by a polemical purpose, and directed against the rationalists of the time, in commendation of the worship of Dionysus, and in recognition of the right of the people, as opposed to the learned few, to have the chief voice in matters of religion[2]. Similarly, K. O. Müller[3] observes

---

[1] Professor Mahaffy's Euripides, p. 85.

[2] p. 623, *fabula dithyrambi quam tragoediae similior totaque ita comparata, ut contra illius temporis Rationalistas scripta videatur, qua et Bacchicarum religionum sanctimonia commendatur* (72 sqq.), *et rerum divinarum disceptatio ab eruditorum judiciis ad populi transfertur suffragia* (426—431), *aliaque multa in eandem sententiam,*

that 'this tragedy furnishes us with remarkable conclusions in regard to the religious opinions of Euripides at the close of his life. In this play he appears,
as it were, converted into a positive believer, or, in
other words, convinced that religion should not be
exposed to the subtilties of reasoning ; that the understanding of man cannot subvert ancestral traditions
which are as old as time, that the philosophy which
attacks religion is but a poor philosophy, and so forth
(200 ff.) ; doctrines which are sometimes set forth with
peculiar impressiveness in the speeches of the old
men Cadmus and Teiresias, or, on the other hand,
form the foundation of the whole piece : although it
must be owned that Euripides, with the vacillation
which he always displays in such matters, ventures,
on the other hand, to explain the offensive story
about the second birth of Bacchus from the thigh of
Zeus, by a very frigid pun on a word which he
assumes to have been misunderstood in the first

quae sive poeta pro se ipse probavit sive alienis largitus est auriculis,
certe magnam vim, magnam auctoritatem apud homines illius aetatis
habuerunt, quae ab impia sophistarum levitate modo ad fanaticas de-
fluxerat superstitiones (*Verius tamen est,* remarks Bernhardy, *eadem*
aetate plebi superstitiones peregrinas, doctis et elegantioribus viris scita
Sophistarum placuisse. Theologumena Graeca III. p. x, and *Hist.*
of Greek Literature I. p. 400). Musgrave viewed it as an attack on
Critias and others on l. 200, *non dubito, quin poeta...Atheniensium*
religiones respexerit quippe quas sollicitare tum - maxime et illudere
coeperunt Critias, Alcibiades aliique, ne Socratem etiam annumerem,
Athenis florentes...Quanquam neque specie caret Tyrwhitti sententia,
poetam ea mente hanc fabulam edidisse, ut gravissimum illud impietatis
crimen, quod cum Socrate et aliis eiusdem sodalitii hominibus commune
habuit, a se amoveret.

[3] *Hist. Gr. Lit.* I. p. 499.

instance' (292). On this hypothesis it would appear that his earlier sceptical temper with its 'obstinate questionings' had, like a troubled stream, run itself clearer with the lapse of time ; and that toward the close of life the 'years that bring the philosophic mind' had led him at last to a calmer wisdom.

In contrast to such a view as that last quoted, which sees in our play a recantation of rationalism and a return to orthodox belief, we have the position taken up, in the first instance, by Hartung[1], who points out that, so far from there being any such alteration of opinion, the moral attitude of the poet in the *Bacchae* is similar to that which he had assumed in the *Hippolytus*,—a work produced in 428 B.C., more than thirty years before. The *rôle* of Pentheus who denies the divinity of Dionysus resembles that of Hippolytus, who disdains the worship of Aphrodite ; the vengeance taken by the god of wine in the former finds its parallel in that exacted by the goddess of love in the latter ; in both alike, the wrath of an offended deity falls on one who sets himself in self-conceited opposition to its power. According to this view, which is further developed by Eduard Pfander[2] and accepted by Mr Tyrrell, we have here, in the language of those critics, no ' change in the point of view from which Euripides regards the old gods of the heathen mythology. As Aphrodite is no mere personal goddess, but a great factor in the order of the world, and a source of happiness and joy ; so

---

[1] *Euripides restitutus*, 1844, II. p. 542.
[2] *Ueber Eur. Bakchen*, p. 2.

Dionysus is not only the god of wine, but a higher
personification of passion in religion, and joy in life;
and the *Hippolytus* as well as the *Bacchae* teaches that
we should not neglect these sources of joy, enthusiasm,
and passion[1].' The *Bacchae*, continues Mr Tyrrell,
'reprobates rationalism' (τὸ σοφὸν, 395); and as the
sentiment referred to comes from a *chorus*, we may
allow it as evidence respecting the poet's opinions at
the time. But we fail to see anything more than a
superficial likeness between the two plays, as regards
their general subject; and we doubt whether the
tracing of such likeness can, with advantage, be pursued into detail by the quotation of single lines from
the *dialogue* of the play; for this, in so far as it must
be kept, more or less, true to character, lends itself
less readily to the expression of the actual views
of the dramatist himself. Thus, even if we admit
that a 'recoil from public opinion' is condemned by
such a line as οἴκει μεθ' ἡμῶν, μὴ θύραζε τῶν νόμων
(331), we can hardly admit as proof of the poet's
opinions the line quoted from the *Hippolytus*, μισεῖν
τὸ σεμνὸν καὶ τὸ μὴ πᾶσιν φίλον (92). The latter, as
the context shews, is only an incidental remark on
the part of the attendant, that it is the rule with all
men to dislike reserve as contrasted with an affable
complaisance, whence he infers that the same law
holds with regard to the gods, and that therefore the
dread goddess Aphrodite will necessarily hate Hippolytus for not deigning to address her. Similarly, we
hesitate to accept lines 467 and 487 of the same play,

[1] Mr Tyrrell's *Introd.* p. xvii.

as 'directed against overwiseness.' In the former the nurse warns her mistress that 'mortals ought not to make an over-serious business of life' (ἐκπονεῖν βίον λίαν); and in the latter, the mistress retorts, that well-ordered states and households have ere now been ruined by over-specious arguments like those she had just heard (οἱ λίαν καλοὶ λόγοι). The second of these lines, so far from confirming, is actually directed against maxims like that of the first; and, even if it were otherwise, we could scarcely regard Phaedra or her nurse as intended by the poet to be the mouth-piece of his own opinions.

But though, for these reasons, we hesitate in accepting all the three passages above quoted, as proof that the poet's disagreement with the Sophistic type of rationalism is not confined to the *Bacchae*, but may also be detected in the *Hippolytus*; we readily concur with Mr Tyrrell in recognising in the poet's later work 'an ethical contentment and speculative calm' which to some extent distinguishes it from his earlier plays, not excluding the *Hippolytus* itself. In the play last mentioned, we have a remarkable passage in which the chorus, while confessing they derive consolation from a belief in the care of the gods, yet declare that, on looking at the chances and changes of human life, they fail to get a clear view of the dealings of providence; and so they are content with the prayer: 'may destiny send me these gifts from the gods, good fortune attended with wealth, and a mind untouched by sorrow; may the thoughts of my heart be not over-precise, not yet marked with the

stamp of a sham' (δόξα δὲ μήτ' ἀτρεκὴς μήτ' αὖ παρά-
σημος ἐνείη, 1102—1119). In the present play, on
the other hand, we have a stronger declaration of a
contented acquiescence in an established order, a
recognition of the existence of a moral government of
the world (392—4, 882—90), and an assurance that
life becomes painless when it cherishes a temper which
befits mortal men, a temper that is prompt in its
obedience to the claims of heaven (1002).

On the whole, we are inclined to hold that, difficult as it is to reconstruct from the writings of a
dramatist, an account of the author's opinions, we
may fairly trace, here and there, in the choral odes of
our play, not exactly a formal palinode of any of the
poet's earlier beliefs, but rather a series of incidental
indications of a desire to put himself right with the
public in matters on which he had been misunderstood. The growth of such a desire may well have
been fostered by the poet's declining years, and the
immature asperities of his earlier manner may have
been softened to some extent by the mellowing
influence of age ; while his absence from Athens may
have still further intensified his natural longing after
a reconciliation with those who had failed to appreciate the full meaning of his former teaching.

§ 7. *The after fame of the play.*

The play, on its exhibition at Athens after the
poet's death, appears to have rapidly acquired a considerable celebrity. It is not improbable that it was
on the occasion of its first representation that the
prize for tragedy, which had seldom fallen to Euripides
in his lifetime[1], was awarded to his posthumous work
with an appreciation that was perhaps all the more
keen now that the poet himself had passed away. It
is referred to in general terms by Plutarch as one of
the plays repeatedly reproduced with lavish expendi-
ture on the Athenian stage[2]. It would also appear to
have become a favourite play in Macedonia ; and the
story already told of the mother of Alexander the
Great shews that so enthusiastic a votaress of Dionysus would have fully entered into its spirit, though,
so far as I am aware, there is no authority for the
statement that 'she openly played the part of the
mother of Pentheus.' It was quoted by Alexander
at his own table (see n. on 266) ; and it supplied Aristippus with an apt reply to Plato at the court of the
second Dionysius (see n. on 317), who had himself
attempted the composition of dramatic poetry, and
testified his admiration for Euripides by paying a
high price for his lyre, his tablets and his pen, and

---

[1] Gellius *N. A.* XVII 4, *Euripidem quoque M. Varro ait, cum
quinque et septuaginta tragoedias scripserit, in quinque solis vicisse, cum
eum saepe vincerent aliquot poetae ignavissimi.*

[2] *de Gloria Ath.* c. 8.

dedicating them in the temple of the Muses in his own capital[1]. It was acted in the camp of the Parthians on the occasion when the actor, playing the part of Agave with the head of Pentheus, held aloft the head of Crassus which had been flung into the tent by the messenger of the Parthian general (n. on 1169). The actor on that historic occasion was a native of Tralles; and a player from another city of Asia Minor, who excelled in the dramatic representation of scenes from our play, is commemorated in the following anonymous epigram :

Εἰς Ξενοφῶντος Σμυρναίου εἰκόνα.

Αὐτὸν ὁρᾶν Ἰόβακχον ἐδόξαμεν, ἡνίκα Ληναῖς
  ὁ πρέσβυς νεαρῆς ἦρχε χοροιμανίης,
καὶ Κάδμου τὰ πάρηβα χορεύματα, καὶ τὸν ἀφ᾽ ὕλης
  ἄγγελον εὐϊακῶν ἰχνελάτην θιάσων,
καὶ τὴν εὐάζουσαν ἐν αἵματι παιδὸς Ἀγαύην
  λυσσάδα. Φεῦ θείης ἀνδρὸς ὑποκρισίης !
                                          (*Anth. Gr.* XVI 289.)

A similar performance in Italy is mentioned with praise in an epigram by Antipater of Sidon on the actor Pylades who practised his art at Rome in the time of Augustus (Suet. *Aug.* 45) :

Εἰς στήλην Πυλάδου ὀρχηστοῦ.

Αὐτὸν βακχευτὴν ἐνέδυ θεὸν, ἡνίκα Βάκχας
  ἐκ Θηβῶν Ἰταλὴν ἤγαγε πρὸς θυμέλην,

---

[1] ψαλτήριον, δέλτον, γραφεῖον (Hermippus in vita Eur. cod. Vindob. ll. 77—82, Nauck).

ἀνθρώποις Πυλάδης τερπνὸν δέος, οἷα χορεύων
δαίμονος ἀκρήτου πᾶσαν ἔπλησε πόλιν.
Θῆβαι γιγνώσκουσι τὸν ἐκ πυρός· οὐράνιος δὲ
οὗτος, ὁ παμφώνοις χερσὶ λοχευόμενος.

(XVI 290.)

The play is referred to by Plato and Aristotle.
It was rendered into Latin by Attius, and was especially familiar to Catullus and Horace, Virgil and
Ovid. Excerpts from its pages appear not only in
the *florilegium* of Stobaeus, but also in the geographical treatise of Strabo, whose subject is one of
those *quae non possunt* ἀνθηρογραφεῖσθαι. It is often
mentioned in later literature by writers such as Plutarch, Polyaenus, Philostratus, Gellius, Athenaeus,
Aelian, and Sextus Empiricus[1]. Clement of Alexandria, besides expressly quoting it in several passages,
borrows from the fate of Pentheus a notable illustration, describing the various schools of Philosophy as
'rending in pieces the one truth, like the Bacchants
who rent the body of Pentheus and bore about the
fragments in triumph[2].' Lucian, again, tells a story
of Demetrius the Cynic, who saw an illiterate person
reading a βιβλίον κάλλιστον, τὰς Βάκχας οἶμαι τοῦ
Εὐριπίδου. He had reached the passage where the
Messenger is reciting the doom of Pentheus and the
awful deed of Agave, when the Cynic seized the book

---

[1] For details, see notes referred to in the Index, under the head
of the names above mentioned.

[2] *Stromateus*, I chap. 13 *init.*, p. 349 (in Milton's *Areopagitica*
a similar image is taken from the mangled limbs of the slaughtered
Osiris). See also note on l. 470.

and tore it into pieces, exclaiming : 'it is better for
Pentheus to be rent asunder once by *me*, than mur-
dered many a time by you[1].' Not a few passages of
the play are paraphrased by Nonnus, the author of
the florid and monotonous epic called the *Dionysiaca,*
who travels over the same ground in books XLIV to
XLVI of his poem ; and lastly, a large number of its
lines were appropriated by the compiler of the dreary
cento known as the *Christus Patiens,* once attributed
to Gregory of Nazianzus.

During the middle ages Euripides appears to have
attracted more attention than Aeschylus or Sophocles.
No mention of either of the latter is made by Dante,
though, in a somewhat arbitrary list, he places Euripides, Antiphon [or Anacreon ?], Simonides, Agathon
and 'other Greeks who once adorned their brows
with laurel,' among the blameless souls, who, by
reason of being unbaptized, haunt the first circle of
his *Inferno*[2]. In the sixteenth century the *Bacchae*
was translated into Latin Prose and into Italian as well
as Latin Verse[3]. In the seventeenth we find Milton
reading Euripides (the 'sad Electra's poet' of one of
his best known sonnets) 'not only with the taste of a
poet, but with the minuteness of a Greek critick[4].'

[1] *adv. indoctum* § 19.

[2] *Purgatorio* XXII. 106 (with *Inf.* IV. 58 ff.).

[3] In L. V., by Coriolanus Martirianus (1556); in Latin by Doro-
theus Camillus (Basil. 1550) and Stiblinus (1562) and Canter (1597); in
Italian by Chr. Guidiccioni (ob. 1582, publ. 1747) and Padre Carmeli
('poor,' 1743—53).

[4] Todd's *Life of M.,* I. p. 158, who refers to Warton's second ed.
of the smaller poems, p. 568. The biographers of Milton have,

We read of Goethe in his old age praising the manner in which our play sets forth the conflict between the might of Godhead and the infatuation of man, and recognising in Dionysus, as here represented, 'the pagan image of an outraged and patient' Deity. The German scholar, who was the first to draw special attention to the poet's criticism, reverently remarks that the play further suggests 'the contrast between the Pagan and the Christian ideal—between repressed menace and gentle firmness—between defiance and reliance[1].'

Even those who, like August W. Schlegel, have no partiality for our poet, and indeed appear to be inspired by an almost personal animosity against him, have nevertheless admitted the excellence of this particular play. Schlegel's critique is as follows :

The *Bacchae* represents the infectious and tumultuous enthusiasm of the worship of Bacchus, with great sensuous power and vividness of conception. The obstinate unbelief of Pentheus, his infatuation, and terrible punishment by the hands of his own mother, form a bold picture. The effect on the stage must have been extraordinary.

---

apparently, not observed that the *Comus*, which contains several Euripidean passages, was written for the autumn of the very year in which the poet bought his copy of the Geneva ed. of Eur. (n. on l. 188).

[1] The words quoted are borrowed from Mr Jebb's review of Mr Tyrrell's ed. in the *Dark Blue* for July, 1871. Goethe's own words are as follows: *Kann man die Macht der Gottheit und die Verblendung der Menschen geistreicher darstellen als es hier geschehen ist? Das Stück gäbe die fruchtbarste Vergleichung einer modernen dramatischen Darstellbarkeit der leidenden Gottheit in Christus mit der antiken eines ähnlichen Leidens, um daraus desto mächtiger hervorzugehen, im Dionysos* (W. Müller, *Göthe's letzte literarische Thätigkeit*, p. 9, quoted by G. H. Meyer, *de Eur. Bacch.* p. 22). Pfander on Eur. p. 37 n. Gruppe, *Ariadne*, p. 381.

Imagine, only, a chorus with flying and dishevelled hair and dress, tambourines, cymbals, &c, in their hands, like the Bacchants we see on bas-reliefs, bursting impetuously into the orchestra, and executing their inspired dances amidst tumultuous music,—a circumstance, altogether unusual, as the choral odes were generally sung and danced at a solemn step, and with no other accompaniment than the flute. Here the luxuriance of ornament, which Euripides everywhere affects, was for once appropriate. When, therefore, several of the modern critics assign to this piece a very low rank, they seem to me not to know what they themselves would wish. In the composition of this piece, I cannot help admiring a harmony and unity, which we seldom meet with in Euripides, as well as abstinence from every foreign matter, so that all the ·motives and effects flow from one source, and concur towards a common end. After the *Hippolytus*, I should be inclined to assign to this play the first place among all the extant works of Euripides[1].

Dean Milman, a more friendly critic, while admitting that there are passages of more surpassing beauty in the *Medea* and the *Hippolytus*, and of greater tenderness in the *Alcestis* and *Iphigeneia*, does ' not scruple to rank the *Bacchae*, on the whole, in the highest place among the tragedies of Euripides.' He also records the fact that his friend Lord Macaulay, notwithstanding the contemptuous depreciation with which he had referred to the poet in his juvenile essay on Milton, nevertheless acknowledged in his maturer years the ' transcendent excellence of the *Bacchae*[2].' In his own copy of our author we find him confessing his change of mind as follows : ' I can hardly account for the contempt which, at school and college, I felt for Euripides. I own that I like him now better than Sophocles '......' The *Bacchae* is a most glorious play.

[1] Schlegel's *Dramatic Lectures*, p. 139.
[2] Milman's *Agamemnon and Bacchanals*, p. 97.

I doubt whether it be not superior to the *Medea*. It is often very obscure ; and I am not sure that I fully understand its general scope. But, as a piece of language, it is hardly equalled in the world. And, whether it was intended to encourage or to discourage fanaticism, the picture of fanatical excitement which it exhibits has never been rivalled[1].'

[1] Trevelyan's *Life of Macaulay*, end of Appendix to vol. i.

BRONZE MIRROR IN THE COLLEGIO ROMANO.

§ 8.   *The textual criticism of the play.*

Of the surviving manuscripts of Euripides, **none**
belong to an earlier date than the twelfth century.
They are divided into two groups, the first of which
contains in all nine plays alone : namely, the *Alcestis*,
*Andromache, Hecuba, Hippolytus, Medea, Orestes, Rhe-
sus, Troades* and *Phoenissae ;* while the second, which
is inferior to the first, further includes tħe remaining
ten.   The MSS of the second group are (1) the Har-
leian MS in the British Museum, of the sixteenth century, commonly designated by the symbol *A* ; (2) the
Palatine MS in the Vatican, a folio on parchment, of
the fourteenth century (*B* or **P**), no. 287 ; and (3) the
Laurentian MS, written on paper, in the library
of San Lorenzo at Florence, also of the fourteenth
century (*C*).   Three of these ten plays, namely the
Helen, Electra and *Hercules furens,* are preserved in
one MS alone (*C*).   The *Bacchae* (with the *Heracleidae,
Supplices,* the two *Iphigenias, Ion* and *Cyclops*) is contained in two MSS only (**P** and *C*), of which the former
alone has the whole play ; the latter, the first 754
lines only, closing with the words οὐ δεσμῶν ὕπο.
Thus, in lines 1—754 inclusive, we have to depend on
two *codices, ' neque boni neque vetusti'* (as Elmsley calls
them); and from 755 to the end of the play on one
only.   Both of these were examined by Elmsley, with
a view to his edition of this play published in 1821,
and a careful collation of the Palatine MS was made
on his behalf by one Jerome Amati.   But our information about the readings of the other manuscript, in

g

the Laurentian library (*C*), with the exception of some few readings noted in the 16th century by the Italian scholar Victorius, mainly depended, until the years 1855—75, on a collation carelessly made for Matthiae's edition by Francesco de Furia (editor of Aesop). This collation proved so untrustworthy, that in the edition of Euripides by Kirchhoff (1855), who was the first to place the textual criticism of our author on a satisfactory footing, an endeavour was made to compensate for the want of a complete account of the readings of this MS, by restoring them with the help of five manuscripts which, to all appearance, were copied from it, three of them in Paris, and the other two in Venice and Florence[1]. Happily, however, both of the MSS with which we are concerned in the *Bacchae* were afterwards most minutely examined by Wilamowitz-Moellendorff, who gives the results of his collation of lines 1—754 in his *Analecta Euripidea*, 1875, pp. 46 ff. He records the readings under the three heads, (1) *loci post novam conlationem congruentes* [29 instances] ; (2) *binae lectiones in altero utro codicum* [18 passages, with the result that *nullo loco C P in binis lectionibus conspirant*] ; (3) *C et P diversa tradunt* [95 variations].

In recording the manuscript readings at the foot of the page in this volume, I have relied in the main on the *apparatus criticus* of Kirchhoff's edition, and wherever the readings there given rest only on the authority of a collator who says nothing to the contrary ('*e silentio collatoris*'), I have added the reading

---

[1] Further details may be found in Kirchhoff's *Praefatio*, p. x.

given by the author of the *Analecta*, whose collation is always intended wherever the phrase *denuo collatus*, or *nuper collatus*, is used. The two MSS were probably derived from the same source ; they have mistakes in common which can hardly be explained on any other hypothesis, though *C* may possibly have been a partially corrected copy of **P**. The mistakes in **P** are more numerous than those in *C*, but on the other hand they are mainly of a trivial character, and, on the whole, we may agree in the opinion that **P** is the better authority of the two[1].

As a partial compensation for the defectiveness of the manuscript authority on which the text of our play is founded, we have the *cento* from Euripides to which reference has been made in a previous section, the *Christus Patiens* (p. lxxxv). Though of little or no value, as far as regards its adaptations of the *Hecuba*, *Hippolytus*, *Medea* and *Orestes*, where our existing MSS are larger in number and better in quality, it is more important in the case of passages borrowed from the *Rhesus*, *Troades* and *Bacchae*, where the evidence for the text is comparatively weak. Most of the places where it materially helps us are pointed out at the foot of the text in this edition, and references to them may be found in the index[2].

The only Greek *scholia* on the play are those in

---

[1] Elmsley, p. 6, remarks *magnopere dolendum est, integras Bacchas in codice Laurentiano non exstare. Nam in priore fabulae parte longe plures bonae lectiones in eo quam in Palatino reperiuntur.* Nauck, p. xl, on the other hand, says of *B* (=**P**) and *C*, '*B prae altero fide dignus est.*' Mr Tyrrell, who gives further details on this point, p. xi, supports the latter view.—On the Laurentian MS. see p. 256 *infra*.

[2] A full list is given on pp. 15—17 by Brambs (Teubner) 1885.

the margin of *C*, most of them unimportant. They may be found in the critical notes on ll. 97, 151, 451, 520, 525, 538 and 709. The only one not recorded there, is that on 611, ὀρκάνας· φυλακάς· ὀρκάνη, κυρίως ἡ ἀγρευτικὴ λίνος (Matthiae's correction for λίνου).

The evidence of later Greek writers who quote from the play, or who, like Nonnus and Philostratus, paraphrase portions of it, is not without value in determining the text. But when all the help that can be got from these various sources is put together, much remains to be restored by conjectural criticism alone. In recording such conjectures as have already been published elsewhere, I have derived some assistance from consulting the critical notes to Mr Tyrrell's recension, and those in Dindorf's last edition of the *Poetae Scenici;* while the labour of collecting others, that are scattered about in foreign periodicals and dissertations, has been lightened in no small measure by the critical appendix to the recent edition of Wecklein. A list of these dissertations and other contributions to the literature of the subject, so far as known to myself, is given at the end of the introduction. I have further compared the texts printed by the nine following editors, and have recorded the principal variations between them: Elmsley, Hermann, Schöne ed. 2, Kirchhoff ed. 1 and 2, Nauck ed. 2, Dindorf ed. 5, Paley ed. 2, Tyrrell, and Wecklein. Wherever any of these are mentioned as supporting one of two readings or conjectures, it is generally to be assumed that the remainder, though not actually mentioned, are in favour of the other.

The first printed edition of the *Bacchae* was that

included in the Aldine text of eighteen plays, printed at Venice in 1503, when the *Electra* was not yet known. It has been proved by Kirchhoff that the editor must have been the learned Greek, Markos Musuros; and that, for his text, he was mainly dependent on the Palatine MS. The editor's tacit corrections of that MS, which at one time were regarded as possibly resting on independent evidence, are now generally considered to be nothing more than his own conjectures. Among the others mentioned in the *apparatus criticus* who have in different degrees contributed towards the correction of the text, the following may be named. (The list is in chronological order, according to the dates of their deaths.) In the *sixteenth* century, Brodaeus (*Jean Brodeau*), W. Canter, Victorius (*Vettori*), J. J. Scaliger, H. Stephanus (*Henri Estienne*); in the *seventeenth*, Milton and Joshua Barnes (ed. 1694); in the *eighteenth*, J. Pierson, B. Heath (of Exeter), J. J. Reiske, J. Markland, Valckenaer, Sir Samuel Musgrave, M.D., Thomas Tyrwhitt, Brunck, and Porson; and in the *nineteenth*, Elmsley (1773—1825), Dobree (1782—1825), Matthiae, Jacobs, Hermann, C. J. Blomfield, F. G. Schoene, J. A. Hartung (ob. 1867), R. Shilleto (1809—1876), W. H. Thompson (1810—1886), and F. A. Paley (1816—1889). Among living scholars, besides those whose editions and dissertations are recorded at the close of this introduction, I may mention the name of Dr Reid, Fellow of Gonville and Caius, whose conjectural emendations, together with those of the late Dr Thompson, I was permitted to publish for the first time in 1880. These conjectures, with a few of my own, may be found by referring to the English index.

THE DEATH OF PENTHEUS.

FROM A RELIEF ON A SARCOPHAGUS IN THE GIUSTINIANI PALACE, ROME.

§ 9. *Euripides and the fine arts. The play in its relation to ancient art.*

From the biographical notices that have come down to us, we learn that Euripides, before devoting himself to poetry and philosophy, cultivated in the first instance the art of painting; and that pictures ascribed to his pencil were to be seen at Megara[1]. This tradition, though in itself resting on slight authority, is nevertheless in accordance with the evidence supplied by his literary work, in which, *veluti descripta tabella,* an artistic training is clearly disclosed. An artist's eye is shewn in the brief touches with which he depicts the beauties of nature[2]; and a keen sense of colour may be discerned in his choice of descriptive epithets[3]. We find him repeatedly referring to works of Architecture, Sculpture and Painting[4]. He alludes to the ancient wooden temples[5], to the 'Cyclopian' walls of Argos and Mycenae[6], and to the stone-built treasuries of the heroic age[7]. He dwells with familiarity

---

[1] *Vita Eur.* l. 16 (ed. Nauck): φασὶ δὲ αὐτὸν καὶ ζωγράφον γενέσθαι καὶ δείκνυσθαι αὐτοῦ πινάκια ἐν Μεγάροις (cf. *ib.* l. 111). Suidas: γέγονε δὲ τὰ πρῶτα ζωγράφος.

[2] *Supra* p. lxx.

[3] e.g. λευκὸς in *Bacch.* 665, 863, *Ion* 221; *H. F.* 573, Δίρκης τε νᾶμα λευκὸν αἱμαχθήσεται. *Hel.* 215, Ζεὺς πρέπων δι' αἰθέρος χιονόχρως κύκνου πτερῷ. *Iph. T.* 399, δονακόχλοα Εὐρώταν. Also epithets such as ποικιλόνωτος, φοινικοφαής, κυανόπτερος, ξουθόπτερος.

[4] Kinkel, *Euripides und die bildende Kunst.* To this nearly exhaustive dissertation I am indebted for many of the above details.

[5] *Fragm.* 475, l. 4—8.   [6] *H. F.* 15, 543; *Tro.* 1087, *Iph. T.* 845, *Iph. A.* 152, 534, 1501.   [7] *Hec.* 1010.

on the structural details of temples and other buildings[1], and borrows appropriate similes from various
forms of handicraft[2].   He refers to the Erechtheum[3],
to the shrine of Aphrodite 'by the rock of Pallas[4],'
and to the temples of Poseidon on the Laconian pro-
montories of Taenarus and Malea, on the Euboean
headland of Geraestus, and the holy place of Athene,
'the silver-veinèd crag' of Sunium[5].   In the domain of
the plastic art, he tells not only of the archaic works of
Daedalus[6], of the Trojan ξόανα of gilded wood[7], and
the awe-inspiring Gorgon's head[8], but also of the
sculptured reliefs on the temple at Delphi[9], the graven
images in the pediment of the sanctuary at Nemea[10],
and the colossal statue of Athene Promachos on the
Acropolis of Athens[11].   In his *Andromeda*, as soon as
Perseus sees the heroine of that play standing chained
to the rock, his first thought is that he must be gazing
on the life-like work of some cunning sculptor[12]; and
in the fine description of the death of Polyxena in
the *Hecuba*, the idealised beauty of the female form,
as represented by the plastic art, is the subject of a
necessarily brief, but none the less happy, allusion :

μαστοὺς τ' ἔδειξε στέρνα θ', ὡς ἀγάλματος,
κάλλιστα   (*Hec.* 560).

---

[1] περικίονας ναούς, *Iph. T.* 405, cf. *Phoen.* 415, *Ion* 185, *fragm.*
370; κρηπίς, *Ion* 38, 510 ; τρίγλυφος, *Bacch.* 1214, *Iph. T.* 113, *Or.*
1366; θριγκός, *Ion*, 156 ; *Iph. T.* 47, *Hel.* 70, *Or.* 1569, *Phoen.* 1158
(Kinkel *u. s.*, p. 37). See also *Bacch.* 591.

[2] See note on l. 1067.   [3] *Phoen.* 1433 ff.   [4] *Hipp.* 30 f.

[5] *Cycl.* 290—6.   [6] *Hec.* 836 ff., (*Eurysth.*) *fragm.* 373, *H. F.* 471.

[7] *Tro.* 1074, *Ion* 1403.   [8] *Alc.* 1118, *El.* 855, *H. F.* 990, *Or.* 1520.

[9] *Ion* 187—223.   [10] (*Hypsip.*) *fragm.* 764, γραπτοὶ τύποι.

[11] *Ion* 9, τῆς χρυσολόγχου Παλλάδος.   [12] *Fragm.* 124.

Among themes of Painting, he refers to ships at sea in the *Troades* (686) and love-scenes in the *Hippolytus* (1005); and, as a mythological subject of pictorial art, he expressly mentions 'Athene entrusting Erichthonius to the daughters of Cadmus' (*Ion* 271). Painting, like Sculpture, supplies him with more than one expressive *simile*, as when Helen, vexed with her fatal gift of beauty, prays that her form might, like a fair picture, be blotted out again, and lose its loveliness;

εἴθ' ἐξαλειφθεῖσ', ὡς ἄγαλμ', αὖθις πάλιν
αἴσχιον εἶδος ἀντὶ τοῦ καλοῦ λάβοιν (*Hel.* 262).

And again, when Hecuba implores the pity of Agamemnon, she asks him to stand back one moment, like an artist viewing his unfinished painting, 'and look and gaze at all that's ill in her':

οἴκτειρον ἡμᾶς, ὡς γραφεύς τ' ἀποσταθείς,
ἰδοῦ με κἀνάθρησον οἷ' ἔχω κακά (*Hec.* 807).

We cannot wonder that a poet who so keenly appreciated the arts that flourished in the Periclean age, should himself in his turn attract the attention of the artists of a later time. Those who came especially under this influence were the artists of the period immediately succeeding the conquests of Alexander. Themes which had won an established reputation through the dramas of Euripides and had been popularised by that poet's art, naturally commended themselves to the painter and sculptor as suitable subjects for their own artistic treatment. Among the recorded works in which the influence of Euripides has, with

more or less probability, been traced, are, in the case of
paintings, the Hippolytus of Antiphilus, the Canace(?)
of Aristeides, the Medea of Aristolaus and Timo-
machus, and the Andromeda of Euanthes and Nicias[1].
The Telephus of Parrhasius, and the Orestes of Timo-
machus, were apparently independent of that influence; while it is only the almost certain spuriousness
of the epilogue to the *Iphigeneia at Aulis* that pre-
vents our supposing that Timanthes, in his celebrated
picture of the sacrifice of Iphigeneia, in which the
head of Agamemnon was veiled because the artist's
pencil could not paint so deep a sorrow, was indebted
for the hint to Euripides himself:

> ἀνεστέναζε κἄμπαλιν στρέψας κάρα
> δάκρυα προῆκεν ὀμμάτων πέπλον προθείς
>
> *(Iph. A.* 1550).

Among works of *sculpture,* the famous group
of the punishment of Dirce, commonly known as the
'Farnese Bull,' by the Rhodian artists, Apollonius
and Tauriscus, may have owed some of its inspiration
to the account of the catastrophe which must have
been given in our poet's *Antiope;* and it seems not
improbable that, even at an earlier time, the 'Maenad
of Scopas' and the 'Dionysus of Praxiteles' may
have been in part suggested by the *Bacchae.*

It is not intended by this to imply that artists
who were great in their own domain sacrificed in any
way the principles of their art to a slavish following
of the treatment of the same theme that had been

---

[1] Kinkel *u. s.,* note 267. See also Vogel's *Scenen Euripideischer
Tragödien in Griechischen Vasengemälden,* 1886.

adopted by the poet. More than a hundred years have now passed since Lessing's *Laokoon* was written, and few things are more clearly recognised in aesthetic criticism than the broad lines of demarcation that distinguish the imitative arts from one another, and in particular the difference between the means whereby the space-arts such as Painting and Sculpture attain their object, and those that are employed by the time-art of Poetry. While Poetry, like Music, is a 'time-art,' an art of vocal utterance depending for its results on the apt expression of certain successive effects in their consecutive evolution in time, Sculpture and Painting have to work under stationary conditions in space. All the three have for their end an idealised imitation of natural objects, but they approximate to nature in different degrees. Thus Sculpture is nearest to nature; in the next degree of distance is Painting; and in the third, Poetry. And the further each of these arts is removed from reality, the wider is its scope[1]. Thus Painting allows of much more combined narration than Sculpture, and the range of resources is still more extensive in Poetry. This greater remoteness from nature is, however, in the *dramatic* species of poetry compensated for by the help of various subsidiary arts, the art of the Scene-painter, the art of Music, which, like Poetry, is a 'Time-art,' and the arts of Dancing and still more that of Acting, the last two being intermediate between 'time-arts' and 'space-arts' and working in time and space at once.

It was not until the time of Praxiteles, who flourished

---

[1] This criticism is due to Professor Colvin.

some forty years after the date of our play, that, in
contrast to the older type of the bearded Dionysus,
which is still to be seen in numerous works of art and
is not unrepresented in the illustrations to this volume
(p. 145),—the youthful, or as he is sometimes called,
the 'Theban,' Dionysus became a favourite theme
of Greek sculpture. Of this later, half-effeminate
type, we have an instance in the bust figured on p. 26.
Praxiteles himself selected his subjects mainly from
the cycles of Dionysus, Aphrodite and Eros. His
group of Maenads, Thyiads, Caryatides and Sileni, is
mentioned by Pliny (XXXVI 23) and praised in an epigram in the Greek Anthology (IX 756). His statue of
Hermes carrying the infant Dionysus, which was seen
by Pausanias at Olympia (V 17 § 3), has been discovered in the recent excavations, and casts of it are
now in our museums[1]. In the Elean temple of Dionysus, near the ancient theatre, the same traveller saw a
statue of the god which was also the work of Praxiteles (VI 26 § 1); and it was possibly this statue that
Callistratus had in view when describing the Dionysus
of Praxiteles as a beautiful youth crowned with ivy
and girt with a fawnskin, his left hand resting on a
thyrsus, with a tender and dreamy expression of
countenance, blended with a fiery glance of the eye;
in which last respect it is distinguished from all the
statues of the god that are now known to us[2]. In
describing this statue, Callistratus remarks that it
resembled the form of the god which is set forth in the

[1] See further in Newton's *Essays on Art and Archaeology*, p. 350;
frontispiece to Overbeck's *Geschichte der gr. Plastik*, II (ed. 1881); also
A. Bötticher's *Olympia*, p. 327, and Perry's *Greek and Roman Sculpture*, p. 456.   [2] Overbeck *u. s.* II p. 40.

Bacchae of Euripides, οἷον αὐτὸν (*al.* αὐτὸς) Εὐριπίδης ἐν Βάκχαις εἰδοποιήσας ἐξέφηνε[1].

The 'Maenad' of Scopas, who flourished during the half century after the death of Euripides, is the subject of another description by the same writer[2]. Scopas was one of the first to represent the enthusiasm of the votaries of Dionysus in a perfectly free and unfettered form; and we may well suppose that a considerable impulse was given to the artistic embodiment of that enthusiasm by so celebrated a masterpiece of literature as our poet's latest play.

It has even been conjectured that this work of Scopas was suggested by the completion of the Theatre of Dionysus under the auspices of the orator Lycurgus in the year 342 B.C.[3] This conjecture, interesting as it is, does not pretend to rest on any foundation of fact; but even if we set it aside, there are other definite points of contact between that Theatre and various works of Greek sculpture, for which we have clear and conclusive authority. The neighbouring temple of Dionysus was adorned, as already mentioned, with reliefs representing the fate of Lycurgus and Pentheus (p. xxiii). Above the theatre itself, on a platform of rock extending along part of the south-east portion of the Acropolis, the munificence of King Attalus I of Pergamos placed at a later time[4] a noble design representing the battle of the giants with Dionysus among the warriors; and

---

[1] *Statuae* 8, partly quoted on p. 132. Perry *u. s.* p. 435—440.

[2] *Stat.* 2 (*infra*, pp. cxli, 188). Overbeck *u. s.* II p. 18.

[3] Urlichs, *Skopas* p. 60.

[4] B.C. 229; Pausan. I 25 § 2, Brunn *Gr. Künstler* I p. 442[1] = 309[2] ff.

just before the Battle of Actium, the figure of Dionysus
in this famous group was blown down by a violent
gust of wind, and fell into his own theatre beneath [1].
And, finally, when that memorable theatre was excavated in and after the year 1862, a series of reliefs
was discovered extending along the front of the stage,
the subjects of which are taken from the legend of
Dionysus (*infra*, p. cxxiii).

The wine-god and his worship long remained
a favourite theme in Greek art [2]. The god himself,
whose ritual began in a rude form of nature-worship,
was in early times represented only by a rustic
image of wood, and the practice of setting up heads
of Dionysus, or mere masks of his features, long continued to be customary; as for example, in the specimen of Roman terracotta on page xlii. Besides these
simpler forms, we have the more artistic types which
fall into two groups, (1) the bearded Dionysus with
majestic mien, luxuriant hair, flowing beard, and
an oriental richness of attire; and (2) the graceful
figure of the youthful Dionysus, with the forehead
bound by the *mitra*, with a crown of vine or ivy-
leaves, his hair falling in curls, the *nebris* over
his shoulder, and the *thyrsus* entwined with ivy in
his hand. He is often attended by his favourite
animal, the panther (*infra*, p. cxxiii); he sometimes
appears as a horned god (p. cxxxii), or even in the
shape of a bull (p. 70). We may also trace on works
of art his marvellous life; his double birth (p. ix

---

[1] Plutarch *Anton.* 60.

[2] For details, see Müller's *Ancient art and its remains* §§ 383—390.

and *infra*, p. 1), his tender affection for his mother
Semele, and his bride Ariadne ; we see him surrounded by his *thiasos* of Maenads and Satyrs, together with Pan and Silenus ; sometimes we view
those Maenads in their wild enthusiasm, with their
dishevelled hair enwreathed with serpents (p. 7),
their heads tossed back (p. 58), their hands beating
the *tympanum*, or grasping the *thyrsus* or sword (p.
238), or the dismembered limbs of the young roe
(p. 86), and with their garments fluttering loosely
in the breeze ; or sometimes reclining in calm slumber, resting from their revels (p. 41). From the time
of Scopas downward, ancient artists vied with one
another in representing an ecstatic elation of mind
by these frenzied Maenads with their light and graceful movements, the purer and severer types being
best exemplified by the designs that are to be
seen on sculptured reliefs, while the more volup-
tuous forms are mainly to be found among engraved
gems and in mural embellishments like those of
Pompeii. But in art, as well as in poetry, the representation of these wild states of enthusiasm was apparently due to the imagination alone, for in prose
literature we have very little evidence, in historic
times, of women actually holding revels in the open
air. Such a practice would have been alien to the spirit
of seclusion which pervaded the life of womankind in
Greece. At Athens, at any rate, nocturnal festivals
by torch-light in which women took part were pro-
hibited by one of the laws of Solon (Plutarch's
Life, cap. 21) ; and even at Thebes we have indica-

tions of the existence of a similar rule of decorum
(Plutarch, *de genio Socr.* 32). The festivals of the
Thyiads were mainly confined to Parnassus, where
they were held once in two years by the Dionysiac
priestesses of Delphi who were joined on this occasion by Thyiads from Attica[1]. The latter proceeded
in a kind of festal march, or θεωρία, from Athens
to Delphi, along the great highway across Cithaeron
and through the Boeotian plain by Thebes, Chaeronea, Panopeus and Daulia. It was at Panopeus,
to the west of Chaeronea, on a rocky hill which
ends the northern spurs of Helicon, that they would
for the first time enjoy an unbroken view of Parnassus ; and it was there, at a place to which Homer
gives the epithet of καλλίχορος, that they apparently
held a sort of rehearsal of the dances and other
festivities that they were shortly to celebrate at
Delphi itself. The passage in Plutarch about Olympias, already quoted on p. xl, implies that the wild
orgies of the Thracian votaries of Dionysus were
regarded by him as an exceptional state of things,
and as a ' barbarous ' departure from the simplicity
of Greek manners[2].

Thus the conclusions we are able to draw from
historical and archaeological literature, with regard
to the actual rites of Dionysus as practised in
Greece, are in many respects inconsistent with what
might be deduced from the representations of the
Maenads which are to be found in Mythology and

---

[1] Pausan. X 4 § 3.

[2] Rapp in *Rheinisches Museum* 1872, pp. 2—14.

Art.   The latter is an imaginative picture which is
portrayed for us not in prose, but in poetry, and the
finest example of its poetic treatment is the play now
before us.   It is this that warrants the attempt which
is made in this volume to set one form of the imaginative treatment of the legend of Dionysus by the
side of another, and, in this particular point, to illustrate the poetry of the Greek drama by means of the
sculpture and painting of Greek art.

For the treatment of the Maenads in ancient art
our principal authorities are the Greek vase-paintings[1].   The vases of the earliest style, with designs
in black, or more frequently brown, on a pale-yellow
ground, are usually decorated with paintings of
animals and various fantastic ornaments, and they
accordingly supply us with few illustrations of our
present subject[2].   On the vases of the next class, with
black figures on a red ground, we find the forms of
the Maenads drawn in a poor and monotonous manner, with violently distorted movements of the body,
but with nothing to indicate that those movements
are in any way connected with extreme excitement of
mind.   On vases of this style where Dionysus himself
is represented, he appears as a bearded form, with a
long robe, with a drinking-horn, or *cantharus*, and
a vine-branch, either standing or sitting, or riding on
a mule, in the midst of Satyrs and Maenads, who

[1] Rapp, *u. s.* p. 562 ff.

[2] The birth of Dionysus is the subject on a vase of this style figured
in R. Rochette, *peint. de Pomp.* p. 73; and Satyrs and Maenads appear
on no. 1626 of the Leyden collection and no. 802 in that of Prince
Canino (quoted by Jahn).

S. B.   *h*

are making merry in music and dancing, or giving
chase to one another[1]. It is not until we reach the
class with red figures on a black ground, that the
coincidence between the artistic and the poetic representation is complete. On vases of this class,
both in the 'strong' and the 'fine' style, Bacchic
subjects assume an important place, and not only do
all the attributes which poets such as Euripides
assign to the Bacchae appear in the design, but the
movements of the body are more free and life-like,
and the expression of the face denotes more suc-
cessfully than before the orgiastic excitement of the
mind[2]. On vases of the 'strong' style Dionysus
himself is still treated in a conventional manner;
with long hair, long beard, and long robe; his *thiasos*
meanwhile is represented under the influence of
ecstatic emotion, which no longer displays itself in
the more unruly forms of revel, but is, in every sense
of the term, less coarsely depicted than on the vases
of the immediately preceding style[3]. In the vase-
paintings in which the 'strong' style of the transi-
tional period has developed into the 'fine' style, in
which the same colours of red upon black are still
used, Dionysiac subjects are very frequent; but side
by side with the bearded Dionysus, we have also
scenes representing the infant-god being entrusted

[1] p. clxiv of Otto Jahn's Introduction to his *Beschreibung der Vasensammlung in der Pinakothek zu München.*

[2] The vase from which the illustration on p. 7 is taken, is an
example of red figures on black ground, designed in the 'strong' style,
before it passed into the 'fine' style.

[3] Jahn *u. s.* p. clxxxv.

to the care of Silenus or the nymphs, and others in which he appears as a lightly-clad youth in the bloom of life[1]. On vases of this 'fine' style, the development of which corresponds in date to the flourishing period of the Greek drama, two types of Maenad may be observed ; the one representing in expression and posture a mood of tender melancholy, the other with a more enthusiastic aspect, with the head tossed back and with streaming hair, swaying the *thyrsus* and beating the *tympanum*[2].

In vases of the 'florid' style, the death of Pentheus is among the subjects represented, and the influence of Greek Tragedy as contrasted with that of Epic Poetry is now more strongly marked. In the representations of Orestes we find reminiscences of Aeschylus; the plays of Sophocles are recalled by 'Teiresias before Oedipus,' and by 'Antigone and Ismene with Creon and Haemon'; while subjects such as 'Hecuba and Polymestor,' 'Bellerophon and Sthenoboea,' and 'Iphigeneia with the tablets in her hand,' besides characters such as Medea and Hippolytus, are as obviously suggested by Euripides[3].

In sculpture as well as in painting we find many representations of the doom of Lycurgus, and also (not less frequently) that of Pentheus. Only three of the artistic representations of the latter were engraved for the first issue of this work, namely those on a sarcophagus in the Giustiniani Palace at Rome, p. xciv

---

[1] *Ib.* p. ccv.

[2] e. g. the four figures on p. xxxii. One of the figures on the other side of the same vase is a good example of the other type.

[3] *Ib.* p. ccxxiv ff.

(described on p. cxxix); on a piece of Calenian pottery at Zurich, p. 69 (cxlv); and on a gem in the British Museum, p. 73 (cxviii, no. 19). In the later editions six more are given, three of them from painted vases and the rest from sculptured reliefs, corresponding to numbers (1), (2), (3), (12), (13) and (15) in the following descriptions:

(1) The moment at which Pentheus is discovered in his hiding-place and attacked by the Maenads is the subject of a vase-painting in the Pinakothek at Munich, no. 1567 (807 in Jahn's *Beschreibung*), first published in Millingen's *peint. de vases* 5, and copied in Jahn's *Pentheus und die Mainaden* taf. II a. The young king is represented not on a tree, as in the *Bacchae*, but in a thicket, which is rudely indicated by a branch before and a branch behind him. On his head is a κυνῆ Βοιωτία; in his right hand he holds a sword behind him, while he stretches forth his left, wrapped in the folds of his *chlamys*, which is thus used as an extemporised shield. He is looking resolutely at the Maenads in front of him; one of them, dressed in a Doric *chiton*, has already caught sight of the intruder and is hastening to the thicket, torch in hand; the next is gazing upward with a fawnskin over her left arm and a short sword in her right; the third, who is drawing near with a *thyrsus* in her right and a *tympanum* in her left, is looking back for a moment at a roughly sketched pillar, possibly a conventional representation of the buildings of the neighbouring town of Thebes. Corresponding to the three Maenads in front of Pentheus, we have three others behind, all of them in Doric *chitons;* the first rushing forward with her hair loose, holding in her hands part of a young roe which she has torn asunder; the next waving the *thyrsus* in her left as she raises the left foot in the dance (see l. 943); the third holding over her head the two ends of a light shawl which is thrown into a graceful curve by the breeze as she hastens forward. All the three Maenads are tastefully drawn, and the flow of the drapery as they move in the dance is well rendered.

The figures in the original vase-painting are yellow. The woodcut opposite is reduced from the copy given by Millingen.

(1) FROM A VASE IN THE PINAKOTHEK AT MUNICH.

(2)   On a vase found in Southern Italy, in the Jatta Collection at Ruvo, a later point in the story is represented. Pentheus, with a *chlamys* flung over his shoulder, with hunting-boots on his feet and two spears in his left and a sword in his right, is here to be seen in actual conflict with the Maenads. One of them, having grasped the right arm of Pentheus firmly by the wrist, so that he is powerless to use his weapon, is on the point of attacking him with her own sword. On the other side of the young king, a second Maenad is rushing forward with *thyrsus* in her right, and with her left extended to seize him by the head. Behind her again is a third, wearing a *nebris*, waving her right hand, and holding up part of the folds of her dress a moment after she has stopped running. These three are probably meant for the daughters of Cadmus, the first with the sword being Agave. Immediately behind her, to the extreme left of the design, is another Maenad in an excited attitude ; the clasp over her right shoulder has become loose, her head is thrown back, and she waves her hand wildly. Behind her is a conventional representation of a vine.

In contrast with the excitement depicted on this side of the vase, we have a scene of repose on the other, where the god himself is seated in calm rest with his head enwreathed in floating ribbands, with a *chlamys* thrown over him, the *thyrsus* in his left, and a *cantharus*, or *carchesium*, extended in his right. A Bacchante is approaching him with her eyes fixed upon the ground, holding a can in one hand and a small pitcher, or καδίσκος, in the other. Behind her, a Satyr, seated on a skin of a panther or fawn, is playing the double flute. To the extreme right, behind the resting god, a Bacchante is standing calmly with the *tympanum* in her left, beckoning with her right. All the Maenads are wearing bracelets of the serpent-pattern. This vase-painting was first published in Jahn's *Pentheus*, taf. 1, whence it is copied on a reduced scale in Müller-Wieseler 11 xxxvii 436.

The original vase is a large *patera*, a foot in diameter and four inches high, with two handles. The figures are red on a black ground. It is described at length by Minervini (*Vas.*

(2) FROM A KYLIX IN THE JATTA COLLECTION AT RUVO.

Jatta vi no. 66 p. 66, and *Bulletino Archeologico Napoletano* an. iv, Dec. 1845 pp. 13—16; also in the *Catalogo del Museo Jatta*, Naples, 1869, no. 1617). In the copies hitherto published the Bacchante with the *thyrsus*, to the extreme left of the obverse of the vase (the part here engraved), is wrongly transferred to the reverse and placed behind the seated Satyr. This mistake, which was first pointed out by Minervini, is here corrected.

(3) On a vase from Ruvo in the National Museum at Naples (Room VI, case iv, no. 1562 in Heydemann's *Vasensammlung*), designed with red (and white) figures on a black ground, we see a youthful form bearing the inscription ΠΕΝΘΕΥΣ, with a shoulder-belt across his chest, a *chlamys* over his left arm, a spear in his right, stumbling over a heap of stones, near which stands a laurel. He is turning towards a Maenad, clad in a *chiton* and with shoes on her feet, who is pursuing him with a sword waving in her right. On the other side a second Maenad, also in a *chiton*, who has already seized in her left the spear of Pentheus, is joining in the struggle. Behind her is a third Maenad in an excited state, hastening to the conflict, brandishing aloft a sword and a scabbard. She is clad in a *chiton* with the right breast bare, and a mantle falling over her left arm. The design, which is here copied, is published in the *Museo Borbonico* 16, 11 and in the *Memorie della Regale Accademia Ercolanense di Archeologia*, vol. ix, 1862 pp. 165—173 (cf. Jahn in *Philologus* 27 p. 11 f.). Like the vase last described it is a *patera* with two handles, standing on a small black pedestal. The diameter is sixteen inches.

(4) Minervini (*Bull. Arch. Nap.*, Dec. 1845, p. 16) describes a fragment of a vase in his own possession found near Avellino. In the midst is a youthful form named ΠΕΝΘΕΥΣ, with a sword hanging on his side and with a double javelin in his left hand. In his right he is brandishing another javelin and part of his fluttering *chlamys* is also to be seen. He is being attacked by a Maenad in tasteful attire, with a *nebris* on her *chiton* and a *tympanum* in her left hand. Her right hand is brandishing some weapon (*thyrsus* or spear) against him. The most important figure in the design is only partially preserved. It is a

(3) FROM A KYLIX IN THE NATIONAL MUSEUM AT NAPLES.

figure seated aloft and pointing to the ground with the left hand with which it is grasping a serpent. It wears a short *chiton* with hunting-boots, and is probably intended for a Fury like that in the Giustiniani sarcophagus (pp. xciv and cxxx, and in the stamp copied on p. 69, cf. p. cxlv).

(5) Pentheus being torn in pieces by the Maenads, while Dionysus looks on, is represented on the lid of a large vase, with yellow figures, formerly in the Campana Collection. One of the Maenads has seized Pentheus by the leg and the left arm, another by his right arm. On the two sides two other Maenads with streaming hair, one of them holding a *thyrsus*, are rushing forward in wild excitement. Dionysus himself is watching the execution of his vengeance, with his dishevelled hair crowned with ivy, a *thyrsus* in his left hand, and with his right hand holding up the *chlamys* which is flung across his shoulder. (Catal. of Musée Campana IV 761.) In an abridged summary of the Campana Catalogue given in the *Archaeologische Zeitung* 1859, p. 109*, the figures are (probably accidentally) described as red instead of yellow. On the dispersion of the Campana Collection, about 1859, most of the vases were bought by France and Russia ; but whether the vase in question is in the Hermitage at St Petersburg, or in the Louvre, I cannot tell. I have failed to find it in the latter, or to trace it to the former.

(6) On a vase with yellow figures of the finest style, found in the Basilicata, and forming part of Barone's collection in Naples, we have on the one side Troilus and Achilles, and in the lower half of the other, the figure of Pentheus with dishevelled hair, wearing a *chlamys*, and holding the sword in his right and two spears in his left. He is rushing forward to the right to meet a woman dressed in a *chiton* and *nebris*, who is attacking him with a dagger. On the left, another woman, with a double *chiton, nebris* and *thyrsus*, is seizing him by the arm (A. Kiessling, in *Bulletino dell' Inst. Archeol.*, 1862, p. 128).

(7) On a small amphora with red figures, very sketchily painted, in a collection belonging to Signor Torrusio which was for sale in Naples in 1869, we find Pentheus fallen on the ground, wearing a *chlamys* and holding aloft a spear in his

right. With his left arm he defends himself against Agave who is seizing his hair with her left hand and brandishing her *thyrsus* in her right. She wears bracelets and is dressed in a *chiton* with a *nebris* flung over it (H. Heydemann, in *Bulletino dell' Inst. Archeol.*, 1869, p. 191).

(8) A *cameo* in the National Museum at Naples, some account of which is given in the note on l. 983, probably represents the espial of Pentheus at the moment when he has just been detected in the disguise of a lion. This form of disguise may either have been suggested to the artist by the passages in our play in which the mother is described as mistaking her son for a lion, or it may have been a conventional way of indicating a spy, which had its origin in the Homeric story of Dolon clad in his wolf-skin (*Il.* 10, 334). There is some difficulty in explaining part of the design in which a Satyr is to be seen holding his hand to his mouth and apparently blowing into a large leather skin, the inflated part of which is held before him by a kneeling Maenad; this may either represent preparations for the form of dancing called the ἀσκωλιασμὸς, or else it may be meant for a wine-skin from which the Satyr is about to take a draught.

(9) A fragment of a relief on a sarcophagus in the Chigi Park at Ariccia, is mentioned by Michaelis in *Bulletino dell' Instituto* 1858 p. 171. It resembles the relief in the Giustiniani Palace, figured on p. xciv, and described on pp. cxxix—cxxxii. Here as there, we have a Fury girt with a *nebris*, though there are in other respects some small points of difference; the tree is larger and Ino is represented as kneeling on *both* knees.

(10) In the National Museum at Naples is a small fragment of a relief, found in the theatre at Capua, and published by Franc. Alvino, *Anfiteatro Campano* tav. xi 2 b. It represents two women in long *chitons*, one of them holding a *tympanum* in her left, and a spear or *thyrsus* in her right. The right arm is held aloft, pointing the weapon downwards to the lower part of the left arm. In front of her is another in a similar attitude, but little is left of her except the upper half of her weapon and the lower half of her dress. This is identified as part of a 'death of Pentheus,' by K. Dilthey in his article on the design

figured on p. 69 (*Archg. Ztg.* 1874 p. 80). In Alvino's work, published in 1842, the above relief is described as coming from one of the lateral parapets of the *vomitoria.* Another fragment belonging to one of the other places of exit represents a female figure with a bow in her left hand, probably Artemis ; a third, part of the legs of a man attacked by a hound, doubtless Actaeon. This increases the probability that the fragment refers to the doom of Pentheus, but the relief is too imperfect to allow of our being absolutely certain on this point.

(11) A relief similar in general design to (10), though with the figures more cramped together. Published in *Marmora Taurinensia* I p. 91, Maffei's *Museum Veronense* p. ccxxvii, 4; Jahn's *Pentheus* t. II b; and minutely described by Dütschke, *Antike Bildwerke in Turin* &c. 1880, no. 118. The lower half has apparently been restored; the indications of the waves in this portion, together with a lyre, (suspiciously resembling a modern violin,) have led some to identify it as a representation of the fate of Orpheus. Another relief at Turin exhibits a group of dancing Maenads with dishevelled hair, one of whom holds in her right hand a *thyrsus* which passes downwards across her shoulders, while in her left she grasps what is sometimes supposed to be the head of Pentheus, but is more probably identified as a tragic mask or an *oscillum* (*Marmora Taurinensia* I p. 29; Maffei, *u. s.*, p. ccxviii, 2, and Dütschke, *u. s.*, no. 132).

(12) In the north cloister of the *Campo Santo* at Pisa there is a sarcophagus with reliefs including a representation of the death of Pentheus. He lies naked on the ground surrounded by the wild Maenads, one of whom standing to the right has violently thrust her foot upon his neck, and is striving with both hands to sever his left arm from his body. To the left is another, resting on her right knee, and her left foot on his left leg, with both hands dragging at his right leg, which she has seized by the foot and also above the knee. Between her and Pentheus stands another, holding in her two hands a knotted staff which she is on the point of bringing down on the head of the unhappy intruder. To the extreme right is another Bacchante who is

(12)   RELIEF ON A SARCOPHAGUS IN THE CAMPO SANTO AT PISA.

hastening to the *melée*, with her garments waving in the wind.
To the extreme left is a curved line, meant perhaps as a rude
representation of a tree. The scene above described forms the
right compartment of the upright portion of the lid of the sarcophagus; the left compartment apparently represents the bringing up of the infant Dionysus by the nymphs. In front of the
sarcophagus itself is Dionysus, with the *cista mystica* and
serpent at his feet. The reliefs which run round the lid, though
much damaged, are full of life, and the movements of the
figures are well designed. Copied from Lasinio's *Raccolta* t. 122,
in Jahn's *Pentheus* t. III b, and fully described by Dütschke,
die Antiken Bildwerke des Campo Santo zu Pisa, 1874, no. 52.
The dimensions of this relief, which I had an opportunity of
examining on the spot in January 1882, are two and a half feet
broad and one foot high. The woodcut is copied from Jahn *u. s.*

(13) A relief on a sarcophagus published in 1782 by Cavaceppi, in vol. III plate 38 of his work entitled *Raccolta d'*
antiche statue busti teste cognite ed altre sculture antiche
scelte restaurate dal Cavaliere Bartolomeo Cavaceppi scultore
Romano. This relief, which was not known to Jahn when he
wrote his monograph on Pentheus in 1841, is incidentally
discussed by Stephani in his elaborate dissertation, *der ausru-*
hende Herakles, pp. 106, 114 (=pp. 358, 366 of the *Mémoires de*
l'Academie Impériale des Sciences de St Pétersbourg, sixième
série, tome viii, 1855). The design falls into three parts, which
however are not sharply separated from one another. (*a*) To
the extreme left is a winged boy with an inverted torch, per-
sonifying Death, as explained in Lessing's interesting essay on
the manner in which Death was represented by the Ancients
(translated in the Prose Works, p. 171—226, of ed. 1879).
Passing to the right, we next see a small altar with a mask
upon it ; then another winged boy, with a staff bound with
ribbands resting on his arm, and a pan-pipe at his feet; next
another, with the double flute and a club at his feet; then a
fourth, with cymbals at his feet, and with a *plectrum* in his right
and a lyre in his left; and, on the ground beneath the lyre, a
mask. (*b*) Next comes a group of two boys supporting a third

RELIEF ON A SARCOPHAGUS IN CAVACEPPI'S RACCOLTA.

who is reeling in a state of mild intoxication, with a *cantharus* in his left and what is perhaps a lantern in his right. Here, as elsewhere, the happiness of the future life is ignobly represented as consisting in an αἰώνιος μέθη (Plato, *Rep.* II 363 C). To the right of this group is a winged boy looking back at the group and holding a wicker basket in his right and a *pedum* in his left. (*c*) The extreme right is filled with a group with which we are immediately concerned. At the foot of a tree kneels a youthful form with a *chlamys* cast over his shoulder. His left arm clasps the trunk of the tree; his right arm is grasped violently by one of the three women who are attacking him. Another is plunging a spear into his breast; the third is seizing him by the hair with her left, and brandishing her *thyrsus* over him. A panther is also springing upon him. From the tree hangs a decorated variety of *tympanum* (cf. Clarac's *Musée*, pl. 132, no. 144, and Campana's *Opere in plastica*, no. 45). The first and second portions of the design, (*a*) and (*b*), closely resemble the relief on a sarcophagus in the Pio-Clementine Museum figured in Millin's *Gallerie Mythologique*, LXIX 272. The third, which undoubtedly represents the fate of Pentheus, may be compared with the designs figured on pages xciv and 69, and opposite p. cxiii. It is here copied, together with one of the winged boys belonging to the second portion of the design, from Cavaceppi's *Raccolta u. s.*, where two sarcophagi are engraved on the same page, with the vague statement that one of them (it does not appear which) was in his own possession.

(14) On a lamp engraved in Passeri's *Lucernae Fictiles* (Pesaro, 1739) II ci, we have a female figure in a long *chiton* and *chlamys* seizing with her right hand the right arm of a youth who is holding a short sword in that hand. Another female is grasping his left wrist with her left hand, and is stretching forth her right to seize him by the hair. His left foot is already off the ground and his fall is imminent. The two women have a ribband tied into a small bow above their foreheads. The letterpress describes it as *Orestes Furiis agitatus;* but a comparison with our other examples almost conclusively proves it to be a Pentheus.

(14 *b*) A Roman bas-relief, found in 1887 in an ancient sepulchre on the *Via Portuensis*, and apparently of the first century of our era, 'represents a naked youth in a condition of much excitement, with long, dishevelled hair. In his right hand he holds a short sword ; a short cloak is wrapped round the left arm. He is defending himself against two young women, one facing him, the other attacking him from behind. They wear each a short *chiton* and *himation*. They brandish *thyrsi*, resembling lances, one with the right hand, the other with the left. A serpent winds itself round the arm of each, in two spirals, and they seem as if about to fling them at the face of the youth. The first impression is that the group represents the tragic story of Orestes haunted by the Eumenides....But the *thyrsi* exclude the possibility of this being a representation of the Orestean doom. The antiquary Luigi Bossari suggests that it more probably represents the fate of Pentheus. A painted vase found in the Basilicata [no. 2, p. cix *supra*] is singularly like this sepulchral tablet, but with points of difference that add to the interest. The material of the tablet seems to be Carrara marble' (Quoted in the *Times*, Sept. 20, 1887, from a correspondent of the *Frankfurter Zeitung*).

(14 *c*) A Pompeian painting in the house of A. Vettius, excavated in 1894—5, represents Pentheus kneeling on his left knee, with his right leg extending forwards, and his *chlamys* floating behind him. He is casting an imploring glance at the Maenad (probably Agave), attacking him on his right. She has seized his hair with her left hand, is holding a *thyrsus* aloft in her right, and has planted her right foot above the knee of Pentheus, who is vainly stretching his arm towards her. On his left, his arm, which is bent upwards to his head, is seized by both the hands of another Maenad, to whom the spear flung on the ground in front of Pentheus probably belongs. In the upper part of the painting appear three other Maenads, those to the extreme left and right brandishing torches and darts, while the one in the middle holds above her head a large flat stone, which she is on the point of dashing down on the head of Pentheus (Mr Talfourd Ely in *Journal of Hellenic Studies*, xvi 1896, with cut on p. 151).

S. B.   *i*

(15) RELIEF ON A MARBLE ALTAR IN THE
UFFIZI AT FLORENCE.

Thus far we have had to deal with representations of the death of Pentheus; the remaining works of art, which we proceed to enumerate, have for their subject the immediately subsequent event, the triumph of Agave.

(15) In the Uffizi at Florence (Dütschke, *die Antiken Marmorbildwerken der Uffizien in Florenz*, 1878, no. 503), in the middle of the right-hand recess of the 'hall of inscriptions,' stands a Roman *cippus* of white marble, on each of the four sides of which is a Bacchante in wild transport, one of whom has the *thyrsus* while two others are clashing cymbals. The one in front is draped in a long semi-transparent *chiton*, her arms are stretched out wide, with a light shawl passing from one to the other and falling loosely between them ; her face looks upwards with an earnest gaze, and the hair is thrown back like that of the Agave on p. 58; in her right she holds a short sword with the point upwards, in her left a youthful head of finely chiselled profile, cut off just below the neck. These figures could hardly have been originally designed for this monument, and are probably, as has been suggested, copied from a lost original representing in a larger design Agave and her Maenads after they had compassed the death of Pentheus. This is rendered probable by the fact that elsewhere we find an altar, (referred to in Zoega's *Bassirilievi* II p. 175,) which represents the three daughters of Cadmus, including Agave with the head of Pentheus; and also a fragment in the Museo Chiaromonti (VII *riquadro* n. 150) on the same theme (Jahn's *Pentheus und die Mainaden* p. 22). The authority last quoted further suggests that the figure of Agave in particular may have been taken from some famous piece of sculpture, which is here combined for the nonce with other Bacchic forms of a conventional type. He cites Welcker (on Zoega's *Bassirel.* p. 163) as referring to a marble slab, in the possession of W. von Humboldt, with a head of Ammon on one side, and Agave with the head of Pentheus on the other ; he also mentions one or two gems on the same sub-

ject in the Berlin collection, and gives a reference to Vivenzio, *gemme antiche ined.* tav. 19, adding however that Gerhard and himself had sought in vain for a copy of that work in Berlin and Kiel respectively. As the work is obviously rare, I may add that Mr King has been good enough to shew me the engraving referred to: it is called *Agave: Calcedonia; Penteo lacerato dalle Baccante;* Pentheus is seen defending himself against three Maenads, the one to the left holding a *thyrsus;* the one in the middle two serpents, while the one on the right has her *thyrsus* thrust forward like a spear. In Mr King's opinion the design is not even *renaissance* work, and he would ascribe it to the last century.—The engraving, opposite p. cxvi, is copied directly from Zannoni's *Reale Galleria di Firenze,* IV 16. The descriptive letterpress in series IV vol i, p. 33—39, states that it was formerly in the *villa Medicea* at Rome.

(16) In Cavaceppi's *Raccolta* I 50, there is an engraving of an Ibis on a pedestal with its base ornamented with winged figures at the corners and floral scrolls between. On the front of the pedestal is a relief representing a female figure dressed in a short *chiton* and a light shawl, standing on tip-toe in an attitude of dancing. On her head is a crown indicated by three spikes radiating upwards to the left, while she looks in profile to the right. In her right she holds a short sword with the point upwards; in her left, she is grasping by the top of the hair a human head which she is holding over the flames of an altar. The pedestal, at the time of Cavaceppi's publication, belonged to 'Sig^r. Cav. Browne,' i.e. Sir Lyde Browne of Wimbledon (Michaelis, *Ancient Marbles in Great Britain,* § 52), from whom it was purchased for the Hermitage at St Petersburg (Stephani, *Mélanges gréco-romains* III p. 361). Guédéonoff, in his catalogue entitled *Musée de sculpture antique de l'Ermitage Impérial,* no. 298, fails to identify as Agave the figure above described. The Ibis is still in England, at Newby Hall (Michaelis *u. s.* p. 534, no. 40).

(17) On one of the three sides of the pedestal of a candelabrum in the British Museum, we have a relief representing Agave in a wild attitude with head thrown slightly back, and

hair dishevelled, holding a human head in one hand, and a sword, with the point upwards, in the other.   The treatment of the feet and the lower folds of the drapery is identical with that in the gem engraved on p. 73 (Combe's *British Museum Marbles* part I plate V, Ellis, *Townley Gallery* II p. 79, and Part II no. 6 in the *Official Guide to the Graeco-Roman Sculptures in the B.M.*, where it is suggested that this type may have been 'derived from some composition by Scopas').

(18) In Welcker's *Alte Denkmäler*, II taf. vi, 11, we have a marble disc, on one side of which is Agave dancing for joy. Her head is tossed back; her right leg is extended far in advance of her left; her arms are stretched widely apart; in her left she is grasping a short sword, pointed upwards; and in her right, she holds before a blazing altar the head of Pentheus.

(19) In the gem-cabinet of the British Museum, we have an antique 'paste' representing Agave with the head of Pentheus. In her right she grasps by the hair the head of her son, in her left a *thyrsus* capped with leaves and trimmed with floating ribbands.   Her head is violently thrown back, and the lower part of the drapery is tossed about as she dances for joy. The engraving of this, enlarged by one-third, from the original gem, is given on p. 73.   No. 559 in Mr A. H. Smith's *Catalogue.*

(20) In Cades' *impronte gemmarie, classe* II A, no. 90, there is a small gem from the Vannutelli collection, figured in Müller-Wieseler II xxxvii 438, in which Agave is holding in her left the head of Pentheus, and in her right a short sword pointed downwards; the lower folds of the dress and the attitude of her head are remarkably like those of the gem on p. 73, to which, however, it is otherwise far inferior.   Now in British Museum, no. 1082.

(21) In Cades *u. s.* II A no. 89, there is another gem nearly identical in composition with the last, except that the sword is pointed upwards; the style is stiffer and the hair hangs down from the back of the head in a somewhat heavy mass.   The light shawl visible in no. 90 is wanting.

(22) and (23)   Two 'pastes' in the Berlin Cabinet.   One of them is described in Tölken's Catalogue III 1074 as an antique 'paste' representing Agave as a wild Maenad, with the head

of her son. It was formerly in the collection of Bartholdy, Prussian consul in Rome.. The colour is a bright green. The other is an antique yellow 'paste' formerly in the Stosch collection (Tölken, IV 5).

Thus far we have been concerned with the *artistic* treatment of the legend of Dionysus and Pentheus, as represented by sculpture and painting, in accordance with their own laws of composition, and with the help of such materials as are at their disposal. The *poetic* treatment of the same subject necessarily differs from the *artistic*, in so far as the former must be in accordance with the laws of poetic composition and the means whereby the effects of poetry are produced. Thus, all that the Second Messenger's Speech in our play brings before the eye of the spectator by means of a rapid narrative, in which the effect is unfolded by a series of successive movements told in due relation of time, is by the art of the painter or the sculptor gathered into the limits of a more confined form of composition in which a single moment is seized and set forth with such resources as those arts can command. As poetry differs from those arts in its method, and its means, and to some extent in its end besides, we must not expect all the details of poetic narrative to be reproduced in the artistic embodiment of the same theme; the points of difference, as well as the points of coincidence in treatment, are both alike instructive. The illustrations in this volume are not intended, as a rule, to help towards the realisation of the manner in which the play was put upon the stage; they are rather meant to supply materials for a comparison between the poetic and the artistic treatment of the same subject. For, in the words of one who was himself a masterly exponent of the principles of Ancient Art,

If we desire to form a lively and true conception of the procedure of an ancient Tragedy upon the stage, we must first divest ourselves entirely of those ideas of the characters in Grecian Mythology, which we derive from ancient works of art, and which from natural causes continually haunt our imagination. There is not the least comparison to be drawn between the *scenic* and the *plastic* costume of the ancient Gods and Heroes; for, as the statements of the old Grammarians and ancient works of art (especially the mosaics in the Vatican) sufficiently prove, there was but one general στολή, or costume for Tragedy. This was nothing more than an improvement on the gay and brilliant apparel worn in the procession at the Dionysian Festivals, and but slight alterations were needed to adapt it to the different dramatic characters[1].

The only work of art at present known to us which has for its subject the *theatrical* representation of the legend of Pentheus, is a design on the back of a bronze mirror in the Collegio Romano at Rome. The scenes were perhaps taken from a lost Latin play which agreed with the *Xantriae* of Aeschylus in representing the Maenads attacking Pentheus with flaming torches, differing in this respect from the treatment of the same subject in the *Bacchae*. This interesting, though somewhat inartistic design, is copied on p. lxxxviii, and described on p. cxxviii.

---

[1] K. O. Müller *on the Eumenides* p. 63.

DESCRIPTION OF THE WOODCUTS.

Frontispiece.

A RELIEF encircling a marble vase, little more than three feet high, of an elegant oval form, with upright massive handles, found in the villa of Antoninus Pius at Lanuvium. The relief represents a scene of Bacchic revelry, in sculptured forms of exquisite workmanship. Beginning from the left, the first group of two consists of a Maenad wearing a *tunica talaris* (χιτὼν ποδήρης), over which falls a ἡμιδιπλοΐδιον (Ar. *Eccl.* 318); she is looking towards a Satyr who is approaching her with a *thyrsus* in his right hand, and the skin of a panther, falling in ample folds, knotted over his left shoulder. The second group is a male Bacchanal, holding an inverted torch in his right hand, and with his left resting on the shoulders of a Maenad looking towards him, clad in loose flowing garments. Next follows a group of three, a bearded Satyr with a panther crouching at his feet, a panther's skin resting on his left arm, his right arm raised, and his whole attitude suggestive of the description in l. 148, 'challenging his errant comrades to running and to dancing, and making them bound again with his revel-shouts.' On either side of him is a Maenad, in a light semi-transparent garment; they are looking towards one another as they dance, the one on the right holding aloft a knife, the one on the left grasping in her left hand part of a dismembered kid, as is clearly seen in the original relief, just as in the cuts on pp. 86 and 238. The last group is composed of a youthful form clad in a short chiton with a panther's skin fastened over his left shoulder, and wearing hunting-boots (ἀρβυλίδες); this figure slightly resembles the second in the relief on p. xciv, and the huntress Maenad or Fury on p. 69. He rests his right hand on a bearded Satyr, slightly intoxicated, and holding a *pedum* in his left hand. The last group closes with the goat-legged Pan, with his right arm vehemently extended and with his left carrying an *amphora* of wine, one of the handles of which appears in the woodcut on the extreme left where the design round the vase is continued.—*Official Guide to the Graeco-Roman Sculptures in the B. M.* Part II no. (55).

The cut is reduced from an engraving in Combe's *British Museum Marbles*, part I, plate vii. There is a somewhat roughly executed copy on a smaller scale in Ellis' *Townley Gallery* II p. 210.

Vignette.

HEAD OF BACCHANTE. A fillet may be seen passing across the brow, a crown of ivy, or of some variety of *smilax*, resting on the hair, and a fawnskin hanging just below the neck. The woodcut is enlarged by one-third from a cast of a sard in the gem-cabinet of the British Museum[1]; but it appears impossible, in any representation on a flat surface, however excellent, to do perfect justice to the exquisitely rounded softness and delicacy of the design. Another copy, by a remarkably skilful artist, Utting, shewing perhaps in a still greater degree the extreme difficulty of the task, may be seen in Munro and King's *Horace* Od. III 25 ; where Mr King, who under the head of 'Bacchic subjects' elsewhere describes the original as 'a gem regarded as the first in this class' (*Antique Gems and Rings* II 56), remarks that 'the face has not by any means the regular beauty of the conventional Maenad-type, but has all the appearance of a portrait from the life.' It is sometimes called an Ariadne, but Mr King suggests that it may either represent some effeminate youth disguised as a Maenad, or some dissolute prince like Ptolemy Philopator (King of Egypt from B.C. 222 to 205), who according to Plutarch, *Cleomenes* § 33, οὕτω διέφθαρτο τὴν ψυχὴν ...ὥστε, ὁπότε νήφοι μάλιστα καὶ σπουδαιότατος αὐτοῦ γένοιτο, τελετὰς τελεῖν καὶ τύμπανον ἔχων ἐν τοῖς βασιλείοις ἀγείρειν (*ib.* § 36, μητραγύρτου βασίλεως σχολὴν ἀναμένων, ὅταν πρῶτον ἀποθῆται τὸ τύμπανον καὶ καταπαύσῃ τὸν θίασον). 'This gem, a noble specimen of Greek art in its full maturity, was found,' he adds, 'in

[1] No. 1066.

Sicily, and presented by the Municipality of Palermo to the Austrian general, Count Salis. It was afterwards bought by Count Wiczay for 300 gold ducats,' and passed through the Pulsky cabinet (which was sold in 1868) into Castellani's hands and thence into the British Museum.

Introduction § 1, p. ix.

THE BIRTH OF DIONYSUS; from a bas-relief in the Vatican. To the left, seated on a rock, is Zeus, a bearded figure with the head bent slightly forward, with a fillet resting on his hair, and with the folds of his mantle passing over from his left shoulder and completely covering his right leg. The left arm is resting against a staff, and the right is pressed down on the rock. From his left leg a vigorous babe, the infant Dionysus, with a band encircling his hair, is leaping upward to the light, while Hermes, who is ready to receive him πήχεϊ κολπωθέντι (Nonnus 9, 17), is leaning forward in a graceful attitude with a panther's skin falling over his hands, a scarf or *chlamys* thrown over his shoulder, a *petasus* on his head, and sandals (faintly indicated) on his feet. Hermes carrying the infant Dionysus is found on reliefs (Müller-Wieseler II 395, 396), once supposed to be copied from the masterpiece of Praxiteles which Pausanias saw at Olympia (V 17 § 1), but the discovery of this very work during the excavations in 1878 disproves this supposition. The figure next to Hermes with the open palm, is almost certainly the goddess of childbirth, Eileithyia (Pausanias VII 23 § 6, Εἰλεί-θυια ἐς ἄκρους ἐκ κεφαλῆς τοὺς πόδας ὑφάσματι κεκάλυπται λεπτῷ… καὶ ταῖς χερσὶ τῇ μὲν εἰς εὐθὺ ἐκτέταται, τῇ δὲ ἀνέχει δᾷδα). The next is hard to identify; Persephone is suggested by Visconti, but it is more probably either Themis or one of the nymphs who nursed the infant god. The last, with the ears of corn in her hand, is obviously the 'counterpart' of Dionysus, Demeter (l. 275 ff.).

It may be interesting to add that among the reliefs, extending along the front of the stage in the theatre of Dionysus at Athens, which were brought to light not many years ago, is one representing the birth of the god; the attitude of Zeus is similar to that in our relief, but it is reversed, being turned to the left instead of to the right; his left hand is resting as here on a block of stone, and his right is extended; Hermes is holding the babe on his arm; and two of the three remaining figures are bearing shields, the Corybantes or Curetes of l. 120, 125 (*Annali dell' Instituto* 1870, vol. 42, p. 97—106, *Mon.* IX tav. 16)[1]. The same subject was treated with far less dignity of style in a painting by a pupil of Apelles, Ctesilochus, *Iove Liberum parturiente depicto mitrato et muliebriter ingemescente inter opstetricia dearum* (Plin. *N. H.* XXXV § 140). We have a vase of the finest style in the British Museum, no. 724, representing his birth from the thigh of Zeus, who seated on an altar, holds the new-born and long-haired infant in his arms. The woodcut is reduced from Visconti's *Musée Pie Clémentin* IV, t. 19.

Page xxxii.

FROM A VASE-PAINTING IN THE MUSEO NAZIONALE AT NAPLES (vase-room IV, no. 2419). On the side of the vase which is here copied, we have four Bacchantes hastening to join in the worship of Dionysus, who is represented, on the other side, in the form described below. All of them are wreathed with leaves of ivy or vine, and are wearing a light head-dress. The first, who is playing the double flute, is robed in a long *chiton* falling to her feet in varied folds and covered with a woollen mantle which leaves the right shoulder and breast free. The second carries in her right a *thyrsus* with a leafy top, and a small branch still unstripped from its stem; in her left is a flaming torch held downwards; she wears a girdled double *chiton;* over her is the name ΘΑΛΕΙΑ. The third, whose head is turned away from the two former, wears a *nebris* over her *chiton* and is beating a *tympanum;* she is named ΧΟΡΕΙΑ (a name mentioned, as it happens, by Pausanias, II 20 § 3, as that of a Maenad who accompanied Dionysus in an expedition against Perseus, and whose tomb the traveller saw near an ancient temple of Τύχη at Argos, at the spot where she was buried apart from the rest of the Maenads slain in battle). The fourth figure, with her head tossed back, has a budding *thyrsus* in her left, while her right is wrapped in the ample folds of the mantle which partly covers her *chiton.*

[1] See Plate in *Papers of American School of Classical Studies at Athens,* i 137.

On the other side of the vase, which is not given here, but may be seen in Müller-Wieseler II xlvi 583 and elsewhere, there is an idol of the bearded Dionysus, decked out with sprays of ivy and laurel, like the figure of the god at Phigalia (Pausan. VIII 39 § 4), or the boy Bacchus of the Homeric Hymn, κισσῷ καὶ δάφνῃ πεπυκασμένος. He has no arms; his *chiton* is bespangled with stars; and his head crowned by a *modius* with seven small pyramids; to the right and left of the head, resting on the shoulders, are two oval objects possibly meant for cymbals; on a light table in front are two large vessels (*hydriae*), and between them a small *cantharus,* a loose ribband and some small white fruits. Beneath the table, laurels are growing up beside the stock of wood on which the idol is set. On each side of the central stock are two female figures; all the four are crowned with ivy or vine-leaves; the one to the extreme left, who holds a thyrsus over her head and a reversed torch in her right, wears a double *chiton* and a *nebris* with a girdle over the latter. The next, whose *nebris* is hanging loosely over her long *chiton* and whose hair is streaming down her back, is dipping a ladle into one of the large vessels on the table, from which she is about to pour into a small two-handled cup or *scyphos* in her left: over her is the name ΔΙΩΝΗ. The next is a female described by the word ΜΑΙΝΑΣ, clad in *chiton* and *nebris*, beating the *tympanum*, and looking away from the idol towards the next figure in the design, who is tossing her head back, and holding a partly inverted torch in the one hand and an upright one in the other; this last figure wears a Doric double *chiton.*

The vase, which is a *Stamnos* with red figures on a black ground, was found at Nocera de' Pagani. It is characterized by Otto Jahn as one of the most beautiful vases now extant and as an example of the finest and freest style of art (*Vasensammlung in der Pinakothek zu München,* lii, cxciii); and by Heydemann, as fine beyond all description, and as a design of surpassing beauty that deserves the highest admiration (*die Vasensammlungen des Museo Nazionale zu Neapel*).

The form of Bacchic worship which it represents has been variously interpreted. An attempt was made, by Panofka, to prove that the women were the *Thyiades* of Delphi holding the *Herois*-festival on Parnassus and worshipping Dionysus περι-κιόνιος or στῦλος; but his conclusions involve a series of fanciful assumptions that do not carry conviction with them. It was also discussed by C. Bötticher in his monograph on Greek tree-worship (*Baumkultus* p. 103, 229), and is referred by him with much probability to the ancient country-festivals of Dionysus δενδρίτης. Lastly, it was suggested by Jahn that it represents the ceremony of the Anthesteria called the ἱερὸς γάμος, which was celebrated by women, and he conjectures that the women may have had a special custom of tasting the new wine corresponding to the men's festival of the χόες on the second day of the Anthesteria (*Annali dell' Instituto* 1862, p. 71). He arrives at this conclusion by comparing with this vase several of similar but in some respects simpler and far less artistic design, two of which may be seen in the British Museum (*Third Vase Room* no. E 140 and E 153). A comparison with those ruder examples would seem to shew that, in this incomparable work, the artist has intended to idealise one of the Dionysiac ceremonials of real life by ascribing to the women of Attica the names and attributes and the ecstatic enthusiasm of the Maenads of Greek mythology; and the contrast between the rude simplicity of the central idol and the artistic beauty of the surrounding worshippers indicates that in the present instance he was consciously blending a scene of actual life with an imaginative representation appropriate to the domain of mythology and art (Rapp, in *Rheinisches Museum* 1872 p. 585).

The figures in the woodcut are taken from Panofka's *Dionysos und Thyaden*, plate 1, 2; the border below is added from a copy in Gargiulo's *Recueil* 1875, pl. 163; in the lettering, the two forms of *epsilon*, which are not distinguished in previous copies, are here discriminated on the authority of a friend who, on a recent visit to Naples, kindly examined the letters at my request.

Page xlii.

MASK OF DIONYSUS BETWEEN THOSE OF A SATYR AND
A SILENUS. The head of Dionysus is decked with ivy leaves
and ribbands; above the brow a fillet binds the hair, which falls
in spiral curls over the forehead and down the cheeks (γένυν
παρ' αὐτὴν κεχυμένος, l. 456). Between this and the bald head of
Silenus on the right, which is crowned with vine-leaves, is a
thyrsus bound with ribbands; on the other side, near the head of
the Satyr, which presents no peculiarity, is a Pan-pipe or *syrinx*
(l. 952), hanging from a *pedum*. The original is a small terracotta mural relief (of one foot seven inches, by six inches) in the
'Etruscan Saloon' of the British Museum, wall-case 14. The
greater part of the mural terra-cottas of this type are probably
the work of Greek artists living about the close of the Roman
Republic (*General Guide*, p. 212).

Page lix.

THE MASKS OF COMEDY AND TRAGEDY CONTRASTED.
In both cases the mouth is wide open (the *hiatus* referred to in
Juvenal III 173 and Persius V 3); in the former, the face, especially the mouth, is grotesquely distorted; in the latter, the
lips are slightly parted, and the profile and general expression
is appropriate to a serene and dignified composure. The comic
mask bears a thick wreath, formed (it has been suggested) of
the flowers of the *narthex* sacred to Dionysus, the god of the
drama; but this is hardly borne out by the passage quoted for
it: Virg. *Ecl.* X 25, *venit et agresti capitis Silvanus honore,
florentes ferulas et grandia lilia quassans*. The original is a
bas-relief in the British Museum, 9½ × 8½ inches; the woodcut is
reduced from the large engraving which forms the vignette of the
Museum Marbles, part II. *Guide to the Graeco-Roman Sculptures*, part II no. (132).

Page lxxii.

BUST OF A YOUTHFUL FAUN. The *nebris* is slung over his
right shoulder, and ivy-leaves are gracefully intermingled with

the curls of his hair. The features are those of 'a handsome rustic boy.' The face, as well as the shoulder, is suggestive of violent effort, blended however with the half-amused air of one who is engaged in a κάματος εὐκάματος. It indicates that the bust belongs to a figure of a Faun in the favourite attitude of supporting a less steady companion. The original is a sard formerly in the cabinet of Mr King, who characterizes it as a 'fine Greek work' (*Antique Gems and Rings*, xxix. 1, and *Horace*, Od. III 18 B).

Page lxxxviii.

SCENES FROM THE TRAGEDY OF PENTHEUS ON A BRONZE MIRROR IN THE COLLEGIO ROMANO. A bronze plate five inches in diameter, bounded by a rim ornamented with wavy lines, is filled with three rows of figures ranging across the plate. The costume of all the figures, the long *chiton* falling in ample folds to the feet, the girdle sitting high on the breast, the upper garment either resting on the shoulders or floating in the air, the ὄγκος on the head, and the *cothurnus* on the feet wherever they are visible ;—all this clearly indicates a series of scenes from a tragedy. The upper row contains four figures, Pentheus with his right arm thrust forward in act to strike, and with his left grasping the arm of one whose hands are tied behind his back and who turns away from the king. This figure, which has a somewhat girlish aspect, must be identified as Dionysus in disguise, wearing a peculiar headdress with loose folds (meant perhaps for curls) falling down the cheeks. To the right of this pair is a figure of gloomy aspect, with a thin staff, or sceptre, in his hand, probably intended for Cadmus. To the left, another holding between the two hands something like a roll or muff. The two extremities of this row of figures are closed by a curious instrument resembling a square table, on which rests a round object with five prominent knobs radiating from its upper part, while some wavy lines are issuing from the foot of the table ; these instruments are probably some kind of musical contrivance, possibly water-organs. The antiquity of the design is doubted by Dierks, *De tragicorum histrionum habitu*, 1883.

In the middle row, we have five figures, four of them armed with torches, crowding round a form intended for Pentheus, whose garb has nothing to distinguish it from that of the women in the same scene. He is helplessly stretching out his arms towards his tormentors.

The third and lowest row represents a figure kneeling on one knee and holding a pair of torches : to the right is another with its back to the former, and with the face hidden by the hand. The kneeling figure is partly supported by another approaching it from behind, and to the left of this is another figure which is somewhat faintly indicated. The kneeling figure is probably Agave, at the moment of her becoming conscious of her deed of horror ; the figure with the face hidden is probably Cadmus. To the extreme right and left are two stands, and on each of them two masks are set up side by side. The style of these masks, as well as that of the water-organs, has suggested the conclusion that the work belongs to late Roman times and that the scenes represented belong to the Roman theatre (Wieseler's *Theatergeb.* p. 99, quoted by Wecklein). The plate is the subject of an article by Otto Jahn in the *Archäologische Zeitung* XXV 1867 taf. CCXXV i no. 225, and a dissertation by B. Arnold, *Festgruss der Philologischen Gesellschaft zu Würzburg an die* XXVI *Versammlung deutschen Philologen u. Schulmänner*, Würzburg 1868, pp. 142—157, where a careful lithograph of the original is given. For the loan of a copy of this pamphlet— Jahn's own copy as it happens—I am indebted to the kindness of Prof. Michaelis. The woodcut here given is reduced by one-third of the diameter of the original, and the ornamental border of the rim has been omitted.

Page xciv.

THE DEATH OF PENTHEUS ; a bas-relief on a sarcophagus in the court of the Giustiniani Palace in Rome. At the extreme left is a female form, fully draped, seated in a sorrowful posture, leaning her head on one side and resting it on her right arm ; her left arm is bent over her head ; from near her left hand a stream of water is issuing. This stream, as well as the serpent coiled about her body, indicates a water-nymph (R. Rochette *Mon. Inéd.* p. 22) lamenting the death of Pentheus. A fountain-nymph girt with a snake is found on coins of Larissa and also on a fine vase referring to the legend of Cadmus (*ib.* 4). She may be identified either as the nymph of the fountain in that part of Cithaeron where both Actaeon and Pentheus were torn asunder (l. 1285, Philostr. *im.* I 14 ; so Wieseler), or more probably, the nymph Dirce (l. 519, Nonnus 44, 10 ; so Jahn). The epithet δρακοντόβοτος is given to Dirce by Nonnus, 4, 356 and 46, 142. The next figure has a short *chiton* reaching nearly to the knee, and a *nebris* which is thrown across half of her chest and bound by a girdle ; her hair falls loosely over her shoulders; a light scarf floats in the air, as it passes from one arm to the other ; the boots and the garb in general are suggestive of a huntress which may be identified as an Erinys (Böttiger *Furien*m. p. 81, and K. Dilthey quoted on page cxlv). Similarly in a bas-relief representing the death of Lycurgus (Müller-Wieseler II 441) we have the figure of a huntress (with apparently a scourge in one hand and a torch in the other).—In the central group is Pentheus, who is lightly clad in a *chlamys*, and is sitting help-lessly on the ground, clasping a tree with his right arm. His left leg is seized by a panther, one of the animals sacred to Dionysus, which is elsewhere to be seen attacking Lycurgus (Müller-Wieseler II 441, also on a mosaic from Herculaneum in the Naples Museum, and on a vase from Canosa, now in Munich, no. 853 in Jahn's *Vasensammlung*). In Oppian, we have a legend describing the god transforming his nurses into panthers and Pentheus into a bull whom they rend in pieces (*Cyneg.* III 78, IV 230); and his fondness for the animal is referred to by Philostratus (*im.* I 19, φιλία δὲ Διονύσῳ πρὸς τὸ ζῷον, ἐπειδὴν θερμότατον τῶν ζῴων ἐστὶ καὶ πηδᾷ κοῦφα καὶ ἴσα εὐάδι). One of the women, who may be identified as Ino (l. 1125 —9), is endeavouring to wrench off his right leg, and another, Agave, his left arm ; the latter is somewhat awkwardly planting her right foot upon his neck. A third, immediately behind Pentheus, is falling on his head, while a fourth is hastening to

S. B.   *k*

join in the fray (Αὐτονόη τ' ὄχλος τε πᾶς ἐπεῖχε Βακχῶν). To the
right of this group are a pair of Centaurs, beings which often
appear in the train of Dionysus (Müller *Ancient Art* § 389,
Jahn's *Pentheus* note 48), one of whom is playing the double
flute, while the other, whose body is wreathed with leaves, is
striking the lyre. To the extreme right is a man with his right
arm bent over his head, who is by some identified as a satyr
(ἀποσκοπεύων), but in the absence of any distinctive satyric attributes it has been suggested that it is intended for Dionysus
himself, who is often represented with his arm over his head, as
here: so Michaelis, who however admits that as the marble is
much damaged, it is uncertain whether it may not, after all, be
one of his attendants. If so, it may be presumed that Dionysus,
if he appeared at all, was riding in a chariot drawn by the
Centaurs whose figures are still preserved in the relief.

The original was first published in the *Galeria Giustiniana*
T. I, plate 104, a tracing of which, from the copy in the Fitzwilliam Library, has been put at my service by the kindness of
Professor Colvin. The engraving is on a large scale, but is
wrongly reversed, and the same mistake runs through all the
smaller reproductions (e.g. the elegant copies in Millin's *Gal.
Myth.* LIII 235, in Jahn's *Pentheus* III a, in Wordsworth's
Greece p. 262, and Milman's *Bacchanals* p. 162). It was first
given correctly, after an original drawing, in Müller-Wieseler II
437. But even this is not perfectly accurate, as is shewn by
Michaelis, who wrote a short article on it in the *Bulletino
dell' Instituto* 1858 p. 170: he has in a most obliging manner
sent me several corrections from his own drawing, which have
happily enabled me to supply, to use his own language, 'a more
trustworthy reproduction than any hitherto published.' Thanks
to his corrections, we can now see (1) the *nebris* on the second
figure which had previously been disregarded; (2) the trunk of the
tree from which Pentheus has fallen, whereas the earlier copies
give us either unintelligible folds of drapery or altogether shirk
the details in this part of the design; and lastly, the position of
the right leg, thrust against the neck of Pentheus, though this
perhaps is still susceptible of a better rendering. Michaelis, in

the article above mentioned, compares our relief with a fragment of a similar design on a sarcophagus in the Chigi park at Ariccia, where the Fury, as here, has a *nebris,* but the tree is larger and the figure corresponding to Ino is kneeling on both knees, and not on one only.

When the original is represented unreversed, we see still more clearly (what Jahn observed even in an incorrect copy) the identity of the general design with the relief in the Campo Santo engraved opposite page cxiii, though the number of figures included there is smaller. All these points of identity, combined with slight diversity, point to an original which is now lost, some famous masterpiece which appears to have been often copied.

Page. clv.

MASK OF SILENUS AND DIONYSUS COMBINED. The original is a red jasper found in May, 1879, by the Rev. Thomas Crowther-Tatham, at Binchester, the ancient *Vinovium,* S. of the Roman wall. With reference to the combinations of masks in gems, it is remarked by Mr King, in his *Handbook of Engraved Gems,* p. 86; that 'the special stone for all such subjects is the red jasper; its colour caused it to be almost exclusively dedicated to the purpose, being that sacred to Bacchus, the "rosy god," whose statues were regularly painted with vermilion, as Pausanias informs us.' This gem, together with all the other antiquities discovered at Binchester, has recently found a permanent home in the University of Durham, owing to the liberality of John Proud, Esq., of Bishop Auckland. It is here figured and described for the first time. For bringing it to my notice, and thus enabling me to publish it in these pages, I am indebted to the kindness of the Rev. S. S. Lewis, F.S.A. The woodcut is enlarged to twice the scale of the original.

On Page I of text, Σεμέλη λοχευθείσ' ἀστραπηφόρῳ πυρί, line 3.

THE DEATH OF SEMELE: from an antique paste in the Berlin Museum. Zeus is here seen 'descending in all his glory, amidst a shower of thunderbolts, upon Semele, who falls lifeless before the insupportable brightness of his advent. The god is represented with wings, that most natural expression of the idea of omnipresence.......Winckelmann (*Pierres Gravées de Stosch*, p. 54) terms this design the perfection of Etruscan art ; remarking that "it would be difficult in any work, of any period, to find the drapery so delicately rendered"' (from Mr King's description in King and Munro's *Horace*, Od. IV xi A). The winged figure was once supposed to represent Θάνατος (Raoul Rochette, *monumens inédits*, p. 218); it is also discussed by Panofka who fancifully calls it ἀγαθὸς θεὸς βροντῶν (*Dionysos und die Thyaden*, p. 377). A cast of this gem, as well as of the *Bacchante* on p. 5, and *Cadmus slaying the serpent* on p. 138, is included in the set of '50 *Gemmen-Abdrücke der Königlichen Sammlung zu Berlin*,' which may be purchased at the Berlin Museum (for 4 *thalers*). The woodcut is borrowed, by permission, from King's *Antique Gems and Rings* I p. 483. It is enlarged to twice the scale of the original.

Page 5.

HEAD OF A MAENAD ; from a red jasper in the gem-cabinet of the Berlin Museum. The band across the forehead and the ivy-crown may be noticed here as in the vignette ; we further see the bacchanal's wand or *thyrsus*, bearing on its top what looks like a bunch of berries, but is possibly only intended for a fir cone ; part of the hair falls in loose and flowing tresses, here and there in the form of curls resembling the serpents which were fancifully represented as twining themselves about the heads of the votaries of Dionysus, as may be seen in a subsequent illustration (on p. 7). The rapt expression and the parted lips finely indicate the wild inspiration of the Bacchante. Mr King characterizes it as 'the most beautiful embodiment of the idea ever produced by the glyptic art' (*Horace* Carm. II xix A). A smaller copy is reproduced in Müller's *Denkmäler* II 560; but a comparison with a cast from Berlin now before me shews it to be less vigorous and even less accurate than the woodcut here given. The latter is borrowed from King's *Antique Gems and Rings* (Plate XXVIII 3). Tölken (III 1062) calls it an *achatonyx*.

Page 7, δρακόντων στέφανοις, lines 101—103.

MAENAD WITH A SERPENT TWINED ABOUT HER HAIR.
In her right, she carries a *thyrsus* partly swathed with ivy ; in
her left, she holds up a live lynx, which she has caught by the
hind leg. She is clad in a long *chiton* falling in fine folds, over
this is a light mantle with a dark border, while the skin of
a panther is clasped across her chest. From a vase-painting,
reduced to the scale of two-thirds of the copy in Müller-
Wieseler's *Denkmäler der Alten Kunst* II XLV 573 (taken from
Abhandlungen der philol.-philos. Cl. der K. Bayer. Akad. IV, I,
München 1844, taf. iv ; Thiersch, *ibid.* p. 80)[1]. The original
design fills the centre of a shallow circular drinking-vessel, or
cylix, in the Pinakothek at Munich. It belongs to the 'strong
style' of vase-painting ; on the outside are Dionysiac subjects
in red figures on black ground, while the internal design, here
copied, is an excellent example of monochrome, drawn with
much care and finish, and coloured with various shades of
brown on a white ground (no. 332 in Jahn's *Beschreibung*).
The vague expression of the face, and the fixed and stony
smile, remind one of the archaic forms of the plastic art, and
these traits, combined with the slight sinking of the head, serve
to heighten the effect of the inspired enthusiasm here represented (Rapp, *Rhein. Mus.* 1872, p. 565). Among the figures
outside the vase is a Maenad, round whose arm is coiled a
snake, with which she is scaring off a rude Satyr ; and on eight
other vases in the same collection (two with black figures, and
the rest with red) Maenads appear with snakes, in their hands
or around their arms. Similarly on a relief figured in Welcker's
Alte Denkm. taf. v 9 (*ib.* p. 572). In the British Museum Vase
Catalogue, no. 815, we have a Bacchic *thiasos* which includes a
dancing Maenad, whose hair is wreathed with a snake with
forked tongue ; and another Maenad holding a snake in both
hands : in no. 816, Dionysus himself is bounding along, brandishing in his right hand a speckled snake.

Page 22, line 370.

MASK FOR A BACCHANTE, in front face, from a very beau-
tifully executed gem (black agate) in Prof. Story-Maskelyne's

[1] There is a coloured copy in Baumeister's *Denkmäler*, fig. 928.

collection; enlarged to twice the scale of the original. The hair, which is bound with ivy, is tied up into a knot, and a double band passes across it, above the forehead; from near the ears, on both sides, hang two strings of large beads, 'which appendage from its constant attachment to similar masks, probably consisted of hollow spheres of metal, and formed the *crepundia* that sounded like bells with every movement of the head' (King on Horace *Epist.* I xx B). The open mouth and the expression of horror in the features may allow of its being used to illustrate the awe-struck and indignant protest of the chorus against the impious language of Pentheus. The engraving is borrowed from King's *Antique Gems and Rings*, Plate XXXI 8.

Page 26, lines 453—9.

HEAD OF YOUTHFUL DIONYSUS; from a marble bust in the Capitoline Museum in Rome. This beautiful head was formerly identified as that of Leucothea, or Ariadne. The characteristic fillet may be clearly seen; the ivy-wreath, which is much damaged in the original, is more faintly indicated, as also the very slightly protuberant horns [?] which first led to its identification as a head of Dionysus, Meyer, *Propyläen* II i 63, and in Winckelmann's *Werken* IV 307, n. 367, *Geschichte der Kunst* I p. 301, II p. 243, n. 314 (from Müller-Wieseler's *Denkmäler* II xxxiii 375). The flowing curls exactly correspond to the poet's description in ll. 453—9, esp. l. 455, πλόκαμος ταναός...γένων παρ' αὐτὴν κεχυμένος, πόθου πλέως, the ἁβρὸς βόστρυχος of l. 493; while the feminine expression of countenance recalls the θηλύμορφος ξένος of l. 353. In the account of the transformations of Dionysus in the Homeric Hymn vii 3, it is in this youthful form that he first appears, ἐφάνη...νεηνίη ἀνδρὶ ἐοικὼς, πρωθήβῃ· καλαὶ δὲ περισσείοντο ἔθειραι κυάνεαι.

Page 34; εὔιππον χώραν, 574.

COIN OF ARCHELAUS I, KING OF MACEDONIA, B.C. 413—399. The metal is silver of the Persic standard. On the obverse, riding a horse, prancing towards the left, is a horseman, wearing the *kausia* and *chlamys*, and carrying two spears, *bina manu lato crispans hastilia ferro;* the border is plain. On the reverse is an incuse square, within which is a linear square enclosing the inscription A PX EΛ AO, in the middle of which is the fore part of a goat turned to the right, kneeling on one knee and looking back. There are earlier Macedonian coins, of the time of Alexander I and Perdiccas II, with a horseman advancing with two spears, or a horse alone, or the head and forelegs of a prancing horse, on the obverse; and on the reverse, the head or forepart of a goat; the goat kneeling on one knee and looking back may also be seen in a coin of Aegae struck by Alexander I (B.C. *circiter* 500—480). The horse on the coin of Archelaus now before us is, however, executed with greater spirit than that on the earlier coinage, and the prancing attitude of the fore-legs in this later design has led to the spear-heads being slightly deflected upwards.

The horseman illustrates the complimentary reference to the dominion of Archelaus as a 'land of noble steeds'; and the goat with reverted head, in the act of lying down, refers to the legend of Caranus, founder of the Argive dynasty in Macedonia, who was led to the place where he fixed his government by following a flock of goats, in accordance with an oracle commanding him 'to seek an empire by the guidance of goats' Hyginus *fab.* 219; Dio Chrys. *Or.* IV p. 70 (163), ἦ οὐκ αἰπόλος ἦν ὁ Ἀρχέλαος καὶ ἦλθεν εἰς Μακεδονίαν αἶγας ἐλαύνων; πότερον οὖν ἐν πορφύρᾳ μᾶλλον ἢ ἐν διφθέρᾳ εἴη τοῦτο ποιεῖν; The place was, according to the legend, named Aegae in commemoration of the event; and the goat's head thus became 'the badge of the royal house of Macedon, and the *type parlant* of their citadel.' The engraving is taken from a cast of a coin in the British Museum; another engraving of the same coin is given in the British Museum Catalogue of Greek Coins, *Macedonia* &c., 1879, p. 163 (cf. *ib.* p. xx, p. 37 and pp. 158 ff.; also Leake's *Numismata Hellenika* p. 1). In the above catalogue it is stated that 'none of the coins attributed to *Aegae* are probably much earlier than the accession of Alexander I (B.C. 498),' while the coins of Aegae itself *with goat types* are 'all probably anterior to B.C. 480.' Its author, Mr Barclay V. Head, has been good enough to inform me that he 'does not think there is any numismatic evidence as to the date of the removal of the seat of government from Aegae to Pella, unless the fact that the goat appears as a coin-type for the last time under Archelaus I may be considered as such.'

Page 41, lines 683—8.

SLEEPING BACCHANTE; in the Museum of the Vatican. The serpent, here twined about the right arm, is a frequent Dionysiac emblem, and it is this that enables us to identify the nymph as a Bacchante (cf. note on l. 100, p. 108—9). The figure is sometimes supposed to represent the nymph of a fountain; it has even been fancifully identified as Olympias, mother of Alexander the Great, in consequence of the story told by Plutarch (*Alex.* 2, quoted on p. 108); but it is probably a sepulcral monument, in which the person commemorated is represented under the form of a sleeping Bacchante. The serpent may also be seen in the bosom of a sleeping nymph with one arm resting on an urn lying on its side, and with the other held above the head, in the attitude of the so-called *Cleopatra* or *Ariadne* of the same collection; also on another nymph figured in the *Statues de Dresde* no. 116, which like the one here engraved has no urn. It is doubtless intended to guard the maiden's slumbers, just as described in the *Dionysiaca* of Nonnus XIV 363—6:

καί τις ὄφιν τριέλικτον ἀπήμονι δήσατο κόλπῳ,
ἐνδόμυχον ζωστῆρα κεχηνότα γείτονι μηρῷ,
μείλιχα συρίζοντα, φιλακρήτοιο δὲ κούρης
ὑπναλέης ἄγρυπνον ὀπιπευτῆρα κορείης.

The original is of marble, about life size, and is placed near the *Gabinetto del Laocoonte* (no. 73). The engraving here given is reduced from the copy in E. Q. Visconti's description of the *Museo Pio-Clementino, Oeuvres*, ed. 1819, III plate xliii (pp. 205—211 and p. 279), whence it is also borrowed in Millin's *Galerie Mythologique* LVI no. 325, and Clarac's *Musée de Sculpture* IV no. 1668, plate 703.

Page 42, lines 699—702.

MAENAD SUCKLING A PANTHER'S CUB; from a Cameo in the 'Marlborough Collection.' The Maenad is represented reclining before the entrance of a rocky den, with her left arm inclined above her head, with her right resting on a wicker-basket, the *cista mystica*, and with a graceful bend of the back which is a favourite attitude in ancient gems (see references in Müller's *Ancient Art* § 388. 4). To the left, a Satyr looks on, playing with the tail of the cub, with his left hand leaning on a *pedum*, and his left leg, which is partly covered by a panther's skin, resting on a rock. To the right, is a second Maenad, with her left hand holding a *tympanum* on her knee, and with her right grasping a veil that flutters in the air. On the ground lie another *tympanum*, a pair of cymbals, and an over-turned *cantharus*. In the 'Marlborough Catalogue' no. 226, Professor Maskelyne describes the gem as follows: 'A bacchanal subject. A cameo antique in character, wrought in a beautiful porcelain white upper stratum of a sardonyx, with a yellow layer. The moulding of the limbs and form of the Maenad in the foreground, is extraordinarily delicate, and the attitudes of the remaining figures, viz. a Satyr teasing a panther, and a second Maenad, who is at hand to beat the tambourine, are artistically drawn. A reserved rim surrounds the design which is set in an enamelled border of tulips and other flowers' [not engraved]. 'The *technique* of this gem resembles the cinque-cento works, but the details betray more of the errors in archaeology so characteristic of a non-critical age; and the work is therefore probably by an ancient artist of a noble school.' The engraving which is enlarged to the scale of eight-sevenths of the original is copied from Müller-Wieseler's *Denkmäler* II xlvi 579, where it is reproduced from the rare work called *Gemmarum antiquarum delectus; ex praestantioribus descriptus, quae in Dactyliothecis Ducis Marlburiensis conservantur,* fol. London, 1780 I pl. 50 [Cambridge Univ. Library Eb 18, 13]. The Marlborough collection, which was mainly formed by the third Duke in the latter part of last century, passed in 1875 into the hands of Mr Bromilow of Battlesden Park, Bedfordshire.

Page 55, lines 920—2

Marble Hermes-bust of horned Dionysus [?] ; from
the Vatican Museum (Bunsen's *Beschreibung* II 2, p. 282, no. 65).
The head resembles that of a satyr ; the hair, which is short
and curly, is bound by a band or μίτρα with its loose ends, or
lemnisci, falling in front of the shoulders. Above the brow, just
in front of this band, two small horns may be seen sprouting
from among the curls. It is these horns that tempt us to
identify the head as that of Διόνυσος κερατοφυής. Compare the
epithet ταυρομέτωπος, in Orphic hymn 45 (44); Athenaeus xi
p. 476, and Tibullus II i 3, *Bacche veni dulcisque tuis e cornibus
uva pendeat,* also Valerius Flaccus *Arg.* II 272, *nivea tumeant
ut cornua mitra;* for other passages see note on l. 100.

On the horned Dionysus there is an interesting passage in
Lessing's *Laokoon,* chap. viii. He is criticising Joseph Spence
[Professor of Poetry at Oxford 1728—38], the author of the
Polymetis, 'An Enquiry concerning the Agreement between the
Works of the Roman Poets and the Remains of the Ancient
Artists,' [ed. 1, 1747]; Spence, he remarks, has the most
curious conceptions about the relations between poetry and
painting, holding as he does that, among the ancients, the poet
never lost sight of the painter or the painter of the poet; and
never thinking that 'poetry is the more comprehensive art, that
beauties wait on its bidding, which painting would in vain attempt to attain'; and 'that it often has good reasons for pre-
ferring inartistic beauties to artistic.' Hence, 'the most trifling
differences that he may observe between the ancient poets and
artists involve him in an embarrassment, by which he is compelled to resort to the strangest expedients.'

For example, 'the ancient poets, for the most part, attributed horns to Bacchus. "Therefore it is surprising," says
Spence, "that these horns are not more commonly seen upon
his statues" (*Polymetis,* Dial. ix p. 129). He first lights on one
reason, then on another, now the ignorance of antiquarians,
now the smallness of the horns themselves, which he thinks
might have been hidden under the grape-clusters and ivy-leaves

which were the constant head-dress of the god. He hovers around the true cause, without for a moment suspecting it. The horns of Bacchus were not natural horns, as were those of fauns and satyrs. They were an ornament of the brow, which he could put on, or lay aside, at his pleasure.

> *Tibi cum sine cornibus adstas*
> *Virgineum caput est,*

is Ovid's festive invocation of Bacchus (*Metamor.* lib. iv 19), so that he could shew himself without horns, and did so whenever he wished to appear in his girlish beauty, in which the artist would naturally represent him, and would therefore be compelled to avoid every addition which might produce a bad effect. Such an addition would these horns have been, which were fastened on the chaplet just as they are seen to be on a head in the Royal Cabinet of Berlin (*Begeri Thes. Brandenb.* vol. iii p. 242). Such an addition was the chaplet itself, which concealed his beautiful forehead, and therefore occurs in the statues of Bacchus as rarely as the horns themselves; while the poets are as continually attributing it to him as its inventor. The horns and the chaplet furnished the poet with neat allusions to the actions and character of the god. To the artist, on the contrary, they were impediments, preventing the display of higher beauties; and if Bacchus, as I believe, obtained the name of *biformis*, Διμορφος, for this very reason, viz. that he could manifest himself in beauty as well as in frightfulness, it is perfectly natural that the artists, from his two forms, should have selected that which best corresponded with the purpose of their art' (mainly from Beasley's trans., ed. 1879). See also chap. ix (with Blümner's notes, esp. p. 122).

Works of art representing the horned Dionysus, though far from common, are, however, less rare than was supposed to be the case when Lessing wrote his masterly essay (1766). Besides the small head of basalt to which he refers (copied in Montfaucon's *Ant.* I ii p. 157, and Hirt's *Bilderb.* 76, 2), now in the 'Old Museum' at Berlin, there is a small bust from Herculaneum in the Museum at Naples (*Bronz.* I, plate v), and a mosaic published by la Causse, *antiche pitture*, plate xx. These examples are quoted by Visconti, *Musée Pie-Clémentin*, VI p. 59, where he also refers to a slightly mutilated bust, then at the Villa Albani, inaccurately restored as a 'youthful Hercules.' Further, on a bronze coin of Nicaea, a horned Dionysus (?), and a goddess, with a *modius* on her head and a *cornucopia* in her hand, are represented driving in a chariot drawn by centaurs (Creuzer's *Dionysus*, plate III 2, Müller-Wieseler II 377). There is also the coin of Bruttium figured in Eckhel's *numi anecdoti*, p. 41, tab. III 21, where a youthful form with two horns projecting from his brow (*delicata cornua e fronte turgentia*) is placing a crown on his head; and a silver coin of Boeotia with the ivy-crowned head of the bearded Dionysus with bull's horns on his brow (Pellerin's *Recueil de Médailles de peuples et de villes*, I p. 152, Pl. XXIV 8, quoted by Streber in the *Abhandlungen der Philosophisch-Philolog. Classe der Bayerischen Akad.* II 1837, p. 482). This last is copied in Müller-Wieseler II 378, and appears to correspond to the *staters* described in Head's *Coinage of Boeotia*, p. 36, and figured in Plate III 4 and 5, a comparison of which makes it probable that the alleged horns are only a projecting portion of the ivy-wreath. Some of the other examples of coins referred to by Streber and Mr R. Brown are open to the objection that the tauriform designs upon them are really intended as representations of river-gods—a subject which has recently been fully discussed by Professor Percy Gardner ('Greek River-Worship,' in *Trans. of the Royal Society of Literature*, vol. XI, part ii, N. S., 1876).

Among the many beautiful illustrations which accompany the same writer's interesting and valuable work on *The Types of Greek Coins*, 1883, may be noticed in Plate XIV, 11, a very satisfactory example of the horned Dionysus on a coin of Seleucus I (B.C. 335—280).

Further, as an instance from another branch of art, we may draw attention to the remarkable bust of red marble figured in the *Archaeologische Zeitung*, 1851, taf. 33, p. 371, representing the head of a boy with a crown of grapes and vine-leaves and with a small bull's head tied on the back of his hair, just above the neck. A head of Dionysus in the Louvre (*Bouillon Mus.* III 9) is also supposed to be an example of the 'horned Dionysus.' Lastly, in the gem-cabinet of the Berlin Museum we have an amethyst formerly in the Stosch collection representing a bearded head of Dionysus with a wild countenance and with the horns and ears of a bull (Tölken III 927). In the same collection we have two examples of the Dionysiac bull (Tölken III 1109, 1110) ; cf. *infra* p. cxlvi.

To the *literary* references to this type of Dionysus quoted on p. 107, may be added the fragment of Nicander's ἑτεροιούμενα preserved by Antoninus Liberalis, chap. x, πρὸς δὲ ταῦτα χαλεπήνας ὁ Διόνυσος ἀντὶ κόρης ἐγένετο ταῦρος, and Nonnus 6, 209, Ζαγρεὺς εὐκέραος ; also Propertius IV 17, 19 *per te et tua cornua vivam virtutisque tuae, Bacche, poeta ferar ;* see also the commentators on Horace *Od.* III 21, 182.

It is highly probable, as suggested to me by Professor Michaelis, that the bust engraved on p. 55 is a representation of a Satyr, and not a horned Dionysus ; a conclusion which is supported by the general cast of countenance and the expression of the features. The subject of similar heads with horns in works of ancient art is elaborately discussed in Wieseler's *Commentatio de Pane et Paniscis atque Satyris cornutis, in operibus artium Graecarum Romanarumque repraesentatis,* Göttingen (Kästner) 1875, in which many works of art hitherto vaguely described as Satyrs are identified as different types of Pan. On p. 19 he throws out a hint which has some bearing on the bust with which we are now concerned : *videndum sintne quaedam capita quae vulgo assignantur Baccho tauriformi potius referenda ad unum ex Satyris. est haec res altioris indaginis de qua alio loco agendum erit accuratius.* The details of the subject are further pursued by the same writer in the Göttingen *Nachrichten* of 1875, pp. 433—478 ; and also by Furtwängler in the *Annali dell' Instituto di Corrispondenza Archeologica,* 1877, p. 208 ff.

But in spite of the Satyr-like expression of the face, the *taenia,* or ribband, falling down the shoulders, is sometimes regarded as in favour of the bust being identified as that of

Dionysus, such an adornment being unsuitable for a Satyr (A. W. Curtius, *Der Stier des Dionysos*, p. 20). This, however, must be regarded as doubtful. The fact is that, even although the earliest art may have represented Dionysus under the form of a bull, in the best period of art the bull became a mere attribute of the god, and the artistic taste as well as the anthropomorphic tendencies of the Greeks led them to shrink from giving undue prominence in the statues of Dionysus to this aspect of the god, although (as we have seen above) it is not unrepresented on gems and coins (cf. R. Brown's *Great Dionysiak Myth*, I p. 364, 374 ff., II 112 ff.).

The woodcut is copied from Müller-Wieseler II xxxiii 376, reduced from Visconti *u. s.*, VI 6, I.

Page 58.

AGAVE IN BACCHIC FRENZY. She is represented dancing; the eyes are gazing upwards, the head is thrown violently back, with the hair wildly streaming from it. The feet and the left arm, which is strongly developed, are displayed to view; the drapery, flung about the rest of the figure and filling nearly the whole field of the design, is tossed about in complex folds which are rendered with a marvellous skill. In this respect it may be compared with the *Atalanta* in the gem-cabinet of the Berlin Museum (catalogue IV 170, figured in King's *Antique Gems and Rings* XLI A 3, and included in the collection of fifty casts already mentioned on p. cxxxiii).

The original is a cameo in *plasma*, formerly in the cabinet of Paulus Praun, patrician of Nuremberg, who died in 1616; and whose collection was ultimately inherited by Madame Martens-Schaafhausen of Bonn and sold by her heirs at Cologne in 1859. The woodcut, which is the actual size of the original, is borrowed from King's *Antique Gems and Rings* XXIX 3.

Page 61, line 1018.

DIONYSOS LEONTOMORPHOS [?]. A lion couchant, in the place of whose head and neck we have the head and the upper part of the body of a bearded man, with winged arms, one of which grasps a myrtle-branch, while the other holds out at full length a Bacchic *crater*. A cast of this gem, taken from a fine sard in the Marquis De Salines' collection, appeared in the series known as Cades' *impronte gemmarie, centuria* III 52, published in 1829 and the following years, by the German Archeological Institute at Rome; in the descriptive letter-press to that series it is mentioned by Gerhard among the examples of Bacchic subjects and is identified, though with some reserve, as a representation of one of the transformations of Dionysus, (*creduto Bacco Leontomorfo ed alato, tiene nelle mani un ramoscello ed un vaso bacchico; la sua testa è calva e di carattere silenico. Corniola molto brugiata in anello d' oro antico. 'Lavoro dei più fini nella collezione del marchese di Salines': Bulletino dell' Instituto di Corrispondenza Archeologica,* 1834, p. 119). The face of a man-lion is to be seen on a terra-cotta from the Berlin Museum (figured in Müller-Wieseler, II xxxiii 384), and a gem representing a lion with the face of a youth is copied from the *impronte gemmarie* II 15, by Müller-Wieseler *u. s.* 385, where the identification of both as forms of Dionysus is submitted as a question for further investigation, references on the subject being also given to Gerhard's *Antike Bildwerke* p. 104 n. 154, and p. 405; and *Etrusk. Spiegel* I i p. 40. Müller-Wieseler 599.

The woodcut is borrowed from King's *Antique Gems and Rings* (XXX 12), where the author, in describing it as 'an exquisite Greek work of the best period,' gives it the alternative title of 'an Andro-Sphinx.' The Male sphinx, half man and half lion, is common in Assyrian and not unfrequent in early Greek art, though the female type afterwards became the exclusive model (King and Munro's *Horace*, p. 411). Even if we prefer identifying it as a Sphinx, instead of as 'Dionysus transformed into a lion,' the illustration may perhaps be regarded as not entirely inappropriate in a drama whose scene is laid at Thebes, and on a page where it faces what has long been considered the most enigmatical passage in the play.

Page 69.

THE DEATH OF PENTHEUS, stamped on a piece of Calenian pottery. The king is here represented as a beardless youth, with a κυνῆ Βοιωτία on his head, a sword in his right hand, a shield on his left. He has fallen on one knee, on some stony ground (cf. ll. 1196, 1138), and is striving in vain to defend himself against the combined attack of a panther who is about to rend him in pieces, and a wild woman who is charging at him with her *thyrsus*, the point of which is capped with an unusually large pine-cone, or bunch of foliage, with ribbands fluttering near it. She wears a short *chiton*, waving in the wind, and over this the skin of a lion or panther. On her feet she has the high hunting-boots known as ἐνδρομίδες, the sole of which may be seen under the left foot and part of the lacing on the other. In the death of Lycurgus on a vase from Canosa in the Munich Museum (no. 853, Jahn), an Erinys appears in a short *chiton*, with a panther at her side and a goad in her hand, striding towards Lycurgus; and a panther and an Erinys, represented as a huntress with ἐνδρομίδες, are to be seen on a sarcophagus at the Villa Taverna, and in the relief already described on p. cxxx, though the attire of the latter is somewhat different. And in all these cases it may fairly be called not a Maenad but a Dionysiac Erinys, with the long stride that reminds us of the σεμνὰς Ἐρινῦς τανυπόδας of *Ajax* 837; a huntress with the panther for her hound and Pentheus for her quarry (cf. θήρ, ἄγρα, λέων in our play). In Lucan, a *Eumenis* incites Agave to the destruction of Pentheus (1 568), and Nonnus mentions an Ἐρινῦς as assisting at his death. The figure in question may in short be regarded as a combination of a Maenad and of the Erinys-like nature exemplified in Lyssa and may briefly be described as a Λύσσα μαινάς.

The woodcut is copied from a lithograph in the *Archäologische Zeitung* 1874, taf. 7, where it is the subject of a long article by K. Dilthey, the owner of the fragment (vol. VI, pp. 78—94), part of the substance of which is incorporated in the above description.

Page 70, line 1159.

DIONYSIAC BULL, girt about with a garland of ivy, and standing on a *thyrsus* decked with ribbands. These accessories sufficiently indicate the Dionysiac character of the design, which represents, not merely an animal sacred to Dionysus, but the god himself in one of his various transformations. In the field of the design we have the word VΛΛΟV, the name of the gem-engraver Hyllus, which also appears on a sardonyx representing Hercules and a cameo of a laughing satyr (both in Berlin), on a sard bearing a female head with a diadem (in St Petersburg), and on a head resembling Sabina and a bust of Zeus, elsewhere. The name, in the opinion of Mr King, 'has been interpolated by a modern hand to enhance the *selling-price* of this magnificent gem' The original is a chalcedony, no. 1637 in the National Cabinet in Paris (Lippert, *Dactyliothek* I no. 231, and Mariette, *Pierres gravées*, I no. 42). The woodcut here given is reduced to the size of the original, from the copy drawn to double that size in King and Munro's *Horace* (Odes II 5), where Mr King remarks that 'Dionysos-Sabazios being always represented with the horns of a bull, it may be inferred that the animal itself was the primitive type of the god.' After referring to *Gan*, the sacred bull of *Siva* in the Indian mythology, he adds that 'the explanation that Dionysos is figured with horns, from having first taught the use of oxen in tillage, may be set down without further enquiry to the account of the *rationalists* of the latest ages of Greece.' The bull is a natural symbol of vigorous vitality.

In another gem (in the St Petersburg Cabinet, Müller-Wieseler, II 383), the Dionysiac bull, standing on a plain staff, perhaps a *narthex*, carries the three Graces between his horns, while in the upper part of the field are the seven stars identified as the *Pleiades*, which form a cluster like a bunch of grapes, in the constellation of *Taurus* (βότρυς, Eustathius on Homer p. 1155). The same animal appears (though in a less aggressive attitude than in the gem here engraved) in the bas-relief figured in the *Mon. inéd. de l'Inst. arch.* t. VI, pl. vi, no. 3.

Page 73.

AGAVE WITH THE HEAD OF PENTHEUS. See p. cxviii (19).

Page 85.

BACCHANALIAN PROCESSION. Foremost of the three figures, here represented as moving onwards in the dance, is a Maenad with her head thrown back and her hair streaming loosely from behind her head, partly clad in a talaric *chiton*, and beating with her right hand the *tympanum* which she holds in her left. Next follows a young Satyr with a panther's skin flung over his left shoulder, playing the double flute, the bass notes being sounded by the *tibia dextra* or αὐλὸς ἀνδρήϊος, and the treble by the *tibia sinistra* or αὐλὸς γυναικήϊος (Herod. I 17, Theophr. *Hist. Plant.* IV 12 and Pliny XVI 66). The straps which bind his head are probably part of the φορβειά, the leathern band or cheek-piece, worn by pipers round the head and face to compress the lips and cheeks, and so give 'a fuller, firmer, and more even tone' to the instrument, as more completely represented in the illustration in Rich's *Dict.* s. v. *capistrum.* The third figure is a youthful Satyr, with the panther's skin held like a buckler on his left arm, and the bent wand of the *thyrsus*, with its pine-cone and ribbands, in his right hand. Beside him walks the panther of Dionysus.

The woodcut is from a bas-relief, rather more than four feet by three, of exquisite workmanship, found on the site of Gabii in 1776, and now in the British Museum (*B.M. Marbles*, II plate xiii; Ellis, *Townley Gallery* II p. 109; photographed, Caldesi no. 30, Harrison no. 861; *Official Guide* (179)). It will be observed that the moulding is deeper at the top and bottom than at the sides; and we may therefore conjecture that it was part of a series of tablets meant to stand side by side, whether actually touching one another or not; a deeper moulding would in this case be avoided, as it would not only appear too heavy, but would also unduly separate it from the corresponding designs in the other compartments. The three figures occur again and again, sometimes in a different order, in other works of sculpture, copied ultimately, no doubt, from some lost masterpiece of ancient art; for example, in the Naples Museum (Ground floor, Hall VII), where the only difference is that the *thyrsus* is held more upright, and the last figure and the panther are not so close to the two others. In the same Museum (Hall VI no. 531), there is a large marble *crater*, much damaged by the boatmen of the bay of Gaeta who used to moor their boats to it, till it was taken to the Cathedral and converted into a font; running round this may be seen a row of eight figures including our three, and also Hermes handing over the infant Dionysus to be nursed by a nymph; it is inscribed with the name of the artist, who is otherwise unknown,—ΣΑΛΠΙΩΝ ΑΘΗΝΑΙΟΣ ΕΠΟΙ-ΗΣΕΝ (copied from *Museo Borbonico* I, 49, in Müller-Wieseler II xxxiv 396).

Page 86.

Βάκχη χιμαιροφόνος, FROM A BAS-RELIEF IN THE BRITISH MUSEUM (140 A). In her left hand she is holding part of a kid that she has slain, in her right she is brandishing a knife over her head. The hair is gathered up into a coif; a *chiton* falls in ample folds down to her feet, which are bare; and an upper garment is thrown over her shoulders, leaving the breasts and both arms uncovered. Behind her, a mantle flutters in the air, with its upper end caught by the hand that holds the knife. The drapery with its sweeping folds is admirably suggestive of swift and energetic movement.

The most memorable instance of the same subject is the masterpiece of Scopas which is the theme of several epigrams of the Greek Anthology (*Anth. Plan.* IV 60, *ib.* 57, 58; and *Anth. Pal.* IX 774, 775), some of which are quoted in the note on l. 739. It is also described by Callistratus, *statuae* 2, from whose account we gather that the Maenad of Scopas was represented with loosely streaming hair; with a slain kid, instead of a *thyrsus*, in her hand; and with the highest enthusiasm expressed in her general appearance. A similar design occurs again and again in ancient reliefs (e. g. in a pseudo-archaic design on a marble vase in the Louvre, inscribed ΣΩΣΙΒΙΟΣ ΑΘΗΝΑΙΟΣ ΕΠΟΙ (Müller-Wieseler II 602[1]); and in Zoega's *Bassirilievi* II plates

[1] The lettering there engraved has O and E instead of Ω and H; but the inscription as here given, rests on the authority of a *facsimile* in Fröhner's *Sculpture Antique du Louvre* ed. 1878, p. 50.

83 and 84, where there is a slight difference in the head-dress and in the angle at which the leg of the animal free from her grasp is extended) ; but, as already observed by Urlichs, in his monograph on *Skopas* p. 62, none of them exactly corresponds to the above description. Thus, the subject of our woodcut, though resembling the work of Scopas, so far as regards the dismembered kid held in the Maenad's hand, and also in its lively attitude of dancing, neverthel ss differs from it in respect to the position of the head and the treatment of the hair. On the other hand, in a relief formerly in the Borghese collection (Winckelmann, no. 81), the head and hair correspond to the description given by Callistratus, but the *thyrsus* appears instead of the slain animal. (See *Appendix.*)

The chief point, then, in which our woodcut is different from what we know of the lost work of Scopas is the tossing back of the head and hair, which was characteristic of the latter and is not unrepresented in several of our other illustrations (pp. 58, 238). It is conjectured by Urlichs (p. 60) that the Maenad of Scopas may have suggested itself to the artist as a theme appropriate to the completion of the Theatre of Dionysus at Athens in B.C. 342. He elsewhere recognises a fresh development of Greek art under the influence of Tragedy, a development which shewed itself not only in the groups of that sculptor but also in single figures like that of his Maenad (p. 216).

The height of the original is 1 foot, 5 inches ; the woodcut is copied from the engraving in the *British Museum Marbles* x plate 35. In the *Official Guide* it is suggested that the relief was probably inserted as a panel in the base of a candelabrum.

Page 109.

BACCHANTE PRYING INTO A CISTA MYSTICA. She is seated under a tree and has just opened the sacred basket, out of which a snake is seen emerging. A young Faun, who has a crook in his right hand, is holding up the left in astonishment. The original is a sard published in *Vidoni's Imp. Gem.* IV 47. The woodcut is borrowed from King's *Antique Gems and Rings* II xxx 12 (also in King and Munro's *Horace* Odes II xix B).

Page 122.

DANCING FAUN, with head tossed back and hair floating in the breeze, bunches of grapes in his right hand, and a panther's skin over his right arm. In his left he holds aloft a thyrsus capped with a pine cone, and a little below this a stick cloven at its upper end is tied to the wand by a single ribband. The original is a 'Florentine gem' first published in Agostini's *Gemme Antiche Figurate* (I pl. 135), and thence copied by Scott for a small illustrated edition of Horace published by Bell and Daldy, 1855; the same woodcut has been used in King's *Antique Gems and Rings* II xxix 9 and in Westropp's *Handbook of Archaeology*, ed. 2, p. 343.

In the cabinet of the British Museum, I have observed a Sardonyx very similar in general design to the above gem, and indeed hardly differing at all, except as regards the position of the overturned wine-vessel[1]. In this gem, which is well accredited, by having been formerly in the Blacas and Strozzi collections, the *thyrsus* is bound by ribbands near the top, and it therefore occurs to me to suggest that the stick given by Agostini is only an inaccurate rendering of one of the two ribbands in the original, which I have at present been unable to trace. Mr King informs me that he doubts the antiquity of the 'Florentine gem,' and he suggests that it may be only a fancy sketch[2].

Page 138.

CADMUS ATTACKING THE SERPENT OF THE FOUNTAIN OF ARES. The fate of his Phoenician comrades is ingeniously indicated by the overturned pitcher. The gem is characterized by Mr King as 'Etruscan work of the most finished kind' (King and Munro's *Horace*, Epod. ix B, from which the woodcut is borrowed). The original is in the Berlin cabinet, and a cast of it is included in the collection mentioned on p. cxxvi. The woodcut is enlarged to double the scale of the gem.

---

[1] No. 1023 of Mr A. H. Smith's *Catalogue* (cf. ib. 1022). In both of these a *cantharus* in the uplifted hand takes the place of the bunches of grapes.　　　　[2] See p. 257.

Page 145.

TELEPHUS CONSULTING THE ORACLE OF DIONYSUS. The
wounded king of Mysia, with his helmet on his head and with
shield and sword beside him, is here bending as a suppliant at
an altar on which stands the oracular head of the bearded
Dionysus. Telephus, according to the legend, had at first
repelled the Greeks; but Dionysus came to their help, and
caused him to be tripped up by a vine, and thereupon wounded
by the spear of Achilles. His wound is here indicated by a
bandage round his ankle and by the 'writhing anguish' expressed in his general attitude. The oracle of the god, who had
caused his fall, replied that only he that had dealt the wound
could cure the same, and the king was healed by Achilles with
the rust of his spear. The weapon is resting against the altar.

The original is a golden sard belonging to the Hon. A. S.
Johnson, Utica, U.S.; the woodcut is borrowed from the
vignette of King's *Antique Gems and Rings*, where the copy is
drawn to twice the actual size of the gem.

Page 238.

TERRACOTTA LAMP FROM CYPRUS. A Maenad with head
tossed back and streaming hair, and with arms violently extended, holding a short sword in her right and part of a slain
animal in her left; she wears the long *chiton*, and over it the
nebris. The lamp was found at *Dali*, the ancient Idalium, in
1871, and was sent by Mr Consul Sandwith to the Rev. S. S.
Lewis, F.S.A., who has kindly permitted its publication, for the
first time, in this volume. The original is slightly larger than
the copy. A lamp with a nearly identical design, discovered at
Athens before 1837, is figured in Stackelberg's *Gräber der
Hellenen* lii 4.

Page 251.

DANCING BACCHANAL, poised on tiptoe, with the left foot
thrown back, and balancing on his left shoulder a *thyrsus* bound
with ribbands. The original is a sard in the Leake Collection
of Gems in the Fitzwilliam Museum (Case II, no. 38), enlarged
to twice the actual size. Mr King's catalogue describes it as
'designed with much spirit in the later Greek style.'

§ 10. *Literature of the play.*

EDITIONS OF EURIPIDES. (1) The Aldine ed. [by Musuros], Venice, 1503; (2) ed. with Latin translation by *Aemilius Portus*, Heidelberg, 1597; (3) *Paul Stephens*, Geneva, 1602 [the ed. used by Milton]; (4)¯*Joshua Barnes*, Cambridge, 1694; 5) *Musgrave*, Oxford, 1778; (6) *Beck*, Leipzig, 1778—88; (7) *Variorum ed.*, Glasgow, 1821 [vol. vi includes the *Bacchae* with the notes of Barnes, Reiske, Musgrave, Heath, Beck, Brunck, Porson and others]; (8) *Matthiae*, Leipzig, 1813—29 [*notae in Bacchas* in vol. viii, 1824]; (9) *Th. Fix*, (Didot) Paris, 1843; (10) *A. Kirchhoff*, (Reimer) Berlin, ed. 1855 [2 vols., with full *apparatus criticus* at the end of each volume]; (11) *A. Kirchhoff*, (Weidmann) Berlin, ed. 1867 [3 vols., with a few of the more important various readings and emendations at the foot of the page]; (12) *Nauck* ed. 2, (Teubner) Leipzig, 1857, [plain text, 2 vols. with introduction 'de Euripidis vita' &c., and 'annotatio critica']; (13) *W. Dindorf* in the 'Poetae Scenici,' ed. 5 (Teubner) Leipzig, 1869; (14) *F. A. Paley* (Bell) London, 3 vols. 8vo. (ed. 2 of vol. ii, 1874).

The above list does not profess to be complete with respect to the earlier editions. Of the editions prior to that of Kirchhoff, (5) and (7) have been consulted more often than the rest. Fuller use has been made of the later editions : (10) to (14).

SEPARATE EDITIONS OF THE BACCHAE. (1) *Brunck* (with *Hec. Phoen. Hipp.*) Strasburg, 1780; (2) *Elmsley*, Oxford, 1821; (3) *Hermann*, Leipzig, 1823; (4) *J. A. Hartung*, with Germ. transl., and notes, Leipzig, 1849; (5) *F. G. Schoene*, ed. 1, 1850, ed. 2 posthumous, (Weidmann) Berlin, 1858, translated into English by the Rev. H. Browne (Rivington) 1853; (6) *F. H. Bothe*, Leipzig, ed. 2, 1854; (7) *R. Y. Tyrrell*, Fellow and Tutor of Trinity College, Dublin, (Longman) London, 1871, [reviewed by R. C. Jebb in the 'Dark Blue' for July, 1871, and by the present writer in the 'Academy,' Apr. 1, 1872, and 'Cambr. Univ. Reporter,' May 31, 1871; (8) *A. Sidgwick* [extracts for beginners], (Rivington), London, 1874; (9) *F. A. Paley* [a school ed.], (Bell), London, 1877; (10) *N. Wecklein*, ausgewählte Tragödien des Eur., für den Schulgebrauch erklärt, drittes

Bändchen, (Teubner) Leipzig, 1879.   (11) *I. T. Beckwith* (Ginn)
Boston U. S., 1885 [mainly founded on Wecklein's ed.].   (12) *E.
Bruhn* (Weidmann) Berlin, 1891.   (13) *R. Y. Tyrrell* (Macmillan)
London, 1892.   (14) *A. H. Cruickshank* (Clarendon Press)
Oxford, 1893.   (15) *N. Wecklein* (Teubner) Leipzig, 1898.
DISSERTATIONS.   (1) *R. P. Joddrell*, M.D., D.C.L., Illustra-
tions of Euripides, on the Ion, Bacchae and Alcestis, London,
1781—89.   (2) *G. H. Meyer*, de Eur. Bacch., Göttingen, 1833.
(3) *E. W. Silber*, de Eur. Bacch., pp. 71 (oeconomia fabulae, de
consilio et ingenio fabulae, de difficilibus quibusdam locis),
Berlin, 1837.   (4) *A. Kirchhoff*, ein Supplement zu Eur. Bakchen
in 'Philologus' vol. 8, pp. 78—93, 1853 (cf. *A. Doering*, die
Bedeutung der Tragödie Χριστὸς πάσχων für die Euripides-
Kritik ib. vol. 25, pages 221—258).   (5) *Reuscher*, de Eur.
Bacch., pp. 34, Perleberg, 1856.   (6) *G. Bernhardy*, Theologu-
menorum Graecorum pars iii, Halle, 1857.   (7) *F. R. L. Adria-
nus*, de Eur. Bacch. vv. 367—426, pp. 35, Görlitz, 1860.   (8) *C.
Middendorf*, Observationes in Eur. Bacch., Münster, 1867.
(9) *F. M. Schulz*, illustratur canticum ex Eur. Bacchis (vv. 64—
169), pp. 43, Halle, 1868.   (10) *E. Pfander*, über Eur. Bakchen,
pp. 41, Bern, 1869.   (11) *J. Bamberger*, de Eur. Bacch., pp. 17,
Bensheim, 1869.   (12) *C. Bock*, de Baccharum prologo (et
parodo) I. pp. 21, Colberg, 1871.   (13) *N. Wecklein*, Studien zu
Eur. in Fleckeisen's Jahrbücher 1874, supplement-band vii,
p. 368 (on ll. 206 f., 235, 859, 982, 1001—5).   (14) *A. Bergmann*,
Kritische u. exegetische Bemerkungen, pp. 20, Würzburg, 1874.
(15) *W. Collmann*, de Baccharum fabulae Euripideae locis nonnullis (vv. 20 ff., 200, 276), pp. 28, Glückstadt, 1875.   (16) *idem*,
emend. Atticarum specimen, pp. 45—51, Kiel, 1869.   (17) *Ulrich
von Wilamowitz-Moellendorff*, Analecta Euripidea, (pp. 46 ff.
'dissensus Laurentiani et Palatini in Bacchis'), Berlin 1875.
(18) *R. Y. Tyrrell*, δεύτεραι φροντίδες, in 'Hermathena,' no. 2,
pp. 292—300, 1876 ; *idem*, no. 4, p. 476 ff. ; *idem*, no. 8, p. 297 on
l. 406 (quoting *Tro.* 825 in defence of his conjecture) and l. 787
(retracting πείσει), 1882.   (19) *A. Palmer*, ib. no. 5, p. 254, 1877
(in l. 778, renders ἐφάπτεται, 'is catching,' 'laying hold of what
is next to it ;' and in l. 1037 adds ἀγήνορας or 'Αγήνορος).   (20)
E. S. Robertson, ib. no. 6, p. 387 ff., on l. 1068, &c.   (21) *S.*

Mekler, Euripidea, text-kritische Studien, (on 38, 181 f., 212, 278, 327, 476, 860 f., 998), pp. 70, Wien, 1879. (22) *Patin*, Études sur les Tragiques Grecs, Euripide, II. pp. 233—272 (les Bacchantes), ed. 5, 1879. (23) *W. H. Thompson*, ' Euripides' a lecture delivered in 1857, privately circulated in 1882 and reprinted in *Journal of Philology*, no. 22. (24) *K. Strobl*, Eur. u. die Bedeutung seiner Aussprüche über göttliches u. allgemein menschliches Wesen, Wien, 1876. (25) *Arnold*, de Eur. re scenica, Pars ii, continens Bacchas (pp. 3—11) et Phoenissas, Nordhausen, 1879. (26) *J. Daehn*, de rebus scenicis in Eur. Bacchis, pars I, Halle, 1880. (27) *S. A. Naber*, Euripidea in ' Mnemosyne ' vol. x (new series) part iii, pp. 273—9, 1882. (28) *Hartmann, ibid.* pp. 309—18. (29) *Herwerden, ibid.* xii 303—317, 1884, and in 'Mélanges Graux,' 187—223. (30) *Althaus*, Coniectanea, 1884, (Bursian's Jahresb. xxxviii 164). (31) *P. J. Meier*, Kritische Bemerkungen, Braunschweig, 1885. (32) *H. Macnaghten*, on ll. 145—9, 506, 678, 859—61, 943, 1005—11, 1063—4, 1174 in ' Classical Review,' ii 224, 1888. (33) *A. Goodwin*, on ll. 235—6, 260—2, 270—1, 278, *ibid.* iii 372, 1889. (34) *H. Stadtmüller* (Blätter f. d. bayr. Gymn. xxviii p. 361 f.). On the problem of the Bacchae (35) *A. W. Verrall*, Classical Review, 1894, 85—9; (36) *A. G. Bather*, Journal of Hellenic Studies, 1894, 244—63; (37) *W. Nestle*, Philologus (1899) 363—400.

In the department of *Art and Archaeology* (with ' sacred antiquities'): (1) *Lobeck*, Aglaophamus, sive de Theologiae mysticae Graecorum causis, Königsberg, 1829. (2) *K. O. Müller*, Ancient Art and its Remains [ed. 1, 1830] transl. by Leitch, 1852, §§ 383 —390, with Müller and Wieseler's Denkmäler der alten Kunst, II, xxxi—xlv. (3) *F. G. Schoene*, de personarum in Eur. Bacchabus habitu scenico, pp. 166, Leipzig, 1831. (4) *E. Gerhard*, auserlesene Vasenbilder vol. I, 1840, Tafel xxxi—xxxix, esp. xxxii ' Dionysos u. Apollo,' xxxiii ' Bacchischer Ap.,' ' Dionysiaka,' xlix—lx esp. l and li ' Bacchischer Feldzug,' also lxiii ' Giganten Kämpfe.' (5) *Otto Jahn*, Pentheus u. die Mainaden, pp. 22 (with 3 pages of illustrations), Kiel, 1841. (6) *Marchese Campana*, opere di plastica, tav. 26—54; 1842—51. (7) *Panofka*, Dionysos u. die Thyaden, in transactions of the ' Königlichen

Akademie der Wissenschaften' pp. 341—390, with three plates, 1852. (8) *L. Stephani*, Compte rendu de la Commission Impériale Archéologique, pp. 161—188 (on representations of Dionysus as a martial god), esp. p. 179 note 4, and 183 note 7, St Petersburg, 1867. (9) *B. Arnold*, Platte mit scenischen Vorstellungen in Collegio Romano pp. 142—157 (Festgruss der Philologischen Gesellschaft·zu Würzburg an d. xxvi Versammlung deutscher Philologen u. Schulmänner), Würzburg, 1868. (10) *G. Kinkel*, Euripides und die bildende Kunst, pp. 98, p. 56 f., Berlin, 1871. (11) *C. W..King's* Antique Gems and Rings, vol. ii, plates xxvii—xxxi, 1872. (12) *A. Rapp* (Stuttgart), die Mänade im griechischen Cultus, in der Kunst und Poesie, in 'Rheinisches Museum' vol. 27, pp. 1—22, and 562—601, 1872. (13) *K. Dilthey*, Tod des Pentheus, Calenische Trinkschale (see woodcut on p. 69), in 'Archäologische Zeitung,' 1874, pp. 78—94. (14) *F. Lenormant*, article on 'Bacchus' in Daremberg and Saglio's Dictionnaire des Antiquités, pp. 591—639, 1875. (15) *idem*, on Dionysos Zagreus, in Gazette Archéologique 1879, pp. 18—37 (with vase-painting called a *scène d'omophagie*, illustrating ll. 1133 f.). (16) *Clarac*, Musée de Sculpture, esp. vol. i plates 123—145, and vol. iv plates 673—728 (various types of Dionysus, Bacchantes, Satyrs &c.), 1826—41. (17) *W. H. Pater*, A Study of Dionysus, Fortnightly Review, Dec. 1876[1]. (18) *R. Brown* jun., 'The great Dionysiak Myth,' 2 vols. pp. 426, 336. The *Bacchae* discussed in vol. i 114—149. (Longmans) London, 1878—9. (19) *M. Ross*, de Baccho Delphico pp. 28, Bonn, 1865. (20) *A. W. Curtius*, der Stier des Dionysos, pp. 36, Jena, 1882. (21) *A. Rapp*, die Beziehungen des Dionysoskultus zu Thrakien und Kleinasien, pp. 37, Stuttgart, 1882. (22) *E. Thraemer*, 'Dionysos,' and *A. Rapp*, 'Mainaden,' in Roscher's Lexikon der Mythologie, Leipzig (Teubner) 1884 f. (23) *A. Baumeister*, 'Dionysos' and 'Mainaden,' in Denkmäler des klassischen Alterthums, Munich, 1885—8. (24) *J. Vogel*, Scenen Euripideischer Tragödien in griechischen Vasengemälden, esp. p. 112—4, Leipzig (Veit) 1886. (25) *Milani*, Dionysos, Eirene e Pluto, 'Bollettino dell' imp. Istituto archeologico germanico' v 2, 92—110, 1890.

---

[1] Reprinted in *Greek Studies* (cp. Verrall, *Class. Rev.* 1895, p. 225 f.).

ΕΥΡΙΠΙΔΟΥ ΒΑΚΧΑΙ.

ΤΑ ΤΟΥ ΔΡΑΜΑΤΟΣ ΠΡΟΣΩΠΑ.

Διόνυϲοϲ.
Χορὸϲ Βακχῶν.
Τειρεϲίαϲ.
Κάδμοϲ.
Πενθεύϲ.
Θεράπων.
Ἄγγελοϲ.
Ἕτεροϲ Ἄγγελοϲ
Ἀγαύη.

ΑΡΙΣΤΟΦΑΝΟΥΣ ΓΡΑΜΜΑΤΙΚΟΥ ΥΠΟΘΕΣΙΣ.

Διόνυσος ἀποθεωθεὶς μὴ βουλομένου Πενθέως τὰ ὄργια
αὑτοῦ ἀναλαμβάνειν εἰς μανίαν ἀγαγὼν τὰς τῆς μητρὸς ἀδελφὰς
ἠνάγκασε Πενθέα διασπάσαι. ἡ μυθοποιία κεῖται παρ᾽ Αἰσχύλῳ
ἐν Πενθεῖ.

Littera **P** indicat codicem Palatinum in bibliotheca Vaticana servatum (no. 287); eundem nonnulli (v. c. Kirchhoffius et Weckleinius)
littera *B* significant.   **C** designat codicem Florentinum in Laurentiana conservatum (xxxii 2) qui post finem versus 755 desinit; ex eodem
(ut videtur) descripti sunt eiusdem bibliothecae codex D (xxxi 1) et
bibliothecae publicae Parisiensis duo (no. 2887 = Par. E, et no. 2817 =
Par. G).   Codicum defectum supplet nonnunquam cento ille partim
e nostra fabula confectus qui Χριστὸς Πάσχων (*Chr. Pat.*), Gregorio
Nazianzeno quondam falso tributus, inscribitur.

E contraria parte, si quando opus est, adieci lectiones editionis
Aldinae anno 1503 Marci Musuri cura editae, quae auctoritate codicis
Palatini plerumque nititur.   Aliorum coniecturas, eas praesertim quas
in textum recepi, primo emendationis uniuscuiusque auctore nominato,
addidi.   Lectiones quas praetulerunt editores recentiores,—Elmsleius
(1821), Hermannus (1823), Schoenius (ed. 2, 1858), Kirchhoffius (1855,
1867), Nauckius (ed. 2, 1860), Dindorfius (ed. 5, 1869), Paleius (ed. 2,
1874), Tyrrellius (1871)*, Weckleinius (1879)†,—ubicumque operae
pretium visum erat, indicavi.

* ed. 2, 1892.   † ed. 2, 1898.

ΕΥΡΙΠΙΔΟΥ ΒΑΚΧΑΙ.

ΔΙΟΝΥΣΟΣ.

Ἥκω Διὸς παῖς τήνδε Θηβαίων χθόνα
Διόνυσος, ὃν τίκτει ποθ᾽ ἡ Κάδμου κόρη
Σεμέλη λοχευθεῖσ᾽ ἀστραπηφόρῳ πυρί·
μορφὴν δ᾽ ἀμείψας ἐκ θεοῦ βροτησίαν
πάρειμι Δίρκης νάματ᾽ Ἰσμηνοῦ θ᾽ ὕδωρ.   5
ὁρῶ δὲ μητρὸς μνῆμα τῆς κεραυνίας
τόδ᾽ ἐγγὺς οἴκων καὶ δόμων ἐρείπια
τυφόμενα Δίου πυρὸς ἔτι ζῶσαν φλόγα,

Εὐριπίδου Βάκχαι P: Εὐριπίδου Πενθεύς C.
1. Θηβαίων PC, schol. Troad. 1 (analecta Ambrosiana apud Keil.
an. gr. p. 10): Θηβαίαν (ab Elmsleio probatum, ab Hermanno in
textum receptum), schol. Hephaestionis p. 183*; Θηβαίαν κατά
Priscianus II p. 151 (=p. 48) quem Θηβαίαν πλάκα legisse suspicatur
Hauptius (*Hermes*, VII 371).   8. σώζοντα Δίου Hartmann.

ib. δίου τε PC : τε delevit Barnesius, quem secuti sunt editores
omnes praeter Tyrrellium, qui testimonio fretus Plutarchi ἁδροῦ πυρὸς
memoriter citantis, ἁδροῦ τε πυρὸς quondam praetulit. δίου τ᾽ ἔτι πυρὸς
Porson.

2 ΕΥΡΙΠΙΔΟΥ

ἀθάνατον Ἥρας μητέρ᾽ εἰς ἐμὴν ὕβριν.
αἰνῶ δὲ Κάδμον, ἄβατον ὃς πέδον τόδε   10
τίθησι θυγατρὸς σηκόν· ἀμπέλου δέ νιν
πέριξ ἐγὼ ᾽κάλυψα βοτρυώδει χλόῃ.
λιπὼν δὲ Λυδῶν τοὺς πολυχρύσους γύας
Φρυγῶν τε, Περσῶν θ᾽ ἡλιοβλήτους πλάκας
Βάκτριά τε τείχη τήν τε δύσχιμον χθόνα   15
Μήδων ἐπελθὼν Ἀραβίαν τ᾽ εὐδαίμονα
Ἀσίαν τε πᾶσαν, ἣ παρ᾽ ἁλμυρὰν ἅλα
κεῖται μιγάσιν Ἕλλησι βαρβάροις θ᾽ ὁμοῦ
πλήρεις ἔχουσα καλλιπυργώτους πόλεις,
εἰς τήνδε πρῶτον ἦλθον Ἑλλήνων πόλιν,   20
κἀκεῖ χορεύσας καὶ καταστήσας ἐμὰς
τελετάς, ἵν᾽ εἴην ἐμφανὴς δαίμων βροτοῖς.

13. τὰς πολυχρύσους PC: τοὺς correxit Elmsleius qui tamen τῶν
πολυχρύσων 'libenter reponeret' (reposuit Wecklein).   γύας P et
corr. C.

v. 14 omisit C.   θ᾽ in δ᾽ mutatum ab Elmsleio delet Wecklein.

15. δύσχειμον PC cum Strabone: correxit Elms.

16. ἐπελθὼν PC et Strabo I p. 27; παρελθὼν auctor Christi
Patientis 1590: ἐπῆλθον Wecklein cum Strabonis loco altero XV
p. 687.   ἀρραβίαν corr. C.

20. versum hunc post 22 transponebat Piersonus (verisimilia p.
122); Piersonum secutus est Wecklein qui praeeunte Schenklio etiam
πόλιν in χθόνα mutat, laudato Chr. Pat. 1601 (1599) εἰς τήνδε πρῶτον
ἦλθες Ἑβραίων χθόνα, et aliis locis commemoratis ubi verba πόλιν et χθόνα
inter se confusa sint, e. g. Alc. 479, Soph. Ant. 187, huius fabulae 961.

versum 20 delet, 23 post 25 transponit Bernhardy (Ind. lect. hib.
Halle 1857) qui post 23 nonnulla excidisse putat.   post versum 22
lacunam indicat Paley.   ordinem vv. 19—20 in MSS traditum defendit
Chr. Pat. l. c.

21. τἀκεῖ scribit Wilamowitz-Moellendorff (Hermes XIV 179).

22. εἴην C; εἴη P.   ἐμφανῶς Chr. Pat. 1564; 'fortasse τελετὰς
ἐδείχθην ἐμφανῶς' Kirchhoff.

πρώτας δὲ Θήβας τῆσδε γῆς Ἑλληνίδος
ἀνωλόλυξα, νεβρίδ' ἐξάψας χροός,
θύρσον τε δοὺς εἰς χεῖρα, κίσσινον βέλος, 25
ἐπεί μ' ἀδελφαὶ μητρός, ἃς ἥκιστ' ἐχρῆν,
Διόνυσον οὐκ ἔφασκον ἐκφῦναι Διός,
Σεμέλην δὲ νυμφευθεῖσαν ἐκ θνητοῦ τινος
εἰς Ζῆν' ἀναφέρειν τὴν ἁμαρτίαν λέχους,
Κάδμου σοφίσμαθ', ὧν νιν οὕνεκα κτανεῖν 30
Ζῆν' ἐξεκαυχῶνθ', ὅτι γάμους ἐψεύσατο.
τοιγάρ νιν αὐτὰς ἐκ δόμων ᾤστρησ' ἐγὼ
μανίαις· ὄρος δ' οἰκοῦσι παράκοποι φρενῶν·
σκευήν τ' ἔχειν ἠνάγκασ' ὀργίων ἐμῶν,
καὶ πᾶν τὸ θῆλυ σπέρμα Καδμείων ὅσαι 35
γυναῖκες ἦσαν ἐξέμηνα δωμάτων·
ὁμοῦ δὲ Κάδμου παισὶν ἀναμεμιγμέναι
χλωραῖς ὑπ' ἐλάταις ἀνορόφοις ἧνται πέτραις.
δεῖ γὰρ πόλιν τήνδ' ἐκμαθεῖν, κεἰ μὴ θέλει,
ἀτέλεστον οὖσαν τῶν ἐμῶν βακχευμάτων, 40
Σεμέλης τε μητρὸς ἀπολογήσασθαί μ' ὕπερ

23. τῆσδε PC: τάσδε Pierson et L Dindorf (G Dindf., Wecklein).
25. θύρσον PC a Wilamowitz-Moellendorffio collati (1875).
κίσσινον μέλος PC: Κίσσινον μέλος quondam Tyrrell: κίσσινον βέλος H. Stephanus.
26. ἥκιστα χρῆν mavult Wecklein.   29. τήνδ' obiter coniecit Paley.
30. εἵνεκα scribit Wecklein; item in vv. 47, 53 (coll. 'curis epigra-phicis' p. 36); idem Tyrrell².
31. ἐξεκαυχώμεθ' libri: ἐξεκαυχῶνθ' H Stephanus.
    ὅτι libri: οὗ Mekler (Krit. Beitr. zu Eur. u. Soph. 1879 p. 5).
32. αὐτάς τ' Wecklein.   οἴστρησ' libri: ᾤστρησ' Elms. (cf. 687, 814, 1285).
38. ἀνορόφοις θ' Wecklein; ἀνορόφους ἧνται πέτρας scribere voluit Elms., ἀνορόφοις στέγαις Mekler (Euripidea p. 19).   ἧνται C, cor-rectum in εἶνται P.

4   ΕΥΡΙΠΙΔΟΥ

φανέντα θνητοῖς δαίμον᾽, ὃν τίκτει Διί.
Κάδμος μὲν οὖν γέρας τε καὶ τυραννίδα
Πενθεῖ δίδωσι θυγατρὸς ἐκπεφυκότι,
ὃς θεομαχεῖ τὰ κατ᾽ ἐμὲ καὶ σπονδῶν ἄπο   45
ὠθεῖ μ᾽ ἐν εὐχαῖς τ᾽ οὐδαμοῦ μνείαν ἔχει.
ὧν οὕνεκ᾽ αὐτῷ θεὸς γεγὼς ἐνδείξομαι
πᾶσίν τε Θηβαίοισιν. εἰς δ᾽ ἄλλην χθόνα,
τἀνθένδε θέμενος εὖ, μεταστήσω πόδα,
δεικνὺς ἐμαυτόν· ἢν δὲ Θηβαίων πόλις   50
ὀργῇ σὺν ὅπλοις ἐξ ὄρους Βάκχας ἄγειν
ζητῇ, συνάψω μαινάσι στρατηλατῶν.
ὧν οὕνεκ᾽ εἶδος θνητὸν ἀλλάξας ἔχω
μορφήν τ᾽ ἐμὴν μετέβαλον εἰς ἀνδρὸς φύσιν.
ἀλλ᾽ ὦ λιποῦσαι Τμῶλον ἔρυμα Λυδίας,   55
θίασος ἐμὸς γυναῖκες, ἃς ἐκ βαρβάρων
ἐκόμισα παρέδρους καὶ ξυνεμπόρους ἐμοί,
αἴρεσθε τἀπιχώρι᾽ ἐν πόλει Φρυγῶν
τύπανα, Ῥέας τε μητρὸς ἐμά θ᾽ εὑρήματα,
βασίλειά τ᾽ ἀμφὶ δώματ᾽ ἐλθοῦσαι τάδε   60
κτυπεῖτε Πενθέως, ὡς ὁρᾷ Κάδμου πόλις.
ἐγὼ δὲ Βάκχαις εἰς Κιθαιρῶνος πτυχὰς
ἐλθών, ἵν᾽ εἰσί, συμμετασχήσω χορῶν.

46. τ᾽ οὐδαμῶς C (Schoenius, Nauck, Dind., Wecklein*); τ᾽ οὐδαμοῦ
P (Elms., Herm., Kirchf., Paley, Tyrrell).   δ᾽ οὐδαμοῦ Chr. Pat. 1571.
52. ζητεῖ correctum in ζητῇ P.   ξυνάψω C; συν- P.
53—54. versum posteriorem delet Hartung, utrumque Bernhardy :
ἀλλάξας ἐγὼ μορφὴν ἐμὴν μετέβαλον coniecit Hermann.   θεῖον pro
θνητὸν Schoenius.
55. λιποῦσα P et a prima manu C: λιποῦσαι corr. C et Chr. Pat.
1602; ἄπτουσαι sec. Elms., (vel ἀποῦσαι sec. Kirchf.,) Strabo p. 469.
57. ἐκόμισ᾽ ὀπαδοὺς coniecit Nauckius.   ξυνεμπόρους P; συν- C.
58. αἴρεσθε PC : ἄρασθε Weckl.²
59. τύμπανα vulgo: τύπανα Nauck (Tyrr.²).
62. πτυχὰς P recte; πτύχας editio Aldina.

* τ᾽ οὐδαμοῦ Wecklein².

ΧΟΡΟΣ.

Ἀσίας ἀπὸ γαίας　　　　　　στροφὴ α΄.
ἱερὸν Τμῶλον ἀμείψασα θοάζω　　65
Βρομίῳ θεῷ πόνον ἡδὺν κάματόν τ᾽ εὐκάματον, Βάκχιον εὐαζομένα.

τίς ὁδῷ τίς ὁδῷ; τίς　　　　ἀντιστροφὴ α΄.
μελάθροις; ἔκτοπος ἔστω, στόμα τ᾽ εὔφημον ἅπας ἐξοσιούσθω· τὰ νομισθέν-　　70
τα γὰρ ἀεὶ Διόνυσον [ὑμνήσω].

64. γᾶς PC: γαίας Hermann.
66. Βρομίῳ πόνον PC : Βρομίῳ θεῷ πόνον ? Nauckius in *annotatione critica* editionis Teubnerianae (1857); in textum recepit Wecklein.
67. εὐαζομένα PC (Kirchf., Nauck, Wecklein); θεὸν omisit P et a prima manu C, τὸν βάκχιον εὐαζομένα θεὸν C a secunda manu (idem omisso τὸν, Elms., Sch.): ἀζομένα θεὸν Hermann (Dind., Paley, Tyrrell).
68. τίς μελάθροις P et C (denuo collatus): τίς δὲ μ. ed. Ald. τίς; μελάθροις ἔκτοπος ἔστω Wecklein Elmsleium secutus; idem Tyrr.[2]
70. ἐξοσιούσθω P et C ante lituram (Elms., Sch., Nauck, Weckl.): ὁσιούσθω C et ed. Ald. (Herm., Dind., Paley, Tyrrell); ἐξοσιούσθω· ὅσιος γενέσθω Hesychius.
71. αἰεὶ PC (Sch., Kirchf., Weckl.); ἀεὶ (Elms., Tyrr., Pal., Dindf.): εὐοῖ Jacobs (Herm.).　　ὑμνήσω PC: κελαδήσω Herm. (Sch., Tyrrell[2]).　κελαδῶ? Nauckius *ann. crit.*

ὦ μάκαρ, ὅστις εὐδαίμων   στροφὴ β'.
τελετὰς θεῶν εἰδὼς
βιοτὰν ἁγιστεύει
καὶ θιασεύεται ψυχάν,   75
ἐν ὄρεσσι βακχεύων
ὁσίοις καθαρμοῖσιν·
τά τε ματρὸς μεγάλας ὄρ-
για Κυβέλας θεμιτεύων
ἀνὰ θύρσον τε τινάσσων   80
κισσῷ τε στεφανωθεὶς
Διόνυσον θεραπεύει.
ἴτε Βάκχαι, ἴτε Βάκχαι,
Βρόμιον παῖδα θεὸν θεοῦ
Διόνυσον κατάγουσαι   85
Φρυγίων ἐξ ὀρέων Ἑλλάδος εἰς
εὐρυχόρους ἀγυιάς, τὸν Βρόμιον·

ὅν ποτ' ἔχουσ' ἐν ὠδίνων   ἀντιστροφὴ β'.
λοχίαις ἀνάγκαισι
πταμένας Διὸς βροντᾶς   90
νηδύος ἔκβολον μάτηρ
ἔτεκεν, λιποῦσ' αἰῶ-
να κεραυνίῳ πληγᾷ·
λοχίοις δ' αὐτίκα νιν δέ-

75. θιασσεύεται P: correxit Elms.   76. ὄρεσι PC: ὄρεσσι Elms.
77. ὁσίοισι P et manu recentiore C: ὁσίοις Elms.
79. θεμιστεύων PC et Strabo p. 469: correxit Musgr.
81. κισσῷ τε στεφανωθεὶς PC, κισσῷ στ. Strabo: κατὰ κισσῷ στ. Herm.,
στεφάνῳ τε στ. Shilleto.   83. ὦ ἴτε βάκχαι ἴτε βάκχαι P (et ante lituram C).
87. εὐρυχώρους P prima manu et C cum Strabone; εὐχυχόρους
P recentiore manu.
93. κεραυνίω C, κεραυνία P; -ίᾳ Kirchf., Nauck; -ίῳ ceteri, cf. 594.
πληγᾶ PC, πλαγᾶ corr. C, πλαγᾷ ed. Ald.   94. An λοχίαις? (cf. 89).

ξατο θαλάμαις Κρονίδας Ζεύς·   95
κατὰ μηρῷ δὲ καλύψας
χρυσέαισιν συνερείδει
περόναις κρυπτὸν ἀφ' Ἥρας.
ἔτεκεν δ', ἀνίκα Μοῖραι
τέλεσαν, ταυρόκερων θεὸν   100
στεφάνωσέν τε δρακόντων
στεφάνοις, ἔνθεν ἄγραν θηρότροφον
Μαινάδες ἀμφιβάλλονται πλοκάμοις.

ὦ Σεμέλας τροφοὶ Θῆ-   στροφὴ γ'.   105
βαι στεφανοῦσθε κισσῷ·
βρύετε βρύετε χλοήρει
μίλακι καλλικάρπῳ
καὶ καταβακχιοῦσθε

95. θαλάμοις PC : θαλάμαις Wecklein collato 561, παλάμαις Jacobs.
97. χρυσέαις P et (cum glossemate συνίζησις) C denuo collatus.
102. θηροτρόφοι P (denuo collatus), θυρσοφόροι C : θηρότροφον coniecit S Allen apud Tyrrellium, dubitanter praeeunte Musgravio; θηροτρόφον probat Wecklein. θηροφόρον Morice.
107. χλοηρεῖ P et C (α, non ον, super ει scripto) : χλοήρει Herm.
108. μίλακι P ; σμίλακι C sed σ a correctore praefixo (Herm., Sch.).

δρυὸς ἢ 'ν ἐλάτας κλάδοισι,　　　　　　110
στικτῶν τ' ἐνδυτὰ νεβρίδων
στέφετε λευκοτρίχων πλοκάμων
μαλλοῖς· ἀμφὶ δὲ νάρθηκας ὑβριστὰς
ὁσιοῦσθ'· αὐτίκα γᾶ πᾶσα χορεύσει,
Βρόμιος εὖτ' ἂν ἄγῃ θιάσους　　　　　　115
εἰς ὄρος εἰς ὄρος, ἔνθα μένει
θηλυγενὴς ὄχλος
ἀφ' ἱστῶν παρὰ κερκίδων τ'
οἰστρηθεὶς Διονύσῳ.

ὦ θαλάμευμα Κουρή-　　　ἀντιστροφὴ γ'.　120
των ζάθεοί τε Κρήτας
Διογενέτορες ἔναυλοι,
ἔνθα τρικόρυθες ἄντροις
βυρσότονον κύκλωμα
τόδε μοι Κορύβαντες ηὗρον·　　　　　125

110. ἢ ἐλάτας κλάδοισιν P (Elms., Herm., Sch., Kirchf., Dind., Paley), ἢ ἐλάτας ἐν κλάδοις C: ἢ 'ν ἐλάτας κλάδοισι Blomfield (*Edinb. Rev.* 34 p. 391, *Mus. Crit.* II 660) quem secutus est Tyrrell; ἢ ἐν Weckl.
111. στικτὰ 'duce stropha' Tyrrell.　　τ' PC (denuo coll.); δ' apographa Parisina.　　ἐνδυκτὰ P, ἐνδυτὰ C: ἐνδυτὰν male ed. Ald.
112. πλοκάμων PC: ποκάδων Reiskius (Tyrrell[1]).
115. ὅτ' ἄγῃ P et a prima manu C, ὅστις ἄγει a manu secunda C: εὖτ' ἂν Elms.
118. ἀφ' ἱστῶν C, ἀμφ' ἱστῶν P, ἀφ' ἱστὸν ed. Ald.　　ἀπὸ κερκίδων Reiskius.
121. ζάθεοι PC: ζαθέου Dindorf.　　κρῆτες P, κρῆτας C (i. e. Κρήτας et Κρῆτες); eodem modo inter se discrepant codices Strabonis p. 469.
123. ἔνθα τρικόρυθες (-ές τ' Ald.) ἐν PC; τρικόρυθες ἀνθοῖς Strabo: ἐν delevit Musgr. (Elms., Herm., Kirchf., Nauck, Wecklein); τρικόρυθες ἔνθ' ἐν transposuit Dobraeus (Sch., Dind., Paley, Tyrrell).
125. ηὗρον P et C (denuo collatus); εὗρον Strabo (Herm., Sch.).

ἀνὰ δὲ †βάκχια συντόνῳ†
κέρασαν ἀδυβόᾳ Φρυγίων
αὐλῶν πνεύματι, ματρός τε ῾Ρέας εἰς
χέρα θῆκαν, κτύπον εὐάσμασι Βακχᾶν·
παρὰ δὲ μαινόμενοι Σάτυροι   130
ματέρος ἐξανύσαντο θεᾶς,
εἰς δὲ χορεύματα
συνῆψαν τριετηρίδων,
αἷς χαίρει Διόνυσος.

ἡδὺς ἐν ὄρεσσιν, ὃς ἂν   ἐπῳδός.   135
ἐκ θιάσων δρομαίων
πέσῃ πεδόσε, νεβρίδος ἔχων

126. βακχεία PC et ed. Ald., βάκχια apogr. Paris., βακχείῳ Strabo:
βακχείᾳ δ᾽ ἀνὰ συντόνῳ κέρασαν (i. e. ἀνεκέρασαν αὐτὸ) Dobraeus.   ἀνὰ
δὲ Βακχάδι συντόνῳ κ. ἡδυβοᾷ Φρυγίων αὐλῶν πνεύματι Herm.   Equidem ἀνὰ δ᾽ ἀράγματα τυμπάνων vel aliud eiusmodi desidero; etiam
Collmanno venerat in mentem συντόνῳ ex τύμπανον esse corruptum,
coniecit enim (ut nuper didici) βακχεῖον δ᾽ ἀνὰ τύμπανον κέρασαν ἀδ.
Φ. αὐ. πνεύματι.   αὐδᾷ βάκχια συντόνῳ κέρασαν ἀδυβοᾶν Φ. αὐ. πνεύματα
Wecklein.

127. ἡδυβόα PC et ed. Ald., κέρας ἀνὰ δύο βοὰν Strabonis codices:
ἀδυβόᾳ Elms. (Kirchf.², Weckl.²), ἀδυβοᾶν Kirchf. ed. 1855 (Tyrrell,
Wecklein¹).

129. ἐν (ἐν τ᾽ C secunda manu) ἄσμασι PC: εὐάσμασι Canterus;
θῆκαν καλλίκτυπον εὔασμα Strabonis codices, ubi καλλ ‘ortum ex praece-
denti καν’ (Dobreé).   131.   θεᾶς PC: ῾Ρέας Strabo (Tyrr.).

133.   συνῆψαν PC (ξυν- Dindf.) : προσῆψαν Strabo.

134.   αἷς PC : οἷς Strabo (Tyrrell).

135.   ἡδὺς PC : ἡδύ γ᾽—πέσῃς maluit Dobraeus; ἀδὺς Dindorf.
ὄρεσιν P, οὔρεσιν C a me collatus; οὔρεσιν e codd. Parisinis admisit
Brunckius (Nauck, Dindf., Wecklein).   ὅταν PC: εὖτ᾽ ἂν Dindorfius
collato v. 115 (Tyrrell, Wecklein*); ἡδύς, ἐν οὔρεσιν, ὅς τ᾽ ἂν Herm.;
-ι χῶταν J S Reid; ‘fortasse ὃς ἂν’ Kirchhoffius; ἡδὺς ἐν ὄρεσσιν ὃς ἂν Sch.

137.   πεύσῃ (littera υ puncto notata) πεδός σε P; πέσῃ πεδόσε C
denuo collatus: σεύῃ Nauck.   νεβρίδ᾽? Nauck. ann. crit.

* ὃς ἂν, fortasse ὅστις ἂν, Wecklein².

ἱερὸν ἐνδυτόν, ἀγρεύων
αἷμα τραγοκτόνον, ὠμοφάγον χάριν,
ἱέμενος εἰς ὄρεα Φρύγια, Λύδια.   140
ὁ δ' ἔξαρχος Βρόμιος, εὐοῖ.
ῥεῖ δὲ γάλακτι πέδον, ῥεῖ δ' οἴνῳ, ῥεῖ δὲ με-
λισσᾶν
νέκταρι, Συρίας δ' ὡς λιβάνου καπνός·
ὁ Βακχεὺς δ' ἔχων   145
πυρσώδη φλόγα πεύκας
ἐκ νάρθηκος ἀίσσει
δρόμῳ καὶ χοροῖς ἐρεθίζων πλανάτας
ἰαχαῖς τ' ἀναπάλλων,
τρυφερὸν πλόκαμον εἰς αἰθέρα ῥίπτων.   150
ἅμα δ' ἐπ' εὐάσμασιν ἐπιβρέμει
τοιάδ'· ὦ ἴτε Βάκχαι,

138. ἀγορεύων P et prima manu C; ἀγρεύων secunda manu C.
140. Λύδιά θ' Elms.
141. εὖ οἴ P; εὖ οἴ C: ὃ δ' ἔξαρχος (sc. ἐστί) 'Βρόμιος εὐοῖ' Wecklein.
143. νέκταρ συρείας P, συρίας δ' ὡς λιβάνου καρπὸς Zonaras p. 1307:
Συρίας δ(ὲ θρ)ώσ(κει) audacius coniecit Wecklein collato *Hec.* 823
καπνὸν...ὑπερθρώσκονθ'.
145. ὁ βακχεὺς δ' ἔχων πῦρ: ἐκ νάρθηκος ἀίσσει | πυρσώδη φλόγα
πεύκας a prima manu C, a sec. manu correctum, deleto πῦρ et transposi-
tionis notis (β α) additis.
148. καὶ χοροῖς PC, 'sed litterae ι in χοροῖς duo puncta subscripta in
P,'* retinuerunt Matthiae, Elms. (in corrigendis), Sch., Kirchhoff, Nauck,
Wecklein; τοὺς χοροὺς reposuit Brunckius, omisso articulo χοροὺς, Herm.,
Dindf., Paley, Tyrrell. ἀίσσει, πλανάτας ἐρεθίζων Wilamowitz.
πλάνας P, πλανάτας C: · forsan πλανάταις· Dobraeus.
149. ἰαχαῖς τ' ἂν ἀπ' ἄλλων C: ἰακχαῖς Dindf. 150. πλόκον Burges.
151. ἐπὶ βρέμει ἐπϊ λίγει· ἤχεῖ cum gl. περισσὸν C, ubi (ut iam
monuit Tyrrellius) tria ista verba ex abundanti addita verbum εὐάσμασιν
interpretantur, περισσὸν autem praepositionem ἐπὶ ex supervacuo itera-
tam indicat. ἐπιβρέμει PC a Wilamowitz-Moellendorffio collati qui in
C ἐπιλέγει ἠχεῖ legit. ἐπ' delet Wilamowitz; idem deleverant Elms.,
Hartung (Weckl.²).

* Non subscripta duo puncta, sed supra scriptus accentus circumflexus in acutum
mutatus.

ὦ ἴτε Βάκχαι,
Τμώλου χρυσορόου χλιδά,
μέλπετε τὸν Διόνυσον   155
βαρυβρόμων ὑπὸ τυμπάνων,
εὔια τὸν εὔιον ἀγαλλόμεναι θεὸν
ἐν Φρυγίαισι βοαῖς ἐνοπαῖσί τε,
λωτὸς ὅταν εὐκέλαδος   160
ἱερὸς ἱερὰ παίγματα
βρέμῃ, σύνοχα φοιτάσιν
εἰς ὄρος εἰς ὄρος· ἡδομένα δ' ἄρα,   165
πῶλος ὅπως ἅμα ματέρι φορβάδι,
κῶλον ἄγει ταχύπουν σκιρτήμασι Βάκχα.

ΤΕΙΡΕΣΙΑΣ.

τίς ἐν πύλαισι; Κάδμον ἐκκάλει δόμων   170
Ἀγήνορος παῖδ', ὃς πόλιν Σιδωνίαν
λιπὼν ἐπύργωσ' ἄστυ Θηβαίων τόδε.
ἴτω τις, εἰσάγγελλε Τειρεσίας ὅτι
ζητεῖ νιν· οἶδε δ' αὐτὸς ὧν ἥκω πέρι
ἅ τε ξυνεθέμην πρέσβυς ὢν γεραιτέρῳ,   175

153. ὦ ἴτε βάκχαι ὦ ἴτε βάκχαι P (ita Elms., Herm., Sch.,
Kirchf., Nauck, Paley, Wecklein); posterius ὦ deletum in C (ita
Dindf., Tyrrell).
154. Τμώλου PC: Πακτωλοῦ Wecklein. χρυσορόα Elms.   χλιδᾷ
ed. Ald. (Kirchf., Nauck, Wecklein); χλιδὰν Seyffert (Schoenius);
χλιδὰ Reiskius (Musgr., Elms., Herm., Dindf., Paley, Tyrrell).
155—156 transponit Wilamowitz.
161. βρέμει supra scripto η P.   162. ἀδομένα Dindf.
169. βάκχου PC: βάκχα Musgravius.
170. ΘΕΡ. C recentiore manu; ΤΕΙΡ. PC; idem ante v. 173 C.
πύλαισι...ἐκκαλεῖ PC: 'non male legeretur πύλαισι; ἐκκάλει'
Elmsleius qui vulgatam tamen scripturam non improbat collato *Hel.*
892. Elmslei coniecturam quam Dobraeus quoque proposuerat, dudum
occupaverat Berglerus; in textum admiserunt Schoenius, Kirchf., Nauck,
Dindf., Tyrrell, Wecklein.

θύρσους ἀνάπτειν καὶ νεβρῶν δορὰς ἔχειν
στεφανοῦν τε κρᾶτα κισσίνοις βλαστήμασιν.

ΚΑΔΜΟΣ.

ὦ φίλταθ᾽, ὡς σὴν γῆρυν ᾐσθόμην κλύων
σοφὴν σοφοῦ παρ᾽ ἀνδρός, ἐν δόμοισιν ὤν·
ἥκω δ᾽ ἕτοιμος τήνδ᾽ ἔχων σκευὴν θεοῦ.   180
δεῖ γάρ νιν ὄντα παῖδα θυγατρὸς ἐξ ἐμῆς,
Διόνυσον ὃς πέφηνεν ἀνθρώποις θεός,
ὅσον καθ᾽ ἡμᾶς δυνατὸν αὔξεσθαι μέγαν.
ποῖ δεῖ χορεύειν, ποῖ καθιστάναι πόδα
καὶ κρᾶτα σεῖσαι πολιόν; ἐξηγοῦ σύ μοι   185
γέρων γέροντι, Τειρεσία· σὺ γὰρ σοφός.
ὡς οὐ κάμοιμ᾽ ἂν οὔτε νύκτ᾽ οὔθ᾽ ἡμέραν
θύρσῳ κροτῶν γῆν· ἐπιλελήσμεθ᾽ ἡδέως
γέροντες ὄντες. ΤΕΙ. ταῦτ᾽ ἐμοὶ πάσχεις ἄρα·
κἀγὼ γὰρ ἡβῶ κἀπιχειρήσω χοροῖς.   190
ΚΑ. οὐκοῦν ὄχοισιν εἰς ὄρος περάσομεν;
ΤΕΙ. ἀλλ᾽ οὐχ ὁμοίως ἂν ὁ θεὸς τιμὴν ἔχοι.
ΚΑ. γέρων γέροντα παιδαγωγήσω σ᾽ ἐγώ.
ΤΕΙ. ὁ θεὸς ἀμοχθὶ κεῖσε νῷν ἡγήσεται.

176. θύρσους: πυρσοὺς Housman. ἀναίρειν Musgr.
178. ᾐσθόμην Musgr.
182. versum ex v. 860 confictum eiecit Dobraeus; etiam Kirchhoffio
et Dindorfio spurius visus est, Tyrrellio et Weckleinio ' iure suspectus'.
πέφην᾽ P et C denuo collati: πέφην᾽ ἐν Tyrrell.   183. δυνατόν.
δαίμον᾽ Naber.
184. ποῦ Wecklein.   δὴ PC: δεῖ correxit ed. Aldina.
188. ἡδέων PC: ἡδέως (1) Miltonus, (2) Barnesius, (3) Brunckius:
Miltoni nostri coniecturam omnes editores in textum receperunt.
Nauckius in ann. crit. 'an ἡδονῇ?'
189. ταῦτά μοι PC: ταῦτ᾽ ἐμοὶ L Dindorfius.
192. ὁμοίως ὁ θεὸς ἂν Porsonus, ὁμοίαν ὁ θεὸς ἂν Elms.   (Weckl.).
ἔχει sed οι superscriptum in P.
194. ἀμοχθεὶ PC (Herm., Sch., Kirch., Nauck): ἀμοχθὶ Elms.
(Dindf., Paley, Tyrrell, Wecklein).   νῶϊν libri.

ΚΑ. μόνοι δὲ πόλεως Βακχίῳ χορεύσομεν; 195
ΤΕΙ. μόνοι γὰρ εὖ φρονοῦμεν, οἱ δ' ἄλλοι κακῶς.
ΚΑ. μακρὸν τὸ μέλλειν· ἀλλ' ἐμῆς ἔχου χερός.
ΤΕΙ. ἰδού, ξύναπτε καὶ ξυνωρίζου χέρα.
ΚΑ. οὐ καταφρονῶ 'γὼ τῶν θεῶν θνητὸς γεγώς.
ΤΕΙ. οὐδὲν σοφιζόμεσθα τοῖσι δαίμοσι. 200
    πατρίους παραδοχὰς ἅς θ' ὁμήλικας χρόνῳ
    κεκτήμεθ', οὐδεὶς αὐτὰ καταβαλεῖ λόγος,
    οὐδ' εἰ δι' ἄκρων τὸ σοφὸν ηὕρηται φρενῶν.
    ἐρεῖ τις ὡς τὸ γῆρας οὐκ αἰσχύνομαι,
    μέλλων χορεύειν κρᾶτα κισσώσας ἐμόν. 205
    οὐ γὰρ διήρηχ' ὁ θεὸς εἴτε τὸν νέον
    χρείη χορεύειν εἴτε τὸν γεραίτερον,
    ἀλλ' ἐξ ἁπάντων βούλεται τιμὰς ἔχειν
    κοινάς, δι' ἀριθμῶν δ' οὐδὲν αὔξεσθαι θέλει.
ΚΑ. ἐπεὶ σὺ φέγγος, Τειρεσία, τόδ' οὐχ ὁρᾷς, 210
    ἐγὼ προφήτης σοι λόγων γενήσομαι.
    Πενθεὺς πρὸς οἴκους ὅδε διὰ σπουδῆς περᾷ.

200. post hunc versum nonnulla deesse putat Kirchhoffius.
201. πατρὸς PC: πατρίους Valckenaer.
202. καταβάλλει C a me collatus (Paley, Tyrrell); -βάλλῃ P: καταβαλεῖ Scaliger (Herm., Schoenius, Kirchf., Nauck, Dindf., Wecklein);
καταβαλεῖ λόγοις Elms. et Dobraeus.
202. ἄκρας—φρενὸς Plutarch. mor. 756. εὕρηται P; ηὕρηται Elms.,
Dind., Paley, Wecklein.
206—207. οὔτε...οὔτε Matthiae et Kirchhoffius.
207. εἰ χρὴ PC (Sch., Kirchf, Nauck): ἐχρῆν ed. Aldina (Elms.,
Herm., Paley?, Tyrrell); θέλει Dindf. χρήζων? Nauckius ann.
crit.; χρῄζει Wecklein, οἱ χρὴ Bergmann, χαίρει χορεύοντ' Usener.
χορεύειν C, χηρεύειν P. χρείη Munro.
209 spurium esse censet Bernhardy (Theologumena Graeca 3 p. ix).
δι' ἀριθμῶν δ' οὐδὲν PC: δι' ἀριθμοῦ? Nauckius ann. crit., διαριθμῶν δ'
οὐδὲν Heathius, διαιρῶν δ' οὐδὲν Bradeius apud Tyrrellium.   Quidni
παραλιπὼν δ' οὐδέν'?   δίχ' εἴργων Lud. Schmidt.   ἀπωθῶν δ' οὐδέν'
F. W. Schmidt.

Ἐχίονος παῖς, ᾧ κράτος δίδωμι γῆς.
ὡς ἐπτόηται· τί ποτ᾽ ἐρεῖ νεώτερον;

ΠΕΝΘΕΥΣ.

ἔκδημος ὢν μὲν τῆσδ᾽ ἐτύγχανον χθονός,   215
κλύω δὲ νεοχμὰ τήνδ᾽ ἀνὰ πτόλιν κακά,
γυναῖκας ἡμῖν δώματ᾽ ἐκλελοιπέναι
πλασταῖσι βακχείαισιν, ἐν δὲ δασκίοις
ὄρεσι θοάζειν, τὸν νεωστὶ δαίμονα
Διόνυσον ὅστις ἔστι τιμώσας χοροῖς·   220
πλήρεις δὲ θιάσοις ἐν μέσοισιν ἑστάναι
κρατῆρας, ἄλλην δ᾽ ἄλλοσ᾽ εἰς ἐρημίαν
πτώσσουσαν εὐναῖς ἀρσένων ὑπηρετεῖν,
πρόφασιν μὲν ὡς δὴ Μαινάδας θυοσκόους,
τὴν δ᾽ Ἀφροδίτην πρόσθ᾽ ἄγειν τοῦ Βακχίου.   225
ὅσας μὲν οὖν εἴληφα, δεσμίους χέρας
σώζουσι πανδήμοισι πρόσπολοι στέγαις·
ὅσαι δ᾽ ἄπεισιν, ἐξ ὄρους θηράσομαι,
Ἰνώ τ᾽ Ἀγαύην θ᾽ ἥ μ᾽ ἔτικτ᾽ Ἐχίονι,
Ἀκταίονός τε μητέρ᾽, Αὐτονόην λέγω.   230
καὶ σφᾶς σιδηραῖς ἁρμόσας ἐν ἄρκυσι
παύσω κακούργου τῆσδε βακχείας τάχα.
λέγουσι δ᾽ ὥς τις εἰσελήλυθε ξένος
γόης ἐπῳδὸς Λυδίας ἀπὸ χθονός,

215 interpolatum esse ex *Hipp.* 281 existimat Baier (*animadv. in poet. tr. gr.*), qui versu proximo scribit κλύω νεοχμὰ...
217. σώματ᾽ P, δώματ᾽ C.
220. διόνυσος P.   222. ἄλλος PC.   223. πτώσσουσαν P.
224 delet Collmannus qui in versu proximo scribit τήν τ᾽ Ἀφροδίτην.
227. πανδήμοις PC...δόμοις P, πανδήμοισι...στέγαις corr. C, πανδό-
μοις...στέγαις ed. Ald.
229. οἰνώ C prima manu.   ἀγαυὴν PC (ὀξυτόνως).
233. ὅστις PC : ὥς τις ed. Aldina.

ξανθοῖσι βοστρύχοισιν εὐόσμοις κομῶν,   235
οἰνωπός, ὅσσοις χάριτας Ἀφροδίτης ἔχων,
ὃς ἡμέρας τε κεὐφρόνας συγγίγνεται
τελετὰς προτείνων εὐίους νεάνισιν.
εἰ δ᾽ αὐτὸν εἴσω τῆσδε λήψομαι στέγης,
παύσω κτυποῦντα θύρσον ἀνασείοντά τε   240
κόμας, τράχηλον σώματος χωρὶς τεμών.
ἐκεῖνος εἶναί φησι Διόνυσον θεόν,
ἐκεῖνος ἐν μηρῷ ποτ᾽ ἐρράφθαι Διός,
ὃς ἐκπυροῦται λαμπάσιν κεραυνίοις
σὺν μητρί, Δίους ὅτι γάμους ἐψεύσατο.   245
ταῦτ᾽ οὐχὶ δεινῆς ἀγχόνης ἔστ᾽ ἄξια,
ὕβρεις ὑβρίζειν, ὅστις ἔστιν ὁ ξένος;
    ἀτὰρ τόδ᾽ ἄλλο θαῦμα, τὸν τερασκόπον
ἐν ποικίλαισι νεβρίσι Τειρεσίαν ὁρῶ
πατέρα τε μητρὸς τῆς ἐμῆς, πολὺν γέλων,   250
νάρθηκι βακχεύοντ᾽· ἀναίνομαι, πάτερ,

235. εὔοσμον κόμην PC et ed. Ald.: εὔκοσμος κόμην H Stephanus
(Matthiae et Elmsl.), εὔοσμος κόμην Brunck (Herm., Paley); εὐόσμοις
κομῶν Badham (Schoenius, Nauck, Dindf., Weckl., Tyrr.²); εὐοσμῶν
κόμης (vel κόμην) Tyrrell¹, εὐόσμου κόμης Collmann.
    236. οἰνῶπάς τ᾽ ὅσοις (manu secunda ὅσσοις) P, οἰνῶπά τ᾽ ὅσσοις C:
οἰνωπὰς ὅσσοις ed. Ald., οἰνῶπας Scaliger (Sch., Weckl.²), οἰνωπὸς Barnesius. εὔοσμον κόμην οἴνῳ γανωθείς, A. Goodwin (Hesych. γανωθείς·
λαμπρυνθείς).   238. προπίνων Valckenaer.
    242—7 post versum 238 transponit Kirchf. ed. 1867, Schoenium
secutus.   242—7 interpolatos esse censet Wecklein.
    243 eiecit Dindorfius.   ἐρράφη PC: ἐρράφθαι Reiskius.
    244. κεραυνίαις PC: -οις Fixius (Dind.); cf. 594. ξὺν Dind. (Tyrrell).
    246. ἔστ᾽ ἄξια PC et ed. Ald. (Schoenius, Kirchf., Nauck, Paley,
Wecklein): ἐπάξια Elms. (Herm., Dindf., Tyrrell). δεινὰ κἀγχόνης Mau.
    251. βακχεύοντας e corr. C, ἀναίνομαι prima littera a correctore
scripta C: βακχεύοντ᾽· ἀναίνομαι, πάτερ, editores fere omnes; πάτερ
metrici ineptum supplementum esse censet Kirchhoffius; praestaret
igitur βακχεύοντας ἀλλ᾽ ἀναίνομαι quod etiam Weckleinio occurrit.
ἀλλ᾽ ἀγαίομαι Naber. βακχεύοντας· αἰδοῦμαι πάτερ, Porsonus; ἀλλὰ
μαίνομαι? Nauckius ann. crit.; βακχεύοντ᾽· ἀναίνομαι [πάτερ] idem in
textu (Tyrrell).

τὸ γῆρας ὑμῶν εἰσορῶν νοῦν οὐκ ἔχον.
οὐκ ἀποτινάξεις κισσόν; οὐκ ἐλευθέραν
θύρσου μεθήσεις χεῖρ᾽, ἐμῆς μητρὸς πάτερ;
σὺ ταῦτ᾽ ἔπεισας, Τειρεσία· τόνδ᾽ αὖ θέλεις   255
τὸν δαίμον᾽ ἀνθρώποισιν εἰσφέρων νέον
σκοπεῖν πτερωτοὺς κἀμπύρων μισθοὺς φέρειν.
εἰ μή σε γῆρας πολιὸν ἐξερρύετο,
καθῆσ᾽ ἂν ἐν Βάκχαισι δέσμιος μέσαις,
τελετὰς πονηρὰς εἰσάγων· γυναιξὶ γὰρ   260
ὅπου βότρυος ἐν δαιτὶ γίγνεται γάνος,
οὐχ ὑγιὲς οὐδὲν ἔτι λέγω τῶν ὀργίων.
ΧΟ. τῆς δυσσεβείας. ὦ ξέν᾽, οὐκ αἰδεῖ θεοὺς
Κάδμον τε τὸν σπείραντα γηγενῆ στάχυν;
Ἐχίονος δ᾽ ὢν παῖς καταισχύνεις γένος;   265
ΤΕΙ. ὅταν λάβῃ τις τῶν λόγων ἀνὴρ σοφὸς
καλὰς ἀφορμάς, οὐ μέγ᾽ ἔργον εὖ λέγειν·
σὺ δ᾽ εὔτροχον μὲν γλῶσσαν ὡς φρονῶν ἔχεις,
ἐν τοῖς λόγοισι δ᾽ οὐκ ἔνεισί σοι φρένες.
θρασὺς δέ, δυνατὸς καὶ λέγειν οἷός τ᾽ ἀνήρ,   270
κακὸς πολίτης γίγνεται νοῦν οὐκ ἔχων.

252. ουν οὐκ ἔχον P, νοῦν οὐκ ἔχων prima manu C. 257. φέρων C.
258. κεἰ μὴ Nauckius ann. crit. 259. καθῇ ἂν, sederes Naber.
261. γίνεται PC. γάνος C cum Etym. magno p. 221, γάμος P.
262. ἔτι λέγω: ἐπλάσω A. Goodwin, omisso v. 261.
263. εὐσεβείας PC (Kirchf., Herm., Schoenius, 'ironice dictum'
Tyrrell): εὐσεβείας... σέβας Fixius, εὐσ... σθένος Musgr.; δυσσεβείας
Reiskius (Elms., Paley, Nauck, Dindf., Wecklein); τῆς ἀσεβείας (sic)
ὦ τάλ᾽ οὐ φοβῇ θεόν; Chr. Pat. 191. εὐσεβοῦς et δυσσεβοῦς confusa in
Hel. 973. 265. καταισχύνειν Herm.
270—1 secludit Dindf.; agnoscit tamen Stobaeus 45, 2.
270. θρασύς τε δυνατὸς P et Stobaeus 45, 2; δὲ ed. Ald. et (denuo coll.) C: θρασύς τ᾽ ἐν ἀστοῖς Badham, δρᾶσαί τε δυνατὸς Heimsoeth,
θρασὺς δὲ γλώσσῃ Wecklein*, θρασὺς δὲ δυνατὸς καὶ λέγειν ὅς ἐστ᾽ ἀνὴρ
Shilleto, θράσει τε δυνατὸς καὶ λέγειν οἷός τ᾽ ἀνὴρ Madvig. δυνατὸς
κακολογεῖν ὁποῖ᾽ ἂν ᾖ, A Goodwin.
271. γίνεται P.

* <γλώσσῃ> Tyrrell²: δυνατὸς Wecklein².

οὗτος δ' ὁ δαίμων ὁ νέος ὃν σὺ διαγελᾷς,
οὐκ ἂν δυναίμην μέγεθος ἐξειπεῖν ὅσος
καθ' Ἑλλάδ' ἔσται. δύο γάρ, ὦ νεανία,
τὰ πρῶτ' ἐν ἀνθρώποισι· Δημήτηρ θεά·   275
γῆ δ' ἐστίν, ὄνομα δ' ὁπότερον βούλει κάλει·
αὕτη μὲν ἐν ξηροῖσιν ἐκτρέφει βροτούς·
ὃς δ' ἦλθεν ἐπὶ τἀντίπαλον ὁ Σεμέλης γόνος
βότρυος ὑγρὸν πῶμ' ηὗρε κεἰσηνέγκατο
θνητοῖς, ὃ παύει τοὺς ταλαιπώρους βροτοὺς   280
λύπης, ὅταν πλησθῶσιν ἀμπέλου ῥοῆς,
ὕπνον τε λήθην τῶν καθ' ἡμέραν κακῶν
δίδωσιν, οὐδ' ἔστ' ἄλλο φάρμακον πόνων.
οὗτος θεοῖσι σπένδεταί θεὸς γεγώς,
ὥστε διὰ τοῦτον τἀγάθ' ἀνθρώπους ἔχειν.   285
καὶ καταγελᾷς νιν, ὡς ἐνερράφη Διὸς
μηρῷ; διδάξω σ' ὡς καλῶς ἔχει τόδε.
ἐπεί νιν ἥρπασ' ἐκ πυρὸς κεραυνίου
Ζεύς, εἰς δ' Ὄλυμπον βρέφος ἀνήγαγεν θεόν,

273. δὴ γελᾷς Naber.   276. ὄνομα C, ὅπομα P nuper collatus.
277. μὲν οὖν?
278. ὅδ' ἦλθεν C, ὅδ' ἦλθ' P e silentio et ed. Ald.: ὃ δ' ἦλθεν Barnesius et Brunckius (Elms., Herm., Schoenius); ὁ δ' Musgr. et Matthiae
(Kirchf., Paley); ὃς δ' Fixius (Nauck, Dindf., Tyrrell, Wecklein); ᾧ δ'
ἦλθες Mekler.   ἡδονὴν ἀντίπαλον Badham; an ἡδονὴν παυσίπονον?*
279. πόμ' PC: πῶμ' Elms.   εὗρε PC; Ald., Nauck, Herm.,
Sch., Kirchf.: ηὗρε Elms., Dind., Paley, Tyrrell, Wecklein.   ex-
pectares κεἰσηγγήσατο (Wecklein).
282. ὕπνον PC (Elms., Herm., Dind., Wecklein), ὕπνου (Ald., Sch.,
Kirchf., Nauck, Paley, Tyrrell); ὕπνῳ? Nauck. ann. crit. utrumque
codicem ὕπνον habere 'post novam conlationem' testatur Wilamowitz-
Moellendorff. idem ego quoque testor.
283. δίδωσ', ἵν' οὐκ ἔστ' Herm.
284—97 eiecit Dindf.; 286—305 Tyrrell; 286—297, 300—1, 305,
Wecklein.   285. διὰ τοῦτον ὥστε numerosius certe Porsonus.
286. κεὶ...μηρῷ, διδάξω conicit Wecklein.   διαγελᾷς Herwerden.
289. δ' omisit P.   θεὸν PC (Kirchf., Nauck, Weck.): νέον ed. Ald.
   * ὃς δ' ἦλθ' ἔπειτ' ἀντίπαλον Housman (Tyrrell²).

"Ηρα νιν ἤθελ' ἐκβαλεῖν ἀπ' οὐρανοῦ· 290
Ζεὺς δ' ἀντεμηχανήσαθ' οἷα δὴ θεός.
ῥήξας μέρος τι τοῦ χθόν' ἐγκυκλουμένου
αἰθέρος, ἔθηκε τόνδ' ὅμηρον ἐκδιδοὺς
Διόνυσον "Ηρας νεικέων· χρόνῳ δέ νιν
βροτοὶ τραφῆναί φασιν ἐν μηρῷ Διός, 295
ὄνομα μεταστήσαντες, ὅτι θεᾷ θεὸς
"Ηρᾳ ποθ' ὡμήρευσε, συνθέντες λόγον.
μάντις δ' ὁ δαίμων ὅδε· τὸ γὰρ βακχεύσιμον
καὶ τὸ μανιῶδες μαντικὴν πολλὴν ἔχει·
ὅταν γὰρ ὁ θεὸς εἰς τὸ σῶμ' ἔλθῃ πολύς, 300
λέγειν τὸ μέλλον τοὺς μεμηνότας ποιεῖ.
"Αρεώς τε μοῖραν μεταλαβὼν ἔχει τινά·
στρατὸν γὰρ ἐν ὅπλοις ὄντα κἀπὶ τάξεσι
φόβος διεπτόησε πρὶν λόγχης θιγεῖν·
μανία δὲ καὶ τοῦτ' ἐστὶ Διονύσου πάρα. 305
ἔτ' αὐτὸν ὄψει κἀπὶ Δελφίσιν πέτραις
πηδῶντα σὺν πεύκαισι δικόρυφον πλάκα,
βάλλοντα καὶ σείοντα Βακχεῖον κλάδον,

292. ἀγκυκλουμένου C.
293. 'interpunge et lege ἔθηκε τόνδ' ὅμηρον, ἐκδιδοὺς Διόνυσον "Ηρᾳ
νεικέων, i.e. ἔθ. τόνδε τὸν ἀπερρηγμένον αἰθέρα ὅμηρον νεικέων, ἐκδιδοὺς
"Ηρᾳ ὡς Διόνυσον. vide *Hel.* 582 ubi confer 34 cum 611 [606?]' Dobraeus.   νείκεσιν Usener.
295. τραφῆναι PC (Elmsl., Herm., Schoenius, Kirchf., Nauck,
Tyrrell, Wecklein): ῥαφῆναι Piersonus (Paley).   ἐν μηρῷ διὸς ed.
Ald. et C (denuo collatus), ἐκ μρος (i.e. μητρὸς) διὸς P.
300—1 suspecti Hartungo, 302—5 Nauckio, 305 iam Piersono
(etiam Weckleinio).
302. ἄρεος P, ἄρεως C.   304. θίγειν PC.
306. δελφοῖσιν P, ἐν δελφοῖς ἔτ' αὐτὸν ὄψει κἀπὶ δελφίσιν πέτραις C.
307. πεύκοισι P, πεύκαισι C.
308. βάλλοντα PC: πάλλοντα Matthiae (Nauck, Kirchf. ed. 1867,
Dindf., Wecklein).   βακχεῖον PC, βάκχιον ed. Ald.

μέγαν τ' ἀν' Ἑλλάδ'. ἀλλ' ἐμοί, Πενθεῦ, πιθοῦ.
μὴ τὸ κράτος αὔχει δύναμιν ἀνθρώποις ἔχειν, 310
μηδ' ἢν δοκῇς μέν, ἡ δὲ δόξα σου νοσεῖ,
φρονεῖν δόκει τι· τὸν θεὸν δ' εἰς γῆν δέχου
καὶ σπένδε καὶ βάκχευε καὶ στέφου κάρα.
οὐχ ὁ Διόνυσος σωφρονεῖν ἀναγκάσει
γυναῖκας εἰς τὴν Κύπριν, ἀλλ' ἐν τῇ φύσει 315
τὸ σωφρονεῖν ἔνεστιν εἰς τὰ πάντ' ἀεί.
τοῦτο σκοπεῖν χρή· καὶ γὰρ ἐν βακχεύμασιν
οὖσ' ἥ γε σώφρων οὐ διαφθαρήσεται.
ὁρᾷς, σὺ χαίρεις, ὅταν ἐφεστῶσιν πύλαις 319
πολλοί, τὸ Πενθέως δ' ὄνομα μεγαλύνῃ πόλις·
κἀκεῖνος, οἶμαι, τέρπεται τιμώμενος.

ἐγὼ μὲν οὖν καὶ Κάδμος, ὃν σὺ διαγελᾷς,
κισσῷ τ' ἐρεψόμεσθα καὶ χορεύσομεν,
πολιὰ ξυνωρίς, ἀλλ' ὅμως χορευτέον,
κοὐ θεομαχήσω σῶν λόγων πεισθεὶς ὕπο. 325
μαίνει γὰρ ὡς ἄλγιστα, κοὔτε φαρμάκοις
ἄκη λάβοις ἄν, οὔτ' ἄνευ τούτων νοσεῖς.

309. μέγαν τὰν P. 311. νοσεῖ PC; νοσῇ ed. Ald., Weckl.

314. οὐχ ὁ διόνυσος σωφρονεῖν P, μὴ σωφρονεῖν Stobaeus 5, 15 et
74, 8; οὐ (οὐχ ὁ manu sec.) διόνυσος σωφρονεῖν C, οὐ γὰρ θεὸς σε σωφρονεῖν Chr. Pat. 262; ἀφρονεῖν Salmasius, ὡς φρονεῖν Porsonus, μὴ φρονεῖν
Herm. (Madvig), μὴ εὖ φρονεῖν? Nauck. ann. crit. ἐντρυφᾶν Naber.
315. ἐν τῇ φύσει PC; εἰς τὴν φύσιν τοῦτο σκοπεῖν χρὴ Stobaeus
74, 8 omisso versu 316; εἰ τῇ φύσει..., τοῦτο σκοπεῖν χρὴ Porsonus
(Paley). v. 316 citavit Stobaeus loco altero 5, 15; versum hunc ex
Hipp. 79 retractum arbitratus, constructionem valde inconcinnam praetulit Kirchhoffius (ἐν τῇ φύσει τοῦτο. σκοπεῖν χρή·), quem secutus est
Wecklein. ἀλλ' ἐν τῇ φύσει τὸ σωφρονεῖν ἔνεστι· κἂν βακχεύμασιν
Bernhardy. ἀλλ' εἰς τὴν φύσιν τούτων σκοπεῖν χρή· Pfander.
320. οὔνομα PC; ὄνομα ed. Aldina. δὴ γελᾷς Naber.
327. ἄνευ του θεῶν Burges; ἄνευ θεῶν Mekler. Fortasse ἀνιάτως.
νοσεῖς PC: νόσου Dobraeus (Weckl.[2]); ἔσει Wieseler (Weckl.[1]).

20 ΕΥΡΙΠΙΔΟΥ

ΧΟ. ὦ πρέσβυ, Φοῖβόν τ' οὐ καταισχύνεις λόγοις,
τιμῶν τε Βρόμιον σωφρονεῖς μέγαν θεόν.

ΚΑ. ὦ παῖ, καλῶς σοι Τειρεσίας παρήνεσεν·   330
οἴκει μεθ' ἡμῶν, μὴ θύραζε τῶν νόμων.
νῦν γὰρ πέτει τε καὶ φρονῶν οὐδὲν φρονεῖς.
κεἰ μὴ γὰρ ἔστιν ὁ θεὸς οὗτος, ὡς σὺ φής,
παρὰ σοὶ λεγέσθω· καὶ καταψεύδου καλῶς
ὡς ἔστι, Σεμέλη θ' ἵνα δοκῇ θεὸν τεκεῖν,   335
ἡμῖν τε τιμὴ παντὶ τῷ γένει προσῇ.
ὁρᾷς τὸν Ἀκταίωνος ἄθλιον μόρον,
ὃν ὠμόσιτοι σκύλακες ἃς ἐθρέψατο
διεσπάσαντο κρεῖσσον' ἐν κυναγίαις
Ἀρτέμιδος εἶναι κομπάσαντ' ἐν ὀργάσιν.   340
ὃ μὴ πάθῃς σύ, δεῦρό σου στέψω κάρα
κισσῷ· μεθ' ἡμῶν τῷ θεῷ τιμὴν δίδου.

ΠΕ. οὐ μὴ προσοίσεις χεῖρα, βακχεύσεις δ' ἰών,
μηδ' ἐξομόρξει μωρίαν τὴν σὴν ἐμοί;
τῆς σῆς δ' ἀνοίας τόνδε τὸν διδάσκαλον   345
δίκην μέτειμι. στειχέτω τις ὡς τάχος,

333—6 suspecti Bernhardyo, Nauckio, Weckleinio, qui (cum Paleio)
expectaret potius κεἰ μὴ γάρ ἐστιν οὗτος, ὡς σὺ φής, θεός.
334. παρὰ σοῦ Herwerden.
335. σεμέλης PC (Herm., Nauck, Paley): Σεμέλη θ' Tyrwhitt.
(Elms., Sch., Kirchf., Dindf., Tyrrell, Wecklein).
336. ἡμῶν Scaliger.   337. ἀκταίωνος P, ἀκτέωνος C a correctore (Wecklein²).
339. κυνηγίαις PC: κυναγ- Matthiae.
341. δεῦρό σοι sive σὸν Herwerden, δεῦρ' ἴθ' ὡς στέψω F W
Schmidt.
343. καὶ βακχεύσεις δ' ἰών C.
345. δ' addidit Matthiae (receperunt praeter Nauckium omnes).
τόνδε P; τήνδε C secundum Furiae collationem; sed uterque codex
denuo collatus τόνδε exhibet.   346. δίκη PC: δίκην Elms.

ἐλθὼν δὲ θάκους τοῦδ' ἵν' οἰωνοσκοπεῖ
μοχλοῖς τριαίνου κἀνάτρεψον ἔμπαλιν,
ἄνω κάτω τὰ πάντα συγχέας ὁμοῦ,
καὶ στέμματ' ἀνέμοις καὶ θυέλλαισιν μέθες 350
μάλιστα γάρ νιν δήξομαι δράσας τάδε.
οἱ δ' ἀνὰ πόλιν στείχοντες ἐξιχνεύσατε
τὸν θηλύμορφον ξένον, ὃς εἰσφέρει νόσον·
καινὴν γυναιξὶ καὶ λέχη λυμαίνεται.
κἄνπερ λάβητε, δέσμιον πορεύσατε 355
δεῦρ' αὐτόν, ὡς ἂν λευσίμου δίκης τυχὼν
θάνῃ, πικρὰν βάκχευσιν ἐν Θήβαις ἰδών.

ΤΕΙ. ὦ σχέτλι', ὡς οὐκ οἶσθα ποῦ ποτ' εἶ λόγων·
μέμηνας ἤδη καὶ πρὶν ἐξέστης φρενῶν.

στείχωμεν ἡμεῖς, Κάδμε, κἀξαιτώμεθα 360
ὑπέρ τε τούτου καίπερ ὄντος ἀγρίου
ὑπέρ τε πόλεως, τὸν θεὸν μηδὲν νέον
δρᾶν. ἀλλ' ἕπου μοι κισσίνου βάκτρου μέτα·
πειρῶ δ' ἀνορθοῦν σῶμ' ἐμόν, κἀγὼ τὸ σόν·
γέροντε δ' αἰσχρὸν δύο πεσεῖν· ἴτω δ' ὅμως· 365
τῷ Βακχίῳ γὰρ τῷ Διὸς δουλευτέον.
Πενθεὺς δ' ὅπως μὴ πένθος εἰσοίσει δόμοις
τοῖς σοῖσι, Κάδμε· μαντικῇ μὲν οὐ λέγω,
τοῖς πράγμασιν δέ· μῶρα γὰρ μῶρος λέγει.

347. τούσδ' PC (Paley): τοῦδ' Musgravius (Matthiae, Elms., Herm., Kirchf., Nauck, cet.). ὀρνιθοσκοπῇ ('nisi hic collatoris error est pro οἰωνοσκοπῇ' Dind.) P; οἰωνοσκοπῇ P denuo collatus, -σκοπεῖ, C a me coll.

348. τριαίνου C; τριαίνης P (denuo collatus), et ed. Aldina.

359. ἐξεστὼς Badham et Herwerden*;ἤδη τῶν πρὶν ἐξεστὼς φρενῶν Baier; librorum lectionem defendit Alciphro 3, 2, μέμηνας, ὦ θυγάτριον, καὶ ἀληθῶς ἐξέστης.

365. γέροντες δ' P, γέροντε C. 368. οὐχ ὁρῶ F W Schmidt.

* idem Tyrrell².

ΧΟ. Ὁσία πότνα θεῶν,   στροφὴ α'.   370
Ὁσία δ' ἃ κατὰ γᾶν
χρυσέαν πτέρυγα φέρεις,
τάδε Πενθέως ἀίεις;
ἀίεις οὐχ ὁσίαν
ὕβριν εἰς τὸν Βρόμιον,   375
τὸν Σεμέλας τὸν παρὰ καλλιστεφάνοις
εὐφροσύναις δαίμονα πρῶ-
τον μακάρων· ὃς τάδ' ἔχει,
θιασεύειν τε χοροῖς
μετά τ' αὐλοῦ γελάσαι   380
ἀποπαῦσαί τε μερίμνας,
ὁπόταν βότρυος ἔλθῃ
γάνος ἐν δαιτὶ θεῶν,
κισσοφόροις δ' ἐν θαλίαις
ἀνδρασι κρατὴρ ὕπνον ἀμφιβάλλῃ.   385

372. χρύσεα PC, recte (ut Dindorfio quidem videtur) modo σκῆπτρα cum Elmsleio scribatur pro πτέρυγα : χρυσέαν Matthiae et Hermannus. χρυσέᾳ πτέρυγι φέρει optime Thompsonus, coll. *H. Fur.* 653, πτεροῖς φορείσθω. 373. τὰ δὲ PC : τάδ' ed. Ald. 375. εἰς C, ἐς P. 379. θιεύσειν P. 383. γάνος ἐν δαιτὶ φίλον conicit Wecklein. 385. ἀμφὶ βάλλη P, ἀμφιβόλη C : ἀμφιβάλλῃ Barnes.

ἀχαλίνων στομάτων   ἀντιστροφὴ α'.
ἀνόμου τ' ἀφροσύνας
τὸ τέλος δυστυχία·
ὁ δὲ τᾶς ἡσυχίας
βίοτος καὶ τὸ φρονεῖν   390
ἀσάλευτόν τε μένει
καὶ συνέχει δώματα· πόρσω γὰρ ὅμως
αἰθέρα ναίοντες ὁρῶ-
σιν τὰ βροτῶν οὐρανίδαι.
τὸ σοφὸν δ' οὐ σοφία,   395
τό τε μὴ θνητὰ φρονεῖν
βραχὺς αἰών· ἐπὶ τούτῳ
δέ τις ἂν μεγάλα διώκων
τὰ παρόντ' οὐχὶ φέροι.
μαινομένων οἵδε τρόποι   400
καὶ κακοβούλων παρ' ἔμοιγε φωτῶν.

389. ἡσυχίας PC : ἀσυχίας Dindorf.

392. συνέχει δώματα πρόσω γὰρ ἀλλ' ὅμως P ; συνέχει δῶμα πρόσω
γὰρ ἀλλ' ὅμως C (post lituram) ut ed. Ald.; ξυνέχει δώματα· πόρρω
(πόρσω e corr. Elms. et Dindf.) γὰρ ὅμως Stobaeus 58, 3.

396. θνητὰ PC : θνατὰ Elms.   τό τε μὴ θν. φρονεῖν βραχὺς
αἰών. ed. Ald., Herm., Schoenius, Kirchf., Tyrrell (δευτεραὶ φροντίδες),
Paley ed. 2.   ...φρονεῖν. βραχὺς αἰών. 'Brodaeo, Heathio Tyrwhit-
toque auctoribus emendavit Brunckius,' quem secuti sunt Elms., Nauck,
Paley ed. 1, Dindf., Wecklein.

397. τούτῳ PC : τούτου Paley.

398. μεγάλα C a me collatus et Stobaeus 22, 17 ; τὰ μεγάλα P :
μακρὰ Heimsoeth.

399. φέρει PC et Stobaeus : φέροι Tyrwhitt. τίς ἂν —φέροι ; 'inter-
rogativa sententia est,' Madvig.

400. μαινομένων P : δ' addit Stobaeus 22, 17 (Nauck); θ' Porson
(Elms.).

401. ἐμοί C, ἔμοιγε C manu recentiore.

24 ΕΥΡΙΠΙΔΟΥ

ἱκοίμαν ποτὶ Κύπρον,   στροφὴ β'.
νᾶσον τᾶς Ἀφροδίτας,
ἐν ᾇ θελξίφρονες νέμον-
ται θνατοῖσιν Ἔρωτες,   405
χθόνα θ' ἂν ἑκατόστομοι
βαρβάρου ποταμοῦ ῥοαὶ
καρπίζουσιν ἄνομβροι.
οὗ δ' ἁ καλλιστευομένα
Πιερία μούσειος ἕδρα,   410
σεμνὰ κλιτὺς Ὀλύμπου,
ἐκεῖσ' ἄγε μ', ὦ Βρόμιε Βρόμιε,
προβακχήιε δαῖμον.
ἐκεῖ Χάριτες, ἐκεῖ δὲ Πόθος·
ἐκεῖ δὲ Βάκχαις θέμις ὀργιάζειν.   415

402. τὰν κύπρον PC: Κύπρον Herm.   νᾶσον τὰν Ἀφρ. E Petersen.
404. ἵνα PC (Kirchf.): ἵν' οἱ Heathius (Elms., Herm., Schoenius,
Dind., Paley); ἐν ᾇ Nauckius (Tyrrell, Wecklein).
406. πάφον θ' PC.   Πάφον, τάν (ἄν) θ' Matthiae.   Πάφον θ'
ἂν θ' Tyrrell: πέδον τ' ἔνθ' Schoenius; γαῖαν θ' Thompson; χθόνα θ'
Meinekius in Philologo 13, 555 (Dind., Nauck, Wecklein*), ἐς τὰν χθόν'
ἂν Hartung, ἐς τ' Ἐπάφον ἂν Bergmann, Φάρον θ' ἂν Reiskius et Em.
Hoffmann; Π...ἀκαματόστομοι Unger, Π...ἐρατόστομοι Musgr.
407. Βωκάρου ποταμοῦ perperam Meursius†.   ἄνομβροι PC:
ἄνομβρον Matthiae (Kirchf., Nauck, Tyrrell); ἄμ' ὄμβρῳ Unger.
409. ὅπου δ' ἁ P et prima manu C (Kirchf.), ὅπου manu secunda C
et ed. Aldina (Elms.): ποῦ δ' ἁ...; Nauckius (Dind., Wecklein, Tyrrell[1]).
οὗ θ' ἁ Schoenius quod Paleio quoque placet (Tyrrell[2]).
410. πιερεία P, πιερία C.   411. κλειτὺς PC: κλιτὺς Canter.
412. ἄγε με, Βρόμιε PC: ἄγε μ' ὦ Βρόμιε Hartungus, quod Hermanno quoque in mentem venerat (ita Wecklein).   ἄγε μ' ὦ
Βρόμιε [Βρόμιε] et in antistropha [φρένα τε] Dindf. (Tyrrell).
413. προβακχήιε PC: πρόβακχ' εὖιε Herm. (Wecklein).
415. βάκχαισι P, βάκχεσι C secundum Furiae collationem: βάκχαις
Kirchhoffius qui in antistropha χρῆταί τε, τόδ' ἂν δεχοίμαν (ita Nauck,
Paley, Wecklein).   βάκχαισιν C a Wilamowitz-Moellendorffio collatus.

* Πάφον ἂν Hermann (Wecklein[2]).
† idem Wecklein[2]. Cf. Louis Dyer, The Gods in Greece, pp. 324—354.

ὁ δαίμων ὁ Διὸς παῖς   ἀντιστροφὴ β΄.
χαίρει μὲν θαλίαισιν,
φιλεῖ δ᾽ ὀλβοδότειραν Εἰ-
ρήναν, κουροτρόφον θεάν.   420
ἴσα δ᾽ εἴς τε τὸν ὄλβιον
τόν τε χείρονα δῶκ᾽ ἔχειν
οἴνου τέρψιν ἄλυπον·
μισεῖ δ᾽ ᾧ μὴ ταῦτα μέλει,
κατὰ φάος νύκτας τε φίλας   425
εὐαίωνα διαζῆν·
σοφὸν δ᾽ ἀπέχειν πραπίδα φρένα τε
περισσῶν παρὰ φωτῶν·
τὸ πλῆθος ὅ τι τὸ φαυλότερον   430
ἐνόμισε χρῆταί τε, τόδ᾽ ἂν δεχοίμαν.

416. πάις Matthiae qui in stropha τὰν Κύπρον retinuit.

419. εἰρήνην P : Εἰρήναν Elms.   εἰρήναν C nuper collatus.

421. ἴσα P et a prima manu C (Herm., Dindf., Kirchf., Nauck, Tyrrell[1], Wecklein); ἴσαν a manu secunda C ut Ald., Elms., Schoenius, Paley (Leo Adrian, Tyrrell[2]).

425. νύκτας θ᾽ ἱερὰς Herwerden.

427. σοφὰν PC: σοφὸν ed. Aldina, quod Kirchhoffio, Nauckio, Weckleinio verum videtur.   σοφὰν δ᾽ ἄπεχε Herm., Elms.; σοφῶν δ᾽ ἀπέχων Paley.   πραπίδα C, παρ᾽ ἀσπίδα P.   φρένα τε delet Hartung, in uncinis secludunt Dind., Tyrrell[1].

428. παρὰ PC : ἀπὸ Reiskius.

430. ὅτιπερ P et prima manu C (quod retinuerunt Dindf., Tyrrell), ὅτι τε secunda manu C et ed. Ald.: ὅτι τι τὸ Brunck.

431. χρῆταί τ᾽ ἐν τῷδε λεγοίμην ἂν P et a primo manu C, χρῆταί τε τόδε τοι λέγοιμ᾽ ἂν manu sec. C ut Ald. *: λεγοίμαν Herm., χρησóν, τόδε τοι λέγοιμ᾽ ἂν Hartung, χρῆταί τε, τόδ᾽ ἂν δεχοίμαν Kirchhoffius (Nauck, Paley, Wecklein); δεχοίμαν iam antea placueat Musgravio.

* eadem Tyrrell.

ΘΕΡΑΠΩΝ.

Πενθεῦ, πάρεσμεν τήνδ᾽ ἄγραν ἠγρευκότες
ἐφ᾽ ἣν ἔπεμψας, οὐδ᾽ ἄκρανθ᾽ ὡρμήσαμεν.   435
ὁ θὴρ δ᾽ ὅδ᾽ ἡμῖν πρᾶος οὐδ᾽ ὑπέσπασε
φυγῇ πόδ᾽, ἀλλ᾽ ἔδωκεν οὐκ ἄκων χέρας,
οὐδ᾽ ὠχρὸς οὐδ᾽ ἤλλαξεν οἰνωπὸν γένυν,
γελῶν δὲ καὶ δεῖν κἀπάγειν ἐφίετο
ἔμενέ τε, τοὐμὸν εὐπετὲς ποιούμενος.   440
κἀγὼ δι᾽ αἰδοῦς εἶπον· ὦ ξέν᾽, οὐχ ἑκὼν
ἄγω σε, Πενθέως δ᾽ ὅς μ᾽ ἔπεμψ᾽ ἐπιστολαῖς.

436. ὅδ᾽ ἦν μὲν scribendum putat Kirchhoffius.

438. οὐδ᾽ ὠχρὸς οὐδ᾽ PC : οὐδ᾽ ὠχρὸς ὤν ? Nauckius *ann. crit.*, οὐκ ὠχρὸς legendum esse censet Kirchhoffius (in textum admisit Tyrrell).

440. εὐπρεπὲς PC : εὐτρεπὲς Canterus, cf. 844 (Elms., Dindf., Paley, Tyrrell*); εὐπετὲς Nauckius (Kirchf. ed. 1867, Wecklein); ἔμενέ τε τοὐμόν, εὐτρεπὲς π. Herm., ἔμενέ τε τοὐμόν, εὐπρεπὲς π. Schoenius.

442. ἐγώ σε P. post hunc versum lacunam suspicatur Schliack, *Philol.* 36, 347.

* εὐπρεπὲς Tyrrell².

ἃς δ' αὖ σὺ Βάκχας εἶρξας, ἃς συνήρπασας
κάδησας ἐν δεσμοῖσι πανδήμου στέγης,
φροῦδαί γ' ἐκεῖναι λελυμέναι πρὸς ὀργάδας 445
σκιρτῶσι Βρόμιον ἀνακαλούμεναι θεόν·
αὐτόματα δ' αὐταῖς δεσμὰ διελύθη ποδῶν,
κλῇδες τ' ἀνῆκαν θύρετρ' ἄνευ θνητῆς χερός.
πολλῶν δ' ὅδ' ἀνὴρ θαυμάτων ἥκει πλέως
εἰς τάσδε Θήβας. σοὶ δὲ τἄλλα χρὴ μέλειν. 450

ΠΕ. μέθεσθε χειρῶν τοῦδ'· ἐν ἄρκυσιν γὰρ ὢν
οὐκ ἔστιν οὕτως ὠκὺς ὥστε μ' ἐκφυγεῖν.
ἀτὰρ τὸ μὲν σῶμ' οὐκ ἄμορφος εἶ, ξένε,
ὡς εἰς γυναῖκας, ἐφ' ὅπερ εἰς Θήβας πάρει·
πλόκαμός τε γάρ σου ταναὸς οὐ πάλης ὕπο, 455
γένυν 'παρ' αὐτὴν κεχυμένος, πόθου πλέως·
λευκὴν δὲ χροιὰν εἰς παρασκευὴν ἔχεις,
οὐχ ἡλίου βολαῖσιν, ἀλλ' ὑπὸ σκιᾶς,
τὴν Ἀφροδίτην καλλονῇ θηρώμενος.
πρῶτον μὲν οὖν μοι λέξον ὅστις εἶ γένος. 460

ΔΙ. οὐ κόμπος οὐδείς· ῥᾴδιον δ' εἰπεῖν τόδε.

444 Nauckio suspectus.
447. ποδῶν PC: πεδῶν Meinekius (Nauck, Kirchf. ed. 1867).
448. κληῗδ' ἐστ' ἀνῆκαν C, τ' post κληῗδες correctori deberi dicitur.
449. ἀνὴρ libri.   450. δέ τ' ἄλλα P, δ' ἔτ' ἄλλα C.
    γρ. λάζυσθε
451. μαίνεσθε χειρῶν τοῦδ' P, quod superscriptum est (γραπτέον
                                                                    ἐμοῦ
λάζυσθε) manifesto e v. 503 sumptum; μαίνεσθε· χειρῶν τοῦδ' C a
Mahaffio collatus (quod recepit Tyrrellius); μαίνεσθε χεῖρον τοῦδ'
Bothius (Schoenius, Kirchf., Nauck); μέθεσθε χειρῶν τοῦδ' Dobraeus et
Burgesius (Herm., Dindf., Paley, Wecklein). μαίνεσθε· χειρῶν PC
denuo collati.   455. οὐ μάλης ὕπο, 'non occulte et furtim,' Madvig.
οὐ πάλης νόμῳ Hartmann.
457. δὲ PC: τε Elms.   εἰς παρασκευὴν PC: ἐς Dind.   ἐκ
παρασκευῆς Kirchf., Wecklein.

28 ΕΥΡΙΠΙΔΟΥ

τὸν ἀνθεμώδη Τμῶλον οἶσθά που κλύων.
ΠΕ. οἶδ᾽, ὃς τὸ Σάρδεων ἄστυ περιβάλλει κύκλῳ.
ΔΙ. ἐντεῦθέν εἰμι, Λυδία δέ μοι πατρίς.
ΠΕ. πόθεν δὲ τελετὰς τάσδ᾽ ἄγεις εἰς Ἑλλάδα; 465
ΔΙ. Διόνυσος ἡμᾶς εἰσέβησ᾽ ὁ τοῦ Διος.
ΠΕ. Ζεὺς δ᾽ ἔστ᾽ ἐκεῖ τις, ὃς νέους τίκτει θεούς;
ΔΙ. οὔκ, ἀλλ᾽ ὁ Σεμέλην ἐνθάδε ζεύξας γάμοις.
ΠΕ. πότερα δὲ νύκτωρ σ᾽ ἢ κατ᾽ ὄμμ᾽ ἠνάγκασεν;
ΔΙ. ὁρῶν ὁρῶντα, καὶ δίδωσιν ὄργια. 470
ΠΕ. τὰ δ᾽ ὄργι᾽ ἐστὶ τίν᾽ ἰδέαν ἔχοντά σοι;
ΔΙ. ἄρρητ᾽ ἀβακχεύτοισιν εἰδέναι βροτῶν.
ΠΕ. ἔχει δ᾽ ὄνησιν τοῖσι θύουσιν τίνα;
ΔΙ. οὐ θέμις ἀκοῦσαί σ᾽, ἔστι δ᾽ ἄξι᾽ εἰδέναι.
ΠΕ. εὖ τοῦτ᾽ ἐκιβδήλευσας, ἵν᾽ ἀκοῦσαι θέλω. 475
ΔΙ. ἀσέβειαν ἀσκοῦντ᾽ ὄργι᾽ ἐχθαίρει θεοῦ.
ΠΕ. τὸν θεὸν ὁρᾶν γὰρ φῂς σαφῶς, ποῖός τις ἦν;
ΔΙ. ὁποῖος ἤθελ᾽· οὐκ ἐγὼ ᾽τασσον τόδε.
ΠΕ. τοῦτ᾽ αὖ παρωχέτευσας εὖ, κοὐδὲν λέγων.
ΔΙ. δόξει τις ἀμαθεῖ σοφὰ λέγων οὐκ εὖ φρονεῖν. 480

466. εὐσέβησ᾽ PC : εἰσέβησ᾽ Abreschius quem fere omnes secuti
sunt, εἰσέφρησ᾽ Burges. 467 sq. Collmanno suspecti.
468. ὃs (ὃ C) σεμέλης ἐνθάδ᾽ ἔζευξεν γάμοις P et ed. Ald. γάμους
Par. G prima manu: ὁ Σεμέλην ἐνθάδε ζεύξας γάμοις Musgr. (Nauck,
Paley, Tyrrell); ὁ Σεμέλης ἐνθάδε ζεύξας γάμους Herm.: ἀλλὰ Σεμέλην
ἐνθάδ᾽ ἔζευξεν γάμοις Canter (Elms., Wecklein).
469. σ᾽ omittit C*. ὄμματ᾽ P et ed. Ald.; ὄμμ᾽ C. σ᾽ ἥγνισεν Reisk.
475. θέλων libri: correxit Victorius.
476. ἀσκοῦνθ᾽ ὄργι᾽ P, -θ᾽ ὄργια C: correxit Ald. ἀσκοῦνθ᾽
ἱερά σ᾽ ἐχθαίρει Mekler.
477. γὰρ ὁρᾶν P (σὺ a correctore super ὁρᾶν scripto) et C; ἦ P,
ὧν (recentiore manu) C: ὁρᾶν γὰρ...ἦν Musgravius ; 'fortasse τὸν θεὸν
ὁρᾶν σὺ φῂς σαφῶς; ποῖός τις ἦ ;' Kirchhoffius.
479. λέγεις Paley. 'legendum εὖ γ᾽ οὐδὲν λέγων' Kirchf.
480. φρονεῖν PC: λέγειν Stobaeus 4, 18.

* om. Wecklein².

ΠΕ. ἦλθες δὲ πρῶτα δεῦρ' ἄγων τὸν δαίμονα;
ΔΙ. πᾶς ἀναχορεύει βαρβάρων τάδ' ὄργια.
ΠΕ. φρονοῦσι γὰρ κάκιον Ἑλλήνων πολύ.
ΔΙ. τάδ' εὖ γε μᾶλλον· οἱ νόμοι δὲ διάφοροι.
ΠΕ. τὰ δ' ἱερὰ νύκτωρ ἢ μεθ' ἡμέραν τελεῖς;   485
ΔΙ. νύκτωρ τὰ πολλά· σεμνότητ' ἔχει σκότος.
ΠΕ. τοῦτ' εἰς γυναῖκας δόλιόν ἐστι καὶ σαθρόν.
ΔΙ. κἀν ἡμέρᾳ τό γ' αἰσχρὸν ἐξεύροι τις ἄν.
ΠΕ. δίκην σε δοῦναι δεῖ σοφισμάτων κακῶν.
ΔΙ. σὲ δ' ἀμαθίας γε τὸν ἀσεβοῦντ' εἰς τὸν θεόν.   490
ΠΕ. ὡς θρασὺς ὁ Βάκχος κοὐκ ἀγύμναστος λόγων.
ΔΙ. εἴφ' ὅ τι παθεῖν δεῖ· τί με τὸ δεινὸν ἐργάσει;
ΠΕ. πρῶτον μὲν ἁβρὸν βόστρυχον τεμῶ σέθεν.
ΔΙ. ἱερὸς ὁ πλόκαμος· τῷ θεῷ δ' αὐτὸν τρέφω.
ΠΕ. ἔπειτα θύρσον τόνδε παράδος ἐκ χεροῖν.   495
ΔΙ. αὐτός μ' ἀφαιροῦ· τόνδε Διονύσου φορῶ.
ΠΕ. εἰρκταῖσί τ' ἔνδον σῶμα σὸν φυλάξομεν.
ΔΙ. λύσει μ' ὁ δαίμων αὐτός, ὅταν ἐγὼ θέλω.
ΠΕ. ὅταν γε καλέσῃς αὐτὸν ἐν Βάκχαις σταθείς.
ΔΙ. καὶ νῦν ἃ πάσχω πλησίον παρὼν ὁρᾷ.   500
ΠΕ. καὶ ποῦ 'στιν; οὐ γὰρ φανερὸς ὄμμασίν γ' ἐμοῖς.

481—2. δεῦρ' ἄγων τάδ' ὄργια ... βαρβάρων τὸν δαίμονα coniecit
Nauckius, in textu tamen vulgatam retinuit.   484. δὲ omittit P.
490. ἀμαθίας ἀσεβοῦντ' P et prima manu C, ἀμαθίας γε κἀσεβοῦντ'
C correctus (quod in textu retinuit Elms.*) : σὲ δ' ἀμαθίας γ' οὐκ εὐ-
σεβοῦντ' obiter ab Elmsleio prolatum ('quae enim facilior emendatio
quam οὐκ εὐσεβεῖν pro ἀσεβεῖν?'), idem protulit nuper Herwerden.
σὲ δ' ἀμ. γε τὸν ἀσεβοῦντ' Porsonus.
496. Διονύσῳ Collmann.   498. ὅταν ἐγὼ καλῶ, propter καλέσῃς in v. proximo positum, conicit Wecklein.
500. καὶ νῦν γ' (collatis El. 1056, Soph. Ai. 1376) Fixius.
501. 'καὶ e superiore versu illatum; scribendum ποῦ δ' ἔστιν;'
Kirchf.   φανερὸς P et corr. C; φανερὸν C.

* item Wecklein, Tyrrell.

ΔΙ.   παρ' ἐμοί· σὺ δ' ἀσεβὴς αὐτὸς ὢν οὐκ εἰσορᾷς.

ΠΕ.   λάζυσθε, καταφρονεῖ με καὶ Θήβας ὅδε.

ΔΙ.   αὐδῶ με μὴ δεῖν σωφρονῶν οὐ σώφροσιν.

ΠΕ.   ἐγὼ δὲ δεῖν γε κυριώτερος σέθεν.   505

ΔΙ.   οὐκ οἶσθ' ὅ τι ζῆς οὐδ' ὁρᾷς ἔθ' ὅστις εἶ.

ΠΕ.   Πενθεὺς Ἀγαύης παῖς, πατρὸς δ' Ἐχίονος.

ΔΙ.   ἐνδυστυχῆσαι τοὔνομ' ἐπιτήδειος εἶ.

ΠΕ.   χώρει· καθείρξατ' αὐτὸν ἱππικαῖς πέλας
φάτναισιν, ὡς ἂν σκότιον εἰσορᾷ κνέφας.   510
ἐκεῖ χόρευε· τάσδε δ' ἃς ἄγων πάρει
κακῶν συνεργοὺς ἢ διεμπολήσομεν
ἢ χεῖρα δούπου τοῦδε καὶ βύρσης κτύπου
παύσας, ἐφ' ἱστοῖς δμωίδας κεκτήσομαι.

ΔΙ.   στείχοιμ' ἄν· ὅ τι γὰρ μὴ χρεών, οὔτοι χρεὼν 515

---

502. αὐτὸς PC : αὐτὸν Elms. (Kirchf. ed. 1867, Wecklein).

503. μου καὶ θήβης P et prima manu C, με καὶ θήβας C correctus et schol. ad Ar. *Ran.* 103.

505 legendum aut 'ἐγὼ δὲ δεῖν γ' ὁ aut κυριώτερος γεγώς' Kirchf.; priorem coniecturam in textum recepit Tyrrell.

506. οὐκ (οὔκ ed. Ald.) οἶσθ' ὅτι ζῆς οὐδ' ὁρᾷς οὔθ' ὅστις εἶ FC*: 'versus a multis tentatus nec tamen emendatus' (Kirchf.). οὐδ' ὅστις εἶ Herm., οὐκ οἶσθ' ὅπου ζῆς, οὐδ' ὁρᾷς ἔθ' ὅστις εἶ legendum suspicatus est Elms., οὐκ οἶσθ' ὃν ἀτίζεις (sic) οὐδ' ὃ ὁρᾷς οὐδ' ὅστις εἶ Reiskius, ὅ τι ζῆς (cetera ut Reisk.) Paley ; ὅ, τι χρῇς (pro θέλεις) Madvig, in ceteris Reiskium secutus ; οὐκ οἶσθ' ἀτίζων (ἔτι ζῶν Hartung) οὔθ' ὃ δρᾷς οὔθ' ὅστις εἶ Wecklein, ὃ τίσεις, οὐδ' ὁρᾷς οὐδ' ὅστις εἶ Schoenius, ἆρ' εἰσέτι ζῆς, οὐδ' ὁρᾷς ἔθ' ὅστις εἶ Tyrrellius (e *Chr. Pat.* 279, ἆρ' εἰσέτι ζῆς δεινὰ ταῦτ' εἰργασμένος ;), οὐκ οἶσθ' ὅ τι ζῆς οὐδ' ὁρᾷς ἔθ' ὅστις εἶ, Nauck, Dind. τοῦθ' ὅστις εἶ H. Macnaghten. οὐκ οἶσθ' ὅτι ζεῖς οὐδ' ὁρᾷς οὔθ' ὅστις εἶ—Munro, coll. *Hec.* 1055, *O. C.* 435, Plat. *Rep.* iv 440 c, ζεῖ τε καὶ χαλεπαίνει. οὐκ οἶσθ' ὃ βάζεις οὔθ' ὃ δρᾷς οὔθ' ὅστις εἶ Cobet, *V. L.*, 449.

513. κτύπους P (Tyrrell), κτύπου C.

514. πάσας C secundum Victorium et Furiam ; idem testatur Wilamowitz-Moellendorff. παύσας P.

515. οὔτε P, οὔτι C, οὔτοι Porsonus.

* Wecklein², qui οἶσθ' ὅπου γῆς conicit.

παθεῖν. ἀτάρ τοι τῶνδ' ἄποιν' ὑβρισμάτων
μέτεισι Διόνυσός σ', ὃν οὐκ εἶναι λέγεις·
ἡμᾶς γὰρ ἀδικῶν κεῖνον εἰς δεσμοὺς ἄγεις.

ΧΟ.   Ἀχελῴου θύγατερ,   στροφή.
πότνι' εὐπάρθενε Δίρκα,   520
σὺ γὰρ ἐν σαῖς ποτε παγαῖς
τὸ Διὸς βρέφος ἔλαβες,
ὅτε μηρῷ πυρὸς ἐξ ἀ-
θανάτου Ζεὺς ὁ τεκὼν ἥρ-
πασέ νιν, τάδ' ἀναβοάσας·   525
ἴθι, Διθύραμβ', ἐμὰν ἄρ-
σενα τάνδε βᾶθι νηδύν·
ἀναφαίνω σε τόδ', ὦ Βάκ-
χιε, Θήβαις ἰνομάζειν.
σὺ δέ μ', ὦ μάκαιρα Δίρκα,   530

516. ἀτάρ τοι PC: 'nescio an legendum ἀτὰρ δὴ' Elms. collatis
Tro. 63, Cycl. 84, H. F. 1353.
518. ἡμᾶς δέων γὰρ Collmann, ἡμᾶς γὰρ ἐκδῶν obiter Wecklein.
519. verba nonnulla quae verbis in antistropha οἵαν οἵαν ὀργὰν
ex altera parte responderent excidisse censuit Musgravius (quem secuti
sunt Elms., Kirchf., Nauck, Dind., Wecklein); placet potius verba in
antistropha, ut correctoris additamentum, eicere.
525. ἥρμοσε legendum putat Kirchhoffius.   ἀναβοήσας C a me
collatus, ἀναβοάσας P: ἀμβοάσας Dindf., ταῦτ' ἀναβώσας Musgr., τᾷδ'
ἀναβώσας Nauck. ann. crit. 'glossam ἀντὶ μιᾶς in vocabula βρέφος et
ἀναβοάσας habet C, quae glossa hoc sibi vult, duas syllabas ita accipi-
endas esse, ut quod attinet ad metrum duntaxat, quasi non duae essent
sed una: minime tamen editoris est ita constituere ut duae syllabae
revera sint una' (Tyrrell).
526. ἴθ' ὦ PC: ἴθι Dobraeus et Herm.
528. ἀναφανῶ PC (Kirchf. ed. 1855): ἀναφάνω Elms. (Tyrrell);
ἀναφαίνω Dobraeus et Herm. (Kirchf. ed. 1867), idem Wecklein.
530. μάκαιρα Θήβα Middendorf.

στεφανηφορους ἀπωθεῖ
θιάσους ἔχουσαν ἐν σοί.
τί μ᾽ ἀναίνει; τί με φεύγεις;
ἔτι ναὶ τὰν βοτρυώδη
Διονύσου χάριν οἴνας   535
ἔτι σοι τοῦ Βρομίου μελήσει.

[οἵαν οἵαν ὀργὰν]
ἀναφαίνει χθόνιον   ἀντιστροφή.
γένος ἐκφύς τε δράκοντός
ποτε Πενθεύς, ὃν Ἐχίων   540
ἐφύτευσε χθόνιος,
ἀγριωπὸν τέρας, οὐ φῶ-
τα βρότειον, φόνιον δ᾽ ὥστε γίγαντ᾽ ἀντίπαλον θεοῖς·
ὃς ἐμὲ βρόχοισι τὰν τοῦ   545
Βρομίου τάχα ξυνάψει,
τὸν ἐμὸν δ᾽ ἐντὸς ἔχει δώ-
ματος ἤδη θιασώταν
σκοτίαισι κρυπτὸν εἱρκταῖς.
ἐσορᾷς τάδ᾽, ὦ Διὸς παῖ   550

531. στεφανηφόρους PC : στεφανα- Dind.
534. ναὶ C ; ἡ (sc. νὴ) superscriptum in P.
537. οἵαν οἵαν ὀργὰν secluserunt Bothius, Herm., Paley, Tyrrell.
adscriptum in C περισσὸν, quod nihil tamen aliud indicare videtur
quam alterum illud οἵαν esse supervacaneum ; cf. notulam criticam in
v. 152.   544. θεοῖς PC denuo collati.
545. ὅς με libri : ὃς ἐμὲ Hartung (Kirchf.); ὃς ἔμ᾽ ἐν post Dobraeum
Dindorfius, cf. infra 615, item Tyrrell, Wecklein².
546. τάχα συνάψει PC : τάχει σ. ed. Ald., τάχα ξ. Brunck.
547. δ᾽ omittit C.
549. σκοτίαις κρυπτὸν ἐν εἱρκταῖς PC (Sch., Paley, Tyrrell): σκοτίαισι
κρυπτὸν εἱρκταῖς Herm. (Kirchf., Nauck, Dind., Wecklein).
550. An ἐφορᾷς?

Διόνυσε, σοὺς προφήτας
ἐν ἀμίλλαισιν ἀνάγκας·
μόλε χρυσῶπα τινάσσων,
ἄνα, θύρσον κατ᾽ Ὀλύμπου,
φονίου δ᾽ ἀνδρὸς ὕβριν κατάσχες.　　　　555

πόθι Νύσης ἄρα τᾶς θη-　　　　ἐπῳδός.
ροτρόφου θυρσοφορεῖς
θιάσους, ὦ Διόνυσ᾽, ἢ
κορυφαῖς Κωρυκίαις·
τάχα δ᾽ ἐν ταῖς πολυδένδρεσ-　　　　560
σιν Ὀλύμπου θαλάμαις, ἔν-
θα ποτ᾽ Ὀρφεὺς κιθαρίζων
σύναγεν δένδρεα μούσαις,
σύναγεν θῆρας ἀγρώτας.
μάκαρ ὦ Πιερία,　　　　565
σέβεταί σ᾽ Εὔιος, ἥξει
τε χορεύσων ἅμα βακχεύ-
μασι, τόν τ᾽ ὠκυρόαν

551. σοὺς C, σὰς P.　　　　552. fuitne ἐν ἀπειλαῖσιν
ἀνάγκας ? Madvig.　　　　553. χρυσωπέ Usener.
554. Ὄλυμπον PC : Ὀλύμπου Kirchhoffius (Tyrrell, Wecklein).
556. νύσης PC : νύσσης ed. Ald. ; Νύσας Elms.　　　　τᾶς erasum in C.
557. θυρσοφορεῖς P, θυρσοφοραισιν C, a me collatus. ποτὶ Νύσας—θυρσοφορεῖς θιάσοις Madvig. 558. ἢ ἐν Wecklein (coll. v. 110). 559. κορυφὲς P.
560. ταῖσι P, ταῖς corr. C.　　　　mox θαλάμοις PC, θαλάμαις Barnesius (quem sequuntur Kirchf. ed. 1867, Dind., Weckl.).　　　　πολυδέν-
δραισιν P, -δένδρεσσιν (alterum σ a manu secunda) C : πολυδένδροισιν
Matthiae (Dind., Tyrrell).
563. σύναγε C, -εν P : συνάγει Dobraeus collato huius fabulae v. 2.
versus suspectus Middendorfio.　　　　564. θήρας PC : θῆρας ed. Ald.
565. μάκαιρ᾽ PC : μάκαρ Dobraeus (collatis Hel. 375, Eubul. ap.
Athen. xv 679 B) et Herm.
567. χορεύων Wecklein.　　　　568. ὠκυρόαν P.

S. B.　　　　3

34   ΕΥΡΙΠΙΔΟΥ

διαβὰς Ἀξιὸν εἰλισ-
σομένας Μαινάδας ἄξει,   570
Λυδίαν τε, τὸν [τᾶς] εὐδαιμονίας
βροτοῖς ὀλβοδόταν
πατέρα [τε], τὸν ἔκλυον
εὔιππον χώραν ὕδασιν
καλλίστοισι λιπαίνειν.   575

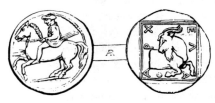

ΔΙ.   ἰώ,
      κλύετ᾽ ἐμᾶς κλύετ᾽ αὐδᾶς,
      ἰὼ Βάκχαι, ἰὼ Βάκχαι.
ΧΟ.   τίς ὅδε, τίς πόθεν ὁ κέλαδος ἀνά μ᾽ ἐκάλεσεν
               Εὐίου;
ΔΙ.   ἰὼ ἰώ, πάλιν αὐδῶ,   580
      ὁ Σεμέλας, ὁ Διὸς παῖς.
ΧΟ.   ἰὼ ἰὼ δέσποτα δέσποτα,
      μόλε νυν ἡμέτερον εἰς

569. ἄξιον P, Ἀξιὸν C.
570. εἰλησσομένας τε P : εἰλισσομένας Heath.
571. λυδίαν PC : Λοιδίαν post Heathium Herm. (quem sequitur
Dind.).   τὸν τᾶς PC : τὸν Herm.
573. τε delevit Bothius (Kirchf.[1], Wecklein[1]); retinet Kirchf. ed. 1867.
574. εὐίον C secundum Furiae collationem.
577. fortasse ἀμᾶς, Wecklein.   578. ὦ βάκχαι, ἰὼ βάκχαι Elms.
579. πόθεν ὅδ᾽ Herm. ; ὅδε πόθεν Wecklein; τίς ὅδε πόθεν...ἐκάλε-
σεν omisso Εὐίου coniecit Nauckius.
583. νῦν libri.   ἡμέτερον PC : ἁμ- Dind.

θίασον, ὦ Βρόμιε Βρόμιε.
πέδον χθονός· ἔνοσι πότνια.　585
ἆ ἆ,
τάχα τὰ Πενθέως
μέλαθρα διατινάξεται πεσήμασιν.
ὁ Διόνυσος ἀνὰ μέλαθρα·
σέβετέ νιν. σέβομεν ὤ.　590
εἴδετε λάινα κίοσιν ἔμβολα
διάδρομα τάδε;
Βρόμιος ἀλαλάξεται στέγας ἔσω.

ΔΙ. ἅπτε κεραύνιον αἴθοπα λαμπάδα·
σύμφλεγε σύμφλεγε δώματα Πενθέως.　595

ΧΟ. ἆ ἆ,
πῦρ οὐ λεύσσεις οὐδ' αὐγάζει
Σεμέλας ἱερὸν ἀμφὶ τάφον, ἄν
ποτε κεραυνόβολος ἔλιπε φλόγα

585. πέδον χθονὸς ἔνοσι πότνια PC (Herm., Kirchf.[1], Tyrrell); πέδου
Elms. (Nauck, Kirchf. ed. 1867, Wecklein).　δαπέδων Schoenius.
'ΧΟ. δ'. πέδον χθονὸς—(sc. σαλεύει). ΧΟ. ε'. ἔνοσι πότνια' Paley. 'versus
non integer, videturque potius verbum aliquod post χθονὸς excidisse,
velut σείεται, quod coniecit Hartungus' (Dindorf). 'scribendum π. χ.
ἔνοσι πιτνεῖ, ἆ, ἆ' Madvig*.　588. διατινάξεται C, -ξεται P.

590. 'verba σέβετέ νιν Baccho tribuit C secundum apographa Parisina. sequentibus hemichorii nota praefixa in Aldina, fortasse etiam in
libris. nam post 590 usque ad finem cantici nullas personarum notas
habet P. nihil monitum de C. certum est haec a singulis chori personis
cantari quas notari nihil attinet' (Kirchhoff, 1855).　'Ημίχ. ante
σέβομεν ὦ PC denuo collati.

591. ἴδετε (+ τὰ P) λάινα PC: εἴδετε...; Dobraeus quem sequitur
Dindorfius.　ἰδὲ τὰ Wecklein.　κίοσιν omittit P.

593 Wilamowitz-Moellendorffio suspectus. Βρόμιος ὅς Musgr.
(Herm., Dind., Tyrrell).　ἀλαλάξεται C, -ξεται P (cf. 588).

594. ΔΙ. addidit Tyrwhitt.　nulla personae nota PC.

596. λεύσεις C.　αὐγάζει PC: αὐγάζεις? Nauckius in ann. crit.
quem sequitur Dindorfius.　597. τόν δὲ Σεμέλας Wilamowitz.

* σεῖε πέδον χθονός, Wilamowitz.

3—2

ἧσσε κἀκέντει φαεννὸν αἰθέρ᾽, ὡς σφάζων ἐμέ.
πρὸς δὲ τοῖσδ᾽ αὐτῷ τάδ᾽ ἄλλα Βάκχιος λυμαί-
νεται·
δώματ᾽ ἔρρηξεν χαμᾶζε· συντεθράνωται δ᾽ ἅπαν
πικροτάτους ἰδόντι δεσμοὺς τοὺς ἐμούς· κόπου
δ᾽ ὕπο
διαμεθεὶς ξίφος παρεῖται. πρὸς θεὸν γὰρ ὢν
ἀνήρ   635
εἰς μάχην ἐλθεῖν ἐτόλμησ᾽· ἥσυχος δ᾽ ἐκβὰς ἐγὼ
δωμάτων ἥκω πρὸς ὑμᾶς, Πενθέως οὐ φροντίσας.
ὡς δέ μοι δοκεῖ, ψοφεῖ γοῦν ἀρβύλη δόμων ἔσω,
εἰς προνώπι᾽ αὐτίχ᾽ ἥξει. τί ποτ᾽ ἄρ᾽ ἐκ τούτων
ἐρεῖ;
ῥᾳδίως γὰρ αὐτὸν οἴσω, κἂν πνέων ἔλθῃ μέγα· 640
πρὸς σοφοῦ γὰρ ἀνδρὸς ἀσκεῖν σώφρον᾽ εὐοργησίαν.

ΠΕΝΘΕΥΣ.

πέπονθα δεινά διαπέφευγέ μ᾽ ὁ ξένος,
ὃς ἄρτι δεσμοῖς ἦν κατηναγκασμένος.
ἔα ἔα·

631. ἧσσε κἀκέντα P, ἧσσε κἀκέντει a corr. C.   αἰθέρ᾽ supplevit Canterus.
632. τὰ δ᾽ libri: τάδ᾽ Victorius et Musgr.
633. συντριαινοῦται δ᾽ ἄφνω coniecit Nauck.
635. παρεῖται om. C.
636. ἐτόλμησ᾽ P, ἐτόλμησε (ν add. manu recentiore) C; ἐτόλμ᾽ ed. Ald.   ἐκ βάκχας ἄγων libri: ἐκβὰς ἐγὼ Bothius; ἧσ. δὲ βασιλικῶν Elms., ἧσ. δ᾽ ἐκ Βακχάδων Herm., εὖχος ἐς βάκχας δ᾽ ἄγων Tyrrell.
638. ψοφεῖ γὰρ Fixius.   640. μέγας Cobet V. L. p. 587² collato Rhes. 323; idem Dawesio placuerat, Misc. Crit. p. 458.
641. ἀσκεῖν C denuo collatus, ἀρκεῖ P.   εὐοργησίαν P; -ία C secundum Victorium et Furiam.

ὅδ' ἐστὶν ἀνήρ· τί τάδε; πῶς προνώπιος 645
φαίνει πρὸς οἴκοις τοῖς ἐμοῖς, ἔξω βεβώς;
ΔΙ. στῆσον πόδ', ὀργῇ δ' ὑπόθες ἥσυχον πόδα.
ΠΕ. πόθεν σὺ δεσμὰ διαφυγὼν ἔξω περᾷς;
ΔΙ. οὐκ εἶπον ἢ οὐκ ἤκουσας ὅτι λύσει μέ τις;
ΠΕ. τίς; τοὺς λόγους γὰρ εἰσφέρεις καινοὺς ἀεί. 650
ΔΙ. ὃς τὴν πολύβοτρυν ἄμπελον φύει βροτοῖς.
ΠΕ. *　*　*　*　*　*
ΔΙ. ὠνείδισας δὴ τοῦτο Διονύσῳ καλόν.
ΠΕ. κλῄειν κελεύω πάντα πύργον ἐν κύκλῳ.
ΔΙ. τί δ'; οὐχ ὑπερβαίνουσι καὶ τείχη θεοί;
ΠΕ. σοφὸς σοφὸς σύ, πλὴν ἃ δεῖ σ' εἶναι σοφόν. 655
ΔΙ. ἃ δεῖ μάλιστα, ταῦτ' ἔγωγ' ἔφυν σοφός.
κείνου δ' ἀκούσας πρῶτα τοὺς λόγους μάθε,
ὃς ἐξ ὄρους πάρεστιν ἀγγελῶν τί σοι·
ἡμεῖς δέ σοι μενοῦμεν, οὐ φευξούμεθα.

ΑΓΓΕΛΟΣ.

Πενθεῦ κρατύνων τῆσδε Θηβαίας χθονός, 660
ἥκω Κιθαιρῶν' ἐκλιπών, ἵν' οὔποτε

645. ἀνὴρ libri.　　647. πόδα libri; τρόπον Musgr. (Wecklein),
βάσιν Blomfield, Fixius, φρένα Middendorf; ἡσυχαίτερον Schoenius.
649. οὐκ ἤκουσας P, ἢ οὐκ ἤκουσας C secundum collatores omnes,
idem apogr. Paris.　　λύσει PC: 'paullo melius esset λύσῃ' Elms.
lacunam unius versus quem post 652 excidisse putaverat Dobraeus,
rectius (ut videtur) post 651 indicandam esse suspicatus est Paleius;
itaque verba ὠνείδισας δὴ τοῦτο Διονύσῳ καλόν ipsi Dionyso reddidi.
653—7. personarum signa confusa in P.
653. κλύειν P et prima manu C, κλείειν corr. C: κλῄειν Elms.
655. σοφὸς εἰ P e silentio, et C inserto γ a manu secunda: σὺ
reddidit textui Porsonus, laudato *Chr. Pat.* 1529, σοφὸς σοφὸς σὺ καὶ
σοφῶς ἔτλης πότμον.　　658. ἀγγελῶν P.
659. φεύξομεθα C prima manu, φευξούμεθα P et recentiore manu C.
661. κιθερῶν' P.

λευκῆς χιόνος ἀνεῖσαν εὐαγεῖς βολαί.

ΠΕ. ἥκεις δὲ ποίαν προστιθεὶς σπουδὴν λόγου;

ΑΓΓ. Βάκχας ποτνιάδας εἰσιδών, αἳ τῆσδε γῆς
οἴστροισι λευκὸν κῶλον ἐξηκόντισαν,   665
ἥκω φράσαι σοὶ καὶ πόλει χρῄζων, ἄναξ,
ὡς δεινὰ δρῶσι θαυμάτων τε κρείσσονα.
θέλω δ᾽ ἀκοῦσαι, πότερά σοι παρρησίᾳ
φράσω τὰ κεῖθεν ἢ λόγον στειλώμεθα·
τὸ γὰρ τάχος σου τῶν φρενῶν δέδοικ᾽, ἄναξ,   670
καὶ τοὐξύθυμον καὶ τὸ βασιλικὸν λίαν.

ΠΕ. λέγ᾽, ὡς ἀθῷος ἐξ ἐμοῦ πάντως ἔσει·
[τοῖς γὰρ δικαίοις οὐχὶ θυμοῦσθαι χρεών·]
ὅσῳ δ᾽ ἂν εἴπῃς δεινότερα Βακχῶν πέρι,
τοσῷδε μᾶλλον τὸν ὑποθέντα τὰς τέχνας   675
γυναιξὶ τόνδε τῇ δίκῃ προσθήσομεν.

ΑΓΓ. ἀγελαῖα μὲν βοσκήματ᾽ ἄρτι πρὸς λέπας
† μόσχων ὑπεξήκριζον, ἡνίχ᾽ ἥλιος

662. χιόνος ἀνεῖσαν PC : ἀνεῖσαν χιόνος G Dindorfius e L Dindorfii
coniectura; idem coniecit Nauckius (Thompson, Weckl.).   εὐαγεῖς PC :
εὐαυγεῖς Musgravius quem sequitur Dind.; ἐξαυγεῖς Wecklein collato
Rhes. 304 χιόνος ἐξαυγεστέρων.

663. δ᾽ ὁποίαν libri : δὲ ποίαν Porsonus. 'fortasse δὲ ποίᾳ προστιθεὶς
σπουδῇ λόγον' Kirchhoff. ποίῳ...λόγῳ Collmann. ποίαν...λόγῳ J S Reid.

664. τῆσδε γῆς in locum τῆς πόλεως irrepsisse suspicatur Wecklein,
collato v. 20.

669. τἀκεῖθεν libri et *Chr. Pat.* 2220: τὰ κεῖθεν Brunck.

673. eiecit Nauckius collato fragm. 289, 1 (Weckl.).

675. τὰς omisit P.   676. προσθήσομεν PC : προήσομεν Hartung.

678. μόσχων neque cum ὑπεξήκριζον neque cum ἀγελαῖα βοσκήματα
recte construi posse ostendunt vv. 734—745 ubi non μόσχοι tantum,
sed πόρις, δαμάλαι, ταῦροι commemorantur; adde quod genitivus a
verbis ἀγελαῖα βοσκήματα nimis remotus est.   suspicor igitur **βόσκων**
esse scribendum, praesertim cum in cursivis codicibus litterae μ et β
saepe inter se simillimae sint; cf. μέλος supra v. 25 e βέλος corruptum.
sed praestat fortasse μοχθῶν (1885); μυχῶν H. Macnaghten, coll. Xen.
Anab. iv 1, 7 ἐν τοῖς ἄγκεσι καὶ μυχοῖς τῶν ὀρέων; sed μυχὸς per se non
vallem sed *recessum* significat.

ἀκτῖνας ἐξίησι θερμαίνων χθόνα·
ὁρῶ δὲ θιάσους τρεῖς γυναικείων χορῶν,   680
ὧν ἦρχ' ἑνὸς μὲν Αὐτονόη, τοῦ δευτέρου
μήτηρ Ἀγαύη σή, τρίτου δ' Ἰνὼ χοροῦ.
ηὗδον δὲ πᾶσαι σώμασιν παρειμέναι,
αἱ μὲν πρὸς ἐλάτης νῶτ' ἐρείσασαι φόβην,
αἱ δ' ἐν δρυὸς φύλλοισι πρὸς πέδῳ κάρα   685
εἰκῇ βαλοῦσαι σωφρόνως, οὐχ ὡς σὺ φὴς
ᾠνωμένας κρατῆρι καὶ λωτοῦ ψόφῳ
θηρᾶν καθ' ὕλην Κύπριν ἠρημωμένας.

ἡ σὴ δὲ μήτηρ ὠλόλυξεν ἐν μέσαις
σταθεῖσα Βάκχαις, ἐξ ὕπνου κινεῖν δέμας,   690
μυκήμαθ' ὡς ἤκουσε κεροφόρων βοῶν.
αἱ δ' ἀποβαλοῦσαι θαλερὸν ὀμμάτων ὕπνον
ἀνῇξαν ὀρθαί, θαῦμ' ἰδεῖν εὐκοσμίας,
νέαι παλαιαὶ παρθένοι τ' ἔτ' ἄζυγες.

680. γυναικίων P.   681. τοῦ δὲ libri: τοῦ Scaliger.
682. τρίτη P et corr. C; τρίτου prima manu C et ed. Ald.   τρίτη
δ' Ἰνὼ τ͵ίτου Herm.
683. εὗδον libri: ηὗδον Elms., Dind., Paley, Tyrrell, Wecklein.
κώμασιν audacius Herm.   684. πρὸς—φόβην, 'corrupta,' Hartmann.
685. πέδῳ PC: πέδον ed. Ald.   687 οἰνωμένας PC: ᾠν- Elmsl.
688. ἠρημωμένας C, ἠρεμωμένας P: ἠρενωμένας ed. Ald., ἠρημω-
μένην Wecklein, ἠνεμωμένας Nauckius laudato Jacobsio in Aeliani Nat.
Anim. 7, 17 p. 260.
694. παρθένοι τε κἄζυγες libri: παρθένοι τ' ἔτ' ἄζυγες e Chr. Pat.
1834 (post Musgravium editores omnes); σύζυγοί τε κἄζυγες Usener.

καὶ πρῶτα μὲν καθεῖσαν εἰς ὤμους κόμας   695
νεβρίδας τ' ἀνεστείλανθ' ὅσαισιν ἀμμάτων
σύνδεσμ' ἐλέλυτο, καὶ καταστίκτους δορὰς
ὄφεσι κατεζώσαντο λιχμῶσιν γένυν.
αἱ δ' ἀγκάλαισι δορκάδ' ἢ σκύμνους λύκων
ἀγρίους ἔχουσαι λευκὸν ἐδίδοσαν γάλα,   700
ὅσαις νεοτόκοις μαστὸς ἦν σπαργῶν ἔτι
βρέφη λιπούσαις· ἐπὶ δ' ἔθεντο κισσίνους
στεφάνους δρυός τε μίλακός τ' ἀνθεσφόρου.

θύρσον δέ τις λαβοῦσ' ἔπαισεν εἰς πέτραν,
ὅθεν δροσώδης ὕδατος ἐκπηδᾷ νοτίς·   705
ἄλλη δὲ νάρθηκ' εἰς πέδον καθῆκε γῆς,
καὶ τῇδε κρήνην ἐξανῆκ' οἴνου θεός·
ὅσαις δὲ λευκοῦ πώματος πόθος παρῆν,

696. ὀμμάτων P, ἀμμάτων C.   698. συνεζώσαντο Blaydes.
ibid. λιχμῶσαν γέναν P, λιχμῶσαν γένυν C, denuo collati: λιχμῶσιν
Heath.

701. ὅσαι P.   μαζὸς PC: μαστὸς Elms.   σπαρτῶν P.
703. ἀνθεσφόρους PC: -ου ed. Brubachiana.
708. πώματος C, πόματος P, denuo collati.

ἄκροισι δακτύλοισι διαμῶσαι χθόνα
γάλακτος ἐσμοὺς εἶχον· ἐκ δὲ κισσίνων   710
θύρσων γλυκεῖαι μέλιτος ἔσταζον ῥοαί.
ὥστ' εἰ παρῆσθα, τὸν θεὸν τὸν νῦν ψέγεις
εὐχαῖσιν ἂν μετῆλθες εἰσιδὼν τάδε.
ξυνήλθομεν δὲ βουκόλοι καὶ ποιμένες,
κοινῶν λόγων δώσοντες ἀλλήλοις ἔριν,   715
ὡς δεινὰ δρῶσι θαυμάτων τ' ἐπάξια·
καί τις πλάνης κατ' ἄστυ καὶ τρίβων λόγων
ἔλεξεν εἰς ἅπαντας· ὦ σεμνὰς πλάκας
ναίοντες ὀρέων, θέλετε θηρασώμεθα
Πενθέως Ἀγαύην μητέρ' ἐκ βακχευμάτων   720
χάριν τ' ἄνακτι θώμεθ'; εὖ δ' ἡμῖν λέγειν
ἔδοξε, θάμνων δ' ἐλλοχίζομεν φόβαις
κρύψαντες αὑτούς· αἱ δὲ τὴν τεταγμένην
ὥραν ἐκίνουν θύρσον εἰς βακχεύματα,
Ἴακχον ἀθρόῳ στόματι τὸν Διὸς γόνον   725
Βρόμιον καλοῦσαι· πᾶν δὲ συνεβάκχευ' ὄρος

709. διαμῶσαι PC: λικμῶσαι Par. E, idem superscriptum in C et apogr. Par. G.

710. ἐσμοὺς libri: ἐσμοὺς Barnes. γάλακτος εἶχον νάματ' Valckenaer; νασμοὺς γ. εἶχον Jacobsius; γ. ἠθμοὺς? Wecklein.

715. καινῶν C secundum Furiam et apogr. Paris. (admisit Musgr.); κοινῶν C sec. Elms. κοινῶν 'post novam conlationem' PC.

716 'versum ex v. 667 (ubi θαυμάτων τε κρείσσονα) huc illatum eiecit Dobraeus' (Dindf.); agnoscit tamen *Chr. Pat.* 2213, ἥκω φράσαι σοι καὶ πόλει πολλὰ ξένα, ὡς καινὰ πάντα θαυμάτων τ' ἐπάξια. ὡς δείν' ὁρῶσι Madwig.

721. θῶμεν PC: vel δῶμεν vel θώμεθ' Elms.; ipse prius praetulit, posterius alii (Bothius, Schoenius, Kirchf. ed. 1867, Tyrrellius, Weckl.).

722. ἐλοχίζομεν P, ἐλλοχίζομεν C: ἐνελοχίζομεν Dind.

726. συνεβάκχευσ' PC: συνεβάκχευεν [Longinus] περὶ ὕψους xv 6, unde συνεβάκχευ' Porsonus.

καὶ θῆρες, οὐδὲν δ' ἦν ἀκίνητον δρόμῳ.
κυρεῖ δ' Ἀγαύη πλησίον θρώσκουσά μου·
κἀγὼ 'ξεπήδησ' ὡς συναρπάσαι θέλων,
λόχμην κενώσας ἔνθ' ἐκρύπτομεν δέμας·   730
ἡ δ' ἀνεβόησεν· ὦ δρομάδες ἐμαὶ κύνες,
θηρώμεθ' ἀνδρῶν τῶνδ' ὕπ'· ἀλλ' ἔπεσθέ μοι,
ἔπεσθε θύρσοις διὰ χερῶν ὡπλισμέναι.
ἡμεῖς μὲν οὖν φεύγοντες ἐξηλύξαμεν
Βακχῶν σπαραγμόν, αἱ δὲ νεμομέναις χλόην   735
μόσχοις ἐπῆλθον χειρὸς ἀσιδήρου μέτα.
καὶ τὴν μὲν ἂν προσεῖδες εὔθηλον πόριν
μυκωμένην ἔχουσαν ἐν χεροῖν δίχα,
ἄλλαι δὲ δαμάλας διεφόρουν σπαράγμασιν.
εἶδες δ' ἂν ἢ πλεύρ' ἢ δίχηλον ἔμβασιν   740
ῥιπτόμεν' ἄνω τε καὶ κάτω· κρεμαστὰ δὲ
ἔσταζ' ὑπ' ἐλάταις ἀναπεφυρμέν' αἵματι.
ταῦροι δ' ὑβρισταὶ κεἰς κέρας θυμούμενοι
τὸ πρόσθεν, ἐσφάλλοντο πρὸς γαῖαν δέμας,
μυριάσι χειρῶν ἀγόμενοι νεανίδων.   745
θᾶσσον δὲ διεφοροῦντο σαρκὸς ἐνδυτὰ

---

727. δρόμου Bergmann. versum interpolatum esse suspicatus est
Baier.   729. ξυναρπάσαι Dind.
731. δρομάδες ἐμαὶ κύνες suspectum Nauckio. 732. τῶνδ' ὕπ'· Weckl.
735. σπαραγμῶν C. νεμόμεναι P, νεμομέναις C, denuo collati.
738. ἔχουσαν—δίκα PC: ἔχουσαν—δίχα Scaliger quem secuti sunt
Herm., Dind. (ἔλκουσαν—δίχα Reiskius, ἄγουσαν—δίχα Musgr.); δίκῃ
Elms. (Schoenius, Paley, Tyrrell); ἀκμαῖς Nauck, βίᾳ Wecklein* (collato
βίαν e διαὶ in Aesch. Cho. 656 ab Hermanno eruto); φέρουσαν—βίᾳ iam
antea coniecerat Collmann.
740. πλευρὰν libri: πλεύρ' Barnes.   743. κἀς Dindorf.
746. 'quod ad accentum attinet, Aldus ἐνδυτὰ dedit nec variare
videntur MSS. Barnesius, quem sequuntur Brunckius et Matthiae,
diserte ἐνδυτὰ' (Elms.).   ἔνδυτα PC denuo collati.

* ἀκμαῖς Wecklein².

ἢ σὲ ξυνάψαι βλέφαρα βασιλείοις κόραις.

χωροῦσι δ' ὥστ' ὄρνιθες ἀρθεῖσαι δρόμῳ
πεδίων ὑποτάσεις, αἳ παρ' Ἀσωποῦ ῥοαῖς
εὔκαρπον ἐκβάλλουσι Θηβαίων στάχυν,   750
Ὑσιάς τ' Ἐρυθράς θ', αἳ Κιθαιρῶνος λέπας
νέρθεν κατῳκήκασιν, ὥστε πολέμιοι
ἐπεισπεσοῦσαι πάντ' ἄνω τε καὶ κάτω
διέφερον· ἥρπαζον μὲν ἐκ δόμων τέκνα,
ὁπόσα δ' ἐπ' ὤμοις ἔθεσαν, οὐ δεσμῶν ὕπο   755
προσείχετ' οὐδ' ἔπιπτεν εἰς μέλαν πέδον,
οὐ χαλκός, οὐ σίδηρος· ἐπὶ δὲ βοστρύχοις
πῦρ ἔφερον, οὐδ' ἔκαιεν. οἱ δ' ὀργῆς ὕπο
εἰς ὅπλ' ἐχώρουν φερόμενοι Βακχῶν ὕπο·
οὗπερ τὸ δεινὸν ἦν θέαμ' ἰδεῖν, ἄναξ.   760

---

747. σὲ ξυνάψαι C (Matthiae, Madvig, Weckl.); σὺ ξυνάψαι prima
manu P, σὺ ξυνάψαις P sec. manu (ita Elms., Herm., Schoenius,
Kirchf., Nauck, Dindf., Paley, Tyrrell).   βασιλικαῖς coniecit Nauck.

749. ἀσωποῦ C, αἰσωποῦ P denuo collatus.

750. Θηβαῖον P (denuo coll.), θηβαίων C: Θηβαίοις Brunckius et
Hartungus.

751. ὑσίας libri: Ὑσιὰς Dind. (Kirchf., Nauck, Wecklein).
θ' omisit P.   Ὑσίας δ' Brunck.

752. 'fortasse ὡς δὲ πολεμίοις' Kirchf.   ὡς δὲ πολέμιοι probavit
Madvig qui v. 754 pro τέκνα scribi voluit τύχᾳ.

754 'aut graviter corruptus aut manca oratio versiculo hausto uno
alterove' (Kirchhoffius). inter 754 et 755 intercidisse nonnulla putavit
Hartungus. ἥρπαζόν <τε χρήματ'> ἐκ δόμων Herwerden.

755. post verba οὐ δεσμῶν ὕπο desinunt C eiusque apographa Parisina
duo. 'in Florentino quae deerant ex Aldina descripta supplevit manus
recentior; in ipso archetypo post illum versum duo folia vacua relicta
sunt a librario' (Kirchhoffius). ante v. 757 lacunam suspicati sunt
Tyrrellius et Middendorfius.

758. ἐκαίεθ' P: ἔκαι ἔθ' Bernhardy, ἔκαιεν Elms. (ἔκαεν Dind.).

τοῖς μὲν γὰρ οὐχ ἥμασσε λογχωτὸν βέλος,
κεῖναι δὲ θύρσους ἐξανιεῖσαι χερῶν
ἐτραυμάτιζον κἀπενώτιζον φυγῇ
γυναῖκες ἄνδρας, οὐκ ἄνευ θεῶν τινος.
πάλιν δ᾽ ἐχώρουν ὅθεν ἐκίνησαν πόδα,   765
κρήνας ἐπ᾽ αὐτὰς ἃς ἀνῆκ᾽ αὐταῖς θεός.
νίψαντο δ᾽ αἷμα, σταγόνα δ᾽ ἐκ παρηίδων
γλώσσῃ δράκοντες ἐξεφαίδρυνον χροός.
τὸν δαίμον᾽ οὖν τόνδ᾽ ὅστις ἔστ᾽, ὦ δέσποτα,
δέχου πόλει τῇδ᾽, ὡς τά τ᾽ ἄλλ᾽ ἐστὶν μέγας,   770
κἀκεῖνό φασιν αὐτόν, ὡς ἐγὼ κλύω,
τὴν παυσίλυπον ἄμπελον δοῦναι βροτοῖς.
οἴνου δὲ μηκέτ᾽ ὄντος οὐκ ἔστιν Κύπρις
οὐδ᾽ ἄλλο τερπνὸν οὐδὲν ἀνθρώποις ἔτι.
ΧΟ. ταρβῶ μὲν εἰπεῖν τοὺς λόγους ἐλευθέρους   775
εἰς τὸν τύραννον, ἀλλ᾽ ὅμως εἰρήσεται·
Διόνυσος ἥσσων οὐδενὸς θεῶν ἔφυ.
ΠΕ. ἤδη τόδ᾽ ἐγγὺς ὥστε πῦρ ὑφάπτεται
ὕβρισμα Βακχῶν, ψόγος ἐς Ἕλληνας μέγας.
ἀλλ᾽ οὐκ ὀκνεῖν δεῖ· στεῖχ᾽ ἐπ᾽ Ἠλέκτρας ἰὼν   780

761. τᾶς P : τοὺς ed. Ald., τοῖς H Stephanus (Elms., Schoenius,
Nauck, Kirchf. ed. 1867, Dindf., Wecklein), τὰς post Brodaeum Barnesius (Herm., Kirchf. ed. 1855, Paley, Tyrrell); τῶν Brunckius quem
sequitur Matthiae.   764. γυναῖκας P : γυναῖκες ed. Ald.
766. κρήναις ἐπ᾽ αὐταῖς ed. Ald.; 'fortasse κρήναις δ᾽ ἐπ᾽ αὐταῖς...
ἔνιψαν αἷμα' Kirchf.   767. νίψαι τὸ σῶμα – ᘯ – ᘯ – ᘯ – | ᘩ
αἱματηρὰς σταγόνας ἐκ παρηίδων...δράκοντες...χρόα (χρόα iam antea coniecerat Porsonus) Hartung.   νίψαι τόδ᾽ αἷμα Herm.   768. δράκοντος P :
-ες Reiskius.   776. πρὸς τὸν τύραννον bis Chr. Pat. (2222, 2244).
778. ἐφάπτεται P : ὑφάπτεται auctor Chr. Pat. 2227, qui versum
integrum suos in usus convertit (ita tres codices a Duebnero collati,
editio Benedictina habuerat ὥσπερ πῦρ ἐφάπτεται).   ὑφάπτεται receperunt Nauck, Kirchf. ed. 1867, Tyrrell (δεύτεραι φροντίδες), Wecklein.

πύλας· κέλευε πάντας ἀσπιδηφόρους
ἵππων τ' ἀπαντᾶν ταχυπόδων ἐπεμβάτας
πέλτας θ' ὅσοι πάλλουσι καὶ τόξων χερὶ
ψάλλουσι νευράς, ὡς ἐπιστρατεύσομεν
Βάκχαισιν· οὐ γὰρ ἀλλ' ὑπερβάλλει τάδε, 785
εἰ πρὸς γυναικῶν πεισόμεσθ' ἃ πάσχομεν.
ΔΙ. πείθει μὲν οὐδέν, τῶν ἐμῶν λόγων κλύων,
Πενθεῦ· κακῶς δὲ πρὸς σέθεν πάσχων ὅμως
οὔ φημι χρῆναί σ' ὅπλ' ἐπαίρεσθαι θεῷ,
ἀλλ' ἡσυχάζειν· Βρόμιος οὔ σ' ἀνέξεται 790
κινοῦντα Βάκχας εὐίων ὀρῶν ἄπο.
ΠΕ. οὐ μὴ φρενώσεις μ', ἀλλὰ δέσμιος φυγὼν
σώσει τόδ'; ἢ σοὶ πάλιν ἀναστρέψω δίκην.
ΔΙ. θύοιμ' ἂν αὐτῷ μᾶλλον ἢ θυμούμενος
πρὸς κέντρα λακτίζοιμι θνητὸς ὢν θεῷ. 795
ΠΕ. θύσω, φόνον γε θῆλυν, ὥσπερ ἄξιαι,
πολὺν ταράξας ἐν Κιθαιρῶνος πτυχαῖς.
ΔΙ. φευξεῖσθε πάντες· καὶ τόδ' αἰσχρόν, ἀσπίδας
θύρσοισι Βακχῶν ἐκτρέπειν χαλκηλάτους.

785. ὑπερβαλεῖ Naber.   787—791. ἄγγελος P: ΔΙ. Tyrwhitt.
πείθει P: πείσει quondam Tyrrell.   790. ἡσύχαζε Elms.   οὐκ
ἀνέξεται P.

791. κινοῦντι P: κινοῦντα Canter. post βάκχας addit σ Lenting
(Wecklein). fortasse οὔ σ' ἀνέξεται (790); idem conicit J S Reid.

793. σώση P: σώσει ed. Ald.   τόδ' P: πόδ' Carolus Dilthey quod
nemo in textum recepit.   δίκην; (interrogative) Kirchf., χέρας Weckl.,
χέρας; Hartmann.   796. ἄξιος Wilamowitz-Moellendorff.

797. πόλεμον ταράξας Collmann et Wecklein, non modo quia
φόνον πολὺν ταράξας inusitatum sit, sed etiam quod verbum θύσω, ex
antecedentis distichi θύοιμ' cum acerbitate quadam iteratum, ita aptius
cum φόνον cohaereat.

vv. 798—9 Pentheo, 800—2 nuntio tribuit P: correxit Tyrwhitt.
798. φευξεῖσθε P: φεύξεσθε Elms.
799. ἐκτρέπειν P: ἐντρέπειν? Nauck. ann. crit., ἐκλιπεῖν Hartung.
Βάκχας scribendum esse suspicamur quod Wackleinius quoque conicit.

ΠΕ. ἀπόρῳ γε τῷδε συμπεπλέγμεθα ξένῳ,   800
  ὃς οὔτε πάσχων οὔτε δρῶν σιγήσεται.
ΔΙ. ὦ τᾶν, ἔτ' ἔστιν εὖ καταστῆσαι τάδε.
ΠΕ. τί δρῶντα; δουλεύοντα δουλείαις ἐμαῖς;
ΔΙ. ἐγὼ γυναῖκας δεῦρ' ὅπλων ἄξω δίχα.
ΠΕ. οἴμοι· τόδ' ἤδη δόλιον εἴς με μηχανᾷ.   805
ΔΙ. ποῖόν τι, σῶσαί σ' εἰ θέλω τέχναις ἐμαῖς;
ΠΕ. ξυνέθεσθε κοινῇ τάδ', ἵνα βακχεύητ' ἀεί.
ΔΙ. καὶ μὴν ξυνεθέμην τοῦτό γ', ἴσθι, τῷ θεῷ.
ΠΕ. ἐκφέρετέ μοι δεῦρ' ὅπλα· σὺ δὲ παῦσαι λέγων.
ΔΙ. ἆ·   810
  βούλει σφ' ἐν ὄρεσι συγκαθημένας ἰδεῖν;
ΠΕ. μάλιστα, μυρίον γε δοὺς χρυσοῦ σταθμόν.
ΔΙ. τί δ' εἰς ἔρωτα τοῦδε πέπτωκας μέγαν;
ΠΕ. λυπρῶς νιν εἰσίδοιμ' ἂν ἐξῳνωμένας.
ΔΙ. ὅμως δ' ἴδοις ἂν ἡδέως ἅ σοι πικρά;   815
ΠΕ. σάφ' ἴσθι, σιγῇ γ' ὑπ' ἐλάταις καθήμενος.
ΔΙ. ἀλλ' ἐξιχνεύσουσίν σε, κἂν ἔλθῃς λάθρᾳ.
ΠΕ. ἀλλ' ἐμφανῶς· καλῶς γὰρ ἐξεῖπας τάδε.
ΔΙ. ἄγωμεν οὖν σε κἀπιχειρήσεις ὁδῷ;
ΠΕ. ἄγ' ὡς τάχιστα, τοῦ χρόνου δέ σοι φθονῶ.   820

801. ὡς P (retinuerunt Herm., Schoenius, Kirchf. ed. 1855, Paley):
ὃς 'legebam olim' Musgr. (in textum receperunt Elms., Nauck, Kirchf.
ed. 1867, Dindf., Tyrrell, Wecklein).   802. ὅταν P : ὦ τᾶν Scaliger.
803 μῶν δούλαισι δουλεύοντ' ἐμαῖς ; coniecit Nauck.
808. μὴ (superscr. ν) P.   ἔστι P (Herm., idem κεἰ μὴ) : ἴσθι
Musgr., ἔς τί Tyrwhitt, ἔς τι Bothius (quod mavult Kirchf., idem Weckl.²).
814. ἐξῳνωμένας P : ἐξων- Elms. τερπνῶς Brunck; λίχνως Metzger.
816. δ' P : γ' Ald.   καθημένας J S Reid, sed adversatur κἂν (817).
817. θέλῃς P : ἔλθῃς Pierson. 'fortasse κἂν θέλῃς λαθεῖν' Paley.
818. τάδε P : τόδε Hermannus solus.   819. ἄγω μὲν Portus (Tyrrell).
820. δέ σ' οὐ P ('σοι puto sequente οὐ posse crasin facere,' Herm.) :
δέ γ' οὐ coniecit Elms. (recepit Schoenius): γὰρ οὐ Paley (Dind.), 'aut
γὰρ οὐ φθονῶ aut δ' οὐδεὶς φθόνος' Kirchhoffius; δ' οὔ σοι Dobraeus, δέ
σοι Nauck (Tyrrell, Wecklein).

ΔΙ. στεῖλαί νυν ἀμφὶ χρωτὶ βυσσίνους πέπλους.
ΠΕ. τί δὴ τόδ'; εἰς γυναῖκας ἐξ ἀνδρὸς τελῶ;
ΔΙ. μή σε κτάνωσιν, ἢν ἀνὴρ ὀφθῇς ἐκεῖ.
ΠΕ. εὖ γ' εἶπας αὐτό καί τις εἰ πάλαι σοφός.
ΔΙ. Διόνυσος ἡμᾶς ἐξεμούσωσεν τάδε.   825
ΠΕ. πῶς οὖν γένοιτ' ἂν ἃ σύ με νουθετεῖς καλῶς;
ΔΙ. ἐγὼ στελῶ σε δωμάτων εἴσω μολών.
ΠΕ. τίνα στολήν; ἢ θῆλυν; ἀλλ' αἰδώς μ' ἔχει.
ΔΙ. οὐκέτι θεατὴς Μαινάδων πρόθυμος εἶ.
ΠΕ. στολὴν δὲ τίνα φῂς ἀμφὶ χρῶτ' ἐμὸν βαλεῖν; 830
ΔΙ. κόμην μὲν ἐπὶ σῷ κρατὶ ταναὸν ἐκτενῶ.
ΠΕ. τὸ δεύτερον δὲ σχῆμα τοῦ κόσμου τί μοι;
ΔΙ. πέπλοι ποδήρεις· ἐπὶ κάρᾳ δ' ἔσται μίτρα.
ΠΕ. ἢ καί τι πρὸς τοῖσδ' ἄλλο προσθήσεις ἐμοί;
ΔΙ. θύρσον γε χειρὶ καὶ νεβροῦ στικτὸν δέρας. 835
ΠΕ. οὐκ ἂν δυναίμην θῆλυν ἐνδῦναι στολήν.
ΔΙ. ἀλλ' αἷμα θήσεις συμβαλὼν Βάκχαις μάχην.
ΠΕ. ὀρθῶς· μολεῖν χρὴ πρῶτον εἰς κατασκοπήν.
ΔΙ. σοφώτερον γοῦν ἢ κακοῖς θηρᾶν κακά.

821. νιν P : νυν Canter.   824. εἶπας αὖ τόδ', ὥς τις εἶ conicit
Wecklein; 824 sq. interpolatos esse putat Collmann.
826. ἀμὲ νουθετεῖς coniecit Elms.   829 εἶ; (interrogative) Nauck-
vv. 828 et 837 interpolatos esse suspicatur Collmann, qui in locum
versus 837 versum 829 transponere vult.
v. 828 etiam Weckleinius seclusit, qui in curis criticis p. 15 versus
827—843 ἄνω κάτω τιθείς, hunc in ordinem redigendos esse censet, 827,
830—33, 836, 829, 834, 835, 842, 837—41, 843.
835. τε P: γε correxit Herm.   δέρος Wecklein collato *Med.* 5,
ubi C habet δέρος [neque aliter scriptum in papyro *Med.* 5—12 ab
H Weilio et F Blassio nuper edita], P (uti hic etiam) δέρας.
vv. 836—9 post v. 823 locat Metzger.
837. αἷμα θήσεις P: δεύσεις Wecklein; coniciet fortasse quispiam
αἷμα θύσεις collato v. 796 θύσω φόνον. εὖ μαθήσει? Nauck. *ann. crit.;*
'fortasse αἱματώσῃ' Kirchf. εὐμαθὴς εἶ συμβαλὼν Housman.

ΠΕ. καὶ πῶς δι' ἄστεως εἶμι Καδμείους λαθών; 840
ΔΙ. ὁδοὺς ἐρήμους ἵμεν· ἐγὼ δ' ἡγήσομαι.
ΠΕ. πᾶν κρεῖσσον ὥστε μὴ 'γγελᾶν Βάκχας ἐμοί.
ἐλθὼν γ' ἐς οἴκους ἂν δοκῇ βουλεύσομαι.
ΔΙ. ἔξεστι· πάντῃ τό γ' ἐμὸν εὐτρεπὲς πάρα.
ΠΕ. στείχοιμ' ἄν· ἢ γὰρ ὅπλ' ἔχων πορεύσομαι 845
ἢ τοῖσι σοῖσι πείσομαι βουλεύμασιν.
ΔΙ. γυναῖκες, ἀνὴρ εἰς βόλον καθίσταται· 848
ἥξει δὲ Βάκχας, οὗ θανὼν δώσει δίκην. 847
Διόνυσε, νῦν σὸν ἔργον, οὐ γὰρ εἶ πρόσω,
τισώμεθ' αὐτόν. πρῶτα δ' ἔκστησον φρενῶν, 850
ἐνεὶς ἐλαφρὰν λύσσαν· ὡς φρονῶν μὲν εὖ
οὐ μὴ θελήσῃ θῆλυν ἐνδῦναι στολήν,

842. γελᾶν P: 'γγελᾶν Reiskius et Piersonus.   κρεῖσσόν ἐστιν
ἢ ἐγγελᾶν? Nauck. ann. crit.   lacunam post hunc v. indicavit
Kirchhoffius; versum ipsum spurium iudicat Middendorfius.   Βάκχας
in ἀστοὺς vel (ut iam antea Jacobsius) Θήβας mutandum esse suspicatur
Wecklein (cf. 854).

843, 845—6 nuntio, 844 Pentheo tribuit P: correxit Heath.

843. ἐλθόντ'—βουλεύσομαι P (Wecklein): ἐλθόντ'—βουλεύσομεν ed.
Ald. (Elms., Herm., Schoenius, Paley); ἐλθών—βουλεύσομαι Kirchf.
(Dind., Tyrrell); ἐλθών γ' Nauck.   ἂν P: ἂν ed. Ald.

844. εὐπρεπὲς P: εὐτρεπὲς Canter.

845. ἢ prima manu P, ἢ secunda.   στείχωμεν Schaeferus.

846. ἢ τοῖς σοῖσι πείθομαι P: ἢ τοῖσι σοῖσι πείσομαι ed. Ald.

vv. 848—7 inverso ordine in P: transposuit Musgr.   848. ἀνὴρ P.
versum damnat Middendorf.   847. βάκχας P: βάκχαις
L Dindorfius (Dind.).   versum 'magistro Byzantino' tribuit Wilamowitz-
Moellendorffius, qui paullo severius adscribit, editores 'Byzantini sapientiam traiecto versu Baccho tradere quam ἦθος artemque tragicam
respicere malle' (Anal. Eur. p. 209).

851. ἐνθεὶς Burges.   852. θελήσει P: correxit ed. Ald.

post 852 ἄρσην πεφυκὼς καὶ γένους ἐξ ἄρσενος temere ex Suida addiderunt Schoenius et Tyrrellius.

ἔξω δ' ἐλαύνων τοῦ φρονεῖν ἐνδύσεται.
χρῄζω δέ νιν γέλωτα Θηβαίοις ὀφλεῖν
γυναικόμορφον ἀγόμενον δι' ἄστεως   855
ἐκ τῶν ἀπειλῶν τῶν πρίν, αἷσι δεινὸς ην.
ἀλλ' εἶμι κόσμον ὅνπερ εἰς "Αιδου λαβὼν
ἄπεισι μητρὸς ἐκ χεροῖν κατασφαγείς,
Πενθεῖ προσάψων· γνώσεται δὲ τὸν Διὸς
Διόνυσον, ὃς πέφυκεν ἐν τέλει θεὸς   860
δεινότατος, ἀνθρώποισι δ' ἠπιώτατος.

ΧΟ.   ἆρ' ἐν παννυχίοις χοροῖς   στροφή.
θήσω ποτὲ λευκὸν
πόδ' ἀναβακχεύουσα, δέραν
εἰς αἰθέρα δροσερὸν   865
ῥίπτουσ', ὡς νεβρὸς χλοεραῖς

853. ἔξω δ' ἀλύων Middendorf.
854. χρῄζω P: θήσω (e *Chr. Pat.* 2311, ὀφλεῖν τ' ἔθηκας τοῖς βροτοῖς
γέλωτά με) mavult Nauckius *ann. crit.*   ὀφλεῖν P.
855—6 transponit Wecklein, ut γέλωτα ὀφλεῖν artius cum verbis ἐκ
τῶν ἀπειλῶν cohaereat.   856. ἃς ἐδέννασεν ? Nauck. *ann. crit.*
860—1 vix sani videntur Kirchhoffio. ἐν τέλει P: ἀνοσίοις Dobraeus, ἐγγελῶσι Meinekius, ἐνστάταις Nauckius *ann. crit.;* ἐλλέροις
audacter in textum recepit Weckleinius, laudato Hesychio, Ἔλλερα· κακά.
ὡς...ἐντελὴς Hirzelius 'deleto versu proximo in quo ineptum est ἀνθρώποισι' (quod ad ὡς attinet, praeiverat Dobraeus*).   861. ἀνθρώποισι:
codicis lectionem e compendio ἄνοισι exortam esse arbitratus, εὐνοοῦσι
coniecit Badhamus†. εὐτρόποισι Musgr.; εὐσεβοῦσι Herwerden qui utrumque versum interpolatum esse existimat; αὐξάνουσι Mekler; ἐννόμοισι
Wecklein; ὁσίοις δ' ἠπιώτατος πέλει Dobraeus.   πέφυκεν] 'πέφηνεν
legit interpolator versus 182,' (Dind.).   v. 861 facile carere pos-
sumus. ἐν (*Hipp.* 1320, *Or.* 754) ἀτελεῖ θεὸς δεινότατος, ἐν ὁμοίοισι
(1302) δ' ἠπιώτατος, coll. *Hymn. Cer.* 481, ὃς δ' ἀτελής, ἱερῶν ὃς ἔτ'
ἄμμορος, οὔποθ' ὁμοίων αἶσαν ἔχει φθιμενός περ Munro.   Equidem
malim ἀτελέσιν ...ἐνσπόνδοισι (924).   ἐν ἀτελεῖ...ἐν θρήσκοισι Verrall.
862. παννυχίοισι P (tertia syllaba fuerat χει) : παννυχίοις ed. Ald.
864. δέρην P : δέραν Elms.
865. εἰς αἰθέρα P : αἰθέρ' εἰς Musgr. (Wecklein, αἰθέρα' ἐς Dind.).

* εἰ (vel ᾧ) θέλει W. T. Lendrum (1883).   † ἀνόσιιν (=ἀνθρώποισιν) revera habet P.

4—2

ἐμπαίζουσα λείμακος ἡδοναῖς,
ἡνίκ᾽ ἂν φοβερὰν φύγῃ
θήραν ἔξω φυλακᾶς
εὐπλέκτων ὑπὲρ ἀρκύων,   870
θωΰσσων δὲ κυναγέτας
συντείνῃ δρόμημα κυνῶν·
μόχθοις τ᾽ ὠκυδρόμοις ἀελλὰς θράσκει πεδίον
παραποτάμιον, ἡδομένα
βροτῶν ἐρημίαις   875
σκιαροκόμου τ᾽ ἐν ἔρνεσιν ὕλας.
τί τὸ σοφὸν ἢ τί τὸ κάλλιον
παρὰ θεῶν γέρας ἐν βροτοῖς
ἢ χεῖρ᾽ ὑπὲρ κορυφᾶς
τῶν ἐχθρῶν κρείσσω κατέχειν;   880
ὅ τι καλὸν φίλον ἀεί.

ὁρμᾶται μόλις, ἀλλ᾽ ὅμως   ἀντιστροφή.

867. ἡδοναῖς P: ἀδ- Elms.   fortasse ἐν νάπαις (collato 1084)
Wecklein.
869. φοβερὰν θήραμ᾽ P: φοβερὸν θήραμ᾽ ed. Ald. (Elms., Schoenius,
Kirchf., Paley, Tyrrell); φοβερὰν θήραν Nauck, Dind., Wecklein
(cf. 1171).
870. 'fortasse legendum εὐπλέκτων θ'' Elms.
872. δράμημα mavult Cobet. V. L. p. 604².
873. μοχθροῖς τ᾽ prima manu P: μόχθοις δ᾽ Fixius; coniunctionem
delet Wecklein.   ὠκυδρόμοις τ᾽ ἀέλλαις P: ὠκυδρόμοις ἀελλὰς Herm.
(Kirch.², Dind., Wecklein).
874. παρὰ ποτάμιον P: correxit Reiskius.   ἡδομένα P: ἀδ- Dind.
876. σκιαροκόμου θ᾽ ἔρνεσιν P: σκιαροκόμου τ᾽ ἐν ἔρνεσιν ed. Ald. et
Nauckius in textu; σκιαροκόμοιὸ τ᾽ ἔρνεσιν Nauckius in ann. crit. (Dind.,
Wecklein).
880. τῶν hic et in antistropha (900) delet Herm.   κρέσσω P.

πιστόν τι τὸ θεῖον
σθένος· ἀπευθύνει δὲ βροτῶν
τούς τ᾽ ἀγνωμοσύναν   885
τιμῶντας καὶ μὴ τὰ θεῶν
αὔξοντας σὺν μαινομένᾳ δοκᾷ.
κρυπτεύουσι δὲ ποικίλως
δαρὸν χρόνου πόδα καὶ
θηρῶσιν τὸν ἄσεπτον. οὐ   890
γὰρ κρεῖσσόν ποτε τῶν νόμων
γιγνώσκειν χρὴ καὶ μελετᾶν.
κούφα γὰρ δαπάνα νομί-
ζειν ἰσχὺν τόδ᾽ ἔχειν,
ὅ τι ποτ᾽ ἄρα τὸ δαιμόνιον,
τό τ᾽ ἐν χρόνῳ μακρῷ   895
νόμιμον ἀεὶ φύσει τε πεφυκός.
 τί τὸ σοφὸν ἢ τί τὸ κάλλιον
παρὰ θεῶν γέρας ἐν βροτοῖς
ἢ χεῖρ᾽ ὑπὲρ κορυφᾶς
τῶν ἐχθρῶν κρείσσω κατέχειν; 900
ὅ τι καλὸν φίλον ἀεί.

εὐδαίμων μὲν ὃς ἐκ θαλάσσας ἐπῳδός.
ἔφυγε χεῖμα, λιμένα δ᾽ ἔκιχεν·

883. τὸ θεῖον P: τό γε θεῖον ed. Ald.; τι τὸ θεῖον Nauck. *ann. crit.*
(Dind., Wecklein).
885. τοὺς τὰν ἀγνωμοσύναν Nauckius *ann. crit.*, servato tamen in
stropha εἰς αἰθέρα (865).
887. συμμαινομένα P: σὺν μαινομένᾳ Barnes. δοξα P: δοκᾷ, praeeunte
J F Daviesio quem secutus erat Tyrrellius, in textum recepit Wecklein[1], collato Aesch. *Ag.* 421, ubi δόξαι in δόκαι (*sic*) ab Hermanno mutatum (Hesych. δόκην (*sic*)· δόκησιν).
 891. γὰρ punctis notatum in P.   893. τ᾽ P: τόδ᾽ Heath.
 902. θαλάσσης P: -ας Brunck.   903. χεῖμα P: κῦμα ed. Ald.

εὐδαίμων δ' ὃς ὕπερθε μόχθων
ἐγένεθ'· ἕτερα δ' ἕτερος ἕτερον   905
ὄλβῳ καὶ δυνάμει παρῆλθεν.
μυρίαι δὲ μυρίοισιν
ἔτ' εἴσ' ἐλπίδες· αἱ μὲν
τελευτῶσιν ἐν ὄλβῳ
βροτοῖς, αἱ δ' ἀπέβησαν·
τὸ δὲ κατ' ἦμαρ ὅτῳ βίοτος   910
εὐδαίμων, μακαρίζω.

ΔΙΟΝΥΣΟΣ.

σὲ τὸν πρόθυμον ὄνθ' ἃ μὴ χρεὼν ὁρᾶν
σπεύδοντά τ' ἀσπούδαστα, Πενθέα λέγω,
ἔξιθι πάροιθε δωμάτων, ὄφθητί μοι,
σκευὴν γυναικὸς μαινάδος Βάκχης ἔχων   915
μητρός τε τῆς σῆς καὶ λόχου κατάσκοπος·
πρέπεις δὲ Κάδμου θυγατέρων μορφῇ μιᾷ.

ΠΕΝΘΕΥΣ.

καὶ μὴν ὁρᾶν μοι δύο μὲν ἡλίους δοκῶ,
δισσὰς δὲ Θήβας καὶ πόλισμ' ἑπτάστομον·

905. ἑτέρα P: ἕτερα Elms.
907. μυρίαι μυρίοισιν ἔτ' εἰσὶν P: μυρίαι δὲ μυρίοισιν | ἔτ' εἴσ' Herm.
(Nauck, Kirchf.², Dind., Tyrrell, Wecklein); μ. δ' ἔτι μυρίοισίν εἰσιν
Schoenius; idem coniecit Paleius nisi quod μυρίοις dedit.
910. ἦμαρ P: ἆμαρ Elms., Dind., Tyrrell.
v. 913 uncinis inclusit Tyrrellius ne Euripides δὶς ταὐτὸν εἰπεῖν videre-
tur; quo fit ut Dionysi orationi totidem versiculis Pentheus respondeat.
σπένδοντα P: correxit Musurus (ed. Aldinae editor).
914. κώφθητί μοι, litterarum concursum parum suavem, praetulit
Herwerden.
916. 'scribendum μητρός γε' Kirchf.   καὶ P: ἐκ Herm., καὶ
χοροῦ Hartung.   versum spurium esse suspicatur Middendorf.
917. μορφῇ P: μορφὴν Musgr. (Dobraeus, Nauck, Kirch.², Paley,
Wecklein).

καὶ ταῦρος ἡμῖν πρόσθεν ἡγεῖσθαι δοκεῖς   920
καὶ σῷ κέρατα κρατὶ προσπεφυκέναι.
ἀλλ᾽ ἦ ποτ᾽ ἦσθα θήρ; τεταύρωσαι γὰρ οὖν.

ΔΙ.   ὁ θεὸς ὁμαρτεῖ, πρόσθεν ὢν οὐκ εὐμενής,
ἔνσπονδος ἡμῖν· νῦν δ᾽ ὁρᾷς ἃ χρή σ᾽ ὁρᾶν.

ΠΕ.   τί φαίνομαι δῆτ᾽; οὐχὶ τὴν Ἰνοῦς στάσιν   925
ἢ τὴν Ἀγαύης ἑστάναι μητρός γ᾽ ἐμῆς;

ΔΙ.   αὐτὰς ἐκείνας εἰσορᾶν δοκῶ σ᾽ ὁρῶν.

921. κέρατα P et schol. Lycophron. 209: κέρᾳ τε ed. Ald. unde
κέρατε Brodaeus (Tyrrell).   922. ἦσθ᾽ ἀνὴρ Middendorf.

923—4 primus Dionyso restituit Tyrwhittus.   925. 'nescio an
legendum τίς᾽ Elms.   926. γ᾽ a correctore additum in P.

927. 'post haec verba versus unus Dionysi, duo Penthei excidisse
videntur Kirchhoffio propter violatam stichomythiam.   eadem de caussa
unius versus defectum post 934 idem notavit' (Dindorf).   Weckleinius,
Middendorfii potius sententiam amplexus versum 929, utpote nequaquam necessarium, damnantis, in versu 931 ἐξ ἕδρας in ἐκ μίτρας mutat,
qua coniectura versus ille suspectus mihi quidem defendi videtur; scilicet
versu ipso servato, nihil inde mutuari necesse est.

ἀλλ' ἐξ ἕδρας σοι πλόκαμος ἐξέστηχ' ὅδε,
οὐχ ὡς ἐγώ νιν ὑπὸ μίτρᾳ καθήρμοσα.

ΠΕ. ἔνδον προσείων αὐτὸν ἀνασείων τ' ἐγὼ   930
καὶ βακχιάζων ἐξ ἕδρας μεθώρμισα.

ΔΙ. ἀλλ' αὐτὸν ἡμεῖς, οἷς σε θεραπεύειν μέλει,
πάλιν καταστελοῦμεν· ἀλλ' ὄρθου κάρα.

ΠΕ. ἰδού, σὺ κόσμει· σοὶ γὰρ ἀνακείμεσθα δή.

ΔΙ. ζῶναί τέ σοι χαλῶσι κοὐχ ἑξῆς πέπλων   935
στολίδες ὑπὸ σφυροῖσι τείνουσιν σέθεν.

ΠΕ. κἀμοὶ δοκοῦσι παρά γε δεξιὸν πόδα·
τἀνθένδε δ' ὀρθῶς παρὰ τένοντ' ἔχει πέπλος.

ΔΙ. ἦ πού με τῶν σῶν πρῶτον ἡγήσει ' φίλων,
ὅταν παρὰ λόγον σώφρονας Βάκχας ἴδῃς ;   940

ΠΕ. πότερα δὲ θύρσον δεξιᾷ λαβὼν χερὶ
ἢ τῇδε, Βάκχῃ μᾶλλον εἰκασθήσομαι ;

ΔΙ. ἐν δεξιᾷ χρὴ χἅμα δεξιῷ ποδὶ
αἴρειν νιν· αἰνῶ δ' ὅτι μεθέστηκας φρενῶν.

ΠΕ. ἆρ' ἂν δυναίμην τὰς Κιθαιρῶνος πτυχὰς   945
αὐταῖσι Βάκχαις τοῖς ἐμοῖς ὤμοις φέρειν ;

ΔΙ. δύναι' ἄν, εἰ βούλοιο· τὰς δὲ πρὶν φρένας
οὐκ εἶχες ὑγιεῖς, νῦν δ' ἔχεις οἵας σε δεῖ.

ΠΕ. μοχλοὺς φέρωμεν ἢ χεροῖν ἀνασπάσω
κορυφαῖς ὑποβαλὼν ὦμον ἢ βραχίονα ;   950

930—1 in margine additos habet P. post 934 unum versum desi-
derat Kirchf.

940. παρὰ λόγον P : παράλογον Porson. sed cf. Shilletonem in
Thuc. I 65.

944. αἴρεινιν P : correxit Ald.   945. πτυχὰς P : πτύχας male
ed. Ald.

946. αὐταῖσι βακχαῖς P : 'καὶ ἐν Βάκχαις, αὐτῆσιν ἐλάταις' schol.
Eur. Phoen. 3, unde αὐταῖσιν ἐλαταῖς in textum receperunt Dind.,
Kirchf.², Wecklein. scholiastam hunc versum respexisse indicaverat
Valckenaer.

ΔΙ. μὴ σύ γε τὰ Νυμφῶν διολέσῃς ἱδρύματα
καὶ Πανὸς ἕδρας, ἔνθ' ἔχει συρίγματα.

ΠΕ. καλῶς ἔλεξας· οὐ σθένει νικητέον
γυναῖκας, ἐλάταισιν δ' ἐμὸν κρύψω δέμας.

ΔΙ. κρύψει σὺ κρύψιν ἥν σε κρυφθῆναι χρεὼν   955
ἐλθόντα δόλιον Μαινάδων κατάσκοπον.

ΠΕ. καὶ μὴν δοκῶ σφᾶς, ἐν λόχμαις ὄρνιθας ὥς,
λέκτρων ἔχεσθαι φιλτάτοις ἐν ἕρκεσιν.

ΔΙ. οὐκοῦν ἐπ' αὐτὸ τοῦτ' ἀποστέλλει φύλαξ·
λήψει δ' ἴσως σφᾶς, ἢν σὺ μὴ ληφθῇς πάρος.   960

ΠΕ. κόμιζε διὰ μέσης με Θηβαίας χθονός·
μόνος γάρ εἰμ' αὐτῶν ἀνὴρ τολμῶν τόδε.

ΔΙ. μόνος σὺ πόλεως τῆσδ' ὑπερκάμνεις, μόνος.
τοιγάρ σ' ἀγῶνες ἀναμένουσιν οὓς ἐχρῆν.
ἕπου δέ· πομπὸς δ' εἰμ' ἐγὼ σωτήριος,   965
κεῖθεν δ' ἀπάξει σ' ἄλλος   ΠΕ. ἡ τεκοῦσά γε.

ΔΙ. ἐπίσημον ὄντα πᾶσιν.   ΠΕ. ἐπὶ τόδ' ἔρχομαι.

ΔΙ. φερόμενος ἥξεις   ΠΕ. ἁβρότητ' ἐμὴν λέγεις.

ΔΙ. ἐν χερσὶ μητρός.   ΠΕ. καὶ τρυφᾶν μ' ἀναγκά-
σεις.

ΔΙ. τρυφάς γε τοιάσδ'.   ΠΕ. ἀξίων μὲν ἅπτομαι.   970

ΔΙ. δεινὸς σὺ δεινὸς κἀπὶ δείν' ἔρχει πάθη,

951. τᾶν (non τῶν) P: τὰ H Stephanus.
952. καπνὸς P; Πανὸς Brodaeus.
955. κρυφῆναι P: κρυφθῆναι ed. Ald.
961. χθονὸς P: πόλεως e Nauckii coniectura Wecklein.
962. εἰμ' (εἰμ' Ald.) αὐτῶν P: αὐτῶν εἰμ' Elms. (Dind., Wecklein).
στῶν coniecit Paley; obiter commemorat Elms., praeiverat Burges.
964. ἐχρῆν P: χρεὼν Hartung, σε χρή Fixius et Wecklein; οὗ
ϲρεὼν mavult Kirchhoffius, οὕς γε χρῆς Bergmann.
965. εἰμ' P: εἰμ' Ald. σωτηρίας J S Reid collato v. 1047.
968. 'nescio an legendum ἐμοὶ λέγεις' Elms.
970. 'vereor ne scripserit ἀξίων γὰρ ἅπτομαι' Herm.

ὥστ' οὐρανῷ στηρίζον εὑρήσεις κλέος.
ἔκτειν', Ἀγαύη, χεῖρας αἵ θ' ὁμόσποροι
Κάδμου θυγατέρες· τὸν νεανίαν ἄγω
τόνδ' εἰς ἀγῶνα μέγαν, ὁ νικήσων δ' ἐγὼ
καὶ Βρόμιος ἔσται. τἄλλα δ' αὐτὸ σημανεῖ.

ΧΟ. ἴτε θοαὶ Λύσσης κύνες ἴτ' εἰς ὄρος, **στροφή.**
θίασον ἔνθ' ἔχουσι Κάδμου κόραι,
ἀνοιστρήσατέ νιν
ἐπὶ τὸν ἐν γυναικομίμῳ στολᾷ
Μαινάδων ἐπὶ κατάσκοπον λυσσώδη.

976. ἔσται P: ἐστι Wecklein. 977. λύσσης P: Λύσσας Elms., Dind., Tyrrell, Wecklein.

981. μαινάδων κατάσκοπον P: M τὸν κ. Meinek., Weckl. – ⏑ M σκοπὸν Matthiae. ‘κατάσκοπον fortasse pro σκοπὸν ab librario positum est ex v. 956, tres autem syllabae vel ante vel post μαινάδων exciderunt’ (Dindorf). ἐπὶ τὸν M σκοπὸν λυσσώδη Hartung, λ. κατάσκοπον M Wilamowitz-Moellendorff (*Hermes* XIV 179). M ἄσκοπον σκοπὸν Fixius; M ἐπὶ κατάσκοπον Thompson.

μάτηρ πρῶτά νιν λευρᾶς ἀπὸ πέτρας ἢ
σκόλοπος ὄψεται
δοκεύοντα, Μαινάσιν δ' ἀπύσει·
τίς ὅδε Καδμείων   985
μαστὴρ ὀριδρόμων
ἐς ὄρος ἐς ὄρος ἔμολ' ἔμολεν, ὦ Βάκχαι;
τίς ἄρα νιν ἔτεκεν;
οὐ γὰρ ἐξ αἵματος γυναικῶν ἔφυ·
λεαίνας δέ τινος ὅδ' ἢ Γοργόνων   990
Λιβυσσᾶν γένος.
ἴτω δίκα φανερός, ἴτω ξιφηφόρος
φονεύουσα λαιμῶν διαμπὰξ
τὸν ἄθεον ἄνομον ἄδικον Ἐχίονος   995
τόκον γηγενῆ·

ὃς ἀδίκῳ γνώμᾳ παρανόμῳ τ' ὀργᾷ   ἀντιστροφή.

982. ᾗ σκόπελος Wecklein, cum alioquin σκόλοπος per abusionem
idem ac δένδρου significaret; ἢ σκοπέλου iam antea coniecerat Hartung.
εὔσκοπος Nauck. ann. crit.—πρῶτα P: an πρώτα ? Thompson.

986. ὀριδρόμων P: οὐριοδρόμων ed. Ald.; οὔριον δρόμον Matthiae
(Herm., Dind., Paley); ὀργίων δρόμῳ Schoenius, ὀρειδρόμων μαστὴρ Καδμείων Nauck. ann. crit.—'an ὀριδρόμων?' (Kirchhoffius et Tyrrellius), quod
verbum, in lexicis nonnullis omissum, a Nonno tamen bis saltem (5, 229
et 25, 194) usurpatum esse iam pridem monui.   ὀρθρεύων Wecklein collatis Supp. 978, Tro. 182.   εἰς...εἰς P: ἐς...ἐς ed. Ald.
alterum ἐς ὄρος delere vult Nauckius.

987. ἔμολεν ἔμολεν P: semel tantum ed. Ald. (Dind.); ἔμολ' ἔμολεν
Elms. (Wecklein).   989. ὅδ' ἔφυ P: ἔφυ ed. Ald.

990. δέ τινος ἢ P: δέ γέ τινος ἢ ed. Ald. (Elms., Paley); δὲ γέγον'
ὅδ' Nauckius; δέ τινος ὅδ' ἢ Herm. (Schoenius, Dind., Tyrrell, Kirchf.²,
Wecklein, sed idem ὅδ' in ὅ γ' mutandum esse conicit).

993, 1014. δαίμων P: λαιμῶν Tyrwhitt.

996. γόνον P*: τόκον e v. 1016 Elms.

in v. 997 ὀργᾷ et v. 998 verba extrema Nauckio suspecta.

* γόνον retinet Tyrrell².

περὶ σά, Βάκχι᾽, ὄργια ματρός τε σᾶς
μανείσᾳ πραπίδι
παρακόπῳ τε λήματι στέλλεται,   1000
σὰν ἀνίκατον ὡς κρατήσων βίαν.
γνώμαν σώφρον᾽, ἃ θνατοῖς ἀπροφασίστοις
εἰς τὰ θεῶν ἔφυ,
βροτείαν τ᾽ ἔχειν ἄλυπος βίος.
τὸ σοφὸν οὐ φθονῶ·   1005
χαίρω θηρεύου-
σα τάδ᾽ ἕτερα μεγάλα φανέρ᾽ ἄγοντ᾽ ἀεί

998. περὶ (+ τὰ Ald.) βάκχι᾽ ὄργια ματρός. τε σᾶς P: περὶ (ἐπὶ W.-
Moellendorff) σά, Βάκχι᾽, ὄργια (ἔργα Elms., ἱρὰ Mekler,) ματρός τε σᾶς
Scaliger (Tyrrell); π. τὰ β. ὀργιά τε θεᾶς ματρὸς Wecklein*; ματρός τε γᾶς
Burges; ὄργιά τε Ματέρος Hartung. 'versus corruptissimus' Kirchhoff.
π. τὰ β. ἱερὰ ματρός τε θεᾶς Weckl. (Phil. Anz. 1879, p. 162).
999. μανεῖσα P: correxit Brodaeus.
1001. τὰν P: τὸν ed. Ald. τἀνίκητον Wilamowitz-M. θεὸν post
Kayserum Schoenius. βία P: βίαν coniecerat quondam Dind., retinuit
tamen βίᾳ. σὰν...βίαν Thompson. τὰν...νίκαν Wecklein.
'Ρείαν ? Nauck. ann. crit.
1002. γνώμαν σώφρονα θάνατος ἀπροφάσιστος εἰς τὰ θεῶν (εἰ τά τε
θεῶν Ald.) ἔφυ P: σώφρον᾽ ἀθάνατον Matthiae et Tyrrell; σώφρονα
θνατοῖς ἀπροφρασίστως Heath; ἃ θνατοῖς ἀπροφάσιστος Herm. (Schoenius, Nauck, Paley). θνατοῖς ἀπροφασίστοις dubitanter conieci, quod
Weckleinio quoque placere nuper didici, sed idem maluit γνώμαν σώφρονα retinere. ἀπροφασίστως Tyrrell. 'fortasse legendum γνώμα
σώφρων ἃ θνατοῖς ἀπροφάσισ-|τος εἰς τὰ θεῶν ἔφυ | βροτείῳ γ᾽ ἔχειν
ἄλυπος βίῳ' Thompson.
1004. βροτείῳ...βίος P: βροτείῳ...βίῳ ed. Ald. (Herm.), βροτείαν...
βίος Elms. (Nauck, Dindf., Paley, Weckl.[1]). βρότειόν Sch. (Weckl.[2],
Tyrrell[2]).
1005. τὸ σοφὸν P: τὸν σοφὸν ed. Ald. φθόνω P: φθόνῳ ed.
Ald. (τὸ σοφὸν οὐ φθόνῳ Elms., Herm., Dind., Paley, Tyrrell).
1007. τὰ δ᾽ P†: τάδ᾽ Heath. θηρεύουσ᾽ ἔτερα (omisso τὰ δ᾽)
Nauck. φανερὰ τῶν ἀεὶ (αἰεὶ Ald.) P: φανερά τ᾽ ὄντ᾽ Musgr.
(Schoenius, Nauck), 'forsan τὸν ἀεὶ' Dobraeus; φανέρ᾽ ἄγοντ᾽ Fix, Weckl.,
Tyrrell[2] (fragm. 651), φανέρ᾽ ἰόντ᾽ Thompson. ἀεὶ ἐπὶ] 'hiatus
vitiosus, nec brevis in fine versus syllaba recte habet' (Dind.).

* Aldinam sequitur Wecklein[2].   † τάδ᾽ in codice revera scriptum.

ἐπὶ τὰ καλὰ βίον,
ἦμαρ εἰς νύκτα τ' εὐαγοῦντ' εὐσεβεῖν,
τὰ δ' ἔξω νόμιμα δίκας ἐκβαλόν-   1010
τα τιμᾶν θεούς.
ἴτω δίκα φανερός, ἴτω ξιφηφόρος
φονεύουσα λαιμῶν διαμπὰξ
τὸν ἄθεον ἄνομον ἄδικον Ἐχίονος   1015
τόκον γηγενῆ.

φάνηθι ταῦρος ἢ πολύκρανος ἰδεῖν   ἐπῳδός.
δράκων ἢ πυριφλέγων
ὁρᾶσθαι λέων.
ἴθ', ὦ Βάκχε, θηραγρευτᾷ Βακχᾶν,   1020

1008. ἐπὶ τὰ κατὰ βίον post Reiskium Herm.   ἐπί: an ποτί?
1009. ἦμαρ P: ἆμαρ post Elmsleium Dind.   εὖ ἄγουντ' P: εὖ
ἄγοντ' ed. Ald. (Schoenius), εὐαγοῦντ' Herm.   1010. τά τ' ἔξω Elms.
1019. ἢ P: 'fortasse ἢ καὶ' Dind., ἤτοι Hartung, ἤπου Tyrrell.

1020. θηραγρότα (ο a correctore) P: θηραγρέτα ed. Ald., θηραγρέτᾳ
Scaliger, et Musgr. (Elms., Herm.).   τῷ θηραγρέτᾳ Brunck; θὴρ
θηραγρέτᾳ Tyrrell.   τὸν θηραγρέταν Matthiae (Paley).   θηρα-
γρεύτα Nauckius (Kirchf.²), θηραγρευτᾷ receperunt Dind. et Wecklein.
θῆρ', ἀγροδότα...πεσόντα Schoenius.   θῆρ' ἀγρεύταν mavult Kirchf.

1018. [δράκων] Tyrrell.

γελῶντι προσώπῳ περίβαλε
βρόχον ἐπὶ θανάσιμον
ἀγέλαν πεσόντι τὰν Μαινάδων.

ΑΓΓΕΛΟΣ.

ὦ δῶμ' ὃ πρίν ποτ' ηὐτύχεις ἀν' Ἑλλάδα,
Σιδωνίου γέροντος, ὃς τὸ γηγενὲς   1025
δράκοντος ἔσπειρ' ὄφεος ἐν γαίᾳ θέρος,
ὥς σε στενάζω, δοῦλος ὢν μέν, ἀλλ' ὅμως.
[χρηστοῖσι δούλοις συμφορὰ τὰ δεσποτῶν]
ΧΟ. τί δ' ἔστιν; ἐκ Βακχῶν τι μηνύεις νέον;
ΑΓΓ. Πενθεὺς ὄλωλε, παῖς Ἐχίονος πατρός.   1030
ΧΟ. ὦναξ Βρόμιε· θεὸς φαίνει μέγας.
ΑΓΓ. πῶς φής; τί τοῦτ' ἔλεξας; ἦ 'πὶ τοῖς ἐμοῖς

1021—3. τὸν θηραγρέταν | γελῶντι προσώπῳ περίβαλε βρόχον θα-
νάσιμον | ἐπ' ἀγέλαν πεσόντα τὰν Μαινάδων, Hartung. verba γελῶντι
προσώπῳ quae metro incommoda esse vidit Dindorfius, glossema esse
putat Weckleinius[1] quod vocabulum aliquod rarius e textu extruserit,
verbi causa χαροπῶς vel χαροπὸς; locum igitur hunc fere in modum
restituere conatur, θανάσιμον βρόχον περίβαλε χαροπῶς | ἐπ' ἀγέλαν πε-
σόντι τὰν Μαινάδων. 1022. ἐπὶ θανάσιμον P: θ. ἐπὶ Fixius (Dindf.).
1023 'fortasse ἐς ἀγέλαν' Kirchf.   πεσόντα P: πεσόντι Scaliger
(Elms., Nauck, Dind., Wecklein).
1024. ηὐτύχεις P: ηὐτύχεις Heath (Elms., Dind., Paley, Tyrrell,
Wecklein). 1026. ὀδόντος ἔσπειρ' Elms., ἔσπειρ' ὀδόντων Hartung.
ὄφεος P: Ἄρεος Elms. (Schoenius). "ὄφεον ex Barnesii coniectura
'etsi non habeo aliud exemplum huius adiectivi' (Hermann); sed ὄφεος
non solum libri [immo vero, codex unicus], verum etiam Gregor. Cor.
p. 402, Theodosius ap. Bekk. Anecdota 981, 13, qui diserte propter
formam ὄφεος h. l. laudant" (Shilleto adv.)   ἐν γύαις Wecklein.
1028. versum hunc, utpote a Med. 54 sumptum, eiciebat Dobraeus
(Kirchf.).   sive τῆς sive τις P: τὰ ed. Ald. ex Med. l. c.
1031. θεὸς φαίνη P: καὶ γὰρ θεὸς φαίνει ed. Ald.   ὦναξ Βρόμιε
θεὸς, θεὸς φ. μ. Herm. (Tyrrell).   θεὸς σὺ φ. μ. Schoenius, Kirchf.
θεὸς φαίνει νῦν μέγας Paley.   ἄναξ ὦ βρόμιε, θεὸς φ. μ. Hartung.

χαίρεις κακῶς πράσσουσι δεσπόταις, γύναι;
ΧΟ.   εὐάζω ξένα μέλεσι βαρβάροις·
οὐκέτι γὰρ δεσμῶν ὑπὸ φόβῳ πτήσσω.   1035
ΑΓΓ. Θήβας δ᾽ ἀνάνδρους ὧδ᾽ ἄγεις * * * *;
ΧΟ.   ὁ Διόνυσος ὁ Διόνυσος, οὐ Θῆβαι
κράτος ἔχουσ᾽ ἐμόν.
ΑΓΓ. συγγνωστὰ μέν σοι, πλὴν ἐπ᾽ ἐξειργασμένοις
κακοῖσι χαίρειν, ὦ γυναῖκες, οὐ καλόν.   1040
ΧΟ.   ἔνεπέ μοι, φράσον, τίνι μόρῳ θνήσκει
ἄδικος ἄδικά τ᾽ ἐκπορίζων ἀνήρ;
ΑΓΓ. ἐπεὶ θεράπνας τῆσδε Θηβαίας χθονὸς
λιπόντες ἐξέβημεν Ἀσωποῦ ῥοάς,
λέπας Κιθαιρώνειον εἰσεβάλλομεν   1045
Πενθεύς τε κἀγώ, δεσπότῃ γὰρ εἱπόμην,
ξένος θ᾽ ὃς ἡμῖν πομπὸς ἦν θεωρίας.
πρῶτον μὲν οὖν ποιηρὸν ἵζομεν νάπος,
τά τ᾽ ἐκ ποδῶν σιγηλὰ καὶ γλώσσης ἄπο
σώζοντες, ὡς ὁρῶμεν οὐχ ὁρώμενοι.   1050
ἦν δ᾽ ἄγκος ἀμφίκρημνον, ὕδασι διάβροχον,
πεύκαισι συσκιάζον, ἔνθα Μαινάδες
καθῆντ᾽ ἔχουσαι χεῖρας ἐν τερπνοῖς πόνοις.
αἱ μὲν γὰρ αὐτῶν θύρσον ἐκλελοιπότα

1032. ἦ P: ἦ Brunck.   1037. Διόνυσος οὐ P: Διὸς παῖς, οὐ Weckl.
1037—8. 'versus ex tribus, ut videtur, dochmiis compositus, sic vel
simili aliquo modo restituendus, ὁ Διόνυσος ὁ Διός, οὐκέτι Θῆβαι, κράτος
ἔχουσ᾽ ἐμόν᾽ (Dindorf).   1039 ἐξειργ. (defunctis) ἐχθροῖσι Hartmann.
1041. ἔννεπε P (Wecklein): ἔνεπε Brunck.   τίνει P: τίνι ed. Ald.
et Chr. Pat. 653, ἄγ᾽, εἰπέ μοι, φράσον, τίνι θνήσκει μόρῳ;
1043. Θεράπνας editores priores (Musgr., Elms., Herm.); θεράπνας
rectius recentiores.   1044. ῥοᾶς P: ῥοὰς ed. Ald.
1048. πικρὸν P: ποιηρὸν ed. Ald.; Chr. Pat. 676, πρῶτον μὲν εἰς
χλοηρὸν ἵζον που νάπος.   1049. ἐκποδὼν P: ἐκ ποδῶν Chr. Pat. 677.
1050. ὁρῶμεν P: ὁρῶμεν Musgr.   1053. κάθηντ᾽ P: καθῆντ᾽ Elms.
1054. ἐκλελοιπότος κισσοῦ Herwerden.

1051. ὑψίκρημνον Schol. B Hephaest. p. 183.

κισσῷ κομήτην αὖθις ἐξανέστεφον,   1055
αἱ δ' ἐκλιποῦσαι ποικίλ' ὡς πῶλοι ζυγὰ
βακχεῖον ἀντέκλαζον ἀλλήλαις μέλος.

Πενθεὺς δ' ὁ τλήμων θῆλυν οὐχ ὁρῶν ὄχλον
ἔλεξε τοιάδ'· ὦ ξέν', οὗ μὲν ἕσταμεν,
οὐκ ἐξικνοῦμαι Μαινάδων ὅσσοις νόθων·   1060
ὄχθον δ' ἐπεμβὰς ἢ ἐλάτην ὑψαύχενα
ἴδοιμ' ἂν ὀρθῶς Μαινάδων αἰσχρουργίαν.

τοὐντεῦθεν ἤδη τοῦ ξένου τι θαῦμ' ὁρῶ·
λαβὼν γὰρ ἐλάτης οὐράνιον ἄκρον κλάδον
κατῆγεν, ἦγεν, ἦγεν εἰς μέλαν πέδον·   1065
κυκλοῦτο δ' ὥστε τόξον ἢ κυρτὸς τροχὸς
τόρνῳ γραφόμενος περιφορὰν ἑλικοδρόμον·

1055. αὖτις P : αὖθις ed. Ald. 1056. ποικίλ' suspectum Nauckio.   inter ἐκλιποῦσαι et ποικίλ' versum unum excidisse suspicatur Wecklein (1879).   ἐμπλέκουσαι ποικίλ' ὡς πῶλοι ζυγὰ Madvig.   αἱ δ', ἐκλιπόντες Weckl. (Phil. Anz. 1881).   inter αἱ δ' et ἐκλιποῦσαι lacunam suspicatur Herwerden.   1060. ὄσοινόθων P : ὄσσοιν νόθων Tyrrell ed. 1. in 'veteribus codicibus' μόθων scriptum fuisse falso affirmavit H Stephanus, cuius mendacio decepti alii alia coniecerunt, ὅποι μόθων Musgr. (Paley), ὅσσοις μόθον Heath (Schoenius), ἐσμὸν μαθεῖν Reiskius; ὅσον ποθῶ Elms., ὅσσοις ὅσον Herm., ὅσσοις ὄχλον Middendorf.   Weckleinius, cui quondam νόσον μαθεῖν arriserat, nunc in scriptura codicis ὅσοι νόθων verbum οἰστρημένων (sc. ᾠστρημένων) latere suspicatur.   ποθεινὸς ὢν Metzger.   An πρόσωθεν ὤν, vel πρόσω σκοπῶν, vel ὅσσοις ἀθρῶν?   ὅσσοις νόθων Tyrrell ed. 2.

1061. ὄχθων δ' ἐπ' ἐμβὰς P : ὄχθον δ' ἐπεμβὰς ed. Ald.   εἰς ἐλάτην P : ἢ 'λάτην Tyrwhittus (Elms., Dind., Paley, Tyrrell); ἢ ἐλάτην Schoenius (Kirchf., Nauck, Wecklein); ἐς ἐλάτην Herm.

1063. τοὐνθένδε δ' ἤδη scribendum videtur Kirchhoffio.   ξένου θαῦμ' ὁρῶ P, τι a correctore inserto : θαυμάσθ' ὁρῶ Nauckius (Kirchf., Tyrrell).   θέαμ' ὁρῶ Wecklein.   1065. κατῆγεν ἠρέμ' ἠρέμ' Naber.

1066. κυκλοῦται P : κυκλοῦτο ed. Ald.   'fortasse κύκλῳ δ' ἄρ',' Kirchf.

1067. περιφοραν ἔλκει (ἔλκη manu sec.) δρόμον P : περὶ φορὰν ἔλκη δρόμον ed. Ald. : ἑλικοδρόμον Reiskius (Dind., Wecklein); ἑλκεδρόμον Scaliger (Tyrrell).   versum delet Schumacher; idem in v. 1061 ὄχθου δ' ἐπ' ἐμβὰς mavult.

ὡς κλῶν' ὄρειον ὁ ξένος χεροῖν ἄγων
ἔκαμπτεν εἰς γῆν, ἔργματ' οὐχὶ θνητὰ δρῶν.
Πενθέα δ' ἱδρύσας ἐλατίνων ὄζων ἔπι,   1070
ὀρθὸν μεθίει διὰ χερῶν βλάστημ' ἄνω
ἀτρέμα, φυλάσσων μὴ ἀναχαιτίσειέ νιν.
ὀρθὴ δ' ἐς ὀρθὸν αἰθέρ' ἐστηρίζετο
ἔχουσα νώτοις δεσπότην ἐφήμενον.
ὤφθη δὲ μᾶλλον ἢ κατεῖδε Μαινάδας·   1075
ὅσον γὰρ οὔπω δῆλος ἦν θάσσων ἄνω,
καὶ τὸν ξένον μὲν οὐκέτ' εἰσορᾶν παρῆν,
ἐκ δ' αἰθέρος φωνή τις, ὡς μὲν εἰκάσαι
Διόνυσος, ἀνεβόησεν· ὦ νεάνιδες,
ἄγω τὸν ὑμᾶς κἀμὲ τἀμά τ' ὄργια   1080
γέλων τιθέμενον· ἀλλὰ τιμωρεῖσθέ νιν.
καὶ ταῦθ' ἅμ' ἠγόρευε καὶ πρὸς οὐρανὸν
καὶ γαῖαν ἐστήριζε φῶς σεμνοῦ πυρός.
σίγησε δ' αἰθήρ, σῖγα δ' ὕλιμος νάπη
φύλλ' εἶχε, θηρῶν δ' οὐκ ἂν ἤκουσας βοήν.   1085
αἱ δ' ὠσὶν ἠχὴν οὐ σαφῶς δεδεγμέναι
ἔστησαν ὀρθαὶ καὶ διήνεγκαν κόρας.
ὁ δ' αὖθις ἐπεκέλευσεν· ὡς δ' ἐγνώρισαν
σαφῆ κελευσμὸν Βακχίου Κάδμου κόραι,
ᾖξαν πελείας ὠκύτητ' οὐχ ἥσσονες   1090

1068, 1073, interpolatos esse censet Herwerden; satis defendit *Chr.*
Pat. 662—3, ὀρθὸς δ' ἐς ὀρθὸν αἰθέρ' ἐστηρίζετο. ἐς κλῶνα δ'.
   1068. ὡς P (Tyrrell): ὡς post Barnesium fere omnes. 1070. ὄχων
ἔπι Hartmann.
   1072. μὴ ἀναχαιτίσειε P: μάναχαιτίσειε Dind.
   1083. ἐστήριζε P: ἐστήριξε ed. Ald. et *Chr. Pat.* 2259, καὶ γαῖαν
ἐστήριξε φ. σ. π.   γαίηθεν ἐστήριξε scribendum videbatur Kirchhoffio.
   1084. εὔλειμος P: ὕλιμος *Chr. Pat.* 2260 (Dind., Tyrrell², Weckl.²).
   1087. ὀρθαὶ P: ὀρθὰ Wecklein (sc. τὰ ὦτα, coll. Soph. *El.* 27).
   1090. ἥσσονες P: ἥσσονα Heath (Elms., Kirchf.²).

ποδῶν ἔχουσαι συντόνοις δρομήμασι,
μήτηρ Ἀγαύη σύγγονοί θ' ὁμόσποροι
πᾶσαί τε Βάκχαι· διὰ δὲ χειμάρρου νάπης
ἀγμῶν τ' ἐπήδων θεοῦ πνοαῖσιν ἐμμανεῖς.

ὡς δ' εἶδον ἐλάτῃ δεσπότην ἐφήμενον, 1095
πρῶτον μὲν αὐτοῦ χερμάδας κραταιβόλους
ἔρριπτον, ἀντίπυργον ἐπιβᾶσαι πέτραν,
ὄζοισί τ' ἐλατίνοισιν ἠκοντίζετο·
ἄλλαι δὲ θύρσους ἵεσαν δι' αἰθέρος
Πενθέως, στόχον δύστηνον· ἀλλ' οὐκ ἤνυτον. 1100
κρεῖσσον γὰρ ὕψος τῆς προθυμίας ἔχων
καθῆστο τλήμων, ἀπορίᾳ λελημμένος.
τέλος δὲ δρυΐνους συγκεραυνοῦσαι κλάδους,
ῥίζας ἀνεσπάρασσον ἀσιδήροις μοχλοῖς.
ἐπεὶ δὲ μόχθων τέρματ' οὐκ ἐξήνυτον, 1105
ἔλεξ' Ἀγαύη· φέρε, περιστᾶσαι κύκλῳ
πτόρθου λάβεσθε, Μαινάδες, τὸν ἀμβάτην
θῆρ' ὡς ἕλωμεν, μηδ' ἀπαγγείλῃ θεοῦ
χοροὺς κρυφαίους. αἱ δὲ μυρίαν χέρα

1091. ἔχουσαι P : τρέχουσαι (Schoenius) vel δραμοῦσαι Hartung collato Chr. Pat. 2015 (in commentario exscripto). versum interpolatum esse suspicatur Wecklein quod Paleio quoque in mentem venerat.

1096. κραταβόλους P : correctum e Chr. Pat. 667, καλάμῳ κραταιβόλῳ ἔβαλλον, ἀντίπυργον εἰσβάντες πέτραν.

1098. δ' P¹ : τ' post Hermannum omnes. versum delet P J Meier (Weckl.²). 1099. ἄλλοι P : ἄλλαι Brodaeus.

1100. τ' ὄχον P : στόχον Reiskius. οὐχ ἤνυτον Elms., auctore Porsono ad Phoen. 463.

1102. τλῆμον P : τλήμων ed. Ald. καθῆσθ' ὁ τλήμων Brunck (quod mavult Tyrrell). λελησμένος P : λελημμένος Musgr.

1103. δρυΐνους συγκεραυνοῦσαι (corruptum Nauckio) κλάδους P : συγκραδαίνουσαι vel συντριαινοῦσαι Piersonus, δρυΐνοις συντριαινοῦσαι κλάδοις Hartung (Wecklein). 1108—9. μηδ'—κρυφαίους secludit Paleius.

προσέθεσαν ἐλάτῃ κἀξανέσπασαν χθονός· 1110
ὑψοῦ δὲ θάσσων ὑψόθεν χαμαιπετὴς
πίπτει πρὸς οὖδας μυρίοις οἰμώγμασι
Πενθεύς· κακοῦ γὰρ ἐγγὺς ὢν ἐμάνθανε.
πρώτη δὲ μήτηρ ἦρξεν ἱερία φόνου
καὶ προσπίτνει νιν· ὁ δὲ μίτραν κόμης ἄπο 1115
ἔρριψεν, ὥς νιν γνωρίσασα μὴ κτάνοι
τλήμων Ἀγαύη, καὶ λέγει παρηίδος
ψαύων· ἐγώ τοι, μῆτερ, εἰμὶ παῖς σέθεν
Πενθεύς, ὃν ἔτεκες ἐν δόμοις Ἐχίονος·
οἴκτειρε δ᾽ ὦ μῆτέρ με μηδὲ ταῖς ἐμαῖς 1120
ἁμαρτίαισι παῖδα σὸν κατακτάνῃς.
ἡ δ᾽ ἀφρὸν ἐξιεῖσα καὶ διαστρόφους
κόρας ἑλίσσουσ᾽, οὐ φρονοῦσ᾽ ἃ χρὴ φρονεῖν,
ἐκ Βακχίου κατείχετ᾽, οὐδ᾽ ἔπειθέ νιν.
λαβοῦσα δ᾽ ὠλέναις ἀριστερὰν χέρα, 1125
πλευραῖσιν ἀντιβᾶσα τοῦ δυσδαίμονος
ἀπεσπάραξεν ὦμον, οὐχ ὑπὸ σθένους,
ἀλλ᾽ ὁ θεὸς εὐμάρειαν ἐπεδίδου χεροῖν.
Ἰνὼ δὲ τἀπὶ θάτερ᾽ ἐξειργάζετο
ῥηγνῦσα σάρκας, Αὐτονόη τ᾽ ὄχλος τε πᾶς 1130

1113 spurium esse censet Nauckius probante Weckleinio.
1114. ἱερεία P: ἱερία correxerunt Dobraeus et Elms. ἱερέα WecklL.[2]
1116. κτάνῃ P: κτάνοι Brunck (Nauck, Kirchf., Dind., Paley,
Tyrrell, Wecklein). 1119. 'fortasse Ἐχιόνι' Wecklein.

1121. σπέρμα σὸν Wecklein, qui ad locum *Med.* 816 provocat ubi
PC σὸν σπέρμα, ceteri codices σὼ παῖδε vel (uti hic P et C) σὸν παῖδα
habent.

1123. χρὴ P (Nauck, Kirchf.[2], Wecklein): χρῆν ceteri omnes
Brunckium secuti. 1124. βακχείου P: βακχίου ed. Ald.

1125. 'an ὠλένης?' Kirchf. ὠλέναισι χεῖρ᾽ ἀριστερὰν Bothius,
ἐν ὠλέναις δ᾽ ἀριστερὰν χέρα Mekler. ὠλένην ἀριστερὰν χερί Minervini.
ὠλέναισι δεξιὰν χέρα Humphreys, *Amer. Journ. of Philology*, ii 220—3.

ἐπεῖχε Βακχῶν· ἦν δὲ πᾶσ' ὁμοῦ βοή,
ὁ μὲν στενάζων ὅσον ἐτύγχανεν πνέων,
αἱ δ' ἠλάλαζον. ἔφερε δ' ἡ μὲν ὠλένην,
ἡ δ' ἴχνος αὐταῖς ἀρβύλαις· γυμνοῦντο δὲ
πλευραὶ σπαραγμοῖς· πᾶσα δ' ᾑματωμένη   1135
χεῖρας, διεσφαίριζε σάρκα Πενθέως.

κεῖται δὲ χωρὶς σῶμα, τὸ μὲν ὑπὸ στύφλοις
πέτραις, τὸ δ' ὕλης ἐν βαθυξύλῳ φόβῃ,
οὐ ῥᾴδιον ζήτημα· κρᾶτα δ' ἄθλιον,
ὅπερ λαβοῦσα τυγχάνει μήτηρ χεροῖν,   1140
πήξασ' ἐπ' ἄκρον θύρσον ὡς ὀρεστέρου
φέρει λέοντος διὰ Κιθαιρῶνος μέσου,
λιποῦσ' ἀδελφὰς ἐν χοροῖσι Μαινάδων.

χωρεῖ δὲ θήρᾳ δυσπότμῳ γαυρουμένη
τειχέων ἔσω τῶνδ', ἀνακαλοῦσα Βάκχιον   1145
τὸν ξυγκύναγον, τὸν ξυνεργάτην ἄγρας
τὸν καλλίνικον, ᾗ δάκρυα νικηφορεῖ.

ἐγὼ μὲν οὖν τῇδ' ἐκποδὼν τῇ ξυμφορᾷ
ἄπειμ', Ἀγαύην πρὶν μολεῖν πρὸς δώματα.
τὸ σωφρονεῖν δὲ καὶ σέβειν τὰ τῶν θεῶν   1150

1132. στυγνάζων P : στενάζων ed. Ald.   ἐτύγχανε πνέων
⟨πλέων a manu prima⟩ P : ἐτύγχαν' ἐμπνέων post Reiskium Dind., quo
recepto etiam ὅσον, uti monuit Weckleinius, in monosyllabon ἕως corri-
gere necessarium fuisset. ἐτύγχανεν πνέων ceteri omnes.

1133. ἀνέφερε P : ἔφερε Duportus.   ἄγε, φέρ' ἡ μὲν Herm·
ἐλένην P : ὠλένην ed. Ald.

1134. γυμνοῦσι δὲ πλευρὰ Piersonus et Porsonus; γυμνοῦτε δὲ πλευ-
ρὰς Herm.   1136. διεσφέριζε σάρκα P : διεσφαίριζε σάρκας ed. Ald.

1137. τυφλοῖς P : στύφλοις Barnes.   1138. φόβω, correctum in φόβῃ, P.

1140. ὄνπερ? Shilleto. ἥπερ Hartmann.   1141. πήξασ' P :
πήξασ' Brodaeus.

1147. 'scribendum aut (cum Heathio) ᾗ (Sch., Weckl.), aut quod
verum puto, ᾗ' Kirchf.[1] ᾧ Reiskius. νικηφορεῖ P : νίκη φέρει Hartung.

1148. τῇδ' addidit Reiskius.

κάλλιστον· οἶμαι δ᾽ αὐτὸ καὶ σοφώτατον
θνητοῖσιν εἶναι χρῆμα τοῖσι χρωμένοις.

ΧΟ.　ἀναχορεύσωμεν Βάκχιον,
　　　ἀναβοάσωμεν ξυμφορὰν
　　　τὰν τοῦ δράκοντος ἐκγενέτα Πενθέως,　　1155
　　　ὃς τὰν θηλυγενῆ στολὰν
　　　νάρθηκά τε πιστὸν "Αιδαν
　　　ἔλαβεν εὔθυρσον,

1151. γ᾽ αὐτὸ P: δ᾽ αὐτὸ Chr. Pat. 1146 et Orion Anth. 4 p. 55:
ταὐτὸ Reiskius (Tyrrell).
1152. χρῆμα P et Chr. Pat. 1147: κτῆμα Orion u. s. (Kirchf.,
Nauck, Wecklein).
1153. βακχείων P: βακχεῖον Ald., βάκχιον post Herm. omnes.
1155. Πενθέως P: τοῦ Π. ed. Ald.　Πενθέος ἐκγενέτα Wilamowitz.
1157. τε πιστὸν Αἴδαν P :　　τε, πιστὸν "Αιδα—ταῦρον Herm.
Βιστονίδων Tyrwhitt, τ᾽ ἐπὶ στοναχαῖς? Kirchf.　κισσοχαίταν collato
1055 Ingram, ἐπακτὸν "Αιδαν Tyrrell.　forsan aut προῦπτον "Αιδαν aut βάκτρον vel κέντρον "Αιδα.　πιστὸν "Αιδα (pignus vel omen mortis)? J S Reid.
ἐπὶ στόμ᾽ "Αιδα N Macnicol, Classical Review, iii 72, coll. 857 et Pind.
Pyth. iv 44 χθόνιον "Αιδου στόμα.　ὃς θηλυγενῆ στολάν τε νάρθηκά θ᾽
ὁπλισμὸν "Αιδα Wilamowitz.

ταῦρον προηγητῆρα συμφορᾶς ἔχων.
Βάκχαι Καδμεῖαι,   1160
τὸν καλλίνικον κλεινὸν ἐξεπράξατε
εἰς γόον, εἰς δάκρυα.
καλὸς ἀγών, ἐν αἵματι στάζουσαν
χέρα περιβαλεῖν τέκνου.

ἀλλ' εἰσορῶ γὰρ εἰς δόμους ὁρμωμένην   1165
Πενθέως Ἀγαύην μητέρ' ἐν διαστρύφοις
ὄσσοις, δέχεσθε κῶμον εὐίου θεοῦ.

ΑΓΑΥΗ.   στροφή.

Ἀσιάδες Βάκχαι,   ΧΟ. τί μ' ὀροθύνεις ὤ;
ΑΓ. φέρομεν ἐξ ὄρεος
ἔλικα νεότομον ἐπὶ μέλαθρα,   1170

1161. ἐξεπράξατυ P*: ἐξεπράξατε Scaliger.
1162. εἰς γόνον P: correxit Canter.
1164. χέρα περιβαλεῖν τέκνον P: 'scribendum χέρα βαλεῖν τέκνῳ'
Kirchf.; (omisso χέρα) περιβαλεῖν τέκνον J F Davies, π. χέρα (omisso
τέκνον vel τέκνου) Tyrrell.   χέρα βαλεῖν τέκνου? Wecklein.
1165. δρόμους P: δόμους H Stephanus.   1167. εὔιον Herm.
1168. γυνή P: ἀγαύη ed. Ald.   τί με (δὴ addit ed. Ald.) ὀρύεις
(ὀρθοῖς H Stephanus, Nauckius) ὤ P: τί με iterare vult Nauckius;
τί μ' ὀροθύνεις ὤ Herm. (Paley, Wecklein[1]); τίνα θροεῖς (Scaliger) αὐδὰν
Hartung; τί με θροεῖς τάδ' ὤ Fixius; τί με δὴ ὄρσεις ὤ Schoenius.
1169. ὀρέων P: ὄρεος Plutarch. v. Crassi 33, Polyaenus 7, 41 (Herm.,
Schoenius, Nauck, Kirchf., Wecklein).

* retinet Tyrrell.

μακάριον θήραν.

ΧΟ. ὁρῶ καί σε δέξομαι σύγκωμον.

ΑΓ. ἔμαρψα τόνδ' ἄνευ βρόχων
λέοντος – ◡ ◡ – νέον ἶνιν,
ὡς ὁρᾶν πάρα. 1175

ΧΟ. πόθεν ἐρημίας;

ΑΓ. Κιθαιρὼν ΧΟ. τί Κιθαιρών;

ΑΓ. κατεφόνευσέν νιν.

ΧΟ. τίς ἁ βαλοῦσα πρῶτα; ΑΓ. ἐμὸν τὸ γέρας.

ΧΟ. μάκαιρ' Ἀγαύη ΑΓ. κληζόμεθ' ἐν θιάσοις. 1180

ΧΟ. τίς ἄλλα; ΑΓ. τὰ Κάδμου ΧΟ. τί Κάδμου;

ΑΓ. γένεθλα
μετ' ἐμὲ μετ' ἐμὲ τοῦδ'
ἔθιγε θηρός. εὐτυχής γ' ἅδ' ἄγρα.

ἀντιστροφή.

μέτεχέ νυν θοίνας. ΧΟ. τί μετέχω τλάμων;

ΑΓ. νέος ὁ μόσχος ἄρ- 1185
τι γένυν ὑπὸ κόρυθ' ἁπαλότριχα

1171. μακάριον θήραμα P et Plutarch. *mor.* p. 501 b; μακαρίαν
θήραν Plutarch. *v. Crassi* 33 (Elms., Dind., Paley, Tyrrell); μακάριον
θήραν Polyaenus *u. s.* (Herm., Sch., Kirchf., Nauck, Wecklein). Cf. 868.
1172. ὁρῶ τε...σύγκωμος, ὦ Herm.   γε et ὦ addidit Ald., om. P.
1173. 'lacunam post βρόχων indicavit Canterus' (Dind.).
1174. νιν P: λῖν Stephanus, rectius λίν Brunck. quem secuti sunt
omnes praeter Weckleinium, qui coniecit λέοντος – ◡ ◡ – νέον ἶνιν
collato *Iph. T.* 1239 ubi φέρει νιν corruptum est e φέρε δ' ἶνιν*.
1179. πρῶτα P: πρῶτά γε Ald.; πρῶτα post Herm. omnes, praeter
Schoenium qui πρῶτά γ' ἐμὸν τὸ γέρας Agavae tribuit.   ἐμὸν ἐμὸν P:
ἐμὸν semel Plut. *Crass.* 33 (quem secuti sunt omnes).
1181. ΑΓΑ. ante τὰ Κάδμου primus addidit Heathius.
γένεθλα bis P: correxit Heathius.
1183. εὐτυχής (εὐτυχεῖς a correctore) τάδ' ἄγρα P: ΧΟ. εὐτυχεῖς τᾳδ'
ἄγρᾳ ed. Ald. (Elms., Herm., Wecklein, ΑΓ... Sch.); εὐτυχής γ' ἅδ' ἄγρα
Nauck (Kirchf.², Dind., Paley, ΧΟ. Tyrrell)†.   1184. τλᾶμον Hartung.

* λέοντος μηλοφόνου νέον ἶνιν, H. Macnaghten, coll. Aesch. *Ag.* 717, 730 μηλο-
φόνοις ἐν ἄταις.   † post hunc versum trimetri duo exciderunt (Wilamowitz).

κατάκομον θάλλει.

ΧΟ. πρέπει γ᾽ ὥστε θὴρ ἄγραυλος φόβῃ.

ΑΓ. ὁ Βάκχιος κυναγέτας
σοφὸς σοφῶς ἀνέπηλ᾽ ἐπὶ θήρᾳ   1190
τοῦδε Μαινάδας.

ΧΟ. ὁ γὰρ ἄναξ ἀγρεύς.

ΑΓ. ἐπαινεῖς; ΧΟ. τί δ᾽ ἐπαινῶ;

ΑΓ. τάχα δὲ Καδμεῖοι

ΧΟ. καὶ παῖς γε Πενθεὺς ματέρ᾽ ΑΓ. ἐπαινέσεται,

ΧΟ. λαβοῦσαν ἄγραν ΑΓ. τάνδε λεοντοφυῆ   1196

ΧΟ. περισσὰν ΑΓ. περισσῶς. ΧΟ. ἀγάλλει; ΑΓ.
γέγηθα
μεγάλα μεγάλα καὶ
φανερὰ τᾷδ᾽ ἄγρᾳ κατειργασμένα.

ΧΟ. δεῖξόν νυν, ὦ τάλαινα, σὴν νικηφόρον   1200
ἀστοῖσιν ἄγραν ἣν φέρουσ᾽ ἐλήλυθας.

1187. βάλλει P: θάλλει Musgr. (Schoenius, Kirchf.[2], Nauck, Dindf., Tyrrell, Wecklein). 1188. ΧΟ. primus addidit Tyrwhitt. πρέπει γὰρ ὥστε θηρὸς ἀγραύλου φόβῳ (φόβῃ Brodaeus, φόβῃ alii) P: πρέπει γ᾽ ὥστε θὴρ ἄγραυλος φόβῃ Kirchf. (Tyrrell, Wecklein). 1189. βακχεῖος P: correxit Ald. 1190. σοφὸς σοφὸς P: σοφὸς σοφῶς post Brunckium omnes. ἀνέπηλεν P: ἀνέπηλ᾽ Dind. (Tyrrell, Wecklein). θήρα τόνδε P: θῆρα τόνδε (Elms., Paley); θήρᾳ τοῦδε Herm. (Schoenius, Nauck, Kirchf.[2], Dind., Tyrrell, Wecklein). 1192. 'qu. ξαγρεὺς' Dobraeus. 1193. τί δ᾽ addidit ed. Ald.; omiserat P: 'vel sic vel τί σ᾽ ἐπαινῶ legendum videtur' Kirchf. 1194. δὲ καὶ P: δὲ Ald. 1195. 'καὶ παῖς—περισσῶς choro, ἀγάλλῃ Agavae, reliqua choro tribuit P: correxit Herm., partim aliis praeeuntibus' (Dindf.). ἐπαινεύσεται P: correxit Ald. 1196. λεοντοφυῆ P: -ᾶ Dind. (Tyrrell). 1197. περισσὰς P: περισσὰν Brodaeus. 1199. τάδ᾽ ἔργα P: τάργ᾽ ἐγὼ Herm.; τᾷδε γᾷ L Dindorfius (G Dind., Schoenius, Paley, Wecklein): τᾷδ᾽ ἄγρᾳ Nauck, Tyrrell. ΑΓ. γέγηθα—φανερὰ τᾷδε ΧΟ. γᾷ κατειργασμένα Kirchf.[1]; ΧΟ. post γᾷ transtulit Wecklein. 1200. νῦν P: νυν ed. Ald.

ΑΓ. ὦ καλλίπυργον ἄστυ Θηβαίας χθονὸς
ναίοντες, ἔλθεθ᾽ ὡς ἴδητε τήνδ᾽ ἄγραν,
Κάδμου θυγατέρες θηρὸς ἣν ἠγρεύσαμεν
οὐκ ἀγκυλωτοῖς Θεσσαλῶν·στοχάσμασιν,   1205
οὐ δικτύοισιν, ἀλλὰ λευκοπήχεσι
χειρῶν ἀκμαῖσι. κᾷτα κομπάζειν χρεὼν
καὶ λογχοποιῶν ὄργανα κτᾶσθαι μάτην;
ἡμεῖς δέ γ᾽ αὐτῇ χειρὶ τόνδε θ᾽ εἵλομεν
χωρίς τε θηρὸς ἄρθρα διεφορήσαμεν.   1210
ποῦ μοι πατὴρ ὁ πρέσβυς; ἐλθέτω πέλας.
Πενθεύς τ᾽ ἐμὸς παῖς ποῦ 'στιν; αἱρέσθω λαβὼν

1203. ἴδετε P : ἴδητε ed. Ald.
1205. ἀγκυλωτοῖς P : ἀγκυλητοῖς? Nauck. *ann. crit.* (Dind., Tyrrell, Weckl.[1]).
1207. κᾷτα κομπάζειν P et editores omnes: malim κᾷτ᾽ ἀκοντίζειν. χρεών...μάτην P : transponit Nauck (Wecklein).
1208. ἔργ᾽ ἀναρτᾶσθαι J Hilberg.
1209. δὲ ταύτῃ P : δέ γ᾽ αὐτῇ Kirchf.[2] (Wecklein). τόδε P : τόνδε ed. Ald.
1210. χωρίς τε θη:ὸς P : χωρὶς σιδήρου τ᾽ Pierson ; χωρίς τέ γ᾽ ἀθέρος (praeeunte Ruhnkenio qui χωρὶς ἄθηρος coniecerat) Wecklein[1] (ἀθήρ· ἐπιδορατίς, ἀκίς, δορίς); χωρίς τε δορίδος Wilamowitz-Moellendorff.
1212. αἱρέσθω P : αἱρέσθω Portus. αἱρέσθω βαλὼν (*Suppl.* 468) Hartmann. ἀράσθω Scaliger (Wecklein[2]).

πηκτῶν πρὸς οἴκους κλιμάκων προσαμβάσεις,
ὡς πασσαλεύσῃ κρᾶτα τριγλύφοις τόδε
λέοντος ὃν πάρειμι θηράσασ᾽ ἐγώ.   1215

ΚΑΔΜΟΣ.

ἔπεσθέ μοι φέροντες ἄθλιον βάρος
Πενθέως, ἔπεσθε, πρόσπολοι, δόμων πάρος,
οὗ σῶμα μοχθῶν μυρίοις ζητήμασι
φέρω τόδ᾽ εὑρὼν ἐν Κιθαιρῶνος πτυχαῖς
διασπαρακτόν, κοὐδὲν ἐν ταὐτῷ πέδῳ   1220
λαβών, ἐν ὕλῃ κείμενον δυσευρέτῳ.
ἤκουσα γάρ του θυγατέρων τολμήματα,
ἤδη κατ᾽ ἄστυ τειχέων ἔσω βεβὼς
σὺν τῷ γέροντι Τειρεσίᾳ Βακχῶν πάρα·
πάλιν δὲ κάμψας εἰς ὄρος κομίζομαι   1225
τὸν κατθανόντα παῖδα Μαινάδων ὕπο.
καὶ τὴν μὲν Ἀκταίων᾽ Ἀρισταίῳ ποτὲ
τεκοῦσαν εἶδον Αὐτονόην Ἰνώ θ᾽ ἅμα
ἔτ᾽ ἀμφὶ δρυμοῖς οἰστροπλῆγας ἀθλίας,

1213. πλεκτῶν P: πηκτῶν ex *Phoen*. 491 Barnesius, quod confir-
mat *Chr. Pat*. 1263, πηκτὰς κλίμακας. πρὸς οἴκῳ Scaliger, πρὸς οἴκοις
Barnes.
1214. τριγλύφοις κάρα τόδε Shilleto (in Thuc. I 14 § 4).
1216. ἄθλιον δέμας? Nauck. *ann. crit*.
1217. δόμων πέλας dubitanter conicit Wecklein collato *H. F.* 139.
1218. μοχθῶν vulgo: μόχθων Wecklein.   1219. κιθερῶνος P.
1220. 'lege πεσὸν cum Reiskio,' Dobraeus.
1221. δυσευρέτῳ P: δυσεύρετον Reiskius, δυσευρέτως Dobraeus et
Hermannus. versus Nauckio et Weckleinio suspectus.
1223. ἔσω P: εἴσω Dind.   1224. πέρι P: πάρα Musgr.
(in textum receperunt editores recentiores praeter Tyrrellium omnes).
1227. ἀκταίων᾽ P: Ἀκτέων᾽ Dind. (Tyrrell). ἀριστέα P: Ἀριστέᾳ
L Dindorfius (Kirchf.¹, Nauck, Dind., Paley, Tyrrell); Ἀρισταίου Miltonus,
Ἀρισταίῳ Heath (Elms., Herm., Schoenius, Kirchf.², Wecklein).

τὴν δ᾽ εἶπέ τίς μοι δεῦρο βακχείῳ ποδὶ 1230
στείχειν Ἀγαύην, οὐδ᾽ ἄκραντ᾽ ἠκούσαμεν·
λεύσσω γὰρ αὐτήν, ὄψιν οὐκ εὐδαίμονα.

ΑΓ. πάτερ, μέγιστον κομπάσαι πάρεστί σοι,
πάντων ἀρίστας θυγατέρας σπεῖραι μακρῷ
θνητῶν· ἁπάσας εἶπον, ἐξόχως δ᾽ ἐμέ, 1235
ἣ τὰς παρ᾽ ἱστοῖς ἐκλιποῦσα κερκίδας
εἰς μεῖζον ἥκω, θῆρας ἀγρεύειν χεροῖν.
φέρω δ᾽ ἐν ὠλέναισιν, ὡς ὁρᾷς, τάδε
λαβοῦσα τἀριστεῖα, σοῖσι πρὸς δόμοις
ὡς ἂν κρεμασθῇ· σὺ δὲ πάτερ δέξαι χεροῖν· 1240
γαυρούμενος δὲ τοῖς ἐμοῖς ἀγρεύμασι
κάλει φίλους εἰς δαῖτα· μακάριος γὰρ εἶ,
μακάριος, ἡμῶν τοιάδ᾽ ἐξειργασμένων.

ΚΑ. ὦ πένθος οὐ μετρητὸν οὐδ᾽ οἷόν τ᾽ ἰδεῖν,
φόνον ταλαίναις χερσὶν ἐξειργασμένων. 1245
καλὸν τὸ θῦμα καταβαλοῦσα δαίμοσιν
ἐπὶ δαῖτα Θήβας τάσδε κἀμὲ παρακαλεῖς.
οἴμοι κακῶν μὲν πρῶτα σῶν, ἔπειτ᾽ ἐμῶν·
ὡς ὁ θεὸς ἡμᾶς ἐνδίκως μέν, ἀλλ᾽ ἄγαν
Βρόμιος ἄναξ ἀπώλεσ᾽ οἰκεῖος γεγώς.

ΑΓ. ὡς δύσκολον τὸ γῆρας ἀνθρώποις ἔφυ 1250

1230. τήνδ᾽ P: τὴν δ᾽ Barnes.
1232. αὐτῆς P (Matthiae, Kirchf.[1], Tyrrell); αὐτὴν, Scaliger, Kirchf.[2], ceteri. Elmsleio 'parum referre' videtur.
1237. μεῖζον P ; Chr. Pat. 163, εἰς μεῖζον ἥξω: μεῖζον' ed. Ald. (Elms., Paley).
1240. ἂν κρεμασθῇ P: ἀγκρεμασθῇ Herm. (Dind., idem Weckl.[2]).
1241. ἐμῆς P : ἐμοῖς ed. Ald.
1245. ἐξειργασμένων, littera ω duobus punctis notata, P : -μένον Ald. versum interpolatum esse existimat Middendorf, probante Weckleinio.
1246. καλὸν πρόθυμα? Wecklein. καλόν γε θῦμα Hartmann.

ἔν τ' ὄμμασι σκυθρωπόν. εἴθε παῖς ἐμὸς
εὔθηρος εἴη, μητρὸς εἰκασθεὶς τρόποις,
ὅτ' ἐν νεανίαισι Θηβαίοις ἅμα
θηρῶν ὀριγνῷτ'. ἀλλὰ θεομαχεῖν μόνον   1255
οἷός τ' ἐκεῖνος. νουθετητέος, πάτερ,
σούστίν. τίς αὐτὸν δεῦρ' ἂν ὄψιν εἰς ἐμὴν
καλέσειεν, ὡς ἴδῃ με τὴν εὐδαίμονα;

ΚΑ.   φεῦ φεῦ· φρονήσασαι μὲν οἷ' ἐδράσατε,
      ἀλγήσετ' ἄλγος δεινόν· εἰ δὲ διὰ τέλους   1260
      ἐν τῷδ' ἀεὶ μενεῖτ' ἐν ᾧ καθέστατε,
      οὐκ εὐτυχοῦσαι δόξετ' οὐχὶ δυστυχεῖν.

ΑΓ.   τί δ' οὐ καλῶς τῶνδ' ἢ τί λυπηρᾶς ἔχει;
ΚΑ.   πρῶτον μὲν εἰς τόνδ' αἰθέρ' ὄμμα σὸν μέθες.
ΑΓ.   ἰδού· τί μοι τόνδ' ἐξυπεῖπας εἰσορᾶν;   1265
ΚΑ.   ἔθ' αὐτὸς ἤ σοι μεταβολὰς ἔχειν δοκεῖ;
ΑΓ.   λαμπρότερος ἢ πρὶν καὶ διιπετέστερος.
ΚΑ.   τὸ δὲ πτοηθὲν τόδ' ἔτι σῇ ψυχῇ πάρα;
ΑΓ.   οὐκ οἶδα τοὔπος τοῦτο, γίγνομαι δέ πως
      ἔννους μετασταθεῖσα τῶν πάρος φρενῶν.   1270
ΚΑ.   κλύοις ἂν οὖν τι κἀποκρίναι' ἂν σαφῶς;

1252. σκυθρωπὸς P : σκυθρωπὸν ed. Ald.   εἰ δὲ P : εἴθε ed. Ald.
1254. ὅτ' ἐν P : ὅπως? Wecklein. ἅμα P: 'probabilius θαμά' (Dindorf).
1257. σοί τ' ἐστίν. τίς P : σούστίν. τίς Kirchhoffius et Nauckius
(Dind., Wecklein); σοί 'στιν· τίς Paley; σοί τ' ἐστὶ κἀμοὶ μὴ σοφοῖς
χαίρειν κακοῖς. ποῦ 'στιν. τίς ed. Ald., quam Tyrrellius solus inter recentiores secutus est. 'locum Musuri [editoris Aldini] libidine turpiter
interpolatum primus me auctore in integrum restituit Nauckius eiectis
ineptis illis additamentis' (Kirchhoff).

1265. τῶν δ' P : τόνδ' H Stephanus.

1268. τόδε τι P : τόδ' ἔτι ed. Ald.

1269—70. unum inter hos duo versus Cadmi versum excidisse, inter-
rupto Agavae sermone, coniecit Nauckius. deleto proximo versu, γιγνώσκω δέ πως Kirchhoffius, κινοῦμαι δέ πως S Allen (ap. Tyrrell.).

1271. σοφῶς P : σαφῶς Reiskius.

ΑΓ. ὡς ἐκλέλησμαί γ᾽ ἃ πάρος εἴπομεν, πάτερ.

ΚΑ. εἰς ποῖον ἦλθες οἶκον ὑμεναίων μέτα;

ΑΓ. σπαρτῷ μ᾽ ἔδωκας, ὡς λέγουσ᾽, Ἐχίονι.

ΚΑ. τί; οὖν ἐν οἴκοις παῖς ἐγένετο σῷ πόσει;   1275

ΑΓ. Πενθεύς, ἐμῇ τε καὶ πατρὸς κοινωνίᾳ.

ΚΑ. τίνος πρόσωπον δῆτ᾽ ἐν ἀγκάλαις ἔχεις;

ΑΓ. λέοντος, ὥς γ᾽ ἔφασκον αἱ θηρώμεναι.

ΚΑ. σκέψαι νυν ὀρθῶς, βραχὺς ὁ μόχθος εἰσιδεῖν.

ΑΓ. ἔα, τί λεύσσω; τί φέρομαι τόδ᾽ ἐν χεροῖν;   1280

ΚΑ. ἄθρησον αὐτὸ καὶ σαφέστερον μάθε.

ΑΓ. ὁρῶ μέγιστον ἄλγος ἡ τάλαιν᾽ ἐγώ.

ΚΑ. μῶν σοι λέοντι φαίνεται προσεικέναι;

ΑΓ. οὔκ· ἀλλὰ Πενθέως ἡ τάλαιν᾽ ἔχω κάρα.

ΚΑ. ᾠμωγμένον γε πρόσθεν ἢ σὲ γνωρίσαι.   1285

ΑΓ. τίς ἔκτανέν νιν; πῶς ἐμὰς ἦλθεν χέρας;

ΚΑ. δύστην᾽ ἀλήθει᾽, ὡς ἐν οὐ καιρῷ πάρει.

ΑΓ. λέγ᾽, ὡς τὸ μέλλον καρδία πήδημ᾽ ἔχει.

ΚΑ. σύ νιν κατέκτας καὶ κασίγνηται σέθεν.

1272. ἐλέλησμαι P : ἐκλέλησμαι ed. Ald.
1273. ὑμεναίων P : ὑμέναιον Scaliger.
1275. 'fortasse σὸς πόσει' Kirchf.
1276. ἐμοὶ P : ἐμῇ ed. Ald.   ἐμῇ...κοινωνίᾳ Hartung.
1279. νῦν P : νυν ('nescio an praestet νιν'), Elms.
1280. φέρομαι P : φέρομεν Elms.
1281. αὖτις Reiskius : αὖθις vel αὖτε Dobraeus.
1283. προσεοικέναι P : προσεικέναι Brunck.
1285. οἰμωγμένον P (Kirchf.[1]) : ᾠμωγμένον post Elms. Dind., Paley, Tyrrell; ἡμαγμένον Musgr. (Herm., Nauck, Kirchf.[2], Wecklein).
1286. ἦλθες P : ἦλθ᾽ εἰς (vel ἐς) χέρας ed. Ald., Weckl.[2]   'non dubitarem reponere ἦλθεν, si certum esset praepositionem recte abesse posse' Elms. ἦλθεν (Herm., Nauck, Kirchf.[2], Dind., Weckl.[1]). ἐμ᾽ ἦλθεν ἐς χέρας Tyrrell.
1289. κασίγνητοι P : κασιγνήτα Barnes, κασίγνηται Markland quod omnes receperunt.

ΑΓ.   ποῦ δ' ὤλετ'; ἢ κατ' οἶκον; ἢ ποίοις τόποις; 1290
ΚΑ.   οὗπερ πρὶν 'Ακταίωνα διέλαχον κύνες.
ΑΓ.   τί δ' εἰς Κιθαιρῶν' ἦλθε δυσδαίμων ὅδε;
ΚΑ.   ἐκερτόμει θεὸν σάς τε βακχείας μολών.
ΑΓ.   ἡμεῖς δ' ἐκεῖσε τίνι τρόπῳ κατήραμεν;
ΚΑ.   ἐμάνητε, πᾶσά τ' ἐξεβακχεύθη πόλις.   1295
ΑΓ.   Διόνυσος ἡμᾶς ὤλεσ', ἄρτι μανθάνω.
ΚΑ.   ὕβριν γ' ὑβρισθείς· θεὸν γὰρ οὐχ ἡγεῖσθέ νιν.
ΑΓ.   τὸ φίλτατον δὲ σῶμα ποῦ παιδός, πάτερ;
ΚΑ.   ἐγὼ μόλις τόδ' ἐξερευνήσας φέρω.
ΑΓ.   ἢ πᾶν ἐν ἄρθροις συγκεκλημένον καλῶς; 1300

* * * * * * *

ΑΓ.   Πενθεῖ δὲ τί μέρος ἀφροσύνης προσῆκ' ἐμῆς;
ΚΑ.   ὑμῖν ἐγένεθ' ὅμοιος, οὐ σέβων θεόν.
       τοιγὰρ συνῆψε πάντας εἰς μίαν βλάβην,
       ὑμᾶς τε τόνδε θ', ὥστε διολέσαι δόμους
       κᾄμ', ὅστις ἄτεκνος ἀρσένων παίδων γεγὼς 1305
       τῆς σῆς τόδ' ἔρνος, ὦ τάλαινα, νηδύος
       αἴσχιστα καὶ κάκιστα κατθανόνθ' ὁρῶ,
       ᾧ δῶμ' ἀνέβλεφ', ὃς συνεῖχες, ὦ τέκνον,
       τοὐμὸν μέλαθρον, παιδὸς ἐξ ἐμῆς γεγώς,
       πόλει τε τάρβος ἦσθα· τὸν γέροντα δὲ 1310

1290.   ἢ 'ν ποίοις τόποις coniecit Wecklein.

1291.   ἀκταίωνα P : 'Ακτέωνα Dind. (Tyrrell).

1297.   ὕβριν P : γ' addiderunt Heathius et Dobraeus (Elms., Schoenius, Kirchf., Dind., Paley, Tyrrell, Wecklein); ὕβρεις Brunck, 'fortasse
ὕβρισμ', Paley; ὑμῖν praeeunte Hermanno Nauck.; ὕβρισεν vel ὕβριξ'
A. Palmer.

1300.   συγκεκλημένον a prima manu P: συγκεκεκλη- omnes praeter
Dind. qui ξυγ- praetulit : συγκεκλειμένον ed. Ald.   lacunam post
hunc versum indicavit Matthiae, praeiverat Victorius.

1302.   ἀφρόνης Housman, Classical Rev., ii 245.

1308.   ᾧ] ὃν superscriptum in P.   ἀνέβλεπεν P : ἀνέβλεφ'
Dobraeus et Elmsleius.

οὐδεὶς ὑβρίζειν ἤθελ' εἰσορῶν τὸ σὸν
κάρα· δίκην γὰρ ἀξίαν ἐλάμβανες.
νῦν δ' ἐκ δόμων ἄτιμος ἐκβεβλήσομαι
ὁ Κάδμος ὁ μέγας, ὃς τὸ Θηβαίων γένος
ἔσπειρα κἀξήμησα κάλλιστον θέρος. 1315
ὦ φίλτατ' ἀνδρῶν, καὶ γὰρ οὐκέτ' ὢν ὅμως
τῶν φιλτάτων ἔμοιγ' ἀριθμήσει, τέκνον,
οὐκέτι γενείου τοῦδε θιγγάνων χερί,
τὸν μητρὸς αὐδῶν πατέρα προσπτύξει, τέκνον,
λέγων· τίς ἀδικεῖ, τίς σ' ἀτιμάζει, γέρον; 1320
τίς σὴν ταράσσει καρδίαν λυπηρὸς ὤν;
λέγ', ὡς κολάζω τὸν ἀδικοῦντά σ', ὦ πάτερ.
νῦν δ' ἄθλιος μέν εἰμ' ἐγώ, τλήμων δὲ σύ,
οἰκτρὰ δὲ μήτηρ, τλήμονες δὲ σύγγονοι.
εἰ δ' ἔστιν ὅστις δαιμόνων ὑπερφρονεῖ, 1325
εἰς τοῦδ' ἀθρήσας θάνατον ἡγείσθω θεούς.

ΧΟ. τὸ μὲν σὸν ἀλγῶ, Κάδμε· σὸς δ' ἔχει δίκην
     παῖς παιδὸς ἀξίαν μέν, ἀλγεινὴν δὲ σοί.

ΑΓ. ὦ πάτερ, ὁρᾷς γὰρ τἄμ' ὅσῳ μετεστράφη

* * * * * * *

1312. ἐλάμβανεν P*: ἐλάμβανες Hermannus ad *Or*. p. 65 (Wecklein); ἐλάμβαν' ἄν Heathius; 'ἄν ἔλαβεν ἄν Elms. *Med*. p. 150, ipse cogi-
tabam de γ' ἄν vel potius τἄν' (Dobraeus).

1317. τέκνων P: τέκνον Reiskius.

1318. θιγγάνω P: θιγγάνων Brodaeus.

1320. τίς σ' ἀδικεῖ P: τίς ἀδικεῖ Barnes.

1329. post hunc versum lacunam versuum haud paucorum primus
indicavit Tyrwhittus qui versum unum e schol. in Ar. *Plut*. 907 Euripidi
reddidit, εἰ μὴ γὰρ ἴδιον ἔλαβον εἰς χέρας μύσος; Agavae orationem
nobis deperditam commemoravit Apsines rhetor a Musgravio primum
laudatus (ed. Walz IX 587, 590); integrum codicem usurpavit *Christi
Patientis* auctor, qui e numero versuum deperditorum complures in usus

* retinet Tyrrell.

Luciani *Pis-* λακιστὸν ἐν πέτραισιν εὑρέσθαι μόρον.
cator § 2.   *   *   *   *   *   *   *

C. P. 1312   πῶς καί νιν ἡ δύστηνος εὐλαβουμένη
1313   πρὸς στέρνα θῶμαι; τίνα (δὲ) θρηνήσω τρόπον ;
Schol. in Ar.   εἰ μὴ γὰρ ἴδιον ἔλαβον εἰς χεῖρας μύσος
Plutum 907.   *   *   *   *   *   *   *

C. P. 1256   κατασπάσασθαι πᾶν μέλος¹‿ ‒ ‿ ‿
1257   κυνοῦσα σάρκας ἅσπερ ἐξεθρεψάμην.
1466   φέρ᾽, ὦ γεραιέ, κρᾶτα τοῦ τρισαθλίου²
1467   ὀρθῶς προσαρμόσωμεν, εὔτονον(?) δὲ πᾶν
1468   σῶμ᾽ ἐξακριβώσωμεν εἰς ὅσον πάρα.
1469   ὦ φίλτατον πρόσωπον, ὦ νέα γένυς,³
   *   *   *   *   *   *   *

1470   ἰδοὺ καλύπτρᾳ τῇδε σὸν κρύπτω κάρα·⁴
1471   τὰ δ᾽ αἱμόφυρτα καὶ κατηλοκισμένα⁵
1472   μέλη
   *   *   *   *   *   *   *

ΔΙΟΝΥϹΟϹ.
   *   *   *   *   *   *   *

1664   εἰς δεσμά τ᾽ ἦλθε καὶ λόγων ὑβρίσματα.⁶
1663   τοιγὰρ τέθνηκεν ὧν ἐχρῆν ἥκισθ᾽ ὕπο.
1667   καὶ ταῦτα μὲν πέπονθεν οὗτος (ἐνδίκως⁷).
1668   ἃ δ᾽ αὖ παθεῖν δεῖ λαὸν (?) οὐ κρύψω κακά.
   *   *   *   *   *   *   *

1674   λιπεῖν πόλιν τήνδ᾽ ἀνοσίου μιάσματος
1675   (ὁσίαν) τινούσας τῷδ᾽ ὃν ἔκτειναν δίκην⁸
1676   καὶ μηκέτ᾽ ἐσιδεῖν⁹ πατρίδ᾽· οὐ γὰρ εὐσεβές.
   *   *   *   *   *   *   *

1690   αὐτὸς δ᾽ ἃ μέλλεις¹⁰ πήματ᾽ ἐκπλήσειν, φράσω.

suos convertit, quorum duo indicavit Porsonus πῶς καί νιν ἡ δύστηνος
εὐλαβουμένη πρὸς στέρνα θῶμαι; τίνα (δὲ) θρηνήσω τρόπον; plures eruere
conatus est Kirchhoffius in *Philologo* VIII 78, quos, habito tamen delectu
quodam, Weckleinius in contextum revocavit.

¹ Auctor *Christi Patientis* more suo scripserat ὅπως κατασπάσαιμι (sic)
καὶ σύμπαν μέλος (cf. ib. 1315), correxit Wecklein. ² τὸν τρισόλβιον auctor
C.P. (correxit Burges). vv. 1466—8, 70, Weckleinius consulto (ut videtur)

δράκων γενήσει μεταβαλών, δάμαρ τε σὴ 1330
ἐκθηριωθεῖσ᾽ ὄφεος ἀλλάξει τύπον,
ἣν Ἄρεος ἔσχες Ἁρμονίαν θνητὸς γεγώς.
ὄχον δὲ μόσχων, χρησμὸς ὡς λέγει Διός,
ἐλᾷς μετ᾽ ἀλόχου, βαρβάρων ἡγούμενος.
πολλὰς δὲ πέρσεις ἀναρίθμῳ στρατεύματι 1335
πόλεις· ὅταν δὲ Λοξίου χρηστήριον
διαρπάσωσι, νόστον ἄθλιον πάλιν
σχήσουσί· σὲ δ᾽ Ἄρης Ἁρμονίαν τε ῥύσεται
μακάρων τ᾽ ἐς αἶαν σὸν καθιδρύσει βίον.
ταῦτ᾽ οὐχὶ θνητοῦ πατρὸς ἐκγεγὼς λέγω 1340
Διόνυσος, ἀλλὰ Ζηνός· εἰ δὲ σωφρονεῖν
ἔγνωθ᾽, ὅτ᾽ οὐκ ἠθέλετε, τὸν Διὸς γόνον
εὐδαιμονοῖτ᾽ ἂν σύμμαχον κεκτημένοι.

omisit.　　³ Maluit Weckleinius, versibus duobus (1469 et 921) in
unum conflatis, ex altero loco ὦ φιλτάτη πρόσοψις adsumere, quae verba
etiam in *Hel.* 636 leguntur.　　⁴ Auctor *Chr. Pat.* σὴν...κάραν (initio
versus ὦ παῖ scripsit Burges.　　⁵ Eur. *Suppl.* 826, κατὰ μὲν ὄνυξιν
ἠλοχίσμεθ᾽.　　⁶ Auctor *Chr. Pat.* λόγους ἐμπαιγμάτων (mutavit Wecklein); etiam in v. 446 εἰς δεσμά τ᾽ ἦλθες.　　⁷ idem οὐκ ἄκων et　　⁹ ἰδεῖν
(utrumque correxit Kirchhoff).　　⁸ Auctor *Chr. Pat.* δίκην τίνοντας
τῷδ᾽ ὃν ἔκτειναν φθόνῳ (θέμις Burges): δίκην transposui et ὁσίαν scripsi,
quod confirmant *Tro.* 1315, ὅσιον ἀνοσίοις σφαγαῖσιν et *Or.* 500, αἵματος
δίκην ὁσίαν διώκοντ᾽.　　¹⁰ idem οὗτος δ᾽ ἃ μέλλει : correxit Kirchhoff.

1330. versum hunc Euripidi primus restituit Matthiae e schol. in
Dionysium Perieg. v. 391, ubi cum sequentibus duobus citatur.

1331—2 inter se transponit Wecklein, praeeunte Schoenio.

1332. ἁρμονίας: correxit Ald.　　　1333. ὄχων P: correxit Ald.

1339. ἐγκαθιδρύσει Burges (*Chr. Pat.* 1754).　　βίον P: δέμας
coniecit Nauckius.

1342. ὅτ᾽ P: ὃν Nauck. *ann. crit.*

1343. εὐδαιμονοῖτ᾽ ἂν P (Elms., Kirchf., Nauck, Wecklein): ηὐδαι-
μονεῖτ᾽ ἂν Musgr. (Dind., εὐ- Herm., Schoenius, Paley, Tyrrell).

ΑΓ. Διόνυσε, λισσόμεσθά σ', ἠδικήκαμεν.

ΔΙ. ὄψ' ἐμάθεθ' ἡμᾶς, ὅτε δ' ἐχρῆν, οὐκ ᾔδετε. 1345

ΑΓ. ἐγνώκαμεν ταῦτ'· ἀλλ' ἐπεξέρχει λίαν.

ΔΙ. καὶ γὰρ πρὸς ὑμῶν θεὸς γεγὼς ὑβριζόμην.

ΑΓ. ὀργὰς πρέπει θεοὺς οὐχ ὁμοιοῦσθαι βροτοῖς.

ΔΙ. πάλαι τάδε Ζεὺς οὑμὸς ἐπένευσεν πατήρ.

ΑΓ. αἰαῖ, δέδοκται, πρέσβυ, τλήμονες φυγαί.   1350

ΔΙ. τί δῆτα μέλλεθ' ἅπερ ἀναγκαίως ἔχει;

ΚΑ. ὦ τέκνον, ὡς εἰς δεινὸν ἤλθομεν κακόν,
σύ θ' ἡ τάλαινα σύγγονοί τε σαὶ [φίλαι],
ἐγώ θ' ὁ τλήμων βαρβάρους ἀφίξομαι
γέρων μέτοικος· ἔτι δέ μοὐστὶ θέσφατον   1355
εἰς Ἑλλάδ' ἀγαγεῖν μιγάδα βάρβαρον στρατόν·
καὶ τὴν Ἄρεως παῖδ' Ἁρμονίαν δάμαρτ' ἐμὴν

1344. λισσόμεθα P et *Chr. Pat.* 2557 ubi trium codicum scripturam in λισσόμεσθα correxit Duebnerus: λισσόμεσθα ed. Ald.

1344, 6, 8. Agavae restituit Elms., Cadmo dederat P.

1345. ἐμέθεθ'...εἴδετε P: ἐμάθεθ'...ᾔδετε ed. Ald.   'ᾔδετε (in codice ᾔδεται scriptum) ex hoc versu attulit Antiatt. Bekkeri p. 98' (Dind.).
δ' ἐχρῆν P: δὲ χρῆν Wecklein (ut antea, 26).

1347. ἡμῶν P; ὑμῶν Victorius.

1349. τάγε P: τάδε ed. Ald.   ἐπήνεσεν P a manu prima, unde ἐμὸς ἐπήνεσεν Nauckius in *ann. crit.*; ἐπένευσεν P correctus, quod omnes in textum admiserunt.

1350. τήλμονες P: correxit Ald.

1351 per incuriam omisit ed. Ald., e codice primus revocavit Elms.

1353. τε σαὶ P: τε σαὶ φίλαι ed. Ald., τε παῖς τε σὸς Hartung (Dind.); παῖς τε σύγγονοί τε σαὶ Herm.; σύγγονοι θ' ὁμόσποροι Wecklein[1], praeeunte Fixio.   versum ipsum spurium esse censet Paleius; post versum lacunam suspicatur Wecklein.   versus in initio < ἄρθην > Tyrrell.

1355. μοι τὸ P: μοὐστὶ Haupt (Dind., Kirchf.[2], Wecklein).
ἔστι γὰρ τὸ θέσφατον *Chr. Pat.* 1670.

δράκων δρακαίνης σχῆμ' ἔχουσαν ἀγρίας
ἄξω 'πὶ βωμοὺς καὶ τάφους Ἑλληνικούς,
ἡγούμενος λόγχαισιν· οὐδὲ παύσομαι   1360
κακῶν ὁ τλήμων, οὐδὲ τὸν καταιβάτην
Ἀχέροντα πλεύσας ἥσυχος γενήσομαι.

ΑΓ. ὦ πάτερ, ἐγὼ δὲ σοῦ στερεῖσα φεύξομαι.
ΚΑ. τί μ' ἀμφιβάλλεις χερσίν, ὦ τάλαινα παῖ,
ὄρνις ὅπως κηφῆνα πολιόχρων κύκνος;   1365
ΑΓ. ποῖ γὰρ τράπωμαι πατρίδος ἐκβεβλημένη;
ΚΑ. οὐκ οἶδα, τέκνον· μικρὸς ἐπίκουρος πατήρ.

ΑΓ. χαῖρ', ὦ μέλαθρον, χαῖρ', ὦ πατρία
πόλις· ἐκλείπω σ' ἐπὶ δυστυχίᾳ
φυγὰς ἐκ θαλάμων.   1370
ΚΑ. στεῖχέ νυν, ὦ παῖ, τὸν Ἀρισταίου

*   *   *   *   *   *

ΑΓ. στένομαί σε, πάτερ. ΚΑ. κἀγὼ σέ, τέκνον,

1358. φύσιν ἔχουσαν ἀγρίαν ed. Ald.; φύσιν om. P : ἀγρίας maluit
Dobraeus collato *Ion*, 992; σχῆμ' ἔχουσαν ἀγρίας Nauckius *ann. crit.*,
quod in textum admisit Wecklein collato *Med.* 1343. φύσιν Tyrrell.

1363. στερηθεῖσα P : στερεῖσα Barnes.

1365. ὄρνις...πολιόχρως κύκνος P (Elms., Herm., Schoenius, Kirchf.,
Nauck, Tyrrell): ὄρνιθ'...πολιόχροα κύκνον Heath. 'si vero sententiae
convenientior videtur accusativus, nescio an potius scribendum ὄρνιν'
(Elms.); ὄρνις...πολιόχρων κύκνος Musgr. (Dind.); ὄρνιν...πολιόχρως κύκνος
Paley; ὄρνιν...πολιόχρων κύκνον Wecklein. scripserim libentius πτεροῖς
ὅπως κηφῆνα πολιόχρων κύκνος.

1367. σμικρὸς Elms.   1368. πατρῷα P : πατρία Elms.

1371. νῦν P. post hunc versum lacunam indicavit Hermannus.

1371—1392 'ab Euripide alienos esse argumentis docemur certis et
indubiis' Nauck.

1372. στέρομαι P : στένομαι Elms.; σὲ post κἀγὼ, addidit Barnes.

καὶ σὰς ἐδάκρυσα κασιγνήτας.
ΑΓ. δεινῶς γὰρ * τάνδ᾽ αἰκίαν
Διόνυσος ἄναξ   1375
τοὺς σοὺς * εἰς οἴκους ἔφερεν.
ΔΙ. καὶ γὰρ ἔπασχον δεινὰ πρὸς ὑμῶν,
ἀγέρατον ἔχων ὄνομ᾽ ἐν Θήβαις.
ΑΓ. χαῖρε, πάτερ, μοι. ΚΑ. χαῖρ᾽, ὦ μελέα
θύγατερ. χαλεπῶς δ᾽ εἰς τόδ᾽ ἂν ἥκοις.   1380
ΑΓ. ἄγετ᾽ ὦ πομποί με, κασιγνήτας
ἵνα συμφυγάδας ληψόμεθ᾽ οἰκτράς.
ἔλθοιμι δ᾽ ὅπου
μήτε Κιθαιρὼν ἔμ᾽ ἴδοι μιαρός
μήτε Κιθαιρῶν᾽ ὄσσοισιν ἐγώ,   1385
μήθ᾽ ὅθι θύρσου μνῆμ᾽ ἀνάκειται·
Βάκχαις δ᾽ ἄλλαισι μέλοιεν.
ΧΟ. πολλαὶ μορφαὶ τῶν δαιμονίων,

1373. κασιγνήτους P : -τας Brunck.
1374. δεινῶς γὰρ τάνδ᾽ αἰκίαν P : τοι inseruit Herm.*; δεινῶς γὰρ δεινῶς τάνδ᾽ αἰκίαν ed. Ald. δεινῶς δεινῶς τάνδ᾽ αἰκίαν Brunck. δεινῶς γὰρ δεινῶς αἰκίαν Δ. ἅ. τοὺς σοὺς τάνδ᾽ εἰς Schoenius. δεινῶς δεινὰν τάνδ᾽ αἰκίαν Wecklein. δεινὴν δεινὸς κτλ. Herwerden. 'locus corruptissimus' Kirchf.
1375. τοὺς σοὺς εἰς οἴκους P : πάτερ inseruit Herm. (Dind.).
1377. ΔΙ. ἔπασχον P : ΚΑ. ἔπασχεν Herm.
1378. ἀγέρατον P : -αστον Barnes†. ὄνομ᾽ ἔχων P : transposuit ed. Ald.
1379. ὦ περ P : πάτερ ed. Aldina.
1380. δ᾽ addidit Reiskius.
1382. ληψώμεθ᾽ P : correxit Elms.
1384. Κιθαιρὼν μιαρὸς P : μ᾽ ἐσίδοι in fine addidit Musgr. (Elms., Herm., Dind.), medium inserit Wecklein; ἔμ᾽ ἴδοι μιαρὸς mavult Kirchhoffius, monente Schoenio (qui ipse ἔμ᾽ ὁρᾷ inseruit) antithesin pronomini ἐγκλιτικῷ repugnare; etiam Tyrrellius ἔμ᾽ ὁρᾷ (modo indicativo).
1387. βάκχαισι P : βάκχαις ed. Ald. et editores omnes. βάκχαι Madvig. τελεταί Hartmann.   1388—1392 uncinis inclusit Wecklein.

* idem Tyrrell.   † idem Wecklein, Tyrrell.

πολλὰ δ' ἀέλπτως κραίνουσι θεοί·
καὶ τὰ δοκηθέντ' οὐκ ἐτελέσθη,   1390
τῶν δ' ἀδοκήτων πόρον ηὖρε θεός.
τοιόνδ' ἀπέβη τόδε πρᾶγμα.

1391. πόρων P: correxit ed. Aldina. εὗρε P: ηὖρε (Elms., Dind.,
Paley, Tyrrell, Wecklein); cf. 125, 279, 683, 1024.

BAS-RELIEF IN THE BRITISH MUSEUM.

Βάκχη χιμαιροφόνος.

(BAS-RELIEF IN THE BRITISH MUSEUM.)

NOTES.

*In Euripidis Bacchabus superest, nisi fallor, non spicilegium,
sed uberrima messis observationum.*

After BERNHARDY, *Theologumena
Graeca*, III p. 11.

1. ἥκω] is also the first word in the *Troades* and *Hecuba*.

Διὸς παῖς] These words in their emphatic position in the opening line strike the key-note of the prologue and indeed of the whole play. The divinity of Dionysus is denied in the very land of his birth, but that land must learn to own him as the true son of Zeus. The object of the prologue in Poetry, as of the exordium in Rhetoric, is as Aristotle says, to 'pave the way for the sequel' (οἷον ὁδοποίησις τῷ ἐπιόντι), and in both, the special aim of the opening words should be to put the audience at the very outset in possession of a ready clue to the whole of the argument (ὁ δοὺς ὥσπερ εἰς τὴν χεῖρα τὴν ἀρχὴν ποιεῖ ἐχόμενον ἀκολουθεῖν τῷ λόγῳ, Ar. *Rhet.* III 14 § 6). In the case of Euripides in particular, this object is usually attained by means of an uninterrupted monologue in which the plot of the play is unfolded with more or less fulness. In the present instance it will be observed that the prologue gives no hint of the final catastrophe.

2. ὃν τίκτει ποθ' ἡ Κάδμου κόρη] The descriptive or, as it is usually termed, the 'historic' present is here used to give a more vivid statement of the past event than could have been expressed by the ordinary aorist, e.g. by the words ὅν ποτ' ἔτεκεν ἡ Κάδμου κόρη. As the present tense is here applied to a time that is past, it is appropriately combined with the particle of past time ποτέ. Cf. Eur. *Suppl.* 640, Καπανέως γὰρ ἦν λάτρις, ὃν Ζεὺς κεραυνῷ πυρπόλῳ καταιθαλοῖ. So also in *Herc. Fur.* 252, ὦ γῆς λοχεύμαθ' οὓς Ἄρης σπείρει ποτέ. Cf. the use in Greek tragedy of ἡ τίκτουσα for 'the mother' (Soph. *O. T.* 1247 and *El.* 342).

3. λοχευθεῖσ' ἀστραπηφόρῳ πυρί] Bore 'by the midwifery of lightning fire' (*inf.* 88). πυρὶ is equivalent to ὑπὸ πυρός, as in *Ion* 455, Προμαθεῖ λοχευθεῖσαν, *infra* 119, οἰστρηθεὶς Διονύσῳ. ἀστραπή-φορον πῦρ = πῦρ ὑπ' ἀστράπης φερόμενον, flame *sped by* lightning. For the mythological reference to the story of Semele, compare *Anthol. Palatina* III 1, τάνδε Διὸς δμαθεῖσαν ἐν ὠδίνεσσι κεραυνῷ | καλλίκομον Κάδμου παῖδα καὶ Ἁρμονίης, | ματέρα θυρσοχαρῆς ἀνάγει γόνος ἐξ Ἀχέροντος | τὰν ἄθεον Πενθεῦς ὕβριν ἀμυνόμενος. This is the first of a series of epigrams describing the sculptures in the temple erected at Cyzicus by Attalus II and Eumenes in honour of their mother. The first birth of Dionysus is repre-sented in a wall-painting copied in Müller and Wieseler's *Denkmäler der alten Kunst* II xxxiv 391; on the right is the lifeless body of Semele lying prostrate after the untimely birth of the babe whose diminutive form is seen above the mother's body; to the left is a lustral vessel with a napkin and a laurel branch, and above these is Zeus, seated on the clouds, with his eagle beside him, with a glowing *nimbus* round his head, and with one hand armed with the flaming thunderbolt, while the other is stretched towards the newborn babe (the same picture is copied in Lenormant's article on *Bacchus* in the *Dict. des Antiquités*, fig. 677, where it is stated that although doubts as to its authenticity had been recently raised by Overbeck, *Gr. Kunstmyth.* I 418, it had been accepted without suspicion by Gerhard, *Hyperb. Röm. Studien* p. 105). No. 392 in Müller-Wieseler u. s. (fig. 679 in Lenormant's article), shews a relief in three compartments; on the right, Semele resting on a couch and in the back-ground Zeus with his thunder-bolt; on the left, Zeus and Eileithyia, a scene intended to indicate the second birth of Dionysus; in the centre, separated by a Hermes-bust on each side from the other two compartments, is the god Hermes carrying off the infant in the folds of his *chlamys*, while in the back-ground lies a prostrate figure that may represent either Semele or Mother Earth. The most notable description of any pictorial representation of the subject is, however, that given by Philostratus, whose account may here be quoted at length, as several of his touches are probably suggested by this play, and therefore serve in their turn as illustrations of it (εἰκόνες, I § 14, p. 785):

Βροντὴ ἐν εἴδει σκληρῷ καὶ Ἀστραπὴ σέλας ἐκ τῶν ὀφθαλμῶν ἱεῖσα πῦρ τε ῥαγδαῖον ἐξ οὐρανοῦ τυραννικῆς οἰκίας ἐπειλημμένον λόγου τοιοῦδε, εἰ μὴ ἀγνοεῖς, ἅπτεται· πυρὸς νεφέλη περισχοῦσα τὰς Θήβας ἐς τὴν τοῦ Κάδμου στέγην ῥήγνυται κωμάσαντος ἐπὶ τὴν Σεμέλην τοῦ Διός, καὶ ἀπόλλυται μέν, ὡς δοκοῦμεν, ἡ Σεμέλη, τίκτεται δὲ Διόνυσος, οἶμαι, νὴ Δία, πρὸς τὸ πῦρ, καὶ τὸ μὲν τῆς Σεμέλης εἶδος ἀμυδρὸν διεκφαίνεται ἰούσης ἐς οὐρανόν, καὶ αἱ Μοῦσαι αὐτὴν ἐκεῖ ᾄσονται, ὁ δὲ Διόνυσος τῆς μὲν μητρὸς ἐκθρώσκει ῥαγείσης τὴν γαστέρα, τὸ δὲ πῦρ ἀχλυῶδες ἐργάζεται φαιδρὸς αὐτός, οἷον ἀστήρ τις, ἀστράπτων. διασχοῦσα δὲ ἡ φλὸξ ἄντρον τι τῷ Διονύσῳ σκιαγραφεῖ παντὸς ἥδιον Ἀσσυρίου τε καὶ Λυδίου, ἕλικές τε γὰρ περὶ αὐτὸ τεθήλασι καὶ κιττοῦ κόρυμβοι καὶ ἤδη καὶ ἄμπελοι καὶ θύρσου δένδρα οὕτω τι ἐκούσης ἀνασχόντα τῆς γῆς, ὡς κἂν τῷ πυρὶ εἶναι ἔνια. καὶ οὐ χρὴ θαυμάζειν, εἰ στεφανοῖτο πῦρ ἐπὶ τῷ Διονύσῳ ἡ γῆ, ἥ γε καὶ συμβακχεύσει αὐτῷ καὶ οἶνον ἀφύσσειν ἐκ πηγῶν δώσει γάλα τε οἷον ἀπὸ μαζῶν ἕλκειν τὸ μὲν ἐκ βώλου, τὸ δὲ ἐκ πέτρας. ἄκουε τοῦ Πανός, ὡς τὸν Διόνυσον ᾄδειν ἔοικεν ἐν κορυφαῖς τοῦ Κιθαιρῶνος, ὑποσκιρτῶν εὔιον. ὁ Κιθαιρὼν δὲ ὀλοφύρεται ἐν εἴδει ἀνθρώπου τὰ μικρὸν ὕστερον ἐν αὐτῷ ἄχη καὶ κιττοῦ φέρει στέφανον ἀποκλίνοντα τῆς κεφαλῆς, στεφανοῦται γὰρ δὴ αὐτῷ σφοδρα ἄκων, ἐλάτην τε αὐτῷ παραφυτεύει Μέγαιρα καὶ πηγὴν ἀναφαίνει ὕδατος ἐπὶ τῷ Ἀκταίωνος, οἶμαι, καὶ Πενθέως αἵματι.

The death of Semele is the subject of the gem placed at the head of the prologue in this edition.

4. μορφὴν ἀμείψας...βροτησίαν] So in l. 53, εἶδος θνητὸν ἀλλάξας. In the sense of *'taking* in change,' the middle is more common. The ambiguous uses of ἀμείβειν as well as ἀλλάττειν may be paralleled by similar ambiguities in the meaning of *muto*.

5. πάρειμι] from εἰμί, *sum.* The sense of motion is here conveyed by the preposition and not by the simple verb. For παρεῖναι with the accusative compare *Cyclops* 95, πόθεν πάρεισι Σικελὸν Αἰτναῖον πάγον, and 106, πόθεν Σικελίαν τήνδε ναυστολῶν πάρει; *Electra* 1278, Ναυπλίαν παρών (= μολών).—Δίρκης νάματ' Ἰσμηνοῦ θ' ὕδωρ] From these two streams the name of διπόταμος πόλις is given to Thebes (*Suppl.* 621); cf. *Phoen.* 825, διδύμων ποταμῶν πόρον ἀμφὶ μέσον Δίρκας, χλοεροτρόφον ἃ πεδίον πρόπαρ Ἰσμηνοῦ καταδεύει, and *Herc. Fur.* 572, νεκρῶν ἅπαντ' Ἰσμηνὸν ἐμπλήσω φόνου, Δίρκης τε νᾶμα λευκὸν αἱμαχθήσεται. The Ismenus was the eastern of the two streams, and the waters of Dirce fall into the former north of the town (Leake's *Northern*

Greece, II 237). For Dirce cf. 519—536 *infra*, and Pindar, *Isthm.* vi = V *ult.*, πίσω σφε Δίρκας ἀγνὸν ὕδωρ, τὸ βαθύζωνοι κόραι χρυσοπέπλου Μναμοσύνας ἀνέτειλαν παρ' εὐτειχέσι Κάδμου πύλαις.

6. **μητρὸς μνῆμα**] 'My mother's monument, the thunder-slain.' This legendary spot was still pointed out to travellers, as late as the second century of our era, when it was seen by Pausanias, who remarks τοῦτον δὲ καὶ ἐς ἡμᾶς ἔτι ἄβατον φυλάσσουσιν ἀνθρώποις (IX 12, 3). A part of the ancient *agora* was supposed to occupy the exact site of the dwelling of Cadmus. Here were shewn ruins of the bed-chambers of Harmonia and Semele, and a piece of wood adorned with brass by one of Semele's brothers, Polydorus, which was called 'Dionysus Cadmeius,' and was said to have fallen from heaven when Semele was struck dead by lightning. Near the gates called Proetides was the theatre, and adjoining to it a temple of Dionysus Lysius, which contained statues of Dionysus and of Semele (Pausanias IX 16, 6; Leake's *Northern Greece*, II 235, 236). For μητρὸς... κεραννίας, cf. Soph. *Ant.* 1139, ματρὶ σὺν κεραυνίᾳ (Schol. κεραυνο-βλήτῳ), *infra* 598, κεραυνόβολος.

8. **τυφόμενα Δίου πυρὸς ἔτι ζῶσαν φλόγα**] 'Smouldering With the still living flame of fire divine.' There seems to be no real difficulty in taking φλόγα as an accusative of cognate sense after the middle (or passive) participle τυφόμενα, the latter being equivalent in general meaning to ἀμυδρῶς φλέγοντα, and the transition between 'smouldering' and 'dimly burning' being quite natural. *Non dubium est autem*, says Hermann, *quin recte τύφεσθαι cum accusativo eius rei construi possit, quam prodit fumus; nam τύφειν φλόγα is dicitur qui excitat ignem: τύφεσθαι autem, quod est* subdito igne fumare, *si additum habet* φλόγα, *necessario significabit* prodere subditum ignem fumando.—The line is in a manner quoted by Plutarch, *Solon* c. 1, παρεφύλαξε τυφομένην ἀδροῦ πυρὸς ἔτι ζῶσαν φλόγα τὴν ἐρωτικὴν μνήμην καὶ χάριν. Hence it is concluded that Plutarch probably read τυφό-μεν' ἀδροῦ τε πυρὸς ἔτι ζῶσαν φλόγα, where the insertion of τε is supported by the fact that the two MSS have δίου τε. As however ἀδρὸς is never used in Greek Tragedy, it seems better to suppose that Plutarch was (whether consciously or not) adapting the passage to his immediate purpose, and to accept Δίου πυρός, striking out τε. Its insertion may be accounted for by its similarity to τι or π, the first letter of the next word. Δίου πυρός, 'the fire of *Zeus*,' is supported by the emphatic reference to Zeus in the first line, and also by the contrast brought out~by Δίου between Zeus in the present line and Hera in the next. The forgers of the thunderbolts of Zeus are called τέκτονας Δίου πυρὸς in *Alc.* 5 (cf. *Alc.* 128, Διόβολον πλῆκτρον πυρὸς κεραυνίου); and at a later point in this play, where the smouldering flame that is here playing around the tomb of Semele is kindled into brightness, that flame is described as the φλόγα Δίου βροντᾶς (599). In Eur. *Suppl.* 860 (on the death of Capaneus), ὁρᾶς τὸ δῖον οὗ βέλος διέπτατο, restored from Polybius, is in the MSS corrupted into ὁρᾶς τὸν ἀβρόν.

9. ἀθάνατον...ὕβριν] 'Hera's immortal despite 'gainst my mother :' immortal, in so far as it was the *enduring* mark of her proud scorn of Semele. This is supported by ἔτι ζῶσαν in the previous line. We have πυρὸς ἐξ ἀθανάτου in 524, and, without excluding the above meaning, there is something to be said in favour of making the line equivalent in sense (as Mr Paley expresses it) to ὕβριν ἀθανάτου θεᾶς εἰς θνητὴν μητέρα.—For the acc. in apposition to the whole of the previous sentence, cf. 30, σοφίσμαθ', 250, πολὺν γέλων, 1100, στόχον δύστηνον, and 1232, ὄψιν οὐκ εὐδαίμονα. It is particularly common in Euripides. Kühner's *Gk. Gr.* § 406. 6.

10. ἄβατον] opp. to βέβηλον. Cf. Pausanias, quoted on l. 6. Places touched by lightning were regarded as sacred. Such spots were sometimes called ἐνηλύσια, as in Aesch. *fragm.* 15, of the place where Capaneus was struck dead; ἐνηλύσια λέγεται εἰς ἃ κεραυνὸς εἰσβέβηκεν ἃ καὶ ἀνατίθεται Διὶ καταιβάτῃ καὶ λέγεται ἄδυτα καὶ ἄβατα (Etym. Magn.). Cf. the Roman *bidental*.

11. σηκόν] a sacred enclosure or τέμενος. Hesychius explains it by τάφος· ναός, referring either to this passage or more probably to *Phoen.* 1752, Βρόμιος σηκὸς ἄβατος ὄρεσι μαινάδων, where the Scholiast says ὁ τάφος τῆς Σεμέλης...σηκὸς δὲ ὁ ναὸς.. —ἐγώ in the next line stands in pointed contrast with Κάδμον above. 'All praise to *Cadmus*, who untrodden keeps This spot,

92 *BACCHAE.* [11

his daughter's chapel; but 'twas *I* That veiled it round with the fresh clustering vine.'

13. Λυδῶν τοὺς πολυχρύσους γύας...] 'Lydia's and Phrygia's tilths that teem with gold.' *Iph. Aul.* 787 (a play of the same date as the *Bacchae*), αἱ πολύχρυσοι Λυδαὶ καὶ Φρυγῶν ἄλοχοι. Cf. 154, Τμώλου χρυσορόου χλιδά, and Herod. v 101, there quoted. —**14. πλάκας**] acc. after ἐπελθών, not after λιπών. Dionysus, after leaving his early haunts in Lydia and Phrygia, and advancing victoriously over Persia, Bactria, Media, Arabia and 'Asia,' comes to Thebes first in all the land of Greece.—**15. δύσχιμον**] The bleak climate of Media is described by Herod. III 8, who in the same chapter refers to the worship of Dionysus in Arabia.—'Asia' is used in its limited sense, referring especially to the west coast of Asia Minor: this is clearly shewn by the context with its mention of the Greek colonies of the sea-board, happily described by Cicero, in a reference to those colonies in general, as a 'fringe upon the robe of barbarism' (*quasi attexta quaedam barbarorum oris, De Rep.* II 4 § 9; Isocr. *Paneg.* § 162). It is an obvious anachronism to make a speaker in the time of Cadmus refer to colonies that were not planted till many generations later.

18. μιγάσιν] A tribrach falling exactly into a single word is rare in Greek tragedy. Cf. however βότρυος (261), ἱερὸς (494), χιόνος (662).—**19. πλήρεις**] here with the instrumental dative, instead of the usual genitive *Herc. Fur.* 372, πεύκαισιν χέρας πληροῦντες, similarly *Or.* 1363, δακρύοισι γὰρ Ἑλλάδ' ἅπασαν ἔπλησε, contrasted with 368, δακρύων δ' ἔπλησεν ἐμέ. Aesch. *S. C. T.* 464, πνεύμασιν πληρούμενοι.

21. κἀκεῖ] i.e. *in Asia also* (with Hermann, *illic quoque*). But κἀκεῖ, it must be admitted, would more naturally be taken as *atque illic,* and this would involve either (*a*) accepting the transposition κἀκεῖ χορεύσας—βροτοῖς, εἰς τήνδε πρῶτον ἦλθον Ἑλλήνων πόλιν (proposed by Pierson and adopted by Elmsley); or (*b*) supposing that a line is lost after 22, e.g. πολλοὺς ἔπεισα τῶν ἐμῶν νόμων κλύειν (as suggested by Mr Paley); or (*c*) transferring to this place line 54, μορφὴν ἐμὴν μετέβαλον εἰς ἀνδρὸς φύσιν (with Mr S. Allen, supported by Mr Tyrrell). The objec-

tion to (*a*) on the ground of its apparent tautology with the line
that would on this supposition follow next in order, πρώτας δὲ
Θήβας τῆσδε γῆς Ἑλληνίδος, is not, I think, insuperable. It
seems not unnatural to take the clause that forms the goal of
the long period immediately preceding, and resume it (with
some slight variation) as the starting-point of a fresh departure.
(*c*), as Mr Paley excellently points out, is open to grave objec-
tions, '(1) the fact would thus be stated three times over; cf. 4
and 53. (2) It is very improbable that, if the verse belonged to
this place, it should have been wrongly transferred after 53.
(3) It is not a tautology in its ordinary place, because εἶδος
θνητὸν is not necessarily a human form.'

24. ἀνωλόλυξα] '*Thebes* have I first Thrilled with glad shouts,'
'filled with the cries of women.' ὀλολυγὴ (unlike *ululatus*) is a
joyous shout, and generally of *women* calling on the gods. In
line 689 where Agave rouses her fellow-Bacchanals from slumber,
the word used is ὠλόλυξεν. The present passage is perhaps the
only place where the word occurs in a causal sense.

νεβρίδ' ἐξάψας χροός] sc. αὐτῶν, the Theban women, implied in
Θήβας. The fawnskin was one of the special characteristics of
Dionysus and his female votaries, while the skin of the panther
was more commonly worn by the Satyrs and other male companions of the wine-god, as well as by the god himself. It is
generally represented in works of ancient art as fastened over
one of the shoulders and slung across the chest, with the larger
portion of its folds falling over the side below the other
shoulder, as may be seen in the illustrations to this volume.
The use of these skins was naturally associated with the mountain haunts and the pursuits of the chase, which were a favourite
pastime of the followers of the god. Cf. *infra*, 111, στικτῶν
νεβρίδων, 137, νεβρίδος ἱερὸν ἐνδυτόν, 249, ποικίλαισι νεβρίσι, 835,
νεβροῦ στικτὸν δέρας, also 176, νεβρῶν δοράς, and 696, νεβρίδας ἀνεστείλανθ' ὅσαισιν ἁμμάτων σύνδεσμ' ἐλέλυτο καὶ καταστίκτους δορὰς
ὄφεσιν κατεζώσαντο. *Hel.* 1375, μέγα τοι δύναται νεβρῶν παμποί-
κιλοι στολίδες, *Phoen.* 1753, Καδμείαν νεβρίδα στολιδωσαμένα ποτ'
ἐγὼ Σεμέλας ἱερὸν θίασον ὄρεσιν ἀνεχόρευσα. The god himself is
called νεβριδόστολος in the Orphic hymn 52, 10; Lucian (III

p. 75, ed. Reitz), *Dionysus* § 1, γυναῖκες νεβρίδας ἐνημμέναι. Cf.
fragment of the *Bacchae* of Attius XIV (12), *tunc silvestrum
exuvias laevo pictas lateri accommodant*, Nonnus *Dionysiaca* XI
233, ὑψόθεν ὤμου νεβρίδα καὶ ψυχροῖσιν ἐπὶ στέρνοισι καθάψας.
(Many other references are given in Schoene, *de personarum
in Euripidis Bacchabus habitu scenico* pp. 79—88 ; also in
Mitchell's n. on Ar. *Ranae*, 1176.)

25. θύρσον] The *thyrsus* was a light wand with its head
covered with a bunch of ivy or vine-leaves, or the cone of a
fir-tree, or with cone and leaves combined. Sometimes a sharp
spike was imbedded in the upper part of the stick, and in this
case the fir-cone would serve as a cap to conceal the point and
to protect the Bacchanal from being hurt by it (the spike is
exposed to view in a bas-relief in the Vatican, Visconti *Museo
Pio-Clementino*, IV pl. 29). In works of ancient art all these
ways of decorating the head of the *thyrsus* are represented,
and the upper part is often bound with ribbands or *fasciae*,
the object of which, apart from ornament, was probably to keep
the stick from being split up by the insertion of the spike or
fir-cone at the top.

The *thyrsus* is often mentioned in the course of the play,
e.g. 80, ἀνὰ θύρσον τινάσσων, 188, θύρσῳ κροτῶν γῆν. Cf. *Herc.
Fur.* 892, κατάρχεται χόρευμα τυμπάνων ἄτερ, οὐ Βρομίῳ κεχα-
ρισμένα θύρσῳ, *Cyclops* 62 (chorus of Satyrs), οὐ τάδε Βρόμιος,
οὐ τάδε χοροί, Βάκχαι τε θυρσοφόροι, οὐ τυμπάνων ἀλαλαγμοί.
Anthol. Pal. VI 165, θύρσου χλοερὸν κωνοφόρου κάμακα, and often
in Nonnus ὀξὺς θύρσος, *id.* IX 122, αὐτὴ δ᾿ ἔπλεκε θύρσον ὁμόζυγον
οἴνοπι κισσῷ, ἀκροτάτῳ δὲ σίδηρον ἐπεσφήκωσε κορύμβῳ, κευθόμενον
πετάλοισιν ὅπως μὴ Βάκχον ἀμύξῃ. Catullus LXIV 256, *tecta
quatiebant cuspide thyrsos*, Statius *Achill.* II 175, *thyrsi teretes*,
Theb. II 665, *fragiles*, Ovid *Met.* VI 594, *levis hasta*, and esp.
Virg. *Aen.* VII 390, *molles tibi sumere thyrsos*, and 396, *pampi-
neasque gerunt, incinctae pellibus, hastas.*

κίσσινον βέλος] *infra* 363, κισσίνου βάκτρου, 710, κισσίνων θύρσων, *Ion* 217, Βρόμιος ἄλλον ἀπολέμοις κισσίνοισι βάκτροις ἐναίρει
γᾶς τέκνων ὁ Βακχεύς. Both the MSS have μέλος, which is
retained in Mr Tyrrell's edition alone; all other editors have

accepted βέλος which is due to Henry Stephens; but instead of honestly putting forward the correction as an emendation of his own, which on its own merits, would have at once carried conviction with it, he actually condescended to the statement that he had found this reading in his 'Italian MSS,' which, it is now generally agreed, had no existence except in his own imagination. In spite of the falsehood which accompanied the first announcement of this correction, we are willing to accept it as a conjecture which supplies a true restoration of the original text. Mr Tyrrell, however, prints Κίσσινον μέλος ἀνωλόλυξα, where the verb is made to govern μέλος as well as Θήβας, the intervening words being parenthetical. But, in the first place, the construction thus gained is harsh; and in the second, there is no ground for his assumption that the Kissian minstrels of Susa 'though generally spoken of as mourners (Aesch. *Pers.* 17, 123, and *Cho.* 415), no doubt sang all kinds of orgiastic strains'; and lastly, beyond the general fact that Dionysus passed through Persia, there is no proof alleged of any connexion whatever between him and the Kissians in particular. Had there been any such point of contact, surely the Kissians would have been named by Nonnus, somewhere or other, in the forty-eight books of his Epic poem on the adventures of Dionysus. While Mr Tyrrell's advocacy of the claims of the manuscript reading μέλος does not appear to be entirely successful, his reasons for not accepting the conjecture βέλος also fail to convince us. His first allegation is that Euripides never applies βέλος to a *thyrsus;* this we at once admit, but what we are defending in the present instance is, the applicability to the *thyrsus*, not of the bare word βέλος, but the full phrase κίσσινον βέλος, where the epithet may be regarded as one of the well-known class of 'limiting' epithets (of which πτηνὸς κύων is an exaggerated instance), in all of which the metaphorical use of the substantive is made possible by the adjective attached to it. Thus the weak wand that is wielded by the votaries of the god is here metaphorically described as a weapon,—a weapon not of war, but wreathed with ivy (cf. ἀπολέμοις κισσίνοισι βάκτροις in the passage quoted above).

The descriptive touch is most natural when we remember that the *thyrsus* is here mentioned for the first time in the play. Again, θύρσοις ὡπλισμένοι, in 733, shews that the poet regarded it as a weapon or missile (cf. 1099); and further in the *Dionysiaca* of Nonnus, a poem of special importance for the illustration of this play, we find in the 43rd book alone, κισσοφόροις βελέμνοις, κισσῆεν ἔγχος, θύρσος ἀκοντιστήρ, and χερείονα θύρσον ἐάσας δίζεό σοι βέλος ἄλλο. Lastly, when Mr Tyrrell states twice over that θύρσος is expressly distinguished from βέλος in line 761, he omits to notice that the *thyrsus* is there contrasted not with βέλος merely, but with λογχωτὸν βέλος. (Part of this criticism has already appeared in my review of Mr Tyrrell's edition in the *Academy* for April 1, 1872, Vol. iii p. 138.)*

In cursive MSS the characters for μ and β are particularly liable to be confounded with one another, β being often written as μ, *minus* the lower part of the first stroke. Thus in a *facsimile* given in Bast's *Commentatio Palaeographica*, βάρβαροι appears as μάρμαροι. So in l. 678 for μόσχων I should prefer to read βόσκων.

29. εἰς Ζῆν' ἀναφέρειν τὴν ἁμαρτίαν λέχους] 'Fathered on Zeus her maidenhood's mischance.' For ἀναφέρειν, in the sense of casting off responsibility from oneself and laying it at another's door, cf. *Or.* 76, εἰς Φοῖβον ἀναφέρουσα τὴν ἁμαρτίαν, *ib.* 432, *Iph. T.* 390, *Ion* 543 and 827; Lysias *contra Eratosthenem* § 64, τὰς ἀπολογίας εἰς ἐκεῖνον ἀναφερομένας, *de olea sacra* § 17, εἴ τις αὐτοὺς ᾐτιᾶτο, εἶχον ἀνενεγκεῖν (τὸ πρᾶγμα), ὅτῳ παρέδοσαν (τὸ χωρίον).†—τὴν ἁμαρτίαν λέχους, instead of the more regular collocation τὴν λέχους ἁμαρτίαν, may be defended (as Mr Tyrrell well observes) on the ground that the two words combine to form one idea, and are therefore treated as practically equivalent to a single word. Paley proposes the tempting, but perhaps needless, correction, ΤΗΝΔ' ἁΜΑΡΤΙΑΝ ; where τήνδε would refer back to νυμφευθεῖσαν ἐκ θνητοῦ τινος in the previous line.
—30. Κάδμου σοφίσμαθ'] The sisters of Semele held that the story of Dionysus being the son of Zeus was a mere tale trumped up by Cadmus to screen his daughter's fall. For the acc. of apposition which is frequent in Euripides, cf. note on l. 9, ὕβριν.

* Prof. Tyrrell has since withdrawn his suggestion.
+ Ar. *Nubes*, 1080, ἐς τὸν Δί' ἐπανενεγκεῖν.

32. νιν αὐτάς] *eas ipsas* (Elmsley), those very sisters of Semele, as contrasted with all the rest of the women of Thebes (πᾶν τὸ θῆλυ σπέρμα Καδμείων). The words ᾤστρησα μανίαις in the present, and παράκοποι φρενῶν in the next line, find their parallel in the *Attis* of Catullus LXIII 4, *stimulatus ibi furenti rabie, vagus animis.* This is one of the many passages in Catullus, which prove his intimate familiarity with this play (a point to which special attention was drawn by Mr George O'Connor). For other instances cf. notes on 59, 472, 506, 987 and 1056, and see especially the fine description in LXIV 251—264.— **35, 36.** These lines are thus translated by Attius; *deinde omni stirpe cum incluta Cadmeide Vagant matronae percitae insania* (Bacchae I (5)).—ὅσαι γυναῖκες ἦσαν is best taken, not as referring to grown-up women (Paley), but as an emphatic repetition of the words πᾶν τὸ θῆλυ σπέρμα (Tyrrell) ; the latter, as was remarked by the late Master of Trinity, is supported by the fact that ἦσαν is written, not εἰσίν. 'And all the womenfolk of Cadmus' race, Aye each and all, I drave from home distraught.'

38. ''Neath the pale firs, on the roofless rocks they sit.' The ἐλάται are not referred to at random, but are part of the accurate local colouring of the play ; even at the present day the silver fir is one of the characteristic trees of mount Cithaeron ; and the modern name of the range is Ἐλατί. In strict keeping with this, the chorus calls on Thebes to play the true bacchanal with boughs of oak and *fir* (110); and hence too, when Pentheus goes to spy out the revellers on the hills, the poet appropriately places him on an ἐλάτη, 1064—74 (Wordsworth's *Athens and Attica*, p. 14). Cf. 684, 816. 'Cithaeron,' says Dodwell, 'is now shrouded by deep gloom and dreary desolation...it is barren or covered only with dark stunted shrubs; towards the summit, however, it is crowned with forests of fir, from which it derives its modern name of Elatea' (quoted in Cramer's *Greece* II 219). So also Col. Leake, *Northern Greece* II 372, after referring to the 'wild rocks and the dark pine-forests of Cithaeron,' states that '*Elatiá* is the name of the two great peaks above *Plataea.*'

42. 'To mortals proved a god, her son by Zeus.' For τίκτει cf. note on l. 2. **43.** γέρας καὶ τυραννίδα] 'his throne and all its rights,' or prerogatives. Thuc. I 13, πρότερον ἦσαν ἐπὶ ῥητοῖς γέρασι πατρικαὶ βασιλεῖαι.

45. θεομαχεῖ] *infra* 325, 1255. The only place besides, in which Euripides uses the word, is in a play of the same date, *Iph. Aul.* 1409, τὸ θεομαχεῖν ἀπολιποῦσα. It is remarked by Donaldson with reference to the *Bacchae* that its 'solemn warning against the dangers of a self-willed θεομαχία seems to have made this drama highly suggestive to those intelligent and educated Jews, who first had a misgiving with regard to the wisdom of their opposition to Christianity' (*Theatre of the Greeks,* p. 151). Cf. Acts V. 39 μήποτε καὶ θεομάχοι εὑρεθῆτε.

46. ἐν εὐχαῖς οὐδαμοῦ μνείαν ἔχει] 'In all his prayers *nowhere* remembers me,' finds no place for me in his petitions, makes no mention of me anywhere, neither in the first nor second nor third place. Aesch. *Supp.* 266, μνήμην ποτ' ἀντίμισθον ηὕρετ' ἐν λιταῖς. οὐδαμοῦ, the reading of one of the MSS (the Palatine), seems better than οὐδαμῶς which is given by the other. The former is confirmed by the author of the *Christus Patiens,* 1571.

49. τἀνθένδε θέμενος εὖ] *Hipp.* 709, ἐγὼ γὰρ τἀμὰ θήσομαι καλῶς, and *Iph. Aul.* 672, θέμενος εὖ τἀκεῖ. The position of εὖ in this verse, coupled as it is in sense with the preceding θέμενος, instead of the succeeding μεταστήσω, weakens the effect of the usual break in the line at the end of the fifth half-foot, and cuts it into two equal portions, a form of verse which is generally avoided. As other instances of εὖ in an exactly similar position we have Soph. *Ai.* 1252, ἀλλ' οἱ φρονοῦντες εὖ | κρατοῦσι πανταχοῦ, and Aesch. *Eum.* 87, σθένος δὲ ποιεῖν εὖ | φερέγγυον τὸ σόν.

52. συνάψω] sc. μάχην, which is expressed in *Phoen.* 1230, συνάψω συγγόνῳ τῷ 'μῷ μάχην, similarly below, 837, συμβαλὼν μάχην. For the dative, μαινάσι στρατηλατῶν, cf. Eur. *El.* 321, Ἕλλησιν ἐστρατηλάτει, and, for the sense as well as the construction, Aesch. *Eum.* 25, ἐξ οὗτε βάκχαις ἐστρατήγησεν θεός.

53, 54. These two lines at first sight mean much the same thing, and we may almost say of Euripides, as Euripides himself in the *Ranae* (1154) says of Aeschylus, δὶς ταὐτὸν ἡμῖν εἶπεν. To remove this tautology, it has been proposed to read ὧν οὕνεκ' εἶδος θνητὸν ἀλλάξας ἐγὼ (for ἔχω) μορφὴν ἐμὴν μετέβαλον εἰς ἀνδρὸς φύσιν (Hermann); it has also been suggested to place the second line after line 22 (by Mr S. Allen, approved by Mr Tyrrell). But, as has already been observed, εἶδος θνητὸν is ambiguous, and ἀλλάξας is uncertain in sense, and thus the second line may very well have been added to clear up the first. Such a redundancy of expression is quite allowable in this particular part of the ῥῆσις, as the two lines in question close a distinctive portion of it with a couplet summing up the general sense of the speech up to this point. The effect of this parallelism of sense is very like that of the parallelism of sound at the end of Shakespeare's speeches, which often close with a rhyming couplet.

55—63. The rest of the prologue is addressed to the Chorus, which is made up of a troop of Asiatic women who have accompanied the speaker during his travels, but regard him only as a fellow-votary of the god and not as the god himself. The god does not reveal himself until line 1340, ταῦτ' οὐχὶ θνητοῦ πατρὸς ἐκγεγὼς λέγω Διόνυσος ἀλλὰ Ζηνός.

Τμῶλον] called ἱερὸς in 65, and ἀνθεμώδης in 462. The mountain was famous for the vines that grew on its slopes, Virg. *Georg.* 2, 98, *Tmolius assurgit quibus et rex ipse Phanaeus;* Ovid *Met.* VI 15, *vineta Timoli*, Seneca *Phoen.* 602 = 240, *nota Baccho Tmolus attollit iuga.*

56. θίασος] specially used of the revel-band of the votaries of Dionysus. *infra* 558, θυρσοφορεῖς θιάσους, 680, 1180. As an example of vowel-change from υ to ι it stands in the same relation to θυιάδες as δρία to δρῦς and σίαλος to σῦς; the root is ΘΥ which appears in θύω, θύελλα, θυά-(δ)-s, θυι-άς. For the termination, cf. πέτ-ασος (G. Curtius *Gk. Etym.* § 320 and p. 671 ed. 3). It thus appears that it is unnecessary to suppose that the word was 'not truly Greek, but Asiatic.'

57. παρέδρους...ξυνεμπόρους] not necessarily synonymous, as the latter expresses companionship in travel, the former in rest and repose. This distinction may be brought out by the rendering 'comrades in rest and march.'

58. 'Take the home-music of your Phrygian land.' πόλει

need not refer to any particular town; in the *Ion* 294, Euripides calls the island Euboea a πόλις. Some however would attempt to identify this πόλις either with Berecynthus, a town of the tribe of Berecyntes which only exists in a late lexicon, or with Pessinus (where the image of Cybele fell from heaven) which has a much better claim.

59. The reading τύμπανα is open to question, as the final *a* would be lengthened before ρ, and the first foot would thus become a cretic. It is therefore probable that we should adopt the less common form τύπανα, making an anapaest in the first foot, as printed by Nauck, and also proposed by Shilleto, '*An* τύπανα?' In a fragment of the Ἠδωνοὶ of Aeschylus, a drama belonging to a tetralogy on the doom of Lycurgus, which owing to its kindred subject must have in several points resembled the present play, we have τυπάνου δ᾽ εἰκὼν ὥσθ᾽ ὑπογαίου | βροντῆς φέρεται βαρυταρβής (fragm. 55), cf. Homeric hymn XIV 3, τυπάνων τ᾽ ἰαχή, Diogenes, quoted below, and *Hel.* 1346, τύπανα (so emended) βυρσοτενῆ. So also in Catullus, who (as already noticed) was specially familiar with the Bacchae, *Attis* (LXIII) 10, *leve typanum, typanum, tubam Cybelles, tua, mater, initia.* The fuller form is found *infra* 156, *Cyclops* 65, 205, and fragm. 589, Θύσαν Διονύσου κόραν, ὃς ἀν᾽ Ἴδαν τέρπεται σὺν ματρὶ φίλᾳ τυμπάνων ἰάκχοις. The last fragment is preserved by Strabo (X p. 470), who quotes it side by side with the present passage and large portions of the following chorus, as an example of the association of the rites of Dionysus with those of Cybele.—The instrument was a kind of timbrel or tambourine, and was made of a 'wooden hoop covered on one side with hide, like a sieve, and [sometimes] set round with small bells or jingles' (Rich, *Dict. Antiq.*)*, cf. Lucr. II 618, *tympana tenta tonant palmis,* and *Anth. Pal.* VI 51, where cymbals and flutes and sounding timbrels (τύμπανα ἠχήεντα) are dedicated to the Mother Goddess; *infra* 126, βυρσότονον κύκλωμα, 507, βύρσης κτύπος, and 159 sqq. Cf. Diogenes tragicus ap. Athenaeum, XIV 636 a, a *locus classicus* on similar instruments too long for quotation in full, καίτοι κλύω μὲν Ἀσιάδας μιτρηφόρους Κυβέλας γυναῖκας, παῖδας ὀλβίων Φρυγῶν, τυπάνοισι καὶ ῥόμβοισι καὶ χαλκοκτύπων βόμβοις βρεμού-

---

* Bartoli and Bellori, *Lucerne Antiche,* 1692, fol. 23; Pacichelli, de Tintinnabulo Nolano 1693, pp. 9, 10 (J. J. Raven).

σας ἀντίχερσι κυμβάλων. The τύμπανον is often represented in works of ancient art, and may be seen in the vase-painting from the Museum at Naples, which supplies one of the illustrations in the introduction to this volume (p. xxxii, cf. p. 85).

60. The scene is laid before the palace of Pentheus.—ὡς ὁρᾷ, 'may come and see.' **62.** πτυχάς] an expressive word for the 'glens' or 'rifted sides' of Cithaeron. The wind-swept mountain-clefts are called πτύχες ἠνεμόεσσαι in the Iliad (11, 77), and ἐν πολυπτύχῳ χθονὶ is applied in *Iph. T.* 677, to the rugged region of Phocis. πτυχάς (from πτυχή, which is certainly the form used by Eur. in lines 797, 1219, and in other plays where πτυχαῖς occurs), is Elmsley's correction for πτύχας, from πτύξ. Mr Paley rightly remarks that 'an undoubted instance of the final -χας made long before a vowel would be an evidence of some weight'; the evidence which he seeks may be found in Soph. fragm. 150, where γραμμάτων πτυχὰς (MS πτύχας) ἔχων closes an iambic line.

64. 'Ασίας] Though Asia has here a wider meaning than in the Homeric poems, it is interesting to notice that south and west of the very Tmolus mentioned in the next line, lay the old 'Asian meadow, around the streams of Cayster' (Il. 2, 461).— On Tmolus, see notes on lines 55 and 154.

65. θοάζω Βρομίῳ πόνον ἡδύν] 'In Bromius' honour I ply in haste my pleasant task, my toilless toil, the Bacchic god adoring.' θοάζειν (θοός, θέω) almost always means 'to speed,' and like its English equivalent is sometimes intransitive, as in line 218, ἐν δὲ δασκίοις ὄρεσι θοάζειν, *Tro.* 307 (and 349), μαινὰς θοάζει δεῦρο Κασσάνδρα δρόμῳ,—sometimes transitive, as here and *Iph. T.* 1141, θ. πτέρυγας, and *Herc. Fur.* 382, θ. σῖτα γένυσιν. One objection to following Elmsley in making it intransitive in the present passage, is that πόνον ἡδὺν κάματόν τ' εὐκάματον thereby becomes an acc. of general apposition, and such a construction, however common in Euripides, is usually more briefly expressed and generally comes at the very end of the sentence, whereas here it would be followed by the words Βάκχιον εὐαζομένα [θεόν]. The word *appears* to be used as equivalent to θάσσειν in Soph. *O. T.* 2, ἕδρας θοάζετε, and Aesch. *Suppl.* 595, and if the double sense of 'speeding' and 'resting' is to be allowed, the word is almost as puzzling to ourselves as our own 'fast,' used of running fast as well as standing fast, is to a foreigner; with this difference, however, that in our English word the notion of firmness and closeness passes off into that of steady swiftness; in the Greek the word that almost invariably indicates rapidity of movement seems conversely to be used in a very exceptional sense of rest. (Buttmann assumes a double root, while Hermann endeavours to bring the exceptions under the same sense as that in ordinary use.)—For the dat. Βρομίῳ, cf. 195, 494, and esp. *Helen.* 1364, βακχεύουσά τ᾿ ἔθειρα Βρομίῳ.— πόνον ἡ- δὺν κάματόν τ᾿ εὐκάματον is a 'labour of love.' So in the *Tempest* III i, *There be some sports are painful, and their labour, Delight in them sets off...These sweet thoughts do even refresh my labours.*

68—71. The chorus solemnly preface their praise of the Bacchic mysteries by warning all profane persons to depart, whether in the highway or in the hall, and by calling for solemn silence. Thus Callimachus begins his hymn to Apollo with the words, οἷον ὁ τὠπόλλωνος ἐσείσατο δάφνινος ὄρπηξ, οἷα δ᾿ ὅλον τὸ μέλαθρον· ἑκάς, ἑκάς, ὅστις ἀλιτρός. Cf. the opening of the μυστῶν χορός in Ar. *Ranae*, a play of about the same date as the present, 355, εὐφημεῖν χρὴ κἀξίστασθαι τοῖς ἡμετέροισι χοροῖσιν ὅστις ἄπειρος τοιῶνδε λόγων, ἢ γνώμῃ μὴ καθαρεύει, ἢ γενναίων ὄργια Μουσῶν μήτ᾿ εἶδεν μήτ᾿ ἐχόρευσεν.—**69.** στόμα τ᾿ εὔφημον, κ.τ.λ.] 'hushed be every lip to holy silence.' For the proleptic epithet, cf. Aesch. *Ag.* 1247, εὔφημον ὦ τάλαινα κοίμησον στόμα; for the sense, *Eum.* 1039, εὐφαμεῖτε πανδαμί, and Horace's *favete linguis.*—**70.** τὰ νομισθέντα ἀεί] 'in ever wonted wise.' For the neuter plural adverbially used, cf. 157, εὔια. Hermann accepts the conjecture of Jacobs, εὐοῖ for ἀεί, and calls it *praeclara atque haud dubie vera...Id ipsum est* τὸ νομισθέν, εὐοῖ *clamari.* ἀεί *quidem neque cum* τὰ νομισθέντα, *neque cum* ὑμνήσω, *apte coniungi potest.* I confess I see little difficulty in either of the last alternatives, and the wild exclamation εὐοῖ, proposed by Hermann, strikes one as out of keeping with the quiet composure that ought to mark an exordium, though quite in place in later parts of the chorus (141, 157), when the enthusiasm of the audience has already been raised to a higher pitch of expectation.—The last word of the antistrophe is doubtful; ὑμνήσω cannot correspond in metre with the strophe ending with ἀζομένα (or εὐαζομένα) [θεόν], unless the first syllable is treated as short. In a play of the same date, *Iph. Aul.* 1573, the MSS give us ᾿Αγαμέμνων, which is corrected by the editors; but there is little difficulty in such a case as that last quoted, or in μεμνῆσθαι (Aesch. *Pers.* 287), as compared with the violence done to the organs of speech in the endeavour to pronounce υ short before a combination of μ and ν; ὑμνωδεῖ in Aesch. *Ag.* 990 is open to grave suspicion, and is altered by Mr Davies into μονωδεῖ. εὔϋμνος is quoted from Epicharmus, 69. In the passage in Pindar *Nem.* IV 83 (135), the first syllable of ὕμνος *need* not be short; and if it were, we should have to assume that Pindar, who makes the first syllable of ὕμνος and its derivatives long about fifty times, breaks the rule in a single instance (cf. Mr Tyrrell's δεύτεραι φροντίδες). It seems best therefore to suppose, with Hermann, that ὑμνήσω is a marginal explanation of some such word as κελαδήσω, which has accidentally found its way into the text. If, however, θεὸν be omitted in the strophe, it is probable that the antistrophe ended with an anapaest, such as κελαδῶ (Nauck).

72—77. This is one of the many passages which ascribe a special happiness to those who are blessed in the full fruition of divine mysteries. The reference in the present instance (as in lines 469—474) is mainly to the sacred rites of Dionysus, but the plural θεῶν proves that a wider meaning is also intended, and that the Eleusinian mysteries of Demeter are not excluded. Several similar passages (Hom. *hymn. ad Cerer.* 480, Pindar *fragm.* 102, Soph. *fragm.* 719, are quoted at length in a note on Isocr. *Paneg.* § 28, τὴν τελετὴν (of Demeter) ἧς οἱ μετασχόντες περί τε τῆς βίου τελευτῆς καὶ τοῦ σύμπαντος αἰῶνος ἡδίους τὰς ἐλπίδας ἔχουσιν. To these may be added Ar. *Ranae*, 455 (χορὸς μυστῶν), μόνοις γὰρ ἡμῖν ἥλιος καὶ φέγγος ἱλαρόν ἐστιν, ὅσοι μεμυήμεθ᾿ εὐσεβῆ τε διήγομεν τρόπον, Plato *Phaedo*, 69 C, ὃς ἂν ἀμύητος καὶ ἀτέλεστος εἰς Ἅιδου ἀφίκηται ἐν βορβόρῳ κείσεται, ὁ δὲ κεκαθαρμένος τε καὶ τετελεσμένος ἐκεῖσε ἀφικόμενος μετὰ θεῶν οἰκήσει. εἰσὶ γὰρ δή, φασὶν οἱ περὶ τὰς τελετάς, ναρθηκοφόροι μὲν πολλοί, βάκχοι δέ τε παῦροι, *Rep.* p. 365 init., Antisthenes ap. Diogen. Laert. VI 4, μυούμενός ποτε τὰ Ὀρφικά, τοῦ ἱερέως εἰπόντος ὅτι οἱ ταῦτα μυούμενοι πολλῶν ἀγαθῶν ἐν ᾅδου μετίσχουσι, τί οὖν, ἔφη, οὐκ ἀποθνήσκεις (other references may be found in Lenormant's *monographie de la voie sacrée Eleusinienne*, 1864, I pp. 58—62). The most masterly book written in modern times on the ancient mysteries is Lobeck's *Aglaophamus*, which may be referred to with advantage as a wholesome corrective to the fanciful theories of our own Warburton and others.

72. ὦ μάκαρ, ὅστις εὐδαίμων, κ.τ.λ.] For the juxtaposition of these almost synonymous terms, cf. 911, Theognis 1013, ἆ μάκαρ εὐδαίμων τε καὶ ὄλβιος, *Cebetis tabula*, caps. 2, 12, 13, and esp. Plato's *Phaedrus*, 250 B, σὺν εὐδαίμονι χορῷ μακαρίαν ὄψιν τε καὶ θέαν...εἶδον καὶ ἐτελοῦντο τῶν τελετῶν ἣν θέμις λέγειν μακαριωτάτην...εὐδαίμονα φάσματα μυούμενοι. **74. βιοτὰν ἁγιστεύει**] Cf. the interesting fragment of the Κρῆτες of Euripides, 475, 10—20, preserved by Porphyry *de abstinentia*, where a βάκχος describes his life of consecration to the worship of Zeus, Dionysus Zagreus, and Cybele (it will also serve to illustrate other passages in this play, references to which are here added) ; ἁγνὸν δὲ βίον τείνομεν, ἐξ οὗ | Διὸς Ἰδαίου μύστης γενόμην | καὶ νυκτιπόλου (486) Ζαγρέως (1192) βροντὰς (σπονδὰς Lobeck) | τάς τ' ὠμοφάγους δαῖτας (139) τελέσας | μητρί τ' ὀρείῳ δᾷδας ἀνασχών, | καὶ Κουρήτων (120) βάκχος ἐκλήθην ὁσιωθείς. **75. θιασεύεται ψυχάν**] i.e. 'joins the Bacchic revel-band in very soul.' The active form occurs in 379.— **78.** Cf. 59 and 129. The metre is *ionic a minore* and Κυβέλας must accordingly be treated as metrically equivalent to two long syllables ; ὅρ- | -γιᾰ Κυβελᾶς | θεμιτεύων| ; cf. 398, δέ τις ἂν μεγα- | -λα διώκων | . *

81. κισσῷ στεφανωθείς] Ivy was used in the worship of Dionysus not only because it could easily be made into wreaths, but also because its leaf is sufficiently like that of the vine to allow of its being used instead, without stripping the vine. Besides, as an evergreen it could be used at times of the year when the vine itself was not in leaf, ὁ ποθῶν χειμῶνος ὥρᾳ τὸν ἀπὸ

---

* **80.** For the *tmesis*, cf. the corresponding line of the antistrophe (96), and 126.

τῆς ἀμπέλου στέφανον, ὡς ἐκείνην ἑώρα γυμνὴν καὶ ἄφυλλον, ἀγαπῆσαι
(δοκεῖ μοι) τὴν ὁμοιότητα τοῦ κιττοῦ, Plutarch *Symp.* III 2. The
very cradle of the infant god is described as having been gar-
landed with ivy, *Phoen.* 651, κισσὸς ὃν περιστεφὴς ἑλικτὸς εὐθὺς
ἔτι βρέφος χλοηφόροισιν ἔρνεσιν κατασκίοισιν ὀλβίσας ἐνώτισεν,
Ovid *Fasti*, 3, 767, *cur hedera cincta est? hedera est gratissima
Baccho... Nysiades nymphae puerum quaerente noverca* (sc.
Hera), *hanc frondem cunis apposuere novis.* In Plutarch *Symp.*
III 1, 3, III 2, there is a discussion over the wine, as to whether
the ivy-wreath was invented by Dionysus to cool the over-heated
brows of his votaries, στεφανοῦσθαι διδάξαι τοὺς βακχεύοντας, ὡς
ἧττον ὑπὸ τοῦ οἴνου ἀνιῷντο, τοῦ κιττοῦ κατασβεννύντος τὴν μέθην τῇ
ψυχρότητι. However that may be, it was one of the primitive
emblems of the god, and he was even worshipped under the
name of Κισσὸς at Acharnae (Pausanias 1, 31, 3). Hence too
such epithets as κισσοκόμης in the Homeric hymns, 26, 1, and
φιλοκισσοφόρος in *Cycl.* 620; cf. Ovid *F.*, 6, 483, *Bacche race-
miferos hedera redimite capillos.*—[*Vide ne rescribendum sit* στεφάνῳ τε, *ut* κισσῷ *glossema sit*] Shilleto, *adv.*

84. **Βρόμιον**] A name descriptive of Dionysus as the god of
boisterous merriment; in the Homeric hymns 25, 8—10, the
account of the infant god 'roaming through the wooded glens,
wreathed with ivy and laurel and attended by the nymphs that
nursed him,' closes with the words βρόμος δ' ἔχεν ἄσπετον ὕλην.

85. **κατάγουσαι**] 'bringing *home.*' See Ar. *Ranae* 1152—65,
and Eur. *Med.* 1015—6.

87. **εὐρυχόρους ἀγυιάς**] Pind. *Pyth.* 8, 77, and oracle quoted
Dem. *Meid.* p. 531, 7, μεμνῆσθαι Βάκχοιο καὶ εὐρυχόρους κατ'
ἀγυιάς, κ.τ.λ.,—the epithet is even used of a district (Elis), in
the Odyssey, 4, 635. It has been supposed that it is only a
poetic form for εὐρύχωρος, but it is often used with a conscious
reference to χορὸς in the sense of a 'place for dancing'; here, of
the 'wide-squared' Grecian towns, with open 'places' for the
dance. This is the only passage where the word occurs in
Tragedy.

88. **ἔχουσ' ἐν ὠδίνων λοχίαις ἀνάγκαισι**] For ἔχουσα cf.
Herod. v 41 (first quoted by Matthiae), καὶ ἡ προτέρη γυνὴ τὸν

πρότερον χρόνον ἄτοκος ἐοῦσα τότε κῶς ἐκύησε, συντυχίῃ ταύτῃ χρη-
σαμένη· ἔχουσαν δὲ αὐτὴν ἀληθέϊ λόγῳ οἱ τῆς ἐπελθούσης γυναικὸς οἰκήϊοι πυθόμενοι ὤχλεον. The whole sentence may be turned
as follows : 'Whom erst, when flew the bolt of Zeus, his mother,
great with child in sorest pangs, brought forth untimely, slain
herself beneath the stroke of thunder.'

94. λοχίοις—θαλάμαις, κ.τ.λ.] 'and anon, unto hollow recesses
of child-birth, Zeus son of Cronos received him.' θαλάμαι refers
metaphorically to the thigh of Zeus, as appears by the next line.
For the application of the word to cavities of the body, cf.
Aristotle περὶ ὕπνου § 3, τῶν ἐν τῇ καρδίᾳ ἑκατέρας τῆς θαλάμης
κοινὴ ἡ μέση. If, however, we retain the manuscript reading,
θαλάμοις, we may render: 'at once, in the very chamber of
birth.' **96.** κατὰ μηρῷ καλύψας, κ.τ.λ.] see 286 ff. Hence the
epithet μηροτραφὴς (Strabo XV p. 687) and εἰραφιώτης (Homeric
hymn 26, *Anth. Pal.* IX 524, 26, and Orphic hymn quoted
below).—χρῦσέαισιν, [*sic* χρύσεα (*vel* χρυσέαν) 372. *vid. Elmsl.
ad Med.* 618] Shilleto, *adv.*

99. ἔτεκεν δ', ἀνίκα Μοῖραι τέλεσαν] 'But, when the Fates
had matured the babe, the father brought forth the bull-
horned god.' For Μοῖραι τέλεσαν, cf. Pindar *Pyth.* III 9, πρὶν
τελέσσαι (of the mother) ματριπόλῳ σὺν Ἐλειθυίᾳ, and *Ol.* VI 42,
where Ἐλευθὼ and the Μοῖραι assist at the birth of Iamos, and
XI 52, ἐν πρωτογόνῳ τελετᾷ παρέσταν Μοῖραι (at the foundation of
the Olympic games). Orph. Hymn. 48 (47), ὃς Βάκχον Διόνυσον.
ἐρίβρομον εἰραφιώτην μηρῷ ἐγκατέραψας ὅπως τετελεσμένος ἔλθοι
μηνὶ περιπλομένοις καί μιν ταχέως ἐκόμισσας Τμῶλον ἐς ἠγάθεον.
So Nonnus 45, 99 calls him ἡμιτέλεστον, and Lucian I, 530,
ἡμιτελής ; cf. Ovid *F.* 3, 717, *puer ut posses maturo tempore
nasci, expletum patrio corpore matris onus.* From the double
birth of Dionysus, we have him called διμήτωρ (Orph. Hymn.
49, 1 ; 51, 9; *bimater* in Ovid *Met.* IV, 12), δισσότοκος (Nonnus
1, 4).

100. ταυρόκερων θεόν] Dionysus is often represented in literature and sometimes also in works of art, either with horns on his
head or even in the form of a bull. See esp. 920—922, 1017,
1159, with the engravings illustrating those passages. Soph.

fragm. 94, τὴν βεβακχιωμένην βροτοῖσι κλεινὴν Νύσσαν (556) ἦν ὁ
βουκέρως Ἴακχος αὐτῷ μαῖαν ἡδίστην τρέφει. So also he has
elsewhere the epithets ταυρωπὸς (Ion Chius, ap. Athen. II 2),
βοόκραιρος (Nonnus 45, 250), κέραος and χρυσοκέρως (*Anth. Pal.*
IX 524), which last exactly corresponds to Horace's description
of him as *aureo cornu decorus* (*Carm.* 2, 19, 30). Cf. esp.
Plutarch *Quaest. Graecae*, 36, "διὰ τί τὸν Διόνυσον αἱ τῶν Ἠλείων
γυναῖκες ὑμνοῦσαι παρακαλοῦσι βοέῳ ποδὶ παραγίνεσθαι πρὸς αὐτάς;
ἔχει δ᾽ οὕτως ὁ ὕμνος· ἐλθεῖν, ἥρω Διόνυσε, ἅλιον ἐς ναὸν ἀγνόν,
σὺν χαρίτεσσιν ἐς ναὸν τῷ βοέῳ ποδὶ θύων. εἶτα δὶς ἐπάδουσιν· ἄξιε
ταῦρε!"—πότερον ὅτι καὶ βουγενῆ προσαγορεύουσιν καὶ ταῦρον
ἔνιοι τὸν θεόν; id. *de Iside et Osiride*, 35, ταυρόμορφα Διονύσου
ποιοῦσιν ἀγάλματα πολλοὶ τῶν Ἑλλήνων, κ.τ.λ. Athenaeus XI 51,
p. 476 (of Dionysus) ἐν δὲ Κυζίκῳ καὶ ταυρόμορφος ἵδρυται. A fine
representation of this kind has been found at Athens, over the
monument of a person named Dionysus (F. Lenormant, *voie
sacrée Eleusinienne*, 1 p. 66). Besides the gem figured in illustration of line 1159, there is another representing the Dionysiac
bull carrying the three Graces between his horns (Müller-
Wieseler, II xxxiii 383).

102. ἔνθεν ἄγραν θηρότροφον Μαινάδες ἀμφιβάλλονται πλοκά-
μοις] 'whence it is that the Maenads fling around their hair the
wild serpents of their prey,' i.e. capture wild serpents to fling
around their hair. ἄγραν has thus a predicative force. θυρσοφόροι (from the Laurentian MS at Florence) was the common
reading up to the time of Mr Tyrrell's edition which was the
first to give an improved text by accepting θηρότροφον, proposed
by (Musgrave and) Mr S. Allen, and founded on the reading of the
other MS (the Palatine), θηροτρόφοι. We thus get rid of a merely
conventional epithet and obtain an appropriate adjective to help
out the meaning of ἄγραν, which Hermann tried to explain by
supplying δρακόντων from the previous clause. The serpent slain
by Cadmus, whose teeth produced the famous crop of armed
warriors, is called in the *Phoen.* 820, θηροτρόφου φοινικολόφοιο
δράκοντος. θηροτρόφος in an active sense occurs in 556, πόθι
Νύσης τᾶς θηροτρόφου θυρσοφορεῖς θιάσους, and in the present
passage the confusion may possibly have arisen from an earlier

MS having had a marginal quotation of the parallel just cited which led to θυρσοφόροι, suggested by the margin, finding its way into the text and taking the place of θηρότροφον (Mr Tyrrell's *introd.* xi).—This is perhaps the only passage where the infant Dionysus is described as entwined with serpents; one of the god's transformations alluded to later in the play (1019), is his appearing as a πολύκρανος δράκων; while the references to his Maenad votaries twining snakes in their hair, and allowing them to curl around their limbs, are common enough : see *infra* 698 and 768. Thus Clemens Alexandrinus (*protrept.* II p. 72 Migne) refers to Βάκχοι ἀνεστεμμένοι τοῖς ὄφεσιν; Philostratus (*imagines*, I § 18) mentions ὄφεις ὀρθοὶ among the accessories of his picture of the Bacchic revels on Cithaeron; Plutarch writes as follows of the mother of Alexander the Great, ἡ δὲ ᾽Ολυμπιὰς μᾶλλον ἑτέρων ζηλώσασα τὰς κατοχὰς καὶ τοὺς ἐνθουσιασμοὺς ἐξάγουσα βαρβαρικώτερον ὄφεις μεγάλους χειροήθεις ἐφείλκετο τοῖς θιάσοις, οἳ πολλάκις ἐκ τοῦ κιττοῦ καὶ τῶν μυστικῶν λίκνων παραναδυόμενοι καὶ περιελιττόμενοι τοῖς θύρσοις τῶν γυναικῶν καὶ τοῖς στεφάνοις ἐξέπληττον τοὺς ἄνδρας (*Alex.* 2); and Lucian, *Dionysus* § 4, says of the battle with the Indians, αἱ Μαινάδες σὺν ὀλολυγῇ ἐνεπήδησαν αὐτοῖς δρακόντας ὑπεζωσμέναι κἀκ τῶν θύρσων ἄκρων ἀπογυμνοῦσαι τὸν σίδηρον. Cf. Catullus LXIV 258, *pars sese tortis serpentibus incingebat, pars obscura cavis celebrabant orgia cistis;* Hor. *Carm.* 2, 19, 19, *nodo coerces viperino Bistonidum sine fraude crines.*

In works of ancient art this characteristic of the Maenads is seldom represented; an example however is engraved in illustration of this passage. The serpent was an important element in the mystic worship of Dionysus and is often represented in reliefs and coins creeping out of a half-opened basket, the *cista mystica;* thus, frequently in Bacchic scenes on sarcophagi, Pan kicks open the *cista* and the snake emerges (e.g. Müller-Wieseler, II, XXXV 412); and on the coins of the kingdom of Pergamus known as *cistophori* (which, as they were not struck till 200 years after the time of Euripides, are cited here not as a contemporary illustration but simply to shew the wide prevalence of the association of the serpent with the mysteries of

Dionysus as well as those of Demeter), we see on the one side, surrounded with a wreath of ivy, the *cista mystica* of Dionysus, half open, with a serpent creeping out of it ; on the other the car of Demeter drawn by serpents. It is the serpent twined about the sleeping nymph figured in illustration of line 683 that has led to her being identified as a resting Bacchante ; and the *cista* and serpent may be seen in the gem engraved below.

105. Thebes, which is here called upon to wear the livery of the god, is similarly personified in Seneca, *Oedipus* 407—12, *effusam redimite comam nutante corymbo mollia Nysaeis armatae bracchia thyrsis...nobiles Thebae.*—On the ivy, see 81 n.

107. χλοήρει μίλακι καλλικάρπῳ] Theophrastus, *hist. plant.* III 18, 11, immediately after describing the ivy, goes on to describe the *smilax* as follows : ἡ δὲ σμῖλαξ ἐστι μὲν ἐπαλλόκαυλον (a creeper), ὁ δὲ καυλὸς ἀκανθώδης καὶ ὥσπερ ὀρθάκανθος, τὸ δὲ φύλλον κιττῶδες μικρὸν ἀγώνιον. (After describing the ribs of the leaves, the joints of the stalk, and also the tendrils, he continues) ἄνθος δὲ λευκὸν καὶ εὐῶδες λείρινον· τὸν δὲ καρπὸν ἔχει προσεμφερῆ τῷ στρύχνῳ (nightshade) καὶ τῷ μηλώθρῳ (bryony) καὶ μάλιστα τῇ καλουμένῃ σταφυλῇ ἀγρίᾳ...ὁ δὲ καρπὸς ἐρυθρός. To the same effect Pliny *Nat. Hist.* XVI 63, who closely follows Theophrastus ; *similis est hederae, e Cilicia primum quidem profecta, sed in Graecia frequentior,...densis geniculata caulibus, spinosis frutectosa ramis, folio hederaceo, parvo, non anguloso, a pediculo emittente pampinos, flore candido, olente*

lilium. This description corresponds exactly with the appearance of the plant called the *smilax aspera* as figured in Sibthorp's *Flora Graeca,* vol. X (1840) p. 49 plate 959, where it is identified with the σμῖλαξ τραχεῖα of Dioscorides and its modern Greek name is said to be ἀκρουδόβατος, while in Cyprus it is known as the ξυλόβατος. It grows abundantly in marshy places and also on rough ground in Greece and the Archipelago, and in Crete as well as Cyprus. Like ivy, it is an evergreen creeper with a dark-green leaf of leathery texture : it bears small white starry flowers with pink stalks, growing in clusters at the tips of the spray ; the berries are of a bright scarlet. The stem and the slightly prominent points of the leaves are in some specimens prickly, in others smooth, having in the latter case *caules fere inermes...folia omnino inermia,* to quote the words of Lindley, who edited the later volumes of Sibthorp's great work, and who also says, *foliorum formâ necnon aculeorum praesentiâ et abundantiâ variare videtur.* (In December, 1881, I frequently saw it growing in rich profusion along the Riviera, mantling the hedges with its dark leaves of glossy green. A large coloured photograph by Guidi of San Remo gives a faithful representation of its bright foliage and its brilliantly scarlet berries.)

Thus we may safely identify the μῖλαξ of the passage now before us with the *smilax aspera* as above described ; the brightness of its berries at once explains the epithet καλλίκαρπος, its clustering flowers account for the epithet ἀνθεσφόρος in l. 703, and its resemblance to ivy would specially commend it to the votaries of Dionysus. It is probably the same plant that is meant in the pleasant picture, in the *Nubes* 1007, of the young athlete running races beneath the sacred olives of Academe, στεφανωσάμενος καλάμῳ λευκῷ μετὰ σώφρονος ἡλικιώτου, σμίλακος ὄζων καὶ ἀπραγμοσύνης καὶ λεύκης φυλλοβολούσης, ἦρος ἐν ὥρᾳ χαίρων ὁπόταν πλάτανος πτελέᾳ ψιθυρίζῃ. Again, in Aelian's charming description of the pass of Tempe, while ivy like the finest vines (δίκην τῶν εὐγενῶν ἀμπέλων) entwines itself about the lofty trees, it is the *smilax* which mantles the rocky walls of the ravine (πολλὴ δὲ σμίλαξ, ἡ μὲν πρὸς αὐτὸν τὸν πάγον ἀνατρέχει καὶ ἐπισκιάζει τὴν πέτραν, *Varia Historia*

III 1). It is not found in the British Isles ; the plant that perhaps most closely resembles it in our own Flora is the Black Bryony, which belongs to the closely allied order of *Dioscoreae*, and (as it happens) derives its name (referring to the quick growth of the stems) from the very same verb (βρύειν) that is here used of the *smilax*. For purposes of translation we must either naturalise the word *smilax* or be content with an approximate rendering such as 'burst forth, burst forth with the green bright-berried bryony.'—This explanation is, I venture to think, better than the conjecture given in Liddell and Scott which makes it the σμῖλαξ λεία and identifies the latter with the bindweed or common convolvulus (*calystegia sepium*), which is too delicate and withers too soon to be suitable for a wreath, and certainly cannot be called καλλίκαρπος. The same name is also sometimes given to the yew (*taxus baccata*), and Mr Paley so understands it in the present passage. But its berries, though as bright as those of the *smilax aspera*, were supposed by the ancients to be poisonous ; it would lend itself less readily than the latter for the purpose of twining into wreaths ; and its foliage, being unlike that of the ivy, and being also of too gloomy a hue, would make it less attractive to the merry Bacchant*.

109. καταβακχιοῦσθε] 'Make a very Bacchanal of thyself' amid branches of oak and fir. On the analogy of verbs in -όω (δηλοῦν, δουλοῦν, ἐρημοῦν = δηλόν, δοῦλον, ἔρημον ποιεῖν), βακχιοῦν means βάκχον ποιεῖν, and the simple verb is here used with the intensifying preposition κατά (as in κατάδηλος, 'very plain') in the ordinary sense of the middle voice, 'make a very Bacchanal of thyself.' This seems better than Lobeck's interpretation of καταβακχιοῦσθαι as *coronari* (quoting Hesych. βακχᾶν· ἐστεφανῶσθαι); his other quotation is more to the point, and is quite as consistent with the sense above given, as with his own view : Schol. on Ar. *Eq.* 409, βάκχον οὐ τὸν Διόνυσον μόνον ἐκάλουν ἀλλὰ καὶ τοὺς τελοῦντας τὰ ὄργια, καὶ τοὺς κλάδους οὓς οἱ μύσται φέρουσι, after which follows a line from the comic poet Xenophanes (as emended by Lobeck), ἑστᾶσιν δ' ἐλατῶν πυκινοὶ περὶ δώματα βάκχοι, where the ἐλατῶν βάκχοι correspond to the ἐλάτας κλάδοι of the text (*Aglaophamus* p. 308, comm. on

* L and S, ed. 1883, quote me as 'connecting' the σμῖλαξ τραχεῖα with our Black Bryony. I only state that they closely resemble one another.

Ajax l. 847). Cf. *Iph. A.* 1058, ἀνὰ δ' ἐλάταισι (Hes. *Scut.* 188, ἐλάτας ἐν χερσὶν ἔχοντες) στεφανώδει τε χλόᾳ θίασυς ἔμολεν … Κενταύρων (quoted by Wecklein).—Liddell and Scott wrongly render, 'in oak leaves ye rave with Bacchic rage.'

The oak and fir are doubtless mentioned because of their being (as already stated on l. 38) the common trees of Cithaeron (cf. 684, ἐλάτης φόβην and 685, δρυὸς φύλλοισι). In 703, the Bacchanals wreathe themselves with crowns of oak-leaves as well as ivy and *smilax*, and in 1103, branches of oak are used to prise up the fir-tree on which Pentheus had climbed to spy out the revellers. Herodotus (IX 31) tells us of a pass of Cithaeron, called Oak-Heads, Δρυὸς κεφαλαί.

111. στικτῶν ἐνδυτὰ νεβρίδων στέφετε λευκοτρίχων πλοκάμων μαλλοῖς] 'Fringe thy livery of dappled fawnskins with woolly tufts of silvery tresses.' The Bacchanals appear to have used tufts of wool or strips of goat's hair to trim their fawnskins and set off their natural colour. Much of the difficulty felt by early editors is excellently cleared up by Lobeck- on *Ajax* l. 847, p. 375, 'significatur…insertio penicillorum ('tufts') diversico-lorum, quibus hodieque pelliones mastrucas ('skins') distinguere solent.' Cf. Tacitus, *Germ.* 17, *eligunt feras et detracta velamina spargunt maculis pellibusque beluarum quas exterior Oceanus atque ignotum mare gignit* (ermine spots are thus imitated in the manufacture of furs into muffs, tippets, &c.) . and Hdt. IV 109, θηρία τῶν τὰ δέρματα περὶ τὰς σισύρας παραρράπτεται. Claudian again (*de quarto cons. Honor.* 228) describes the fawn-skin of Bacchus as bespangled with pearls, *Erythraeis intextis nebride gemmis Liber agit currus.* But, while using these illustrations, we need not assume that in the present passage the fawnskins were *studded* with artificial spots, as this would give στέφετε a sense which it can hardly bear ; it is enough to understand a *fringe* or *trimming*, which that word may very well express. According to Müller, *Ancient Art* § 386, 5, the 'roe-skin covered with tufts of wool, is also to be recognised on vases.' For the use of wool in sacred rites cf. Aesch. *Eum.* 45, ἐλάας ὑψιγέννητον κλάδον λήνει μεγίστῳ σωφρόνως ἐστεμμένον ἀργῆτι μαλλῷ.

λευκοτρίχων πλοκάμων μαλλοῖς presents some difficulty ; there
would be little awkwardness in the apparent combination of
'hair' and 'wool,' in the first and last words of the phrase, as
the compound λευκόθριξ need not mean much more than λευκός ;
but the addition of πλοκάμων makes it less easy to get rid
of the full meaning of the adjective ; and unless we suppose
that Euripides uses the three words as a condensed and con-
fused expression for tufts of wool and bunches of goat's hair
combined, it is hard to make sense of the passage, especially
as πλόκαμος is not, so far as I can find, used elsewhere of
the hair of animals, but is constantly applied to the flowing
locks of men and still oftener of women.   Reiske (once followed
by Mr Tyrrell) proposes ποκάδων (sometimes said to mean
'sheep,' but only found in the sense of 'hair' or 'wool' in Ar.
Thesm. 567, ἀλλ' ἐκποκιῶ σου τὰς ποκάδας, which apparently
means 'I'll tear your hair out,' 'give you a good combing').
Elmsley suggests προβάτων, with misgivings, as the word is
never used in Euripides, nor indeed (he might have added)
by any of the Tragedians (though Strabo p. 784, speaking of
the Nabataean Arabs, says they have πρόβατα λευκότριχα).   On
the whole, I think it best to regard μαλλοῖς as a metaphor taken
from tufts of wool and applied by an easy transition to bunches
of hair, and to understand λευκοτρίχων πλοκάμων, 'white-haired
tresses,' as an ornamental phrase for the tufts of hair which
the Bacchae may have taken to trim their fawn-skins from the
goats killed by them in the chase.   In l. 139, αἷμα τραγοκτόνον
is mentioned immediately after the words, νεβρίδος ἔχων ἱερὸν
ἐνδυτόν.   (See further in *Supplementary Notes.*)

113. ἀμφὶ νάρθηκας ὑβριστὰς ὁσιοῦσθε] 'be reverent in thy
handling of the saucy (or 'wanton') ferule.'   The νάρθηξ was the
light wand supplied by the pithy stem of the giant fennel.   It is
the Latin *ferula*, of which Pliny XIII 42 (cf. Theophr. *Hist.
Plant.* VI 2 §§ 7, 8) writes, *nulli fruticum levitas maior. ob id
gestatu facilis baculorum usum senectuti praebet;* cf. Nonnus
XI 354, γηροκόμῳ νάρθηκι δέμας στηρίζετο βάκτρῳ, and Ovid *Met.*
IV 26.   Its lightness would make it very suitable for the female
votaries of Dionysus ; and, if we adopt the notion naïvely sug-

gested by Diodorus, IV p. 149, it was to prevent serious conse-
quences arising from the abuse of clubs on occasions of boisterous merriment, that the god himself graciously enjoined on
his worshippers the use of the light and comparatively harmless
weapon (similarly Plutarch, *Symp.* 7, 10, 3, ὁ θεὸς τὸν νάρθηκα
τοῖς μεθύουσιν ἐνεχείρισε κουφότατον βέλος καὶ μαλακώτατον ἀμυντή-
ριον, ὅπως ἐπεὶ τάχιστα παίουσιν, ἥκιστα βλάπτωσι).

Tournefort (in his *Voyage du Levant* I p. 245, quoted by
Joddrell) says it grows plentifully in the island of Skinosa [Σίκινος,
one of the *Sporades*]——modern Greeks call it Nartheca; 'it bears
a stalk five feet high, three inches thick, with a knot every ten
inches, branched at every knot and covered with a hard bark of
two lines thick: the hollow of the stalk is filled with a white
marrow, which when well dried catches fire just like a match.'
It was in the *narthex* that Prometheus stole the fire from heaven
(Aesch. *P. V.* 109, ναρθηκοπληρώτου πυρός, Hesiod *Works and
Days* 52), cf. Phanias Epigr. 2, πυρικοίταν νάρθηκα κροτάφων
πλάκτορα νηπιάχων.

Strictly speaking, the νάρθηξ was different from the θύρσος,
the former being a plain light staff, the latter usually swathed
with ivy, or trimmed with ribbands, and armed with a sharp point
capped with a fir-cone. Eur. however in the course of the play
sometimes uses the words indifferently. Thus Cadmus has a
νάρθηξ in line 251, which is called a θύρσος three lines after;
and in 1155 we have νάρθηξ εὔθυρσος applied to the θύρσος of
Pentheus (835, 941).

118. Cf. 1236, τὰς παρ' ἱστοῖς ἐκλιποῦσα κερκίδας.

120. 'O vaulted chamber of the Curetes! O holy haunts of
Crete, birth-place of Zeus; where, in yon caves, the Corybantes,
with helms of triple rim, first framed for my joy this round timbrel
of hide.' According to Strabo, 10, 11 p. 468, the Curetes saved
the infant Zeus from being devoured by his father Cronos, by
sounding the *tympanum* and other instruments, and by martial
and boisterous dances which drowned the cries of the babe and
prevented his being discovered. He suggests two derivations
for the name, ἤτοι διὰ τὸ νέοι καὶ κόροι (cf. κοῦροι) ὄντες ὑπουργεῖν
ἢ διὰ τὸ κουροτροφεῖν τὸν Δία.—The common tradition placed

the home of the Curetes in Crete, and that of the Corybantes in Phrygia, but Euripides in the present passage clearly assigns the Corybantes also to Crete, and either identifies them with the Curetes, or at any rate gives them a Cretan origin. The lore of the subject has been collected and discussed by Lobeck, *Aglaophamus* p. 1111—55 (esp. 1144, 1150, 1155), whose conclusion is as follows: 'satis confirmatum videtur Corybantum et nomen et cultum ad sacra Phrygia pertinere, plurimumque interesse inter hunc barbarum Κορυβαντισμὸν et Graecorum Cretensium Κουρητισμὸν discriminis, quamvis Corybantes et Curetes a poetis et mythographis propter generalem similitudinem saepe confusi sint.' Cf. Lucr. ii 629, 633.

Lobeck on *Ajax* l. 847, p. 374, refers the epithet τρικόρυθες, here used of the Corybantes, to the 'triple rim of their helmet which gave the effect of three helmets placed in succession on one another,'—not unlike the papal tiara. Strictly speaking, it was the Curetes who wore a helmet, while the Corybantes wore a κυρβασία or tiara (Hdt. v 49, 7; vii 62, 2); but they are here confounded with each other, and the epithet properly applicable to the former is thus transferred to the latter. In works of art the Corybantes are represented as dancing not only around the infant Zeus (according to the common legend), but also, in one instance, around the new-born Dionysus (relief in the Vatican, copied in Müller-Wieseler ii xxxv 412).

The reading of the MSS is ἔνθα τρικόρυθες ἐν ἄντροις. The metre is restored either (1) by writing ἔνθα τρικόρυθες ἄντροις where ἄντροις is a dative of place, a construction which except in the case of names of places is almost confined to poetry, esp. Epic poetry, though it also occurs in Sophocles and more frequently in Euripides and the Lyric poets; or (2) by accepting Dobree's conjecture τρικόρυθες ἔνθ' ἐν ἄντροις.

126. βάκχια] is certainly harsh in sense, as it implies that, *before* the Satyrs borrowed the *tympanum* from Rhea, to introduce it into the worship of Dionysus, the sounds of that instrument could be called Bacchic sounds, which would be a strong instance of a truly proleptic epithet. Of βάκχιος Hermann says 'rara omnino haec forma est, ubi non de ipso Baccho aut vino

usurpatur sed ut adiectivum additur nominibus';...'verum qui
Βάκχια aut τὰ Βάκχια dixerit, id ut Bacchica sacra significaret,
novi neminem.' Further, he rejects the possibility, of taking
ἀνὰ βάκχια together, in the sense 'in the Bacchic rites'; and even
assuming its possibility, holds that such an anticipatory use of
the epithet is logically absurd. He rightly insists on taking ἀνὰ
with κέρασαν, *per tmesin;* but it is difficult to follow him when in
place of βάκχια he conjectures βακχάδι, an adjective for which
(as he admits) there is no authority. If βάκχια is wrong, the
text must have been corrupted at an early date, as Strabo
testifies to the reading βακχείῳ in his very inaccurate quotation
of parts of this chorus (10 p. 469). συντόνῳ is also open to
suspicion, as the meaning 'intense,' 'impetuous,' 'keen,' is not
quite in harmony with ἀδυβόᾳ; and it is possibly a corruption of
τυμπάνων. The requirements of the sense would be met by some
such emendation as ἀνὰ δ' ἀράγματα τυμπάνων κέρασαν ἀδυβόᾳ
Φρυγίων αὐλῶν πνεύματι (cf. Eur. *Cycl.* 205).

129. κτύπον εὐάσμασι Βακχᾶν] put in apposition to βυρσότονον
κύκλωμα, 'to sound in loud accord with the revel-shouts of the
Bacchae.' Even here, as above in the manuscript reading
βάκχια, the reference to the βάκχαι seems premature, as it is not
till the next sentence that the passing of the *tympanum* into the
worship of Dionysus is described; but the present instance is
less harsh than the former; even *there* however, the harshness
of the *prolepsis* is to some extent softened by μοι (=ταῖς βάκχαις)
in the previous line. Cf. also l. 59, where the instrument is
described as the joint invention of Rhea and Dionysus.

131. ἐξανύσαντο, 'won it for their own,' stronger than ἠνύσαντο,
which means to 'attain,' 'get at,' as in Aesch. *P. V.* 700, χρείαν
ἠνύσασθε. Liddell and Scott, less adequately, explain it in the
present passage as meaning 'to gain one's end.'*–συνῆψαν, not
ἑαυτούς, 'joined in the dance,' but τὸ τύμπανον, 'wedded it
(mingled it) with the dances of the triennial festivals, which
gladden Dionysus.' τριετηρίδες, i.e. festivals returning *every
other year*, once in every cycle of two years, for this is what the
Greeks meant by a τριετηρίς (*alternis annis*, says Macrobius,
quoted on 306), just as the Olympic πενταετηρίς was what we

---

* Corrected in ed. 1883:—' Med. to obtain, borrow.'

should call a cycle of four full years. Ovid *F.* 1, 393, *festa corymbiferi celebrabas Graecia Bacchi, tertia quae solito tempore bruma refert;* Virg. *Aen.* IV 300, *saevit inops animi, totamque incensa per urbem bacchatur; qualis commotis excita sacris Thyias, ubi audito stimulant trieterica Baccho orgia, nocturnusque vocat clamore Cithaeron.*

135. ὅταν πέσῃ standing without any subject is awkward, and the same objection applies to εὖτ' ἄν. It is therefore not improbable that for ὅταν we should read ὃς ἄν (which has occurred to Kirchhoff and doubtless to others). Even ἡδύς, though found in the sense of 'well-pleased,' 'glad,' in Soph. *O. T.* 82, and elsewhere, has been altered into ἧδος, *voluptas in montibus* (Musgrave), and into ἡδύ γ' (Dobree); the latter may be supported by a fragment of the *Archelaus*, a play so named out of compliment to the king at whose court the *Bacchae* was written, frag. 265, ἔστι (+τι Meineke) καὶ παρὰ δάκρυσι κείμενον ἡδὺ βροτοῖς, ὅταν ἄνδρα φίλον στενάχῃ τις ἐν οἴκῳ (vel οἴκτῳ), where however it will be noticed that τις is expressed. A further extension of Dobree's conjecture was suggested by Dr Thompson, late Master of Trinity College, ἁδύ γ' ἐν ὄρεσίν ὃς ἄν, which he supported by Soph. fragm. 326, ἥδιστον δ' ὅτῳ πάρεστι λῆψις ὧν ἐρᾷ καθ' ἡμέραν. This is not open to the objection raised above, viz. the absence of a subject to the verb πέσῃ. Hermann, who prints ἡδύς, ἐν οὔρεσιν, ὅς τ' ἄν...πέσῃ πεδόσε, renders 'laetitiae plenus est, in montes, quique ex velocibus thiasis in campos se contulerit,' thus introducing a contrast between οὔρεσιν and πεδόσε. He makes merry over the absurdity of the god, or his votary, being described as 'happy on the mountains when he hunts on the plain,' but neither in the manuscript reading nor in any proposed correction, is Euripides really responsible for such a statement; for πεδόσε must mean, not πρὸς πεδία (much less ἐν πεδίοις) but πρὸς πέδον, 'to the ground,' just as in 600, δίκετε πεδόσε τρομερὰ σώματα compared with 605, πρὸς πέδῳ πεπτώκατε; cf. *Troad.* 99, ἄνα, δυσδαίμων, πεδόθεν κεφαλήν. Some such correction as ἡδὺς ἐν οὔρεσιν οὔρεσίν ἐσθ' ὃς ἄν would be open to no exception on the ground of construction, or of·metre, coinciding as it does with a form of verse used four times in this epode; e.g. εἰς ὄρος, εἰς ὄρος ἀδομένα δ' ἄρα, where the characteristic repetition of οὔρεσιν also finds its parallel. Such a repetition would easily drop out of the MSS and ἐσθ' or ἐστὶν might be lost after the last syllable of οὔρεσιν. As an alternative might be suggested ἡδὺς ἐν οὔρεσίν ἐσθ' ὅταν τις, a logaoedic verse like the last line of an Alcaic stanza, and equivalent to the next verse in this chorus with a dactyl prefixed. A still simpler course would be to keep closer to the MSS and to accept ἡδὺς ἐν ὄρεσσιν ὃς ἂν, a paeonic dimeter, $-\smile\smile\smile \mid -\smile\smile\smile \mid$. This is Schöne's emendation, and it has the advantage of giving us the same form ὄρεσσιν as has been already adopted in 76, and altering only one letter in the rest of the line.

The sense thus gained is: 'Oh! happy on the hills is he, whoe'er from amid the revel-bands sinks to the ground.' So Propertius 1, 3, 5, *assiduis Edonis fessa choreis qualis in herboso concidit Apidano, talis visa mihi mollem spirare quietem Cynthia, non certis nixa caput manibus.* The resting Maenad is well represented in the sleeping nymph, engraved in this book in illustration of line 683. In modern sculpture the resting Bacchante is one of Bartolini's works in the gallery of the Duke of Devonshire at Chatsworth. (See *Supplementary Notes.*)

138. ἀγρεύων αἷμα τραγοκτόνον ὠμοφάγον χάριν] 'chasing the goat to the death, for the raw banquet's relish,' lit. 'hunting after a goat-killing slaughter, as a raw-eating delight.' For αἷμα = φόνος, cf. *Orest.* 285, 1139, and esp. 833 and 1649, ματροκτόνον αἷμα, 'matricidal murder.' With τραγοκτόνος in this active sense Elmsley compares μητροκτόνος (u. s.), ἀνθρωποκτόνος (*Cycl.* 127), and βροτοκτόνος (*Iph. T.* 384).

ὠμοφάγον χάριν] in app. to αἷμα, = χάριν ὠμοφαγίας, 'for the enjoyment of a raw banqueting.' So *Herc. F.* 384, χαρμοναῖσιν ἀνδροβρῶσι = χαρμοναῖς ἀνθρωποφαγίας. Cf. Eur. fragm. of *Cretes*, ὠμοφάγους δαῖτας, quoted on 74, which might appear in favour of printing ὠμόφαγον (passive) here; but even there, 'raw-eaten banquets,' though a more obvious, seems a less poetical idea than 'raw-eating banquets.'

For the sacrifice of the he-goat to Dionysus (as a foe to the vine [?] or for other reasons) Virg. *G.* 2, 380, *Baccho caper omnibus aris caeditur;* Ovid *F.* 1, 357, *rode caper vitem, tamen hinc, cum stabis ad aram, in tua quod spargi cornua possit, erit.* On a painted vase (copied from *Mon. ined. del. Inst.* 1860 pl. xxxvii in Daremberg and Saglio's *Dict. des Antiq.* s.v. *ara*) there is a representation of an altar with the head of an ox carved upon it, and beside the altar a priestess with a fawnskin across her robe holding a knife in one hand, and a goat, which she is on the point of sacrificing, in the other. At Potniae, near Thebes, there was still standing in Pausanias' day a temple to Dionysus Αἰγοβόλος (IX 8, 1). It was probably as an animal sacred to Dionysus, and *not* as an enemy of the god, that the goat was sacrificed to him; the Maenads sometimes wore the goat-skin (Hesychius s.v. αἰγίζειν and τραγηφόροι); and in the masterpiece of Scopas known as the βάκχη χιμαιροφόνος (the original of many representations on ancient monuments, one of which is copied among the illustrations to this ed., p. 86), a Maenad was to be seen holding in her hands part of a dismembered kid. The rites of ὠμοφαγία were connected with the cult of Dionysus Zagreus (the hunter), and the animals captured and pulled to pieces by the Bacchanals are supposed to have taken the place of the human victims of an earlier time (Paus. IX 8, 2, Porphyr. *de abstinentia,* II 55); thus even Themistocles, before the battle of Salamis, sacrificed three young Persian prisoners to Dionysus Omestes (Plutarch *Them.* 13). There is an interesting article on the subject by F. Lenormant in the *Gazette Archéologique* 1879, pp. 18—37, *Dionysos Zagreus.*

141. **ἔξαρχος...εὐοῖ**] ἐξ. of the *coryphaeus* of a chorus, here of Dionysus himself as the invisible inspirer of the revels. Dem. *de cor.* p. 313 § 260, τοὺς ὄφεις (cf. 103, 698) τοὺς παρείας θλίβων καὶ ὑπὲρ τῆς κεφαλῆς αἰωρῶν καὶ βοῶν εὐοῖ σαβοῖ καὶ ἐπορχούμενος ὑῆς ἄττης ἄττης ὑῆς, ἔξαρχος καὶ προηγεμών...προσαγορευόμενος. Lucian *Dionysus* § 4, III p. 78 (Reitz), τὸ σύνθημα (watchword) ἦν ἅπασι τὸ εὐοῖ, Hor. *Carm.* 2, 19, 5 *evoe! recenti mens trepidat metu...evoe parce, Liber, parce gravi metuende thyrso.*

142. These marvellous streams of wine, milk and honey are dwelt upon with more detail in 697—704, 750 ff. It was doubtless descriptions like these that Plato had in mind when writing

the fine passage on poetic inspiration in the *Ion*, 534 A, esp.
the words, βακχεύουσι καὶ κατεχόμενοι ὥσπερ αἱ βάκχαι ἀρύττονται
ἐκ τῶν ποταμῶν μέλι καὶ γάλα κατεχόμεναι. So Horace *Carm.*
2, 19, 10, *vinique fontem lactis et uberes cantare rivos atque
truncis lapsa cavis iterare mella;* Ovid tells of streams of milk
and nectar flowing in the golden age, *Met.* I, 111. Elmsley
quotes the Septuagint version of Exodus III. 8, εἰς γῆν ῥέουσαν
γάλα καὶ μέλι. For the dat. γάλακτι, where the acc. might have
been used as well, just as in the passage above quoted, cf. *Iliad*
22, 149, ἡ μὲν (πηγὴ) ὕδατι λιαρῷ ῥέει, and 4, 451.

144. 'There (breathes) a reek as of Syrian incense.' To fill
up the ellipse, we may supply either ἐστὶ or some such word as
πνεῖ, implied by the general sense of ῥεῖ in the preceding clause.
For Συρίας λιβάνου, cf. Aesch. *Ag.* 1312, οὐ Σύριον ἀγλάϊσμα δωμάτων λέγεις, and Orphic hymn to Aphrodite, 54, 17, εὐλιβάνου
Συρίης.

145. ὁ Βακχεὺς δ' ἔχων πυρσώδη φλόγα πεύκας ἐκ νάρθηκος
ἀΐσσει δρόμῳ καὶ χοροῖς ἐρεθίζων πλανάτας ἰακχαῖς τ' ἀναπάλλων,
τρυφερὸν πλόκαμον εἰς αἰθέρα ῥίπτων. This is a somewhat per-
plexing passage. The above words seem to give the best text
that can be got by keeping closely to the MSS, without resorting
to a considerable amount of emendation. Both MSS have καὶ
χοροῖς, but in the Palatine there are two accents over ι in χοροῖς
which seem to point to χορούς. If we strike out καὶ and read
δρόμῳ, χορούς—we are almost compelled to take ἀΐσσει δρόμῳ
together, in the most obvious intransitive sense, 'rushes along
at full speed,' 'speeds along in the race,' though there is a strong
temptation to make it transitive (with Paley) who renders the
whole sentence as follows: 'and the follower of Bacchus, holding the ruddy blaze of pine-wood on his wand, waves it about in
his course, rousing the scattered bands as he goes.' The torch,
he adds, seems to have been placed at the end of the wand,
for the purpose both of holding it aloft, and of giving it a wider
range in brandishing it about. This last suggestion as to the
way in which the torch may have been attached to the ferule is
very likely to be right; and, if we accept it, we may understand
ἐκ νάρθηκος to mean, either (1) 'hanging down from,' or (2) 'pro-

jecting from near the end of the ferule to which it was attached'; or possibly (3) from a socket formed by removing the pith of the νάρθηξ, letting the torch in and tying it fast with ribbands round the bark. I rather incline to the first, because in the present sentence it would appear that after the rest from the chase and the refreshment of the honey, milk and wine, the chorus passes, by the transition supplied in the reference to the 'reek of Syrian incense,' to the description of the Bacchant himself rising from his repose and refreshment, and holding aloft the newly kindled pine-torch, which, before being carried separately in full blaze, would not unnaturally be suspended from the ferule with the flame downwards ; (this could easily have been managed with strings or ribbands like those which may often be seen in works of art representing the pine-coned thyrsus with ribbands fluttering about its upper part.) The leader next rouses his companions, rallies the scattered revel-bands, and calls upon them to sound the praise of Dionysus on the timbrel and the flute.

ἐκ νάρθηκος in the sense of 'hanging from the ferule,' without any participle or similar word to introduce it, is not entirely free from suspicion; and it is this that leads some to prefer making ἀΐσσει transitive. The sense then would be, ' the Bacchanal holding the ruddy flame of the pine-torch, shoots it forth from his ferule as he runs,' or rather 'by his running'; but if we thus take the verb in a transitive sense, it seems clearly better to separate δρόμῳ from ἀΐσσει and read δρόμῳ καὶ χοροῖς ἐρεθίζων πλανάτας, 'challenging his truant (or 'errant') comrades by his coursing and his dances' (the usual construction of ἐρεθίζειν as in *Iliad* 4, 5, κερτομέοις ἐπέεσσιν and *Od.* 17, 394, μύθοισιν χαλεποῖσιν), or 'to racing and dancing' (the construction found with a similar verb in *Il.* 7, 218, προκαλέσσατο χάρμῃ). Cf. Ar. *Nubes* 312, εὐκελάδων τε χορῶν ἐρεθίσματα, καὶ μοῦσα βαρύβρομος αὐλῶν. For the trans. use of ἀΐσσειν, cf. *Ajax* 40, and *Or.* 1416. See *Supplementary Note.*

The only representation of anything like a torch attached to the ferule, which I have been able to find, is the following engraving, taken from what purports to be a copy of a Florentine gem. Though I have some suspicions as to the correctness of the original copy from which it is taken (as I have observed on pp. cl, 270, in the description of the engravings), I nevertheless give it here as at any rate a representation of one of the various ways in which a torch may have been attached to the Bacchanal's wand.

ἐκ νάρθηκος has ere now been understood of the tinder-like stem of the ferule in which fire was commonly carried about, as is still the custom in Greece, *Bacchus habens* (i.e. gestans) *igneam* (igniferam) *flammam taedae ex ferula orientem* (emicantem) *ruit* (F. M. Schulz). Nonnus, by the way, has in 7, 340, πυρσοφόρῳ νάρθηκι καταχθέα πῆχυν ἐρείσας; but this interpretation would almost require ἐκ νάρθηκος ἀνάπτει (kindles), and, besides, the minute detail thus introduced is too trivial to be tolerated in a vigorous and rapid description of the wild revels on the hills.

It once occurred to me that the right reading might possibly be ἐκ νάρθηκας ἀίσσει ('shooteth forth ferule after ferule') = νάρθηκας ἐξαίσσει, by a tmesis twice exemplified in this chorus, ἀνὰ θύρσον τε τινάσσων (80), and κατὰ μηρῷ δὲ καλύψας (96); this would be parallel in sense to βάλλοντα καὶ σείοντα βακχεῖον κλάδον in 308, but the only evidence I can find in favour of the compound ἐξαίσσειν being transitive, is its use in the passive in one passage of Homer, *Il.* 3, 368, ἐκ δέ μοι ἔγχος ἠΐχθη παλάμηφιν (which also exemplifies the *tmesis* proposed).

The pine-wood torch described in l. 146 as borne by the Bacchanal, and often so represented in works of art, is sometimes mentioned as waved about by the god himself (see on 306—8).

151. 'And withal, to swell his revel-shouts, he thunders forth such calls as these: On! On! my Bacchanals, bright grace of Tmolus and his streams of gold.' On mount Tmolus see note on 55. The epithet χρυσορόας is here applied to it, because it was the source of the small stream of the Pactolus, a tributary of a far larger river, the Hermus, which is itself called *auro turbidus* (Virg. *Georg.* 2, 137): Herod. V 101, ἐπὶ τὸν Πακτωλὸν ποταμόν, ὅς σφι ψῆγμα χρυσοῦ καταφορέων ἐκ τοῦ Τμώλου διὰ μέσης τῆς ἀγορῆς ῥέει καὶ ἔπειτα ἐς τὸν Ἕρμον ποταμὸν ἐκδιδοῖ, Ovid *Met.* XI, 87 (of Bacchus) *cumque choro meliore sui vineta Timoli Pactolonque petit; quamvis non aureus illo tempore, nec caris erat invidiosus arenis.* Nonnus, 43, 442, Πακτωλοῦ παρὰ πέζαν, ὅπη χρυσαυγέϊ πηλῷ ἀφνειοῦ ποταμοῖο μέλαν φοινίσσεται ὕδωρ.

156. βαρυβρόμων ὑπὸ τυμπάνων] 'to the sound of the deep-toned drums.' The same epithet is applied elsewhere by Eur. to the notes of the flute, the sound of thunder and the roar of the waves (*Hel.* 1305, 1351, *Phoen.* 183).—For ὑπὸ, which is often used c. gen. to indicate a musical accompaniment, cf. ὑπ' αὐλοῦ χορεύειν, ὑπὸ φορμίγγων. Herod. I 17, ἐστρατεύοντο ὑπὸ σαλπίγγων.

157. εὔια] 'glorifying the Evian god *in right Bacchic sort.*' Cf. τὰ νομισθέντα in 70. **160.** λωτὸς εὐκέλαδος] *El.* 716, λωτὸς δὲ φθόγγον κελάδει κάλλιστον, Μουσᾶν θεράπων. Cf. *Alc.* 346 and *Hel.* 170. The λωτὸς Λίβυς (*celtis australis*) was one of the common materials for flutes, Theoph. *H. P.* IV 314 (Wecklein).

164. σύνοχα φοιτάσιν εἰς ὅρος] 'in apt accord with the wild bands trooping to the mountain' (=φοιτώσαις εἰς ὄρος). We cannot construe εἰς ὄρος with ἴτε βάκχαι (Musgrave) or with κῶλον ἄγει (Elmsley).—Βάκχα in 169 is Musgrave's excellent correction of the manuscript reading Βάκχου.

170. τίς ἐν πύλαισι; Κάδμον ἐκκάλει] The older editions, including Elmsley's, had τίς ἐν πύλαισι Κάδμον ἐκκαλεῖ (fut.) δόμων. Elmsley himself however suggests, but does not adopt, the reading printed in the text, quoting in its support *Hel.* 437, τίς πρὸς πύλαισι; *Phoen.* 1067, ὠή, τίς ἐν πύλαισι δωμάτων κυρεῖ; ἀνοίγετ᾽, ἐκπορεύετ᾽ Ἰοκάστην δόμων. To these may be added Eur. fragm. 625ᵃ (*Peleus*) βοάσομαι τἄρα τὰν ὑπέρτονον βοάν· ἰώ, πύλαισιν ἢ τίς ἐν δόμοις; and Ar. *Plutus* 1103, (A) σὺ τὴν θύραν ἔκοπτες;—(B) ἀλλ᾽ ἐκκάλει τὸν δεσπότην.

171. πόλιν—ἄστυ] In πόλις the city is primarily regarded as an association of men, a body of citizens; in ἄστυ, as a place of dwelling, a group of buildings. The former is connected with the Sanskrit *pur, pura, purī*, still frequently found as an element in the name of Indian cities and villages, e.g. *Cawnpore, Serampore, Midnapore. Pur* or *puri* (πόλις) and *puru* (πολύς) are doubtless connected, as both sets come from the root PĂR, 'to fill.' The latter, ἄστυ, is connected with the Indo-European root VĂS, 'to dwell,' whence the Sanskrit *văs-tya, vāstu*, 'dwelling-place,' 'house'; the Greek ἑσ-τία, Ϝεστία; and the Latin *Vesta* and possibly *ves-ti-bulum.*—Thus the walls and towers are the ἄστυ only, while the citizens are the true πόλις, and the famous words of Nicias to his Athenian soldiers in Sicily are, even etymologically, strictly true, ἄνδρες οὐ τείχη πόλις.*—In the passage before us the exact sense of ἄστυ is kept up by the use of ἐπύργωσε.

176. θύρσους ἀνάπτειν] Some supply χερὶ and make it = λαβεῖν εἰς χεῖρα (Schöne), but it is perhaps better to render it 'to swathe (lit. to fasten) the thyrsus,' i.e. 'to dress it with ivy,' after the manner described in 1054—5 (so Elmsley). Cf. *Herc. F.* 549, θανάτου περιβόλαι᾽ ἀνήμμεθα and ib. 1012, δεσμὰ σειραίων βρόχων ἀνήπτομεν πρὸς κίονα. Mr Tyrrell well quotes Hesychius ἀνάπτειν, περιθεῖναι. The thyrsus-wand was not always capped with the pine-cone only, but often finished off at the top or swathed along the stem with ivy or vine-leaves. Virg. *Ecl.* 5, 31, *thiasos inducere Bacchi et foliis lentas intexere mollibus hastas*, and Nonnus 9, 122, quoted in note on i. 25 (paragraph 2).

* Thuc. VII 77 *ad fin.*

178. 'Dearest of men! for e'en within the house I heard thy words, wise as the man that speaks them.' ὡς = *nam* gives the reason why Cadmus at once comes out and addresses Teiresias, without waiting for the porter to open the door and announce the visitor. *Hec.* 1114, ὦ φίλτατ', ἠσθόμην γάρ, 'Aγά-μεμνον, σέθεν φωνῆς ἀκούσας. Elmsley also quotes *Rhes.* 608, *Oed. Col.* 891.—For ἠσθόμην, ἠδόμην and ἠσθήμην [sic] (from ἥδομαι) have been suggested, but the plupf. of that verb would be ᾖσμην, and the aorist or present would have been more natural than either the plupf. or impf. The line is borrowed, just as it stands here, by the author of the *Christus Patiens,* 1148.

183. αὔξεσθαι μέγαν] 'wax to greatness,' a proleptic epithet.—

184. ποῖ (for ποῦ) δεῖ χορεύειν is due to the implied idea of motion, *Herc. F.* 74, ποῖ πατὴρ ἄπεστι γῆς ;

185. ἐξηγοῦ σύ μοι γέρων γέροντι] 'Expound to me as an old man to his fellow.' In Soph. *O. C.* 1284, καλῶς γὰρ ἐξηγεῖ σύ μοι, we have a coincidence of expression, but the sense is somewhat different. In the present passage, and not unfrequently elsewhere, the word is used of priestly interpretations; e.g. Andocides, *de myst.* § 116, ἐξηγῇ, Κηρύκων ὤν, οὐχ ὅσιον σοὶ ἐξηγεῖσθαι (i.e. *you* have no right to expound the sacred rites, as you are not one of the priestly Eumolpidae, but only one of the hereditary Heralds of Eleusis). Cf. ἐξηγητής, *interpres religionum.*

188. ἐπιλελήσμεθ' ἡδέως γέροντες ὄντες] The manuscript reading is ἡδέων, and the sense thus given, 'we in our old age have forgotten our pleasures,' 'are not alive to the pleasures still open to us,' does not tally with the reply of Teiresias, 'Then you feel as *I* do, I too feel young again and shall essay the dance.' Hence all editors now accept the emendation ἡδέως, due in the first instance to Milton. The same easy alteration afterwards occurred, possibly independently, to Barnes (ed. Cambridge, 1694) and to Brunck (ed. Strasburg, 1780). The former says 'mendam hic nemo ante est suspicatus'; the latter 'mirum est id non adsecutos fuisse viros doctissimos...nostra emendatione nihil certius.' But Dobree is perhaps not entirely justified in his severe epigram: 'palmariam emendationem ἡδέως Miltono surripuit Barnesius, Barnesio Brunckius' (Kidd's *Miscellaneous tracts*

p. 224). Milton's emendations were known to Dr Joddrell whose 'illustrations of the *Ion* and *Bacchae*' appeared in 1781 (II p. 335" and 572) and all of them were printed in the *Museum Criticum* in 1814. They were written in the margin of his copy of the edition of Euripides printed by Paul Stephens at Geneva in 1602, 2 vols. 4to. now in the possession of William Wyman Vaughan, Esq., of Upton Castle, Pembroke. Milton bought it in 1634, the very year in which he wrote the *Comus,* which was acted at Michaelmas of that year, and shews in several points special familiarity with this and other plays of Euripides (cf. esp. *Comus* 297—301 with *Iph. T.* 264—274, and notes on 235 and 317 *infra*). For the sense, cf. Ar. *Ran.* 345 sqq. (χορὸς μυστῶν).

192. ἀλλ' οὐχ ὁμοίως ἂν ὁ θεὸς τιμὴν ἔχοι] Elmsley (approved by Shilleto) suggests a somewhat more rhythmical line, ἀλλ' οὐχ ὁμοίαν ὁ θεὸς ἂν τιμὴν ἔχοι, remarking that 'in tragic iambics, a monosyllable which is incapable of beginning a verse, as ἂν, γὰρ, δὲ, μὲν, τε, τις, is very rarely employed as the second syllable of a tribrach or dactyl.' But Hermann shews that τιμὴν ἔχειν being equivalent to τιμᾶσθαι, ὁμοίως will stand, and that although ὁ θεὸς is found elsewhere as a tribrach in the same place as in Elmsley's line, with the *ictus* on the article (206, 333), it is better in the present instance to keep the manuscript reading which allows the *ictus* to fall on θεός, the emphatic word.

193. 'The old man then shall be the old man's guide.' Gellius *N. A.* XIII 19, 3, *sed etiam ille versus non minus notus* γέρων—ἐγὼ *et in tragoedia Sophocli scriptus est cui titulus est* Φθιώτιδες *et in Bacchis Euripidi.* **194. ἀμοχθί**] v. Ar. *Ran.* 400, ἄνευ πόνου. **197. μακρὸν τὸ μέλλειν**] 'delay is tedious.' **198.** 'There now ! clasp hands and link your hand with mine.'

200. οὐδὲν σοφιζόμεσθα τοῖσι δαίμοσι] 'we don't philosophise (do not rationalise) about the gods.' οὐδὲν, lit. 'in no respect.' Some of the earlier scholars (Scaliger, Valckenaer, Brunck) favoured the alteration οὐδὲν σοφιζώμεσθα, forgetting to challenge it on the obvious ground that with the conj. Eur. would have written μηδέν. τοῖσι δαίμοσιν appears to be a dative of hostile direction, 'against the gods,' which Elmsley compares with the common construction of πολεμεῖν and ἐπιβουλεύειν, '*nihil argute commi-*

niscimur in deos'; so also with ἀγωνίζεσθαι, μάχεσθαι, ἀντιλέγειν, ἀνθίστασθαι. Mr Tyrrell however refers to 683, σώμασιν παρειμέναι, thus shewing that he would rather take it as meaning 'in the matter of.'—σοφίζεσθαι is only once used elsewhere by Eur., and that in a play of the same date, *Iph. A.* 744, σοφίζομαι δὲ κἀπὶ τοῖσι φιλτάτοις τέχνας πορίζω. In the sense of 'speculating,' 'rationalising,' 'subtly explaining away' a received belief, it is well illustrated by Plato *Phaedr.* 229 (in part already quoted by Paley), "Tell me, Socrates," says Phaedrus, "was it not from somewhere hereabouts on the Ilissus that Boreas, as the story runs, carried off Orithyia?...Do you believe the legend (μυθολόγημα) to be true?" "Why" (answers Socrates), "I should be doing nothing extraordinary, if, like the learned (οἱ σοφοὶ), I were to disbelieve the tale ; and if, in a rationalising mood (σοφιζόμενος), I went on to say that as the girl was playing ...she was blown over the cliffs just here, by a blast of the wind Boreas, and that having thus met her end, she was fabled to have been carried off by the god Boreas... But I have no leisure for such studies... I therefore leave them alone and acquiesce in the received opinion regarding them" (χαίρειν ἐάσας ταῦτα, πειθόμενος...τῷ νομιζομένῳ περὶ αὐτῶν). The mental attitude thus described is remarkably parallel with that expressed in the present and several other passages in the play (427—31, 395, 882—95). But just as Plato in the *Republic* and elsewhere rejects myths of an immoral tendency, so the vulgar stories with which the Greek Theogony was rife (whatever explanation of them may in the present day be made possible by the light of comparative mythology) were again and again condemned by Euripides (*Iph. T.* 386, *H. F.* 1341). Yet this position of remonstrance does not prevent his allowing expression to be given here and elsewhere, by characters in his plays, to a feeling of contented and unquestioning submission to traditional and time-honoured beliefs. Such passive compliance is dramatically appropriate in the lips of the aged prophet, and is not unsuitable to the declining years of the poet himself; but we must be careful not to assume that the poet himself actually held the sentiments which a sense of dramatic fitness leads him to ascribe to the characters in his plays. It was an assumption of this kind that led Aristophanes and others to make an unwarrantable charge against him founded on a line wrested from its context, ἡ γλῶσσ᾽ ὀμώμοχ᾽, ἡ δὲ φρὴν ἀνώμοτος (*Hipp.* 612), a line which is dramatically most defensible ; and, if read in its proper place, is justly recognised as a sudden outburst of self-reproach on the part of a youth of stainless purity, indignant at having been entrapped into a verbal oath of whose true meaning he was at the time utterly innocent, an oath whose binding force he acknowledges immediately after, and which he keeps at the cost of losing his life.

201—3. πατρίους παραδοχὰς...φρενῶν] 'Our fathers' heir-loom of time-honoured faith, No reasoning shall cast down, not though the lore Hath been the invention of the keenest wit.' This passage is referred to by Plutarch *Mor.* II p. 756 (*Amatorius* 13, 3), μεγάλου μοι δοκεῖς ἅπτεσθαι καὶ παραβόλου πράγματος, μᾶλλον δὲ ὅλως τὰ ἀκίνητα κινεῖν, τῆς περὶ θεῶν δόξης ἣν ἔχομεν, περὶ ἑκάστου λόγου ἀπαιτῶν καὶ ἀπόδειξιν· ἀρκεῖ γὰρ ἡ πατρία καὶ παλαιὰ πίστις, ἧς οὐκ ἔστιν εἰπεῖν οὐδ᾽ ἀνευρεῖν τεκμήριον ἐναργέστερον, οὐδ᾽ εἰ δι᾽ ἄκρας τὸ σοφὸν εὕρηται φρενός, ἀλλ᾽ ἕδρα τις αὕτη καὶ βάσις ὑφεστῶσα κοινὴ πρὸς εὐσέβειαν, ἐὰν ἐφ᾽ ἑνὸς ταράττηται καὶ σαλεύηται τὸ βέβαιον αὐτῆς καὶ νενομισμένον, ἐπισφαλὴς γίνεται πᾶσι καὶ ὕποπτος. This quotation (as was first pointed out by Valckenaer) shews that for the manuscript reading πατρός, we should read πατρίους. It is acutely suggested by Mr Tyrrell that Plutarch paraphrases καταβάλλει ('gets the better of') as if he had read ὑπερβαλεῖ ('will be better than').— πατρίους] Plat. *leges* 793 B, πάτρια καὶ παντάπασιν ἀρχαῖα νόμιμα.— ὁμήλικας χρόνῳ] This may mean either (1) traditions '*coeval in time*' (with ourselves), which we have not only inherited from our ancestors (πατρίους) but have looked upon as familiar friends who have grown up with us from our very infancy ; in this case we may compare Soph. *O. C.* 112, χρόνῳ παλαιοί, 374, χρόνῳ μείων, 875, χρόνῳ βραδύς (so Hermann); or (2) '*coeval with time*,' as old as time itself, like the unwritten ordinances of the gods in Soph. *Antig.* 456, οὐ γάρ τι νῦν γε κἀχθές, ἀλλ᾽ ἀεί ποτε ζῇ ταῦτα, κοὐδεὶς οἶδεν ἐξ ὅτου 'φάνη. The latter interpretation is sometimes held to be supported by Plutarch's παλαιὰ in the passage quoted above, but that epithet seems equally applicable to the former sense, in which the traditions are spoken of as φίλοι παλαιοί, *veteres amici;* had he used ἀρχαία πίστις, *antiqua fides, prisca fides*, he might have been appealed to with greater confidence as in favour of the second rendering; his paraphrase of the passage is however too loose and cursory to admit of our relying upon it for the determination of so nice a point. 'Old as time itself' is a spirited expression which may appear too bold for Euripides, but it must be remembered that he personifies time in this very play, as well as in a line from a lost play quoted by Aristophanes to raise a laugh at his expense (χρόνου πόδα, 889 n.). Had he meant the first sense, he would probably have written ἅς θ' ὁμήλικας πάλαι κεκτήμεθα.—αὐτά] (used instead of αὐτὰς) refers to the general sense of the previous line, as in Thuc. v, 10, σπονδαὶ ἔσονται· οὕτω γὰρ ἔπραξαν αὐτὰ (*sc.* τὰ περὶ τὰς σπονδάς).

εὕρηται is best taken not as aor. conj. mid., but as perf. indic. passive. Hermann however says, ' neque vero εἰ εὕρηται indicativo perfecti dictum hic aptum est, ut in re incerta. itaque aut τὶς intelligendum, aut εὕρηται perfecto passivo, sed modi coniunctivi habendum *.'—In thought and expression alike, the passage appears to be directed against the Sophists, the first of whom, Protagoras, wrote a treatise under the title, Καταβάλλοντες (sc. λόγοι). One of his sayings was, περὶ μὲν θεῶν οὐκ ἔχω εἰδέναι οὔθ' ὡς εἰσὶν οὔθ' ὡς οὐκ εἰσίν, Diog. L. ΙΧ 51 (Usener).

204. ἐρεῖ τις] *At enim, 'fortasse dixerit quispiam.'* 'Some one may say, I have no regard for eld (no self-respect), In going to dance, with ivy round my head; *Not so*, for the deity hath not defined, &c.'—εἰ χρὴ χορεύειν implies the copyist took the syntax to be, οὐ διῄρηκεν εἴτε τὸν νέον εἴτε τὸν γεραίτερον, εἰ χρὴ χορεύειν = εἴτε τὸν νέον χρὴ χορεύειν εἴτε τὸν γεραίτερον. Mr Munro suggests χρείη for εἰ χρὴ : 'the corruption would arise from χρὴ being written for χρείη and then εἰ added in the margin or above. This opt. is common enough, and yet it is constantly corrupted (*e.g.* O. T. 162, 555).'

209. δι' ἀριθμῶν] This difficult phrase, about which almost the only point that is clear is that it is intended to stand in

* See *Supplementary Notes.*

sharp contrast to ἐξ ἁπάντων in the previous line, is supposed
to mean, 'by certain fixed numbers,' i.e. by certain circum-
scribed classes of men, young alone or old alone, only poor
or only rich. The god will have no compromise; he claims a
honour from all classes indefinitely, without respect of age or
other circumstances, and cares not to be worshipped by any
narrow number, to be honoured by instalments, *by halves,* as
Elmsley expresses it. In short, he expects of the state in
general what Wordsworth in a strain of higher mood says
of the unreserved self-sacrifice of the individual, 'Give all
thou canst; high Heaven rejects the lore Of nicely calculated
less or more' (*Ecclesiastical Sonnets* 43). Mr G. O'Connor comes
near the sense of this last parallel, when understanding it "with
employment of calculations" and translating it "by rule and
measure." Mr Brady (quoted by Mr Tyrrell) proposes διαιρῶν,
suggested doubtless by διήρηκε and already anticipated by Dr
Joddrell; but Mr Tyrrell himself has since deserted that proposal in favour of διαριθμῶν, (suggested by Heath as well as by
himself,) which he takes with οὐδέν, '*making no distinction,*' though
he allows that, in this sense, the middle is more usual. I own
I am not satisfied with the above explanation of δι' ἀριθμῶν or
with any of the proposed corrections. What is obviously
wanted for the restoration of the text is a phrase exactly parallel
to ἐξ ἁπάντων in the previous line; the most obvious equivalent
to *including all* among those by whom the god expects to be
honoured is *omitting no one,* and the most natural Greek for this
would be οὐδένα παραλιπὼν; the sense would therefore be satisfied
by some such correction as παραλιπὼν δ' οὐδέν' αὔξεσθαι θέλει.

οὐδὲν...θέλει] 'in no wise wishes.' There seems to be practically little, if any, difference in sense between θέλει in the
present and βούλεται in the previous line. In *Iph. Aul.* 338, we
have τῷ δοκεῖν μὲν οὐχὶ χρῄζων τῷ δὲ βούλεσθαι θέλων, *Alc.* 281,
λέξαι θέλω σοι πρὶν θανεῖν ἃ βούλομαι, and in Dem. *fals. leg.*
§ 23, οὔτ' ἀκούειν ἠθέλετε οὔτε πιστεύειν ἐβούλεσθε. βούλομαι
(according to Donaldson *New Crat.* § 463) 'refers to the desire
or wishing for a thing;' while θέλω 'is restricted to the mere
will or willingness.'

211. προφήτης] 'myself shall be the prompter of thy words.'
Had not Teiresias been blind, he would have ended his speech
by announcing the approach of Pentheus in some such words as
καὶ μὴν (*Antig.* 526, 1180) πρὸς οἴκους ὅδε διὰ σπουδῆς περᾷ Πενθεύς.
As it is, Cadmus prepares the audience and the soothsayer, for
the coming of the king, by taking up the speech instead,
and this is why he is called προφήτης λόγων. So Teiresias himself is called Διὸς προφήτης (Pind. *Nem.* I. 91) as one who
speaks instead of Zeus and interprets his will to man; so also in
Aesch. *Eum.* 19, Διὸς προφήτης ἐστι Λοξίας πατρὸς, Apollo is the
revealer of the will of Zeus, and the Delphic priestess in her
turn is Φοίβου προφῆτις *Ion* 321, cf. esp. 91—93. The notion of
foretelling is only subordinate; and in the line before us we
cannot (with Bothe and Schöne) understand Cadmus to be
predicting a coming conversation.

214. ὡς ἐπτόηται] 'how flushed he is!', 'how wild his mien!'
1269, τὸ πτοηθέν, 304, διεπτόησε (struck with panic), and in a play
of the same date, *Iph. A.* 1029, στείχουσαν ἐπτοημένην. Cf. *Med.*
1120, πνεῦμα δ' ἠρεθισμένον δείκνυσιν ὥς τι καινὸν ἀγγελεῖ κακόν.

215. τυγχάνω, with the participle, often expresses coincidence in time apart from any notion of chance. 'Though at the
moment absent from this land, I hear of strange ills in the city
here. Our women as we find (ἡμῖν) have left their homes In
feigned orgies; on the shadowy hills They frisk it.' Θοάζειν, here
intrans. (cf. n. on 65), 'hurry hither and thither,' *Troad.* 307,
μαινὰς θοάζει δεῦρο Κασσάνδρα δρόμῳ, and *ib.* 349.—**221.** θιάσοις
ἐν μέσοισιν, not, 'in the midst of the festal groups,' but 'in the
midst of each festal group.'—ἑστάναι κρατῆρας, Paus. VII 27, 3,
at Pallene, τούτῳ (Διονύσῳ Λαμπτῆρι) καὶ Λαμπτήρια ἑορτὴν ἄγουσι
καὶ δᾷδάς τε ἐς τὸ ἱερὸν κομίζουσιν ἐν τῇ νυκτὶ καὶ οἴνου κρατῆρας
ἱστᾶσιν ἀνὰ τὴν πόλιν πᾶσαν, and Oracles quoted in Dem. *Mid.*
§§ 51, 53; also Statius *Theb.* II 75 (of Theban votaries of Bacchus)
*effusi passim per tecta, per agros Serta inter vacuosque mero
crateras.*

224. πρόφασιν μέν] Ar. *Eq.* 466, πρόφασιν μὲν Ἀργείους
φίλους ἡμῖν ποιεῖ, ἰδίᾳ δ' ἐκεῖ Λακεδαιμονίοις συγγίγνεται, Thuc. VI
33 and Lysias Or. 13 § 12 (cf. 12 § 6), πρόφασιν μέν...τὸ δ' ἀληθές.

—ὡς δὴ sc. οὔσας. For this ironical use of ὡς δὴ, cf. *Androm.*
235, ὡς δὴ σὺ σώφρων τἀμὰ δ᾽ οὐχὶ σώφρονα, where as here the
participle is omitted.—θυοσκόους] also used in *Rhesus* 68, τῶν
ἐμῶν θυοσκόων βουλάς, and *Iliad* 24, 221, ἢ οἱ μάντιές εἰσι θυοσκόοι
ἢ ἱερῆες. The verb is found in Aesch. *Ag.* 87, θυοσκεῖς.—**226**.
δεσμίους χέρας] χέρας is the 'acc. of closer definition.'—**227**.
πανδήμοισι στέγαις] 444, πανδήμου στέγης, the 'public buildings,'
as a euphemism for the prison; cf. οἴκημα, δήμιος and δημόκοινος.

229. So in Idyll XXVI of Theocritus, on the doom of Pentheus, (Λῆναι ἢ Βάκχαι), Ἰνὼ κ᾽ Αὐτονόα χ᾽ ἁ μαλοπάραος Ἀγαύα
τρεῖς θιάσους ἐς ὄρος τρεῖς ἄγαγον αὐταὶ ἐοῖσαι.

234—6. 'A wizard sorcerer from the Lydian land, With
fragrant golden curls, and ruddy face, And eyes that beam
with Aphrodite's charms.' The whole picture reminds one of
Milton's 'Vermeil-tinctured lip, Love-darting eyes or tresses like
the morn' (*Comus* 753); words written, it is to be remembered,
for the autumn of the very year in which he bought the copy of
Euripides described in a previous note, l. 188.

It is doubtless to the present passage, and to 453—459, that
Callistratus refers in his graceful description of a statue of
Dionysus, the work of Praxiteles, (*Stat.* 8), ἦν δὲ ἀνθηρὸς, ἁβρό-
τητος (493) γέμων, ἱμέρῳ ῥεόμενος, οἷον αὐτὸν Εὐριπίδης ἐν Βάκχαις
εἰδοποιήσας ἐξέφηνε...ὡς κισσὸς ἦν ὁ χαλκὸς εἰς κλῶνας καμπτύ-
μενος καὶ τῶν βοστρύχων τοὺς ἑλικτῆρας ἐκ μετώπου κεχυμένους
ἀναστέλλων.

γόης ἐπῳδός] It seems best to understand the latter word as
a separate substantive and not as an adjective to the former.
The words are used as substantives in *Hipp.* 1038, ἐπῳδὸς καὶ
γόης, Plat. *Symp.* 203 D, δεινὸς γόης καὶ φαρμακεὺς καὶ σοφιστής
(a clever wizard, sorcerer and charlatan). The notion that the
strange visitant was a wizard might easily arise from vague
reports of his mystic mummeries, the τελεταὶ εὔιοι of 238, and
of the marvellous streams of milk and honey and wine referred
to in 142.

235. ξανθοῖσι βοστρύχοισιν] *Cyclops* 75, ὦ φίλος, ὦ φίλε Βάκχιε,
ποῖ οἰοπολεῖς ξανθὰν χαίταν σείων, Seneca *Oed.* 421 (of Bacchus),
crine flaventi simulata virgo.—εὐόσμοις κομῶν (as in *Iliad* 8, 42 ;

13, 24; χρυσέῃσιν ἐθείρῃσιν κομόωντε) is Badham's conjecture for εὔοσμον κόμην (of the MSS and Ald. ed.). εὔοσμος κόμην (Brunck's conjecture, adopted by Paley) has the advantage of being a slighter departure from the MSS. εὐοσμῶν κόμης (proposed by Mr Tyrrell) is not conclusive, for in that case κόμης would not be wanted at all as a genitive after βοστρύχοισιν; and, partly for this reason, his alternative εὐοσμῶν κόμην seems better.

239—241. The sense would perhaps be improved by transferring these lines to a place between lines 247 and 248. We should thus get the stranger's misdemeanours mentioned first, with the threats of punishment immediately following. This suggestion is due to Kirchhoff.

242. ἐκεῖνος εἶναί φησι Διόνυσον θεόν] Not *ille se dicit esse Dionysum deum* (Barnes), which would obviously have required the nominative after εἶναι, on the principle which is well illustrated by Thuc. IV 28, οὐκ ἔφη αὐτὸς ἀλλ' ἐκεῖνον στρατηγεῖν. The nom. is actually printed in the editions of Reiske and Matthiae, who forget that Dionysus has not yet revealed his deity, as the plot of the play implies that at present the god represents himself as a votary only of Dionysus, and not as the god himself. The repetition of ἐκεῖνος in the next line, the genuineness of which has been perhaps unnecessarily suspected, is intended to intensify the contempt conveyed by the pronoun; ''Tis *he* (this Lydian impostor with his own unsupported assertion), that says Dionysus is a god; 'tis *he*, forsooth, that says that Dionysus was sewn up in the thigh of Zeus; the babe that was really blasted to death by the flaming thunderbolt.'—**244.** ἐκπυροῦται, present of vivid description, as in line 2. For the verb, cf. *Troad.* 301, αὐτῶν ἐκπυροῦσι σώματα, *Herc. F.* 421, ὕδραν ἐξεπύρωσεν, and *Iph. A.* 1070, Πριάμοιο κλεινὰν γαῖαν ἐκπυρώσων.—**245.** Δίους ὅτι γάμους ἐψεύσατο, see lines 26—31.

246—7. 'Do not these wrongs call for the awful halter, This stranger's outrages—whoe'er he be?' ἔστ' ἄξια] The same words end the line in *Orest.* 615, but both passages are perhaps unnecessarily altered by Elmsley into ἐπάξια, because, as he says, *nullum senarium apud tragicos exstare puto qui in initio quinti pedis ἔστ' vel ἐστ' habeat.*—ἀγχόνης] Soph. *O. T.* 1374, ἔργα

κρείσσον' ἀγχόνης, Eur. *Heracl.* 246, τάδ' ἀγχόνης πέλας, Ar.ʼ*Ach.*
125, ταῦτα δῆτ' οὐκ ἀγχόνη ; In all these cases hanging is referred
to, not as a punishment, but as a form of suicide ; and it has
been suggested that the present passage is no exception, but
that Pentheus here virtually exclaims ʻ This is as bad as bad can
be—it is enough to make one hang oneself.' On this supposition,
it is urged that the transcriber, mistaking the sense of this line,
and wrongly supposing it referred to the hanging of the impostor,
added the next line (247) to explain it ; but the retention of the
next line is not inconsistent with the above suggestion.   Those
who understand the halter to be here a form of punishment,
may notice that (according to the ordinary printing of the
passage) Pentheus has already threatened to cut the stranger's
head off, in which event he might dispense with threats of
hanging ; but it is open to them to rejoin that the king's rage
makes him incoherent, and leads to his blurting out one punishment after another in an ungovernable fit of passion ; in a later
passage, 356, he threatens him with neither decapitation nor
hanging, but with death by stoning.—ὕβρεις ὑβρίζειν] As the only
other instance of the plural of ὕβρις in Tragedy is *Herc. F.* 741,
ὕβρεις ὑβρίζων εἰς ἀμείνονας σέθεν, it has been proposed to alter
it in both instances to ὕβρισμ' (Elmsley, who quotes *Heracl.* 18,
ὕβρισμ' ἐς ἡμᾶς ἠξίωσεν ὑβρίσαι), but (as Hermann justly remarks) *raritas non est idonea damnandi caussa.* ὕβρισμα *hic, mea
sententia, alienum foret, quia non de una, sed de multiplici con-
tumelia sermo est.*   The singular is much more common as in
Hel. 785, ὕβριν θ' ὑβρίζειν εἰς ἔμ' ἦν ἔτλην ἐγώ, *Herc. F.* 708, ὕβριν
θ' ὑβρίζεις ἐπὶ θανοῦσι τοῖς ἐμοῖς, *Iph. Aul.* 961, ἀλλ' ὕβριν ἐς
ἡμᾶς ὕβρισ' 'Αγαμέμνων ἄναξ.   In all these cases the cognate
acc., contrary to the general rule, has apparently no adjective
or pronoun joined with it, though it has what may be regarded
as an adjectival phrase instead.   In the present passage, the
absence of any adjectival element condemns the conjecture
ὕβρισμ' ὑβρίζειν, but this objection does not apply to the manuscript reading, as the use of the plural, ὕβρεις, gives a fuller
meaning to what would otherwise have been a bare repetition of
the same sense.   (Further details on this construction may be

found in Lobeck, *de figura Etymologica*, p. 506, and in G. Günther, *de obiecti quod dicitur interioris usu Euripideo*, p. 22).

251. νάρθηκι βακχεύοντ'] It is uncertain whether this stands for the dual or the singular accusative. Though both are alike arrayed in the Bacchic garb, Teiresias is specially described as dressed in fawnskins; so it may be Cadmus alone that is represented 'with a ferule masquerading.' At the same time, it is not improbable that as a single fawnskin is all that is usually ascribed to the votaries of Dionysus, the poet is thinking of Cadmus as well as Teiresias in using the plural νεβρίσι (cf. however Nonnus 45, 86, χρύσεα πέπλα φέρων οὐ νεβρίδας).—The reading of the Laurentian MS is corrected into βακχεύοντας, both MSS have ἀναίνομαι, while πάτερ may be an interpolation, added to eke out the metre. As, however, the first reading of the Laurentian MS was ναίνομαι, we may suggest that this points not to ἀλλὰ μαίνομαι, as has been proposed, but to an original reading νάρθηκι βακχεύοντας· ἀλλ' ἀναίνομαι, the accidental omission of ἀλλὰ accounting for the mutilated form ναίνομαι. νάρθηκι βακχεύοντας· αἰδοῦμαι πάτερ is proposed by Porson (*advers.* p. 264), and this is supported by Nonnus, 45, 73 (referred to by Hermann, who, however, does not accept the alteration), where Pentheus says to Teiresias, αἰδέομαι σέο γῆρας, ἀμετροβίων δὲ καὶ αὐτῶν μάρτυρα σῶν ἐτέων πολιὴν πλοκαμῖδα γεραίρω. For ἀναίνομαι, see *Iph. Aul.* 1502, θανοῦσα δ' οὐκ ἀναίνομαι, 'it pains me not to die'; 'proprie est *recuso, detrecto,* quod quoniam est eius, qui quid invitus facit, significat *piget me*' (Hermann).—If we retain πάτερ we must be careful to translate ὑμῶν so as to shew that it is plural, 'father, I am pained for thee, At seeing *your* old age so reft of sense.' Cf. Soph. *O. C.* 1102, 1104.

253—9. Nonnus expands this speech after his diffuse manner, 45, 67, Κάδμε, μιαινομένης ἀποκάτθεο κισσὸν ἐθείρης, κάτθεο καὶ νάρθηκα νοοπλανέος Διονύσου...νήπιε Τειρεσία στεφανηφόρε, ῥῖψον ἀήταις σῶν πλοκάμων τάδε φύλλα, νόθον στέφος. In the next line but one, follows the passage above quoted, and then the further imitation, 75, εἰ μὴ γὰρ τόδε γῆρας ἐρήτυε καὶ σέο χαίτη, καί κεν ἀλυκτοπέδησιν ἐγὼ σέο χεῖρας ἑλίξας δέσμιον ἀχλυόεντι κατεσφρήγισσα μελάθρῳ, κ.τ.λ.

255—7. We have an equally strong invective against Teiresias from Oedipus in Soph. *O. T.* 387, μάγον ... μηχανορράφον, δόλιον ἀγύρτην, ὅστις ἐν τοῖς κέρδεσιν μόνον δέδορκε, and in *Antig.* 1055, Creon taunts him with venality, τὸ μαντικὸν γὰρ πᾶν φιλάργυρον γένος. The function of soothsayer seems to have been held in small repute among the contemporaries of the Greek tragic poets, and passages like these reflect the general feeling of the day. Euripides in particular enters with special zest into attacking the whole tribe of μάντεις, e.g. *Hipp.* 1059, *Ion* 374—8, *Hel.* 744—757, *El.* 400, *Phoen.* 772, *fragm.* 793, τί δῆτα θάκοις μαντικοῖς ἐνήμενοι σαφῶς διόμνυσθ' εἰδέναι τὰ δαιμόνων; οὐ τῶνδε χειρώνακτες ἄνθρωποι λόγων, and (in a play of the same date as this) *Iph. A.* 520, τὸ μαντικὸν πᾶν σπέρμα φιλότιμον κακόν. The taunts of venality, which Euripides here allows to be flung at Teiresias by Pentheus, taunts to which he offers no reply, may well make us hesitate in accepting the prophet as the exponent of the poet's opinions in the often-quoted line, οὐδὲν σοφιζόμεσθα τοῖσι δαίμοσι (200).

262. οὐδὲν ὑγιές] is very common in prose and comedy, but is less suited to the dignity of tragedy. It is however found in Eur. *Hel.* 746, *Phoen.* 201, *Androm.* 448, 952, and three passages in the fragments 496, 660, 821, in all of which allusion is made to current proverbs or opinions of the day; hence it is that Euripides, while referring to these proverbs and opinions, falls into the use of a phrase of every-day life (οἰκεῖα πράγματ' εἰσάγων, οἷς χρώμεθ', οἷς σύνεσμεν, *Ranae* 959): Aeschylus, on the other hand, never uses it, and Sophocles only once, *Phil.* 1006, and even there without any loss of dignity, ὦ μηδὲν ὑγιὲς μηδ' ἐλεύθερον φρονῶν.—In the previous line, for βότρυος, a tribrach consisting of a single word, see 18, μιγάσιν.

263. The MSS have τῆς εὐσεβείας, which, if retained, is most naturally taken in an ironical sense (as by Barnes, Matthiae, and Tyrrell). But irony is out of keeping with the general character of the chorus in Greek Tragedy, and least of all is it appropriate in the case of Asiatic women addressing a Theban king. Hermann, while retaining εὐσεβείας, suggests καταισχύνειν in the third line, and gives an explanation which strikes one as highly artificial and unconvincing: "constructio verborum haec est, οὐκ αἰδῇ θεούς, τῆς εὐσεβείας Κάδμον τε καταισχύνειν, iam dicere debebat καὶ τὸ σὸν αὐτοῦ γένος...sed continuat orationem...'Εχίονος δ' ὢν παῖς καταισχύνειν γένος," i.e. 'Are you not ashamed before the gods at disgracing not only Cadmus on account of his piety (*propter pietatem*), but also (as son of Echion) disgracing your own lineage.' A clearer sense is given by adopting the emendation τῆς δυσσεβείας suggested by Reiske, and apparently approved by Porson (*Kidd's tracts*, p. 225). Hermann's objection to treating the first two words of the line as a separate exclamation on the ground that *exclamatio non nisi familiari colloquio convenit* may be met by admitting that such an exclamation is more common in Aristophanes than in the tragedians, but by pointing out at the same time that in the very last line we find a colloquialism in the phrase οὐδὲν ὑγιές. This kind of gen. is found sufficiently often in tragedy, preceded by φεῦ, ὦ πόποι or οἴμοι (e.g. *Herc. F.* 1374, οἴμοι δάμαρτος καὶ τέκνων οἴμοι δ' ἐμοῦ), and also (as here) without any interjection, as in *Med.* 1051, ἀλλὰ τῆς ἐμῆς κάκης τὸ καὶ προέσθαι (*sc. ἐμὲ*) μαλθακοὺς λόγους φρενί, and *Iph. A.* (a contemporary play) 327, ὦ θεοί, σῆς ἀναισχύντου φρενός.—The two next verses (264—5) are transposed by Musgrave, the effect of which is to bring Κάδμον under the influence of καταισχύνεις, leaving θεοὺς alone to be governed by αἰδεῖ. This is not a bad arrangement, but one that probably did not occur to Euripides, who adopts the natural order of time, mentioning the gods first, then Cadmus the grandfather, and next Echion the father of Pentheus.—For the reference to the crop of armed warriors that sprang up from the serpent's teeth sown by Cadmus, cf. 1315 and see esp. *Phoen.* 657—75, 818—21 and 939. The teeth, as the legend ran, were those of the serpent that guarded the fountain of Ares and killed the men sent to draw water by Cadmus who slew the serpent and sowed the teeth. The armed men who thus sprang into life forthwith began to kill one another; of the five survivors one was Echion, who became the father of Pentheus by Agave, daughter of Cadmus. The following gem represents Cadmus at the fountain attacking the serpent which had slain his companions, whose fate is indicated by the overturned pitcher.

265. καταισχύνεις γένος;] *Od.* 24, 508, Plato *Laches* 187 A.

266—7. This couplet from a play written (it will be remembered) at the Macedonian court, was afterwards quoted by no less a successor of Archelaus than Alexander the Great, after listening to an eloquent speech by the philosopher Callisthenes in praise of the men of Macedon (Plutarch, *Alex.* 53, 2). The king next called upon him to show his powers as an orator by discoursing on a more difficult theme, the *faults* of the Macedonians, and the philosopher indiscreetly consenting, at the close of the second speech the king remarked that Callisthenes had given the Macedonians a proof not of his eloquence but of his enmity. Plutarch, after giving another instance of the indiscretion of Callisthenes, adds that his relative Aristotle had therefore well remarked of him, ὅτι Καλλισθένης λόγῳ μὲν ἦν δυνατὸς καὶ μέγας, νοῦν δὲ οὐκ εἶχεν. Here we may note the coincidence of expression with the context of Alexander's quotation, where δυνατὸς and νοῦν οὐκ ἔχων occur in the same short sentence. Were the words less common, the identity of expression would better deserve notice ; but if it is admitted that Aristotle was thinking of the context when he made his remark, it would be an argument of some slight weight in favour of retaining the manuscript reading δυνατὸς instead of accepting Dr Badham's tempting conjecture ἐν ἀστοῖς.—For ἀφορμὰς cf. *Herc. F.* 236, ἆρ' οὐκ ἀφορμὰς τοῖς λόγοισιν ἀγαθοὶ θνητῶν ἔχουσι κἂν βραδύς τις ᾖ λέγειν ; and *Hec.* 1239, βροτοῖσιν ὡς τὰ χρηστὰ πράγματα χρηστῶν ἀφορμὰς ἐνδίδωσ' ἀεὶ λόγων, also Lucian, *Rhetorum praeceptor* c. 18, ἐπειδὰν δέῃ λέγειν καὶ οἱ παρόντες ὑποβάλωσί τινας ὑποθέσεις καὶ ἀφορμὰς τῶν λόγων.—268. εὔτροχον γλῶσσαν] fragm. 442 (Hippol.), εὐτρόχοισι στόμασι τἀληθέστατα κλέπτουσιν, ὥστε μὴ δοκεῖν ἃ χρὴ δοκεῖν. *This tongue that runs so roundly in thy head* (*Rich. II* ii, 1).

270—1. ' But the rash man, if strong and eloquent, Makes a bad citizen, because he's senseless.' This couplet is placed in brackets by Dindorf, who does not perhaps attribute sufficient weight to the fact that it is quoted by Stobaeus, 45. 2, from the ' Pentheus ' of Euripides (as also the previous couplet in 36. 9). On the same page (45. 5) he cites a passage from *Orest.* 907, which is closely parallel to it, ὅταν γὰρ ἡδὺς τοῖς λόγοις φρονῶν κακῶς πείθῃ τὸ πλῆθος, τῇ πόλει κακὸν μέγα. This last quotation is supposed to have been directed against Cleophon, a demagogue of influence between B.C. 410 and 405. The couplet, inspired perhaps by the poet's remembrance of some such notable member of the Athenian democracy, would have been less in place at any representation of the play at the court of King Archelaus, than before the Athenian audience that heard it after the poet's death.—νοῦν οὐκ ἔχων] states the fact, ' destitute, as he is, of sense' and repeats in another form the notion already expressed by θρασύς ; had the sense been ' *if* destitute of sense,' the negative particle which implies a supposition would have been used, and we should have had some phrase equivalent to μὴ ἔχων.—[*legendum* θρασὺς δέ, δυνατὸς καὶ λέγειν ὅς ἐστ' ἀνήρ. Dem. *Androt.* p. 601 § 33, ἢ δεινοὺς ἢ θρασεῖς...τοῖς θρασέσι καὶ δυνατοῖς λέγειν] Shilleto.—Cf. *Or.* 889, *Ion* 596.

272—3. οὗτος ὁ δαίμων κ.τ.λ., instead of being placed after ὅσος, on which it depends, is for rhetorical emphasis put at the very beginning of the sentence, without being altered into the acc. after ἐξειπεῖν. So in Xen. *Anab.* 2, 5, 41, Πρόξενος καὶ Μένων ἐπείπερ εἰσὶν ὑμέτεροι εὐεργέται, πέμψατε αὐτοὺς δεῦρο.

273. οὐκ ἂν δυναίμην μέγεθος ἐξειπεῖν ὅσος, is rendered by Attius, *Bacchae* IX (2), ...*neque sat fingi neque dici potest | pro magnitate.*

274. δύο] sc. Δημήτηρ and Διόνυσος. Nonnus, 45, 101, in the corresponding speech of Teiresias, says of the god, οὗτος ἀμαλλοτόκῳ Δημήτερι μοῦνος ἐρίζει ἀντίτυπον σταχύεσσιν ἔχων εὔβοτρυν ὀπώρην. The identification of Δημήτηρ with γῆ is in accord-

ance with the old etymology, which made it an old form of γῆ
μήτηρ, cf. δᾶ for γῆ in *Phoen.* 1296 (rejected by Ahrens *Dor.*
p. 80, who connects δᾶ with the root of δῖος, Διός, Δάν for Ζάν
&c.; and by Curtius, *Gk. Etym.* p. 492 ed. 5). For **276**, Paley
aptly quotes Aesch. *P. V.* 217, Γαῖα πολλῶν ὀνομάτων μορφὴ μία.
—**278.** By accepting the correction ὃς δ' we get an easier
transition to the next line than that supplied by ὃ δ', (which,
however, comes nearer the MSS, which have ὅδ'). ὃ in the
latter correction is used as a demonstrative pronoun ; ' in bonis
codicibus ubi ὁ non articulus, sed pronomen demonstrativum
est accentu notatur' (Hermann).

As an extension of Badham's ingenious conjecture ἡδονὴν
ἀντίπαλον, we may propose ἡδονὴν παυσίπονον, which comes
very near the manuscript reading τἀντίπαλον. This is suggested by an expression in one of the Orphic hymns, 50 (49),
addressed to Dionysus, παυσίπονον θνητοῖσι φανεὶς ἄκος. The
word is found in *Iph. T.* 451, and in the parody of Euripides
in Ar. *Ranae*, 1321, οἰνάνθας γάνος ἀμπέλου, βότρυος ἕλικα παυσίπονον. ἀντίτυπον, however, in the passage above quoted from
Nonnus, seems to shew that in *his* time, at any rate, the manuscript reading was probably ἀντίπαλον.

282. Some edd. print ὕπνου, making a double gen., the notion
of 'oblivion arising from sleep' being coupled with 'oblivion of
ills.' 'He gives in sleep, from all our daily ills Oblivion, that
sole simple for all toils.' ὕπνου was supposed to be the reading
of P (the Palatine MS); Milton suggested ὕπνον, which happens
to be the reading of the other MS (the Laurentian), and (according to the latest collation) it is found in the Palatine MS
also.

284. σπένδεται] used in a double sense, being grammatically
applicable in the middle voice to the god himself, who 'makes
peace with' the other gods ; but also involving a reference to his
gift of wine which 'is poured out' in libations.

286—297. The genuineness of this whole passage is open to
serious doubt. It professes to give an explanation of the legend
that Dionysus was sewn up in the thigh of Zeus, a story which
had its origin, according to Teiresias, in a confusion between the

words ὅμηρος and μηρός. Against the genuineness of the lines
may be urged, (1) the absurdity of the explanation ; (2) the
intricacy of part of the language in which it is expressed ; (3)
the inconsistency between the present account and the popular
legend accepted unreservedly by the chorus (96—100, 519—29) ;
(4) the incongruity of placing this attempt to do what looks very
like explaining away the traditional belief, in the lips of the very
prophet who has shortly before exclaimed, οὐδὲν σοφιζόμεσθα
τοῖσι δαίμοσι (200).   On the other hand, it may be observed that
(1) absurd as is the explanation, the popular legend is at least
equally absurd ; (2) the explanation finds a partial parallel in the
legend preserved by Apollodorus, according to which Zeus
deceived Hera by changing the infant Dionysus into a kid
(III 4, 3 *ad fin.*) ; (3) the clearing up of a confusion arising from
two words being similar in sound is apt in any case to be
intricate, especially in poetry ; (4) a fondness for etymologising
is one of the characteristics of Euripides ; (5) Pentheus had
made an emphatic reference to the current story of the god's
birth (243), and in accordance with the constant rule of
Euripidean rhetoric, this point had to be met in the prophet's
reply ; (6) it is not necessary to have a perfect consistency of
opinion between all the characters of the play, and a chorus of
Asiatic women may well be represented as accepting with
unquestioning trust a popular legend which is indignantly rejected by the young king, who is unconscious of the inner
meaning which it is the prophet's task to unfold in his reply ;
and lastly (7), as to the supposed inconsistency of Teiresias, it
has been well remarked, that "The form of the popular story
is, he allows, absurd.   But the story itself is essentially true.
Dionysus *is* the son of Zeus ; Zeus did save him from Herê ;
a jumble of μηρὸς and ὅμηρος was the source of the grotesque
popular legend.   Now, this is not incongruous with the character of Teiresias : it is a rationalism which, holding to the
substance of faith, seeks to purge it of gross accidents ; it is
in perfect harmony with the office of the prophet, the ἐξηγητής,
at need, of esoteric truth" (Mr Jebb, in the *Dark Blue* for July,
1871).

In Dindorf's *Poetae Scenici*, lines 284 to 297 inclusive (*i. e.* the passage now under discussion, together with the preceding couplet,) are all placed in brackets; Mr Tyrrell allows the couplet in question to stand, but brackets all the lines down to 305 inclusive, he also brackets 243, to which part of this passage is a reply, pointing out that unless emended it interrupts the construction; he holds that the passage now before us "must have been interpolated either by the younger Euripides, or, as is far more probable, by some Alexandrian learned in mythology, and in the etymology of the time... The interpolator of vv. 298—305 was perhaps reminded by the mention of Delphi in v. 306 of the word μάντις, and, being in the etymologising vein, wished to make out an affinity between μάντις and μανία. The etymologising in v. 520 *seqq.* is quite in the allusive style of Euripides, and strongly contrasts with the ponderous exegesis of the spurious passage." (*Introduction*, p. xxix.) I am not prepared to go so far as this myself, for the part referring to the oracular and martial powers of Dionysus is finely written and is quite worthy of Euripides; I am less clear about the preceding portion (286—297), but even here it is an undue exaggeration to say, as Dindorf does, *dictio inepta confusa omninoque non Euripidea.* With regard to the relative length of the two speeches, that of Pentheus contains 48 (or if, as by Dindorf, 243 is rejected, 47) lines; the reply of Teiresias as given in the MSS has 62, as in Dindorf's text 48 (more accurately 46, as he also brackets 270 and 271), while in Mr Tyrrell's it is reduced to 42; but the defence made by the aged prophet would naturally be longer than the speech of accusation delivered by the youthful king, and the general law of symmetry is rather in favour of only rejecting as much as is bracketed by Dindorf, though we can hardly regard that law alone as conclusively in favour of rejecting any portion of the text. In the following notes attention will be drawn to any parallels that appear to shew that the Greek of the passage in dispute is such as might have been written by Euripides, and such evidence as is supplied by adaptations or quotations by later writers will be duly recorded.

Lines 285, 287, 289, 291 are recognised by the author of

NOTES.

Christus Patiens (569—580), but this recognition is, of course, consistent with an early interpolation.

286. καταγελᾷς νιν, ὡς ἐνερράφη] καταγελᾶν (like καταφρονεῖν and ὀλιγωρεῖν) usually take the genitive of the person ridiculed ; here, however, we have the accusative, as also in 503 κατα-φρονεῖ με. The acc. in the present passage, however, may be explained as used by anticipation in the principal sentence, instead of the nom. in the subordinate clause. So in Thuc. v, 36, 2, τὸ μέντοι Πάνακτον ἐδέοντο Βοιωτοὺς ὅπως παραδώσουσι Λακεδαιμονίοις, Ar. *Av.* 652, ἐστὶν λεγόμενον δή τι τὴν ἀλώπεχ᾽ ὡς φλαύρως ἐκοινώνησεν ἀετῷ ποτέ, and 1269, δεινόν γε τὸν κήρυκα ...εἰ μηδέποτε νοστήσει πάλιν (see further in Shilleto's *adversaria*, in Vol. III p. 225 of Cope's *Rhetoric*).—For ἐνερράφη Dr Thompson would prefer the older Attic form ἐνερράφθη. The 2nd aor. ἐρράφην is found in the Ionic Greek of Hippocrates, 3, 524, and ῥαφῆναι in the later Attic of Dem. *Conon* (54) § 41.—Hdt. II 146 Διόνυσον ἐς τὸν μηρὸν ἐνερράψατο Ζεύς.

288. For the expression ἥρπασ᾽...εἰς δ᾽ Ὄλυμπον ἀνήγαγεν, cf. Theognis 1347, (of *Zeus* as here) ἁρπάξας δ᾽ ἐς Ὄλυμπον ἀνήγαγε, καί μιν ἔθηκε δαίμονα (of Ganymede). ἀνήγαγεν θεὸν, the manuscript reading, is in some slight measure supported by the latter part of the passage just quoted ; θεὸν, if retained, is equivalent to ἅτε θεὸν ὄντα, and gives the reason for the babe being carried off to Olympus ; cf. θεὸς a few lines later (296), referring almost certainly to Dionysus, and not to Zeus.

288 sqq. The explanation offered by the prophet appears to be that when Semele was struck dead by lightning, Zeus rescued the babe from the flames and took him to Olympus ; Hera, in her jealousy, wished to cast the infant out of heaven, but Zeus thwarted her design by removing the real Dionysus, and palming off upon her in the form of the infant, a wraithe, which he placed in her keeping as a pledge of his fidelity to her for the future.—**291.** οἷα δὴ θεὸς] devised a counter-plot ʻ with godlike skill.' οἷα δὴ like ἅτε, ἅτε δὴ, ὡς, is often used as a causal particle, its relative force being nearly lost. For the omission of ὤν with such particles, contrast Xen. *Cyrop.* I, 3, 3, ὁ Κῦρος ἅτε παῖς ὢν καὶ φιλόκαλος, with the preceding words, ὁ Κῦρος οἷα δὴ παῖς φύσει φιλόστοργος.—Plato *Critias* p. 113 E, οἷα δὴ θεὸς εὐμαρῶς.

292. Hermann makes the construction run as follows: τόνδε (*sc.* αἰθέρα = αἰθέρος μέρος τόδε) ἔθηκε Διόνυσον, ἐκδιδοὺς ὅμηρον Ἥρας νεικέων. This is particularly harsh, as it removes Διόνυσον from the influence of the participle ἐκδιδοὺς which may naturally be expected to govern it. Schöne prints ἔθηκ' ἐν τῷδ', understanding that Zeus ' rent off a portion of the aether, and therein put Dionysos (enveloped him therewith), giving him up as a hostage, a pledge, against the contention of Hera.' In preference to either of these courses, we would take ἐκδιδοὺς Διόνυσον together, and without altering the text construe ἔθηκε τόνδε ὅμηρον with Ἥρας νεικέων, understanding τόνδε to be masc. either by attraction into the gender of ὅμηρον, or by reason of αἰθὴρ being referred to instead of αἰθέρος μέρος. The rendering would thus be : 'made *that* a pledge against the strife of Hera,' the while 'entrusting Dionysus to safe keeping,' 'putting him out' to be nursed by the nymphs; or possibly 'by way of surrendering D.' This is substantially Paley's view, only he translates ἐκδιδοὺς Δ., ' palming it off as the real D.'

292. τοῦ χθόν' ἐγκυκλουμένου αἰθέρος] fragm. 935, ὁρᾷς τὸν ὑψοῦ τόνδ' ἄπειρον αἰθέρα καὶ γῆν πέριξ ἔχονθ' ὑγραῖς ἐν ἀγκάλαις; and 911, ὁ πέριξ χθόν' ἔχων αἰθήρ.

295. ῥαφῆναι, instead of τραφῆναι, is a conjecture proposed with some hesitation by Pierson (*verisimilia* p. 126, quoted by Elmsley). It is suggested by the description in 96 and by the words ἐρράφθαι (ἐρράφη) in 243, and ἐνερράφη in 286. *Nunc tamen dubito*, he adds, *anne Bacchus etiam dici possit* τραφῆναι ἐν μηρῷ Διός.

297. ὡμήρευσε = ὅμηρος ἐγένετο, θεὸς being Dionysus. This seems better than taking it as trans., as in Liddell and Scott. Had it been active (as in *Rhes.* 434), we should almost certainly have had the object expressed, e.g. νιν instead of πόθ'.—συνθέντες λόγον] = ψευδῶς. Aesch. *P. V.* 686, συνθέτους λόγους.

298. μάντις] It was in Thrace in particular, in the neighbourhood of which this play was written, that Dionysus was regarded as a god possessed of oracular power. Herod. VII, 111, οὗτοι (the Thracian tribe of Satrae) οἱ τοῦ Διονύσου τὸ μαντήϊόν εἰσι ἐκτημένοι (and Pausan. IX 30 § 9), *Hec.* 1267, ὁ Θρῃξὶ μάντις εἶπε Διόνυσος τάδε (in the same play 123, Cassandra, though inspired by *Apollo*, is yet called a μαντίπολος βάκχα); Macrobius *Sat.* I 18, 1, *Aristoteles, qui Theologumena scripsit,...apud Ligyreos ait in Thracia esse adytum Libero consecratum ex quo reddantur oracula.* But the reference is also appropriate to the scene where the action of the play is laid, in so far as at Amphicleia, in the adjoining district of Phocis, Dionysus was specially worshipped as a μάντις, Pausanias X 33 § 10, Διονύσῳ δρῶσιν ὄργια... λέγεται δὲ ὑπὸ τῶν Ἀμφικλειέων μάντιν τέ σφισι τὸν θεὸν τοῦτον καὶ βοηθὸν νόσων καθεστηκέναι...πρόμαντις δὲ ὁ ἱερεύς ἐστι, χρᾷ δὲ ἐκ τοῦ θεοῦ κάτοχος. Similarly, in the gem engraved below, Telephus the wounded king of Mysia may be seen consulting the oracle of Dionysus.

299. 'For Bacchic frenzy And madness have no small prophetic power.' Cic. *de divin.* I, I, *huic praestantissimae rei* (sc. *divinationi*) *nomen nostri a divis, Graeci ut Plato* (Phaedrus 244 C) *interpretatur, a furore duxerunt.* ib. 31 § 67, *vaticinari furor vera solet.* The present passage is twice quoted by Plutarch, *de defectu oraculorum*, p. 432 F, τὸ γὰρ **βακχεύσιμον καὶ τὸ μανιῶδες μαντικὴν πολλὴν ἔχει,** κατ᾽ Εὐριπίδην, ὅταν ἔνθερμος ἡ ψυχὴ γενομένη καὶ πυρώδης ἀπώσηται τὴν εὐλάβειαν, and *quaest. conviv.* p. 716 B, οἱ παλαιοὶ τὸν θεὸν Ἐλευθερᾷ καὶ Λύσιον ἐκάλουν καὶ μαντικῆς πολλὴν ἔχειν ἡγοῦντο μοῖραν οὐ διὰ τὸ **βακχεύσιμον καὶ μανιῶδες,** ὥσπερ Εὐριπίδης εἶπεν, κ.τ.λ.

300. **εἰς τὸ σῶμ᾽ ἔλθῃ πολύς**] For the construction cf. *Hipp.* 443, (Κύπρις) ἦν πολλὴ ῥυῇ, and for a close parallel to the expression, *Anth. Pal.* VII 105, on the death of Lacydes (Diog. Laert.

4, 61), καὶ σέο Λακύδη φάτιν ἔκλυον, ὡς ἄρα καὶ σὲ βάκχος ἑλὼν
ἀΐδη ποσσὶν ἔσυρεν ἄκροις· ἢ σαφὲς ἦν· Διόνυσος ὅταν πολὺς
εἰς δέμας ἔλθῃ λῦσε μέλη· διὸ δὴ μήτι Λυαῖος ἔφυ. πολὺς, 'in full
force,' 'in the plenitude of his power.'

302. 'He also shares a part of Ares' rights.' Cf. βρόμιε,
δορατοφόρε, ἐννάλιε, πολεμοκέλαδε, poet ap. Dionys. *de comp. verb.*
1, 17, and Macrobius *Sat.* I 19, 1, *plerique Liberum cum Marte
coniungunt, unum deum esse monstrantes. unde Bacchus* Ἐννά-
λιος *cognominatur quod est inter propria Martis nomina. coli-
tur etiam apud Lacedaemonios simulacrum Liberi patris hasta
insigne, non thyrso.*—In the following lines we find ascribed
to Dionysus those sudden *panics* which as their name implies
are elsewhere ascribed (though not exclusively) to Pan, one of the
most constant attendants on Dionysus ; *Rhes.* 36, ἡ Πανὸς
τρομερᾷ μάστιγι φοβεῖ; *Med.* 1172, δόξασά που ἢ Πανὸς ὀργὰς ἢ
τινος θεῶν μολεῖν (Polyb. 5. 96, 3; 20. 6, 12, Cic. *ad Att.* V 20,
3), *Hipp.* 141, ἔνθεος εἴτ' ἐκ Πανὸς εἴθ' Ἑκάτας, ἢ σεμνῶν Κορυβάν-
των φοιτᾷς, ἢ ματρὸς ὀρείας. To the power of Pan was attributed
the flight of the Medes at Marathon (cf. Πᾶνα τροπαιοφόρον in
Anth. Gr. XVI 259); Pan appears as shield-bearer to Dionysus
in the exquisite fragment of ancient sculpture figured in Zoega's
Bassirilievi, plate 75 (copied in Müller-Wieseler, II xxxviii 445,
and in Lenormant's article on *Bacchus,* fig. 692); the same type
is to be seen on a sarcophagus in the Vatican (Müller-Wieseler
u. s. 4 14) where the victorious Dionysus is receiving the submission of an Indian king.—On the coins of Maronea, Dionysus is
to be seen with a bunch of grapes and two javelins (*ib.* 357); on a
fine Italian vase (now in St Petersburg), he is represented arming
himself in the midst of his Maenads, who bring him his shield
and helmet; while in several others he may be seen warring
against the Giants*(Lenormant *u. s.* notes 613 and 623, and
fig. 637).—For φόβος διεπτόησε (304) cf. Plato *Rep.* 336 B, δεί-
σαντες διεπτοήθημεν.

306. 'Even on Delphi's rocks thou *yet* shalt see him, With
pine-torch bounding o'er the twin-peaked height, Tossing and
shaking his own bacchic wand.' ἔτι, frequent in prophetic denunciations, 'the day will come when &c.' *infra* 534—6. Hence

* See also British Museum Vase Cat., no. 788*, and Millingen's *Anc.
Uned. Mon.* pl. xxv (described in R. Brown's *Dionysiak Myth* I 330);
and cf. Eur. *Cycl.* 5—8.

Shilleto's emendation of Aesch. *Eum.* 851, ὑμεῖς δ' ἔτ' (for ἐς)
ἀλλόφυλον ἐλθοῦσαι χθόνα γῆς τῆσδ' ἐρασθήσεσθε.— κἀπὶ Δελφίσιν
πέτραις, even on the heights of Parnassus, sacred at present to
Apollo only. This alliance of the old Dorian worship of Apollo
with the more recently imported cult of Dionysus was typified
in the design on the two pediments of the Delphic temple, one
of them representing Artemis, Leto, Apollo and the Muses, the
other [?] the setting of the Sungod and Dionysus and his attendant
Thyiades (Paus. x 19, 4). Macrob. *Sat.* 1, 18, 6, *Euripides in
Licymnio Apollinem Liberumque unum eundemque deum esse
significans scribit,* δέσποτα φιλόδαφνε Βάκχε, παιὰν Ἄπολλον
εὔλυρε (fragm. 480). *ad eandem sententiam Aeschylus* ὁ κισσεὺς
Ἀπόλλων ὁ Βακχεῖος ὁ μάντις (fragm. 394). *Ib.* § 3, *item Boeotii
Parnassum montem Apollini sacratum esse memorantes simul
tamen in eodem et oraculum Delphicum et speluncas Bacchicas
uni deo consecratas colunt...quod...etiam Euripides his docet*
(fragm. 752, *Hypsipyle,* also quoted in Ar. *Ranae* 1211), Διόνυσος
ὃς θύρσοισι καὶ νεβρῶν δοραῖς κάθαπτος ἐν πεύκαισι Παρνασσὸν κάτα
πηδᾷ χορεύων (+ παρθένοις σὺν Δελφίσιν Schol. Ar. *l. c.*).   *In hoc
monte Parnasso Bacchanalia alternis annis aguntur.*

   307—8. Hermann punctuates these lines as follows : πηδῶντα
σὺν πεύκαισι, δικόρυφον πλάκα βάλλοντα, καὶ σείοντα βακχεῖον
κλάδον. This compels him to understand πεύκαισι with βάλλοντα,
nam facibus collustrare bicipitem rupem dicitur Bacchus. It
seems better, however, to make the pause in the sense coincide
with the close of the line, placing a comma after πλάκα and
taking it as acc. after πηδῶντα by exactly the same construction
as in Soph. *Ajax* 30, πηδῶντα πεδία σὺν νεορράντῳ ξίφει, first
quoted by Brunck, to whom in particular Hermann is referring
when he says, *solent critici, si quid alicubi exquisitius dictum
viderint, id etiam alienis locis inferre.* Nevertheless, the parallel is very much to the point, and the construction defended by
it is not really so rare as to be called *exquisitius;* e.g. Aesch.
Eum. 76, τὴν πλανοστιβῆ γῆν βεβώς, *Hel.* 598, πᾶσαν πλανηθεὶς
τήνδε βάρβαρον χθόνα, *ib.* 1130, ἔδραμε ῥόθια; and in 873 *infra,*
θρώσκει πεδίον is better taken in this than in any other way. *At
quid tum est βάλλοντα?* asks Hermann ; *quatiebant thyrsum*

bacchantes, non ut missilia iaculabantur. To this we may reply that in this very play and elsewhere the *thyrsus* is often represented as a missile (762, 1099), and Dionysus may very well be here described as shooting his wand through the air on the Delphic heights. This is probably only a poetic way of referring to the sunbeams darting from point to point athwart the crest of Parnassus. The brilliant cloud-effects at and after sunset, while the light lingers on the mountain-peaks, are still more vividly represented by the pine-torches which poetic fancy describes as held aloft by the god, in the present passage and elsewhere:— e.g. *Phoen.* (the scene of which is laid at Thebes) 226, ὦ λάμπουσα πέτρα πυρὸς δικόρυφον σέλας ὑπὲρ ἄκρων Βακχείων Διονύσου, *Ion* 716, Παρνασοῦ...ἵνα Βάκχιος ἀμφιπύρους ἀνέχων πεύκας λαιψηρὰ πηδᾷ νυκτιπόλοις ἅμα σὺν Βάκχαις, ib. 550, 1076, 1125, Soph. *O. T.* 213, Βάκχον...φλέγοντ᾽ ἀγλαῶπι πεύκᾳ, *Antig.* 1126, Βακχεῦ...σὲ δ᾽ ὑπὲρ διλόφοιο πέτρας στέροψ ὄπωπε λιγνύς, Ar. *Nubes* 603, Παρνασίαν θ᾽ ὃς κατέχων πέτραν σὺν πεύκαις σελαγεῖ Βάκχαις Δελφίσιν ἐμπρέπων κωμαστὴς Διόνυσος, and fragm. *Hyps.* quoted on p. 147. These lines are translated as follows by Attius *Bacchae* X (1), *laetum in Parnaso inter pinus tripudiantem in circulis | ludere...atque taedis fulgere.*—In the twain-crested height, the poet refers to 'the two lofty rocks which rise perpendicularly from Delphi... anciently known by the names of Hyampeia and Nauplia (Hdt. VIII 39);...the celebrated Castalian fount pours down the cleft or chasm between these two summits, being fed by the perpetual snows of Parnassus' (Cramer's *Greece* II 170). The true summit of Parnassus (8000 ft. above the sea) lies several thousand feet above the double cliff (*bicipiti Parnasso*), which however, is a most prominent object in the landscape (as may be seen in the views on pp. 236, 240, 249 of Wordsworth's *Greece*), and makes the site of Delphi easily identified at a great distance (Leake's *Northern Greece* II 568).—πλάκα, often of lofty ridges, tablelands or (as in 718) mountain-terraces; in Soph. *Ajax* 1220, of the level top of Sunium, *Phil.* 1430, of the height of mount Oeta.—The construction βάλλειν κλάδον is quite admissible, and when it is objected that 'the Greeks say βάλλειν τινα λίθῳ, not βάλλειν λίθον,' the objector loses sight of passages where the missile is

put in the acc., as in *Iliad* 5, 346 χαλκὸν βαλὼν, *Od.* 9, 495, βαλὼν
βέλος, *Phoen.* 1375, δὸς ἔγχος ἡμῖν καλλίνικον ἐκ χερὸς ἐς στέρν'
ἀδελφοῦ τῆσδ' ἀπ' ὠλένης βαλεῖν, *Iph. T.* 1376, πέτρους (MSS,
πέτροις Paley) ἐβάλλομεν,—though the dat. is undoubtedly more
common, as in fragm. 566, πυκνοῖς ἔβαλλον Βακχίου τοξεύμασιν
κάρα γέροντος τὸν βαλόντα δὲ στέφειν ἐγὼ 'τετάγμην, ἆθλα κοσσάβων
διδούς.—**βάλλοντα** is altered by Matthiae into **πάλλοντα**, which
though applicable to a spear strikes one as somewhat too strong
a word for the Bacchic wand in the present passage, esp. as the
same general idea recurs in σείοντα : yet it may be right, after all.

310. 'Vaunt not that might alone (e.g. thy royal sway) hath
power with men, Nor, if thou think it (though thy thought's
unsound) Think thou art wise in aught.' **μὲν** in the principal
clause is answered by **δὲ** in the clause which is incidentally
introduced immediately after but is not influenced by **ἤν**.

314—6. Teiresias here attempts to rebut the scandalous
rumours referred to by Pentheus (221—5), by representing that
the god is not himself responsible for the conduct of the women
who are his votaries; *that* depends on their inborn nature ; if
they are naturally immodest, the god will not *drive* them into
the path of decorum ; if again they are truly modest, they will
not be corrupted by association with his revelries.   The former
part of this plea is hollow enough ; but with its later portion we
may compare the noble speech on 'Saintly Chastity' in Milton's
Comus (418—475).   The dramatic description of 'the lady' in
that play, surrounded (but not by her own seeking, as in the case
of the revellers of Cithaeron) by the riotous crew of Comus, could
not have a fitter motto than the words, καὶ γὰρ ἐν βακχεύμασιν οὖσ'
ἥ γε σώφρων οὐ διαφθαρήσεται, and it is not unlikely that Milton
had this passage before him in writing his play (cf. n. on 188).
(The sense is well given by Mr Shuckburgh : 'Not Dionysus makes
or mars the chaste, But chaste thoughts and sweet nature inly
bred ; She that is truly chaste will never lose This flower in
Bacchic orgies.')—The passage has a further literary interest in
connexion with the story told of Plato and Aristippus, the he-
donist of Cyrene, when both were present at a banquet given by
Dionysius II of Syracuse.   The king asked Aristippus to put aside

his cloak (τρίβων) and put on a purple shawl instead (πορφυροῦν ἱμάτιον); Aristippus consented; the king asked Plato to do the same, but was met with a refusal expressed in an apt quotation from this play, οὐκ ἂν δυναίμην θῆλυν ἐνδῦναι στολήν (834) : whereupon Aristippus rejoined with the present passage which, according to the version of the anecdote given in Suidas, was quoted in the adapted form, καὶ γὰρ ἐν βακχεύμασιν ὁ νοῦς ὁ σώφρων οὐ διαφθαρήσεται (the rest cite it as in Eur., *viz.* Diog. Laert. II 78, Stobaeus 5. 46, and Sextus Empiricus, all quoted in full in Elmsley's note on 834).

σωφρονεῖν] One of the MSS (Pal.) adds μὴ above the word σωφρονεῖν ; Stobaeus (5. 15, and 74. 8) quotes it twice with the negative ; while on the other hand, μή is omitted in MS Laur., and the author of the *Christus Patiens* 262 has οὐ γὰρ θεός σε σωφρονεῖν ἀναγκάσει. The insertion of the μὴ was apparently due to a misunderstanding of the drift of the passage, as explained above ; and we need not build upon it any alteration of the text such as μὴ φρονεῖν (suggested by Musgrave and Hermann). Porson (*Kidd's Tracts* p. 225) proposed ὡς φρονεῖν ἀναγκάσει...ἀλλ' εἰ τῇ φύσει τὸ σωφρονεῖν ἔνεστιν εἰς τὰ πάντ' ἀεὶ τοῦτο σκοπεῖν χρή, *Porsonum sequor*, says Shilleto, *adv.*, and Mr Paley, in stating that in his own judgment no change is required than εἰ for ἐν, supports the latter part of Porson's proposal by the quotation in Stobaeus 74. 8, ἀλλ' εἰς τὴν φύσιν | τοῦτο σκοπεῖν χρή. Here Stobaeus omits the line τὸ σωφρονεῖν ἔνεστιν εἰς τὰ πάντ' ἀεί, but he does not do so in his other quotation of the passage (5. 15) where he concludes with that line, and thus stops short of τοῦτο σκοπεῖν χρή. The passage is similar to that in *Hipp.* 79—81, ὅσοις διδακτὸν μηδέν, ἀλλ' ἐν τῇ φύσει τὸ σωφρονεῖν εἴληχεν εἰς τὰ πάνθ' ὁμῶς (πάντ' ἀεί in one MS Par.), τούτοις δρέπεσθαι· τοῖς κακοῖσι δ' οὐ θέμις, lines which Dindorf puts into brackets, thinking them made up from the present passage, but even on that hypothesis they are evidence in favour of ἐν as against εἰ. Euripides may well have repeated in one of his latest plays a phrase occurring in a play whose general drift is not unlike that of the *Bacchae*. The next three lines (319—321) also find a close parallel in *Hipp.* 7, ἔνεστι γὰρ δὴ κἂν θεῶν γένει τόδε τιμώμενοι χαίρουσιν ἀνθρώπων ὕπο. For ἐν τῇ φύσει, cf. *Hel.* 1002, [Dem.] *Aristog.* i § 35.

322. ὃν σὺ διαγελᾷς] The acc. after διαγελᾶν is not uncommon. So in Theocr. 20, 1, Εὐνείκα μ᾽ ἐγέλαξε, *derisit.* On καταγελᾷς νιν, see note on 286.

326. κοῦτε φαρμάκοις ἄκη λάβοις ἄν, οὔτ᾽ ἄνευ τούτων νοσεῖς] i. e. 'Thou art sorely frenzied, yet no healing drugs Could cure a mind, not without drugs diseased.' 'Significat mentem ipsi pharmacis corruptam esse' (Musgrave, in whose view Elmsley acquiesces). The prophet hints (but not too darkly) that Pentheus is under a spell which is leading him on to a doom beyond all remedy. This is a fairly simple way of understanding the passage, but Hermann is not content; "mihi nihil," he says, "neque argutius neque putidius dicere potuisse videtur Teiresias. Immo vero praeclara est, et dignissima sapientissimo vate sententia, quum dicit: *insanis tristissima insania, et nec remediis sanari potes, nec sine remedio aegrotas.* Hoc enim significat, neque esse, quod illum ad sanam mentem revocare queat, neque insanire eum ita, ut non finem isti insaniae crudelissima, quae ei immineat, mors impositura sit." This is certainly sufficiently oracular to give fresh point to the remark of the chorus, that the prophet's words did no dishonour to Phoebus, yet Hermann's interpretation of the general drift of the passage may be right; but if so, it may be questioned whether the irony of the words as they stand is not too obscurely expressed to be fairly intelligible, and it may be worth suggesting that ἄνευ τούτων may be a corruption of ἀνιάτως, due possibly to ἀνίατον having been written by a copyist, and then altered by adding -τως, a correction which would lead to the unintelligible ανιατοντως which would readily pass into ἄνευ τούτων. ἀνίατος, however, it must be admitted is a Platonic rather than a Tragic word; and if any difficulty is felt on this ground, οὔτ᾽ ἀνήκεστον νοσεῖς would make equally good sense; 'Thou art sorely frenzied, and no medicine Could cure thee, *yet thy malady hath a cure.*' (The reviewer of my first ed. in the *Athenaeum,* 11 Dec. 1880, supposes τούτων to refer to the Thebans generally : 'nor does thy disease fail to affect the state.' Cf. 362.)

328. The remark of the chorus need not be narrowed into a reference to the last words of Teiresias ; it applies rather to the general attitude taken up by the whole speech, which proves

that Teiresias can shew due reverence to the new god Dionysus without dishonouring the older deity whose prophet he is.

330. 'My son! right well Teiresias counsels thee, Dwell thou with us, within the pale of wont, For now thou'rt flighty, senseless in thy senses.' For νόμων, customary and conventional laws, cf. 891, κρεῖσσον τῶν νόμων γιγνώσκειν. For πέτει, of fitful, inconstant, flighty pursuit of wild vagaries, cf. Ar. *Aves*, 1445, ἀνεπτερῶσθαι καὶ πεποτῆσθαι τὰς φρένας. φρονῶν οὐδὲν φρονεῖς, i.e. 'your wisdom is very foolishness.'

334. καταψεύδου καλῶς] 'tell of him the splendid (the ennobling) falsehood,' cf. Soph. *Ant.* 74, ὅσια πανουργήσασα and Horace's *splendide mendax.* For καταψεύδεσθαι, 'to speak falsely *of*,' cf. κατηγορεῖν in the sense 'to tell *of*' which gives us κατηγορία, in the sense of *category;* so also καθ᾽ ὑμῶν ἐγκώμιον, 'praise bestowed on you,' Dem. Or. 6 § 9.

337. ὁρᾷς] 'You see before you,' or 'are familiar with.' Plato, *Gorg.* 470 D, (Polus) Ἀρχέλαον δήπου τοῦτον τὸν Περδίκκου ὁρᾷς ἄρχοντα Μακεδονίας; (Socrates) εἰ δὲ μὴ ἀλλ᾽ ἀκούω, &c. Actaeon, it will be remembered, was Pentheus' own cousin (228), and was torn in pieces by his hounds near Thebes, according to the present passage in the meadows of the Asopus where he had boasted he was braver than Artemis in the hunt. ἐν ὀργάσιν, though probably meant as the scene of the doom as well as of the boasting of Actaeon, is better taken with the nearer κομπάσαντ᾽, rather than with the somewhat distant διεσπάσαντο. [*De ὀργάσιν* vid. *Schneider* ad Xen. *venat.* IX. 2] Shilleto, *adv.*

341. ὃ μὴ πάθῃς σύ, δεῦρο...στέψω] 'And lest *thou* meet his doom, come! let me crown Thy head with ivy.' ὃ μὴ πάθῃς σὺ is sometimes taken separately, as an imperative (not unlike Dem. *Lept.* § 50, ὃ μὴ πάθητε νῦν ὑμεῖς), but the clause is so short that it seems better to take it with the subsequent sentence. στέψω is aor. coni., the *coniunctivus adhortativus*, with which φέρε or ἄγε is often expressed. *Herc. F.* 529, φέρ᾽ ἐκπύθωμαι, Theopompus apud Athen. 470 F (quoted by Elmsley), χώρει σὺ δεῦρο (addressing a wine-cup)...δεῦρο δὴ γεμίσω σ᾽ ἐγώ, where if the future had been meant, we should, have had γεμιῶ.

343. οὐ μὴ προσοίσεις χεῖρα...δὲ...μηδὲ...] 792, οὐ μὴ φρενώσεις μ' ἀλλά... *Hipp.* 606, οὐ μὴ προσοίσεις χεῖρα μηδ' ἄψη πέπλων. Donaldson, *Gk. Gr.* § 544, would explain the construction of such a passage as the present by making it mean literally ' will you not *not* apply your hand, but go to your revels; and *not* wipe off your folly upon me?', i.e. ' Hands off! I charge thee! get thee to thy mummeries! And smear not off thy senselessness on me.' Kühner, *Gk. Gr.* § 516, 10, objects to the interrogative punctuation of such sentences, and explains them by understanding οὐ (δεινόν ἐστι) μή, an explanation founded on such passages as Xen. *Mem.* II 1 § 25, οὐ φόβος μή σε ἀγάγω, but this theory (as is remarked by Goodwin, *Moods and Tenses*, § 89, 1, note 2), while applicable to οὐ μή with the conjunctive, leaves οὐ μή with the future indic. entirely unexplained. Conversely, Donaldson's treatment of the fut. indic. with οὐ μή as an interrogative construction (suggested by Elmsley), is inapplicable to οὐ μή c. *coni.* It seems best therefore to consider οὐ μή c. *coni.* as ' a relic of the common Homeric subjunctive,' used in independent sentences in a future sense, and to explain οὐ μή with *fut. ind.* as expressing a stronger prohibition than μή c. *imp.*—' οὐ μή having the same force of a strong single negative in both constructions' (Goodwin, *u. s.* § 89, remark 1)*. οὐ μή προσοίσεις is in any case equivalent in sense to a strong form of μὴ προσενέγκῃς χεῖρα. ἐξομόρξει. Sen.*Ep.*7 §2 *vitium adlinit*...§ 7 *adfricuit.*

346. δίκην μέτειμι] c. acc., Elmsley's excellent correction of δίκη. He quotes *Eum.* 230, δίκας μέτειμι τόνδε φῶτα. Cf. Isaeus VII § 10, δίκας εἶλεν Εὔπολιν δύο.

347. The proximity implied in the manuscript reading θάκους τούσδε seems inconsistent with the impression of distance conveyed by the context, στειχέτω τις ὡς τάχος, ἐλθὼν δέ. I accordingly prefer the emendation τοῦδε which is accepted by several editors, though (as is remarked by Mr Paley) the word τόνδε has already been used once, and is sufficient to mark the person meant. For Teiresias' seat of augury, cf. Soph. *Antig.* 999—1004, *Phoen.* 840, θάκοισιν ἐν ἱεροῖσιν οὗ μαντεύομαι. The legendary site of the οἰωνοσκοπεῖον Τειρεσίου was still pointed out in the time of Pausanias (IX 16, 1).

348. μόχλοις τριαίνου] *Herc. F.* 946, στρεπτῷ σιδήρῳ συν-

---

* See New Edition, 1889, §§ 297—301, and pp. 389—397.

τριαινώσω πέδον, and Ar. *Pax* 570, τριαινοῦν τῇ δικέλλῃ ... τὸ
γήδιον, Plato Comicus, Ἑλλ. 2, ταῦτα πάντα συντριαινῶν ἀπολέσω.

349. 'Mingling them pell-mell in one general ruin,' cf. 602,
741, 753, and Aesch. frag. 321, ὗς ... δονοῦσα καὶ τρέπουσα τύρβ'
ἄνω κάτω. **351. δήξομαι**] 'shall wound, nettle, gall him.' *Med.*
1370, οὐκέτ' εἰσί· τοῦτο γὰρ σὲ δήξεται.

357. πικρὰν βάκχευσιν...ἰδών] 'Having bitterly rued his revelry in Thebes.' πικρὸς is often (as here) used with an empha-
tically predicative force, *Med.* 1388, πικρὰς τελευτὰς τῶν ἐμῶν
ἰδὼν γάμων, 'having seen how bitter is my wedding's end,'
Androm. 384, πικρὰν κλήρωσιν αἵρεσίν τέ μοι βίου καθίστης, 'how
bitter is this choice· 'twixt life and death,' Soph. *El.* 1504, φυ-
λάξαι δεῖ με τοῦτό σοι πικρόν (quoted by Prof. Campbell, *Soph.*
p. 30, as an instance where the adj. expresses the chief part of
the predicate and is more emphatic than the verb).

358. οὐκ οἶσθα ποῦ ποτ' εἶ] C. J. Blomfield (*Museum Criticum*
2, 663) proposed οἶσθ' ὅπου, which is the common form in cases
where a direct becomes an indirect interrogative (*Rhes.* 689,
οἶσθ' ὅποι, *Hipp.* 1091, οἶδα δ' οὐχ ὅπως φράσω); but the text is
defended not only on rhythmical grounds but also by other
passages where the direct is used instead of the oblique interrogative. In the following passage, the direct and indirect
interrogatives are curiously intermingled : Xen. *Anab.* II 5, 7,
οὐκ οἶδα, οὔτ' ἀπὸ ποίου ἂν τάχους οὔτε ὅποι ἄν τις φεύγων ἀπο-
φύγοι οὔτ' εἰς ποῖον σκότος ἀποδραίη οὔθ' ὅπως ἂν εἰς ἐχυρὸν
χωρίον ἀποσταίη (Kühner, *Gk. Gr.* § 587. 4).

359. 'Foolish thou wast before, but now stark mad.'

365. ἴτω δ' ὅμως] *Med.* 798, ἴτω· τί μοι ζῆν κέρδος, 819, ἴτω·
περισσοὶ πάντες οὖν μέσῳ λόγοι, lit. 'let it go,' i.e. 'let it pass,'
used in setting aside a distressing thought, and passing on to
something else in spite of it, like our conversational 'well,
well ! no matter.' Cf. also *Heracl.* 454, οὐ φιλεῖν δεῖ τὴν ἐμὴν
ψυχήν· ἴτω.

367. Πενθεὺς...πένθος] *infra* 508 and Theocr. 26, 26, ἐξ ὄρεος
πένθημα καὶ οὐ Πενθῆα φέροισαι. 'Take heed, lest Pentheus
make your mansion a pent-house of grief,' is the far from
felicitous rendering suggested by Donaldson, who rightly re-

marks that translators 'are not always very happy in their
substitution of English for Greek in reproducing such plays
upon words' (*Theatre of the Greeks*, p. 136, ed. 7). It would
perhaps be more in accordance with modern taste in such
matters, to be content with some such paraphrase as follows:
'Beware, lest Pentheus bring into thy house His namesake
Sorrow.' Instances of similar plays on words are found in Euripides, in the names of Aphrodite, Atreus, Capaneus, Dolon,
Helen, Ion, Meleager, Theoclymene, Theonoe, Thoas; and not in
Euripides alone, but also in Aeschylus, who deals in like manner with the names of Apollo, Io, Prometheus, and Polynices,
as well as that of Helen; so also in Sophocles, in the case of
Ajax and Sidero. These are not to be regarded as mere plays
on words, as the Greeks 'read in the significant name the
character or destiny of its bearer; and thus employed they
have a true tragic interest' (Cope on *Rhet.* II 23 § 29, where
Aristotle quotes from Chaeremon, Πενθεὺς ἐσομένης συμφορᾶς
ἐπώνυμος. Cf. Farrar's *Chapters on Language*, XXII p. 272—7).

370. 'Queen in heaven, goddess holy, holy goddess who to
earth thy golden pinion bendest.' Ὁσία] The chorus calls
upon the goddess of Sanctity to listen to the impious language
of Pentheus. So Demosthenes, of the ὕβρις of Meidias, p. 556,
§ 126, ὁ θεὸς (sc. Διόνυσος) ᾧ χορηγὸς ἐγὼ καθειστήκειν, καὶ τὸ
τῆς ὁσίας, ὁτιδήποτ' ἐστίν, τὸ σεμνὸν καὶ τὸ δαιμόνιον, συνηδίκηται.
Ὁσία is a personification created apparently by Euripides himself; at any rate not mentioned elsewhere, though it may be
assumed that in her general attributes she closely corresponds
to Θέμις. As the daughters of Θέμις, Hesiod, *Theog.* 902, mentions Εὐνομίη, Δίκη and Εἰρήνη, called by Pindar, *Ol.* 13, 6—10,
χρύσεαι παῖδες εὐβούλου Θέμιτος. So in Statius, *Silv.* 3, 3, 1,
*summa deum Pietas, cuius gratissima caelo rara profanatas
inspectant numina terras; huc vittata comam, niveoque insignis
amictu, qualis adhuc praesens nullaque expulsa nocentum fraude
rudes populos atque aurea regna colebas* (Joddrell). Among
similar personifications of abstract notions, we have Πόθος (414)
and Εἰρήνη (419) in the present chorus; so also Πίστις, Νίκη,
Ὁμόνοια, Ἔλεος; similarly in Latin *Fides, Mens, Virtus, Con-*

passage in *Iph. T.* 1122, τὸ δὲ μετ᾽ εὐτυχίας κακοῦσθαι βαρὺς αἰών. Just as βαρὺς αἰὼν there means βαρὺν ποιεῖ τὸν αἰῶνα, so here βραχὺς αἰών, with its similar sequence of sound and its exactly corresponding position in the sentence, means βραχὺν ποιεῖ τὸν αἰῶνα. This parallel, which has apparently escaped the attention of previous editors, seems conclusive, and when occasion was taken to point it out in a notice of Mr Tyrrell's ed. (in the *Cambridge University Reporter,* May 31, 1871), it convinced both Mr Paley and Mr Tyrrell of the erroneousness of the ordinary punctuation. (3) It is also supported by the construction found in 1004, where ἄλυπος βίος means, 'makes life painless:' For the sense, Hermann quotes *Iliad* 5, 407, ὅττι μάλ᾽ οὐ δηναιὸς ὃς ἀθανάτοισι μάχηται, which refers to the life of Lycurgus (like that of Pentheus in the present play) being cut short by his opposition to Dionysus.

397. ἐπὶ τούτῳ] *hac condicione* (Hermann), i.e. 'on this condition of a shortened existence.' 'And whosoever, on this frail tenure, aims at things too great for him, may miss the boons within his reach.' So in Browning's *Grammarian's funeral,* 'this high man, aiming at a million, misses a unit.' Paley proposes ἐπὶ τούτου in the sense, 'in the time of this' (short life): but it may be questioned whether ἐπὶ τούτου can mean more than 'during this man's time' (*in huius memoria* as Mr Tyrrell puts it).

401. παρ᾽ ἔμοιγε, *meo quidem iudicio*, Hdt. 1, 86, τοὺς παρὰ σφίσι αὐτοῖσι δοκέοντας ὀλβίους, Dem. 11 § 3, θαυμαστότερος παρὰ πᾶσι νομίζεται, *El.* 737, λέγεται, τὰν δὲ πίστιν σμικρὰν παρ᾽ ἔμοιγ᾽ ἔχει.

402. Anacr. fr. 2 (to Dionysus), ὦναξ ᾧ δαμάλης Ἔρως...πορφυρίη τ᾽ Ἀφροδίτη συμπαίζουσι.

404. θελξίφρονες...θνατοῖσιν] Elmsley well paraphrases the line, ἔνθα διατρίβουσιν οἱ ἔρωτες οἱ θέλγοντες τὰς φρένας τῶν θνητῶν, 'the haunt of the love-gods who soothe the heart of man,'—'where for man's joy the gentle love-gods dwell.'

406. The manuscript reading Πάφον θ᾽ ἂν appears to present insuperable difficulties. By the ἑκατόστομοι βαρβάρου ποταμοῦ ῥοαὶ ἄνομβροι which 'fertilise' Paphos, we cannot understand any stream in Cyprus, for in the days of Euripides, (as at the present time,) the description given by one of our own travellers must

have held good. *that the brookes (for rivers it hath none) rather
merite the name of torrents, being often exhausted by the Sunne*
(George Sandys, *Travels*, p. 221, ed. 1615, quoted by Joddrell).
We can apply them to the Nile alone, as described in the
opening words of the *Helen*, Νείλου μὲν αἵδε καλλιπάρθενοι ῥοαί,
ὃς ἀντὶ δίας ψεκάδος Αἰγύπτου πέδον λευκῆς τακείσης χιόνος ὑγραίνει
γύας, and in fragm. 230 (Archelaus), Νείλου λιπὼν κάλλιστον ἐκ
γαίας ὕδωρ ὃς ἐκ μελαμβρότοιο πληροῦται ῥοὰς Αἰθιοπίδος γῆς, ἡνίκ᾽
ἂν τακῇ χιών. This involves us in a geographical difficulty, to
remove which Mr Paley is driven to conjecture that 'Euripides
may have supposed the fertilizing current of the Nile reached even
to Phoenicia, and that Paphos and Cyprus were parts of that
country.' The only other passage, so far as I am aware, which gives
us any hint as to the extent of the poet's knowledge with respect
to the position of Cyprus, is in *Hel.* 148, where Teucer, who
has sailed from the island of Salamis to the delta of the Nile,
informs Helen that he proposes to consult an oracle with a view
to getting a fair wind to take him to Cyprus, ὅπη νεὼς στείλαιμ᾽
ἂν οὔριον πτερὸν εἰς γῆν ἐναλίαν Κύπρον,—on which it may be
remarked that had the outflow of the Nile been sufficiently
strong to 'fertilise' Paphos, Teucer might have trusted himself
to the current alone, without waiting for the breeze to fill his
sails. Hermann, who omits τε and makes Πάφον depend on
νέμονται, meets the difficulty by understanding καρπίζουσιν of the
enriching of Paphos by its trade with Egypt ('opes indicat
omnigenas, quas *trabe Cypria mercator* Paphi congerat, per
Nilum cum orientis regionibus commercia exercens'). Reiske
proposes Φάρον, suggested probably by its mention in the prologue to the *Helen*, but in no way specially connected with the
worship of Dionysus or Aphrodite. Schöne conjectures πέδον τ᾽
ἔνθ᾽, and Meineke, χθόνα θ᾽ ἂν, both referring to Egypt; Mr
Tyrrell Πάφον θ᾽, ἂν θ᾽, but it may fairly be asked whether in
such a case we can understand ἂν as equivalent to τήν τε γῆν ἥν,
though the harshness of the ellipse is undoubtedly softened
to a certain extent by the further alteration of ἄνομβροι to
ἄνομβρον, while it is almost paralleled in *Tro.* 825, ἁ δέ σε γειναμένα
πυρὶ δαίεται. Dr Thompson's suggestion γαῖαν θ᾽ ἂν gives ex-

cellent sense, but appears open to the objection that it would involve making the first syllable of ἴσαν (in the antistrophe) *long;* an Epic usage, not found in Greek Tragedy (v. Ellendt).

409. καλλιστευομένα] 'deemed most beautiful', pass. as in *Med.* 947. 'The Muses' famed Pierian haunt, the hallowed slope of Olympus' (Μοῦσαι 'Ολύμπια δώματ' ἔχουσαι, *Il.* 2, 484). Pieria, the district north of the σεμνὰ κλιτὺς 'Ολύμπου, bounded towards the north by the Macedonian river Haliacmon, was the birth-place of Orpheus (Apollonius Rhod. 1. 23) and of the Muses (Hesiod, *Theog.* 53). This region formed part of the Macedonian dominions of Archelaus, at whose court the play was composed, and who himself established "Olympian" festivals in honour of Zeus and the Muses. These were celebrated with peculiar splendour by one of his successors, Alexander the Great, who according to Diodorus Sic. XVII 16, θυσίας μεγαλο- πρεπεῖς τοῖς θεοῖς συνετέλεσεν ἐν Δίῳ τῆς Μακεδονίας καὶ σκηνικοὺς ἀγῶνας Διὶ καὶ Μούσαις οὓς 'Αρχέλαος ὁ προβασιλεύσας πρῶτος κατέδειξε, cf. Arrian *Anab. Alex.* 1, 11, τῷ τε Διὶ τῷ 'Ολυμπίῳ τὴν θυσίαν τὴν ἀπ' 'Αρχελάου ἔτι καθεστῶσαν ἔθυσε καὶ τὸν ἀγῶνα ἐν Αἰγαῖς διέθηκε τὰ 'Ολύμπια· οἱ δὲ καὶ ταῖς Μούσαις λέγουσιν ὅτι ἀγῶνα ἐποίησε. καὶ ἐν τούτῳ ἀγγέλλεται τὸ 'Ορφέως τοῦ Οἰάγρου τοῦ Θρακὸς ἄγαλμα τὸ ἐν Πιερίδι ἱδρῶσαι ξυνεχῶς. For another com-plimentary reference to the dominions of Archelaus, see 560—75.—The massive breadth of Olympus, rising to 9754 feet above the level of the sea, would stand out boldly in the Pierian land-scape towards the southern part of his dominion.

412. προβακχήιε] a word invented for the occasion. The effect of the exceptional word in Greek may be kept up in English by some such rendering as 'Vancourier (in the sense of 'leader') of the Bacchic throng.' **414.** Πόθος, an abstract divinity (cf. 'Οσία, 370) personified as son of Κύπρις in Aesch. *Suppl.* 1040, and mentioned (as here) with the Graces in Ar. *Aves* 1320, Σοφία, Πόθος, ἀμβροσίαι Χάριτες. Cf. Gray, 'the bloom of young Desire, and purple light of Love.'

419. Εἰρήναν κουροτρόφον] This epithet of Peace who is here described as 'tender nurse of youth, boon goddess of increase,' comes from Hesiod, *Works and Days* 226, Εἰρήνη δ' ἀνὰ γῆν κουροτρόφος. The poet's love of peace may be illustrated by numerous passages, e.g. the fine fragment of the *Cresphontes*, 462, Εἰρήνα βαθύπλουτε (cf. ὀλβοδότειραν) καὶ καλλίστα μακάρων θεῶν, ζῆλός μοι σέθεν, ὡς χρονίζεις. ὑπερβάλῃ με γῆρας, πρὶν σὰν χαρίεσσαν ὥραν προσιδεῖν καὶ καλλιχόρους ἀοιδὰς φιλοστεφάνους τε κώμους. ἴθι μοι, πότνα, πόλιν, τὰν δ᾽ ἐχθρὰν στάσιν εἴργ᾽ ἀπ᾽ οἴκων τὰν μαινομέναν τ᾽ ἔριν θηκτῷ τερπομέναν σιδάρῳ (rendered by Browning in Arist. *Apol.* p. 179). Cf. Ar. *Pax* 308 (Εἰρήνην) τὴν θεῶν πασῶν μεγίστην καὶ φ ι λ α μ π ε λ ω τ ά τ η ν.

Εἰρήνη, here described as loved by Dionysus, is also associated with him in works of ancient art; e.g. in a vase-painting copied in Müller-Wieseler II, 585, among the figures surrounding Dionysus are ΕΙΡΗΝΗ, a winged boy named ΙΜΕΡΟΣ, and a seated form with a torch resting on one of her hands and a *rhyton* in the other. Similarly another vase-painting, *ib.* 584, represents Dionysus seated, caressing ΙΡΗΝΗ who is softly approaching him: among the figures in the upper part of the same vase is a winged boy beating the *tympanum*, bearing the name of ΠΟΘΟΣ (also in O. Jahn's *Vasenbilder* III, plate 2).

421. ἴσα, or ἴσαν, 'in equal measure,'—both to the wealthy and to the lowly. 423. τέρψιν ἄλυπον] fragm. 889, (ἔρως) ἄλυπον τέρψιν τιν᾽ ἔχων εἰς ἐλπίδ᾽ ἄγει, *supra* 280, παύει...λύπης.

427. σοφὸν δ᾽ ἀπέχειν πραπίδα φρένα τε περισσῶν παρὰ φωτῶν] ''tis wise to hold aloof the thought and mind that come from those who are over-clever.' σοφὰν is the manuscript reading (altered into σοφόν, with the Aldine edition). ἀπέχειν is sometimes used where we should expect ἀπέχεσθαι, e.g. Aesch. *Ag.* 350, ἀθανάτων ἀπέχειν χέρας, while in *Od.* 22, 316, we have κακῶν ἀπὸ χεῖρας ἔχεσθαι (L. and S.); and in the present passage ἀπέχειν may mean 'keeping off from oneself.' σοφὰν δ᾽ ἄπεχε is the correction printed by Elmsley and Hermann, the latter of whom gives the rendering *procul habe sapientiam a nimium doctis hominibus profectam.* περισσῶν παρὰ φωτῶν, *perhaps* c. ἀπέχειν, 'to keep the mind aloof from...' For the sense, cf. fragm. 916, μή μοι λεπτῶν θίγγανε μύθων, ψυχή· τί περισσὰ φρονεῖς ; εἰ μὴ μέλλεις σεμνύνεσθαι παρ᾽ ὁμοίοις.—πραπίδα, though rare in singular, also occurs *infra* 999, μανείσᾳ πραπίδι, and in a fragment of

S. B.   11

Pindar.—Of the last words of the chorus Hermann justly remarks: 'quomodo τόδε τοι λέγοιμ' ἂν significare possit, τόδε τοι ἄριστον εἶναι λέγοιμ' ἂν, neque ego video, neque facile aliis persuadeatur.' He himself prefers λεγοίμαν (pass.), i. e. τόδε τοι λεγοίμην νομίζειν καὶ χρῆσθαι. I prefer accepting Kirchhoff's conjecture, τόδ' ἂν δεχοίμαν. For the sense, cf. fragm. 642 (Polyeid.), πλουτεῖς, τὰ δ' ἄλλα μὴ δόκει ξυνιέναι· ἐν τῷ γὰρ ὄλβῳ φαυλότης ἔνεστί τις, πενία δὲ σοφίαν ἔλαχε διὰ τὸ δυστυχὲς (v. l. συγγενές).

436. 'A gentle creature too we found our quarry.' The word θὴρ is used to keep up the notion of ἄγρα in the first line of the speech. Cf. also *infra*, 922.—**439.** ἀπάγειν is almost a technical term here ; it is constantly used in the Attic orators, of summary arrest, *rapere in ius.* So also in Plato, *Gorg.* 486 A, εἴ τις σοῦ λαβόμενος...εἰς τὸ δεσμωτήριον ἀπαγάγοι.—It is apparently the present passage that is rendered as follows by Attius *Bacchae* XI (18)...*praesens praesto irridens* [*leniter*] *Nobis stupe*[-*factis sese*] *ultro ostentum obtulit.* From a similar scene in the *Lycurgus* of Naevius XI (25), we have the line *dic quo pacto eum potiti* [*sitis*]: *pugna*[-*ne*] *an dolis?*

440. τοὐμὸν εὐπρεπὲς ποιούμενος] 'making my task a seemly one,' instead of causing an unseemly scuffle by his resistance. This would seem to be a tolerable explanation of the manuscript reading, but several editors (Elmsley, Paley, Tyrrell) accept the alteration εὐτρεπὲς, though in the three passages in Eur. where the phrase εὐτρεπῆ, or εὔτρεπες, ποιεῖσθαι occurs (*Iph. T.* 245, *Herc. F.* 497, *Electra* 689), it implies 'getting something ready for one's own use' (Paley). Another punctuation is that given by Hermann, ἔμενέ τε τοὐμόν, εὐτρεπὲς ποιούμενος, *exspectabat, ut ego meum officium facerem, paratum id mihi reddens: ego vero pudore tactus* (δι' αἰδοῦς), *invitum me eum abducere dixi.* I have thought it best, on the whole, to accept the emendation εὐπετὲς (Nauck). An equally good sense would be given by εὐχερὲς or εὐμαρὲς (Paley).—**442.** Aesch. *P. V.* 3, σοὶ δὲ χρὴ μέλειν (450) ἐπιστολὰς ἅς σοι πατὴρ ἐφεῖτο (439).

447-8. 'Their bonds were burst asunder of themselves, And the gates unbarred by more than mortal hand.' Nonnus 44, 21, αὐτόματοι κληῖδες ἀνοίγνυντο πυλάων, καὶ δολιχοὺς πυλεῶνι

μάτην ἐπέβαλλον ὀχῆας ἠερίοις θεράποιτες ἐριδμαίνοντες ἀήταις, *ib.*
45, 278—83, ὑπὸ στροφάλιγγι δὲ ταρσῶν χαλκοβαρὴς τροχόωσα
ποδῶν ἐσχίζετο σείρη...καὶ σκοτίου πυλεῶνες ἀνεπτήσσοντο βερεθρου
αὐτόματοι, Ovid *Met.* III 700 (of the release of Acoetes, imprisoned
by Pentheus, like Dionysus in the play before us) *sponte sua
patuisse fores, lapsasque lacertis sponte sua fama est nullo
solvente catenas.* Acts of the Apostles XII. 7 (of the miraculous
release of St Peter) ἐξέπεσον αὐτοῦ αἱ ἁλύσεις ἐκ τῶν χειρῶν, 10
(πύλη) αὐτομάτη ἠνοίχθη αὐτοῖς, XVI. 26 (of St Paul and Silas at
Philippi) ἄφνω δὲ σεισμὸς ἐγένετο μέγας, ὥστε σαλευθῆναι τὰ θεμέ-
λια τοῦ δεσμωτηρίου· ἀνεῴχθησάν τε παραχρῆμα αἱ θύραι πᾶσαι, καὶ
πάντων τὰ δεσμὰ ἀνέθη. Beda, *Hist. Eccl.* IV 22, *vincula soluta,*
with Mayor's n. p. 357. The manuscript reading δεσμὰ...ποδῶν
(altered sometimes into πεδῶν) is defended by Homeric hymn 7, 13,
τὸν δ᾽ οὐκ ἴσχανε δεσμὰ, λύγοι δ᾽ ἀπὸ τηλόσε πίπτον χειρῶν ἠδὲ ποδῶν.

451. The manuscript reading μαίνεσθε gives a fair sense: it
makes Pentheus say that the account just given of the escape of
the Maenads and the reference to the miracles of their captive
companion, prove that the attendants themselves are mad.
In the Laurentian MS (C), examined by Mr Mahaffy for Mr
Tyrrell, 'the regular space for a stop' may be seen 'between
the words μαίνεσθε and χειρῶν, and in that space the mark of
punctuation'; and, in accordance with this way of stopping the
passage, that MS has the explanation ἐμοῦ written over τοῦδε.
'This', as Mr Tyrrell admits, 'would put γὰρ out of its place.
However, γὰρ occurs in the sixth place in Soph. *Phil.* 1451,
καιρὸς καὶ πλοῦς ὅδ᾽ ἐπείγει γὰρ, and in the fourth place in v. 477.'
λάζυσθε, the correction written above the text in the Palatine
MS, is obviously suggested by 503, and is as obviously refuted by
that line, as Pentheus would not have been made to exclaim
'seize him!' in the later passage, if he had already given orders
for him to be bound in the present. Closest to the manuscript
reading is the ingenious conjecture μαίνεσθε χεῖρον τοῦδ᾽ (Bothe,
followed by Kirchhoff and Nauck), 'Ye are more mad than he';
but the prisoner himself (whatever may be said of his captors)
has shewn no signs of madness; on the contrary, he has proved
himself uncommonly calm; the warmth however of the king's

language may be defended by 'the keen resentment (τοὖξύθυμον) and right royal temper' assigned to him in 671 ; and this applies equally to the abrupt exclamation μαίνεσθε, the reading of the Laurentian MS. But I feel some hesitation in supporting that reading, as there seems no sufficient reason why we should not have had the obvious words χειρῶν τῶνδ' instead of τοῦδ'. Besides, the plural μαίνεσθε, addressed to *all* the attendants, seems out of place when only *one* has shewn his 'madness' by his speech. This objection does not apply to the ingenious correction proposed by George Burges, μέθεσθε χειρῶν τοῦδ', because more than one were holding the prisoner fast, as is seen from λάζυσθε already referred to ; cf. *Iph. T.* 468, μέθετε τῶν ξένων χέρας, ὡς ὄντες ἱεροὶ, μηκέτ' ὦσι δέσμιοι. This conjecture (which I venture to accept) admirably suits the context : 'let loose his hands !' the king exclaims, 'for hemmed in as he is, by my toils, he is not swift enough to escape from me.' Then, after a pause, during which he takes a survey of the stranger's figure, which would have been out of the question, had not the prisoner been let loose first, he continues : 'So then, you are fairly handsome in your form,' &c.

453. So in fragm. XII (14) of the translation by Attius, *formae figurae nitiditatem hospes geris* and similarly line 455 finds its parallel in XIII (9) *nam flori crines video ei propessi iacent.*

455. 'Thy hair flows gracefully from lack of wrestling.' οὐ— πάλης must be taken as one idea, equivalent to ἀγυμνασίας (Porson on *Eccl.* 115), as in *Hipp.* 197, δι' ἀπειροσύνην ἄλλου βιότου κοὐκ- ἀπόδειξιν (=κάλυψιν, κρύψιν) τῶν ὑπὸ γαίας, where Monk quotes *Hec.* 12, μὴ σπάνις and *Or.* 931, οὐ σπάνις (=*abundantia*). Cf. *infra* 1288, ἐν οὐ-καιρῷ, and Thuc. I 137, 7 τὴν τῶν γεφυρῶν οὐ-διάλυσιν. The athlete's hair would naturally be kept short, as it would other-wise get in the way in wrestling, and be oppressively hot for the shoulders. Wearing long hair was not an Athenian but a *Spartan* fashion, and it was only as an affected imitation of the Spartan mode that it came into vogue at Athens after the end of the Peloponnesian war. In the present passage the flowing locks betray that the wearer of them is no wrestler. In *El.* 527, the strong growth of Orestes' hair is contrasted with the hair of his sister, ἔπειτα χαίτης πῶς συνοίσεται πλόκος, ὁ μὲν παλαίστραις ἀνδρὸς εὐγενοῦς τραφείς, ὁ δὲ κτενισμοῖς θῆλυς.

In Greek art *ephebi* and athletes are usually represented with short hair, slightly curled. ' Palaestra,' as personified in Philostratus *imagines* 11 § 32, has short hair. Cf. Lucian *Dial. Mer.* 5, 3, ἐν χρῷ ἀποκεκαρμένος ὥσπερ οἱ σφόδρα ἀνδρώδεις τῶν ἀθλητῶν (K. O. Müller, *Ancient Art* § 330).

457. 'Thy skin too is, for a set purpose, white   Not with the sun's rays but beneath the shade,   In quest of Cypris by thy loveliness,' 688, θηρᾶν καθ' ὕλην Κύπριν, Plat. *Phaedr.* 239 C, Stobaeus 97, 17, χειμῶνί τ' ἀσκεῖν σῶμα θερμά θ' ἡλίου τοξεύματ' αἰνεῖν μὴ σκιατροφουμένους.— εἰς παρασκευήν] *i.e.* 'for the furtherance of your object,' namely Ἀφροδίτην θηρώμενος. Antiphon, or. 6 § 19, μὴ ἐκ προνοίας μηδ' ἐκ παρασκευῆς γενέσθαι τὸν θάνατον, Lysias, or. 31 § 30, ἵν' ἀγαθοὶ προθυμῶνται γίνεσθαι ἐκ παρασκευῆς, Thuc. 1, 133, ἀπὸ παρασκευῆς.— εἰς παρασκευὴν *pro* ἐκ παρασκευῆς *dictum videtur* (Elms.) *.

460. Aesch. fr. 56, ποδαπὸς ὁ γύννις; τίς πάτρα; τίς ἡ στολή; p. xxv.

461. '*That* may be lightly told ; 'tis no grand tale : Haply thou know'st, by hearsay, flowery Tmolus.' Virg. *Georg.* 1 56, *croceos ut Tmolus odores...mittit.* The range of Tmolus runs from east to west, and mainly lies to the south of Sardis ; only a spur of the mountain-range faces that place on the west, while along the north extends the plain of the Hermus ; so that the poet's reference to its 'surrounding' Sardis is not very accurate.

465. πόθεν] not 'from what place?' but, as the answer shews, ' on whose prompting?' '*How came you* then to bring these rites to Greece?' (cf. 648). The only way in which a *local* sense can be here given to πόθεν is to suppose that Pentheus takes the Lydian Sardis for the *birthplace* only of the stranger, and wants to know what the place was which he had left last on his way into Greece ; but if so, the answer scarcely fits the question.

466. εἰσέβησ'] not εἰς τὴν Ἑλλάδα (as taken by Abresch, to whom the emendation is due), but εἰς τὰς τελετὰς = *initiavit;* so εἰσιτήρια, *initia.* Orph. *Arg.* 470, ἔνθα καὶ ὄργια φρικτὰ θεῶν, ἄρρητα βροτοῖσιν, ἄσμενοι εἰσεπέρησαν, Ammianus XVI 3, 365, *in-*

---

* Paley however explains ἐς π., 'to a degree that shows art ' (cf. ἐς κάλλος, *El.* 1073, *Tro.* 1201 ; ἐς πλησμονὰς, *Tro.* 1211), 'too white to be natural.'

ducendum=initiandum (Lobeck, *Aglaophamus*, 74 note). Cf. Virg. *Ecl.* 5, 30, *thiasos inducere Bacchi.*

467. Pentheus in his reply catches up the last words of the previous line, ὁ τοῦ Διός, with the enquiry, 'Have you a Zeus *there*, who begets new gods?'—to which the stranger replies, '*No*, but 'twas he who wedded Semele *here*,' not another Zeus, but the Zeus of your own local legend. *Hel.* 489, Διὸς δ᾽ ἔλεξε παῖδά νιν πεφυκέναι. ἀλλ᾽ ἤ τίς ἐστι Ζηνὸς ὄνομ᾽ ἔχων ἀνὴρ Νείλου παρ᾽ ὄχθας ; εἰς γὰρ ὅ γε κατ᾽ οὐρανόν.

469. ἠνάγκασεν] 'pressed thee into his service.' 'By night, or openly, did he *impress* thee.' Thuc. VII 58, 3, ἀναγκαστοὶ στρατεύοντες, and VIII 24, 2, ἐπιβάτας τῶν ὁπλιτῶν ἐκ καταλόγου ἀναγκαστούς.

470. ''Twas face to face, and he gave me sacred rites.' Clement of Alexandria, who uses the strongest language against the mysteries of Dionysus elsewhere (*Protrept.* II), fancifully applies this line and 471, 472, 474, 476, to the mysteries of the Christian religion (*Stromateus* IV 25, p. 1372 Migne).

472—4. Theocr. 26, 14, ὄργια Βάκχου...τὰ δ᾽ οὐχ ὁρέοντι βέβαλοι. Catullus 64, 259, *pars obscura cavis celebrabant orgia cistis, orgia quae frustra cupiunt audire profani;* Statius, *Ach.* II 137, *Bacchea ferentes orgia.*

475. 'A pretty tale, to make me to long to hear.' It is hard to keep up the literal metaphor from base coinage contained in ἐκιβδήλευσας ; the words 'tinselled,' 'gilded,' varnished,' give the same general sense in English.

476. *i.e. You* may not hear them, 'for the rites of the god hate him who lives in sin.' Diodorus, *Sic.* III 64, καταδεῖξαι δὲ καὶ τὰ περὶ τὰς τελετὰς καὶ μεταδοῦναι τῶν μυστηρίων τοῖς εὐσεβέσι τῶν ἀνθρώπων καὶ δίκαιον βίον ἀσκοῦσι. Naevius, *Lycurgus* XIV (9), *oderunt di homines iniuros.*

477. 'As you clearly saw the god, what like was he?' **478.** 'What like he pleased ; 'twas not for *me* to dictate.'

479. παρωχέτευσας] a metaphor from an ἀνὴρ ὀχετηγὸς, diverting a channel of water from one part of a garden to another. Suidas, παροχετεύει: ἀπὸ ἑτέρου ὑδρηγοῦ εἰς ἕτερον ἐπιβάλλει, ἢ μεταφέρει τὸ ὕδωρ. The corresponding metaphor with ourselves

would probably be one borrowed from fencing, 'Well parried
there again ! yet answering naught.'—480. Fragm. 891, ...οὐκ
ἂν δυναίμην μὴ στέγοντα πιμπλάναι, σοφοὺς ἐπαντλῶν ἀνδρὶ μὴ σοφῷ
λόγους.—485. [Maetzner ad Antiphont. p. 221] Shilleto, adv.

486. νύκτωρ] Hence the epithet ἐννύχιος applied to Dionysus in Anth. Pal. IX 524, νυκτέλιος in Plutarch de EI in Delphis,
p. 389, and Ovid Met. IV 15 ; according to Pausanias I 40,· 6,
there was a temple of Dionysus, under the latter name, at
Megara.—487—8. Fragm. 528 (Meleager), ἡ γὰρ Κύπρις πέφυκε
τῷ σκότῳ φίλη τὸ φῶς δ' ἀνάγκην προστίθησι σωφρονεῖν, the former
of which lines justifies the fears of Pentheus, while the latter
disposes of the sophistical reply of Dionysus. In Orphic hymn
54, we have ὄργια νυκτιφαῆ τελεταῖς ἁγίαις ἀναφαίνων (of Silenus).

491. ' How bold our Bacchant ; how well trained in word-
fence !' βάκχος is here simply the votary of Dionysus, and not
the god himself, whose identity with his follower is not made
known till near the close of the play, 1340.   The word βάκχος
does not occur in Homer or Aeschylus (who however has βάκχαι):
and the god was not commonly called by that name till a comparatively late period.   In Soph. the word is found only once,
O. T. 211, τὸν χρυσομίτραν...οἰνῶπα Βάκχον εὔιον, as a name it occurs in the oracle quoted in Dem. Meid. § 52, μεμνῆσθαι Βάκχοιο,
Hipp. 560, Διογόνοιο Βάκχου, Iph. A. 1061, κρατῆρα Βάκχου, Iph. T.
161, Βάκχου λοιβάς.

492. This and some of the following lines are fancifully
interpreted by Horace, Ep. I 16, 73, vir bonus et sapiens audebit
dicere 'Pentheu, rector Thebarum, quid me perferre patique
indignum coges ?' 'adimam bona.' 'nempe pecus, rem, lectos,
argentum. tollas licet.' 'in manicis et compedibus saevo te sub
custode tenebo' (497). 'ipse deus, simul atque volam, me solvet'
(498). opinor hoc sentit, 'moriar.' mors ultima linea rerum
est. Cf. Arrian Epictet. dissert. 18, 17, ἀλλ' ὁ τύραννος δήσει· τί;
τὸ σκέλος. ἀλλ' ἀφελεῖ· τί; τὸν τράχηλον, and ib. 19, 8.

493. ἁβρὸν βόστρυχον] Cf. Callistratus quoted on 235.—494.
The practice of consecrating the hair to a god and cutting it off
at a solemn season in his honour is also referred to in Aesch.
Choeph. 6, πλόκαμον Ἰνάχῳ θρεπτήριον, Philostratus imagines

1 7 § 1, of Memnon, ὁ τῶν βοστρύχων ἄσταχυς οὓς (οἶμαι) Νείλῳ ἔτρεφε, Pausanias, VIII 20, 2, ἔτρεφεν ὁ Λεύκιππος κόμην τῷ Ἀλφειῷ. The Athenians used to dedicate their hair to Apollo, Plut. *Thes.* 5. Diphilus, ap. Athenaeum, p. 225 B (quoted by Elmsley), ἐνταῦθα γοῦν ἔστιν τις ὑπερηκοντικὼς, κόμην τρέφων μὲν πρῶτον ἱερὰν τοῦ θεοῦ, ὡς φησίν· οὐ διὰ τοῦτο γ᾽, ἀλλ᾽ ἐστιγμένος, πρὸ τοῦ μετώπου παραπέτασμ᾽ αὐτὴν ἔχει. (Becker's *Charicles*, sc. XI.) The words ἱερὸς ὁ πλόκαμος are quoted in a difficult epigram of Callimachus, XLIX (48), *Anth. Pal.* VI 310, which apparently describes the dedication to the Muses of a mask, or other representation of Dionysus, by Simus, possibly the actor of that name ; εὐμαθίην ᾔτεῖτο διδοὺς ἐμὲ Σῖμος ὁ Μίκκου ταῖς Μούσαις· αἱ δὲ Γλαύκος ὅκως ἔδοσαν | ἀντ᾽ ὀλίγου μέγα δῶρον. ἐγὼ δ᾽ ἀνὰ τήνδε κεχηνὼς κεῖμαι τοῦ Σαμίου διπλόον, ὁ τραγικὸς | παιδαρίων Διόνυσος ἐπήκοος. οἱ δὲ λέγουσιν, 'ἱερὸς ὁ πλόκαμος,' τοὐμὸν ὄνειαρ ἐμοί (see Otto Schneider, *Callimachea*, I p. 438). Virg. *Aen.* VII 390, *molles tibi sumere thyrsos, te lustrare choro, sacrum tibi pascere crinem.*

494. ἱερὸς] is here necessarily trisyllabic. There is no passage in Greek tragedy where we cannot scan it as three syllables, and there are several where that is the only scansion possible, *e.g.* ἱερὰ, at the beginning of an iambic line, in Soph. *Phil.* 943, *Herc. F.* 922, and *Ion* 1317 ; ἱερὸς in the same place in *Iph. T.* 1452, and lastly *Phoen.* 840, θάκοισιν ἐν ἱεροῖσιν. Hence it appears that the disyllabic spelling ἱρὸς, often found in Dindorf's *Poetae Scenici*, is never necessary and is best avoided, being inadmissible in the above passages, whereas the trisyllabic spelling, ἱερὸς, will always stand (R. Shilleto).

499. 'Not till thou call'st him, 'mid thy Bacchanals,' i.e. 'Never.' ἐστάθην in Tragedy is used in the same sense as ἔστην, 'I stood,' but in prose it is a true passive and is limited to inanimate objects, *e.g.* buildings, trophies, statues.

502. Callimachus *Apollo* 11, ὡπόλλων οὐ παντὶ φαείνεται ἀλλ᾽ ὅτις ἐσθλός κ.τ.λ.

503. καταφρονεῖ με. The usual construction has occurred in 199: the exception is noticed by the Scholiast on Ar. *Ran.* 103, σὲ δὲ ταῦτ᾽ ἀρέσκει· ἀντὶ τοῦ σοὶ Ἀττικῶς. σημειωτέον τοίνυν

ὅτι Ἀττικοὶ κέχρηνται τῷ τοιούτῳ σχηματισμῷ. καὶ Εὐριπίδης ἐν
Βάκχαις· καταφρονεῖ με καὶ Θήβας ὅδε (Elmsley).—505. κυριώτερος
σέθεν, 'But *I* who have better right than thou say, *Bind!*' σέθεν
is gen. not after κύριος, but after the comparative.

506. 'Thy life thou know'st not, see'st no more e'en who thou
art,' i e. you little know the full import of your life, no nor even
of your very existence.   Persius III 67, *quid sumus aut quid-
nam victuri gignimur;* Persius as a careful student of Horace
would have his attention directed to this play by his predecessor's paraphrase of the context of this passage (note on 492);
hence the words above-quoted are probably a direct imitation of
the line before us.   A fainter reminiscence may possibly be
traced in Catullus, who specially studied this play, XVII, 22, *ipse
qui sit, utrum sit an non sit, id quoque nescit.*   The only emendation of the line which appears to be necessary is Elmsley's
ἔθ' for οὖθ' ὅστις εἶ. * Pentheus, not grasping the full meaning
of the remark, thinks that it only implies that he does not know
who he is, and accordingly gives his *name* in answer, whereupon
he is reminded of its ill-omened significance : see note on 367 and
Chaeremon there quoted, also (with Herm.) Nonnus XLVI 73,
addressed to Pentheus, σοὶ τάχα μᾶλλον ἔθεντο προμάντιες οὔνομα
Μοῖραι ὑμετέρου (wrongly used for σοῦ) θανάτοιο προάγγελον.

508. ἐνδυστυχῆσαι] 'a very proper name to bring bad omen,'
lit. 'in name thou art fit indeed *to be luckless therein.' Phoen.* 727,
ἐνδυστυχῆσαι δεινὸν εὐφρόνης κνέφας.   The verb is one of many
instances in which the compound in Greek has to be split up
into its component parts in translating into English.   This is
often the case with verbs compounded with ἐν; e.g. Herod. IX 1,
ἐπιτηδεώτερος ἐνστρατοπεδεύεσθαι, ib. 25, ib. 7, ἐπιτηδεώτατόν ἐστι
ἐμμαχέσασθαι τὸ Θριάσιον πεδίον, VI 102, ἐπιτηδεώτατον ἐνιππεῦ-
σαι, Pl. *Phaedr.* 228 F, ἐμαυτόν σοι ἐμμελετᾶν (to practise *upon*)
παρέχειν (many other instances are collected by Cope on Aristot.
Rhet. II 4 § 12, ἡδεῖς συνδιαγαγεῖν καὶ συνδιημερεῦσαι).   Cf. also
the exceptional use of ἐλλείπειν in Soph. *El.* 736, ἐλλελειμμένον
(left in), Eur. *El.* 609, οὐδ' ἐλλέλοιπας ἐλπίδ', and Thuc. V 103,
ἐν ὅτῳ ἔτι φυλάξεταί τις αὐτὴν γνωρισθεῖσαν οὐκ ἐλλείπει.

509. ἱππικαῖς φάτναισιν] 'On the left of the palace, but in

* See *Supplementary Notes.*

close contiguity to it (Julius Pollux IV § 125, εἰρκτὴ δὲ ἡ λαιά), and between it and a κλίσιον representing the stable, was seen the entrance to a dark and gloomy dungeon (550, σκοτίαις ἐν εἰρκταῖς, 611, ἐς σκοτεινὰς ὀρκάνας).' *Theatre of the Greeks*, p. 294. The stable, however, was probably itself used as a dungeon (618), as in *Orest.* 1448.

510. σκότιον εἰσορᾷ κνέφας] Soph. *O. T.* 419, βλέποντα... σκότον, and Eur. *Phoen.* 377, σκότον δεδορκώς. Seneca Ep. 57 (of the *Piedigrotta*, the great tunnel between Naples and Puteoli), *nihil illo carcere longius, nihil illis faucibus obscurius, quae nobis praestant non ut per tenebras videamus sed ut ipsas.* Milton *P. L.* 1 63, 'No light, but rather darkness visible.'

513. καὶ βύρσης κτύπου] explanatory of δούπου.—**ἄποινα** (516) in general apposition to μέτεισι Διόνυσός σε. So in Pindar *Isthm.* VIII 6, ἀνεγειράτω κῶμον, Ἰσθμιάδος τε νίκης ἄποινα, *Alc.* 7, θητεύειν...τῶνδ' ἄποιν' ἠνάγκασεν, *Iph. T.* 1459, ὅταν ἑορτάζῃ λεὼς τῆς σῆς σφαγῆς ἄποινα, *El.* 1180, ἄποιν' ἐμῶν πημάτων, *supra* 346.

519. 'Hail! Achelous' daughter, lady Dirce, happy maiden.' The nymph of the fountain is addressed as daughter of the Achelous, because that river was 'the patriarch and eponyme hero of the whole fresh-water creation of Hellas' (Mure's *Tour*, 1 p. 102, where it is described as 'a noble river, by far the finest in Greece'); cf. Acusilaus (*fl.* B.C. 530) Müller's *fragm. histor.* p. 101, Ὠκεανὸς δὲ γαμεῖ Τηθὺν ἑαυτοῦ ἀδελφήν· τῶν δὲ γίγνονται τρισχίλιοι ποταμοί· Ἀχελῷος δὲ αὐτῶν πρεσβύτατος καὶ τετίμηται μάλιστα (quoted by Macrobius *Sat.* 5, 18, 10); see further, on l. 625. So Herodotus tells us that a tributary of the Asopus, the stream Oëroë, had the local name Ἀσωποῦ θυγάτηρ or ἡ Ἀσωπίς. On Dirce, in whose waters the newborn Dionysus was dipped, cf. *Hipp.* 555—562, *Phoen.* 645, καλλιπόταμος ὕδατος ἵνα τε νοτὶς ἐπέρχεται ῥυτὰς Δίρκας χλοηφόρους βαθυσπόρους γύας, Βρόμιον ἔνθα τέκετο, and *ib.* 825, quoted on l. 5.—**523. πυρὸς ἐξ ἀθανάτου**] Cf. 8—9. 'When, from the undying flame, Zeus his sire rescued him (and placed him) in his thigh.' **μηρῷ**, a local dat.

526—9. 'Come, my Dithyrambus, come, Enter thou thy father's womb, Lo! to Thebes I now proclaim, Bacchic boy, be this thy name.' By the name is meant Διθύραμβος, a word of

doubtful derivation, which Eur. here apparently connects with
δὶς or Διός, θύρα and βαίνειν, referring it either to the babe being
shut up in the thigh of Zeus, or to the double birth by which he
twice passed the doors of life ; Etymologicum Magnum, *s. v.*,
...ᾗ ἀπὸ τοῦ δύο θύρας βαίνειν, τήν τε κοιλίαν τῆς μητρὸς Σεμέλης
καὶ τὸν μηρὸν τοῦ Διός· ἀπὸ τοῦ δεύτερον τετέχθαι...ἵν᾽ ᾖ ὁ δὶς
θύραζε βεβηκώς (Schöne). But the quantity of the first syllable
is against deriving it in any way from δὶς, and is in favour of
connecting it with Διί, as in Δι-πόλια, Δί-φιλος. Donaldson,
New Cratylus § 319, after a long discussion comes to the conclusion that the word came to mean 'a chorus or song celebrating the birth of Bacchus,' from originally signifying 'the
bringing to Jupiter of the θρῖον or leaf-enveloped heart or body
of the god.' However improbable his explanation of the word
may be, one thing is certain that the name was elsewhere, as
here, specially connected with the marvellous birth of the god,
e.g. Plat. *leg.* III 700 B, ἄλλο (εἶδος ᾠδῆς) Διονύσου γένεσις, οἶμαι,
διθύραμβος λεγόμενος.

526. ἄρσενα νηδύν] Nonnus 1, 10 (of Dionysus), ἄρσενι
γαστρὶ λόχευε πατὴρ καὶ πότνια μήτηρ. 532. ἐν σοί cannot be
taken literally, even if we understand it of the stream whose
nymph is here invoked ; it appears rather to be used of the
surroundings of the stream which the chorus invokes instead of
calling on Thebes itself.

533. τί μ᾽ ἀναίνει;] 'Why disown me?' For another use of
ἀναίνομαι cf. 251. 534—6. 'The day will come, I swear by the
clustered grace of Dionysus' vine, the day will come when
Bromius shall find a place in thy heart.' For ἔτι cf. 306.

537. οἵαν οἵαν ὀργὰν have nothing answering to them in the
corresponding strophe, hence it has been sometimes supposed
that the first line of the chorus has been lost ; but it seems
better to regard the line before us as an interpolation due to a
copyist who, mistaking the construction and supposing that χθόνιον γένος ἐκφύς τε δράκοντός ποτε Πενθεύς was nom. to ἀναφαίνει,
thought it necessary to supply an acc. after that verb. By
omitting the words, we have a perfectly intelligible construction,
'Pentheus betrays his earth-born descent, betrays that (lit. 'and

that') he sprang from a dragon of old, Pentheus begotten by earth-born Echion to be a monster of savage mien, no mortal wight, but like to an ensanguined giant, foe of heaven.' The constr. of ἀναφαίνει ἐκφύς is like that of δηλοῦν c. particip., e.g. Soph. *Ant.* 20, δηλοῖς γάρ τι καλχαίνουσ' ἔπος, cf. Soph. *El.* 24, σαφῆ σημεῖα φαίνεις ἐσθλὸς εἰς ἡμᾶς γεγώς.

In the Laurentian MS (C) this line has written above it the word περισσὸν, which at first sight might be taken to mean that the whole line is superfluous, whereas it more probably refers to the unnecessary repetition of οἵαν.

Pentheus is compared to one of the Giants, γίγαντι γηγενέτᾳ προσόμοιος (as some one else is called in *Phoen.* 128), not only as son of the earth-born (χθόνιος) Echion, but also as a foe of heaven. The battle between the gods and the giants (who are sometimes wrongly confounded with the Titans) was the subject of a piece of sculpture at Delphi, described by Euripides himself in *Ion* 206—18, where Enceladus and Mimas and other giants are at war with Zeus, Pallas and Dionysus.

550. 'Dost thou look on this, O Dionysus, son of Zeus, dost thou see how thy prophets are in conflict with oppression?' ἐσορᾷς may possibly be a corruption of ἐφορᾷς, used often of standing calmly by, looking on with indifference, at the troubles of others, e.g. Soph. *Trach.* 1269, θεῶν οἱ φύσαντες καὶ κληζόμενοι πατέρες τοιαῦτ' ἐφορῶσι πάθη, and id. *El.* 825, εἰ ταῦτ' ἐφορῶντες (Ζεὺς καὶ Ἥλιος) κρύπτουσιν ἔκηλοι.—For προφήτας, referring to the votaries of Dionysus, cf. *Rhes.* 972, where Orpheus is called Βάκχου προφήτης.— For ἀνάγκας, cf. 643, δεσμοῖς κατηναγκασμένος.

553. χρυσῶπα θύρσον] 'Down from Olympus, come! O king! Thy golden thyrsus brandishing.' The thyrsus is exceptionally described as gleaming with gold, because Dionysus is addressed as a king (ἄνα) and the thyrsus is his sceptre. This is better perhaps than understanding it of the *hederae flores quorum croceus color est* (Hermann). So in the account of the gorgeous procession held in honour of Dionysus by Ptolemy Philadelphus, the god, on his victorious return from India, is described as στέφανον κισσοῦ καὶ ἀμπέλου χρυσοῦν ἔχων, εἶχεν ἐν ταῖς χερσὶ θυρσόλογχον χρυσοῦν (Callixenus ap. Athen. p. 200).

554. ἄνα is best taken as voc. of ἄναξ, and not with τινάσσων (as in 80), nor as = ἀνάστηθι.—κατ' 'Ολύμπου, 'down from Olympus,' (one of the haunts where the chorus suppose the god to be lingering), makes better sense than κατ' 'Ολυμπον.

556. 'O where, I marvel, in Nysa, the lair of wild beasts, art thou wielding thy wand o'er thy revel-bands?' Several places of the name of Nysa are mentioned in connexion with Dionysus; a mountain in India, in Aethopia, in Arabia felix, besides places in Cappadocia, in Caria, in Lycia, in Thrace, in Helicon, in Boeotia, and in Euboea. Hence it was once happily described in a professorial lecture as 'in fact, a mountain which attended Dionysus on his travels.' The very name of the god is sometimes connected with Nysa. According to the Homeric hymn 26, 2, it was there that the Nymphs nursed the infant Dionysus, καὶ ἐνδυκέως ἀτίταλλον Νύσης ἐν γυάλοις. Cf. Soph. fragm. 94, quoted on l. 100, and Virg. *Aen.* 6, 805, *Liber agens celso Nysae de vertice tigres*, Lucan 1, 65, *Bacchumve avertere Nysa.*

557. θυρσοφορεῖς θιάσους] So in Herod. II 168, ἐδορυφόρεον τὸν βασιλέα (*ib.* III 127); Kühner, *Gk. Gr.* II § 409 p. 260.

559. By κορυφαὶ Κωρύκιαι are meant the rocky heights near one or other of the famous caverns of that name, either that on mount Parnassus, or that on the coast of Cilicia. The latter is referred to by Strabo as Κώρυκος ἄκρα (XIV p. 670), and is elaborately described by Pomponius Mela, I c. 13, *grandi hiatu patens montem litori appositum..aperit....rursus specus alter aperitur...terret ingredientes sonitu cymbalorum divinitus et magno fragore crepitantium. totus autem augustus et vere sacer, habitarique a dis et dignus et creditus, nihil non venerabile, et quasi cum aliquo numine se ostentat* (ap. Joddrell). The coins of Corycus in Cilicia sometimes represent Dionysus on the one side and the Corycian cavern on the other. If we suppose that by Nysa a mountain in Asia is meant, it would be not unnatural to understand the poet to be here referring to the Cilician promontory; especially as, according to the prophecy of Teiresias (306), the god has still to take possession of Parnassus, and it was not till *after* the doom of Pentheus that, according to Aesch. *Eum.* 22—7, he claimed the Corycian cave on that mountain as one of his haunts; σέβω δὲ νύμφας, ἔνθα Κωρυκὶς πέτρα κοίλη, φίλορνις, δαιμόνων ἀναστροφή· Βρόμιος δ' ἔχει τὸν χῶρον, οὐδ' ἀμνημονῶ, ἐξ οὗτε βάκχαις ἐστρατήγησεν θεός, λαγὼ δίκην Πενθεῖ καταρράψας μόρον. Nevertheless, it is more probable that, as the scene is laid at Thebes, the poet means the well-known cave on the not far distant mount of Parnassus, thus referring by anticipation to a haunt of the god which in after times was frequently associated with him, cf. Soph. *Antig.* 1125, (of Parnassus) ἔνθα Κωρύκιαι νύμφαι στείχουσι βακχίδες, and Strabo IX p. 417 A (quoted by Schöne), ἱεροπρεπὴς δ' ἐστὶ πᾶς ὁ Παρνασσὸς, ἔχων ἄντρα τε καὶ ἄλλα χωρία τιμώμενά τε καὶ ἁγιστευόμενα, ὧν ἐστι γνωριμώτατον καὶ κάλλιστον τὸ Κωρύκιον νυμφῶν ἄντρον, ὁμώνυμον τῷ Κιλικίῳ. The cavern on the way up to the heights of Parnassus, the actual summit of which is nearly five hours' climb above the cave, is a vaulted chamber, 300 feet long by nearly 200 wide and about 40 high in the middle,—large enough to give shelter to the greater part of the inhabitants of Delphi at the Persian invasion (Hdt. 8, 36). It was formerly dedicated to Pan and the Nymphs, though the inscription to that effect can now be seen no longer.

560—4. 'Or haply, in the teeming forest-haunts of Olympus, where in the olden time Orpheus struck his harp, and by his music gathered the trees around him, gathered around him the beasts of the field.' In another play, acted at Athens at the same time as the *Bacchae*, we have similarly an allusion to the legend of Orpheus, *Iph. A.* 1211, εἰ μὲν τὸν Ὀρφέως εἶχον, ὦ πάτερ, λόγον, πείθειν· ἐπᾴδουσ', ὥσθ' ὁμαρτεῖν μοι πέτρας, κηλεῖν τε τοῖς λόγοισιν οὓς ἐβουλόμην, ἐνταῦθ' ἂν ἦλθον.

With the epithet πολυδένδρεσσιν, cf. Virg. *Georg.* 281, *frondosum Olympum*, and Hor. *Carm.* 3, 4, 52, *opacus Olympus.* The mountain, as already remarked (on 411), lay to the south of the dominions of Archelaus, and the view from the site of his ancient capital 'embraces not only the mighty mass of the snowy Olympus, but the wide plain of lower Macedonia.' Tozer's *Geography of Greece* p. 203.

θαλάμαις, the regular word for 'lairs of wild beasts' (Hesychius explains θαλάμη by τρώγλη, κατάδυσις). The fact that the

manuscript reading θαλάμοις is a corruption of θαλάμαις is proved
by ταῖς in the preceding line.

565. For **μάκαρ** fem. (Hermann's correction of the manuscript reading μάκαιρα), cf. *Hel.* 375, μάκαρ... Καλλιστοῖ. The
mention of Orpheus and his μοῦσαι naturally leads up to the
complimentary reference to Pieria, part of the southern dominions of Archelaus already alluded to in 409, and to the subsequent mention of the swift stream of Axius, and the river
Lydias, on the heights above which, that king's capital was
situated. For the Axius, cf. *Il.* 21, 158, Ἀξιοῦ ὃς κάλλιστον
ὕδωρ ἐπὶ γαῖαν ἵησι, 2, 849, τηλόθεν ἐξ Ἀμυδῶνος ἀπ᾽ Ἀξίου εὐρὺ
ῥέοντος Ἀξίου οὗ κάλλιστον ὕδωρ ἐπικίδναται αἶαν. Just as Homer
calls it κάλλιστος, so Eur. in his complimentary allusion refers
to the swiftness of the stream, while the matter-of-fact Strabo
assures us that it was a turbid river (ἐκ πολλῶν πληρούμενος
ποταμῶν θολερὸς ῥέει, Eustathius on *Il.* β 850, Strabo VII Epitome
§§ 20—23). Leake, crossing it in Nov., describes it as 'rapid,
deep and swollen with rain, though not so high as it usually is
in winter,' *Northern Greece* III 259. Philostratus, *imag.* II 8
ad fin. (thinking probably of Homer's lines), gives it the epithet
πάγκαλος.

For the river Lydias, cf. Herod. VII 127, Λυδίεώ τε ποταμοῦ
καὶ Ἀλιάκμονος, οἳ οὐρίζουσι γῆν τὴν Βοττιαιΐδα καὶ Μακεδονίδα,
ἐς τωὖτὸ ῥέεθρον τὸ ὕδωρ συμμίσγοντες. On this stream lay
Aegae (or Edessa) the ancient capital of Macedonia, identified by Leake with *Vodhená*, which 'in the grandeur of its
situation, in the magnificence of the surrounding objects, and
the extent of the rich prospect which it commands, is not
inferior to any situation in Greece,' *u. s.* III 272 ; reference
is also there made to its 'rocks, cascades, and smiling valleys,' and to 'its lofty, salubrious and strong position.' Though
Aegae still continued to be the royal burial-place, the seat of
government was afterwards transferred by Philip [?] to Pella,
where he was himself brought up, and where Alexander was born.
The later capital stood on a height about halfway between
Aegae and the sea, but separated from the Lydias by a muddy
marsh referred to in the epigram in which Aristotle is attacked

by Theocritus of Chios for leaving the Academia to live at the Macedonian court ; ὃς διὰ τὴν ἀκρατῆ γαστρὸς φύσιν εἵλετο ναίειν ἀντ' Ἀκαδημείας Βόρβορον ἐν προχοαῖς (Plutarch, de exilio c. 10).

571—5. 'Father and giver of wealth and blessing to man; who, they tell me, enriches with fairest waters a land of noble steeds.' The reference in the latter part of this sentence, even if we read πατέρα τε, is probably to the Lydias, otherwise it is possible to explain it of the Haliacmon, a much larger river, which is joined by the Lydias shortly before falling into the sea. Nearly the same language is used elsewhere of the great Thessalian river Apidanus, *Hec.* 451, Φθιάδος, ἔνθα καλλίστων ὑδάτων πατέρα φασὶν Ἀπιδανὸν γύας λιπαίνειν. The Apidanus however cannot be referred to in the present passage, as Dionysus is here described as coming from the north to Pieria, and thus crossing the rivers of *Macedonia*, first the Axius, next the Lydias, and possibly also the Haliacmon.—ὕδασι καλλίστοις is a complimentary phrase, since the stream was really muddy and turbid, as is shewn by the reference to its fertilising effects (λιπαίνειν). Similarly κάλλιστον ὕδωρ is used of the Nile in a play of Eur. named 'Archelaus' out of compliment to the king (fragm. 230). The modern names of the Lydias, both in Turkish and in Greek (*Mauronero*), mean 'Black Water.'

The reference to the noble horses of Macedonia is illustrated by the coin of Archelaus engraved in the text, where a horseman may be seen on the one side, and a goat, in allusion to the name of the king's capital (Αἰγαί), on the other. The horses of Archelaus are mentioned in Thuc. II 100 § 2.

576—603. The choral portions of this κομμὸς between the chorus and Dionysus may be either distributed among the fifteen members of the chorus (as in Paley's Edition) ; or, better perhaps, assigned (with Wecklein) as follows : lines 579 and 591—3, to the leader of the first ἡμιχόριον ; 582—4 and 596—9 to that of the second ; 585—590, and 600—4, to the *Coryphaeus*, whose call in 590, σέβετέ νιν, is, according to this arrangement, answered by the whole chorus in the words σέβομεν ὤ. The MSS, however, indicate a somewhat different distribution by assigning these last words to a ἡμιχόριον.

579. Scaliger supposed that this passage was the original of a fragment in Varro :—(Cho.) *quis me iubilat?* (Bacch.) *vicinus tuus antiquus;* and that the reply of the chorus was to be found in a fragment of the *Bacchae* of Attius (V 17) preserved by Macrobius (VI 5, 11), *o Dionyse pater optime vitisator Semela genitus Euhie;* but the resemblance is too distant to allow of our being at all confident as to his conjecture.

585. πέδον χθονός· ἔνοσι πότνια] 'Oh! floor of earth! oh! awful earthquake.' It seems better to treat these words as two separate exclamations, than to assume (with Hermann) that πέδον is acc. after the substantive ἔνοσι.

588. 'Soon will the palace of Pentheus be shaken to its fall.' διατινάξεται, fut. mid. in passive sense, like φυλάξεται (Soph. *Phil.* 48), στερήσεται (Soph. *El.* 1210), τιμήσεται and διδαξόμεσθα (*Ant.* 210, 726).

591. 'Did ye mark how yonder the marble imposts on the pillars were parting asunder?' ἔμβολα is followed by κίοσιν, in the same construction as the corresponding participle ἐμβεβλημένα. It refers to the marble entablature in general, including the architrave or ἐπιστύλιον. Horace *Carm.* 2, 19, 15, *tectaque Penthei disiecta non leni ruina.* For διάδρομα Milton' needlessly conjectured διάτρομα (cf. 188 n).

594. 'Light the lurid levin-torch, wrap in flame the halls of Pentheus.' So the King's palace is doomed to the flames in the *Lycurgus* of Naevius XX (23)...*ut videam Volcani opera haec flammis flora fieri.* With αἴθοπα λαμπάδα, cf. *Suppl.* 1019, αἴθοπι φλογμῷ. The epithet κεραύνιος points to the flame, here kindled afresh, as having first been lighted by the thunderbolt of Zeus, when Semele was slain, as is shewn by the first four following lines of the chorus, cf. also *supra* 6—9.—With Δίου βροντάς in 599, cf. 8, Δίου πυρὸς, and for ἄνω κάτω in 602, see 349.

606. The MSS have the unmetrical line διατινάξαντος δῶμα Πενθέως· ἀλλ' ἐξανίστατε, which is corrected by Musgrave into τὰ Πενθέως δώματ'· ἀλλ' ἀνίστατε. The present line and the next are bracketed by Nauck, partly on the ground of the corruptions they contain and partly perhaps because they spoil the symmetry of the dialogue; if they are left out, we get the conversation of

Dionysus and the chorus, from 604—615 inclusive, into exact correspondence. Nevertheless, as the chorus is prostrate in fear, some words of reassurance are wanted to encourage them to rise to their feet, and we are therefore unable to reject the lines in question, especially as the alterations required to correct them are very slight.

612. τίς μοι φύλαξ ἦν, εἰ σὺ συμφορᾶς τύχοις;] This sentence does not fall exactly into any of the common types of conditional construction; but it is readily explained by the consideration that the chorus is here referring to the fear they had felt in the past, which, if expressed at the time, would have naturally taken the form, τίς μοι φύλαξ μέλλει ἔσεσθαι, ἐὰν σὺ συμφορᾶς τύχης. In repeating in the present time this expression of fear in the past, the conditional part is slightly altered, and the tense in the principal sentence is changed into the imperfect (without ἄν): 'who, methought, would be my guardian, if *thou* wert to meet with woe.' Cf. *Iph. A.* 1405, μακάριόν μέ τις θεῶν ἔμελλε θήσειν, εἰ τίχοιμι σῶν γάμων, and *Herc. F.* 467, σὺ δ' ἦσθα (= ἔμελλες ἔσεσθαι) Θηβῶν τῆς φιλαρμάτων ἄναξ.

617. ἔθιγεν...ἥψατ'] 'Dr Elmsley observes *idem significant* ἔθιγεν *et* ἥψατο. Not exactly, we think. θιγγάνειν is *to touch* simply, ἅπτεσθαι is *to take hold of, to fasten one's hand to anything*, Iliad 2, 181' (C.J. Blomfield, *Museum Criticum* 2, 664).

ἐλπίσιν δ' ἐβόσκετο] 'but on idle fancies fed.' Similar in verbal expression, though different in general sense, is *Phoen.* 396, αἱ δ' ἐλπίδες βόσκουσι φυγάδας, ὡς λόγος.

618. The delusion of Pentheus which leads him to mistake a bull for his prisoner has some colour lent it by the fact that that was one of the forms assumed by Dionysus (100, 920, 1017). Cf. the delusion of Ajax, ἐν ἐλίκεσσι βουσὶ πεσὼν (*Aj.* 375).

619. περὶ βρόχους ἔβαλλε] The *tmesis* is here worth noticing, as the division of περιέβαλλε into two words makes it possible to use a form which would have been otherwise inadmissible, compounds of περὶ and ἀμφὶ followed by a vowel being avoided in Greek tragedy ; thus ἠμφιεσμένος, however tempting a word in Greek verse composition, is really a Comic, not a Tragic form

(Ar. *Eccl.* 879). But for this principle, Eur. might easily have written τῷδε περιέβαλλε δεσμά. **620.** *Ajax* 10, κάρα στάζων ἱδρῶτι.

623. ὁ **Βάκχος**] is probably used by Dionysus with intentional ambiguity, meaning either (1) the Bacchant (as in 491) or (2) Dionysus himself, in which sense the word is used by Soph. *O. T.* 211, quoted on that line. Porson's remark, *Euripidis aetate non utebantur v.* βάκχος *hoc sensu* (1); *forsan* βακχεύς (*Kidd's tracts* p. 225), is refuted by the line already quoted from this play.

625. 'Αχελῷον] Here the name of the great river of Acarnania, the largest in Greece, is used of water in general. So in *And.* 167, (in Thessaly) ἐκ χρυσηλάτων τευχέων χερὶ σπείρουσαν 'Αχελῴου δρόσον. Macrobius, *Sat.* v 18 §§ 2—12, in illustration of Virg. *Georg.* I 9, *poculaque inventis Acheloia miscuit uvis,* quotes a parallel from Aristoph. fragm. 130, οὐ μίξας πῶμ' 'Αχελῴῳ, and a passage from Ephorus ascribing this use to the influence of the oracle of Dodona, not far from the source of the river: σχεδὸν γὰρ ἐν ἅπασιν αὐτοῖς (sc. τοῖς χρησμοῖς) προστάττειν εἴωθεν 'Αχελῴῳ θύειν ὥστε πολλοὶ νομίζοντες οὐ τὸν ποταμὸν τὸν διὰ τῆς 'Ακαρνανίας ῥέοντα ἀλλὰ τὸ σύνολον ὕδωρ 'Αχελῷον ὑπὸ τοῦ χρησμοῦ καλεῖσθαι, μιμοῦνται τὰς τοῦ θεοῦ προσηγορίας. σημεῖον δὲ ὅτι πρὸς τὸ θεῖον ἀναφέροντες οὕτω λέγειν εἰώθαμεν. μάλιστα γὰρ τὸ ὕδωρ 'Αχελῷον προσαγορεύομεν ἐν τοῖς ὅρκοις καὶ ἐν ταῖς εὐχαῖς καὶ ἐν ταῖς θυσίαις, ἅπερ πάντα περὶ τοὺς θεούς. *Didymus* (he continues) *grammaticorum omnium facile eruditissimus, posita causa quam superius Ephorus dixit, alteram quoque adiecit his verbis;* ἄμεινον δὲ ἐκεῖνο λέγειν [ὅτι] διὰ τὸ πάντων τῶν ποταμῶν πρεσβύτατον εἶναι 'Αχελῷον τιμὴν ἀπονέμοντας αὐτῷ τοὺς ἀνθρώπους πάντα ἁπλῶς τὰ νάματα τῷ ἐκείνου ὀνόματι προσαγορεύειν. ὁ γοῦν 'Ακουσίλαος διὰ τῆς πρώτης ἱστορίας δεδήλωκεν ὅτι 'Αχελῷος πάντων τῶν ποταμῶν πρεσβύτατος. ἔφη γάρ· Ὠκεανὸς δὲ γαμεῖ Τηθὺν ἑαυτοῦ ἀδελφήν, τῶν δὲ γίνονται τρισχίλιοι ποταμοί, 'Αχελῷος δὲ αὐτῶν πρεσβύτατος καὶ τετίμηται μάλιστα. He concludes with a line from Eur. fragm. 753, (of a river far from Acarnania) δείξω μὲν 'Αργείοισιν 'Αχελῴου ῥόον. Servius ad Georg. *l. c. sicut Orpheus dicit generaliter omnem aquam veteres Acheloum nominant* (where however it may be suggested that *Orpheus* is a misreading for *Ephorus*).

Something like it is to be noticed in the passages in English literature where the name of an important river is put for 'water,' as in Shakespeare, *Cor.* II 1, 53, *A cup of hot wine with not a drop of allaying Tiber in it*, imitated by Lovelace, 'To Althea from prison,' *When flowing cups run swiftly round With no allaying Thames*.

630. φάσμ' is an emendation for φῶς. In the Homeric hymn 7, 45, quoted *infra* 1019, σήματα φαίνων is used of the god's successive transformations into the form of a lion or a bear.

633. συντεθράνωται] 'lies in ruin,' shivered to pieces; a word never used elsewhere, (explained by Hesychius, συμπέπτωκε); —the sense however is shewn by ἔρρηξεν, and by the analogy of συνθραύω, e.g. *Orest.* 1569, τῷδε θριγκῷ κρᾶτα συνθραύσω σέθεν. Lycophron 664 has θρανύσσειν, 'to break in pieces.' The supposition that -θρανοῦν and θραύειν mean the same thing (Elmsley) is doubted by C. J. Blomfield, *Mus. Crit.* 2, 664, who says "θρανοῦν is to level with the ground, from θρᾶνος 'a footstool,' or possibly 'to beat,' cf. θράνιον a form or bench upon which curriers stretched their hides."—On πικροτάτους cf. 357 n.

635. παρεῖται] Cf. σώμασιν παρειμέναι in 683.

636. ἐκβὰς ἐγώ is a good and sufficient correction of the corrupt reading ἐκ βάκχας ἄγων, and it is supported by ἔξω βεβὼς, *infra* 646.

638. 'And methinks, at least I hear his sounding footfall in the house, He will soon come to the forefront.' For ψοφεῖ ἀρβύλη, cf. Theocr. 7, 26, πᾶσα λίθος πταίοισα ποτ' ἀρβυλίδεσσιν ἀείδει. προνώπια, followed shortly after by προνώπιος, 645, reminds one of a similar word which Eur. was (according to Aristophanes) over-fond of using, namely ἐξώπιος *Thesm.* 881.

641. 'Lightly can a wise man's temper keep a sober self-control.' *Hipp.* 1039, τὴν ἐμὴν πέποιθεν εὐοργησίᾳ ψυχὴν κρατήσειν τὸν τεκόντ' ἀτιμάσας.

647. 'Stay! let thy rage advance with gentler step.' Lit. 'suggest to your anger a quiet step.' The repetition of πόδα may possibly be a carelessness due to the play not receiving the poet's final revision. ἥσυχον βάσιν has been proposed, for which we may compare Aesch. *Cho.* 452, ἡσύχῳ φρενῶν βάσει.

648. For πόθεν 'how came you to...,' cf. 465.

650. τοὺς λόγους γὰρ εἰσφέρεις καινοὺς ἀεί] a good instance of what has been called 'the tertiary predicate'; Donaldson *Gk. Gr.* § 489—[*Ion*, 1340, ὁ μῦθος εἰσενήνεκται νέος] Shilleto, *adv.*

652. ὠνείδισας δὴ τοῦτο Διονύσῳ καλόν] It is clear from the στιχομυθία that a line has here been lost. It seems best (as suggested in passing, by Paley) to assign to Dionysus the line that has been preserved: it gives a very suitable answer to some random taunt of Pentheus at the evil effects of the juice of the grape, which had been suggested by the previous words of Dionysus, who now parries the taunt with the line that is usually wrongly assigned to Pentheus. *Iph. A.* 305, λίαν δεσπόταισι πιστὸς εἶ | καλόν γέ μοι τοὔνειδος ἐξωνείδισας, and *Med.* 514.

661—2. 'where the bright flakes of white snow never cease.' *Phoen.* 803, ὦ ζαθέων πετάλων πολυθηρότατον νάπος, Ἀρτέμιδος χιονοτρόφον ὄμμα Κιθαιρών. ἀνεῖσαν appears to mean, 'never pass away,' i.e. there was always some unmelted snow resting on it. It has been remarked by Col. Mure, *Tour in Greece* I, 264, that 'unless the climate of Greece has greatly changed since the days of Euripides, he must be presumed to have taken a slight liberty in describing the snow as lying throughout the year on Cithaeron. In summer or even in the more advanced stage of spring, it now disappears from every part of the mountain.'

εὐαγεῖς] 'pure,' 'clear,' 'bright,' possibly the same word as that used in Parmenides ap. Clement Alex. 732, εὐαγέος ἠελίοιο. In *Suppl.* 652, πύργον εὐαγῆ λαβών, and Aesch. *Pers.* 466, ἕδραν εὐαγῆ στρατοῦ, the sense passes from 'clear' to 'conspicuous.' εὐαγής in the sense of ὅσιος is generally regarded as a separate word, connected with ἅγιος, ἅγος, Soph. *O. T.* 921, *Ant.* 521; and a third word is sometimes recognised in the sense of 'quickly-moving'; but brightness and rapid movement are closely connected with one another, and the meaning 'bright' is applicable to two of the passages quoted under this third head

in L and S ; viz those where it is an epithet of μέλισσαι (*Anth. Pal.*
IX 404, 7, Antiphilus, χαίροιτ' εὐαγέες, καὶ ἐν ἄνθεσι ποιμαίνεσθε),
and of ὄφθαλμοι (Aretaeus); but not to the third, where Hippocrates uses it of ἄνθρωποι.—To improve the rhythm, λευκῆς
ἀνεῖσαν χιόνος has been proposed, but we have several other
instances in this play of the tribrach being exactly coextensive
with a single word, cf. 261 n.

663. προστιθεὶς] sc. πρὸς τὸ ἥκειν, ' of what important tidings
may you be the bearer?'

664. ποτνιάδας] *Or.* 317 ; Hesych. αἱ βάκχαι· ἀντὶ τοῦ Μαινάδες
καὶ Λυσσάδες. It was at Potniae in Boeotia that the mares of
Glaucus were seized with madness and tore their master in
pieces ; the epithet is thus specially appropriate in its application
in the present passage to the wild revellers of the same district.

'Who from this land, With frenzy stung, shot forth with
gleaming limb.' The bare white feet of the Bacchanals would
be displayed to view, as they ran wildly to the hills. *Cycl.* 73,
('Αφροδίταν) θηρεύων πετόμαν βάκχαις σὺν λευκόποσιν, and *infra*
863. For κῶλον ἐξηκόντισαν cf. *Iph. T.* 1369, κῶλ' ἀπ' ἀμφοῖν τοῖν
νεανίαιν ἅμα ἐς πλευρὰ καὶ πρὸς ἧπαρ ἠκοντίζετο (of a violent kick).

667 is rendered by Attius IX (2 , *neque sat fingi neque dici
potest | pro magnitate;* unless perhaps this comes from his
translation of 273, οὐκ ἂν δυναίμην μέγεθος ἐξειπεῖν ὅσος καθ'
Ἑλλάδ' ἔσται.

669 φράσω...στειλώμεθα] For the combination of singular
and plural, cf. *Iph. T.* 348—9, ἠγριώμεθα δοκοῦσα, *Ion* 108, 251,
321, 391, 548, 596—7, 1250, Kühner § 430 1. d; Cic. *pro imp.
Cn. Pomp.* § 47 (these references are due to Prof. J. E. B. Mayor).
For the met. from striking sail, cf. *Or.* 607 and Dem. *F. L.* § 237.

671. [*Qu.* Plat. *Prot.* 338 A, τὸ κατὰ βραχὺ λίαν] Shilleto *adv.*

673. For τοῖς γὰρ δικαίοις οὐχὶ θυμοῦσθαι χρεών (rejected by
Nauck) cf. fragm. 289, τοῖς πράγμασιν γὰρ οὐχὶ θυμοῦσθαι χρεών.

677—774. Here follows a brilliant description of the revels
of the Bacchanals, one of the finest passages in Greek Tragedy.

678. ὑπεξήκριζον] The general structure of the context is
somewhat in favour of taking this as first person singular,
which would thus correspond to ὁρῶ in l. 680; while the use of

ἐξακρίζειν in *Or.* 275, ἐξακρίζετ' αἰθέρα πτεροῖς, and ἀκρίζων in
fragm. 574, = ἄκροις ποσὶν ἐπιπορευόμενος (Hesychius), is somewhat in favour of making it intransitive. The ordinary way of
taking the passage, while regarding the verb as intransitive,
makes it a *third* person plural with βοσκήματα for the nom.
'The herds of pasturing kine had just begun to scale Cithaeron's
steep, what time the sun shoots forth his rising rays to warm
the earth, when, &c.' It was just as the herdsman and his
charge were passing along one of the ridges dividing the upland
dells of Cithaeron from one another, that he caught sight of the
Bacchanals in the dell beneath. The pl. instead of sing. after
βοσκήματα is defensible by the rule of usage stated by Porson,
'veteres Attici hanc licentiam...nunquam usurpabant, nisi ubi
de animantibus ageretur' (*Hec.* 1141, cf. Jebb's note on Soph. *El.*
438). But μόσχων seems too far removed from βοσκήματα to be
taken as gen. dependent upon it, and we either expect some
gen. after λέπας, or after ὑπὸ in ὑπεξήκριζον; hence Paley suggests that the meaning may possibly be the "'herds of cows
were making their way uphill away from their calves'; thus
μόσχοις in v. 736 will refer to the calves that had been left in the
pastures." I doubt, however, whether this distinction can be
drawn, as Eur. there mentions the πόρις, the δάμαλαι and the
ταῦροι in the same context as the μόσχοι, which seems to shew
that the calves had *not* been left alone in the lowland pastures.
Hence I conclude that the calves were not separated from the
rest of the cattle, and that therefore μόσχων cannot be a gen.
after ὑπεξήκριζον; I also conclude that the herds which the
herdsman was driving to the upland pastures did not consist of
calves alone, and that therefore the words ἀγελαῖα βοσκήματα are
a sufficient description of the herded cattle, and that μόσχων is
unnecessary, besides being (as already remarked) too far removed from the word usually supposed to govern it.

I accordingly propose instead of μόσχων to read βόσκων
which at once removes all difficulty. In cursive MSS the difference between μ and β is often extremely slight, as has been
already noticed in the case of μέλος and βέλος in l. 25. The
Tragedians, it is true, seem fonder of the metaphorical than the

literal sense of βόσκειν (as in l. 617, ἐλπίσιν δ' ἐβόσκετο); but the use of the active voice in its literal sense is fully established by such passages as *Il.* 15, 548, εἰλίποδας βοῦς βόσκ' ἐν Περκώτῃ, and the cognate acc. proposed is exactly parallel to that in *Cycl.* 27, ποίμνας...ποιμαίνομεν. Musgrave must have been feeling his way towards some such emendation as that which I now venture to propose, when he suggested ἀγελαῖ' ἄγων βοσκήματα, observing: *boum in collem ascensio praeter necessitatem et descriptionis ornandae causa commemoratur; quod...in poeta dramatico parum venustum est.* The *structure* of the passage as now restored (ἀγελαῖα μὲν βοσκήματα βόσκων ἄρτι...ὑπεξήκριζον ...ὁρῶ δὲ) exactly corresponds with that of the beginning of Pentheus' speech, ἔκδημος ὢν μὲν τῆσδ' ἐτύγχανον χθονὸς, κλύω δὲ κ.τ.λ. (215).—Hesychius has ὑπεξήκριζον· ὕβριζον [?].*

679. Naevius *Lycurgus* XXII (11) *iam solis aestu candor cum liquesceret.*

680. Theocr. XXVI, quoted on l. 29, and Prop. IV 17, 24, *Pentheos in triplices funera grata greges.*

683. σώμασιν παρειμέναι] 'They all lay slumbering with languid limbs,' lit. tired *in* their bodies; for the dat. where the acc. is more common, cf. Soph. *O. T.* 25, φθίνουσα μὲν κάλυξιν ἐγκάρποις χθονὸς, Xen. *Mem.* II 1, 31, τοῖς σώμασιν ἀδύνατοι, ταῖς ψυχαῖς ἀνόητοι compared with IV 1, 2, τῶν τὰ σώματα,...τῶν τὰς ψυχὰς εὖ πεφυκότων.

684. The constr. is νῶτ' ἐρείσασαι πρὸς ἐλάτης φόβην, i.e. either reclining on the piled-up branches of the fir, or more probably leaning against the lower boughs that sweep the ground in the way that is common with trees of this kind. Theocr. 3, 38, ἀσεῦμαι ποτὶ τὰν πίτυν ὧδ' ὑποκλινθείς. The fir and the oak are mentioned with perfect accuracy of local colouring, as the characteristic trees of Cithaeron, cf. 110.

687. An instance of σύλληψις, the common term ὠνωμένας being combined in a literal sense with κρατῆρι, and in a metaphorical sense with λωτοῦ ψόφῳ. *Heracl.* 311, δώματ' οἰκήσητε καὶ τιμὰς πατρός (see Cope on *Rhet.* A 4 § 6). The 'intoxicating' effect here ascribed to the flute is illustrated by Aristot. *Pol.* VIII 6, 9, οὐκ ἔστιν ὁ αὐλὸς ἠθικὸν ἀλλὰ μᾶλλον ὀργιαστικόν, and Soph.

* 1880. Possibly μοχθῶν is better than βόσκων [1885].

Trach. 217, ἀείρομ' οὐδ' ἀπώσομαι τὸν αὐλὸν, ὦ τύραννε τᾶς ἐμᾶς φρενός. ἰδοῦ ἰδού μ' ἀναταράσσει, εὐοῖ, ὁ κισσὸς ἄρτι βακχίαν ὑποστρέφων ἅμιλλαν.

688. 'Alone amid the woods, in quest of Cypris.' ἠρημωμέ- νας has been unnecessarily altered into ἠνεμωμένας, one of the MSS having ἠρεμωμένας, by a slip of the pen easily made, while the other has ἠρημωμένας, which is clearly confirmed by 222, ἄλλην ἄλλοσ' εἰς ἐρημίαν πτώσσουσαν.

692. θαλερὸν ὕπνον] 'refreshing sleep' (Elmsley), 'balmy sleep,' 'somnus, qui est in ipso flore, i.e. altus sopor' (Hermann). The idea of fresh and flourishing growth that underlies the word (cf. θάλλω), and the use of the word in the present passage, may be illustrated by the Latin *alma quies.*

693. 'a sight of wondrous grace,' lit. a wonder to look upon by reason of their modest mien.

695. 'Tied up their fawnskins, where the fastening bands
       Had been unloosed, and girt the spangled fells   With
zones of serpents that e'en licked their cheeks.' ὅσαισι is best
taken not after νεβρίδας, but as the relative to the subject of
ἀνεστείλαντο, lit. 'all those for whom,' 'in whose case,' so *infra*
761. The following are the corresponding lines in the *Bacchae*
of Attius IV (12), *Tunc silvestrum exuvias laevo pictas lateri
accommodant* and XV (10), *deinde ab iugulo pectus glauco pam-
pino obnexae tegunt.* The fawnskin would be fastened above
the shoulder on one side, passing across the chest and falling
below the waist on the other side; it would thus have to be
fastened both at the shoulder and near the waist, the former
is expressed by ἀνεστείλαντο, the latter by κατεζώσαντο. The
serpents are represented as harmlessly coiling about the upper
part of the Maenad's body from the waist upwards and even
licking the women's cheeks, cf. 767—8. Nonnus 14, 233 (of
Dionysus himself) καρήνου ἄπλοκον ἐσφήκωσε δρακοντείῳ τρίχα
δεσμῷ, 216 (of the Nymphs), ἐμιτρώθησαν ἐχιδναίοισι κορύμβοις,
340 (a Bassaris) ἐχιδναίῳ κεφαλὴν ἐζώσατο δεσμῷ, 356, ὠμοβόρων
ἔζευξεν ἐπ' αὐχένι δεσμὰ δρακόντων, and 44, 410, κεφαλὴν κυκλώ-
σατο Κάδμου πρηὺς ὄφις καὶ γλῶσσα πέριξ λίχμαζεν ὑπήνην. Cf.
Naevius *Lycurgus* II (17), *alte jubatos angues in sese gerunt.*

699—701. Nonnus 14, 361, ἄλλη σκύμνον ἔχουσα δασυστέρνοιο
λεαίνης ἀνδρομέῳ γλαγόεντι νόθῳ πιστώσατο μαζῷ, 45, 304, πολλαὶ
δ᾽ ἀρτιτόκοιο μετοχλισθέντα τεκούσης τέκνα δασυστέρνοιο τιθηνήσαντο
λεαίνης. Fragm. XVI (20) of the *Bacchae* of Attius, *indecorabi-
liter alienos alunt*, is possibly a rendering of the present passage.

703. On the ivy crown, see 81 n; on the oak, 110 n; and on
the *smilax*, 108 n.

706—710. 'Another shot her ferule to the ground   And
the god shot up for her a fount of wine.' For the passages in
Plato and Horace, referring to these miraculous streams, see
note on 142, and cf. Nonnus 45, 306, ἄλλη δίψιον οὖδας ἐπέκτυπεν
ὀξέι θύρσῳ ἄκρον ὄρος πλήξασα νεοσχιδές· αὐτοτελὴ δὲ οἶνον ἐρευγο-
μένη κραναὴ πορφύρετο πέτρη (cf. 48, 575—7), λειβομένου δὲ
γάλακτος ἀρασσομένης ἀπὸ πέτρης πίδακες αὐτοχύτοισιν ἐλευκαί-
νοντο ῥεέθροις, Diodorus Sic. III 66 (in Teos), τεταγμένοις χρόνοις
ἐν τῇ πόλει πηγὴν αὐτομάτως ἐκ τῆς γῆς οἴνου ῥεῖν εὐωδίᾳ διαφέροντος,
Pausan. VI 26 § 2 (in Andros), παρὰ ἔτος ῥεῖν οἶνον αὐτόματον ἐκ
τοῦ ἱεροῦ (Pliny *N. H.* II § 231, XXXI § 16), also Philostratus
quoted on l. 3 and 1136.

704—5. Pausanias IV 36 § 7 (of a fountain between Pylos
and Cyparissiae in Messenia), ῥυῆναι δὲ Διονύσῳ τὸ ὕδωρ λέγουσι
θύρσῳ πλήξαντι ἐς τὴν γῆν, καὶ ἐπὶ τούτῳ Διονυσιάδα ὀνομάζουσι τὴν
πηγήν.

710. γάλακτος ἐσμούς, 'rich store of milk.' Philostratus, *vit.
Sophist.* I 19 (quoted by Porson), τὰς δ᾽ ἐννοίας ἰδίας τε καὶ παρα-
δόξους ἐκδίδωσιν ὥσπερ οἱ βακχεῖοι θύρσοι τὸ μέλι καὶ τοὺς ἐσμοὺς
τοῦ γάλακτος. A metaphor from the hive, like our colloquial use
of the word 'swarms.' In late Greek this metaphor became common, e.g. Lucian *Lexiphanes* § 17, κατακλείσας εἶχες τοσοῦτον
ἐσμὸν (sic)...ὀνομάτων. Dobree quotes σμῆνος σοφίας (Plato *Crat.*
401 E), ἐσμὸς λόγων (*Rep.* 450 A—B), and πάντα ἐσμὸν ἡδονῆς ἐξηρτημένον ἄγειν (Basil, *de leg. Gr. libr.* p. 92, 2, where Grotius
renders the word *apparatum*).

711. Aelian *de nat. animal.* V 42, ἐν Μηδίᾳ δὲ ἀποστάζειν τῶν
δένδρων ἀκούω μέλι, ὡς ὁ Εὐριπίδης ταῖς Βάκχαις ἐν τῷ Κιθαιρῶνι
φησὶν ἐκ τῶν κλάδων γλυκείας σταγόνας ἀπορρεῖν, and Virg. *Ecl.* 4, 30.

717. 'Then one, oft truant in town, and skilled in speech.'

This description of the herdsman, whose short speech is on the point of being quoted, is thrown in to lead up to the rhetorical flourish with which he addresses his brother-herdsmen in the words: 'O ye who dwell On the dread mountain-terraces'; it also accounts for his taking a prominent part in the debate of the rustics. In the debate described in the *Orestes*, after an account of the speech delivered by an ἀνὴρ ἀθυρόγλωσσος, the rustic orator who follows next is described in the words, ὀλιγάκις ἄστυ κἀγορᾶς χραίνων κύκλον (219).

721. χάριν...θῶμεν] Either δῶμεν or θώμεθ' (as Elmsley remarks) would be a more usual expression, but as διδόναι χάριν is 'to grant a favour,' and θέσθαι χάριν 'to do a kindness,' the latter is more suitable in the present passage (*Museum Criticum* 2, 665). Cf. *Hec.* 1211, χάριν θέσθαι, *El.* 61, χάριτα τιθεμένη πόσει.

722. αὐτούς for ἡμᾶς αὐτούς. ' Hoc pronomen omnium personarum commune est' (Porson on *Or.* 626); for examples in Aesch. and Soph. see Jebb's note on Soph. *El.* 285, or Kühner *Gk. Gr.* § 455, 7 b, where Thuc. 1 82, τὰ αὐτῶν ἅμα ἐκποριζώμεθα, and other instances are quoted.

723. τὴν τεταγμένην ὥραν] 'at the set *time*,' Aesch. *Eum.* 109, ἔθυον ὥραν οὐδένος κοινὴν θεῶν. In the sense of *hour* the word is not used till the time of the Alexandrian astronomer, Hipparchus, B.C. 140. **725.** ἀθρόῳ στόματι, 'in pealing chorus.'

726. (Longinus) περὶ ὕψους 15 § 6 (speaking of φαντασία), παρὰ μὲν Αἰσχύλῳ παραδόξως τὰ τοῦ Λυκούργου βασίλεια κατὰ τὴν ἐπιφάνειαν τοῦ Διονύσου θεοφορεῖται, ἐνθουσιᾷ δὴ δῶμα, βακχεύει στέγη, ὁ δὲ Εὐριπίδης τὸ αὐτὸ τοῦθ' ἑτέρως ἐφηδύνας ἐξεφώνησε, πᾶν δὲ συνεβάκχευ' ὄρος.

730. ἐκρύπτομεν] The correction ἐκρυπτόμην (suggested by Barnes, approved by Musgrave and accepted by Brunck) is unnecessary ; the plural obviously refers to the whole body of herdsmen (722), and there is no difficulty in the use of the singular δέμας (cf. 744, ἐσφάλλοντο...δέμας).—**731.** For δρομάδες, a tribrach coextensive with a single word, cf. 18, μιγάσιν.

736. χειρὸς ἀσιδήρου μέτα] So Naevius *Lycurgus* XIX (16)

sine ferro pecua ut manibus ad mortem meant (J. Wordsworth's
Specimens of Early Latin p. 578).

737. εὔθηλον πόριν] 'a cow with swelling udder.' The same
adj. is found in a play of the same date, *Iph. A.* 580, εὔθηλοι δὲ
τρέφωντο βόες. **738.** τὴν μὲν appears to refer to Agave in particular, hence the dual χεροῖν, which would probably have been
plural had τὴν μὲν been only general in its meaning. ἐν χεροῖν
δίκα is the reading of the MSS, for which it has been proposed
to read δίκᾳ or δίχα. In the latter case we may render : 'Herself you might have seen with her twain hands   Hold a deep-
uddered heifer's legs asunder,   Bellowing the while.'

ἔχειν δίχα is apparently to be understood *divisam tenere*,
διειλημμένην, not '*torn* asunder,' διασπαρακτὸν (1220).   The latter
sense seems more than can fairly be got out of the words and is
less easy to reconcile with μυκωμένην, as we cannot suppose that
the bellowing cow would continue to expostulate when her limbs
were already 'rent asunder.'   Yet something very like this meaning is intended in the following passage of Arnobius, V, 19 pr.,
*Bacchanalia etiam praetermittamus immania, quibus nomen
Omophagiis Graecum est, in quibus furore mentito, et sequestrata
pectoris sanitate, circumplicatis vos anguibus, atque ut vos
plenos Dei numine ac maiestate doceatis, caprorum* reclamantium
viscera, cruentatis oribus dissipatis.

739. For the general description, cf. Catullus 64, 257, *pars e
divulso iactabant membra iuvenco.*   Lucian III 77 *Dionysus* § 2,
τὰς δ᾽ οὖν ποίμνας διηρπάσθαι ἤδη ὑπὸ τῶν γυναικῶν καὶ διεσπάσθαι
ἔτι ζῶντα τὰ θρέμματα· ὠμοφάγους γάρ τινας αὐτὰς εἶναι. *Anth.*
Pal. VI, 74, βασσαρὶς Εὐρυνόμη σκοπελοδρόμος, ἥ ποτε ταύρων
πολλὰ τανυκραίρων στέρνα χαραξαμένη, | ἡ μέγα καγχάζουσα λεοντο-
φόνοις ἐπὶ νίκαις παίγνιον ἀτλήτου θηρὸς ἔχουσα κάρη, IX 774 (on
the Maenad of Scopas) ἁ βάκχα Παρία μὲν ἐνεψύχωσε δ᾽ ὁ γλύπτας
τὸν λίθον· ἀνθρώσκει δ᾽ ὡς βρομιαζομένα. | ὦ Σκόπα, ἁ θεοποιὸς
[ἄπιστον] ἐμήσατο τέχνα θαῦμα, χιμαιροφόνον Θυιάδα μαινομέναν.
Callistratus *Stat.* 2, p. 892 = 147 (on the same statue), ἀλλά
τι σφάγιον ἔφερεν ὡς εὐάζουσα, πικροτέρας μανίας σύμβολον—
τὸ δὲ ἦν χιμαίρας τι πλάσμα. Nonnus 14, 377—80, and 43,
40—51 the conclusion of which is taken from 740, δίχηλοι

ἔμβασιν κ.τ.λ., πολυστροφάλιγγι δὲ ῥιπῇ ὄρθιον ἐσφαίρωσεν ἐς ἠέρα δίζυγα χηλήν. For representations in works of ancient art, see description on p. cxlviii of the woodcut on p. 86.

743. 'the wanton bulls That erstwhile glanced along their maddened horns, Fell tumbling, with their bodies dragged to earth By the multitudinous hands of the young women.' Cf. the passage in *Hel.* 1558, κυρτῶν τε νῶτα κεῖς κέρας παρεμβλέπων. εἰς κέρας θυμοῦσθαι, imitated by Virgil *G.* 3, 232 and *Aen.* 12, 104, *irasci in cornua;* cf. Aelian *hist. anim.* 2, 20 and 4, 28, ὑβρίζειν εἰς κέρας. Donaldson, who refers to the above passages (*New Crat.* § 170), thinks the preposition in all such instances may be explained from the idea of 'looking towards'; which undoubtedly suits the passage in the *Helen.* Here, however, it may possibly imply the gathering and concentrating of the rage 'into' the horn.

746. 'And the flesh that clothed their limbs was stripped asunder Ere thou could'st drop the lids on thy royal eyes.'

σαρκὸς is explanatory of ἐνδυτά, like ἐνδυτὰ νεβρίδων (111). This seems to be better than understanding it 'the skin that clothed their flesh.' ἐνδυτὰ in either case is literally acc., as δέμας in 744.

θᾶσσον...ἢ σὺ ξυνάψαις (without ἂν) is supported by *Hipp.* 1186, καὶ θᾶσσον ἢ λέγοι τις* (Elmsley). Cf. Aristot. *hist. anim.* IX 12, μένει χρόνον οὐκ ἐλάττονα ἢ ὅσον πλέθρον διέλθοι τις. One of the MSS however has σὲ ξυνάψαι (accepted by Matthiae and Madvig), as in 1286, πρόσθεν ἢ σὲ γνωρίσαι: and this I prefer.

748. ὥστ᾽ ὄρνιθες ἀρθεῖσαι] The Maenads are compared to birds, because in their hovering flight they scarcely seem to touch the ground; like Virgil's Camilla, *illa vel intactae segetis per summa volaret gramina* (Aen. 7, 808).

749. The fertile plains, stretching along the streams of Asopus, north of the range of Cithaeron, are elsewhere spoken of as πυροφόρα...Ἀόνων πεδία, *Phoen.* 643. Hysiae and Erythrae, here described as 'nestling 'neath Cithaeron's crag,' are mentioned by Herodotus in connexion with the movements of the allied Greeks against the Persians under Mardonius immediately before the battle of Plataea: IX 15, παρῆκε δὲ αὐτοῦ

---

* Wecklein conjectures ἢ λόγοισιν, comparing *Iph. T.* 837.

(sc. Μαρδονίου) τὸ στρατόπεδον ἀρξάμενον ἀπὸ Ἐρυθρέων παρὰ
Ὑσιάς· κατέτεινε δὲ ἐς τὴν Πλαταιίδα γῆν, παρὰ τὸν Ἀσωπὸν
ποταμὸν τεταγμένον, *ib.* 19, ὡς δὲ ἄρα ἀπίκοντο (*sc.* the allied
Greeks) τῆς Βοιωτίας ἐς Ἐρυθράς, ἔμαθόν τε δὴ τοὺς βαρβάρους
ἐπὶ τῷ Ἀσώπῳ στρατοπεδευομένους, φρασθέντες δὲ τοῦτο ἀντετάσ-
σοντο ἐπὶ τῆς ὑπωρείης τοῦ Κιθαιρῶνος. Erythrae was noted
for its bread, Archestratus ap. Athen. III 77, ἐν δὲ φερεσταφύλοις
Ἐρυθραῖς ἐκ κλιβάνου ἐλθών, λευκός, ἁβραῖς θάλλων ὥραις τέρψει
παρὰ δεῖπνον. νέρθεν, here adv., 'below,' i.e. in the vale (L and S).

752. The emendation ὡς δὲ πολεμίοις (Kirchhoff), would place
Ὑσιάς τ' Ἐρυθράς θ' in apposition to πεδίων ὑποτάσεις. The
text, as it stands, involves making them acc. after ἐπεισπεσοῦσαι,
and coupling διέφερον to χωροῦσι by means of the first τε after
Ὑσιάς.

754. ἥρπαζον ἐκ δόμων τέκνα, κ.τ.λ.] Imitated and expanded
by Nonnus 45, 294, ἄλλη δὲ τριέτηρον ἀφαρπάξασα τοκῆος ἄτρομον
ἀστυφέλικτον ἀδέσμιον ὑψόθεν ὤμων ἵστατο κουφίζουσα μεμηλότα
παῖδα θυέλλαις, ἑζόμενον γελόωντα καὶ οὐ πίπτοντα κονίῃ. This
parallel shews that Nonnus read τέκνα and disposes of the
emendation τύχᾳ proposed by Madvig.

ὁπόσα may be intended to *include* the τέκνα, but cannot
apply exclusively to them (as Nonnus appears to have thought);
as we find in partial apposition to it the words, οὐ χαλκὸς οὐ
σίδηρος. It is not improbable that something may be lost before
the latter words (Tyrrell), or more probably before ὁπόσα
(Hartung).

755. οὐ δεσμῶν ὕπο] These words close the Laurentian MS
at Florence and the copies in the library at Paris. For the rest
of the play we have to depend on one MS only (the Palatine MS
in the Vatican).

757. ἐπὶ δὲ βοστρύχοις πῦρ ἔφερον] Virgil *Aen.* 2, 686, *ecce
levis summo de vertice visus Iuli fundere lumen apex, tractuque
innoxia molli lambere flamma comas et circum tempora pasci.*

760. *Iph. T.* 320, οὗ δὴ τὸ δεινὸν παρακέλευσμ' ἠκούσαμεν.

761—4. Nonnus 14, 394 (of the battle of Dionysus against
the Indians), βάκχη δ' ἀμφαλάλαζε, καὶ ἀμπελόεσσαν ἀκωκὴν βασσαρὶς ἠκόντιζε, μελαρρίνου δὲ γενέθλης ἄρσενα πολλὰ κάρηνα δαΐζετο

θήλει θύρσῳ...πολυσταφύλῳ δὲ πετήλῳ κέντορα κισσὸν ἔπεμπεν ἀλοιητῆρα σιδήρου.

767. νίψαντο δ' αἷμα] This is the first instance, in the present play, of the omission of the syllabic augment. With the exception of a very few passages which are probably corrupt (Aesch. *P. V.* 305, *Cho.* 917, Soph. *Phil.* 371, Eur. *Hec.* 580, *Alc.* 839), all the instances of this omission are to be found in *Messengers'* *speeches* (ἀγγέλων ῥήσεις): (1) once in the middle of the iambic line, but at the beginning of a sentence, viz. *infra* 1134, ἡ δ' ἴχνος αὐταῖς ἀρβύλαις· γυμνοῦντο δὲ: (2) oftener at the beginning of the line, as here and *infra* 1066, κυκλοῦτο, 1084, σίγησε, similarly in Aesch. *P. V.* 368, τροποῦντο, 408, παίοντ', 450, κυκλοῦντο, 498, πῖπτον, Soph. *O. T.* 1249, γοᾶτο, *O. C.* 1606, κτύπησε, 1624, θώυξεν, *Trach.* 915, φρούρουν: also (3), in the following instances, where however the previous line ends with a long vowel or a diphthong, and thus allows of the possibility of explaining the omission of the augment by *aphaeresis*, Soph. *O. C.* 1607, ῥίγησαν, *El.* 715, φορεῖθ', 716, φείδοντο *Trach.* 904, βρυχᾶτο and Eur. *Hec.* 1153, θάκουν. (Kühner, *Gk. Gr.* I p. 503). It has been suggested that this omission may be due to the Epic colouring of the messengers' narratives, but if so, we should expect examples of the omission of the temporal augment as well.   The subject is discussed at length in Hermann's preface to the *Bacchae*, where he endeavours to reduce it to a question of rhythm and emphasis, and comes to the following conclusions: (1) *verbum fortius, in quo augmenti accessio anapaestum facit, in principio versus positum, addi augmentum postulat:* ἐγένοντο Λήδᾳ Θεστιάδι τρεῖς παρθένοι (*Iph. A. init.*).   (2) *verbum fortius, in quo augmenti accessio non facit anapaestum, in principio versus positum, carere potest augmento:* σίγησε δ' αἰθήρ· κτύπησε μὲν Ζεὺς χθόνιος· παίοντ', ἔθραυον· πῖπτον δ' ἐπ' ἀλλήλοισιν. (3) *eiusdemmodi verbum, si incipit sententiam videtur etiam in medio versu carere augmento posse: quale foret illud, ea, qua supra dictum est condicione:* γυμνοῦντο δὲ πλευραὶ σπαραγμοῖς. (4) *verbum minus forte, sive facit augmenti accessio anapaestum, sive non facit, in principio versus positum, si ultra primum pedem porrigitur, caret augmento:* γοᾶτο· θώυξεν.   (5) *eiusdem-*

modi verbum si non ultra primum pedem porrigitur, ut detracto augmento parum numerosum, aut vitatur, ut κάνες (ἔκανες *Choeph.* 930), *aut cum alia forma commutatur, ut* κάλει *cum* καλεῖ. But in rule (1) we can hardly admit that ἐγένοντο is a *verbum fortius* unless we understand by that term an ordinary verb in an accidentally prominent position with no true emphasis of sense; and the chief value of the rest of these rules is that they bring out clearly the fact, that all the instances of omission are at the beginning of the sentence and almost all at the beginning of the line as well.—In the present passage Hermann unnecessarily alters the text into νίψαι τόδ' αἷμα, objecting that νίψαντο ought to have been νίπτοντο, and also remarking: 'si finem factum dicere voluisset poeta, πάλιν ἐχώρησαν scripsisset.' But we may reply, that the imperfect ἐχώρουν well describes the slow and gradual retreat of the Bacchanals to the spot from which they suddenly started forth (ἐκίνησαν πόδα), that νίψαντο expresses the momentary plunge into the fountain which washed off nearly all the blood, while the subsequent imperfect ἐξεφαίδρυνον indicates the continued process by which slowly 'from their cheeks snakes licked the gore-drop clean from off the skin.'

775. τοὺς λόγους ἐλευθέρους] 'I fear to utter forth the words of freedom'; lit. words that are free, the position of the article shewing that a predicative sense must be given to the adjective; cf. Donaldson *Gk. Gr.* § 489 and *supra* l. 650.

778. ὥστε πῦρ ὑφάπτεται] (1) 'To set on fire' in *Or.* 621, ὑφῆψε δῶμ' ἀνηφαίστῳ πυρί (and *ib.* 1618) and *Tro.* 1274, πόλις ὑφάπτεται πυρί : (2) 'to kindle a fire' (as here) in Ar. *Thesm.* 730. This reading is restored from the author of the *Christus patiens*, and makes better sense than the manuscript reading, ἐφάπτεται, which would naturally mean either 'is impending' or 'is reaching us.' The latter sense is however not impossible in the present passage.

779. ἐς Ἕλληνας] 'a great disgrace to us in the eyes of Greece. ['aliter scribendum foret Ἕλλησι. eadem ratione Plato *Gorg.* 526 B, ἐλλόγιμος εἰς τοὺς ἄλλους Ἕλληνας, *Sympos.* 179 B ubi vid. Stallbaum. Thucyd. VI 31, ἐς τοὺς ἄλλους Ἕλληνας ἐπί-

δειξιν, VII 56, καλὸν σφίσιν ἐς τοὺς Ἕλληνας τὸ ἀγώνισμα φανεῖσθαι]
Shilleto, *adv.*

780. The Electran gates were south of the city, and therefore
on the way to Cithaeron. It was by this approach that in the
time of Pausanias, as at the present day, the traveller from
Plataea entered Thebes, Pausan. IX 8 § 7; so Sir Thomas
Wyse, *Impressions of Greece*, p. 295, describes a drive from
Athens through 'Cithaeron's woody folds,' down into the Pla-
taean plain, and so 'by the Electra gate into Thebes.'

782. ἀπαντᾶν] i.e. 'to muster.' The verb, though reserved
for the second clause, has to be taken with the former clause as
well.*

785. οὐ γὰρ ἀλλ'] 'Nay but this is past endurance!' See
Shilleto on Dem. *Fals. Leg.* App. C *ad finem*, Ar. *Ran.* 58, 192, 498.

786. πεισόμεσθ'...πάσχομεν...πείθει] The last verb, though
different in sense, seems to have been suggested by the sound of
the first. [πείθει post πεισόμεσθ'. Dem. *de F. Leg.* p. 368 § 98,
Arist. *Eth. Nic.* III 7 = 5 § 7, Xen. *Anab.* I 3 § 6] Shilleto, *adv.*

791. 'Bromius will not brook thee   Driving his Maenads
from the hills of revel.' Cf. *And.* 711, οὐκ ἀνέξεται τίκτοντας
ἄλλους. For εὐΐων ὁρῶν, cf. mount Εὔας in Messene, Pausan. IV
31 § 4. τελετὰς εὐΐους has occurred in 238.

792. 'Don't lecture me! thou hast escaped from bonds, So
be content!—else I must once more doom thee.' On οὐ μή, see
note on 343. σώσει τόδ'] Soph. *El.* 1257, μόλις γὰρ ἔσχον νῦν
ἐλεύθερον στόμα. ξύμφημι κἀγὼ τοιγαροῦν σώζου τόδε.

794. 'I would slay him victims, rather than in rage
Kick 'gainst the goad, a man at war with god.' Pind. *Pyth.* II
173, ποτὶ κέντρα λακτίζεμεν ὀλισθηρὸς...οἶμος, Aesch. *P. V.* 323,
πρὸς κέντρα κῶλον ἐκτενεῖς, *Ag.* 1633, Eur. fragm. 607, πρὸς κέντρα
μὴ λάκτιζε τοῖς κρατοῦσί σου, Ter. *Phorm.* I 2, 27, *nam quae
inscitia est advorsum stimulum calces*, Plaut. *Truc.* IV 2, 59;
and Acts of the Apostles, xxvi 14.—For the general sense, cf.
Naevius *Lycurgus* XIII (18), *cave sis tuam contendas iram
contra cum ira Liberi.*

798. ἀσπίδας θύρσοισι Βακχῶν ἐκτρέπειν] Explained in L
and S, 'to turn shields *and flee before* the thyrsus.' We may

* On l. 783, see *Supplementary Notes.*

accordingly render, "'twere shame to turn away Shields wrought of bronze, before the revellers' wands.' It has been suggested, however, that 'the sense of the passage is, *it is disgraceful that they with the thyrsi of Bacchanals should beat down and turn away your brazen shields*' (C. J. Blomfield, *Mus. Crit.* 2, 666). The easiest way of clearing up the passage is to alter βακχῶν into βάκχας, which would thus become the acc. before ἐκτρέπειν.

800. 'An awkward stranger this, we are hampered with.' Donaldson, *Gk. Gr.* § 491.

802. ὦ τᾶν] Soph. *O. T.* 1145, *Phil.* 1387, Eur. *Cycl.* 536, and frequently in Aristophanes and Plato. ὦ 'τᾶν· πρόσρημα τιμητικῆς λέξεως· λέγεται δὲ καὶ ἐπ' εἰρωνείᾳ πολλάκις (Hesychius). It is supposed to stand for ἐτᾶν=ἐτᾶεν, voc. of ἐτάεις (ἐτήεις), connected with ἔτης, a 'relative,' or 'friend.'*

814. Dionysus, by asking Pentheus why he is so eager to see the Bacchanals grouped upon the mountain-side, arouses misgivings on the part of the king, who replies; 'With sorrow would I see them drunk with wine.' Dionysus enquires once more; 'Yet, would'st thou see with joy what thou must rue?' Here the words ἅ σοι πικρά (like much besides in this dialogue) are intentionally ambiguous; to Pentheus, they are only an echo of his own word λυπρῶς; to the audience, they point to the bitter end of the king's espial.

819. ἄγωμεν like φέρωμεν (949). [ἄγωμεν...ἄγ' (820), *sing. et plur.* 512, 514; 616, 617; *Hel.* 990, 1010] Shilleto *adv.*

820. The manuscript reading is τοῦ χρόνου δέ σ' οὐ φθονῶ, in which case σ' would have to stand for σοι, which cannot be thus elided. Hence the emendations, (1) τοῦ χρόνου δέ σοι (Nauck) i. e. 'I grudge delay,'—'we must lose no time about it'; (2) τοῦ χρόνου δ' οὔ σοι (Dobree) i. e. 'Lead me there with all speed, *but* I do not grudge you the time,'—'you are welcome to take your own time, eager though I am to go'; (3) τοῦ χρόνου γὰρ οὐ φθονῶ or ὃ οὐδεὶς φθόνος (Kirchhoff). Cf. with (2) and (3), *Hec.* 238, ἔξεστ', ἐρώτα· τοῦ χρόνου γὰρ οὐ φθονῶ.

821. βυσσίνους πέπλους] 'Array thee, then, in robes of finest lawn.' Theocr. 11 73, ὡμάρτευν βύσσοιο καλὸν σύροισα χιτῶνα. These robes were not of 'cotton' (as sometimes supposed), but

* See *Supplementary Notes.*

of 'fine linen.' *Byssus* or 'fine flax' did not grow in Greece (except in Elis, Pausan. v 5 § 2); it was imported through the Phoenicians 'from the Hebrews' (one of whose names for it was *bûtz*), and from Egypt. Herodotus, ιι 86, says the Egyptian mummies were wrapped round with σινδόνος βυσσίνης τελαμῶσι, which are now ascertained to be bandages of fine linen, not of cotton. For the latter (Pliny's *gossipion*), the Greek writers have no special word. In Hdt. ιιι 47, linen and cotton are mentioned side by side, θώρηκα λίνεον κεκοσμημένον χρυσῷ καὶ ἐρίοισι ἀπὸ ξύλου.

822. Nonnus 46, 82, φάρεα καλλείψας βασιλήϊα τέτλαθι, Πενθεῦ, θήλεα πέπλα φέρειν, καὶ γίνεο θῆλυς (*v.l.* θυιὰς) 'Αγαύη. τελῶ; *future.* A metaphor from the *census,* as in *O. T.* 222, εἰς ἀστοὺς τελῶ; cf. εἰς ἱππῆς τελεῖν.

828. θῆλυν.] In poetry, θῆλυς is not unfrequently of common gender, *Med.* 1084 γενεὰν θῆλυν, *Iliad* 19, 97, Ἥρα θῆλυς ἐοῦσα.

833. πέπλοι ποδήρεις] Aesch. fr. 64 b, *Edoni,* ὅστις χιτῶνας βασσάρας τε Λυδίας ἔχει ποδήρεις, Nonnus 46, 115 (of Pentheus) χειρὶ δὲ θύρσον ἄειρε· μετερχομένοιο δὲ βάκχας ποικίλος ἰχνευτῆρι χίτων ἐπεσύρετο ταρσῷ.

μίτρα] Hence Dionysus himself is called θηλυμίτρης in Lucian ιιι p. 77, *Dion.* § 3, and χρυσομίτρης in Soph. *O. T.* 209. The word has a variety of meanings; here it appears to be either (1) a band or snood, carried through the hair and across the forehead, like that with which Dionysus himself is often represented in works of ancient art; or, more probably, (2) a light cap, like the head-dress of the Bacchanals in the vase painting copied in the introduction, p. xxxii. *Hec.* 923, πλόκαμον ἀναδέτοις μίτραισιν ἐρρυθμιζόμην, *infra* 929. It is sometimes used of a royal diadem, and also (especially in Latin, as in *Aen.* 4, 216; 9, 616) of the Phrygian head-dress.

836. The line quoted by Plato in the story already referred to in the note on 317.

837. αἷμα θήσεις] So in *Ion* 1225, ἐν τ' ἀνακτόροις φόνον τιθεῖσαν, 1260, τοῖς ἀποκτείνασί σε προστρόπαιον αἷμα θήσεις, and *Iph. A.* 1418, διὰ τὸ σῶμα μάχας ἀνδρῶν τιθεῖσα καὶ φόνον, in which last passage however (as suggested by Wecklein) the poet may have been thinking of the common phrase ἀγῶνα τιθέναι. Also *Or.* 833, μητροκτόνον αἷμα χειρὶ θέσθαι. Several emendations have been suggested, such as αἷμ' ἀφήσεις (Reiske), εἷμα θήσεις (Tyrwhitt), αἷμα δεύσεις (Wecklein), even αἷμα θύσεις might be supported by 796, but none of these alterations seems absolutely necessary.

839. κακοῖς θηρᾶν κακά] 'quest of endless ills,' pursuing evil ends by evil means. *Herc. F.* 1076, πρὸς κακοῖς κακὰ μήσεται, 1213, κακὰ κακοῖς συνάψαι, Soph. fr. 75, κακοῖς ἰᾶσθαι κακά.

843. The manuscript reading ἐλθόντ' (dual), followed by βουλεύσομαι, involves an *anacoluthon*, which may possibly be explained by supposing that Pentheus, after referring to their returning *together* to his palace, reserves for himself *alone* the duty of deliberating as to the best course to be pursued on their return.

848. Pentheus having left the stage to array himself for his adventure, Dionysus tells the chorus that the toils are fast closing round their prey : 'women ! our man comes within cast of net.' Cf. *Rhes.* 730, ἴσως γὰρ εἰς βόλον τις ἔρχεται. So of a fisherman with his net, ready for a cast [?], Theocr. 1 40, μέγα δίκτυον ἐς βόλον ἕλκει. Cf. Hesiod *Scut. Herc.* 213, εἶχε δὲ χερσὶν ἰχθύσιν ἀμφίβληστρον, ἀπορρίψοντι ἐοικώς (and Aesch. *Ag.* 1382 ; see however *Persae* 425, and Eur. *El.* 582).

847. ἥξει δὲ Βάκχας οὗ θανὼν δώσει δίκην] This extension of the acc. of the *place to which*, to that of the *persons to whom* one goes, is somewhat rare (1354) : the fact that it *is* an extension of the same principle, is proved by the subsequent οὗ. The slight harshness of this collocation may, however, be removed by conjecturing ἥξει δὲ Βάκχαις οὗ θανὼν δώσει δίκην, 'he will go there where, by dying, he will pay the penalty to the Bacchanals,' as in line 62, ἐγὼ δὲ Βάκχαις εἰς Κιθαιρῶνος πτυχὰς ἐλθών, ἵν' εἰσί, συμμετασχήσω χορῶν.—Cf. also *Herc. F.* 740, ἦλθες χρόνῳ μὲν οὗ δίκην δώσεις θανών.

851. ἐνεὶς ἐλαφρὰν λύσσαν] 'instilling flighty madness.' ὅταν δ' ὁ δαίμων ἀνδρὶ πορσύνῃ κακά, τὸν νοῦν ἔβλαψε πρῶτον ᾧ βουλεύεται (*Trag. incert. ap. schol. ad Soph. Ant.* 622).

852. οὐ μὴ θελήσῃ] A strong negative ; see Goodwin's *Moods and Tenses*, § 89, 1 (quoted in note on 343, *supra*).

853. ἔξω δ' ἐλαύνων τοῦ φρονεῖν] Aesch. *Cho.* 1022, ὥσπερ ξὺν ἵπποις ἡνιοστροφῶ δρόμου ἐξωτέρω· φέρουσι γὰρ νικώμενον φρένες δύσαρκτοι· and *P. V.* 883, ἔξω δὲ δρόμου φέρομαι λύσσης πνεύματι μάργῳ.

860. ἐν τέλει] 'Who is in the end' (i.e. if provoked) 'A god most dread, though unto man most gentle.' We should have expected a more sharply contrasted pair of clauses like that in *Med.* 809, βαρεῖαν ἐχθροῖς καὶ φίλοισιν εὐμενῆ. This contrast is gained by the conjecture, ὃς πέφηνεν ἀτελέσιν θεὸς δεινότατος, ἐνσπόνδοισι δ' ἠπιώτατος. For the sense, cf. Plut. *Ant.* 24 § 3.

862. 'Oh! shall I ever in the night-long dances plant my gleaming step in Bacchic revelry.' λευκὸν πόδα, cf. note on 665. In the dance the 'gleaming step' would be especially displayed, a point which is happily caught in the Homeric phrase μαρμαρυγὰς θηεῖτο ποδῶν (*Od.* 8, 265).

864. δέραν...ρίπτουσα] 'Tossing my neck into the dewy air.' As the chorus compares itself to a fawn, this expression is quite allowable; so in Pindar *fragm.* 224, μανίαι τ' ἀλαλαί τ' ὀρινομένων ῥιψαύχενι σὺν κλόνῳ (apparently of horses tossing their necks in an excited procession), where ῥιψαύχην supports the text against the proposed alteration δορὰν, since revoked by its proposer; cf. also Sen. *Troad.* 473, *cervice fusam dissipans iacta comam*, and Catullus 63, 23, *ubi capita Maenades vi iaciunt hederigerae.*

866. χλοεραῖς λείμακος ἡδοναῖς] by *enallage* for χλοεροῦ, 'like a fawn disporting herself in the joyance of green pastures.' *El.* 859, θὲς εἰς χορὸν ἴχνος ὡς νεβρὸς οὐράνιον πήδημα κουφίζουσα σὺν ἀγλαΐᾳ.—φοβερὸν θήραμ' would be descriptive of νεβρὸς, and nom. to φύγῃ; 'what time the trembling quarry flees out of watch, over the well-meshed nets.' But I prefer the other alternative, φοβερὰν θήραν, leaving νεβρὸς itself as the subject, 'flees from the fearful chase.'

869. ἔξω φυλακᾶς, i.e. 'away from the watch set upon it,' Xen. *Venat.* VI 12, συνιστάναι τὰς ἄρκυς καὶ τὰ δίκτυα, ὡς εἴρηται· μετὰ δὲ τοῦτο, τὸν μὲν ἀρκυωρὸν εἶναι ἐν φυλακῇ.

872. συντείνῃ δρόμημα κυνῶν] 'braces his hounds to the top of their speed,' cf. συντόνοις δρομήμασιν (1091). **873.** If we retain μύχθοις τ' ὠκυδρόμοις τ' ἀέλλαις we may render: 'while she, with labouring steps and fitful bursts of speed, boundeth along the level river-lawn.' With ὠκυδρόμοις ἀέλλαις, compare the epithet ἀελλόπος used (of Iris) in the *Iliad* (8, 409; 24, 77 and 159), and once in Tragedy, Eur. *Hel.* 1314, κοῦραι ἀελλόποδες. But this gives an unusual sense to ἄελλα, though in *Hel.* 1498, we have ἄστρων ὑπ' ἀέλλαισι; on the whole, I prefer accepting the emendation μόχθοις τ' ὠκυδρόμοις ἀελλὰς, an adjective found in Soph. *O. T.* 466 ἀελλάδων ἵππων and Soph. *fragm.* 614, ἀελλάδες φωναί. For θρώσκει πεδίον, cf. note on πηδῶντα πλάκα (307).

875—6. 'rejoicing in solitudes by man unbroken, and amid the leafy branches of the shady forest.' Adjectives compounded with -κομος are favourite forms with Eur., ἀκρόκομος, δενδρόκομος, χλωρόκομος, ὑλόκομος, ὑψίκομος, ἀβροκόμης (Wecklein).

877—881. These five lines recur as a refrain below (897 sqq.). 'What is the (truest) wisdom, or what among mortals is the boon of heaven, that is fairer than waving the hand victorious, over a fallen foe? What is fair is ever dear.' The words last quoted by the chorus gain fresh point from the legend that they were the burden of the song of the Muses at the marriage of the founder of Thebes, Theognis v. 15, Μοῦσαι καὶ Χάριτες κοῦραι Διὸς, αἵ ποτε Κάδμου ἐς γάμον ἐλθοῦσαι, καλὸν ἀείσατ' ἔπος· ὅττι καλὸν, φίλον ἐστί, τὸ δ' οὐ καλὸν οὐ φίλον ἐστί, cf. Plato *Lysis* p. 216 C, κινδυνεύει κατὰ τὴν παλαιὰν παροιμίαν τὸ καλὸν φίλον εἶναι.

882. 'Slowly, yet surely withal, the might of heaven advances.' Eur. *fragm.* 223, δίκα τοι δίκα χρόνιος, ἀλλ' ὅμως ὑποπεσοῦσ' ἔλαθεν, ὅταν ἔχῃ τιν' ἀσεβῆ βροτῶν, *ib.* 797, (θεοὶ) ὡς πᾶν τελοῦσι κἂν βραδύνωσιν χρόνῳ, *Ion* 1615 and *Or.* 420.   **844.** ἀπευθύνει, κολάζει (Hesych.).

888. 'In cunning wise, they lie in wait, for a long lapse of time, and hunt down the impious one,' *fragm.* 969, (ἡ Δίκη) σῖγα καὶ βραδεῖ ποδὶ στείχουσα μάρψει τοὺς κακοὺς, ὅταν τύχῃ. For ποικίλως, 'craftily,' rather than 'in varied wise,' cf. *Hel.* 711, ὁ θεὸς ἔφυ τι ποικίλον, and Ar. *Eq.* 196. κρυπτεύουσι, intr. as in Xen. *Cyr.* IV 5, 5. δαρὸν χρόνου πόδα] The same metaphor occurs in *fragm.* 43, καὶ χρόνου προὔβαινε πούς, and as the *Bacchae* is not referred to in the *Ranae* (which was probably exhibited before the present play was put on the stage at Athens, after the poet's death in Macedonia), it is the fragment above quoted and not the passage before us which Aristophanes finds fault with, as an over-bold form of expression : *Ranae* 100, ὅστις φθέγξεται τοιουτονί τι παρακεκινδυνευμένοι; αἰθέρα Διὸς δωμάτιον ἢ χρόνου πόδα, and 311, τίν᾽ αἰτιάσωμαι θεῶν μ᾽ ἀπολλύναι; αἰθέρα—ἢ χρόνου πόδα. Modern taste would probably be on the side of Euripides ; in Shakespeare, at any rate, a large part of a scene in *As you like it*, III 2 320—351, consists of variations on the very same metaphor : *the lazy foot of Time... the swift foot of Time...Time travels in divers paces with divers persons. I'll tell you who Time ambles withal, who Time trots withal, who Time gallops withal, and who he stands still withal.*

891. Cf. the legal maxim, *Neminem oportet sapientiorem esse legibus.* Soph. *Ant.* 454—5. **892.** γιγνώσκειν and μελετᾶν are here contrasted as 'thought' and 'practice' respectively.

893. 'It costs but little to hold, that *that* has (sovereign) power, whate'er it be that is more than mortal, and in the long ages is upheld by law and grounded in nature.' For κούφα γὰρ δαπάνα (sc. ἐστὶ) cf. Pind. *Isth.* I, 61, ἐπεὶ κούφα δόσις ἀνδρὶ σοφῷ...ἔπος εἰπόντ᾽ ἀγαθὸν ξυνὸν ὀρθῶσαι καλόν. φύσει πεφυκὸς, cf. Soph. *Phil.* 79, ἔξοιδα, παῖ, φύσει σε μὴ πεφυκότα τοιαῦτα φωνεῖν.

902. 'Happy is he who from out the sea hath fled the storm and found the port; happy also is he who has reached the crown of all his toils.' The first clause introduced by μὲν appears simply to compare the happiness of victory over toils, to the happiness of finding a safe haven from the storm; just as in fragm. 1034, ἅπας μὲν ἀὴρ ἀετῷ περάσιμος, ἅπασα δὲ χθὼν ἀνδρὶ γενναίῳ πατρίς,—and it is perhaps too fanciful to trace (with Lobeck, *Aglaophamus* p. 648) a reference here to the form of words used on the occasion of initiation into the mysteries, ἔφυγον κακὸν εὗρον ἄμεινον (Dem. *de cor.* § 259).

909. ἀπέβησαν] often used of 'turning out' well or ill; also absolutely, of 'succeeding,' here exceptionally of 'failing,' lit. 'passing away.' Something like it is *Andr.* 1021, ἀπὸ δὲ φθίμενοι βεβᾶσι, of the kings of Ilium who are 'dead and gone.'

910. ' Him do I call blessed whose life is happy day by day.'
τὸ κατ᾽ ἦμαρ, an adverbial expression, also found in *Ion*, 123.
Cf. *Hec.* 627, κεῖνος ὀλβιώτατος, ὅτῳ κατ᾽ ἦμαρ τυγχάνει μηδὲν κακόν.
εὐδαίμων and μακαρίζω are combined in 72, μάκαρ...εὐδαίμων.

913. σπεύδοντά τ᾽ ἀσπούδαστα] The same phrase occurs in
Iph. T. 201 ; this combined with the fact that the speech of
Dionysus is a line longer than that of Pentheus has led to the
suggestion that the present line may be an interpolation
(Tyrrell). If the line is omitted, the construction of the acc. is
like that in Soph. *Ant.* 441, σὲ δή, σὲ τὴν νεύουσαν ἐς πέδον κάρα,
φῄς, and Eur. *Hel.* 546, σὲ τὴν ὄρεγμα δεινὸν ἡμιλλημένην...μεῖνον·
if retained, it is like *Herc. F.* 1215, σὲ τὸν θάσσοντα δυστήνους
ἕδρας αὐδῶ, φίλοισιν ὄμμα δεικνύναι τὸ σόν.*

916. μητρός τε τῆς σῆς καὶ λόχου κατάσκοπος] λόχου may
stand without the article, just as in *Herc. F.* 140, τὸν ῾Ηράκλειον
πατέρα καὶ ξυνάορον, where as here, καὶ couples an anarthrous word
to one which cannot refer to the same person. In such cases the
repetition of the article, though often found, is not necessary.

917. πρέπεις]=ὅμοιος εἶ. *Herc. F.* 548, νερτέροις πρέπων, *Alc.*
1121, Aesch. *Suppl.* 301. μορφῇ, '*in* shape,' though close to μιᾷ,
obviously does not go with it; to get rid of this very slight
ambiguity, which would readily be removed by a very little care
in the delivery, μορφὴν has been suggested (by Musgrave).

918—9. Referred to by Lucian *Pseudolog.* III 177, τοῦτο δὴ
τὸ ἐκ τῆς τραγῳδίας δύο μὲν ἡλίους ὁρᾶν δοκοῦσι δισσὰς δὲ Θήβας.
Cf. Virg. *Aen.* 4, 468, *Eumenidum veluti demens videt agmina
Pentheus et solem geminum et duplices se ostendere Thebas;*
where, in the first line, Virgil has applied to Pentheus what
would have been more appropriate to an Orestes (Aesch. *Cho.*
1057) and it has therefore been ingeniously suggested that for
Eumenidum we should read *Euiadum* (S. Allen, ap. Tyrrell).—
This scene is also alluded to by Sextus Empiricus *adv. Logicos*
I 192, ὅτε δὴ μεμηνὼς δισσὰς ὁρᾷ τὰς Θήβας καὶ δισσὸν φαντάζεται
τὸν ἥλιον, and by Clemens Alexandrinus (*Protrept.* xii p. 240
and *Paedag.* II 2 p. 417 ed. Migne), who, somewhat carelessly,
speaks of Pentheus, not as mad, but as intoxicated.

* l. 913 makes the personal reference in the previous line still
clearer to the audience : if any line is left out, it should be 916.

919. καὶ πόλισμ' ἑπτάστομον] 'that city of seven gates,' καὶ
introducing an expansion of Θήβας. *Herc. F.* 15, Ἀργεῖα τείχη
καὶ Κυκλωπείαν πόλιν.

920—2. The king's fancy that his escort has assumed the
form of a bull was probably suggested to the poet by the legends
of the transformations of Dionysus which are more directly
alluded to elsewhere, e.g. 1017, φάνηθι ταῦρος, cf. note on 100.
τεταύρωσαι γὰρ οὖν, 'thou hast, at any rate, a bull-like mien.' The
horned Dionysus is a form under which he is sometimes represented in works of ancient art, as in the engraving given in the
text. Cf. however p. cxlii.

923. εὐμενής] a term usually applied as here to the 'gracious-
ness' of a deity, as contrasted with the kindly feelings of man
for man which is expressed by εὔνους, εὔνοια, &c.   **924.** *Ion* 558,
νῦν ὁρᾶς ἃ χρή σ' ὁρᾶν.

925. *P.* 'What like am I, then? Have I not the port Of
Ino, or Agave my own mother? *D.* When I see *you*, methinks
I see themselves.' (The sense of these lines is strangely missed
in Milman's rendering.)

929. This line is slightly in favour of understanding μίτρα
not of a 'snood' or ribband passing through the hair, but of
a cap resting upon it. See note on 833, and cf. 1115.

The line is sometimes suspected (e.g. by Wecklein) on the
ground that it breaks the regularity of the *stichomythia.* But it
may be suggested that, after the first line of the reply of Dionysus
(927), the player is possibly intended to make a pause, of about
one line in length, during which he takes a leisurely view of the
king's attire. Thus, the duration of the single line in which he
replies would, including this interval, be equivalent to that of the
two lines of the king's question. *After* this pause, Dionysus
starts the conversation afresh, with a couplet (928—9); to which
Pentheus answers with the same number of lines. Similarly,
after 934, where Pentheus has only one line assigned to him,
there was probably a pause equivalent to one line's duration,
while his head-dress is put right by Dionysus.

936. στολίδες] 'folds.' Pollux VII 54, εἴη δ' ἄν τις καὶ στολι-
δωτὸς χιτών· στολίδες δέ εἰσιν αἱ ἐξεπίτηδες ὑπὸ δεσμοῦ γινόμεναι

κατὰ τὰ τέλη τοῖς χιτῶσιν ἐπιπτυχαί, μάλιστα ὑπὸ λινῶν χιτωνίσ-
κων (See *Supplementary Notes*).

938. ὀρθῶς παρὰ τένοντ'] 'straight along the step,' or 'ankle,'
of the left foot. Cf. *Med*. 1166, τένοντ' ἐς ὀρθὸν ὄμμασι σκοπου-
μένη.

943. In using a stick, the most natural movement would be
to advance the *left* foot, while the stick is held forward in the
right hand; Dionysus, for the sake of humouring Pentheus in
his fancy that the Bacchic wand must be held in some special
manner, tells him to do just the opposite, and advance his *right*
foot instead.

In 114, we have some slight reference to 'the reverent handling of the narthex,' but I have observed nothing elsewhere,
in literary or artistic representations of Bacchanals, to confirm
the directions here given by Dionysus; it is probably a pure
fancy of the poet, to put Pentheus into an attitude calculated
to excite the pity, or the amusement, of the spectators.

951. 'Nay! prithee do not ruin the shrines of the nymphs,
　　　And the haunts of Pan, where he doth hold his pipings.'
The reference is to the little shrines carved out in the face of
the rocks (as notably on the north-western side of the Acropolis
at Athens, *Ion* 492—502), in which images of Pan and the
nymphs were placed: Pl. *Phaedrus* 230 B, (on the Ilissus)
νυμφῶν τέ τινων καὶ Ἀχελῴου ἱερὸν ἀπὸ τῶν κορῶν τε καὶ ἀγαλμάτων
ἔοικεν εἶναι. In Plutarch, *Aristides* § 11, the Delphic oracle
promises the Athenians victory at Plataea, on condition of their
offering prayers to Zeus, to the *Cithaeronian* Hera, and to Pan and
the Nymphs called σφραγιτίδες. Cf. Pausan. IX 3 § 9, ὑπὸ δὲ τῆς
κορυφῆς (τοῦ Κιθαιρῶνος), ἐφ' ᾗ τὸν βωμὸν ποιοῦνται, πέντε που
μάλιστα καὶ δέκα ὑποκαταβάντι σταδίους νυμφῶν ἐστιν ἄντρον
Κιθαιρωνίδων, Σφραγίδιον (? Σφραγιτίδων) μὲν ὀνομαζόμενον, cf. I
34 § 3 (of the altar of Amphiaraus at Oropus), πέμπτη (sc. τοῦ
βωμοῦ μοῖρα) πεποίηται νύμφαις καὶ Πανὶ καὶ ποταμοῖς Ἀχελῴῳ καὶ
Κηφίσῳ. See also Wordsworth's *Athens and Attica*, chap. xii.

955. In form, the line resembles *Iph. A.* 1182, δεξόμεθα
δέξιν ἥν σε δέξασθαι χρεών. 'Thou shalt be hidden where thy
doom shall hide thee.' This line, like many others in this scene,

is spoken in stern irony, not merely referring to the king's
hiding-place while spying out the Bacchanals, but also darkly
hinting at his impending doom.

957—8. 'in love's sweet snares, like birds amid the copses'
(*supra* 223 and *Hec.* 829).   **959.** φύλαξ = κατάσκοπος.

960. ἢν σὺ μὴ ληφθῇς πάρος] may be regarded as an *Aside*.
This trick of the stage is far from common in Greek Tragedy.
If we suppose that Pentheus is intended to hear it, it can only
convey to him a warning that he must go in his present disguise,
as otherwise he will only increase the risk of being detected
in his reconnaissance.

963. ὑπερκάμνεις] here as before, a double sense is intended;
to Pentheus, 'thou only toilest for thy country's good;' to the
spectators, 'thou only sufferest on the land's behalf.'

Similarly ἀγῶνες in the next line means, to Pentheus, the
pitched battles with the Maenads which are to follow his
reconnaissance; to the spectators, his own struggle for life when
torn asunder by the Bacchanals. The emphatic repetition of
μόνος at the beginning and end of 963 is paralleled by *Alc.* 722,
Hipp. 327, *Rhes.* 579.

968. Pentheus, misunderstanding the ambiguous statement
that, on his return, he would be 'borne aloft,' supposes Dionysus
to refer to his being carried in triumph and replies, 'That will
be daintiness indeed!'—ἀβρότητ' ἐμὴν λέγεις is altered into ἐμοὶ by
Elmsley, who compares Ar. *Plut.* 637, λέγεις μοι χαράν· λέγεις
μοι βοάν.—Even when Dionysus adds, that he will be borne 'in
his mother's hands' on his return, the king is still in the dark,
and answers, 'You will force me even to luxury'; 'Strange
luxury, indeed!', is the ironical reply, to which Pentheus
responds; ''Tis my desert,' lit. 'I am taking in hand a worthy
task.'

971. δεινός] 'Thou'rt wondrous, wondrous, doomed to wondrous woes'; πάθη meaning (1) the sufferings inflicted by the
king, (2) those which he is himself about to undergo.

972. οὐρανῷ στηρίζον is also used of the great wave described
in *Hipp.* 1207, and in *Iliad* 4, 443, Ἔρις...οὐρανῷ ἐστήριξε κάρη.
The prophecy of the glory of Pentheus, 'towering high as

heaven,' is fulfilled in another sense in the sequel, where the
branch of the fir-tree on which he is placed soars up into the
air (1073, ἐστηρίζετο), and where the god "twixt heaven and
earth, raises a pillar high of awful fire' (1083, ἐστήριζε).

976. 'The rest the event will shew.' Plato *Theaet.* 200 E,
αὐτὸ δείξει, *Protag.* 324, αὐτό σε διδάξει, Eur. *Phoen.* 623, αὐτὸ
σημανεῖ.

977. θοαὶ Λύσσης κύνες] The chorus calls upon the hounds
of Lyssa, the personification of madness. Just as in the Ξάντριαι
of Aeschylus, so in the *Herc. furens*, Λύσσα is one of the characters in the play: in the latter she makes a vigorous speech comparing herself, while doing the bidding of Hera and Iris, to the
hounds that attend the huntsman (860, ὁμαρτεῖν ὡς κυνηγέτῃ κύνας).
So the Erinyes are called κύνες in Aesch. *Cho.* 1054, Soph. *El.* 1388.
It is impossible to suppose that the chorus can here be addressing any of their own body. The *Asiatic* votaries of Dionysus,
who form the chorus of the play, however spirited and enthusiastic their songs and dances may be, are never allowed to
break out into the frenzy which is characteristic of the *Theban*
bacchanals.

981. 'Against him that is arrayed in woman's feigned garb,
that frenzied spy on the Maenads.'* We may supply ὄντα with
ἐπὶ τὸν ἐν γυναικομίμῳ στολᾷ, and in apposition to this we have
the phrase Μαινάδων κατάσκοπον λυσσώδη (Donaldson, *Gk. Gr.*
§ 407 (δ) (a)). The only other way of explaining the position
of the article ἐπὶ τὸν...κατάσκοπον λυσσώδη is to give λυσσώδη
a predicative force, in which case the general sense would be:
'On! ye hounds of frenzy, rouse the daughters of Cadmus
against that spy who himself is frenzied.'

The corresponding line to Μαινάδων κατάσκοπον λυσσώδη is
τὰν ἀνίκατον ὡς κρατήσων βίᾳ, which shews that a long syllable is
lost after Μαινάδων; hence τὸν (or ἐπὶ) κατάσκοπον, and ἄσκοπον
σκοπόν, have been proposed to satisfy the metre: in the latter half
of the line ‒ ‒ ‒ ‒ ‒ corresponds to ‒ ‒ ‒ ‒ ‒ (the normal form of
the dochmiac), just as in Soph. *Ant.* 1308, τί μ᾽ οὐκ ἀνταίαν has
in the antistrophe, ὁ κάλλιστ᾽ ἐμῶν, and *ib.* 1319, ἐγὼ γάρ σ᾽
ἐγὼ = 1341, σέ τ᾽ αὖ τάνδ᾽ ὤμοι (Dindorf, *Poet. Sc.* ed. v p. 46 b).

* A rendering of the manuscript reading. I now accept ἐπὶ in l. 982.

982. 'First shall his mother behold him, as he watches from smooth rock or withered tree.' λευρᾶς πέτρας and σκόλοπος partially correspond to ὄχθος and the ἐλάτη which Pentheus is described as proposing to climb in 1061. σκόλοψ answers apparently to *stipes* in the following much mutilated fragment of the *Bacchae* of Attius, as restored by Ursinus, XIX (ed. Ribbeck) ap. Festum, p. 314 M.—'[stipes fustis terrae] de-fixus — — — [Accius] in Bacchis : ec-[quem stipitem abi-]-eg[n]um aut al [neum.........] us.'—In the National Museum in Naples there is a cameo, almost certainly representing the Espial of Pentheus at the moment of his detection ; in which Satyrs and bacchanals appear in the fore-ground, while in the back-ground a man crouching on all fours, with a lion's skin over him, may be seen on the smooth and level top of a stone structure shaped like an altar (copied in Jahn's *Pentheus*, pl. 1 (d), Tassie's *Gems*, 4867, and Gargiulo's *Musée National*, p. 90).

985. The MS has ὀριοδρόμων, for which ὀριδρόμων is con-jectured by Kirchhoff. As the word is omitted in Liddell and Scott, I may mention that it is used by Nonnus 25, 194, Ἀρκάδα κάπρον ὀρίδρομον and 5, 229 (of Aristaeus hunting on the hills). As Nonnus was very familiar with the *Bacchae* and often imitates it, his evidence is of special value in confirmation of the above conjecture. The metre however is not satisfied unless we transpose Καδμείων and ὀριδρόμων, and read τίς ὅδ' ὀρειδρόμων μαστὴρ Καδμείων (i.e. 'as a hunter after the Theban revellers on the hills,' the βάκχαι Καδμεῖαι of l. 1160) which corre-sponds exactly to τὸ σοφὸν οὐ φθονῶ· χαίρω θηρεύουσ'.

987. The reiteration ἐς ὄρος ἐς ὄρος ἔμολ' ἔμολεν is in keeping with the excitement of the scene. A similar repetition has already occurred in 165, and it is a device of which Eur. is perhaps over-fond (see *Or.* 1414—29, *Phoen.* 1030 sqq, 1567 sqq., and esp. the parody in Ar. *Ran.* 1352—5). But Aeschylus also resorts to it, in some excited lines in the *Persae*, 981—1000.

990. Theocr. 3, 16, νῦν ἔγνων τὸν ἔρωτα· βαρὺς θεός· ἦ ῥα λεαίνας μασδὸν ἐθήλαζε and Virg. *Aen.* 4, 365.

[Similis divisio Dochmiaci (λεαίνας δέ γέ τιν|ος) *Ion* 723, si Dindorfii l. vera. Fortasse in *Ion* 676 legendum ὁρῶ δάκρυα μέλε|α καὶ πένθιμος (libri enim μὲν) et in antistr. φίλαι, πότερα, πότερ' ἐμᾷ δεσποίνᾳ] Shilleto *adv.* Dindorf's last ed. follows Hermann.

992. 'Let Justice advance in visible form, advance with sword in hand, to slay with a stroke, right through the gullet, the godless, the lawless, the reckless one—the earth born son of Echion.' Ἐχίονος τόκον γηγενῆ is in apposition to the clause containing the article, otherwise the order would have been γηγενῆ τόκον, cf. 981 n. **997.** ἀδίκῳ and παρανόμῳ echo the epithets ἄνομον and ἄδικον already applied to Pentheus (995).

998. The MS has περὶ βάκχι' ὄργια ματρός τε σᾶς, the Aldine edition prints περὶ τὰ answering to the three short syllables of θίασον in the corresponding line (978); βάκχι' ὄργια ought similarly to answer to ἔνθ' ἔχουσι in the strophe, and ὄργια must therefore be pronounced as two syllables by *synizesis*. The words ματρός τε σᾶς unless altered into γᾶς (which once occurred to me, but is open to objection on account of γηγενῆ preceding), compel us to take βάκχι' as a vocative, and this further suggests the insertion of σὰ before it, instead of the τὰ of the Aldine edition. The reference in this case must be to the orgies of Dionysus and of Semele, as in Theocr. 26, 6; where the Bacchanals set up three altars to Semele and nine to Dionysus. Hermann, who prints the line περὶ τὰ Βάκχι' ὄργι' ᾶς ματέρος, thus making it unnecessary to resort to *synizesis* in the scansion of ὄργια, explains the last two words as a reference to Agave, who has been prominently mentioned in the former part of the chorus ; Schöne, keeping closer to the MS, prints περὶ τὰ βάκχι' ὄργια τὰ ματρὸς ᾶς, where a long syllable in the strophe is answered by two short syllables in the antistrophe. But βάκχιος is almost always used as a synonym of Dionysus (see *index*); as an adj. (= βακχεῖος) it is hardly ever found, except in *Phoen.* 655, βάκχιον χόρευμα.

999. The rare singular πραπίδι has already occurred in 427.

1001. The MS has τὰν ἀνίκατον ὡς κρατήσων βίᾳ, the Aldine ed. τὸν, Schöne (after Kayser) θεὸν, which is metrically equivalent to the first syllable of Μαινάδων in 981 ; σὰν ἀνίκατον ὡς κρατήσων βίαν makes good sense.

1002. The MS has γνώμαν σώφρονα θάνατος ἀπροφάσιστος εἰς τὰ θεῶν ἔφυ βροτείῳ τ᾽ ἔχειν ἄλυπος βίος, the Aldine ed. εἰ τά τε θεῶν, and some later edd. (e.g. Matthiae's) εἰς τά τε θεῶν. The restoration of the true text appears impossible, though the manuscript reading cannot be far wrong as it nearly corresponds to the metre of the strophe. To obtain something equivalent in metre to πρῶτα νιν λευρᾶς, we have only to read σώφρον᾽ ἃ θνατοῖς (with Heath and Hermann); we also read βροτείαν for βροτείῳ (with Elmsley, Nauck, Paley and Wecklein); the sense would then be, if we invert the clauses for convenience of translation: "'Tis a painless life to keep a temper that is mortal and which amongst mortal men makes no excuses with regard to things divine.' For an exact equivalent to l. 982, we may propose θνατοῖς ἀπροφασίστοις, in the following sense : 'life becomes painless if we keep a temper befitting mortals, a temper which belongs to mortal men who are prompt in their obedience to things divine.' This emendation has, I observe, independently occurred to Wecklein (1879). The constr. of ἄλυπος βίος (sc. ἐστι) = ἄλυπον ποιεῖ τὸν βίον, is the same as that of βραχὺς αἰών as explained in note on 397. Hermann, who follows the Aldine ed. in having no full stop before γνώμαν σώφρονα and reads βροτείῳ—βίῳ (with Scaliger), gives the following far from satisfactory rendering : *ut invictam vi superaturus piam mentem* (Bacchi sacra scilicet celebrantium), *quae mortalibus nullo praetextu in rebus divinis detrectanda, ad humanamque vitam expers mali est, eam habet.* 'Quid sit γνώμην βροτείαν ἔχειν docet noster *Alc.* 802, ὄντας δὲ θνητοὺς, θνητὰ καὶ φρονεῖν χρεών' (Elmsley).[*] We may contrast with this, the loftier view of Aristotle ; οὐ χρὴ δὲ κατὰ τοὺς παραινοῦντας ἀνθρώπινα φρονεῖν ἄνθρωπον ὄντα οὐδὲ θνητὰ τὸν θνητὸν (e.g. Epicharmus ap. *Rhet.* II 21 § 6), ἀλλ᾽ ἐφ᾽ ὅσον ἐνδέχεται ἀθανατίζειν (*Eth. N.* X. 7 § 8).

1005. The MS has τὸ σοφὸν οὐ φθονῶ (so Schöne, Kirchhoff, Nauck, Wecklein) ; i.e. 'I envy not (false) wisdom,' the wisdom referred to in l. 396, τὸ σοφὸν οὐ σοφία. Others prefer

---

[*] Cf. rather Aesch. *Pers.* 820, and Pind. fr. (33), οὐ γὰρ ἔσθ᾽ ὅπως τὰ θεῶν βουλεύματ᾽ ἐρευνάσει βροτέᾳ φρενί. θνατᾶς δ᾽ ἀπὸ ματρὸς ἔφυ.

φθόνῳ, in which case τὸ σοφὸν comes after θηρεύουσα and οὐ φθόνῳ = ἀφθόνως, ' I delight in the unstinted quest of knowledge.'

1007. τὰ δ' ἕτερα μεγάλα φανερὰ τῶν ἀεὶ is the reading of the MS, altered by Musgrave into φανερά τ' ὄντ' ἀεὶ (followed by Schöne, who however has τάδ'). τὰ δ' ἕτερα μεγάλα φανέρ' ἰόντ' ἀεὶ is proposed by Dr Thompson, in the following sense : ' but those other matters are great and manifest, that one should ever be going in pursuit of noble ends, living day and night a life of piety and holiness, and honouring the gods by rejecting all the ordinances that are beyond the pale of justice.' This he supports by Thuc. VIII 92, ἰέναι ἐπὶ τὰ πράγματα, *Iph. A.* 413, ἰέναι ἐπὶ μηχάνας, and a passage from Plato (where however the phrase occurs *passim*) οἱ δειλοὶ οὐκ ἐθέλουσιν ἰέναι ἐπὶ τὸ κάλλιόν τε καὶ ἥδιον, *Protag.* 360 A. This suggestion I formerly accepted ; (except that for τὰ δ' I adopted τάδ', which is required, if we retain the manuscript reading φθονῶ, 1005). A simpler construction is, however, obtained by accepting Wecklein's emendation ἄγοντα (*frag.* 671, εἰς τὸ σῶφρον ἐπ' ἀρετήν τ' ἄγων ἔρως). The sense of τάδ' ἕτερα—βίον is further explained in the two following clauses, as in 424-6, where as here the acc. c. inf. is used. As the sentiment is a general one, the participles are masc. in spite of the preceding fem. θηρεύουσα*.

1009. εὐαγοῦντ' εὐσεβεῖν] Theocr. 26, 30 (on the doom of Pentheus), αὐτὸς εὐαγέοιμι καὶ εὐαγέεσσιν ἄδοιμι. For τὰ ἔξω νόμιμα δίκας, cf. 331, θύραζε τῶν νόμων, and 896 ; also *Androm.* 787.

1017. Dionysus is here called upon to appear in one or other of his favourite transformations, either as a bull (cf. note on ταυροκέρων θεὸν, 100, and passages there quoted), or as a serpent like the hundred-headed hydra, or lastly as a lion. In reference to these transformations, the god is elsewhere called αἰολόμορφος (Orph. hymn 50), ἀλλοπρόσαλλος (Nonnus 14, 170), μυριόμορφος (Anth. Pal. IX 524, 13) ; cf. Homeric hymn VII 45 (on Dionysus and the Tyrrhenian pirates), ὁ δ' ἄρα σφι λέων γένετ' ἔνδοθι νηὸς δεινὸς ἐπ' ἀκροτάτης μέγα δ' ἔβραχεν, ἐν δ' ἄρα μέσσῃ ἄρκτον ἐποίησεν λασιαυχένα, σήματα φαίνων. It is highly probable that by the 'lion' in these passages a panther is really meant, for that is the animal usually represented in works of ancient art referring to

Dionysus; as may be seen in the two representations of the doom of Pentheus in this volume (e. g. on p. 68).

For πυριφλέγων ὁρᾶσθαι λέων cf. Milton's *P. L.* 4, 399—402, where in the account of the transformations of Satan into a lion, a tiger, a toad, and a serpent, the first is described in the words :—*about them round A lion now he stalks with fiery glare.* The resemblance may of course be accidental, but Milton was a careful student of Euripides and may possibly have been thinking of the present passage.

Mr Tyrrell brackets δράκων, and thereby places between the definite references to the 'bull' and 'lion' a vague allusion to '*some* many-headed monster,' a collocation which strikes one as particularly improbable.

For λέων, cf. Hor. *Carm.* 2, 19, 23, *Rhoetum retorsisti leonis unguibus horribilique mala ;* also Nonnus, 40, 43—60, ἀντὶ Λυαίου πόρδαλιν αἰολόνωτον ἐπαΐσσοντα κιχάνω· μαινομένου δὲ λέοντος ἐπείγομαι αὐχένα τέμνειν, καὶ θρασὺν ἀντὶ λέοντος ὄφιν δασπλῆτα δοκεύω, and the following lines; where his transformation into a bear, a boar, a bull, and even into fire and water, are given in full detail, in an account of his contest with king Deriades.

1020. The MS has θηραγρότα, the Ald. ed. θηραγρέτα, Schöne, θὴρ' ἀγροδότα, Nauck θηραγρεύτα (gen.?), while Kirchhoff says, 'malim θὴρ' ἀγρεύταν.' Mr Tyrrell with much probability suggests the insertion of θὴρ, which might easily have dropt out before the following word; this is supported by the preceding reference to the various transformations in which the god was expected to appear, and by the contrast thus brought out between the θὴρ (Dionysus) and Pentheus the huntsman of the Bacchanals. Paley considers γελῶντι προσώπῳ a 'gloss' on some such word as γελῶν, and proposes the following dochmiacs as satisfying the sense and the metre ;[*]ἴθ', ὦ βάκχε, θὴρ' ἀγρεύταν βακχᾶν | γελῶν περίβαλε βρόχον θανάσιμον | ἐς ἀγέλαν πεσόντα τὰν μαινάδων. We should thus be able to take θανάσιμον naturally with βρόχον, cf. Aesch. *Suppl.* 788, μορσίμου βρόχου.—I cannot understand θηραγρεύτα βακχᾶν (Nauck) if it is taken as Dor. gen.; it is possibly meant for a voc. ; but if so, the last syllable would be short.— πεσόντα is the reading of the MS and may be understood as acc.

[*] The second line, however, is metrically unsatisfactory.

after the general sense of περίβαλε βρόχον = αἴρει, Matthiae (or ἅλισκε, Hermann). 'Cf. Aesch. *Pers.* 914, ἐσιδόντα, and *Choeph.* 411, Soph. *El.* 480, Ar. *Av.* 47' (R. Shilleto).

1026. ὄφεος] We should naturally expect a genitive after γαίᾳ, which seems rather bald if left standing by itself. Hence Elmsley, who holds that, if the text is sound, the order is, ὃς ὄφεος ἐν γαίᾳ ἔσπειρε τὸ γηγενὲς δράκοντος θέρος, 'who in the land of the serpent sowed the dragon's earth-born crop,' proposes ῎Αρεος ἐν γαίᾳ, comparing Aesch. *S. C. T.* 105, προδώσεις, παλαί-χθων ῎Αρης, τὰν τεὰν γᾶν; also *Phoen.* 661 δράκων ῎Αρεος (which however would be rather in favour of making ῎Αρεος genitive after δράκοντος), and *ib.* 941, Κάδμῳ παλαιῶν ῎Αρεος ἐκ μηνιμάτων, ὃς γηγενεῖ δράκοντι τιμωρεῖ φόνου. Paley and others (comparing συσὶ κάπροισι) take δράκοντος ὄφεος together, and consider the combination to be all the more admissible on the ground that δράκων was originally a participial epithet of the snake. γένος μὲν ὁ ὄφις, εἶδος δὲ ὁ δράκων, Schol. on *Orest.* 479.

1028. χρηστοῖσι δούλοις συμφορὰ τὰ δεσποτῶν is also found in *Med.* 54, where it is followed by the words, κακῶς πίτνοντα καὶ φρενῶν ἀνθάπτεται. τὰ δεσποτῶν, standing by itself, is vague, and requires some such expression as that in the Medea, to help it out; hence it is not improbable that the line is an interpolation. There is no difficulty in the ending ἀλλ' ὅμως, standing by itself, as may be seen by comparing *Hec.* 842, *Or.* 1023, Ar. *Ach.* 956, 402, 408 (where Euripides, in reply to the words ἀλλ' ἀδύνατον, gives the answer ἀλλ' ὅμως).

1031. Probably a dochmiac line; the metre may be restored by printing either θεὸς σὺ (with Schöne) or repeating θεὸς (with Hermann). **1034—5,** dochmiacs; ξένᾱ is fem. sing.

1036. The conclusion of the line is lost, unless we suppose it is intentionally cut short by the excited protest of the chorus. The drift of the messenger's remark is that the women of the chorus need not exult over the death of Pentheus, as though Thebes could boast no men beside *him*, to make slaves of them, now that the king himself was dead. Cf. Soph. *O. C.* 917, καί μοι πόλιν κένανδρον ἢ δούλην τινὰ ἔδοξας εἶναι κἄμ' ἴσον τῷ μηδενί. **1038.** ἐμὸν = ἐμοῦ, power, authority, 'over me.' **1039.**

ἐπ' ἐξειργασμένοις, 'we must forgive thee; save, it is not noble, Ye dames, to joy o'er ills past all repair.' Aesch. *Ag.* 1379, Soph. *Ai.* 377.

1042. At this point begins the second Messenger's speech, one of the most brilliant pieces of narrative in all extant Greek poetry. Its opening portion has before now been referred to as a 'description of scenery disclosing a deep feeling for nature' (Humboldt's *Cosmos* II note 12); it will be observed, however, that the element of the picturesque is confined to a line and a half, ἦν δ' ἄγκος ἀμφίκρημνον ὕδασι διάβροχον, πεύκαισι συσκιάζον (1051). But as a vigorous and rapid narrative, displaying great powers of clear and graphic description, it would be hard to find its rival. See further in *Introd.* § 5.

1043. θεράπνας, 'homesteads'; αὐλῶνες, σταθμοί (Hesychius). So also in *Tro.* 213, τὰν ἐχθίσταν θεράπναν Ἑλένας, *Herc. F.* 370, Πηλιάδες θεράπναι. It was also the name of a place in Boeotia, mentioned in Strabo IX 409 A, (of the parts about the Asopus,) ἐν δὲ τῇ Θηβαίων εἰσὶ καὶ αἱ Θεράπναι καὶ ὁ Τευμεσσός,—in Müller and Grove's Ancient Atlas it is doubtfully placed not far from the road from Thebes towards the pass of Phyle and near a small northern tributary of the Asopus, along which a route is marked leading across the Asopus and ascending a southern tributary of the stream, and thus reaching a 'little rocky table height overlooking the river,' which is identified by Leake with Scolus; it was near this last place, according to Strabo (p. 408), that Pentheus met his doom. There were other places named Therapne (e. g. in Laconia), and some prefer considering it to be a name of a place here; but it may be remarked that there is no authority for such a place in Boeotia except the passage of Strabo, who may be thinking of the very passage before us; if however we take it as the name of the place, τῆσδε Θηβαίας χθονὸς becomes superfluous, as the rustic messenger cannot be supposed to be anxious to prevent the Asiatic women, whom he is addressing, from supposing that he could possibly mean a place in any other part of Greece, such as Laconia.

1044. ἐξέβημεν ῥοάς] so in *Herc. F.* 82, γαίας ὅρι' ἂν ἐκβαῖμεν, Sallust *Iug.* 110, 8, *flumen non egrediar,* Liv. III 57, 10, *priusquam urbem egrederentur,* Tac. *Ann.* I 51, *evasere silvas.*

1048. ποιηρὸν ἔξομεν νάπος] 'we halted in a grassy glade,' described as a εὔλειμος νάπη in 1084. 'The lower region of Cithaeron here [i.e. above Plataea] consists, partly of steep swelling banks, covered with green turf of a richness and smoothness such as I scarcely recollect having observed in any other district of rugged Greece, or with dense masses of pine forest; partly of rocky dells, fringed with brushwood or stunted oaks' (Col. Mure's *Tour in Greece* I 264). Doubtless many a spot might be found on the slopes of Cithaeron corresponding with sufficient closeness to the scene described by Euripides; the writer just quoted, after translating the first ten lines of this speech, adds: 'here we have as graphic a description as can be desired of the site of the little village of Kokla, immediately above the ruins of Plataea, in the centre of an open bank of smooth green turf, overhung with pine forest,' *u. s.* p. 266. The legendary scene of the doom of Pentheus was, however, more to the East, in the lonelier parts of the mountain-side; according to Strabo, above quoted, at Scolus.

1049. τά τ᾽ ἐκ ποδῶν...καὶ γλώσσης ἄπο.

'With noiseless footfall and with silent tongues,
    That we might see, unseen the while ourselves.'

Instead of καὶ, we might have expected a repetition of τά τε.

1051. 'There was a rock-girt glen, with rivulets watered, With stone-pines over-shadowed.' Cf. Seneca *Oedipi fragm.* 12—18, *ibo ibo qua praerupta protendit iuga meus Cithaeron... qua per obscurum nemus silvamque opacae vallis instinctas deo egit sorores mater et gaudens malo vibrante fixum praetulit thyrso caput;* id. *Oedipus* 543, *est procul ab urbe lucus ilicibus niger, Dircaea circa vallis irriguae loca;* and, for Ovid's description of the scene, *Met.* III 707, *monte fere medio est, cingentibus ultima silvis, purus ab arboribus spectabilis undique campus.*

1052. συσκιάζον] lit. 'thick-shading,' with no acc. actually expressed. The participle is thus virtually equivalent to an adjective, just as we find *umbrans* for *umbrosus* in Seneca, *Herc. furens* 722, *ingens domus umbrante luco tegitur.*—Mr Paley well contrasts the 'spiry pyramidal outline of the silver-fir' (ἐλάτη) with the 'wide and dense crown' formed by the spreading boughs of the stone-pine (πεύκη).

The pines of Cithaeron are often mentioned by travellers; e.g. Leake's *Northern Greece* II 369 (after indicating the probable site of Scolus), 'we soon afterwards' (while still ascending the steep side of Cithaeron) 'enter a ravine between two ridges of the mountain, answering exactly to the description given by Euripides...except that the pine-forests do not now extend below the higher parts of the mountain.' With the description of natural scenery in the text, we may compare part of fragm. 1068, (of Laconia) πολλὴν μὲν ἄροτον, ἐκπονεῖν δ' οὐ ῥᾴδιον· κοίλη γὰρ ὄρεσι περίδρομος τραχεῖά τε δυσείσβολος δὲ πολεμίοις..., (of Messenia) καλλίκαρπον...κατάρρυτόν τε μυρίοισι νάμασι. This passage was probably in the mind of the Scholiast on Hephaest. p. 87. 32, Pauw, who quotes the present line, ἥδ' ἄγκος ὑψίκρημνον, ὄρεσι περίδρομον. Cf. Ar. *Thesm.* 995 ff., ἀμφὶ δὲ σοὶ κτυπεῖται Κιθαιρώνιος ἠχώ, μελάμφυλλά τ' ὄρη δάσκια καὶ νάπαι πετρώδεις βρέμονται.

1055. κισσῷ κομήτην, proleptic, 'were garlanding afresh A faded thyrsus till it curled with ivy,' fragm. 202, ἔνδον δὲ θαλάμοις βουκόλον...κομῶντα κισσῷ στῦλον εὐίου θεοῦ.

1056. Madvig, *adv.* I 235, writes: 'mira comparatio Baccharum cum pullis iugum relinquentibus (et labore fessis); et quo pertinet in hac comparatione iugi (veri) cognomen ποικίλα? scribendum αἱ δ' ἐμπλέκουσαι ποικίλ' ὡς πῶλοι ζυγά, hoc est multiplices variosque serentes ordines.' But a troop of young colts let loose from the yoke, might be fresh and frisky enough to warrant the simile in the text, and the text is defended by *Or.* 45, πηδᾷ δρομαῖος, πῶλος ὡς ἀπὸ ζυγοῦ. ποικίλα is only an ornamental epithet, as in ἅρματα ποικίλα χαλκῷ, often found in Homer, *Il.* 4, 226; 10, 322, 393, and (without χαλκῷ) 5, 239; 13, 537; 14, 431; 10, 501, ποικίλου ἐκ δίφροιο· An Epic usage need not surprise us in an ἀγγέλου ῥῆσις.

1060. The MS has ὅσοι νόθων, and Henry Stephens' fraudulent statement that he found ὅσον and μόθων in his pretended "Italian MSS" has led critics astray and suggested a number of emendations founded on the supposition that there was real authority for those readings. Mr Tyrrell has done good service by restoring the reading of the only existing

MS and proposing the emendation ὄσσοιν for ὄσοι, pointing out
that the same copyist has seven times in this play made the
same mistake of writing σ for σσ, or ν for νν. His emendation
presupposes that οσοινοθων was mis-written for οσσοιννοθων. For
the use of the word νόθος, he quotes Nonnus 46, 207, where
Pentheus says : μηδὲ δαμῆναι Βασσαρίδων τεὸν υἶα νόθαις παλά-
μῃσιν ἐάσῃς, and compares πλασταῖσι βακχείαισι (218), to which
I may add from the same speech of Pentheus, πρόφασιν μὲν
ὡς δὴ Μαινάδας θυοσκόους (224). Provisionally, I accept this,
with a slight preference however in favour of ὄσσοις νόθων, as
being a more frequent form than ὄσσοιν, and a more euphonious
combination than that given by the concurrence of the double ν,
which might cause a slight difficulty in the delivery of the passage.—There is much however in favour of ὅποι μόθων (φορτικὸν
ὀρχήσεως εἶδος Schol. on Ar. *Eq.* 697). It makes fair sense and
keeps nearer to the MS than most of the emendations.

1064. On the silver-fir, a characteristic tree of Cithaeron, cf.
note on 38. At Corinth, Pausanias was shewn two rude images
of Dionysus, gilded all over except the face, which was dyed
red : these, he was assured, were made at the command of an
oracle, from the wood of the tree which Pentheus climbed when
he went to spy out the Maenads (III 2 §§ 6, 7).

1065. κατῆγεν, ἦγεν, ἦγεν] 'He caught by the tip a soaring
branch of fir, And tugged it down, down, down, to the dark
ground.' In Greek where the sense of a compound verb has
to be given afresh, it is often only the simple verb that is
actually repeated (*Hec.* 168, ἀπωλέσατ' ὠλέσατ', *Med.* 1252).
The repetition of ἦγεν where *we* should probably prefer to
repeat the preposition, well expresses (as already remarked by
Reiske and Paley) the successive efforts to bend the branch
down to the earth ; so in Nonnus 46, 152, κόρυμβον χειρὶ
πιέζων εἰς πέδον εἰς πέδον εἷλκε. Cf. *Christus patiens* 660, οὐρανοδρόμῳ ξύλῳ ἀνῆγον, ἦγον, ἦγον εἰς ἄκρον τέλος, where οὐρανοδρόμῳ and ἄκρον have been apparently suggested by οὐράνιον
ἄκρον in 1064.

Fronto *de eloquentia*, p. 148 Naber (thinking apparently of
this scene, as represented by some such rendering as that of
Attius), *quin erige te et extolle, et tortores istos, qui te ut*

*abietem aut alnum proceram incurvant et ad chamaetorta
detrahunt, valido cacumine excute* (Ribbeck on Attius *Bacchae*
XIX, quoted on 982).

1066.— On κυκλοῦτο, cf. note on 767, νίψαντο.—' E'en like
a bow it bent, or rounded wheel, When peg and cord mark
out its curvèd disk.' The τόρνος is an instrument used to mark
out a circumference by means of a string, with one end made
fast at a centre, and a piece of chalk or lead at the other. The
passage refers to the gradual process by which the circumference is described. It is important to notice the present
participle γραφόμενος, as this allows us to conceive of only an
arc of the whole circumference being marked out on the wood
of the future wheel; the tip of the lofty branch is brought
down not to the roots of the tree, but to the ground at some
distance from the stem. In a fragment, however, of the
Theseus, 385, an unlettered slave describes the shape of Θ in
the lines, κύκλος τις ὡς τόρνοισιν ἐκμετρούμενος, οὗτος δ' ἔχει
σημεῖον ἐν μέσῳ σαφές, where the present participle appears to
be somewhat loosely used. Mr Tyrrell in a long, but particularly serviceable, note has collected passages bearing on the
meaning of τόρνος (*Cycl.* 661, τόρνευ' ἕλκε, Hdt. IV 36 and Plat.
Phil. 51 C); to these may be added Plat. *Critias*, 113 D, δύο μὲν
γῆς θαλάττης δὲ τρεῖς (τροχοὺς) οἷον τορνεύων ἐκ μέσης τῆς
νήσου, *Tim.* 33 B, διὸ καὶ σφαιροειδές, ἐκ μέσου πάντη πρὸς
τὰς τελευτὰς ἴσον ἀπέχον, κυκλοτερὲς αὐτὸ ἐτορνεύσατο, Aristot.
de mundo p. 391 *b* 22, τοῦ δὲ σύμπαντος οὐρανοῦ τε καὶ κόσμου
σφαιροειδοῦς ὄντος καὶ κινουμένου…ἐνδελεχῶς, δύο ἀκίνητα ἐξ
ἀνάγκης ἐστὶ σημεῖα καταντικρὺ ἀλλήλων, καθάπερ τῆς ἐν τόρνῳ
(*a lathe-chisel*, here and below) κυκλοφορουμένης σφαίρας, and
Aesch. fragm. 54, βόμβυκες τόρνου κάματος. Also, Theognis 805,
τόρνου καὶ στάθμης καὶ γνώμονος ἄνδρα θεωρόν, Plat. *Phil.* 56 B,
where it is mentioned, with the κανὼν, διαβήτης and στάθμη,
among the tools of the builder's art in general and of ξυλουργικὴ
in particular. Hesychius has τόρνος· ἐργαλεῖον τεκτονικὸν ᾧ τὰ
στρόγγυλα σχήματα περιγράφουσιν (in Blümner's *Technologie* II
232, a reference is further given to 'Dionys. Perieg. 157 and
Eust. ad h. l.'). For acc. after γραφόμενος, cf. 746.

ἕλκει (corrected into ἕλκῃ) δρόμον is the reading of the MS, which is altered by Reiske into ἑλικοδρόμον (accepted by Dindorf and Nauck) and into ἑλκέδρομον by Scaliger, who is followed by Tyrrell. The former of these compounds finds its parallel in such words as ἑλικοβλέφαρος (Hes.), ἑλικοβόστρυχος (Ar.), and ἑλίκωψ (Iliad), and it actually occurs in Orph. H. 8, 10; the formation of the latter, of the actual use of which there is no example, is supported by ἑλκεχίτων, often used in the Iliad (e.g. 13, 685); and both of these epithets, supported as they are by Epic analogies, may be defended on the ground that in messengers' speeches an Epic colouring is quite in place. The author of the *Christus patiens* in the line already cited has the epithet οὐρανοδρόμῳ, which was suggested to him partly by οὐράνιον in l. 1064, and partly possibly (as Mr Tyrrell suggests) by some compound epithet of the same formation in the present line. The main objection to ἕλκει δρόμον is, that accepting it involves taking ὥστε with a finite verb (this use being chiefly Epic), and that, even so, the verb applies to the wheel alone and not to the bow. The only instance I can find in Tragedy is Soph. *Trach.* 112, ὥστ᾽ ἀκάμαντος ἢ Νότου ἢ Βορέα τις κύματα...ἴδῃ, οὕτω.

For similar comparisons in Euripides, suggested by various forms of handicraft, cf. *Hipp.* 468 (κανὼν), *Cycl.* 460 (τρύπανον), and fragm. *Erechth.*, 362, 12, ἁρμὸς πονηρὸς ὥσπερ ἐν ξύλῳ παγείς.

The latest suggestion as to the interpretation of the passage is that made by Mr E. S. Robertson in *Hermathena* III p. 387, where the instrument referred to is understood to be probably a *lathe* of the kind still in use in the North-west provinces of India, the working of which he describes as follows: A stout pole of some elastic wood is fixed into the wall, so as to project at right angles, with its thinner end free. To this end is attached a string, which is brought down and fastened to a pin in the drum of the lathe. The workman then attaches the block of timber which is to be turned into a wheel; and he drags this round...until the string is coiled round the drum as many times as it will go. This of course bends down the pole, which is the process described by κυκλοῦτο...His sug-

gestion is that the simile in the text is taken from the slow
bending of the pole in the process of coiling the string.

1068. ὥs] An Epic and Ionic use, not frequent in Tragedy.
Aesch. *Ag*. 930, εἰ πάντα δ᾽ ὡς πράσσοιμεν, Soph. *O. C.* 1242,
ὥs τις...ὡς καὶ (chor.), Eur. *El.* 155, οἷα δέ τις...ὡς σὲ (chor.).
Mr Tyrrell however prefers ὥs, taking it as equivalent to ὅτε,
but this would give us a somewhat straggling sentence.

κλῶν᾽...ἔκαμπτεν] cf. Σίνις ὁ πιτυοκάμπτης, Pausan. II 1 § 4, ὁ
λῃστὴς Σίνις λαμβανόμενος πιτύων ἦγεν ἐς τὸ κάτω σφᾶς· ὁπόσων
δὲ μάχῃ κρατήσειεν, ἀπ᾽ αὐτῶν δήσας ἀφῆκεν ἂν τὰ δένδρα ἄνω
φέρεσθαι.

1072. 'Gently, for fear the steed should throw his rider,'
ἀναχαιτίσειε, which is strictly applicable to a horse rearing and
throwing off his rider (*Hipp.* 1232, *Rhes.* 786), is here metaphorically applied to the tree on which Pentheus was seated.
The same metaphor is kept up in 1074, νώτοις and 1107, τὸν
ἀμβάτην.

1073. 'It slowly rose aloft to the lofty air.' The epithet
ὀρθὴ is thoroughly applicable to the ἐλάτη and has already been
applied to the βλάστημα (1071); but it is only by a kind of attraction used of the αἰθήρ. Similarly, for the sake of symmetry,
we find in Soph. *El.* 742, ὠρθοῦθ᾽ ὁ τλήμων ὀρθὸς ἐξ ὀρθῶν
δίφρων, where Jebb quotes *Phil.* 682, ἴσος ὢν ἴσοις ἀνήρ.

1076. ὅσον οὔπω δῆλος ἦν...καὶ] 'He was all but seen upon
his lofty seat, *when...*' This use of καὶ, for ὅτε, is a construction
common in the simple style of Epic poetry, as *infra* 1082, καὶ
πρὸς οὐρανόν.

1080. We may regard ὄργια as acc. either after τιθέμενον,
with γέλων in apposition to it; or (better) after the single notion
comprised in the words γέλων τιθέμενον.

1083. ''Twixt heaven and earth He raised a pillar bright of
awful flame.' Cf. *supra* 972, n.

1084. σίγησε δ᾽ αἰθήρ] An undoubted instance of the omission of the augment, which Porson endeavoured to remove

by the suggestion, '*transpositione leni repone,* αἰθὴρ δ' ἐσίγα' (Kidd's *tracts* p. 190). Cf. *supra* 767, n.

1084. ὕλιμος νάπη] 'the forest glade,' cp. 1048, 1138. The MS reading, εὔλειμος, not found elsewhere, was deemed equivalent to Homer's εὐλείμων (*Od.* 4, 607). But the author of the *Christus patiens,* 2260, who includes this line in his cento, has ὕλιμος νάπη. This is accepted by Dindorf (1869), Tyrrell (1892) and Wecklein (1898). It is supported by a fragment of the *Melanippe* of Eur. published by Blass in 1880, no. 495, 34 Nauck, εἶδον δὲ τὸν μὲν ὄρεος ὑλίμῳ φόβῃ κρυφθέντα.

1087. διήνεγκαν κόρας, 'stared this way and that'; oddly enough, κόραι is immediately after used in another sense.

1090. ἥσσονες...ἔχουσαι are the readings of the MS. The former makes fair sense. lit. 'they rushed forth, not inferior to any dove in swiftness,' and ἔχουσαι may then be taken absolutely, 'holding on their way, with eager runnings of feet.' To simplify the constr. of ἔχουσαι, ἥσσονα has been proposed (by Heath), and as an alternative we have the obvious suggestion, τρέχουσαι, or δραμοῦσαι (Schöne and Hartung), supported by *Chr. pat.* 2015, οἶμαι, πελείας ὠκύτητ' οὐχ ἥσσονες ποδῶν δράμωσι συντόνοις δρομήμασιν.

The simile was perhaps suggested by *Iliad* 5, 778, αἱ δὲ βάτην τρήρωσι πελειάσιν ἴθμαθ' ὁμοῖαι, cf. Soph. *O. C.* 1081, ἀελλαία ταχύρρωστος πελειάς.—For συντόνοις δρομήμασι, cf. 872 συντείνῃ δρόμημα.

1093. 'Through the torrent-glen, O'er the rocks they leapt, inspired by heaven-sent madness.' Cf. Aesch. *P. V.* 884, λύσσης πνεύματι μάργῳ. Sir Thomas Wyse says, in describing the route from Plataea to Athens through 'the inner foldings of Cithaeron,' 'various small torrent-beds seam the green of the fir-forest, yet in vigour here. Now and then we caught sight of a dizzy pathway and...sundry mysterious recesses ran up the glens, amidst half-burnt trunks and knotted roots. Later, the mountain faces began to close upon each other, and to present scenery, in its more forest-like character of rock and tree, for the legends of Oedipus and Pentheus' (*Impressions of Greece* p. 198).

1096. αὐτοῦ...ἔρριπτον] *Cycl.* 51, ῥίψω πέτρον τάχα σου, *Iph.*
T. 362, ὅσας γενείου χεῖρας ἐξηκόντισα.

1099. θύρσους ἵεσαν..Πενθέως, στόχον δύστηνον] The constr. of
the gen. is the same as that illustrated in the last note.   στόχον
(Reiske's excellent emendation for τ' ὄχον) δύστηνον, is in general
apposition to the sense of the previous sentence. Cf. 9, 30, 250,
1232, *Or.* 499, 727, *H. F.* 323, *Hipp.* 815 (Kühner *Gk. Gr.* § 406, 6).

1101.   'For far aloft, beyond their eager reach, He sat, a
poor, perplexed and helpless captive.' Aesch. *Ag.* 1376, ὕψος
κρεῖσσον ἐκπηδήματος.

1103.   'At last they strove by shattering (riving) oaken boughs,
To up-tear the roots, with bars—but not of iron.' συγκεραυνοῦσαι,
Archil. 79, συγκεραυνωθεὶς, 'thunder-stricken'; Cratinus ap.
Athen. 494, τοὺς καδίσκους συγκεραυνώσω σποδῶν.—ἀσιδήροις is a
'limiting epithet' which makes it possible to transfer μόχλοις
from its primary meaning of 'iron crowbars' to its metaphorical
application to the boughs of tough oak here used to prise up the
roots of the fir tree on which Pentheus is seated.   On such
epithets see Cope on Arist. *Rhet.* III 6 § 7.

1106.   φέρε...λάβεσθε] This combination of the singular with
the plural imperative is also found with ἄγε, ἰδέ, and εἰπέ, and
may be explained by regarding the singular imperative as a
stereotyped form which, owing to constant use in everyday life,
came to be treated as an uninflected interjection.   *Od.* 3, 475,
παῖδες ἐμοὶ, ἄγε Τηλεμάχῳ καλλίτριχας ἵππους ζεύξατε, Soph. *Trach.*
821, ἴδ' οἷον ὦ παῖδες κ.τ.λ., Ar. *Ach.* 318, εἰπέ μοι, τί φειδόμεσθα
τῶν λίθων, ὦ δημόται (Kühner *Gk. Gr.* § 371, 4 α).

1108.   Agave's fanciful description of the spy as some beast
astride the silver-fir, is intended to lead up to the sequel where,
in her growing frenzy, she regards the head of her own son as
that of a lion.   For 1110, cf. Hor. *Carm.* 3, 25, 15—16.

1113.   For rhetorical effect, the name of Pentheus is reserved
to the end of the sentence, and the pause, at so early a point as
the end of the first foot of the line, is admirably adapted to
express the sudden fall.   Milton *P. L.* 6, 912 (quoted by Jod-
drell), *Firm they might have stood,* | *Yet fell.*

1114.   ἱερία] *infra* 1246, καλὸν τὸ θῦμα... For the μίτρα, cf. 833.

1120. 'Do not, for all *my* errors, slay *thy son.*'

1124. οὐδ' ἔπειθέ νιν] The subject of the preceding and the succeeding clauses here becomes the object of the short intervening sentence.

1125—1130. Imitated by Theocritus 26, 22, Ἰνὼ δ' ἐξέρρηξε σὺν ὠμοπλάτᾳ μέγαν ὦμον λὰξ ἐπὶ γαστέρα βᾶσα, Nonnus 44, 68 ἡμιτόμου Πενθῆος ἐρεισαμένη πόδα λαιμῷ κ.τ.λ.

1128. 'But the god himself lightened her handiwork'; this is added to shew that it was only by supernatural power that she was able to wrench the shoulder off the body. 'No human force,' observes Dr Joddrell, 'unaided by artificial instruments can ever detach the tenacious adhesion of the sinews and tendons of the human body.'

1129. Ovid *Met.* III 722, *dextramque precantis abstulit; Inoo lacerata est altera raptu.*

1131. 'Nihil ex illo ἐπεῖχε efficias ad Bacchas reliquas aptum. Scrib. ἐπεῖγε [*sic*], urgebat et incitabat' (Madvig). The Attic form would of course have been ἤπειγε, and the middle ἠπείγετο would have been more natural than the active. ἐπεῖχε, *instabat* (*Heracl.* 847, Hom. *Od.* 22, 72, ἐπὶ δ' αὐτῷ πάντες ἔχωμεν), makes good sense :—'Autonoe and all the crowd Of Bacchanals pressed on.'

1132. In apposition to the sense implied in ἦν δὲ πᾶσ' ὁμοῦ βοή (=ἐβόων ὁμοῦ), we have ὁ μὲν στενάζων, and (by a slight change of construction, as in *Heracl.* quoted below) αἱ δ' ἠλάλαζον, instead of αἱ δ' ἀλαλάζουσαι. For examples of the implied subject split up into its component parts, and each of those parts placed in the nom. in apposition to that implied subject, cf. Aesch. *P. V.* 201, στάσις τ' ἐν ἀλλήλοισιν ὠροθύνετο, οἱ μὲν θέλοντες...οἱ δὲ τοὔμπαλιν σπεύδοντες, Soph. *Ant.* 260, λόγοι δ' ἐν ἀλλήλοισιν ἐρρόθουν κακοί, φύλαξ ἐλέγχων φύλακα, Eur. *Heracl.* 40, δυοῖν γερόντοιν δὲ στρατηγεῖται φυγή, ἐγὼ μὲν...καγχαίνων...ἡ δ' αὖ... σώζει, *Phoen.* 1462, Xen. *Hell.* II 2 § 3, οἰμωγὴ...εἰς ἄστυ διῆκεν, ὁ ἕτερος τῷ ἑτέρῳ παραγγέλλων (Kühner *Gk. Gr.* § 493, 2).

1134. γυμνοῦντο] on the omission of the augment, see note on 767. For αὐταῖς ἀρβύλαις, cf. 946.

1136. διεσφαίριζε] Nonnus 43, 51, πολυστροφάλιγγι δὲ ριπῇ
ὄρθιον ἐσφαίρωσεν ἐς ἀέρα δίζυγα χηλήν (cf. 740).

Philostratus, under the title Βάκχαι, describes a picture
which had for its subject the revels on Cithaeron; I extract
his account of that portion of the painting in which the death
of Pentheüs was represented (εἰκόνες I, 18, p. 394 = 790):

γέγραπται μέν, ὦ παῖ, καὶ τὰ ἐν τῷ Κιθαιρῶνι, Βακχῶν χοροὶ καὶ
ὑποινοι πέτραι καὶ νέκταρ ἐκ βοτρύων καὶ ὡς γάλακτι τὴν βῶλον ἡ γῆ
λιπαίνει, καὶ ἰδού, κιττὸς ἕρπει καὶ ὄφεις ὀρθοὶ καὶ θύρσοι καὶ δένδρα,
οἶμαι, μέλι στάζοντα. καὶ ἥδε σοι ἡ ἐλάτη χαμαὶ γυναικῶν ἔργον ἐκ
Διονύσου μέγα, πέπτωκε δὲ τὸν Πενθέα ἀποσεισαμένη ταῖς Βάκχαις ἐν
εἴδει λέοντος, αἱ δὲ καὶ ξαίνουσι τὸ θήραμα μήτηρ ἐκείνη καὶ ἀδελφαὶ
μητρὸς αἱ μὲν ἀπορρηγνῦσαι τὰς χεῖρις, ἡ δὲ ἐπισπῶσα τὸν υἱὸν τῆς
χαίτης. εἴποις δ᾽ ἄν, ὡς καὶ ἀλαλάζουσιν, οὕτως εὔιον αὐταῖς τὸ ἆσθμα.
Διόνυσος δὲ αὐτὸς μὲν ἐν περιωπῇ τούτων ἕστηκεν ἐμπλήσας τὴν παρειὰν
χόλου, τὸν δὲ οἶστρον προσβακχεύσας ταῖς γυναιξίν· οὔτε ὁρῶσι γοῦν τὰ
δρώμενα, καὶ ὁπόσα ἱκετεύει ὁ Πενθεύς, λέοντος ἀκούειν φασὶ βρυχωμένου.

On the death of Pentheus as a theme of ancient art, see the
descriptions of the illustrations, printed on p. cvii ff. of the *Introd.*

1139. οὐ ῥᾴδιον ζήτημα] For the acc. in apposition to the
previous sentence, cf. 1100.

1140. Hor. *Sat.* 2, 3, 304, *quid? caput abscissum demens
cum portat Agave nati infelicis sibi tum furiosa videtur.*
Agave with the head of Pentheus is a not unfrequent subject in
works of ancient art; she is generally represented as grasping it
by the hair, instead of holding it aloft transfixed on the point of
her thyrsus as in the present passage. See woodcut on p. 73.

1144. *Antiatt.* p. 87, 29. γαυριᾶν· καὶ τοῦτο μέμφονται. Δημ.
περὶ τοῦ στεφάνου, Εὐρ. Βάκχαις. This may be a careless reference either to γαυρουμένη here or to γαυρούμενος in 1241, or else
some actual part of γαυριᾶν may have been used in the lost
portion of the play (*infra* 1300).—Attius *Bacch.* fr. XVII (3),
quanta in venando adfecta est laetitudine.

1146. 'Her fellow-huntsman, who had shared victorious
A chase where tears are all the victor's meed.' The MS has ᾗ
(referring to ἄγρας), for which Schöne (after Heath) proposed
ᾗ, referring to Agave. He objects to the manuscript reading on
the ground that it throws together the words τὸν ξυνεργάτην ἄγρας
τὸν καλλίνικον which ought (as he thinks) to be taken separately,

but it may be remarked that if we remove τὸν καλλίνικον from τὸν ξυνεργάτην ἄγρας, we leave the latter not sufficiently distinguished in sense from τὸν ξυγκύναγον.—δάκρυα is acc.

1150. 'But sober sense, and awe of things divine,
I deem the noblest course, and wisest too,
For mortals who indeed that path pursue.'

σοφώτατον κτῆμα, which is accepted by Nauck and Dindorf (from Orion), seems to me less intelligible than the manuscript reading χρῆμα.—The concluding lines of this brilliant ῥῆσις may strike some readers as tame by comparison with the rest of the speech; but we here find the same law holding good as that which has been observed in the speeches of the Attic Orators, where the part immediately *before* the peroration is marked by an outburst of eloquence which in the present instance finds its climax in the words ᾗ δάκρυα νικηφορεῖ, while the conclusion itself is characterized by a calm and severe self-control (cf. note on Ar. *Rhet.* III 19 § 1 in Cope's ed.). 'In a Greek speech,... wherever pity, terror, anger, or any passionate feeling is uttered or invited, this tumult is resolved in a final calm; and where such tumult has place in the peroration, it subsides before the last sentences of all.' Jebb's *Attic Orators*, I p. ciii.

1153. Elmsley ingeniously suggests that the part of Agave as well as that of the 'Second Messenger' may have been assigned to the same actor, and that the short chorus following may have been introduced to give him time to change his dress. In any case, it is clearly a dramatic gain for the messenger to retire before Agave appears, as he would otherwise either become a κωφὸν πρόσωπον, or be compelled to enter into a tedious dialogue with Agave, at a point in the play when the interest of the spectator is excited to the highest pitch.

1157. πιστὸν "Αιδαν] This is explained to mean 'a sure pledge of doom,' and as parallels Schoene quotes *Ag.* 1086, δίκτυον "Αιδου (of the garment in which Agamemnon was entangled when he received his death-blow), and Soph. *Ant.* 1190, νυμφεῖον "Αιδου κοῖλον (of the vault in which Antigone was imprisoned). But the difficulty is really in the word πιστὸν, which.

in such a connexion, has no parallel except Homer's σῶς αἰ‑
πὺς ὄλεθρος, *Il.* 13, 773 (quoted by Mr Tyrrell). κόσμον Ἄιδου
might be suggested by 857 ; but, though this would suit τὰν
θηλυγενῆ στολὰν, it is less applicable to the νάρθηξ with which
it is more closely connected ; βάκτρον Ἄιδου would be less open
to objection, as the Bacchic wand is called κισσίνου βάκτρου
in 363. If an adj. is preferred, προῦπτον Ἄιδαν (suggested by
O. C. 1440) would make better sense than πιστόν. Mr Tyrrell
proposes ἐπακτὸν Αἴδαν (a doom brought on one's self). κέντρον
Ἄιδου might also be proposed as not inapplicable to the ταῦρος
mentioned below ; the 'ferule with fair shaft' is in the hands
of Pentheus a 'fatal ox-goad' before which the phantom form
of the bull Dionysus advances, leading him onward to his doom
(cf. 920). Cf. Nonnus, 14, 243, κέντωρ θύρσος, and *anon.* in
Etymologicum magnum (MS Flor.) κέντορι Βασσαρίδων. For
προηγητῆρα, Eur. fragm. 813, τυφλὸν...προηγητῆρος ἐξηρτημένον.

1161. τὸν καλλίνικον] sc. ὕμνον. *H. F.* 180 ; Pind. *Ol.* 9, 3 ; *Nem.*
4, 16. 'Glorious is the triumph-song which ye have achieved,
ending in wailing and tears ; 'tis goodly sport to bathe the
hand in the blood of a son till it drips again*.' **1166.** ἐν διαστρό‑
φοις ὅσσοις] a peculiar use of ἐν where σύν might have been
expected, or where no preposition need have been used. Some‑
thing like it is found in Soph. *Phil.* 60, σ' ἐν λιταῖς στείλαντες,
ib. 102, ἐν δόλῳ ἄγειν, *Trach.* 886 (θάνατου ἀνύσασα) ἐν τομᾷ
σιδήρου (Kühner *Gk. Gr.* § 431 p. 404).

1168. For ὀρθοῖς (used in frag. 337, τί μ' ἄρτι πημάτων
λελησμένην ὀρθοῖς ;) Hermann proposes τί μ' ὀροθύνεις ὦ ; The
Epic word ὀροθύνειν is found in Aesch. *P. V.* 200.

1169. 'Lo! from the mountain we bring to the hall a shoot
but newly cut, our happy quarry.' The mother in her frenzy
mistakes the head of her son for a freshly-cut branch of ivy
or vine. This passage is famous in connexion with the his‑
torical anecdote told by Plutarch, *Crassus* 32, 33 :—[The Par‑
thian general] Surena sent the head and hand of Crassus to
Hydrodes in Armenia'... (c. 33) 'When the head of Crassus
was brought to the door, the tables were taken away, and an
actor of tragedies, Jason by name, a native of Tralles, chanted

* See *Supplementary Note.*

that part of the Bacchae of Euripides which relates to Agáve. While he was receiving applause, Sillaces, standing by the door of the apartment, and making a reverence, threw the head of Crassus before the company. The Parthians clapped their hands with shouts of joy, and the attendants, at the command of the king, made Sillaces sit down, while Jason handed over to one of the members of the chorus the dress of Pentheus, and laying hold of the head of Crassus, and putting on the air of a bacchant (ἀναβακχεύσας), he sang these verses with great enthusiasm :—

> φέρομεν ἐξ ὄρεος
> ἕλικα νεότομον ἐπὶ μέλαθρα
> μακαρίαν θήραν.

This delighted all the company ; and while the following verses were being chanted, which are a dialogue with the chorus,

A. τίς ἐφόνευσεν ;   B. ἐμὸν τὸ γέρας,

Pomaxathres [the Parthian who had killed Crassus] springing up (for he happened to be at the banquet), laid hold of the head, deeming it more appropriate for *him* to say this than for Jason. The king was pleased, and made Pomaxathres a present, according to the fashion of the country, and he gave Jason a talent. In such a farce (ἐξόδιον) as this, it is said, that the expedition of Crassus terminated, just like a tragedy' (George Long's transl., slightly altered).

1180. **μάκαιρ' 'Αγαύη**] Sen. *fragm. Phoen.* 1, *Felix Agave : facinus horrendum manu Qua fecerat gestavit ut spolium caput Cruenta nati Maenas in partes dati.* If μάκαιρ' 'Αγαύη is assigned to the chorus, we must understand the sense to be continued in the reply **κληζόμεθ' ἐν θιάσοις**, ' so they call me amid the revellers.'

1185. 'The whelp is yet young and is just blooming with a downy cheek beneath its crest of delicate hair.' It is either this passage, or part of the description of Dionysus in l. 235, that is translated by Attius *Bacch.* 8, *ei lanugo flora nunc* [*genas*] *demum inrigat.* Nonnus 46, 201, δέρκεο ταῦτα γένεια νεότριχα. Philostratus in his account of the picture already referred to

(1139 n.), describes the head of Pentheus as νεωτάτη καὶ ἁπαλὴ τὴν γένυν καὶ πυρσὴ τὰς κόμας.

θάλλει is Musgrave's conjecture for βάλλει, which is intelligible in itself (= ἐκβάλλει, φύει, 'putting forth,' Paley), though I cannot find an exact parallel. For the general sense, cf. Aesch. *S. C. T.* 534, στείχει δ' ἴουλος ἄρτι διὰ παρηίδων, ὥρας φυούσης, ταρφὺς ἀντέλλουσα θρίξ. Pindar has δένδρε' (acc.) ἔθαλλε χῶρος, *Ol.* 3, 23.

1192. ὁ γὰρ ἄναξ ἀγρεύς] 'For the king (Dionysus) is a very captor,' referring perhaps to Dionysus Ζαγρεύς, cf. fragm. quoted on l. 74.

1195. It seems unnatural to assign to the chorus this reference to Pentheus; exultant as they are at the death of the king, they are not so heartless as to feel no pity for the mother who has unconsciously caused his death. They call her τλάμων in 1184, and τάλαινα in 1200.

1197. περισσὰν περισσῶς] *Cho.* 'booty strange.' *Ag.* 'in strangest wise.'   **1204.** θηρὸς depends on ἦν (ἄγραν).

1205. 'Not with the looped darts of Thessaly.' Θεσσαλῶν γὰρ εὕρημα τὸ δόρυ (Schol. on *Hipp.* 221, Θεσσαλὸν ὄρπακα). *Or.* 1477, ἀγκύλας...ἐν χεροῖν ἔχων (where the thong of the javelin, *amentum*, is used for the javelin itself). Aesch. *fragm.* 14, καὶ παλτὰ κἀγκύλητα καὶ χλῆδον βαλών, poet. ap. Ath. 534 Ε, ἔρως κεραυνὸν ἠγκυλημένος. "The two ends of the strap were tied round the shaft several times and arranged in a loop, through which the fingers were put (διηγκυλωμένοι, Ovid, *Met.* 12, 326, *inserit amento digitos*). At the moment of throwing the spear the loop was pulled violently, by means of which the strap, in being unwound, conveyed to the spear a rotating movement, similar to that of the missiles of our rifled guns" (Guhl and Koner, *Life of the Gks. and Romans*, p. 242).

1206. λευκοπήχεσι χειρῶν ἀκμαῖσι] a somewhat redundantly ornate phrase for 'the fingers of our fair hands.' *Phoen.* 1351, λευκοπήχεις κτύπους χεροῖν, where the adj. logically belongs to the genitive, as in Aesch. *Cho.* 21, ὀξύχειρ κτύπος = κτύπος ὀξὺς χειρῶν (Kühner, *Gk. Gr.* § 402, 3).

S. B.   15

1207. κᾆτα κομπάζειν χρεὼν καὶ λογχοποιῶν ὄργανα κτᾶσθαι μάτην;]
Nauck, feeling the difficulty of κομπάζειν, transposes μάτην and
χρεών (cf. *Hipp.* 978, κομπάζων μάτην), but an easier, and, I
venture to think, a more conclusive correction would be to
suppose that ΚΔΙΤΑΚΟΜΠΑΖΕΙΝ is an error of the copyist for
κᾆτ' ἀκοντίζειν, ΚΔΙΤΑΚΟΝΤΙΖΕΙΝ. 'Must one then hurl the dart,
and get one armourers' weapons, all in vain? Why *we*' (in
contrast to those who hunt with darts and lances with such
poor success) 'have, with the bare hand alone, captured our
quarry and torn his limbs asunder.' The general sense however may simply be (as maintained in Wecklein's review) 'what
avails all the boasting in brazen weapons? *Our* deed has
turned the prowess of armed men into an idle boast.'

1210. χωρὶς intensifies the idea of separation in διεφορήσαμεν.
θηρὸς however is open to suspicion, as, if expressed at all, we
should have expected it in the former clause (cf. however 781—
2). χωρὶς σιδήρου τ' has been suggested with much probability.
But χωρὶς has already been used adverbially in 1137.

1212. Πενθεύς τ' ἐμὸς παῖς ποῦ 'στιν;] ' C'est le trait de notre
Thyeste, s'écriant, l'horrible coupe dans la main ....*mais cepen-
dant je ne vois point mon fils*' (Patin, *Eur.* II 261).

1213—5. *Phoen.* 489, προσφέρων πύργοισι πηκτῶν κλιμάκων
προσαμβάσεις. Nonnus 44, 78, σὺ δὲ σύμβολα παιδὸς Ἀγαύης
πῆξον ἀριστοπόνοιο τεοῦ προπάροιθε μελάθρου, 46, 230, παρὰ
προπύλαια δὲ Κάδμου πήξατε τοῦτο κάρηνον, ἐμῆς ἀναθήματα νίκης.
'The marble *lion-head* antefixa, which terminate the northern
angles of the western pediments of the Parthenon, and are
usual ornaments in other parts of such a building, indicate
that Euripides has not neglected one of the most pathetic
features of madness—its partial saneness and sense of pro-
priety,' Wordsworth's *Athens and Attica,* p. 100, where Vitr. 3,
in cymis *capita leonina sunt scalpenda*, is quoted.—For the
custom of setting up the spoils of the chase, or the heads of
slaughtered enemies, outside a building, cf. *Iph. T.* 73—5, ἐξ
αἱμάτων γοῦν ξάνθ' ἔχει θριγκώματα, θριγκοῖς δ' ὑπ' αὐτοῖς σκῦλ'
ὁρᾷς ἠρτημένα ; τῶν κατθανόντων γ' ἀκροθίνια ξένων, Aesch. *Ag.*
578, θεοῖς λάφυρα ταῦτα τοῖς καθ' Ἑλλάδα δόμοις ἐπασσάλευσαν
ἀρχαῖον γάνος. Eur. is probably thinking of the parts between·

* *simis* p. 82, 25 ed. Rose.

the triglyphs, the square spaces known as metopes, and usually
adorned with images in relief, representations of ζῷα, which
led to this part of the entablature being called the ζωφόρος.
It has however been suggested that, owing to the reference
to the nailing up of the head, *wooden* triglyphs are here meant,
and this is all the more probable as the triglyphs were originally nothing more than vertically fluted beam-ends, while the
metopes were the vacant spaces between. *Iph. T.* 113, εἴσω
τριγλύφων ὅποι κενόν, and *Or.* 1366, πέφευγα...κεδρωτὰ παστάδων
ὑπὲρ τέρεμνα Δωρικάς τε τριγλύφους (Müller's *Ancient Art,*
§ 52, 3).

1216. ἄθλιον βάρος] Also used by Soph., in *El.* 1140, of
the remains of Orestes.

1218. In support of the perhaps unnecessary alteration
μόχθων, for μοχθῶν, Wecklein quotes *Iph. A.* 1230, Aesch. *P. V.*
900, and Soph. *Ai.* 888, in all which passages the possessive
genitive πόνων is used in a 'qualitative' sense.

1221. ὕλη...δυσευρέτῳ] 'the trackless wood,' a more poetic
reading than Reiske's δυσεύρετον, or Hermann's δυσευρέτως
(an adverb like δυσεκλύτως in Aesch. *P. V.* 60).

1226. κατθανόντα being virtually the passive of κατακτείνω
(which has no aor. pass. of its own in good Greek) is naturally
followed by Μαινάδων ὕπο.—**1229.** δρυμοῖς] For the oak copses
of Mount Cithaeron, cf. 685.

1231. *Iph. T.* 520, ἔστιν γὰρ οὕτως οὐδ' ἄκραντ' ἠκούσατε.—
1232. ὄψιν οὐκ εὐδαίμονα] in apposition to λεύσσω αὐτὴν (*Orest.*
727) Scaliger's excellent correction of the prosaic αὐτῆς.—**1236,**
Cf. 118.

1240. ὡς ἂν κρεμασθῇ] Hermann's proposal ὡς ἀγκρεμασθῇ gives us the same constr. as in 1214, ὡς πασσαλεύσῃ. Cf.
fragm. 270 *Erechth.* πέλταν πρὸς Ἀθήνας περικίοσιν ἀγκρεμάσας
θαλάμοις. Hermann's objection to the ordinary text is that ἂν is
out of place, *ut in re minime dubia.* "Mihi nondum exploratum
est," replies Matthiae, "ἂν in dubiis tantum rebus coniunctivo
addi. supra v. 483 verba ὡς ἂν σκότιον εἰσορᾷ κνέφας reddere
nolim cum Hermanno, *ut, si libet, tenebras adspiciat.* nam
qui in obscuro carcere inclusus est, tenebras adspicere debet."

15—2

sive ei libeat, sive non libeat. et hoc loco negare tamen poterat pater, quod filia petebat."

1251. δύσκολον] 'crabbed'; the line is quoted by Stobaeus.

1253—5. εὔθηρος εἴη...ὅτ'...θηρῶν ὀριγνῷτ'] 'Oh that my son might be as lucky as his mother whene'er amid (a troop of) Theban youths he goes a hunting.' "Quum dicit ὀριγνῷτο, non ὀριγνᾶται, ipso verbi modo indicat, non esse Pentheum venationis studiosum. itaque non opus habuit adiicere, *at ille non it* venatum" (Hermann). The optative is found, as here, dependent on an optative expressing a wish, in Aesch. *Eum.* 297, ἔλθοι...ὅπως γένοιτο τῶνδ' ἐμοὶ λυτήριος, Soph. *Ajax*, 522, γενοίμαν...ὅπως προσείποιμεν, *Trach.* 955, εἴθε γένοιτ'...αὔρα, ἥτις μ' ἀποικίσειεν, and Eur. *Hel.* 433. Eur. sometimes violates this rule, as in *Ion*, 672, εἴη...ὡς μοι γένηται, where subj. follows the opt. of prayer, and in *Hel.* 176, πέμψειεν ἵνα λάβῃ (R. Shilleto). —At the end of the line ἅμα is redundant after ἐν; so in *Ion*, 716, ἅμα σὺν βάκχαις. **1255.** For θεομαχεῖν, cf. 325.

1257. [*Hel.* 435, τίς ἂν...μόλοι, ὅστις διαγγέλειε...] Shilleto *adv.*

1259. φρονήσασαι ['when ye come to your senses,' Plat. *Phaedr.* 231 D, ὥστε πῶς ἂν εὖ φρονήσαντες ταῦτα καλῶς ἔχειν ἡγήσαιντο] Shilleto *adv.*

1264—70. Cadmus begins by making trial of Agave's outward senses: he finds that her sense of sight is becoming true again, as her clouded vision passes away, and the sky seems brighter to her than before; he next leads her on, step by step, till her inward sense returns, and she is at last conscious that the head she is holding in her hand is that of her own son.

1267. καὶ διιπετέστερος, ἀντὶ τοῦ διαυγέστερος (*Etym. Magn.* referring to this passage). In Homer διιπετής is an epithet applied to rivers alone (*Il.* 16, 174; 17, 263; 21, 268 and 326; *Od.* 4, 477), 'fed by, swollen with, rain from heaven.' Here Euripides, while keeping the Homeric quantity of the second syllable, departs from the Homeric meaning of the word. He might easily have written κἄτι διαφανέστερος instead. The word is also found in an obscure fragm. of Eur. 812, διιπετῆ κτείναι, and in *Rhes.* 43, διιπετῆ δὲ νεῶν πυρσοῖς σταθμὰ, while Erotianus, *gloss. Hippocr.*, explains it διαυγὴς καὶ καθαρός. (On this and other Homeric words apparently misused by Attic poets, προθέλυμνος, ἔμπαιος, ἀμφίγυος, see Shilleto in *Journal of Cl. and S. Philology*, IV 315—8.) The following fragment of the *Bacchae* of Attius was supposed by Scaliger to be a careless rendering of the present line, XVIII (15),...*splendet saepe, ast idem nimbis interdum nigret.*—**1268.** τὸ πτοηθὲν, cf. 214, ὡς ἐπτόηται.

1269—70. As the symmetry of the στιχομυθία is broken by Agave replying in two lines instead of one only, it has been proposed to strike out the second and read γιγνώσκω δέ πως in the first; but it is worth while suggesting, that the exceptional length of her reply, which was probably delivered very slowly, is intended to express the gradual dawning of her slowly return-, ing senses.

1274. On σπαρτῷ, which is to be taken with ὡς λέγουσι, see note on 264.

1281. ἄθρησον κ.τ.λ.] 'Now scan it keenly and more clearly mark it.' ἀθρεῖν is used of earnest gaze, and thus denotes an advance in emphasis on the preceding synonyms, σκέψαι, εἰσιδεῖν, λεύσσω. G. Curtius *Gk. Etymology*, book I § 13, has some interesting pages on several of the Greek words for 'sight,' as distinguished from one another by the aid of Comparative Philology.

1283. προσεικέναι] for the manuscript reading προσεοικέναι, is also found in Ar. *Eccl.* 1161; among the other parts used in Attic Greek are ἔοιγμεν, εἴξασιν and εἰκώς (see Veitch, *Gk. Verbs*).

1285. The MS has οἰμωγμένον, which is best corrected into ᾠμωγμένον, i.e. 'bewailed by me ere *thou* couldst recognise it.' Musgrave (followed by Nauck) has ἠμαγμένον, which seems less easy to understand. **1286.** *Heracl.* 931, χεῖρας ἵξεσθαι σέθεν.

1287. ἐν ου καιρῷ=ἀκαίρως, cf. οὐ πάλης ὕπο, 455; Thuc. 3, 95, τὴν οὐ—περιτείχισιν, 5, 50, τὴν οὐκ—ἐξουσίαν, 7, 34, τὴν τῶν Κορινθίων οὐκέτι ἐπαναγωγὴν (Kühner *Gk. Gr.* § 461, 6 *d*); also without the article, as in *Hipp.* 196 quoted on l. 455.

1288. τὸ μέλλον is acc. either 'of respect,' or after the transi-

tive sense implied in καρδία πήδημ' ἔχει. Cf. Aesch. *Ag.* 788,
'Ιλίου φθοράς...ψήφους ἔθεντο = ἐψηφίσαντο,—Soph. *Trach.* 997,
οἴαν μ' ἄρ' ἔθου λώβαν,—*O. C.* 583, τὰ δ' ἐν μέσῳ ἢ λῇστιν ἴσχεις
ἢ δι' οὐδενὸς ποιῇ,—Eur. *H. F.* 709, ἃ χρῆν σε μετρίως σπουδὴν
ἔχειν, *Or.* 1069, ἐν μὲν πρῶτά σοι μομφὴν ἔχω,—*Ion* 572, τοῦτο
κἄμ' ἔχει πόθος (Kühner *Gk. Gr.* § 411, 4). To these may be
added Soph. *El.* 123—5, τίν' ἀεὶ τάκεις οἰμωγὰν...'Αγαμέμνονα;
Dem. p. 53, 11, p. 366, 26, τεθνήκασι δέει τοὺς Φιλίππου ξένους.

1291. Cf. 337.—**1295.** ἐμάνητε...ἐξεβακχεύθη, cf. 36, ἐξέμηνα.
[*Suppl.* 1001, ἐκβακχευσαμένα, Plato VIII *Rep.* 561 A, ἐκβακχευθῇ]
Shilleto *adv.* **1296.** ἄρτι μανθάνω] *Alc.* 940.

1300. ἐν ἄρθροις συγκεκλημένον] Cf. Philostratus εἰκόνες I § 18
(Βάκχαι), (after passage quoted on l. 1139) ταῦτα μὲν τὰ ἐν τῷ
ὄρει, τὰ δὲ ἐγγὺς ταῦτα, Θῆβαι ἤδη καὶ Κάδμου στέγη καὶ θρῆνος ἐπὶ
τῇ ἄγρᾳ καὶ συναρμόττουσιν οἱ προσήκοντες τὸν νεκρόν, εἴ πη
σωθείη τῷ τάφῳ. At this point a line is lost containing the reply
of Cadmus, as was first pointed out by Matthiae.—**1303.** συνῆψε]
sc. ὁ θεός.—**1305.** ἄτεκνος ἀρσένων παίδων] *Phoen.* 324, ἄπεπλος
φαρέων λευκῶν.—**1306.** τόδ' ἔρνος κατθανόνθ'] constr. κατὰ σύνεσιν,
Troad. 740, ὦ φίλτατ', ὦ περισσὰ τιμηθεὶς τέκνον.

1308. ἀνέβλεφ'] Elmsley's correction for ἀνέβλεπεν, which
would give us an anapaest in the third place, as a short vowel
before βλ is always lengthened except in the case of βλαστάνω
and its derivatives. In *fragm.* 1002, τὸ μὲν τέθνηκε σῶμα· τοῦτο
δ' ἀναβλέπει is altered by Cobet and Nauck into αὖ βλέπει,
which is better than ἀμβλέπει. The short vowel apparently
remains short in Ar. *Vesp.* 570, τὰ δὲ συγκύπτονθ' ἅμα βληχᾶται,
where however Shilleto would read ἀμβληχᾶται, or βληχᾶται
alone. In the Tragic poets there are thirty-three instances (in
Eur. alone twenty-four) of the short vowel being lengthened
in compounds before βλ; ten instances in which the vowel
of the augment or of reduplication is lengthened before βλ,
as against three in which it is left short (S. *Phil.* 1311, *El.* 440,
and *fragm.* 491); twice is a short vowel lengthened before βλ in
the middle of a word, once only left short (Aesch. *Supp.* 761,

βύβλου); lastly, the short vowel is eighteen times lengthened before βλ in the following word, and only five times left short, Aesch. *Suppl.* 317, Soph. *O. T.* 717, *O. C.* 972, *fragm.* 124, 491.

The accurate study of the lengthening of short vowels before combinations of mutes and liquids in Greek Iambics has been much advanced by the Rev. H. E. Savage's elaborate tables of statistics printed in the *Memoranda* of the Cambridge Philological Society for May 9, 1878, from which the numerical statements above quoted are borrowed.

1308—9. ὃς συνεῖχες, ὦ τέκνον, τοὐμὸν μέλαθρον] cf. 392 ; *Iph. T.* 57, στῦλοι γὰρ οἴκων εἰσὶ παῖδες ἄρσενες ; Pliny *Ep.* 4, 21, 3, *unus ex tribus liberis superest domumque pluribus adminiculis paulo ante fundatam desolatus fulcit ac sustinet*, Virg. *Aen.* 12, 59.

1312. Those who keep δίκην ἐλάμβανεν are compelled to render it : 'he (sc. any one who insulted me) got his deserts.' This involves an interchange of δίκην λαμβάνειν, which is generally used of the person who punishes, with δίκην διδόναι, which is the corresponding term for the person punished. Another instance of the exceptional use is found in Hdt. I, 115, εἰς ὃ ἔλαβε τὴν δίκην. But it would seem better on the whole to print ἐλάμβανες. 'No one ever dared to insult me, while he saw your presence, for you were certain to exact from him the proper penalty' (=ἔμελλες λαμβάνειν). δίκην διδόναι is frequently used by Eur. in its ordinary sense, and we have already had it twice in this play (479, 847); again, in a recently discovered fragment attributed to him, δίκην λαμβάνειν is used in the opposite meaning (papyrus edited by Weil and Blass l. 7, ἐκεῖνος εἰ μὲν μεῖζον ἠδίκηκέ τι, οὐκ ἐμὲ προσήκει λαμβάνειν τούτων δίκην). It is therefore extremely improbable that the poet interchanged the two senses in the present passage.

1315. Cf. note on 264.—**1317.** τῶν φιλτάτων ἀριθμήσει] For the gen., cf. Hor. *Ep.* I 9, 13, *scribe tui gregis hunc.*—**1327.** [vid. Elmsl., aliter *Androm.* 1063] Shilleto *adv.*

1329. After this line there is a considerable *lacuna* in the MS, only one line of Agave's speech having been preserved, and the earlier part of the speech of Dionysus being also lost. This was first indicated by Tyrwhitt, who pointed out that the verse cited from the *Bacchae* by the scholiast in Ar. *Plut.* 907, εἰ μὴ γὰρ ἴδιον ἔλαβον εἰς χεῖρας μύσος, must have been part of the lost speech of Agave. We gather the purport of that speech from two references to it in the rhetorician Apsines, *Rhet. Gr.* I p. 399 ed. Spengel (= IX p. 587 ed. Walz, where the treatise according to Ruhnken's view is ascribed to Longinus), ἔτι κινήσομεν ἔλεον αὐτοὶ κατηγοροῦντες ἑαυτῶν. τοῦτό ἐστι μὲν εὑρεῖν καὶ παρὰ τοῖς τραγικοῖς ποιηταῖς, ἀμέλει παρὰ τῷ Εὐριπίδῃ ἡ τοῦ Πενθέως μήτηρ Ἀγαυὴ ἀπαλλαγεῖσα τῆς μανίας καὶ γνωρίσασα τὸν παῖδα τὸν ἑαυτῆς διεσπασμένον κατηγορεῖ μὲν αὐτῆς, ἔλεον δὲ κινεῖ. Also p. 401 Sp (= 590 W), τοῦτον τὸν τόπον κεκίνηκεν Εὐριπίδης οἶκτον ἐπὶ τῷ Πενθεῖ κινῆσαι βουλόμενος. ἕκαστον γὰρ αὐτοῦ τῶν μελῶν ἡ μήτηρ ἐν ταῖς χερσὶ κρατοῦσα καθ' ἕκαστον αὐτῶν οἰκτίζεται (he also refers to Hecuba's speech over the dead body of Astyanax, *Tro.* 807). The compiler of the *Christus Patiens* appears to have had the speech in the MS which he used, as several lines are to be found in his *cento* which cannot be traced to any of the other plays from which he borrowed, but which are particularly suitable to such a speech as that described by Apsines. Two of these were detected by Porson (*Kidd's Tracts*, p. 169), καὶ πῶς νιν ἡ δύστηνος εὐλαβουμένη πρὸς στέρνα θῶμαι; τίνα (*sic*) θρηνήσω τρόπον. George Burges, who made preparations towards editing the play and allowed Elmsley to have access to his proposed recension of the text*,wrote two sets of Greek verses, of slight critical value, to fill up the *lacuna* (they may be seen in the *Gentleman's Magazine* for Sept. and Dec. 1832). A partial endeavour to restore the loss was afterwards made by Hartung, *Euripides Restitutus* II (1844) p. 556; but it was reserved for Kirchhoff to found, on a careful examination of the *Christus Patiens*, a more systematic restoration of the lost portion (*Philologus* (1853) 8, 78—93). In the 34 more or less complete verses which he prints, there is much that can hardly have been written by Euripides, and one of his fragmentary lines from the *Chr. Pat.* 1473, πᾶσαν ἡματωμένην, cannot have belonged to this portion of the play as it is obvi-

* See p. 265—7.

ously borrowed from l. 1135, πᾶσα δ' ἡματωμένη. ,His restoration
has been judiciously revised (with considerable retrenchments)
by Wecklein in his recent edition (1879). Wecklein's first line
(which is not accepted by Kirchhoff) is taken from a passage in
Lucian, *Piscator* § 2 (first pointed out by Musgrave), but it does
not necessarily refer to the *Bacchae*, and is quite as applicable to
the fate of Orpheus as to that of Pentheus : καὶ μὴν ἄριστον ἦν
καθάπερ τινὰ Πενθέα ἢ Ὀρφέα λακιστὸν ἐν πέτραισιν εὑρέσθαι
μόρον.

1330. The mutilated remainder of Dionysus' speech begins
with a prophecy of the transformation of Cadmus and Harmonia
into serpents. In another play, Eur. actually represented on the
stage the commencement of the change, as is shewn by the
following somewhat ludicrous lines, *fragm.* 922, οἴμοι, δράκων
μοι γίγνεται τὸ γ' ἥμισυ· τέκνον, περιπλάκηθι τῷ λοιπῷ πατρί.
Cf. Ovid *Met.* 4, 584, *me tange manumque accipe dum manus
est, dum non totum occupat anguis;* and Milton *P. L.* 9, 505,
*never since of serpent kind Lovelier, not those that in Illyria
changed, Hermione* (sic) *and Cadmus.*

The close of Philostratus' description of the picture of the
revels in Cithaeron (εἰκόνες 1 § 18, already quoted in part on
1139) shews that he had in mind the above fragment, as well as
the lost line restored above from the Schol. on Ar., εἰ μὴ γὰρ
ἴδιον ἔλαβον εἰς χείρας μύσος.

ἡ δ' Ἀγαυὴ περιβάλλειν μὲν τὸν υἱὸν ὥρμηκε, θιγεῖν δὲ ὀκνεῖ. προσμέ-
μικται δ' αὐτῇ τὸ τοῦ παιδὸς αἷμα τὸ μὲν ἐς χεῖρας, τὸ δὲ ἐς παρειάν, τὸ δὲ
ἐς τὰ γυμνὰ τοῦ μαζοῦ. ἡ δὲ Ἁρμονία καὶ ὁ Κάδμος εἰσὶ μέν, ἀλλ' οὐχ
οἵπερ ἦσαν, δράκοντε γὰρ ἤδη ἐκ μηρῶν γίγνονται, καὶ φολὶς αὐτοὺς ἤδη
ἔχει, φροῦδοι πόδες, φροῦδοι γλουτοί, καὶ ἡ μεταβολὴ τοῦ εἴδους ἕρπει ἄνω.
οἱ δὲ ἐκπλήττονται καὶ περιβάλλουσιν ἀλλήλους, οἷον ξυνέχοντες τὰ λοιπὰ
τοῦ σώματος, ὡς ἐκεῖνα γοῦν αὐτοὺς μὴ φύγοι.

1333. ὄχον δὲ μόσχων] First explained by Musgrave, who
quoted the following passage of the *Etym. Magn.*, Βουθόη· πόλις
Ἰλλυρίδος· εἴρηται ὅτι Κάδμος ἐπὶ βοῶν ζεύγους ἐκ Θηβῶν ταχέως
(sc. θοῶς) εἰς Ἰλλυρικοὺς παραγενόμενος ἔκτισε πόλιν. The legendary city founded by Cadmus is still called *Budua* (in Dalmatia
near Montenegro).

1334. βαρβάρων, sc. the tribe of *Encheleis.* On the legend of Cadmus, so far as referred to in the latter part of this play, cf. Apollodorus III 5, 4, ὁ δὲ Κάδμος μετὰ Ἀρμονίας Θήβας ἐκλιπὼν πρὸς Ἐγχελέας παραγίνεται. τούτοις δὲ ὑπὸ Ἰλλυριῶν πολεμουμένοις, ὁ θεὸς ἔχρησεν Ἰλλυριῶν κρατήσειν, ἐὰν ἡγέμονα Κάδμον καὶ Ἀρμονίαν ἔχωσι· οἱ δὲ πεισθέντες ποιοῦνται κατὰ Ἰλλυριῶν ἡγεμόνας τούτους καὶ κρατοῦσι· καὶ βασιλεύει Κάδμος Ἰλλυριῶν .. αὖθις δὲ μετὰ Ἀρμονίας εἰς δράκοντα μεταβαλὼν εἰς Ἠλύσιον πεδίον ὑπὸ Διὸς ἐξεπέμφθησαν.—**1336.** The plundering of the shrine of Delphi, which was fated to bring destruction on the plunderers, is referred to in Herod. 9, 41, ἔστι λόγιον ὡς χρεών ἐστι Πέρσας ἀπικομένους ἐς τὴν Ἑλλάδα διαρπάσαι τὸ ἱρὸν τὸ ἐν Δελφοῖσι, μετὰ δὲ τὴν διαρπαγὴν ἀπολέσθαι πάντας...τοῦτον δ᾽ ἔγωγε τὸν χρησμὸν, τὸν Μαρδόνιος εἶπε ἐς Πέρσας ἔχειν, ἐς Ἰλλυριούς τε καὶ τὸν Ἐγχελέων στρατὸν οἶδα πεποιημένον, ἀλλ᾽ οὐκ ἐς Πέρσας.

1341—3. εἰ σωφρονεῖν ἔγνωθ᾽...εὐδαιμονοῖτ᾽ ἄν] As the protasis contains εἰ with the aor. indic., the indicative aor. or impf. with ἄν would have been the normal construction ; accordingly it has been proposed to read εὐδαιμονεῖτ᾽ ἄν. This alteration however cannot be regarded as certain ; the optative refers to the future, and means, ' Still for all that, if you have the son of Zeus for your ally, you may *yet* be happy.' In other words, instead of using the impf. indic., which would have rudely told Agave that under certain circumstances she *might* have been happy, but is *not*, the god shews himself not a θεὸς δεινότατος alone, but also ἠπιώτατος (861), by referring to a future possibility of her being restored to happiness. Two conditional sentences, the first referring to the past and the second to the future, are here condensed into one, which may be expanded as follows : εἰ δὲ σωφρονεῖν ἔγνωτ᾽, ὅτ᾽ οὐκ ἠθέλετε, τὸν Διὸς γόνον σύμμαχον ἂν εἴχετ᾽, εἰ δ᾽ ἔχοιτέ νιν φίλον, εὐδαιμονοῖτ᾽ ἄν. In the text, the *apodosis* of the first is suppressed, and the true *protasis* of the second is expressed in the participle κεκτημένοι.

[exemplis ab Hermanno laudatis adde sis Soph. *Electr.* 797—8, πολλῶν ἂν ἥκοις, ὦ ξέν᾽, ἄξιος τυχεῖν, εἰ τήνδ᾽ ἔπαυσας τῆς πολυγλώσσου βοῆς. Plat. *Phaedr.* 251 A, καὶ εἰ μὴ δεδίει τὴν τῆς σφόδρα μανίας δόξαν, θύοι ἂν ὡς ἀγάλματι καὶ θεῷ τοῖς παιδικοῖς. ubi nollem editores nuperi monstrum illud, sane in libris paucis inventum, recepissent (δεδίει plusperfectum est indicativi, δεδιείη ad notissimum librariorum errorem refertur, η post ει temere irrepente). ceterum miror Hermannum, qui rectissime de reliquis disputavit, non hoc loco item optativum retinuisse. vult enim Bacchus id ostendere, posse etiam nunc Thebanos felicitate frui. quid sibi voluerit Matthiae parum intelligo. de Latinis cf. Plaut. *Mil. Glor.* IV 8, 46, 'etsi ita sententia *esset,* tibi servire *mavelim,*' cuius loci vim perspexit Lindemann] Shilleto *adv.* **1347.** Cf. 1298.

1345. ἤδετε] This is one of the three passages in the Greek drama, where editors follow Elmsley in admitting forms of the pluperfect with a short penultimate in the *first* or *second* person plural. The others are Ar. *Lys.* 1098, δεινά κα 'πεπόνθεμες, and Soph. *O. T.* 1232, ἤδεμεν, where there is no difficulty in retaining the reading of the MSS, ἤδειμεν. In the present instance, ἤδετε is an emendation, but it makes better sense than the manuscript reading εἴδετε. See G. Curtius, *On the Greek Verb,* p. 432 of translation by Wilkins and England.

1348. πρέπει...ούχ ὁμοιοῦσθαι] *hyperbaton* for οὐ πρέπει, otherwise μή might have been expected. [vid. Thucyd. VI 16] Shilleto *adv.* Cf. *Alc.* 682, *Hel.* 1448.

1350. δέδοκται...τλήμονες φυγαί] An Attic instance of what is called the *schema Pindaricum* (Pind. *Ol.* X 6, ἀρχαὶ λόγων τέλλεται, *Pyth.* X ult. κεῖται κυβερνάσιες, and *fragm.* 45 βάλλεται ...φόβαι. ἀχεῖται ὀμφαί,....χοροί). In Attic Greek, the use of the singular verb with the plural or dual subject is generally confined to the verbs εἶναι and γίγνεσθαι (e.g. Soph. *Trach.* 520, ἦν...κλίμακες, Eur. *Ion,* 1146, ἐνῆν...ὑφαί, Plato *Symp.* 118 B γίγνεται, *Rep.* 363 A, γίγνηται...,—also in *Gorg.* 500 D and Ar. *Vesp.* 58, ἔστι followed by dual). Cf. Plato *Theaet.* 173 D, σπουδαὶ δ' ἑταιρειῶν...καὶ σύνοδοι καὶ δεῖπνα καὶ σὺν αὐλητρίσι κῶμοι οὐδὲ ὄναρ πράττειν προσίσταται αὐτοῖς· In almost all the above examples, as here, the verb stands first. In the present instance the singular is probably used because of the awkwardness of the circumlocution δεδογμέναι εἰσὶν, especially as τλήμονες φυγαὶ is virtually equivalent to a singular in sense. As additional examples in *lyrical* passages, we have *Hel.* 1358, μέγα τοι δύναται...στολίδες κ.τ.λ. and *Phoen.* 349, ἐσιγάθη σᾶς ἔσοδοι (so one MS) νύμφας. Cf. Abbott's *Shakespearian Grammar,* §§ 333, 335.

1358. *Ion* 992, ποῖόν τι μορφῆς σχῆμ᾽ ἔχουσαν ἀγρίας.

1361. τὸν καταιβάτην Ἀχέροντα] 'The nether Acheron,' the river descending to the under-world, explained in L. and S. 'that to which one descends.' But in the *Odyss.* 13, 110 we have the gates *by* which men descend from the land into the sea called θύραι...καταιβαταὶ ἀνθρώποισι.—The river Acheron in Thesprotia, after rushing through a deep, dark, chasm, passed into the sea through the *Acherusia palus*, which has now almost vanished ; the stream did not disappear underground like some of the rivers of Greece, yet it was supposed to be in communication with the under-world; thus, Pluto under the name of Aïdoneus was said to have once reigned in that region (Pausan. *Att.* 17), and on its banks there was an oracle which was consulted by evoking the dead, νεκυομαντεῖον (Hdt. 5, 92). The gloomy gorge of the river, and the malaria said to be still prevailing in the neighbouring plain of *Phanári* (Cramer's *Greece* I 112), would naturally account for the ancient superstition which thus connected the stream of Acheron with the realm of the dead.

1365. The MS has ὄρνις ὅπως κηφῆνα πολιόχρως κύκνος, which is retained by Nauck and by Hermann, who places a comma before and after κηφῆνα ; Musgrave however alters πολιόχρως into πολιόχρων, which is adopted by Dindorf, as πολιόχρως seems more applicable to the aged Cadmus than to Agave ; we thus get, instead of three nominatives to one acc., two of each in pairs, ὄρνις κύκνος and κηφῆνα πολιόχρων. For κηφῆνα cf. *Tro.* 191, γραῦς κηφήν ; for πολιόχρως, *Herc. F.* 110, πολιὸς ὄρνις, 692, κύκνος ὡς γέρων ἀοιδὸς πολιᾶν ἐκ γενύων. Similarly in *El.* 153, Electra lamenting her father compares herself to a swan, which πατέρα φίλτατον καλεῖ ὀλόμενον δολίοις βρόχων ἕρκεσιν.

Swans, as well as storks, were regarded by the ancients as notable for their affection toward their parents, Cic. *de fin.* II 33 (*indicia pietatis*). In the present passage, the daughter flinging her arms round the neck of her aged father, is compared to a swan folding its wings about the feeble form of its parent. Cygnets, especially at the time when they are losing their dark plumage, may be often observed flapping their young wings vigorously in the presence of the parent birds ; and some such action as this appears to have suggested the simile in the text.

The combination ὄρνις...κύκνος may be defended by *Hel.* 19, κύκνου μορφώματ' ὄρνιθος, and *Iph. T.* 1089, ὄρνις...ἀλκυών. But ὄρνις seems too far removed from κύκνος, and the absence of a word corresponding to χερσὶν in the previous line, leads one to suggest that ὄρνις, which is not wanted, may have taken the place of a lost word such as πτεροῖς.

1371. τὸν 'Αρισταίου] Unless, as is very probable, some lines have been lost after this, we must understand οἶκον, a doubtful ellipse. In the passage formerly quoted to confirm it, Ar. *Ach.* 1222, θύραζέ μ' ἐξενέγκατ' ἐς τὸν Πιττάλου, where Elmsley proposed τὰ, the editors now prefer τοῦ.

As the Greek law required one who was guilty of homicide to go into exile, Agave is naturally represented as leaving Thebes ; her going to the house of Aristaeus, the husband of her sister Autonoe, is not inconsistent with this, as the legend describes him as wandering from place to place, in Thessaly, Thrace, &c.

1374. The solemn movement of the successive long syllables is apparently intended to serve as an echo to the sense.

1380. εἰς τόδ'] sc. χαίρειν, implied in the preceding χαῖρε. 'Fare thee well, father.' 'Fare thee well, my sorrowing daughter ; and yet 'twere hard for thee to fare well.' *Hec.* 426, (*Polyx.*) χαῖρε...(*Hec.*) χαίρουσιν ἄλλοι μητρὶ δ' οὐκ ἔστιν τόδε, Aesch. *Ag.* 538, (*Cho.*) χαῖρε...(*Herald*) χαίρω· τεθνάναι δ' οὐκέτ' ἀντερῶ. Cf. *Alc.* 511.

1384. The personification of Cithaeron reminds one of Soph. *O. T.* 1391, ἰὼ Κιθαιρών, τί μ' ἐδέχου.

1387. Βάκχαις δ' ἄλλαισι μέλοιεν] "sed neque quid aliis Bacchis cordi esse velit, apparet (nam Cithaeron et thyrsus mire coniunguntur), neque quas alias significet Bacchas, quae omnes perosa sit. Aliis, non sibi Bacchas earumque res cordi esse iubet : Βακχαι δ' ἄλλαισι μέλοιεν," Madvig, *Adv.* I p. 54.

1388—1392. These last five lines occur at the end of four other plays (*Androm. Hel. Med. Alc.*), with the exception that in *Med.* the first line runs πολλῶν ταμίας Ζεὺς ἐν 'Ολύμπῳ.

Hermann suggests a curious reason for this repetition which is worth quoting :

... '*Scilicet, ut fit in theatris, ubi actorum partes ad finem deductae essent, tantus erat surgentium atque abeuntium strepitus, ut quae chorus in exitu fabulae recitare solebat, vix exaudiri possent. Eo factum, ut illis chori versibus parum curae impenderetur.*'

It will however be remarked that this conventional conclusion is not entirely appropriate either to the present play, or to the *Medea.* Possibly (as suggested in Wecklein's ed. of the latter play) their transfer from one play to another was due to the actors, and not to the poet himself. The *Iph. Taur., Orestes* and *Phoenissae*, all close with the following sentence : ὦ μέγα σεμνὴ Νίκη, τὸν ἐμὸν βίοτον κατέχοις καὶ μὴ λήγοις στεφανοῦσα.

ANTIQUE TERRACOTTA LAMP FROM CYPRUS.

CONSPECTUS OF CHORAL METRES.

For information on Greek choral metres, the student may refer either to Linwood's *Greek Tragic Metres*, or to Dr J. H. H. Schmidt's *Introduction to the Rhythmic and Metric of the Classical Languages* [1869], translated by Dr J. W. White, 1879 (some references to the metres of this play may be found on pp. 71, 75, 130—132). An elementary outline for beginners is given in the preface to Badham's English ed. of the *Ion*, and in Anthon and Major's *System of Greek Prosody*, 1845. Among books of special research on this subject may be mentioned Rossbach and Westphal, *Metrik der griechischen Dramatiker u. Lyriker nebst den begleitenden musischen Künsten*, esp. part iii, 1856; J. H. H. Schmidt, *Die Kunstformen der griechischen Poesie* (the third vol., 1871, includes the text and *schemata* of all the lyric parts of Euripides, pp. xlvi—lxxxi); and W. Christ, *Metrik der Griechen u. Römer*, 1874; also H. Buchholtz, *Tanzkunst des Eur.*, 1871, and R. Arnoldt, *Die chorische Technik des Eur.*, 1878.

In the following schemes, I have not considered it worth while to give the precise technical name of each line after the manner of writers on Greek metre of the school of Hermann; this has been carefully done in the editions of Schöne and Tyrrell. I have thought it enough (with Wecklein) to give a symmetrical conspectus of the metres, indicating, however, in the case of each chorus, the general character of the rhythm used, and adding a few notes where necessary. The symbol ⏤ (often in the penultimate place in the series) denotes a long syllable that is specially lengthened, being usually equivalent to a long followed by a short syllable ; in other words, to three short syllables.

πάροδος **64—169.**

[Other arrangements may be found in Westphal, *u. s.* III p. 320, and Schmidt, *u. s.* III p. xlvi—li.]

στροφὴ α΄ 64—67 = 68—71.

Ionic a minore verses, with the last syllable of the Ionic foot sometimes omitted. The following scheme involves ending l. 71 with some such word as κελαδῶ. Some, however (as Schmidt), decline to regard the verses as antistrophic and retain the manuscript reading ὑμνήσω.

64	⏑⏑ –	⏑⏑ – –		68
65	⏑⏑ – –	⏑⏑ – –	⏑⏑ – –	69
66	⏑⏑ – –	⏑⏑ – –	⏑⏑ – –	70
67	⏑⏑ – –	⏑⏑ – –	⏑⏑ –	71

στροφὴ β΄ 72—87 = 88—103.

Choriambic followed by *Ionic a minore* rhythms (as in Soph. *O. T.* 483 ff.). The Ionic measure is also used in the invocation of Iacchos by the chorus of μύσται in Ar. *Ranae* 324—353. It is specially suited for the expression of strong excitement. A still more vehement degree of emotion is expressed by the choriambic rhythm.

72	– ⏑⏑ – ⏑ – – –	88
	⏑⏑ – ⏑ – – –	
	⏑⏑ – ⏑ – – –	

75   − ‿‿ − ‿ − − −   91
       ‿‿ − ‿ − − −
       ‿‿ − ‿ − − −

       ‿‿ − −   ‿‿ − −
       ‿‿ ‿‿ −   ‿‿ − −
80   ‿‿ − −   ‿‿ − −   96
       ‿‿ − −   ‿‿ − −
       ‿‿ − −   ‿‿ − −
       ‿‿ − −   ‿‿ − −
       ‿‿ − −   ‿‿ − −
85   ‿‿ − −   ‿‿ − −   101
       ‿‿ − −   ‿‿ − −   ‿‿ −

87   − ‿‿ − ‿   − − −   ‿‿ −   103

στροφὴ γ′ 105—119 = 120—134.

Choriambic rhythms.

105   − ‿‿ −   ‿ − −   120
             − ‿‿ −   ‿ − −
             ‿‿ ‿‿ ‿‿   ‿ − −
             − ‿‿ ≋   ‿ − −
             − ‿‿ −   ‿ − ‿
110   ‿‿ − ‿‿ −   ‿ − ≍   125

        ‿‿ ‿   − ‿‿ −   ‿ −
        ‿‿ ‿   − ‿‿ −   ‿‿ −
        − −   − ‿‿ ⌐   − ‿‿ − −
        ‿‿ ⌐   − ‿‿ ⌐   − ‿‿ − −
115   ‿‿ ‿   − ‿‿ −   ‿‿ −   130
        − ‿‿   − ‿‿ −   ‿‿ −
        − ‿‿   − ‿‿
        ‿ ⌐   − ‿‿ −   ‿ −
119   − −   − ‿‿ ⌐   −   134

S. B.   16

ἐπῳδός 136—169.

Various measures of a lively and animated character including paeonic (e. g. 135, 160), dactylic (139, 159, 165 ff.), choriambic (136) and dochmiac rhythms (145).

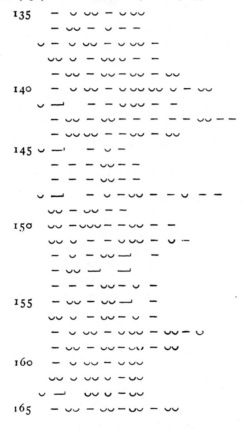

στάσιμον πρῶτον.

[Westphal, *u. s.* and Schmidt, p. liii.]

στροφὴ α΄ 370—385 = 386—401.

Ionic a minore alternating with *choriambic* rhythms

370	⏑⏑ — — ⏑⏑ —	386
	⏑⏑ — — ⏑⏑ —	
	⏑⏑ — ⏕ ⏑⏑ —	
	⏑⏑ — — ⏑⏑ —	
	⏑⏑ — — ⏑⏑ —	
375	⏑⏑ — — ⏑⏑ —	391
	— ⏑⏑ — — ⏑⏑ — — ⏑⏑ —	
	— ⏑⏑ — — ⏑⏑ —	
	— ⏑⏑ — — ⏑⏑ —	
	⏑⏑ — — ⏑⏑ —	
380	⏑⏑ — — ⏑⏑ —	396
	⏑⏑ — — ⏑⏑ — —	
	⏑⏑ — ⏕ ⏑⏑ — —	
	⏑⏑ — — ⏑⏑ —	
	— ⏑⏑ — — ⏑⏑ —	
385	— ⏑⏑ — — ⏑⏑ — ⏑ — —	401

στροφὴ β΄ 402—415 = 416—433.

Glyconean verses (consisting as usual of a choriambus and, under certain limitations, two dissyllabic feet). Combined with these are instances of the pherecratean (e.g. 402, 403, 405), a variety of the same type (being a glyconean with the choriambus in the middle, and with the last syllable omitted from the following dissyllabic foot). A graceful measure.

402   ∪ – – ∪∪ – –   416
     – – – ∪∪ – –
     ∪ – – ∪∪ – ∪ –
405   – – – ∪∪ – –   420
     ∪∪ – ∪∪ ·· ∪ –
     – ∪ – ∪∪ – ∪ –
     – – – ∪∪ – –
     – – – – – ∪∪ –
410   ⊽ ∪∪ – – – ∪∪ –   425
     – – – ∪∪ – –
     ∪ – ∪∪ – ∪∪ ∪∪ ∪∪
     ∪ —– – ∪∪ – ⊽

     ∪ – ∪∪ ∪∪ – ∪∪ ∪
415   ∪ ⊽ ∪ —– – ∪∪ – ∪ —– –   431

στάσιμον δεύτερον.

[Westphal, p. 322, Schmidt, p. lvi.]

στροφὴ β′ 519—536 = 538—555.

Ionic rhythm (with one or two resolved syllables).

     ∪∪ – – ∪∪ –
520   ∪∪ – – ∪∪ – –   539
     ∪∪ – – ∪∪ – –
     ∪∪ –   ⊽ ∪∪ ∪
     ∪∪ – – ∪∪ – –
     ∪∪ – – ∪∪ – –
525   ∪∪ – ⊽ ∪∪ – –   544
     ∪∪ – ∪ – ∪ – –
     ∪∪ – ∪ – ∪ – –
     ∪∪ – – ∪∪ – –
     ∪∪ – – ∪∪ – –

530   ◡◡ – ◡ – ◡ – –   549

        ◡◡ – ◡ – ◡ – –

        ◡◡ – ◡ – ◡ – –

        ◡◡ – – ◡◡ – –

        ◡◡ – – ◡◡ – –

535   ◡◡ – – ◡◡ – –   554

        ◡◡ – – ◡◡ – ◡ —' –

ἐπῳδός 556—575.

Ionic rhythms (556—570), followed by *choriambic* (571, 572), and closing with a glyconean (574) and pherecratean (575). The metre of 573 is uncertain (perhaps two dactyls with the first syllable resolved ≃ ◡◡ – ◡◡). On metrical grounds, Westphal, approved by Schmidt, regards the first word of l. 572 (βροτοῖς) as an interpolation.

556   ◡◡ – – ◡◡ – –

       ◡◡ – – ◡◡ –

       ◡◡ – – ◡◡ – –

       ◡◡ – – ◡◡ –

560   ◡◡ – – ◡◡ – –

       ◡◡ – – ◡◡ – –

       ◡◡ – – ◡◡ – –

       ◡◡ – – ◡◡ – –

       ◡◡ – – ◡◡ – –

565   ◡◡ – – ◡◡ –

       ◡◡ – – ◡◡ – –

       ◡◡ – – ◡◡ – –

       ◡◡ – – ◡◡ –

       ◡◡ – – ◡◡ – –

570   ◡◡ – – ◡◡ – –

− ∪ − ∪∪ − − − ∪∪ −

∪ — − ∪∪ −

∪ ∪∪ ∪ ∪∪ ∪ πατέρα τὸν ἔκλυον

− − − − − ∪∪ −

575   − − − ∪∪ — −

κομμὸς between the Chorus and Dionysus, **576—603.**

[Westphal, p. 378, Schmidt, p. lxi.] Irregular rhythms, mainly *dochmiac* and *dactylic*, well adapted for a scene of tumultuous excitement.

576   ∪ −

∪∪ ∪ − ∪∪ − −

∪ − − − ∪ − − −

∪∪ ∪ − ∪ ∪∪∪∪∪∪ ∪∪∪∪ ∪ − ∪ −

580   ∪∪ ∪ − ∪∪ − −

∪∪ ∪ − ∪∪ − −

∪∪ ∪ − − ∪∪ − ∪∪

∪∪ ∪ − ∪∪ ∪ −

∪∪ ∪ − ∪∪ ∪ ∪∪ ∪

585   ∪ − ∪∪∪∪ ∪ ∪∪ ∪

− −

∪∪ ∪ − −

∪∪ ∪ ∪∪ ∪ − ∪ − ∪ − ∪ − ∪ ≙

∪∪ ∪ − ∪ ∪∪ ∪ − ∪

590   ∪∪ ∪ − ∪∪ ∪ −

− ∪∪ − ∪∪ − ∪∪ − ∪∪

∪∪ ∪ ∪∪ ∪

∪∪ ∪ ∪∪ − ∪ − ∪ − ∪ −

− ∪∪ − ∪∪ − ∪∪ − ∪∪

595   − ∪∪ − ∪∪ − ∪∪ − −

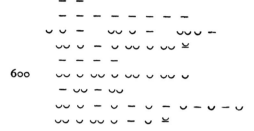

στάσιμον τρίτον 862—911.

[Schmidt, p. lxii, who describes the two strophes as 'an uncommonly beautiful piece of composition,' divides each of them into 3 periods corresponding to ll. 862—872 ; 873—7 ; 878—882.]

στροφὴ 862—881 = 882—901.

Glyconean rhythms.

865   885

870   890

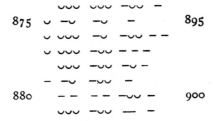

875   895

880   900

ἐπῳδός 902—911.

Mainly *glyconean*, combined with *trochaic* rhythms.

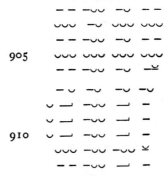

905

910

στάσιμον τέταρτον 977—1016.

[Schmidt, p. lxvi, proposes to add δή after Μαινάδων in 981, and omit θανάσιμον in 1022.] Mainly *dochmiacs*, in 992 we have a senarius; 993, a bacchius; 1017, an iambelegus.

στροφή 977—996 = 997—1016.

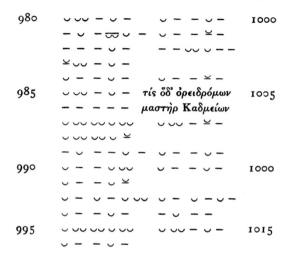

980   1000

985   τίς ὅδ᾽ ὀρειδρόμων   1005
       μαστὴρ Καδμείων

990   1000

995   1015

ἐπῳδός 1017—1023.

1020

κομμός of Chorus, interrupted by trimeters spoken by the Messenger, **1030—1042**.

[Schmidt, p. lxii.] *Dochmiacs.*

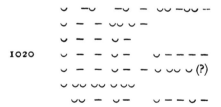

1031
θεὸς   [σύ]

1034   − − − ◡ −   ◡ ◡◡ − ◡ −

       − ◡◡ − − −

1037   ◡ ◡◡ − ◡ ◡◡   ◡ − ◡ − − − (?)

       ◡ ◡◡ − ◡ −

1041   ◡ ◡◡ − ◡ −   ◡ ◡◡ − − −

       ◡ ◡◡ ◡◡ ◡ −   ◡ − − − ◡ −

In 1037 Schmidt suggests that the second Διόνυσος may have its penultimate short; but it would be better to alter it (as has been suggested) into Διὸς παῖς, rather than allow such a license.

χορικὸν (Monostrophic ode) 1153—1164.

[Schmidt, p. lxxiv, makes 1155 an Iambic trimeter (like 1159 and 1161), τὰν τοῦ δράκοντος ἐκγενέτα (τοῦ) Πενθέως. This involves having an anapaest in the fourth place.]

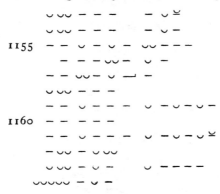

κομμὸς between the Chorus and Agave, 1168—1199.

στροφὴ 1168—1183 = 1184—1199.

Mainly *dochmiacs :* in 1173—4, we have *iambi* followed by anapaests; in 1175, trochees; in 1177, a pherecratean;

1179—80, *iambelegi;* and 1181, *bacchius.* Schmidt, p. lxxix, makes 1169—1170 a double *bacchius* repeated, as in 1180—1, and 1177 : he also gets a *senarius* in 1174 by prefixing κᾶνευ σθένους, and proposing in the antistrophic line 1190, σοφὸς ἀνέπηλ᾽ ἐπὶ θῆρα τόνδε Μαινάδας.

1368—end.

Concluding March in Anapaests.

APPENDIX.

Introduction, p. x—xii. (*The Legend of Dionysus.*)

ON the etymological signification of the name of Dionysus Professor Max Müller writes as follows in the *Academy* for Aug. 5, 1882, p. 95. There can be 'little doubt that Dionysos corresponds to a Sanskrit prototype Dyu-niṣ-ya, lit. the child of Dyu-niṣe, of Day and Night, or of Heaven and Earth, one of the most natural and intelligible names of the sun... A few of the epithets of Dionysos...may here be pointed out in order to show how well they agree with the solar character of the god, and with his descent from the two parents, or the two mothers, Heaven and Earth, Day and Night. He is called *Protogonos, Pyrigenes, Antauges, Chrysokomos, Lampter, Philodaphnos, Brisaios, Erikapaios,* &c. In the epithet *Nyktelios* we have a mere repetition of the second part of *Dio-nyxos'* [a dialectic form of *Dionysus*]; 'and in *Dimeter* (Sanskrit *dvimâtâ*), *Dimorphos, Diphyes* we read the story of his double descent and his double character, the bright and the dark, the diurnal and the nocturnal god. The epithet of *Hyes* shows that from an early date Dionysos represented the Sun in his character of rain-bringer, which accounts for his becoming afterwards an *Antheus, Karpios, Dendritcs,* a vivifying and genial god, and, lastly, the representative of that most genial and vivifying beverage with which his name became in the end most intimately connected—the juice of the grape.'

p. xciii. (*Textual criticism of the play.*)

Since the publication of my first edition, I have met with a recension of the text of the *Bacchae*, together with Idyll xxvi of Theocritus, by George Burges, of Trinity College, Cambridge (1786—1864). It was probably printed in 1818, but never published. For an opportunity of examining this text I am indebted to the kindness of the late Dr Luard, Registrary of the University, who in 1881 lent me his presentation copy. It is a small pamphlet of 64 pages ; marginal references to the *Christus Patiens* are printed systematically throughout the play, and many unnecessary alterations and additions are introduced from that source. The play is thus extended to more than 1700 lines, about 300 more than appear in our ordinary editions. Most of the emendations are extremely improbable, and to print the whole of them would be no real service to the criticism of the play. I have only selected those that appear to me to have some slight value or interest, although even this selection includes many, of which ι sober judgment could not possibly approve. It is of this recension that Elmsley says on p. 10 of his preface : *Textus sui inspiciendi copiam mihi fecit vir amicissimus. Multa in eo optime constituta reperi. Sed pruritum illum corrigendi, etiam ubi omnia integerrima sunt, quem in me reprehendit Hermannus, ego quoque nequeo non reprehendere in Burgesio.* Two of the following emendations are already known to scholars through Elmsley's edition, namely those in lines 451 and 998. Among the rest may be found two or three which are of special interest, in so far as they anticipate suggestions which have independently occurred to other editors at a later date (cf. 479, 678, 962).

2 ὅν ποτ' ἔτεκεν. 8 τεφρούμεν', ἀμύδρου τ' ἔτι πυρὸς ζῶσαν φλόγα. *versum* 20 *post* 22 *posuit Burgesius, mutato* πρῶτον *in* πρῶτος ; *idem initio v.* 23 πρῶτος *legit.* 22 (ἐμφανὴς) ἐν φάναις. 32 (αὐτὰς) αὐτὸς. 38 ἐν ὀρόφοις τ' (*sic*) ἧνται πέτρας. 43 ὅτ' ἐγήρασκε. 67 εὐὰν ἀζομένα. 68 τίς ὁδῷ ποῦς ; 89 (ἀνάγκαισι) ἀνειλιθυίαις. 92 (ἔτεκεν) ἔδικε (*servato in antistropha* ὄρεσι, l. 76). 93 κεραυνοπλῆγα. 95 παλαμαῖς. 99 (ἔτεκεν δ') ἀνέψξ'. 102 (ἄγραν) ὕδραν. 106 κισσοὶ...χλοηραὶ σὺν μίλακι. 111 ἐνδύντα στικτῶν νεβρίδων στέφετε. 113 νάρθηχ' ἀβρογυίοις ποσὶ σοῦσθ'. 115 Βρόμιος αὐτὸς ἄγει. 126 ἐν δὲ βακχείαν συντονὴν κέρασεν. 145 ὁ βακχεὺς δ', ἔρπιν ἔχων εὐώδη, ἔξαρχος φλογὶ πεύκας. 148 θοάζων. 169 (ἄγει) ἄγω. 178 *cum Musgravio* ἡδόμην. 180 (θεοῦ)

τάχει. 190 κἀπιχαιρήσω. 201 Κρόνῳ κεκτήμεθ᾽, οὐκ ἀνατί.
209 οἴνης δι᾽ ἀριθμὸν ληνὸς (!) αὔξεσθαι θέλει. 218 νήστῃσι. 223
πτήσσουσαν. 224 μαινάδ᾽ ἢ θυοσκόον. 235 cum Stephano
εὔκοσμος κόμην. 252 τὸ γῆρας ὠμὸν εἰσορῶν νοῦν σ᾽ οὐκ ἔχειν.
264—5 cum Musgravio transponit. 270 λέγειν θ᾽ ὁ δυνατὸς καὶ
θρασὺς· τοιόσδ᾽ ἀνὴρ κακὸν πολίταις γίγνεται. 284 οἶνος θεοῖσι
σπένδεται θεοῦ γάνος. 293 ἔθηκ᾽ αὐτοῦ σφ᾽. 308 retinet βάλλοντα. 340 ἐν τ᾽ ὀργάνοις. 378 ὅς γ᾽ ἔλαχεν. 396 τί
δὲ μὴ θνητὰ φρονεῖ βραχὺς αἰών; 406 cum Reiskio Φάρον θ᾽ ἄν.
413 τρὶς Βάκχ᾽ εὔιε. 451 μέθεσθε χειρῶν τοῦδ᾽. 479 Kirchhoffii
coniecturam (εὖ γ᾽ οὐδὲν λέγων) praeripuerat Burgesius. 490 σὲ
δ᾽ ἀμαθίας γ᾽ οὐκ .εὐσεβοῦντ᾽ Burgesio debetur. 499 ταθείς.
506 ὅ, τι (ὅτι PC) ζῆς. reliquum versum a plurimis tentatum, Bur-
gesium qui tot locos temere tentaverit, prorsus intactum praeterisse,
nemini non mirum videbitur. Post v. 518 ὦ καλλίνοτις
κρήνη. 645 ἐμοῖς ; ΔΙ. ἔξω βεβώς. 677—8 ἀγελαῖα μὲν μοσ-
χεύματ᾽ (βοσκήματ᾽) ἄρτι πρὸς λέπας βόσκων (μόσχων) ὑπεξήκριζον.
Quarum emendationum posteriorem quidem primus, ut mihi videbar, in
editione priore indicavi, nesciens nostratem nostra ante nos dixisse.
709 διακλῶσαι χθόνα γάλακτος εἶχον νασμόν. 746 διεφόρουν τὰ.
853 ἀλαίνων. 860 πέφυκε θεός, εἴ τις, πολὺ δεινὸς σκυθρωποῖς,
ἠπίοισι δ᾽ ἤπιος. 873 ἴσα τ᾽ ὠκυδρόμοις ἀέλλαις θρώσκῃ πέδον παρὰ
ποτάμιον. 915 γυναικόμιμον ὡς Βάκχης. 946 αὐταῖσιν ἐλαταῖς recepit.
962 ἀστῶν quod Paleio quoque placuit. 976 αὐτά. 998 περὶ τὰ,
Βάκχε, σ᾽ ὄργια ματρός τε Γᾶς. 1042 ἀδικά τ᾽ ἔμ᾽ ἐξορίζων.
1056 ἐκλιποῦσα ἐπὶ χιλὸν (!) ὡς πῶλος ξυγά. 1060 οὐκ ἔστιν ἀκοή
τ᾽ ὄμμα τ᾽ οὐδ᾽ ὅσον μαθεῖν. 1062 ἀρθείς (ὀρθῶς). 1103 συγκραδαίνουσαι edidit. 1134 ὤγνυντο (γυμνοῦντο). 1147 νίκη φέρει
quod etiam Hartungius coniecit. 1192 ζαγρεὺς quod Dobraeus
quoque obiter commemoravit. 1210 χωρίς τ᾽ ἀθῆρος. 1308
ὃν δῶμ᾽ ἀνέβλεφ᾽. P. 80, Christi patientis l. 1466, κρᾶτα τὸν
τρισαθλίου. Ibid. l. 1470 ἰδοὺ servat quod postea (anno 1832) mutavit.
1361 νεκυοβάτον (καταιβάτην). 1365 ΑΓ. ὄρνις ὅπως ἀπτὴν γε—
ΚΑ. πολιόχρων κύκνον. 1388—1392 (πολλαὶ μορφαὶ κ.τ.λ.)
Fabulae versus postremi quinque, a Weckleinio nuper uncinis inclusi,
² Burgesio iam pridem prorsus exclusi sunt.

Readings of the Laurentian MS. C.

The following notes represent nearly all the results of a careful examination of the above MS during a visit to Florence in the spring of 1883.

107 χλοηρεῖ, *super ultimam syllabam non* ου, *sed* α, *scripto ; quod Elmsleius quoque vere testatur.* 125 *circa vocabulum* ἔνθα *circulus atramento subrufo scriptus est.* 135 οὔρεσιν, *non* ὄρεσιν. *Illud in ipso codice Elmsleius quoque vidit : hoc codici temere tribuit Analectorum Euripideorum scriptor.* 151 *non* 'supra versum,' *ut a collatore quodam dictum est, sed in paginae columna dextrorsum proxima, inter ipsa poetae verba, legitur additamentum istud* ἐπ̇ιλιγειῆχεῖ : *deinde statim sequitur* τοιάδε. *huius autem versus supra vocabulum primum* (ἐπὶ) *scriptum est per compendium* περισσόν. 154 χλιδᾷ, *vel fortasse,*

χλιδᾷ 182 πεφηναν̇θρωποι̇σθεός· *signo elisionis supra* ν *addito, et* εν *supra scripto ; quod Tyrrellii nostri coniecturae* (πέφην' ἐν) *favere videtur.* 202 καταβάλλει. 292 ἀγκυκλουμένου, *quod quondam Furiae tantum testimonio nitebatur, nunc revera in codice scriptum esse constat.* 315—7 ἀλλ' ἐν τῇ φύσει τὸ σωφρονεῖν ἔνεστιν εἰς τὰ πάντ' ἀεί· τοῦτο σκοπεῖν χρή· *inter* ἀεί *et* τοῦτο *signo interpunctionis posito.* 332 πέτῃ τε καὶ φρονῶν, οὐδὲν φρονεῖς. 335 ὡς ἐστὶ σεμελῆς, *interpunctione atramento subrufo addita.* 338 τὸν *correctum in* ὄν, *littera* τ *prope omnino erasa et* ο *mutata in* °Ο. 345 *luce clarius apparet* τόνδε. *ne vestigium quidem apparet lectionis* τήνδε *quam solita incuria codici nostro tribuit Furia.* 346 δίκῃ *potius quam* δίκη. 347 *utrumque codicem* οἰωνοσκοπῇ *habere testatur Analectorum Euripideorum auctor ; revera autem in Laurentiano legitur* οἰωνοσκοπεῖ.

372 χρύσε πτέρυγαφέρεις. : τάδε *In vocabulo.* χρύσεα, *in litterae* ε *particula superiore correctoris manus atramento subrufo indicatur. post* φέρεις *spatium litterarum duarum capax litura notatum.* 385 ἀμφῒβάλῃ : 392 δ ῶ μ α. πρόσω γὰρ. ἀλλ' ὅμ ω ς αἰθέρα ναί· (οντες *in altera columna addito). litteras aliquatenus litura inquinatas typis diductis indicavi.* 395—7 τὸ σοφόν:δ':οὐ σοφία : τό τε μὴ θνητὰ φρονεῖν : βραχὺς αἰών. ἐπὶ τούτω δέ τις ἂν μεγάλα *supra verbum ultimum recentiore manu monitum metricum* ἀντὶ μιᾶς *per compendium scriptum. idem supra* τὰν κύπρον *in v.* 402, *et* βρέφος *in v.* 522.

421 ἴσαδ'εἶς, *littera* ν *pallidiore atramento supra scripta.* 431 τὸ

πλῆθος ὅτι᾿ τ᾿φαυλότερον ἐνόμισε· χρῆταί τ᾿, τόδε λέγοιμ᾿ ἄν: *post* ὅτι *puncta duo superiora atramento subrufo picta.* deinde τε, *quanquam in litura, nigro tamen atramento scriptum.* ante τόδε *et* ἄν *litterarum duarum spatium.* 468 οὔκ᾿ ἀλλ᾿ ὁ *litterae* ὁ *parte dextra colore rubro leviter tacta et ante verbum proximum linea evanida* (ι) *interposita.* 477 *supra* θὲ (θεὸν) *scriptum est* ─῀῀ῆ. 490 σὲ δ᾿ ἀμαθίας γε κάσεβοῦντ᾿ *nihil vidi quod indicaret codicem quondam* ἀμαθίας ἀσεβοῦντ᾿, *litteris nullis interpositis, habuisse.* 502 αὐτὸς ὤν, *signo interpunctionis a correctore addito.* 525 νιν, τάδ᾿ ἀναβοήσας *omnia post* νιν *litteris subrufis scripta sunt.* 537 περισσὸν *superadditum potius quam adscriptum.* ante hunc versum μεσῷδος *notatur, ante v.* 547 (!) ἀντιστροφή. *unde colligere licet* περισσὸν *non versum, quod ad metrum attinet, supervacaneum ; sed* οἴαν *ex abundanti iteratum indicare.* 537 *inter* ἐμὸν *et* ἐντὸς *colore subrufo litura, ubi in codice altero* δ᾿ *insertum.* 556

ἄραθη ροτρόφονθυρσοφορ. *inter* α θη *et* ρ, *quae ipsa liturae vestigiis notata sunt, trium litterarum spatium relictum* (=τᾶς). *prima manu scriptum* θυρσοφοραῖσιν (*non* -ραις). 574 *diserte legitur* εὖϊ.ππ (*sc.* εὔιππον) *lectionem* εὔιον *codici tribuit nil nisi incuria Furiae.* 590 σέβετέ νιν *Dionyso,* σέβομεν ὢ *hemichorio tributum.* 596 *Hemichorio tributum* ἄ ἄ: πῦρ οὐ λεύσεις· οὐδ᾿ αὐγάξῃ (*sic*), *supra scripto* ὁρᾷς? 631 ἤισσε *in medio verbo non legitur* σ, *sed* σσ *per compendium scriptum.* ὗτε *a correctore supra scriptum.* 641 εὐοργησίαν *potius quam* εὐοργησία. *scilicet post* σϊ *per compendium scriptum, sequitur paullum supra versum littera quae speciem fert litterae* α *cum* ν *vel* γ *coniunctae.* 677—8 β *et* μ *in* βοσκήματ᾿ *et* μόσχων *ita scripta ut, in Laurentiano saltem, nequaquam inter se confundi possint ; sed idem in v.* 25, *cum Palatino, diserte habet* μέλος *pro* βέλος. *Utriusque igitur codicis in archetypo fortasse litterae istae fere eandem formam habuerunt.* 715 κοινῶν. ο (*non* α) *et* ι *prope in unum coniuncta.* 755 *post hunc versum paginae quinque vacuae.*

Description of the Woodcuts, p. cxlix. (*The Maenad of Scopas*).

The statuette from Smyrna in the Millingen collection at Florence (figured in *Archaeol. Zeit.* VII taf. 1, 2, and in Perry's *Greek and Roman Sculpture* p. 384), which was formerly considered the nearest approximation to the Maenad of Scopas (Urlichs p. 63), is now ascertained to be not made of marble at all but only of biscuit-porcelain (Overbeck, *Gr. Plastik* ed. 3, II, note 20).

Description of the Woodcuts, p. cl. (*Dancing Faun*).

During a visit to Florence in April 1883, I tried to find the original of this 'Florentine gem.' I looked through the whole of the gem-cabinet of the Uffizi without success; the nearest approach to it which I could discover being a large gem in case VIII, part i, row 2, between nos. 3046 and 3052. This, however, though closely resembling the Blacas and Strozzi gem referred to in the text, turns out to be a modern fabrication. In the same cabinet there is a genuine gem of much smaller size representing a dancing Satyr, gazing upwards, with his head tossed far further back than in the engraving on p. 122; the right arm held higher, with the panther's skin falling from it in graceful folds; and the left hand holding aloft a thyrsus only. On the ground, behind the foot on which he is moving on tip-toe, and far below the foot that is raised in the dance, lies a small cup overturned, with what is probably meant for a few drops of wine in front of it. For a cast of this gem (an enlarged copy of which may be seen in Gori's *Museum Florentinum* I lxxxvii 4) I am indebted to Prof. L. A. Milani, of the Archaeological Museum, Florence, who has most courteously assisted me in my enquiries. He suggests with great probability that Agostini's engraving does not represent any actual gem, but is an imitation borrowed in part from the one just mentioned and from two others (nos. 2 and 7 in the same page of Gori, *u. s.*). In none of these is there any trace of the blades of grass with which Agostini has embellished his design; nor is there anything like the stick tied by a ribband to the uplifted *thyrsus*, which first led to my drawing attention to the engraving. All of them justify my own suspicion that the stick is only an inaccurate rendering of a ribband fluttering in the air; and confirm Mr King's opinion that the engraving does not represent a genuine antique.

102. ἄγραν θηρότροφον] Mr F. D. Morice ingeniously suggests ἄγραν θηροφόρον, 'booty (consisting) of beasts worn (as wreath)', comparing Soph. *Fragm.* 16, καταστίκτου κυνὸς σπολὰς Λίβυσσα, παρδαληφόρον δέρος, 'hide of leopard-skin worn' (May, 1885).

112. λευκοτρίχων πλοκάμων μαλλοῖς] πλόκαμος is used in Xen. *Cyneg.* ix 12 of the 'twisted cord' of a deer-trap, which by the way is to be made of the σμῖλαξ (l. 107). This shews that πλόκαμος need not always mean 'human hair'; and of course the word itself, as is implied by its derivation from πλέκω, means merely a twist or plait of any material. If then, as suggested in the latter part of the note on p. 113, μαλλοῖς is to be regarded as applied metaphorically to bunches of *hair*, there seems no difficulty in the view there taken, as πλοκάμων in itself may mean 'plaits,' or 'tresses' of any kind, the actual material being defined by the latter part of the epithet λευκοτρίχων (C. S. Jerram). With regard to Elmsley's suggestion προβάτων, it may be remarked that, although the word itself is not used by the Tragedians, the compound form προβατογνώμων is found in Aesch. *Ag.* 795.

124. βυρσότονον κύκλωμα] *Hel.* 1347, τύπανα βυρσοτενῆ, already quoted in note on line 59. The whole of the Second Strophe and Antistrophe of the Helen, from which the above parallel is taken, should be referred to in connexion with the present passage and other portions of this play.

135. To the passage from Propertius quoted on p. 118, add Ovid, *Amores* I. 14, 19, *saepe etiam, nondum digestis mane capillis, purpureo iacuit semisupina toro; tum quoque erat neglecta decens, ut Threcia Bacche, cum temere in viridi gramine lassa iacet.* This parallel is quoted by Helbig in his *Untersuchungen über die Campanische Wandmalerei,* where reference is made to several ancient paintings found on the walls of Pompeii, in which resting Maenads are represented (no. 542 ff., 559 ff., and 566). There are engravings of similar subjects in ancient sculpture, in Clarac's *Musée de Sculpture* IV pl. 703 no. 1667—9.

145. In the *Classical Review*, ii 224, Mr Hugh Macnaghten objects to the translation on p. 121 on the ground of the sudden change of object. ἔχων governs φλόγα, ἐρεθίζων governs πλανάτας, and ἀναπάλλων again governs φλόγα. This appears to him awkward in the extreme. He therefore takes πλανάτας to be nominative and supplies φλόγα as the acc. to all three participles. His translation is as follows : ' The Bacchanal holding the ruddy blaze of pine wood on his wand rushes forward, fanning it by his running and dances as he roams, and waving it with cries.' For the meaning here given to ἐρεθίζων, he compares Ar. *Ach.* 669, φέψαλος ἐρεθιζόμενος ῥιπίδι.—In the late Dr Thompson's interleaved copy of Elmsley's *Bacchae* I find the rendering : ' challenging to the race and the dance his errant followers.'

203. ηὕρηται] The form εὕρηται printed in Hermann's text, and elsewhere, is obviously ambiguous. Hermann himself refuses to take it either as an aorist conj. mid., or as perf. indic. passive, but insists on regarding it as perf. *conjunctive* passive. But (1) it may well be doubted whether there is such a form as εὕρωμαι, the only ones in use appearing to be κέκτωμαι and μέμνωμαι ; and (2) it seems *not* to be here (as Hermann holds) a *res incerta*. The passage implies rather that ' keen wit *has been* tried upon the ancient creeds ' (C. S. Jerram).

506. οὐκ οἶσθ' ὅ τι ζῆς οὐδ' ὁρᾷς ἔθ' ὅστις εἶ] ' I would not, for reasons to be given presently, adopt even Elmsley's ἔθ' for οὔθ'. Nor do I think ὅ τι ζῆς suited to the context or to a general Athenian audience. Persius got his *Quid sumus cet.* from the Porch, not being led to the Bacchae by his friend Horace. My correction is diplomatically almost as slight as ζῆς for ζῆς : I would read

ουκ οἶσθ' ὅτι ζεῖς οὐδ' ὁρᾷς οὔθ' ὅστις εἶ—

ζέω, like *ferveo*, means to boil with passion of any sort. θυμός is generally added, as in *Hec.* 1055 θυμῷ ζέοντι Θρῃκὶ δυσμαχωτάτῳ : *Oed. Col.* 435 ἔζει θυμός : but not always as Plato will shew : *Rep.* IV, 440 C ὅταν ἀδικεῖσθαί τις ἡγῆται, οὐκ ἐν τούτῳ ζεῖ τε καὶ χαλεπαίνει ; Pentheus' answer is anyhow abrupt, not to say somewhat inane. But this inanity is I think increased, if you suppose Dionysus' speech to be complete.

I assume it to be broken off by -Pentheus' sudden retort. Generally, when a speaker is interrupted in a stichomythia, he afterwards completes his sentence ; but not always, as for instance in *Alcestis* 1088.' (Mr Munro in *Journal of Philology* XI p. 279.)

783. πέλτας ὅσοι πάλλουσι] The contemporary coins of Thebes often have, on the one side, the characteristic shield, 'the so-called Boeotian buckler, a round or oval shield with a semicircular opening at either side'; and, on the other, the ivy-crowned head of the bearded Dionysus. See *Select Greek and Roman Coins of the British Museum*, III B 29, and Head's *Coinage of Boeotia*, Plate III 4, 5, 6.

802. ὦ τᾶν] 'Whether τᾶν has anything to do with ἔτης is very doubtful. Buttmann's view, that τᾶν means *thou*, finds support in the Sanskrit *tvam* and τᾶν· σύ 'Αττικῶς, Hesych.' (G. Curtius, *Greek Etymology*, p. 675, translated by Wilkins and England).

935—6. Mr A. S. Murray of the British Museum suggests to me that the couplet, in which Dionysus describes the girdle of Pentheus as being still loose and the folds of his robe falling unevenly, may in a manner be illustrated by the beautiful group of the youth with the boy standing immediately behind him, at the N.W. angle of the Panathenaic frieze. The youth's girdle is just fastened and the boy and himself are engaged in pulling down the folds from under it. The group may be easily found in the Museum or in any of the casts or other reproductions of the frieze (figures 133 and 134 of the North frieze in the plates to Michaelis' *Parthenon ;* Ellis, *Elgin Marbles*, I p. 198 ; or Perry's *Greek and Roman Sculpture*, p. 279, fig. 109). The dress of the disguised Pentheus is of course a woman's robe that falls as far as the ankles instead of only reaching to the knees, as in the figure of the youth above referred to.

1005—9. "I should accept from Elmsley τὸ σοφὸν οὐ φθόνῳ χαίρω θηρεύουσα and, retaining τῶν ἀεὶ, translate as follows : ' I delight in the ungrudging quest of knowledge, but the other course has been approved to be great, consisting as it does in those eternal ordinances that a man in pursuit of noble ends should be holy and pious in life by day and by night.' Taken thus I see in this passage a reference to *Antigone* 450—457 and especially to the lines : οὐ γάρ τι νῦν γε κἀχθὲς ἀλλ' ἀεί ποτε ζῇ ταῦτα, κοὐδεὶς οἶδεν ἐξ ὅτου 'φάνη. And in these lines I find the key to the interpretation of the present passage. The question raised in the *Antigone* seems to me admirably to illustrate the point which is here insisted on" (H. Macnaghten, *Classical Review*, ii 224).

1097. ἀντίπυργον...πέτραν] either 'a rock that served as tower' (cf. ἀντίδουλος, Aesch. *Cho.* 135, ἀντίμολπος, *Ag.* 17); or better 'rock that towered before him' (Aesch. *Eum.* 658, 690).

1163—4. The translation in the note is virtually identical with that given by the late Dr Thompson in his professorial lectures ; but Mr H. Macnaghten (perhaps rightly) thinks it untenable. Retaining the manuscript reading τέκνον, which is naturally governed by περιβαλεῖν, he renders the passage thus : "'Tis a glorious contest to embrace one's child with a hand that reeks with blood.' 'This,' he adds, 'is Agave's obvious meaning, but there is also a sense in which the words are fulfilled already, and of which she knows nothing. At this moment she is literally embracing her son's head with a hand that reeks with blood. As to the construction χέρα περιβαλεῖν τέκνον Attic usage is certainly against it, but it is found in Herodotus [i. 163 τεῖχος περιβαλέσθαι τὴν πόλιν], and there seems to me no insuperable difficulty in supposing that it is found here' (*Classical Review*, ii 225).

GREEK INDEX,

MAINLY TO THE TEXT.

The numerals refer to the *lines* of the play.—Figures preceded by p. refer to the *pages* of the book.—Abbreviations such as 8n refer more particularly to the English notes.

Words not used elsewhere by *Euripides*, are denoted by *. Words not yet found elsewhere in *any* author, by ** (Vater's *Rhesus* p. cix)

ENGLISH INDEX,

MAINLY TO THE INTRODUCTION AND NOTES.

Roman numerals, and all arabic numerals preceded by p., refer to the PAGES of the book. All other figures refer to the *lines* of the play, with the notes upon them.

S. B.   18

Lightning Source UK Ltd.
Milton Keynes UK
UKOW05f1539070314

227741UK00001B/23/P